"*The Art that is Life*":
The Arts & Crafts Movement
in America, 1875-1920

" *The Art that is Life* ":
The Arts & Crafts Movement in America, 1875-1920

by Wendy Kaplan

with contributions by
Eileen Boris, W. Scott Braznell, Robert Judson Clark,
Edward S. Cooke, Jr., Ellen Paul Denker, Bert Randall Denker,
Robert Edwards, Jonathan L. Fairbanks, Sally Buchanan Kinsey,
Gillian Moss, Cheryl Robertson, Susan Otis Thompson,
Richard Guy Wilson, and Catherine Zusy

A New York Graphic Society Book
Little, Brown and Company, Boston

Museum of Fine Arts, Boston

The exhibition is sponsored by the Fidelity Foundation, a charitable foundation funded by Fidelity Management & Research Company, investment adviser to Fidelity Investments, and by the National Endowment for the Humanities, a Federal agency. The Luce Fund for Scholarship in American Art, a project of the Henry Luce Foundation, made possible the research for the exhibition and catalogue and supported a portion of the publication. Additional support for publication of the catalogue was provided by the J. Paul Getty Trust.

Printed and typeset by Acme Printing Co., Wilmington, Massachusetts
Bound by Acme Bookbinding Co., Charlestown, Massachusetts
Designed by Carl Zahn

Exhibition dates:

Museum of Fine Arts, Boston
March 4 – May 31, 1987

Los Angeles County Museum of Art
August 16 – November 1, 1987

The Detroit Institute of Arts
December 9, 1987 – February 28, 1988

Cooper-Hewitt Museum, New York
April 5 – June 26, 1988

Cover and jacket illustration:
Wallpaper frieze, 1900-1905 (no. 193)
H.B.H. Company (origin unknown)
Cooper-Hewitt Museum, the Smithsonian Institution's National Museum of Design, New York. Gift of Paul Franco

Frontispiece: From *War is Kind* by Stephen Crane, 1899 (no.46)
Illustrator: Will H. Bradley (1868 - 1962)
Department of Rare Books and Special Collections, Princeton University Library

New York Graphic Society books are published by Little, Brown and Company (Inc.).

Published simultaneously in Canada by Little, Brown & Company (Canada) Limited.

Contents

Foreword

The Fidelity Foundation, a charitable foundation funded by Fidelity Management & Research Company, investment adviser to Fidelity Investments, is pleased to sponsor the exhibition and catalogue "*The Art that is Life*": *The Arts and Crafts Movement in America, 1875-1920*. We believe that a renewed interest in the crafts today makes this an especially appropriate time to look back at the period and its distinctive architecture and handcrafted decorative arts.

In assembling the exhibition, the Museum of Fine Arts draws on a rich local heritage, as well as that of numerous other regions, including New York and California, where Arts and Crafts ideals flourished. It is especially appropriate that the exhibition was organized in Boston, a city that provided the model for Arts and Crafts societies and exhibitions throughout the country. We hope that as audiences from New England to the west coast view the art of this era, they will gain a better appreciation of the stylistic and philosophic considerations behind the objects; the movement's emphasis on individualism and quality is a fascinating study for contemporary viewers.

The arts play a vital role in the community, which must be supported by corporations, foundations, government agencies, and individuals. For this reason, Fidelity is pleased to join with the National Endowment for the Humanities, the Henry Luce Foundation, and the J. Paul Getty Trust in funding this critical reexamination of turn-of-the-century culture.

EDWARD C. JOHNSON 3D
Chairman, Fidelity Investments
Trustee, Museum of Fine Arts, Boston

Director's Preface

The exhibition and accompanying catalogue *"The Art that is Life": The Arts and Crafts Movement in America, 1875-1920* presents pioneering research into one of the most significant but least understood areas of American art history. In response to the harsh conditions of modern life and industrialization, the movement's proponents advocated reforms on many different levels – reforms in how objects were made, how they looked, and how they were marketed; reforms in education; and reforms in the fundamental ways people lived with their possessions.

It is particularly appropriate that the Museum of Fine Arts has organized this project, since its own founding was tied to the educational ideals of the Arts and Crafts movement. Like those of the South Kensington Museum in London (now the Victoria and Albert Museum), the collections at the Museum of Fine Arts were intended to serve as inspiration for contemporary designers. The School of the Museum was an early leader in "affording instruction in the Fine Arts" and in following William Morris's dictate that the decorative arts were to be considered equal to painting and sculpture. Classes in decorative design were introduced a few years after it was established in 1877. Evening courses titled "Practical Application of Artistic Principles" were given by a member of the Museum's staff in 1914 for employees of several of Boston's large stores; objects from the stores were brought in and compared with objects from the Museum. Furthermore, the Museum demonstrated its support for raising standards of contemporary craftsmanship by hosting several exhibitions of the Boston Society of Arts and Crafts until the time of the first world war. A commitment to contemporary crafts continues through active collecting and through programs such as "Please Be Seated," whereby visitors can sit in furniture designed by some of today's leading American cabinetmakers while examining the art of the past.

Research for "The Art that is Life" began in the autumn of 1982 and was supported initially by a planning grant from the National Endowment for the Humanities. The Museum is appreciative of N.E.H. support given at that time and again in 1985 with the awarding of a major grant for the exhibition. We also acknowledge the generous sponsorship of the Fidelity Foundation, a charitable foundation funded by Fidelity Management & Research Company, investment adviser to Fidelity Investments, which has for many years demonstrated its commitment to furthering scholarship in American art.

The Luce Fund for Scholarship in American Art, a project of the Henry Luce Foundation, provided a generous grant that made possible extensive research and travel for examination of objects, photography, honorariums for catalogue contributors, and publication costs. Additional funds for catalogue production costs were given by the J. Paul Getty Trust.

JAN FONTEIN
Director

Curator's Preface

Throughout the half century that followed America's post-civil-war reconstruction, fundamental changes took place at all levels of society. Pervasive during this era (1875-1920) was a popular quest for unity in government, in the new middle class, and among progressive thinkers. This mindset is basic to the understanding of the present catalogue. The differences were not merely the result of Americans' post-Civil-War aspirations, nor did they derive only from the taming of the frontier and the linkage of an extended nation through great railroad systems completed in the late 1870s. Reflecting a nation in transition, the Philadelphia Centennial Exposition of 1876 marked a moment of achievement in technology and a turning point in the arts. As the reality of daily life for many Americans shifted in the late nineteenth century from the farm to the city, the nature of work was altered by new sources of energy, by highly specialized divisions of labor, and through large factory systems, which produced consumer goods in quantity at low cost. Such improvements took their toll, with wealth and power concentrated in the hands of a few. In the workplace decisions about the design and making of objects were made by individuals other than those who actually processed material. Rhythms of life and work once governed by changing seasons and by daylight were changed through the employment of artificial illumination and by continuous productivity through alternating shifts of workers. This catalogue deals with many of the questions raised by such issues, and with the artistic and social responses of those who were concerned for unity in the arts and in society. The central focus is upon arts of the home and upon the democratization of the artistic impulse believed to be inherent in every human being.

A leading revolutionary a century ago was the Englishman William Morris, whose work as an artist, designer, printer, and intellectual reflected a search for a new social order. He persuaded many of the necessity for change, even if few Americans were converted to his brand of socialism. In a lecture entitled "Art and Beauty of the Earth" given in October 1881, Morris observed degraded humanity on the waterfront outside his window at Hammersmith and detailed with compassion the basic human needs: "I know by my own feelings & desires what these men want, what would have saved them from this lowest depth of savagery; Employment which would foster their self-respect and win the praise and sympathy of their fellows, and dwellings which they could come to with pleasure, surroundings which would soothe and elevate them; reasonable labour, reasonable rest. There is only one thing that can give them this, and it is art." For Morris art was broadly defined to include all social improvement and his views had great impact upon those who had just emerged from an era of mid-Victorian Romantic classicism. As documented by this catalogue, Arts and Crafts ideals were embraced by a wide range of individuals who shared a kinship of ideals rather than a recognizable academic style. The integration of physical and mental labor and the recognition that art is a source for regeneration available to all was the basic ideology of turn-of-the-century reformers. Their legacy is apparent in the crafts movement that arose after the second world war; that it continues to flourish is attested by the opening of a new museum for American crafts in New York City in 1986.

Since its founding in 1971, the Department of American Decorative Arts and Sculpture has generated an important series of exhibitions about American crafts and decorative arts. In 1975, Boston's bicentennial year, the department mounted two exhibitions: "Frontier America: The Far West" and "Paul Revere's Boston." These displays offered the viewer insight into the arts of the common man of the nineteenth-century west and the arts of the mercantile elite of eighteenth-century Boston. In 1982 the department celebrated the founding of New England with an exhibition entitled "New England Begins: The Seventeenth Century." New analysis of this remote period of time and culture changed fundamental misconceptions about the culture. The present exhibition recorded by this catalogue expands the visitors' panorama of three-dimensional American arts into the late nineteenth and early twentieth century.

Expanding themes introduced in "The Arts and Crafts Movement in America, 1876-1916," an exhibition at the Princeton University Art Museum in 1972, "The Art that is Life" places the Arts and Crafts movement in its social and intellectual context. The first major section, "Reform in Aesthetics," concerns the development of styles and forms – reform in the way objects looked. The second section, "Reform in Craftsmanship," examines the various methods by which objects were made, while the third, "Spreading the Reform Ideal," considers the organizations, communities, and schools through which Arts and Crafts principles were disseminated. The fourth section, "Reform of the Home," addresses the impact of the movement on domestic life and the creation of a harmonious Arts and Crafts interior.

A significant area of reexamination, one particularly relevant in New England, is the colonial revival. It is manifest as Hispanic in Florida, California, and New Mexico; as imaginary "frontier" log buildings and stick furniture in the Adirondacks and in Yellowstone; and as an evocation of the first New England colony. In Boston, the work of such prominent local silversmiths such as George Gebelein, Katherine Pratt, Frans Gyllenberg, and Henry Swanson (see nos. 65-67) tended to be adaptations of seventeenth-, eighteenth-, and early-nineteenth-century forms. Gebelein became renowned for his services inspired by the teapots of Paul Revere, to whom he was linked by a succession of apprenticeships.

Although the original impulse that had fueled the creative energies of the Arts and Crafts movement waned in the 1920s, the legacy was perpetuated in superb works by individual craftsmen. It is still apparent today after sixty years of modernism, and thus "The Art that is Life" provides a valuable perspective for the crafts movements that constitute our ongoing history.

JONATHAN L. FAIRBANKS
Katharine Lane Weems Curator
of American Decorative Arts and Sculpture

Lenders

Morton Abromson and Joan Nissman
Mr. and Mrs. John M. Angelo
The Art Institute of Chicago
The Athenaeum of Philadelphia
Francis E. Condit Ballard, M.D.
Rosalie M. Berberian
Berea College, Appalachian Museum, Berea, Kentucky
Michael Bernstein, Pieces of Tyme Antiques
Richard Blacher
Sonia and Walter Bob
Henry Scripps Booth
Mr. and Mrs. Peter M. Brandt
Andrew S. Braznell
Jennifer Braznell
Gary Breitweiser
The Brooklyn Museum
Don and Rosemary Burke
Cambridge City Public Library, Cambridge City, Indiana
Chicago Historical Society
Cincinnati Museum of Art
Mr. and Mrs. Robert Judson Clark
Robert F. Cohn
Columbia University (New York), Avery Architectural and Fine Arts Library, School of Library Service Library, and Rare Books and Manuscript Library
The Connecticut Historical Society, Hartford
Charles J. Connick Associates, Boston
Cooper-Hewitt Museum, The Smithsonian Institution's National Museum of Design, New York
The Cranbrook Academy of Art Museum, Bloomfield Hills, Michigan
The Dana-Thomas House, The Illinois Historic Preservation Agency, Springfield
Mr. and Mrs. Daniel Dietrich
D.P. Magner Arts & Crafts
Robert Edwards
Martin Eidelberg

Elizabeth's Olden Days
Everson Museum of Art, Syracuse
The Frank Lloyd Wright Memorial Foundation, Taliesin West, Scottsdale, Arizona
Mr. and Mrs. Henry E. Fuldner
Gebelein Silversmiths, East Arlington, Vermont
The Glessner House, Chicago Architecture Foundation
William and Marcia Goodman
Gordon William Gray
Stephen Gray
Greenville College, The Richard W. Bock Sculpture Collection, Greenville, Illinois
Conrad and Marsha Harper (courtesy of Jordan-Volpe Gallery)
Harvard University, Cambridge
Mary Kane and Ted Hendrickson
William and Mary Hersh
High Museum of Art, Atlanta
Hingham Historical Society, Hingham, Massachusetts
Historic Deerfield, Inc., Deerfield, Massachusetts
Betty and Robert A. Hut
Indianapolis Museum of Art
Frederick R. Innes
Mr. and Mrs. A.A. Jaussaud
Cynthia Lang
Library of Congress, Washington, D.C.
Lillian Nassau, Ltd.
Los Angeles County Museum of Art
Luther Collection
Boice Lydell, The Roycroft Arts Museum, East Aurora, New York
Malden Public Library, Malden, Massachusetts
Marie Zimmermann Archives
James and Janeen Marrin
The Metropolitan Museum of Art, New York
Marilee B. Meyer
Minneapolis Institute of Arts
"The Mission Inn" National Historic Landmark Hotel, Riverside, California

Moravian Pottery and Tile Works, Bucks County
Department of Parks and Recreation,
Doylestown, Pennsylvania
The Museum of Art, Rhode Island School of
Design, Providence
Museum of Fine Arts, Boston
Museum of Fine Arts of Houston
John H. Nally
National Museum of American History,
Smithsonian Institution, Washington, D.C.
Scott H. Nelson
New York Public Library, Rare Books and
Manuscripts Collection and the Spencer
Collection
David Norris
North Andover Historical Society, North
Andover, Massachusetts
Northwestern University, The Mary and Leigh
Block Gallery, Evanston, Illinois
Tazio Nuvolari
The Oakland Museum
Max Palevsky
P.G. Pugsley & Son Antiques
Lachlan Pitcairn
Pocumtuck Valley Memorial Association,
Memorial Hall Museum, Deerfield,
Massachusetts
Princeton University Library, Rare Books and
Special Collections
John R. Rivers
The Ross C. Purdy Museum of Ceramics,
Columbus, Ohio
Allan Sacks and Barbara Taff
San Diego Historical Society
San Diego Museum of Art
School of the Museum of Fine Arts, Boston
The Shack Collection
Mr. and Mrs. Andrew Shapiro
Sigma Phi Society, Alpha of Wisconsin, Madison
Edgar O. Smith
Society for the Preservation of New England

Antiquities, Boston
Southern Illinois University at Edwardsville,
University Museums
The State Historical Society of Wisconsin,
Madison
The Strong Museum, Rochester
Syracuse University, American Costume
Collection
Eleanor McDowell Thompson
Kenneth R. Trapp
University of California, Architectural Drawing
Collection, Santa Barbara
University of California, College of
Environmental Design, Documents Collection,
Berkeley
University of Chicago, Joseph Regenstein Library,
Special Collections
University City Public Library, University City,
Missouri
University of Minnesota, Northwest
Architectural Archives, Minneapolis
University of Pennsylvania, Architectural
Archives, Philadelphia
University of Rochester Library, Rochester
University of Southern California, Greene and
Greene Library, The Gamble House, Pasadena
The Van Briggle Art Pottery Company, Colorado
Springs
Jean-François Vilain and Roger S. Wieck
Wadsworth Atheneum, Hartford
Barbara V. Wamelink
Stan and Rilda Webb
Mr. and Mrs. Mark Willcox
Robert Winter
Worcester Art Museum
Yale University Art Gallery, New Haven
Mrs. Harvey Z. Yellin

Acknowledgments

First, I wish to thank Jan Fontein, Director, and Jonathan Fairbanks, Katharine Lane Weems Curator of American Decorative Arts and Sculpture, for giving me the opportunity to organize this exhibition and catalogue. The entire project owes a great deal to members of the Department of American Decorative Arts, whose chief curator gave his support, encouragement, and expert advice to every aspect of the project. In addition to writing many of the catalogue entries, the assistant curator Edward S. Cooke, Jr., reviewed other scholars' contributions, helped develop the exhibition story line, and contributed his wide-ranging knowledge of both materials and their meaning. The exhibition would not have been possible without the tireless efforts of the research assistant, Catherine Zusy. Her expertise was essential in the selection of objects for the exhibition, her management ability ensured that deadlines were met, and her design sense contributed greatly to the installation. Jennifer Dragone, National Museum Act intern, spent much of her year at the museum providing invaluable assistance for the exhibition, and Rachel Camber, Lauretta Dimmick, Paula Kozol, and Joy Cattanach Smith kindly took time from their other responsibilities to help with the myriad details of organization.

I am grateful to Ross W. Farrar, Deputy Director, and all his colleagues, including G. Peabody Gardner III, Janet Spitz, Kathy Duane and Drew Knowlton, for overseeing the administrative aspects of the project and the four generous grants that support it.

The assistance of volunteers and interns made an important contribution to the exhibition. Jane Becker helped to assemble the many components of the N.E.H. grant and wrote entries for the catalogue, Edith Alpers contributed meticulous bibliographic and proofreading skills, and Tracy Rubin assisted with many aspects of research and photography. Jeannine Fallino, Isabel Taube, Leslie Bodenstein, Sarah Giffen, and Nancy Spiegel also deserve appreciation.

Grateful acknowledgment is extended also to colleagues in other departments of the Museum. Francine Flynn and Lynn Herrmann Traub coordinated the complicated registration procedures. Janice Sorkow, assisted by Sandra Mongeon, Jane Hankins, and Ann Petrone, oversaw the administration of photography. The Museum photographers – John Woolf, John Lutsch, and Gary Ruuska – provided outstanding images, as did the freelance photographers Rick Echelmeyer, Lynn Dianne De Marco, and others. With "The Art that is Life" Carl Zahn added to his long list of superbly designed museum catalogues. Wendy Moran's word processing and organizational skills were invaluable, as was her unfailing good humor. Janet O'Donoghue and Kathy Dusenbury in the Publications office also helped in many ways.

The museum conservators generously gave their time and expertise in the preparation of objects for display. We would like to thank especially Robert Walker and Sue Odell in Furniture Conservation; Arthur Beale, Pamela Hatchfield, Merville Nichols, and Margaret Leveque in the Research Laboratory; Leslie Smith, Monica Vroon and Kathleen Dardes in Textile Conservation; Karin Bengtson in the Textile Department; and Roy Perkinson, Gail English, and Elizabeth Lunning in Prints Conservation.

The Education department – especially William Burback, Barbara Martin, Joan Hobson, Vishakha Desai, and Nancy Howard – contributed much to the success of special programs and exhibition interpretation. Linda Patch and Joan Norris did an outstanding job generating publicity. Special thanks must go to Nancy Allen, librarian; Patricia Chappell, director of special events; Chuck Thomas, director of membership; Carl Beck, assistant director of membership, and Russell Hamilton, whose conscientiousness helped ensure the safe arrival of objects.

Bringing to the project a great sensitivity to the interpretation of objects, Elroy Quenroe and David Mihaly of Quenroe Design Associates created an imaginative and beautiful installation.

The interdisciplinary skills required to examine the breadth and complexity of the Arts and Crafts movement were contributed by a number of scholars outside the Museum: Robert Judson Clark, Associate Professor of Art and Archaeology at Princeton University, coauthored the essay on style; Richard Guy Wilson, Associate Professor of Architectural History at the University of Virginia, contributed entries and the essay on architecture; Eileen Boris, Assistant Professor of History at Howard University, analyzed the social history of the movement; Robert Edwards, editor of the journal Tiller, examined the nature of work process; Cheryl Robertson, Associate Curator of Education at the Winterthur Museum, wrote about the Arts and Crafts home; and Sally Buchanan

Kinsey, Associate Professor of Costume and Textiles at Syracuse University, wrote entries and the essay on dress reform. W. Scott Braznell, a metals scholar, wrote the entries on metals; Ellen Paul Denker, a ceramics history scholar, and Bert Randall Denker, librarian of the Decorative Arts Photographic Collection at the Winterthur Museum, wrote the entries on ceramics; Gillian Moss, Assistant Curator of Textiles at the Cooper-Hewitt Museum, wrote the textile entries; and Susan Otis Thompson, Associate Professor of Library Science at Columbia University, wrote those concerning books.

In addition to writing essays and entries for the catalogue, the consultants to the exhibition were invaluable in the process of selecting objects: W. Scott Braznell, metals; Ellen and Bert Denker, ceramics; Robert L. Edwards, furniture; Sally Buchanan Kinsey, costumes; Gillian Moss, textiles; Cheryl Robertson, various media; Susan Thompson, books; and Richard Guy Wilson, architectural drawings. Robert Judson Clark, Ellen and Bert Denker, Robert Edwards, and Cheryl Robertson also donated countless hours to help structure the themes and organization of the exhibition. Eileen Boris's comments and suggestions for the essays made this a better book. Robert Edwards shared his furniture research with Catherine Zusy and thoughtfully critiqued her entries.

Betty and Robert A. Hut provided special assistance with the selection of ceramics for the exhibition. Their expertise in the field of art pottery and knowledge of collections across the country were important contributions. Jean-François Vilain generously gave his knowledge and editorial skills as a reader for the pottery and book entries. Sharon Darling, Martin Eidelberg, and Kenneth R. Trapp shared both their erudition and research.

It is a pleasure to thank colleagues at other institutions who have assisted with research and made their collections available. The following individuals are among the many who have helped: Milo M. Naeve, Anndora Morginson, John Zukowsky, Pauline A. Saliga, and Susan Glover Godlewski at The Art Institute of Chicago; Sandra Tatman, Bruce Laverty, Roger Moss, and Herbert Mitchell at The Athenaeum of Philadelphia; John Lewis at the Berea College Appalachian Museum in Berea, Kentucky; Sinclair Hitchings, and all of the Fine Arts Reference Department at the Boston Public Library, especially Noreen M. O'Gara; Dianne H. Pilgrim, Kevin Stayton, and Christopher Wilk at

The Brooklyn Museum; Louise Braunschwinger at the California Historical Society in Los Angeles; Douglas Haller at the California Historical Society in San Francisco; Sarah M. Addison at the Cambridge City Public Library in Indiana; Phillip Johnston and Sarah Nichols at the Museum of American Art of The Carnegie Institute in Pittsburgh; Sharon Darling, Olivia Mahoney, Janice McNeill, and Elizabeth Jachimowicz at the Chicago Historical Society; Martha Bickel at Christ Church in Cranbrook, Michigan; Anita Ellis, Carol Schoelkopf, and Mona L. Chapin at the Cincinnati Museum of Art; Henry H. Hawley at the Cleveland Museum of Art; Virginia Raguin at the College of the Holy Cross in Worcester; Janet Parks at the Avery Architectural and Fine Arts Library, Ohla della Cava at the School of Library Service Library, and Kenneth Lohf at the Rare Books and Manuscripts Library, all of Columbia University; Robert Trent and Christopher P. Bickford at the Connecticut Historical Society in Hartford; Orin E. Skinner, Rebecca Breymann, and Marilyn Justice at Charles J. Connick Associates in Boston; Lisa Taylor, Elaine Evans Dee, Lucy Commoner, and Konstanze Bachmann at the Cooper-Hewitt Museum of The Smithsonian Institution's National Museum of Design in New York; Susan Waller and Mark Coir at The Cranbrook Academy of Art Museum in Bloomfield Hills, Michigan; Donald Hallmark at The Dana-Thomas House of The Illinois Historic Preservation Agency in Springfield; Tina Hess at the Darien Library in Connecticut; Ann C. Madonia at The Davenport Art Gallery in Iowa; David A. Hanks of David A. Hanks & Associates; Electa Kane Tritsch and Kathy L. Kottaridis at The Dedham Historical Society; Tom Beckman at The Delaware Historical Society in Wilmington; Nancy Shaw and Sarah Towne Hufford at the Detroit Institute of Arts; Jeanine M. Head and Judith Endelman at the Edison Institute and Michael Ettema at the Henry Ford Museum and Greenfield Village in Dearborn, Michigan; Anne Farnam at the Essex Institute in Salem; Barbara Perry and John Rexine at the Everson Museum of Art in Syracuse; Marilynn Johnson at the Fashion Institute of Technology in New York; Richard Wattenmaker at the Flint Institute of Arts in Michigan; Bruce Pfeiffer and Indira Berndtson at The Frank Lloyd Wright Memorial Foundation, *Taliesin West*, in Scottsdale, Arizona; Edgard Moreno at Gebelein Silversmiths in East Arlington, Vermont; Amy S. Doherty, Mark Weimer, and others at the George Arents Research

Library of Syracuse University; Elaine Harrington and William Brubaker at The Glessner House, Chicago Architecture Foundation; Gordon Olson, Pamela D. Boynton, and Helen Bisbee at the Grand Rapids Public Library; Nancy S. Powell at the Grand Rapids Public Museum; Teren Duffin at The Historical Society of the Town of Greenwich, Inc.; Guy Chase of The Richard W. Bock Sculpture Collection at Greenville College in Illinois; Nancy Finlay, Eleanor Garvey, and Lawrence Dowler at the Houghton Library and Louise Todd Ambler and Ada Bortuluzzi at the Harvard University Art Museums, Cambridge; Donald Peirce, Woodrow Mankin, Elizabeth Bacchetti and Frances Francis at the High Museum of Art in Atlanta; Evelyn C. Cheney at the Hingham Historical Society; Donald R. Friary, J. Peter Spang, and Phil Zea at Historic Deerfield, Inc.; Catherine Ricciardelli Davis and Katherine Lippert at the Indianapolis Museum of Art; Mary E. Carver at the J.B. Speed Art Museum in Louisville; Mimi Henson Rogers at the Jekyll Island Museum in Georgia; Phyllis Danielson at the Kendall School of Design in Grand Rapids; Robert J. Sullivan at Lenox China in Trenton; Donna Elliot at the Library of Congress; Leslie Greene Bowman, Anita Feldman, and John Passi at the Los Angeles County Museum of Art; Harold Schlackman at Marcus and Co. of Kay Jewelers; Marianne Curling at the Mark Twain Memorial in Hartford; James Blackaby at The Mercer Museum in Doylestown, Pennsylvania; Morrison H. Heckscher, Alice Cooney Frelinghuysen, Frances Gruber Stafford, Craig R. Miller and Mary Lawrence at The Metropolitan Museum of Art, New York; Euloda L. Fetcha, Town Historian in Mexico, New York; Terry Marvel at the Milwaukee Art Museum; Michael Conforti and Francis J. Puig at the Minneapolis Institute of Arts; Amy Ryan at the Minneapolis Public Library and Information Center; Theresa Hanley and Pam Young at "The Mission Inn" National Historic Landmark Hotel in Riverside, California; Charles Yeske and Mandy Sallade at the Moravian Pottery and Tile Works, Bucks County Department of Parks and Recreation in Doylestown, Pennsylvania; David P. Donaldson at The Morse Gallery of Art in Winter Park, Florida; Katherine Howe and Carl Venable at The Museum of Fine Arts in Houston; Christopher Monkhouse and Thomas S. Michie at The Museum of Art of the Rhode Island School of Design in Providence; Susan Meyers, Sheila Machlis Alexander, Regina Blaszczyk, and Spencer R. Crew at the National Museum of American History of the Smithsonian Institution in Washington, D.C.; Ulysses Dietz and Margaret Di Salvi at The Newark Museum; Robert Rainwater, Roberta Waddell, Daniel Tierney, Joseph Arkins, and others at the New York Public Library; Martha Hamilton at the North Andover Historical Society in Massachusetts; Kathy Kelsey Foley and Jim Riggs-Bonamici at The Mary and Leigh Block Gallery of Northwestern University in Evanston, Illinois; Christine Droll, Harvey Jones, and Inez Brooks-Myers at The Oakland Museum; Conrad Weitzel and Gary Arnold at the Ohio Historical Society in Columbus; Betsy Fahlman at Old Dominion University in Norfolk, Virginia; Terrance M. Prior at the Oswego County Historical Society in New York; William L. Dulaney at The Pennsylvania State University in State College; Beatrice Garvan and Wendy Christie at the Philadelphia Museum of Art; Suzanne L. Flynt at the Memorial Hall Museum and David R. Proper at the Library of the Pocumtuck Valley Memorial Association in Deerfield; Peter Bunnell and Maria B. Pellerano at Princeton University and Richard Ludwig in the Rare Books and Special Collections of the Princeton University Library; Gregg Fisher at The Ross C. Purdy Museum of Ceramics in Columbus, Ohio; Kitty Turgeon and Robert Rust at The Roycroft Inn in East Aurora, New York; Christina Nelson, Doris Sturzenberger, and Kristan McKinsey at The Saint Louis Art Museum; Bruce Kammerling and Cathleen Crawford at the San Diego Historical Society; William S. Chandler and Louis Goldrich at the San Diego Museum of American Art; Bruce MacDonald at the School of the Museum of Fine Arts in Boston; Dr. Samuel Moore of Sigma Phi Society, Alpha of Wisconsin, in Madison; staff at the Skaneateles Historical Society in Skaneateles, New York; Richard Nylander and Elinor Reichlin at the Society for the Preservation of New England Antiquities in Boston; Michael Mason, David Huntley and Eric Barnett at the University Museums of Southern Illinois University in Edwardsville; Anne Woodhouse at The State Historical Society of Wisconsin in Madison; Mary-Ellen Earl Perry, Melissa A. Morgan, Lynette Francisco, and Susan Williams at The Strong Museum in Rochester; Terry Jones at the Syracuse University American Costume Collection; Janet Zapata at Tiffany and Co., New York; staff at the Bancroft Library of the University of California in Berkeley; David Gebhard and Gavin Townsend at the Architectural Draw-

ing Collection of the University of California in Santa Barbara; Margaret Wong, Annemarie Adams, Stephen Tobrinder, and Elizabeth Byrne at the Documents Collection, College of Environmental Design, of the University of California in Berkeley; Jeffry Abt in the Special Collections at the Joseph Regenstein Library of the University of Chicago; Linda Ballard at the University City Public Library in University City, Missouri; Alan Lathrop at the Northwest Architectural Archives of the University of Minnesota in Minneapolis; Julia Converse at the Architectural Archives of the University of Pennsylvania in Philadelphia; Mary H. Huth at the University of Rochester Library; Randell L. Makinson and James Benjamin at the Greene and Greene Library, The Gamble House in Pasadena and Alison Clark, also of the University of Southern California in Los Angeles; Deborah Fulton at the University of Virginia in Charlottesville; Ken Stevenson at The Van Briggle Art Pottery Company in Colorado Springs; staff at the Art Library of the Victoria and Albert Museum in London; William Hosley, Gregory Hedberg, and David H. Parrish at the Wadsworth Atheneum in Hartford; Nancy Perry Fetterman at the Washington Cathedral in Washington, D.C.; Richard Longstreth at George Washington University in Washington, D.C.; Barbara Ward, Nancy G. Evans, and Neville Thompson at the Winterthur Museum; Susan E. Strickler, Elizabeth Roessel, and Sally R. Freitag at the Worcester Art Museum; Patricia E. Kane, Janine Skerry, David Barquist, and Michael Komanecky at the Yale University Art Gallery in New Haven.

By sharing their collections and providing unpublished information concerning designers and craftsmen, many individuals were of great assistance to this project. They include: Susan H. Anderson-Hay, Jack Andrews, Al Audi, Arthur E. Baggs, Jr., Florence Balasny-Barnes, James Benjamin, Catherine Little Bert, Carey W. Bok, Curtis Bok, William Bowers, Charles H. Carpenter, Jr., Barbara Carson, Henry L. Caulkins, Elenita C. Chickering, Maurice J. Clifford, M.D., Alan Crawford, Stephen Dennis, the late Henry Dubois, Joseph R. Dunlap, Michael Ettema, Paul Evans, Jean France, Roy Frangiamore, Herman W. Glendenning, Alexander Yale Goriansky, Frank Grebe, George Grillo, Knut Günther, Henry Lyon Hall, Wilbert Hasbrouck, Barry Haynes, Margery B. Howe, Michael James, Kathleen and Gregory Johnson, Edward Kattel, Barbara Kramer, Susan Larkin, Wendy Lehing, Robert Aaron Levy, Andy Lopez, Anne

B. Loring, Robie Macauley, Don Marek, Larry Marsh, David Mason, Ellsworth Mason, L.J. McElroy, Mavina McFeron, Mr. and Mrs. William McGuire, Mr. and Mrs. James McWilliams, Derek Ostergard, Andrew Passeri, Gordon Pfeiffer, Mr. and Mrs. Christopher Pullman, Cleota Reed, Barbara Rimer, Sonia Richardson, William Rubin, Ronald Saarinen Swanson, Mr. and Mrs. Robert J. Sallick, Viktor Schreckengost, Randy Sandler, Mr. and Mrs. Jerome Shaw, Earle Shettleworth, Jr., Jerome E. Sikorski, Rollo Silver, Ira Simon, Stanley Skwarek, Mary Anne Smith, Philip Sperling, Ronald Saarinen Swanson, Diana Stradling, Ed Teitelman, Susan Tunick, Michael J. Weller, Peg Weiss, Linda Welters, Robert Winter, Don Williams, M.D., and Philip Zucker.

Auction houses and art dealers helped to locate objects and contributed their expert knowledge – in particular, Michael J. Weller of Argentum Antiques, Ltd.; Rosalie Berberian of Ark Antiques; James Bakker of Bakker on Broadway; Michael Carey; D. Roger Howlett of Childs Gallery; J. Alastair Duncan and Nancy McClelland of Christie, Manson and Woods International, Inc.; L. Meyer at Greystone Gardens Vintage Clothing; Scott Elliott of Kelmscott Gallery; Beth Cathers, Vance Jordan, and Todd Volpe of the Jordan-Volpe Gallery; Don Magner, Arts and Crafts; Paul Nassau of Lillian Nassau, Ltd.; Bryce R. Bannatyne, Jr., of P.G. Pugsley and Son; David Rago; Andrew Shapiro of Phillips, Son and Neale; Marilee Meyers of Robert W. Skinner, Inc.; and Roger Williams.

The deepest appreciation and gratitude must be extended to both public and private lenders to "The Art That is Life," who are listed separately. Private collectors shared not only their objects but also their research and knowledge. They kindly cooperated with our photography and transport schedules and generously agreed to part with cherished possessions for the eighteen-month run of the exhibition.

Finally, Philip Rodney, Ellen Rothman, and Joseph Ayoub, Jr., were always willing to read and critique the seemingly endless drafts of the catalogue. They and other friends offered the support and encouragement essential to the completion of this work.

WENDY KAPLAN
Exhibition Director

Color Plates

1. *Six-paneled window for William Watts Sherman house, Newport, Rhode Island, 1877-1878*
Designer: John La Farge (1835-1910) ⟩

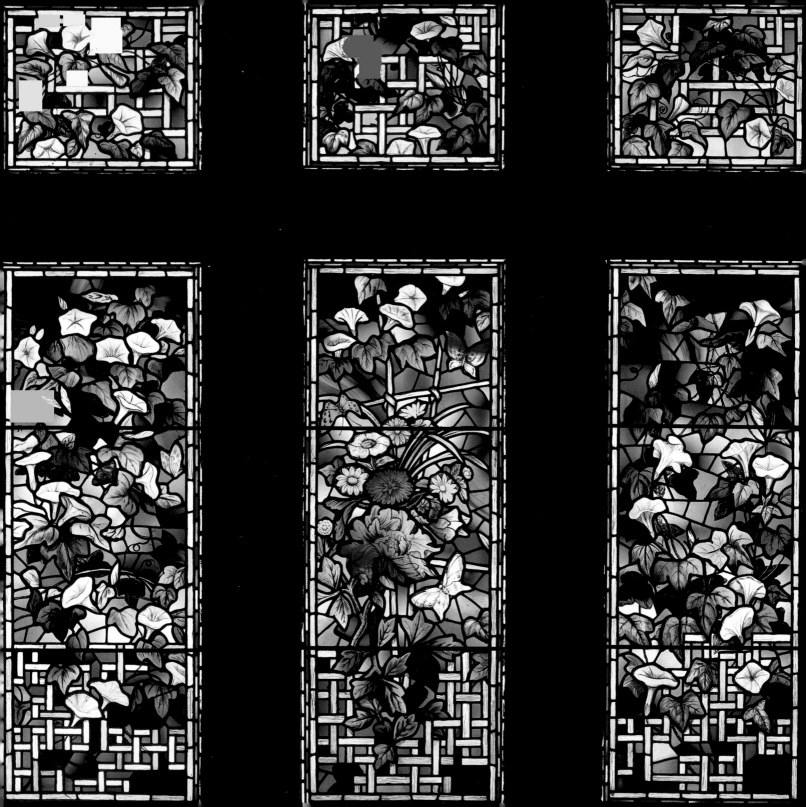

9. *Tiles, 1881/83-1895*
Low Art Tile Works (1878-1907), Chelsea,
Massachusetts

⟨ **3.** *Portière, ca. 1885*
Associated Artists, New York (Candace Wheeler,
director)
Maker: probably Cheney Bros., South
Manchester, Connecticut

10. *Pitcher, ca. 1878*
Tiffany & Co., New York (1837 to present)

12. *Center table, for the James J. Goodwin house, Hartford,*
ca. 1874–1878
Herter Brothers, New York (1865-1905) ⟩

14. *Standing desk,* 1876
Designer and carver: Mary Louise McLaughlin,
Cincinnati (1847-1939)

15. *Armchair, ca. 1876*
Maker unknown, possibly from Gardner,
Massachusetts

31 a and b. *Two vases, ca. 1888*
Chelsea Keramic Art Works (1872-1889), Chelsea,
Massachusetts
Hugh C. Robertson (1845-1908)

⟨ **20.** *Alms basin,* 1914
George Ernest Germer (1868-1936)

32. *Vase*, 1899
Rookwood Pottery Company (1880-1960),
Cincinnati
Decorator: Kataro Shirayamadani (1865-1948)

35. *Armchair, ca. 1894-ca. 1920s*
David Wolcott Kendall (1851-1910)
Phoenix Furniture Company, Grand Rapids,
Michigan (founded in 1870) ⟩

36. *Center table from the William Prindle house, Duluth, Minnesota, ca. 1905*
Designer: John Scott Bradstreet (1845-1914), Minneapolis
Maker: John S. Bradstreet and Co., Minneapolis

37. *Lighting fixture for H.M. Robinson house, Pasadena 1906*
Designers: Charles Sumner Greene (1868-1957) and Henry Mather Greene (1870-1954)
Manufacturer: Emil Lange, Los Angeles (wooden fixture made by Peter Hall) ⟩

38. *Three-panel screen, ca. 1900*
Tiffany Studios, New York

42. *Vase*, 1902-1907
Weller Pottery Company (1872-1949), Zanesville,
Ohio
Decorator: Jacques Sicard (active in U.S 1902-
1907; d. in France 1923)

72. *Presentation drawing: aerial perspective for expansion of Glenwood Mission Inn, Riverside California (between Main and Orange and 6th and 7th Streets [undergoing restoration currently]),* 1908
Architect: Arthur Burnett Benton (1857-1927)
Renderer: William A. Sharp (1864-1944)

85. *Presentation rendering: front perspective for Ward W. Willits house, Highland Park, Illinois (1445 Sheridan Road),* 1902-1903
Frank Lloyd Wright (1867-1959)

84. *Architectural ornament for Henry Babson residence, Riverside, Illinois,* 1908-1909 (destroyed)
Designers: Louis H. Sullivan (1856-1924) and George A. Elmslie (1871-1952)
Modeler: probably Kristian Schneider)

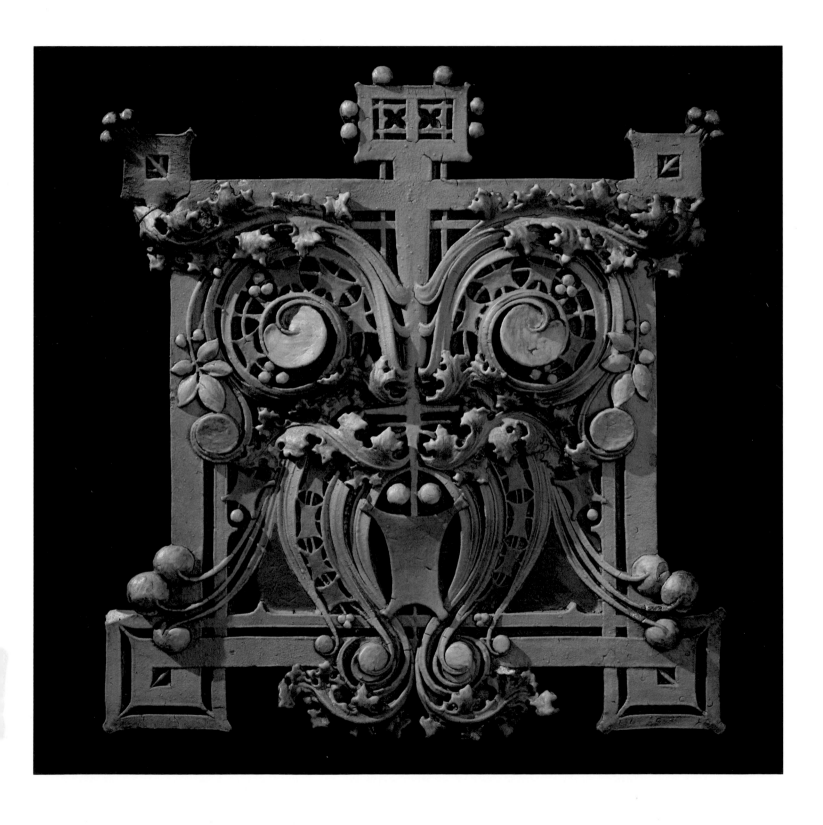

80. *Rectangular box with lid, 1929*
Designer: Lucia Kleinhans Mathews (1870-1955)

106. *China cabinet, ca. 1906*
The Shop of the Crafters, Cincinnati (1904-1920) ⟩

108. *Vase*, 1908
Adelaide Alsop Robineau (1865-1924), Syracuse

110. *Vase*, ca. 1900
Biloxi Art Pottery (1878-1884 - ca. 1909) of George
E. Ohr (1857-1918), Biloxi, Mississippi

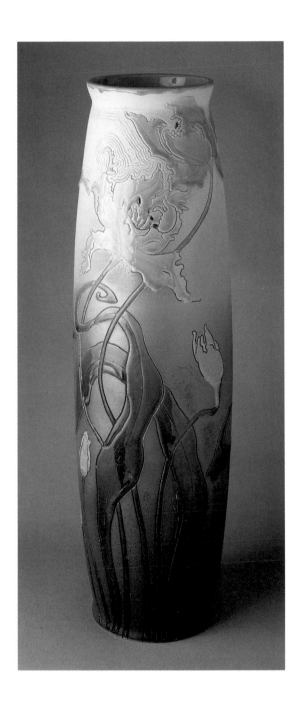

114. *Vase, ca.* 1929
Pewabic Pottery (1903-1961), Detroit
Mary Chase Perry Stratton (1867-1961)

123. *Vase, ca.* 1905
Roseville Pottery Company (1892-1954),
Zanesville and Roseville, Ohio
Designer: Gazo Fudji (also Fujiyama, Foudji)
(working ca. 1905)

117. *Vase*, 1899-1912
Grueby Faience Company (1897-1909) or Grueby
Pottery Company (1907-1913), Boston
Designer: attributed to George Prentiss Kendrick
(active with Grueby 1897-1901)
Decorator: Gertrude Stanwood

119. *Tile*, 1906-1920
Grueby Faience Company (1897-1909), Grueby
Pottery Company (1907-1913), or Grueby Faience
and Tile Company (1909-1920), Boston
Designer: Addison B. LeBoutillier (1872-1951) ⟩

129. *Box*, 1922
Elizabeth E. Copeland (1866-1957), Boston

126. *Brooch*, 1904–1905
A. Fogliata (active ca. 1903-1905), Hull-House
Shops (ca. 1898-ca. 1940), Chicago

133. *Tea and coffee set, ca. 1910*
Designer: Louis Rorimer (1872-1940)
The Rokesley Shop, at Rorimer-Brooks Studios
Co., Cleveland

144. *Jardinière, ca. 1902*
Arthur J. Stone (1847-1938), Gardner,
Massachusetts

⟨ **137.** *Table lamp, probably 1911-1915*
Dirk Van Erp (1859-1933), San Francisco (probably after a design by Eleanor D'Arcy Gaw [active
ca. 1900-1920])

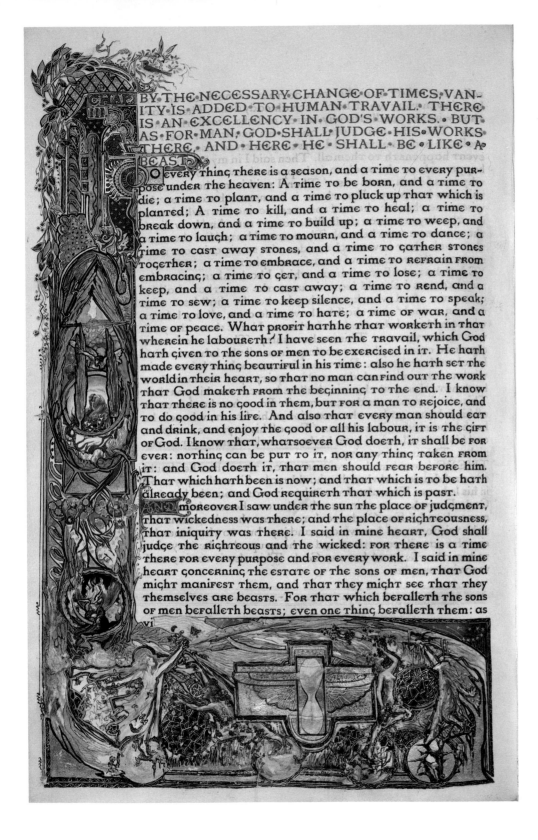

BY·THE·NECESSARY·CHANGE·OF·TIMES, VAN-
ITY·IS·ADDED·TO·HUMAN·TRAVAIL· THERE
IS·AN·EXCELLENCY·IN·GOD'S·WORKS· BUT·
AS·FOR·MAN, GOD·SHALL·JUDGE·HIS·WORKS
THERE· AND·HERE· HE· SHALL·BE· LIKE· A·
BEAST

TO every thing there is a season, and a time to every purpose under the heaven: A time to be born, and a time to
die; a time to plant, and a time to pluck up that which is
planted; A time to kill, and a time to heal; a time to
break down, and a time to build up; a time to weep, and
a time to laugh; a time to mourn, and a time to dance; a
time to cast away stones, and a time to gather stones
together; a time to embrace, and a time to refrain from
embracing; a time to get, and a time to lose; a time to
keep, and a time to cast away; a time to rend, and a
time to sew; a time to keep silence, and a time to speak;
a time to love, and a time to hate; a time of war, and a
time of peace. What profit hath he that worketh in that
wherein he laboureth? I have seen the travail, which God
hath given to the sons of men to be exercised in it. He hath
made every thing beautiful in his time: also he hath set the
world in their heart, so that no man can find out the work
that God maketh from the beginning to the end. I know
that there is no good in them, but for a man to rejoice, and
to do good in his life. And also that every man should eat
and drink, and enjoy the good of all his labour, it is the gift
of God. I know that, whatsoever God doeth, it shall be for
ever: nothing can be put to it, nor any thing taken from
it: and God doeth it, that men should fear before him.
That which hath been is now; and that which is to be hath
already been; and God requireth that which is past.
AND moreover I saw under the sun the place of judgment,
that wickedness was there; and the place of righteousness,
that iniquity was there. I said in mine heart, God shall
judge the righteous and the wicked: for there is a time
there for every purpose and for every work. I said in mine
heart concerning the estate of the sons of men, that God
might manifest them, and that they might see that they
themselves are beasts. For that which befalleth the sons
of men befalleth beasts; even one thing befalleth them: as
vi

149. *Ecclesiastes, or the Preacher; and the Song of Solomon,*
1902
Ballantyne Press, London. Printed under the
supervision of Charles Ricketts
Designer and illuminator: da Loria Norman
(1872-1935)

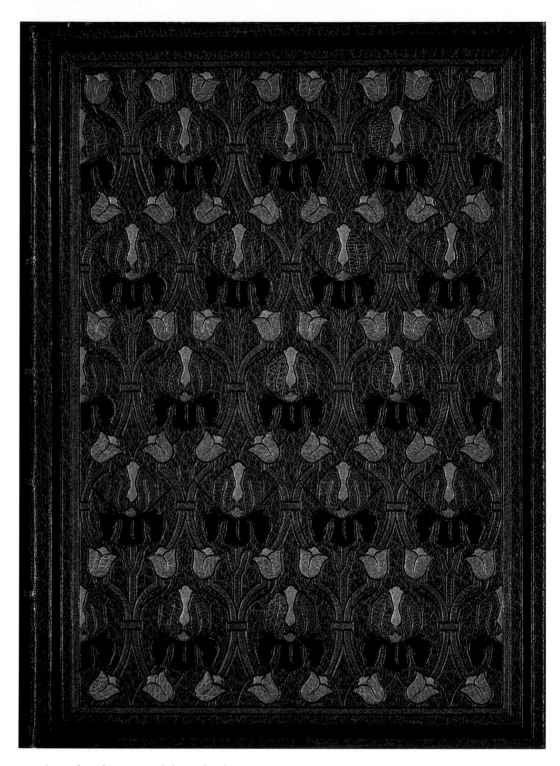

150. *Flowers of Song from Many Lands*, by Frederick
Rowland Marvin, 1902
Pafraets Book Company, Troy, New York (printed
at the Merrymount Press, Boston)
Designer of binding: Mary Crease Sears (executed
by Agnes St. John)

164. *Vase,* 1915
Paul Revere Pottery (1911-1942) of the Saturday
Evening Girls' Club, Boston/Brighton,
Massachusetts
Decorator: Sarah Gelner (1894-1982)

⟨ **157.** *Poster for Bradley, His Book,* 1896
Wayside Press, Springfield, Massachusetts
Artist: Will Bradley (1868-1962)

165. *"Linen Press" cabinet, ca.* 1904
Byrdcliffe Colony, Woodstock, New York
Panel designer: Zulma Steele

167. Crib, 1922
Frank Jeck (dates unknown), Bryn Athyn,
Pennsylvania

178. *Lamp*, 1904
Newcomb Pottery (1895-1940), New Orleans
Decorator: Mary Gavin Sheerer (1865-1954)

179. *Vase*, 1909
Newcomb Pottery (1895-1940), New Orleans
Decorator: Sarah Agnes Estelle Irvine (1887-1970)

183. *Vase*, 1911
University City Pottery (1910-1912), University
City, Missouri
Decorator: Frederick Hurten Rhead (1880-1942)

193. *Wallpaper frieze, 1900-1905*
H.B.H. Company (origin unknown)

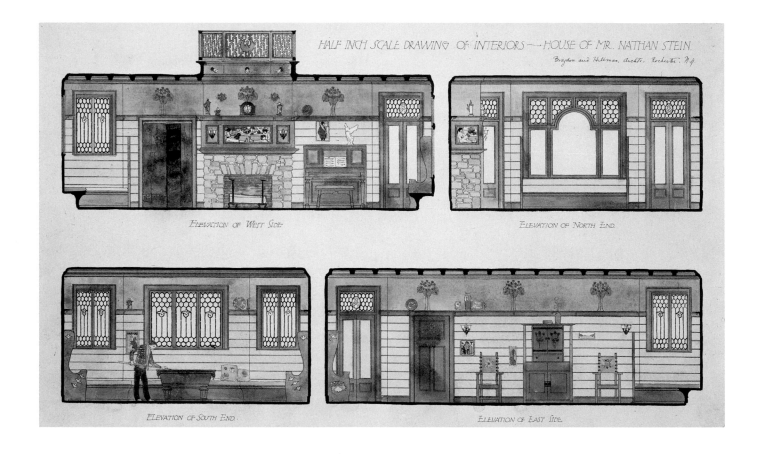

195. Elevations of living room (west and east sides, north and south ends) for Nathan Stein summer house, Ontario Beach, New York, 1897-1899
Architects: Bragdon and Hillman (Claude Fayette Bragdon [1866-1946] and James Constable Hillman (1863-1932)

199. *Presentation perspective: "Casas Grandes" project for*
Homer Laughlin, Hollywood, California, ca. 1912-1915
(never built)
Architect: Irving John Gill (1870-1936)

200. *Cushion cover, early 20th century*
Embroiderer: Annie May Hegeman, New York
City (after a design by Morris & Co., London)

205. *Morris chair, ca. 1910*
The Craftsman Workshops, Eastwood (near
Syracuse), New York ⟩

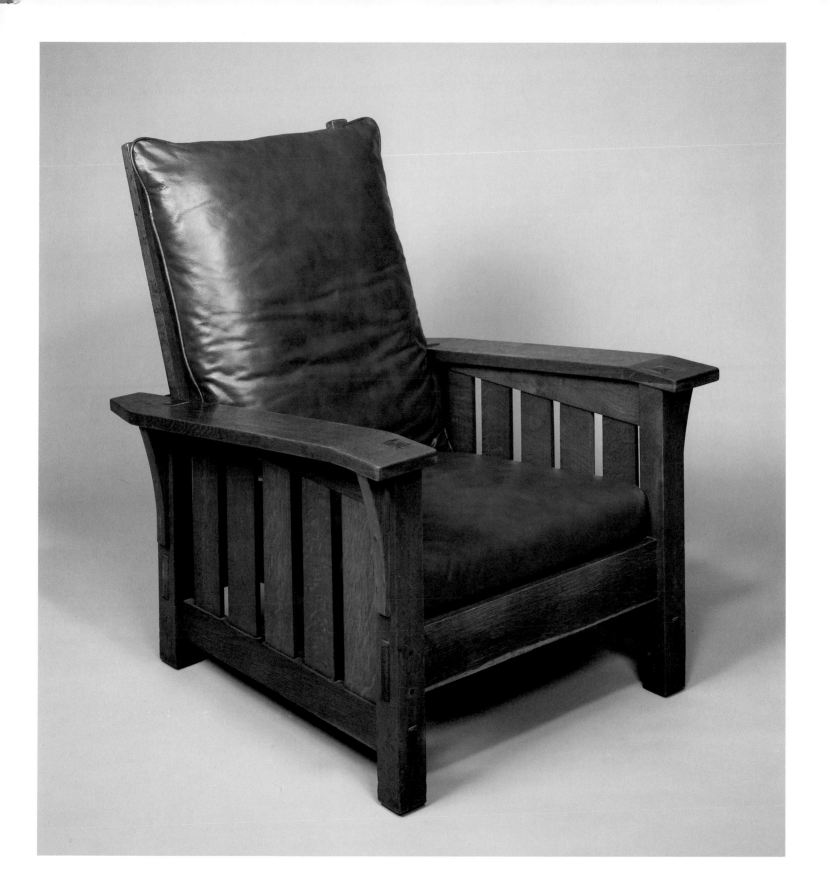

213. *Rendering for the dining room of the Susan Lawrence Dana house, Springfield, Illinois, ca. 1903*
Architect: Frank Lloyd Wright (1867-1959)

214. *Window for Susan Lawrence Dana house, Springfield, Illinois, 1903*
Designer: Frank Lloyd Wright (1869-1959)
Manufacturer: Linden Glass Company, Chicago ⟩

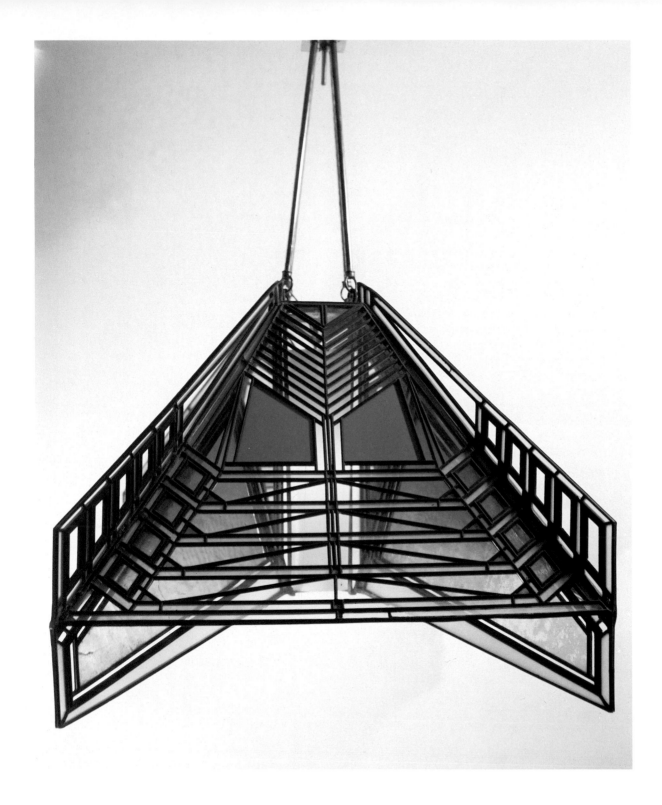

215. *Hanging lamp for the Susan Lawrence Dana house,*
Springfield, Illinois, 1903
Designer: Frank Lloyd Wright (1869-1959)
Manufacturer: Linden Glass Company, Chicago

217. *Armchair for Rockledge, Homer, Minnesota, ca. 1912*
Designer: George Washington Maher (1864-1926) ⟩

219. *Table lamp for Rockledge, Homer, Minnesota, ca.*
1912
Designer: George Washington Maher (1864-1926)

222. *Writing table, from the Robert R. Blacker house,*
Pasadena, 1907
Designers: Charles Sumner Greene (1868-1957)
and Henry Mather Greene (1870-1954)
Maker: Peter Hall Manufacturing Company,
Pasadena ⟩

223. *Arm chair from the Robert R. Blacker house, Pasadena, 1907*
Designer: Charles Sumner Greene (1868-1957)
and Henry Mather Greene (1870-1954)
Maker: Peter Hall Manufacturing Company,
Pasadena

Introduction:
Origins of the Movement

The Lamp of British Precedent: An Introduction to the Arts and Crafts Movement

Wendy Kaplan

William Price's phrase "the art that is life," used as the subtitle of his periodical *The Artsman*, was a succinct expression of the ideal underlying the Arts and Crafts movement.[1] Convinced that industrialization had caused the degradation of work and the destruction of the environment, Arts and Crafts reformers created works with deliberate social messages. Their designs conveyed strong convictions about what was wrong with society and reflected prescriptions for living. Passionately committed to righting social ills, groups of English and American reformers chose art as their medium. Some advocated a return to medieval craft systems; others retreated to utopian communities; and still others established schools of design, sought new ways to organize industry, and initiated crafts philanthropies.

The Arts and Crafts ideal was not so much a style as an approach, an attitude toward the making of objects. Neither the British nor the American movement was monolithic; both included people of varying convictions. A rigid definition of those who belonged, based solely on criteria of style, method and quantity of production, or attitude toward the machine would exclude many of its adherents. Participation in the movement is therefore being defined broadly enough to include all those who shared its goals of rationalizing, simplifying, and unifying work and environment.

Alan Crawford designates the 1880s as a beginning date for the Arts and Crafts in Britain, when the movement became "aware of itself" and gave itself a name.[2] Other art historians assign the 1890s as the time of inception in the United States. Both dates are limiting, since they consign major figures such as John Ruskin and William Morris to the position of forerunners and make the work of such architect-designers as H.H. Richardson and Frank Furness (nos. 13 and 16) "Arts and Crafts before its time."[3] This catalogue treats the 1870s and 1880s as the first Arts and Crafts period. By this time, sufficient consensus existed on both sides of the Atlantic about the need for reforms. In America, however, the zenith of the Arts and Crafts movement took place a generation later, between 1890 and 1910, and was characterized by the dramatic blossoming of societies, guilds, and classes, all of which had direct roots in England.

One early-nineteenth-century British reformer, A.W.N. Pugin (1812-1852), looked to preindustrial England for inspiration. Deploring classical styles, he favored the asymmetry and naturalism of Gothic ornamentation. Pugin did not pioneer the revival of the Gothic, but he was among the first to imbue it with a moral dimension, asserting that its use would restore values that had been corrupted by the modern world. A convert to Catholicism, Pugin idealized the medieval for its most important artistic venture – the building of the great cathedrals. They were for him evidence of an order and stability, sense of community, and joy in labor missing from nineteenth-century life. His *Contrasts* (1836) compared the medieval and Victorian worlds and found the latter wanting (fig. 1). In its seeming lack of design standards he saw a deteriorating quality of life. Only by espousing Gothic principles, he believed, would standards be restored: "The two great rules for design are these: 1st, that there should be no features about a building which are not necessary for convenience, construction, or propriety; 2nd, that all ornament should consist of enrichment of the essential construction of the building."[4] Pugin did not advocate mere aping of Gothic forms; rather, he urged selective adaptation to combat "the present decay of taste."[5] Such adaptation is seen in a sideboard of 1835 (fig. 2),

THE SAME TOWN IN 1840.

1. St Michaels Tower, rebuilt in 1750. 2. New Parsonage House & Pleasure Grounds. 3. The New Jail. 4. Gas Works. 5. Lunatic Asylum. 6. Iron Works & Ruins of St Maries Abbey. 7. Mr Evans Chapel. 8. Baptist Chapel. 9. Unitarian Chapel. 10. New Church. 11 New Town Hall & Concert Room. 12. Wesleyan Centenary Chapel. 13. New Christian Society. 14. Quakers Meeting. 15. Socialist Hall of Science.

Catholic town in 1440.

1. St Michaels on the Hill. 2. Queens Cross. 3. St Thomas's Chapel. 4. St Maries Abbey. 5. All Saints. 6. St Johns. 7. St Peters. 8. St Alkmunds. 9. St Maries. 10. St Edmunds. 11. Grey Friars. 12. St Cuthberts. 13. Guild hall. 14. Trinity. 15. St Olaves. 16. St Botolphs.

Fig. 1. Plates from A.W.N. Pugin, *Contrasts*, second edition (London, 1841), showing the same town in the middle ages and in Victorian times.

Fig. 2. Design for a sideboard, illustrated in A.W.N. Pugin, *Gothic Furniture in the Style of the Fifteenth Century* (London, 1835).

Fig. 3. William Morris (designer), Jeffrey and Company (manufacturer). "Trellis" wallpaper (sample), 1864. Trustees of the Victoria and Albert Museum, London.

which features Gothic cusps and vaulting scaled down from a building; the roundels are reminiscent of heraldry.[6]

Pugin's critique of contemporary life, his search for simpler and more functional design, and the inspiration he derived from the Gothic past all influenced the next generation of design reformers.[7] His goal of reuniting art and labor, designer and craftsman, and the spiritual with the everyday provided the ideological foundations of the Arts and Crafts movement. Giving provisional sanction to the use of machinery, Pugin stated, "We do not want to arrest the course of inventions, but to confine these inventions to their legitimate uses . . . "[8] – a viewpoint that would be echoed by later Arts and Crafts leaders who were not against technological innovation, but who believed that machines should be be used only to relieve the tedium of mindless, repetitive tasks.

John Ruskin (1819-1900), the first professor of art history at Oxford University and the most influential art critic of his day, shared Pugin's disgust with the classical world, not because it was "pagan" but because its aesthetic was based on symmetry and regulation. For Ruskin, the opposite qualities – asymmetry, irregularity, and roughness – made Gothic architecture superior, permitting the craftsman freedom of expression. One of the sternest critics of industrialization and the only Arts and Crafts reformer to reject the use of machinery altogether, Ruskin declared that "all cast and machine work is bad; as work . . . it is dishonest."[9] He believed that factory work had disturbed the natural rhythms of life, that it turned once creative craftsmen into mere cogs in the wheel of machinery so that they, like their products, lost uniqueness. For Ruskin, the industrial revolution made designers become anonymous laborers. Only by returning to handwork would indi-

viduality and, with it, quality be restored. Accordingly, Ruskin was an indefatigable proselytizer for the dignity of labor and its essential contribution to the quality of human life. He gave innumerable lectures, penned many essays, and in 1871 established the Guild of St. George, the first of many influential utopian Arts and Crafts communities. His two most famous books, *The Seven Lamps of Architecture* (1849) and *The Stones of Venice* (1851 and 1853), established criteria for judging art that were followed well into the twentieth century.

In *The Seven Lamps of Architecture*, Ruskin declared that architecture was distinguished from mere building by the application of ornament, which was legitimate only if it adhered to his strict rules of "honesty." Ornament had to be derived from nature and could not violate qualities inherent in the material from which it was made. In "The Lamp of Truth" he asserted that architectural deceit was "as truly deserving of reprobation as any other moral delinquency; it is unworthy alike of architecture and of nations."[10] The craftsmen who made the tracery on Gothic churches "as yielding as a silken cord"[11] earned his censure.

Ruskin was as fervent about work process as he was about style. In the renowned essay "The Nature of Gothic" (a chapter in *The Stones of Venice*), he demanded that labor be permitted only when it gave pleasure to the worker, that nothing be produced unless it was "absolutely necessary," and that exact copying of existing works be forbidden.[12] Only by reuniting art and labor could moral regeneration take place, he argued, because present social conditions dictated that "one man . . . always [be] thinking, and another . . . always working, and we call one a gentleman and the other an operative; whereas the workman ought often to be thinking, and the thinker often to be working, and both should be gentlemen, in the best sense."[13]

While Ruskin was one of the most widely read English authors, William Morris (1834-1896) was more far reaching in his influence. He too was a prolific lecturer and writer whose works were popular on both sides of the Atlantic, but his stature as the protean figure of the Arts and Crafts movement came from the example he set as a consummate craftsman. Morris read *The Stones of Venice* in 1853 as an undergraduate at Oxford. Having gone there to study for the ministry, he encountered Ruskin's ideas and instead committed his life to reforming society through craftsmanship. After experimenting with architecture and painting, Morris devoted himself to the decorative arts. In 1861 he established the firm of Morris, Marshall, Faulkner and Co. as a collaborative venture with the goal of uniting all the arts.[14] The Pre-Raphaelite painters Dante Gabriel Rossetti, Edward Burne-Jones, and Ford Madox Brown and the architect Philip Webb were also founding members. Their diverse talents combined to produce furniture, stained glass, wall-painting, painted tiles, embroidery, table glass, and metalwork. Morris's interest in pattern design also led to the production of chintzes and wallpapers and – after the firm was reorganized as Morris and Co. in 1875 – tapestry and carpets as well.[15]

To his admiring public and to the younger generation of architect-designers who followed him, Morris was the embodiment of the Arts and Crafts movement, blending art, ideals, and business. His work – in patterns derived from the underlying geometry of flowers and plants – was characterized by natural materials. When commercial dyes for his textiles failed to meet his exacting standards, he made his own, using only vegetable coloring and tradi-

tional recipes. His wallpapers and textile designs, handprinted from woodblocks (fig. 3), were available in department stores throughout Europe and America and were purchased by people as diverse as the Belgian architect Henry van de Velde and the Chicago art patron Frances Glessner (see nos. 5 and 126).

Although Morris's wall coverings were available to a fairly broad clientele in Europe and America, only the wealthy could afford products such as the firm's painted furniture. The contradictions between his ideals concerning the democracy of art and his actual products led him to the question "What business have we with art at all, unless all can share it?"[16] Furthermore, Morris recognized that the organization and division of labor at his own firm were not very different from others in the period and required much tedious and repetitive work. By the 1880s he had begun to seek a political solution to the central paradox of craft reform and in 1883 he allied himself formally to socialism. For the next ten years much of his energy was devoted to advancing socialist causes. Other Arts and Crafts leaders such as Philip Webb, Walter Crane, and W.R. Lethaby also became socialists, but most did not and were careful to separate Morris the socialist from Morris the ideal craftsman. (This was particularly true in America, where the Arts and Crafts movement had even fewer links to political radicalism.)

One of the many organizations to emulate Morris's example was the Century Guild, founded in 1882 by architect-designer A.H. Mackmurdo and designer-illustrator Selwyn Image in London. It professed "to render all branches of art the sphere no longer of the tradesman, but of the artist," and to "restore building, decoration, glass painting, pottery, wood-carving and metal to their rightful places beside painting and sculpture."[17]

Fig. 4. Arthur H. Mackmurdo (designer), Collinson and Lock (manufacturer). Dining chair, ca. 1882 - 1883. Trustees of the Victoria and Albert Museum, London.

Mackmurdo, moved by Ruskin's *Fors Clavigera*,[18] journeyed to Oxford in 1873 to hear him lecture. Ruskin became his mentor, and they traveled together to Italy the following year. Mackmurdo later met Morris, and established aims for the Century Guild that were similar to those of the Morris company. Unlike most Arts and Crafts leaders, however, Mackmurdo was influenced more by the Renaissance than by the Gothic. His patterning was more stylized than naturalistic and many of his designs, such as the fretwork back of a dining chair (fig. 4), are considered early examples of Art Nouveau.

In 1884 Mackmurdo began publishing

The *Hobby Horse*, a magazine that was the first in a long line of journalistic efforts to combine the most advanced artistic and literary thought of the day. His periodical was the inspiration for *Knight Errant* (see p. 113, fig. 12) in Boston (1892) and was the forerunner of *The Studio* (1893), the journal most responsible for disseminating Arts and Crafts work.[19] Mackmurdo himself, although cognizant of his debt to Morris, asserted that the influence was not all one way and that his own *Hobby Horse* had inspired Morris's last great venture, the founding of the Kelmscott Press in 1890.[20]

The Century Guild, although seminal, was both small and short lived. In contrast, the Art Workers' Guild, founded in 1884 in London, had a much more broadly based membership and exists to this day. Under the motto "The Unity of the Arts," the Guild brought together architects, painters, and designers for lectures, debate, and demonstrations of craft processes. Although the Guild was a private organization with elected members, many of them believed that a public forum was necessary to change the status of the applied arts. Throughout 1886 and 1887, designers from the Guild met in order to establish an organization to display their crafts. During these discussions the bookbinder T.J. Cobden-Sanderson suggested "Arts and Crafts" as the title for the new society, thereby creating a name for the movement as well.[21]

Over five hundred objects selected by the Arts and Crafts Exhibition Society were displayed to great public acclaim at the New Gallery in London in October of 1888. After two further annual exhibitions, the Society limited its shows to triennial events. To inveterate reformers like George Bernard Shaw, the first exhibition heralded a brave new world wherein the handicrafts not only equaled the fine arts but were superior

to them: "Perhaps the beginning of the end of the easel-picture despotism is the appearance in the New Gallery of the handicraftsman with his pots and pans, textiles and fictiles [pottery], and things in general that have some other use than to hang on a nail and collect bacteria. Here, for instance, is Mr. Cobden Sanderson, a gentleman of artistic interests. Does Mr. Cobden Sanderson paint wooden portraits of his female relatives, and label them Juliet or Ophelia, according to the color of their hair? No: he binds books, and makes them pleasant to open and shut, pleasant to possess, and as much of a delight as the outside of a book can be."[22]

Nine years after this successful display of the "useful" arts, the first organization modeled after the Exhibition Society was established in America. The Boston Society of Arts and Crafts, founded in June of 1897, was followed by similar organizations in Chicago, New York, Minneapolis, and Detroit. Within a decade hundreds of societies had been formed and were disseminating Arts and Crafts ideals across the country through exhibitions, salesrooms, periodicals, and classes.

Although smaller in numbers, Arts and Crafts workshops were equally influential, and none more so than C.R. Ashbee's Guild of Handicraft. Ashbee (1863-1942), began his architectural training in 1886 at the office of G.F. Bodley while living at Toynbee Hall, a pioneering university settlement house in one of the poorest sections of London. There he started a Ruskin reading class and soon added an art class. Out of this group of working-class laborers came the School of Handicraft in 1887; the Guild of Handicraft followed a year later. In his proposal for the establishment of the Guild, Ashbee acknowledged its debt to Morris and Company.[23] Like Morris, he developed an aesthetic

Fig. 5. C.R. Ashbee and the Guild of Handicraft. Muffin dish, ca. 1900, silver. Trustees of the Victoria and Albert Museum, London.

that was inseparable from his goals of social and industrial reform, but he was even more emphatic about man's need to take joy in his work. Since Ashbee believed the most important product of work was pleasure, he expected members of his guild not to be expert craftsmen but to share his principles; aptitude would evolve from the right attitude. He and his workers taught themselves a variety of crafts, becoming best known for furniture, metalwork, and books (fig. 5).

Ashbee moved the Guild of Handicraft to the rural Cotswold village of Chipping Campden in 1902. For a few years his craftsmen followed Ashbee's ideal of "the simple life," one characterized by the making of beautiful objects in a bucolic setting, where activities such as calisthenics, drama, and music formed an integral part of the daily routine, and where profit-sharing contributed to the spirit of comradeship. Commercially successful before its move, the Guild had to disband for economic reasons after five years in the Cotswolds. While it flourished, however, the Ashbee colony provided a model for crafts organizations abroad. In Vienna,

Josef Hoffmann and Koloman Moser based the Weiner Werkstätte on the methods of production they had observed at the Guild. In America, the influence was felt in numerous ways: the Handicraft Shop of the Boston Society of Arts and Crafts moved to rural Wellesley Hills for a few years, inspired by Ashbee's belief in rural living (see no. 135); Ernest Batchelder (see no. 181) traveled to Chipping Campden in 1905, chronicling his experience in *The Craftsman*;[24] and the University of Chicago professor Oscar Lovell Triggs, although he probably never met Ashbee, devoted an essay, "Ashbee and the Reconstructed Workshop,"[25] to the subject.

While Britain affected the development of the American Arts and Crafts ideal in significant ways, America provided some influential figures for the British movement. Ashbee's journals, for example, document the importance of the transcendentalists. He wrote of a visit to Concord: "Thoreau and the Walden Woods, the teachings of Ralph Waldo Emerson, . . . and the Brook Farmers, have become very much a part of one's life, and life's work in England."[26] Ashbee was also a great admirer of Walt Whitman, as evidenced by his title *Where the Great City Stands*, taken from a passage in Whitman's poem "Song of the Broad Axe."[27] Other prominent Americans he encountered include Will Price, Frank Lloyd Wright, and Charles Sumner Greene; his journals are filled with accounts of meetings and incidents from frequent trips and lecture tours between 1896 and 1915, when he made a point of visiting many centers of Arts and Crafts activities – communities, societies, presses, and settlement houses.

Ashbee was the most significant member of the Anglo-American cultural exchange, but many other leaders of design reform also visited the United States. As early as 1876 Christopher Dresser gave a series of lectures ("Art Industries," "Art Schools," and "Art Museums") in Philadelphia and Oscar Wilde lectured frequently on a subject entitled "The House Beautiful" during his tour of 1882-1883. In 1891, when the Boston Museum of Fine Arts was the first of several American cities to exhibit Walter Crane's work, the artist came to promote both his work and his socialist convictions (the former being better received than the latter). William Morris's daughter May arrived in 1909 to lecture on costume and pattern designs, embroidery, and jewelry. For many British craftsmen who emigrated to America, the exchange became permanent. Some, such as Joseph Twyman of the Tobey Furniture Company (see no. 100), were active movement spokesmen. (Twyman established a William Morris room in the company's showrooms and founded the William Morris Society in Chicago.) Others, for example the silversmith Arthur Stone (see nos. 143-145), spread Arts and Crafts ideals through exemplary craftsmanship and enlightened shop conditions.

New ideas about design, craft communities, and philanthropy resulted from reciprocal visits by Americans to Britain. Charles Eliot Norton, Harvard's first professor of the fine arts and an influential taste-maker of the last quarter of the nineteenth century, established a forty-five-year friendship with John Ruskin that had a significant effect upon his ideas about the role of art in society. A promoter of the craftsman ideal, Norton became the first president of the Boston Society of Arts and Crafts[28] and, like his English counterparts, was involved in a wide range of activities – from manual training and model housing for the poor to writing books on medieval architecture and supervising the design of new typefaces.[29]

Both Elbert Hubbard and Gustav Stickley, the two best-known promoters of the Arts and Crafts movement in America (see nos. 168-171 and 101-103, 204, and 205), reached the turning points of their careers during visits to Britain. Hubbard, claiming to have met William Morris at the Kelmscott Press in 1894, returned to found the Roycroft press and community.[30] Stickley introduced Craftsman furniture shortly after his visit to England in 1898, during which time he had seen furniture designs of C.F.A. Voysey and Ashbee. By way of acknowledging his indebtedness to the English movement, Stickley devoted the first and second issues of his *Craftsman* magazine (1901) to articles about Morris and Ruskin, respectively.

Jane Addams, a pioneer in social work, was one of many Americans to model her activities after the example of Toynbee Hall in London. Hull House, established in 1889, was the most successful American settlement house of its time and Ashbee considered it to have surpassed its English prototype. Her cofounder, Ellen Gates Starr, studied bookbinding with T.J. Cobden-Sanderson (1897-1898) and then set up a hand bindery at Hull House (see no. 159).

Philanthropy through the crafts was an important aspect of Anglo-American exchange. The British Home Arts and Industries Association, founded in 1884, was inspired by the work of an American, Charles Godfrey Leland, who had established a manual training program for the Philadelphia school system.[31] The Association's goal was "to encourage the practice of handicrafts and revive old ones, more especially in village and country places out of touch with the organizations for art and technical instruction enjoyed by large towns."[32] On the premise that culturally deprived working-class people would be given an "uplifting" activity and women, in particular, would be given a skill they could market, the Association established craft classes all over Britain. The textile arts – embroidery, sewing, and weaving – were the most typical courses, but metalwork, bookbinding, pottery, and woodworking were taught as well. Nostalgia for the handicrafts of a preindustrial period, combined with efforts to give those in poverty a respectable way of earning a living, appealed enormously to upper-middle-class women, who became the chief sponsors of the movement's attempts to save lost arts and lost souls.

America provided particularly fertile ground for such crafts philanthropy at the turn of the century. Appalachian coverlets and Italian lace – just two of the many home crafts that idealized the rural and primitive and also appealed to both aesthetic and humanitarian sensibilities – found a ready market among movement enthusiasts. In the rural south concerted efforts were made to retain and revive Appalachian crafts. A contemporary account of the Berea Fireside Industries (see no. 161) noted that "for many of the mountain families the spinning wheel and loom are the principal sources of cash income."[33] Some immigrant women had brought highly developed embroidery and lacemaking skills, which were channeled and marketed through settlement houses such as Boston's South End House and organizations such as New York's Scuola d'Industrie Italiane (see no. 162). At some settlement houses, crafts programs were seen as a way for immigrants to retain pride in their native heritage (figs. 6 and 7) or as a creative outlet to alleviate the tedium of factory work. The psychological benefits of handwork were such that the line between professional training for the craftsman and therapeutic activity for the hobbyist was often unclear (see nos.

Fig. 6. "A Corner in the Hull House Labor Museum," illustrated in *The Chautauquan*, May 1903. Hull House Collection Archives, University of Illinois, Chicago.

187 and 202). This became a troubling issue for Arts and Crafts programs in both Britain and America. The glorification of any work executed by hand led to judging an object by its maker's intention rather than by its quality, and thus to charges of amateurism and a downgrading of professional standards. Many organizations, such as the Deerfield Society of Blue and White Needlework (see nos. 60 and 61), were very concerned about hobbyists penetrating their ranks and they tried to exclude them. Other professional craftsmen objected to exhibiting their work alongside more amateur products.[34]

A problem raised by Ernest Batchelder in *Craftsman* magazine – "The Arts and Crafts Movement in America: Work or Play?"[35] – was complicated further by the establishment of crafts communities. Their ideal of unity of all the crafts could lead either to each specialist contributing his best effort or to the well-meaning dilettante executing any number of crafts with no great skill. The former was the case at Rose Valley (see no. 166), where professional furniture makers did not participate in lectures, plays, and publications that constituted the cultural life of the larger community.

The latter was to be found at the Roycroft community, where craftsmen "in the intervals of bookmaking lend a hand to spread mortar or adjust a corner stone." Such working methods produced "queer stuff . . . all colors and types and papers and bindings with now and then a successful fluke."[36]

Although C. R. Ashbee had little use for such commercial communities as the Roycrofters, he justified grass-roots working conditions on the Ruskinian grounds that the goal of craftsmanship was to bring joy to the maker. He wrote of the metal shop at the Elverhöj Colony in New York that "the real thing is the life; and it didn't seem to matter so very much if their metal work was second-rate. Give them their liberty of production and they'll do it better. It's quite a simple proposition. We cannot measure the out-put of these personal shops by the high standards of the best. That is what we in England have been doing, and have thus made of a great social movement a narrow and tiresome little aristocracy working with high skill for the very rich."[37] Ashbee, in other words, was confronted with the same paradox described by Morris: how to blend artistic and political ideals.

The Arts and Crafts movement has often been identified with various others – stylistically with the Art Nouveau and Aesthetic, politically with Progressivism and (to a lesser extent) socialism. Such connections are accurate to a point, since all movements overlap with others, but there are distinctions to be made among them. In the 1870s and '80s both the Aesthetic and Arts and Crafts movements drew from many of the same stylistic sources, Oriental and Gothic being the most significant. As the Aesthetic movement waned, the Arts and Crafts broadened its scope to encompass vernacular design. A new seriousness replaced the Aesthetic "sweet-

Fig. 7. Basket making class, Denison House, Boston, ca. 1910. The Schlesinger Library, Radcliffe College.

ness and light''; a focus on form and structure replaced the emphasis on surface decoration.[38] In contrast to the earlier Aesthetic goal of "art for art's sake," the aim of Arts and Crafts reformers was to incorporate art into everyday activity – espousing "art for life's sake" – and thus to democratize it. Arts and Crafts concerns were more social – for example, with improving conditions for the working classes – but it had neither a sufficiently developed agenda nor enough of a consensus to be fully linked to Progressive politics in America. Instead, it became identified with an emerging nationalism that, at best, brought architecture and the decorative arts to a new level of comfort and practicality and, at worst, could turn into insular, narrow-minded chauvinism. As

such, it belonged to an international response to each country's particular geographic, climatic, and historical conditions.

The English Arts and Crafts movement overlapped with a widespread search for a national identity. This search drew from many arts and was characterized by the revival of folk traditions: vernacular architecture, native crafts, ethnic costumes, and peasant literature. In Germany, the revival of rural art and architecture became known as "Heimatkunst" (homeland-art); in Austria, "Provinzkunst" (art of the provinces). In Ireland, where leaders of crafts industries were often members of the Gaelic League and the Irish Literary Society,[39] the growth of Irish nationalism was combined with a longing for what was

perceived as a purer, less complicated era. The revival of Celtic metalwork, manuscript illumination, jewelry, and carving evoked the glories of former independence. In the United States, Appalachian coverlets and Navajo blankets (see nos. 161 and 208) recalled rural independence and individual accomplishment.

This element of nostalgia for a simpler time that probably never existed has led many to conclude that the Arts and Crafts movement was deeply conservative and anti-modernist. Others, however, have viewed it as the crucial link between the Victorian and International styles, contributing to the modernism of the 1920s through the principles of simplicity, abstraction, and utility and the rejection of academic styles.[40] At the turn of the century in America these forces – the conservative and the progressive – were not mutually exclusive but in the next two decades they were to become polarized. The more conservative elements, for whom the Arts and Crafts had been chiefly an expression of longing for the stability of a pre-industrial past, turned to various revival styles – Tudor, Spanish, and especially colonial. The adaptation of the architecture and furnishings of pre-1840 America, which had begun as a search for native traditions, evolved by the 1920s into a nationalistic quest to preserve the values represented by the colonial past. Progressives like Frank Lloyd Wright, on the other hand, believed that for designers to produce a truly democratic art they must learn not only to accept the machine but also to embrace it. Wright led the way with his declaration "my god is machinery." He declared that the art of the future must be determined by the machine's superior capabilities, but always under the artist's creative control.[41]

Thus, the Arts and Crafts movement

in the late teens and early twenties had developed in two clear directions – one an evocation of the past, the other accepting the challenge of the future. Regardless of its final evolution, the movement had, by World War I, made a major impact on American art and American life. In altering attitudes toward the fabrication and use of objects, it changed fundamental perceptions regarding design, the home, and work.

1. "The art that is life" was printed on the cover of each issue of *The Artsman*, the journal of Will Price's Rose Valley community (see no. 166) in Moylan, Pennsylvania. *The Artsman* was published from October 1903 to April 1907.

2. Alan Crawford, *C.R. Ashbee: Architect, Designer, and Romantic Socialist* (New Haven and London: Yale University Press, 1985), p. 31.

3. Alan Crawford, ed., *By Hammer and Hand: The Arts and Crafts Movement in Birmingham* (Birmingham: Birmingham Museums and Art Gallery, 1984), p. 20.

4. A.W.N. Pugin, *The True Principles of Pointed Christian Architecture* (London: Henry G. Bohn, 1853; first published in 1841), p. 1.

5. Quoted in Gillian Naylor, *The Arts and Crafts Movement* (London: Studio Vista Publishers, 1971), p. 13.

6. I am grateful to Robert Judson Clark for this analysis of the sideboard.

7. As the architect J.D. Sedding proclaimed in 1888, "We should have had no Morris, no Street, no Burges, no Shaw, no Webb, no Bodley, no Rossetti, no Burne-Jones, no Crane, but for Pugin," quoted in Naylor 1971, p. 15.

8. A.W.N. Pugin, *An Apology for the Present Revival of Christian Architecture in England* (London: J. Weale, 1843), p. 41.

9. Quoted in Peter Davey, *Architecture of the Arts and Crafts Movement* (New York: Rizzoli, 1980), p. 14.

10. John Ruskin, *The Seven Lamps of Architecture* (London: Smith, Elder and Co., 1849), p. 31.

11. Quoted in Robert Hewison, *John Ruskin: The Argument of the Eye* (Princeton: Princeton University Press, 1976), p. 134.

12. John Ruskin, "The Nature of Gothic" (from *The Stones of Venice*), in John D. Rosenberg, ed., *The Genius of John Ruskin: Selections from His Writing* (Boston, London, and Henley: Routledge & Kegan Paul, 1980; first published in 1853), pp. 180-181.

13. Ibid., p. 182.

14. Nikolaus Pevsner emphasized Morris's legacy in the observation: "If we, in this century of ours are once more convinced . . . of the fact that the designer of furniture or lamps or textiles is just as important an artist as the painter, we should realize that it is William Morris to whom we owe this revelation. The new conception of art, though theoretically established by Pugin and Ruskin, was first put to the test of practical applicability when . . . Morris decided to found [his] firm." See "Fifty Years of Arts & Crafts," *Studio* 116 (November 1938), p. 225.

15. Peter Stansky, *Redesigning the World: William Morris, the 1880s and the Arts and Crafts* (Princeton: Princeton University Press, 1985), p. 34.

16. Quoted in Berry B. Tracy et al., *19th-Century America: Furniture and Other Decorative Arts* (New York: Metropolitan Museum of Art, 1970), cat. no. 210.

17. Quoted in Crawford 1985, p. 31.

18. *Fors Clavigera* (subtitled *Letters to the Workmen and Labourers of Great Britain*) was first published in 1871 and issued monthly until 1878, then intermittently through 1884. See Rosenberg 1980, pp. 362-455.

19. *Hobby Horse* has been called "the first piece of printing laid out and produced as conscientiously and beautifully as Morris planned and produced his textiles." See Pevsner 1938, p. 227.

20. Mackmurdo's account of his own influence on Morris is related in Lionel Lambourne, *Utopian Craftsmen: The Arts and Crafts Movement from the Cotswolds to Chicago* (London: Astragel Books, 1980), p. 50.

21. Crawford 1984, p. 9.

22. George Bernard Shaw "In the Picture Galleries," reprinted in *Studio* 116 (November 1938; first published in 1888), pp. 229-230.

23. Crawford 1985, p. 31.

24. Ernest Batchelder, "Why the Handicraft Guild at Chipping Campden Has Not Been a Business Success," *Craftsman* 15 (November 1908), pp. 173-175.

25. Oscar Lovell Triggs, *Chapters in the History of the Arts and Crafts Movement* (Chicago: Bohemian Guild of the Arts and Crafts, 1902).

26. "The Ashbee Memoirs" (typescripts made about 1934 from parts of Ashbee's handwritten journals, now in Victoria and Albert Museum Library), entry for January 1901, p. 289.

27. Crawford 1985, p. 169.

28. At least a third of the architects who were later connected with the Boston Society of Arts and Crafts traveled or studied in Britain or on the continent between 1897 and 1917. See Beverly Kay Brandt, " 'Mutually Helpful Relations': Architects, Craftsmen and The Society of Arts and Crafts, Boston" (Ph.D. thesis, Boston University, 1985), p. 23.

29. For Norton's influence, see T.J. Jackson Lears, *No Place of Grace: Antimodernism and the Transformation of American Culture, 1880-1920* (New York: Pantheon Books, 1981), pp. 243-247 and 258-260; and Brandt 1985, pp. 28-36. For the Ruskin-Norton friendship, see Charles Eliot Norton, ed., *Letters of John Ruskin to Charles Eliot Norton*, 2 vols. (Boston and New York: Houghton Mifflin, 1905).

30. Elbert Hubbard, *The Roycroft Shop, Being a History* (East Aurora, N.Y.: Roycrofters, 1908), p. 19.

31. Eileen Boris, *Art and Labor: Ruskin, Morris and the Craftsman Ideal in America* (Philadelphia: Temple University Press, 1986), pp. 84-85 and 123-124.

32. Anthea Callen, *Women Artists of the Arts and Crafts Movement, 1870-1914* (New York: Pantheon, 1979), p. 5.

33. Max West, "The Revival of Handicraft in America," U.S. Bureau of Labor Bulletin 55 (November 1904), p. 1582.

34. The jury of the Boston Society of Arts and Crafts railed against "tyroish" work: "The jury is certainly right in calling into strict account the dabblers whose work, if unchecked, or at least if too charitably embraced, would inevitably promote only the discredit of the movement." See "Current Art Events," *International Studio* 29 (September 1906), p. 87.

35. Ernest Batchelder, "The Arts and Crafts Movement in America: Work or Play?" *Craftsman* 16 (August 1909), pp. 548-552.

36. The observation was made by C.R. Ashbee's wife Janet in "The Ashbee Memoirs," December 18, 1900, pp. 267 and 264.

37. Ibid., June 1915, p. 201.

38. For a comprehensive study of the Aesthetic movement, see Doreen Bolger Burke et al., *In Pursuit of Beauty: Americans and the Aesthetic Movement* (New York: The Metropolitan Museum of Art and Rizzoli, 1986).

39. Nicola Gordon Bowe, "The Arts and Crafts Society in Ireland (1894-1925) with particular reference to Harry Clarke," Decorative Arts Society Journal, no. 9 (1985), p. 31.

40. English Arts and Crafts leaders such as Mackmurdo and C.F.A. Voysey, who were still alive in the 1930s, did not consider themselves harbingers of modernism. Voysey was reported to have been annoyed that he was to be included in a book on modern architecture, "in which he appeared among those who had pioneered the break-away from nineteenth-century academic conventions. He objected indignantly to being included among the originators of an architecture he heartily disliked. He was unable to understand . . . how buildings . . . which had discarded the traditional – the individual – craftsmanship on which he placed such value, could be linked with his buildings in any way." See Sir James Richards, preface to Duncan Simpson's *C.F.A. Voysey: An Architect of Individuality* (London: Lund Humphries, 1979), p. 7.

41. "Ashbee Memoirs," December 8, 1900, p. 242. See also Frank Lloyd Wright, "The Art and Craft of the Machine" in Edgar Kaufmann, Jr., and Ben Raeburn, eds., *Frank Lloyd Wright: Writings and Buildings* (New York: New American Library, 1974), pp. 55-73.

Explanatory Notes

ENTRY AUTHORS

Jane S. Becker	JSB
W. Scott Braznell	WSB
Edward S. Cooke, Jr.	ESC
Ellen Paul Denker	EPD
Bert Randall Denker	BRD
Jennifer Dragone	JD
Wendy Kaplan	WK
Sally Kinsey	SK
Gillian Moss	GM
Joy Cattanach Smith	JCS
Susan Thompson	ST
Richard Guy Wilson	RGW
Catherine Zusy	CZ

The catalogue is divided according to four major Arts and Crafts themes: reform of aesthetics, reform of craftsmanship, dissemination of reform ideals, and reform of the home. "Reform in Craftsmanship" is the only section organized by media. The goal of improving the way in which objects were made not only led to the proliferation of individual craftsmen's studios and small shops; it also had an effect on factory production. Therefore, furniture, ceramics, silver, and books follow a sequence beginning with the most one-of-a-kind studio production and ending with multiple or mass production.

Dimensions are taken at the widest point, unless otherwise stated. Dimensions of architectural drawings and books are given with height preceding width.

1 (color plate, p. 3)

Six-paneled window for William Watts Sherman house, *Newport, Rhode Island, 1877-1878*

Designer: John La Farge (1835-1910)

Manufacturer: Page, McDonald and McPherson, Boston

Leaded stained glass

H: 86½ in. W: 72 in.

Museum of Fine Arts, Boston. Gift of James F. and Jean Baer O'Gorman. 1974.498a-f

The revival of American interest in stained glass owes much to the efforts of John La Farge, who developed new techniques in the production of leaded-glass windows. Following his painting studies abroad, La Farge returned to America in 1857 and worked for some years as a painter of landscapes and murals before beginning to experiment with glass in the 1870s.[1] His interests would seem to have evolved during exposure to European traditions, especially the English revival of medieval and Gothic stained-glass techniques.

La Farge's most innovative work came in the development of opalescent glass in which several colors are fused together to create an irregular texture that suggests variations in density and shade. Working with the glassmakers Thill and Heidt, both of Brooklyn, he received a patent for the glass in 1880.[2] Early successes encouraged La Farge to open his own glass shop in New York City in 1879; four years later it became the La Farge Decorative Art Company. Although the firm went bankrupt in 1885 and La Farge ceased to manufacture glass, he continued to make windows, contracting work through the Decorative Stained Glass Company, a firm founded by one of his former assistants.

La Farge received his most significant commission as a painter from the architect H.H. Richardson, who asked him to design and paint the murals for Trinity Church in Boston in 1876. It was apparently this association that led to La Farge's commission to design a six-paneled window for the living room of Richardson's house for William Watts Sherman in Newport. The project represents one of the earliest American attempts to integrate stained glass into the overall architectural scheme in a domestic setting.

La Farge's "morning glory" window documents his early experimentation with opalescent glass in stained-glass designs, perhaps the earliest such use in America. While the panels are composed primarily of traditional pot-metal glass, opaque opalescent glass is used for the white flower petals.[3] The artist was particularly attracted to the subtleties in texture inherent in this versatile glass, which could simulate such effects as shading, folds in fabric, and other textures; it allowed him to abandon older techniques such as painting directly on the surface. While La Farge did some painting and cross-hatching here, the work represents a deliberate effort to exploit the natural properties of the material in fashioning the design, an Arts and Crafts ideal.

La Farge used the leadwork of the window as an integral part of the design as well, delineating the latticework of the bamboo trellis design with the leaden cames necessary to support individual pieces of glass in the panels. The lattice design reflects La Farge's interest in Japanese art, shared by other late-nineteenth-century American designers.

JSB

1. For information regarding La Farge's work see Henry B. Adams, "The Stained Glass of John La Farge," *American Art Review* 2 (July-August 1975), pp. 41-63; Helene B. Weinberg, "The Early Stained Glass Work of John La Farge," *Stained Glass* 67 (Summer 1972), pp. 4-16; and idem, "John La Farge and The Invention of American Opalescent Windows," *Stained Glass* 67 (Autumn 1972), pp. 4-11.

2. While Louis Comfort Tiffany is often associated with the discovery and use of opalescent glass, scholars point out that La Farge received his patent for the glass in 1880 while Tiffany's was issued in 1881. (See Adams 1975, p. 41; and Dianne H. Pilgrim, "Decorative Art: The Domestic Environment," in *The American Renaissance* [New York: Pantheon Books, 1979], p. 131.)

3. La Farge recognized the unique qualities of such glass while working on a window using onyx and other stones, when he found a piece of opalescent glass that he thought might be used to substitute for onyx. See Kirk Henry, "American Art Industries - Stained Glass Work," *Brush and Pencil* 7 (December 1900), p. 154.

2

Presentation drawing: interior perspective for William Watts Sherman house, *Newport, Rhode Island (2 Shepard Avenue [altered]), 1874-1875*

Architect: Henry Hobson Richardson (1838-1886) with Stanford White (1853-1906)

Renderer: attributed to Stanford White

Graphite and ocher wash on paper

6¾ x 8½ in.

Houghton Library, Harvard University, Cambridge

The William Watts Sherman house illustrates the adaptation of the advanced "Old English" manner of the Aesthetic movement to the American resort scene.[1] Popularized by Richard Norman Shaw in the late 1860s and early 1870s, the style would have been known to Richardson and White through books and English architectural journals and by the first-hand observation of colleagues such as Charles Follen McKim, who was in the office from 1870 to 1872 and had traveled in England in 1869. The design of the house was apparently a joint effort by Richardson and his office ornamentalist, Stanford White. White did two other drawings for the project, views of the exterior (see fig. 4) and the main hall.[2] Concentrating on atmosphere, texture, and forms bathed and dissolved in light, he gave his drawings an "impressionistic" freedom.

The Sherman house is as important for its interior as for its exterior. The main living hall, an imitation of the English prototype, dominates the ground floor. At each end of the hall, large windows, partially filled with La Farge stained glass of semitropical birds and plant life, filter the light (no. 1). On the second-floor landing in the front is a window seat recess with small-paned handpainted windows in Morris-type patterns of sunflowers.

The fireplace inglenook became one of the signposts of the Aesthetic movement and was featured frequently in interiors by William Morris and by Shaw and his partner, W. Eden Nesfield. (An inglenook designed by Nesfield had been published in Eastlake's *History of the Gothic Revival* in 1872.[3]) While indebted to more recent revivals, Richardson and White's use of Gothic detailing and paneling indicates that they probably looked also at Joseph Nash's *Mansion of England in the Olden Time* (1839), the four volumes of which were in Richardson's library. The cozy inglenook with its tiled fireplace and pot hook would become prime symbols of the developing Arts and Crafts movement in America.

RGW

1. Henry Russell Hitchcock, *The Architecture of H.H. Richardson and His Times* (rev. ed., Cambridge: MIT Press, 1966), pp. 156-160; Vincent Scully, Jr., *The Shingle Style and the Stick Style* (rev. ed., New Haven: Yale University Press, 1971), pp. 15-18; James F. O'Gorman, *H. H. Richardson and His Office: Selected Drawings* (Cambridge: Harvard College Library, 1974), pp. 95-96; Jeffrey Karl Ochsner, *H. H. Richardson: Complete Architectural Works*

FIRE·PLACE·IN·DINING·ROOM

FOR·C·W·WATTS·SHERMAN·ESQ

2

(Cambridge: MIT Press, 1982), pp. 133-139; and Richard Guy Wilson (entry on Sherman house), in William H. Jordy and Christopher P. Monkhouse, eds., *Buildings on Paper: Rhode Island Architectural Drawings 1825-1945* (Providence: Bell Gallery, List Art Center, Brown University; Rhode Island Historical Society; Museum of Art, Rhode Island School of Design, 1982), pp. 146-147.

2. They were both published in *New York Sketch Book of Architecture* 2 (May 1875), pp. 18-19.

3. Charles L. Eastlake, *A History of the Gothic Revival* (London: Longmans, Green, 1872), p. 345.

3 (color plate, p. 4)
Portière, ca. 1885
Associated Artists, New York (Candace Wheeler, director)
Maker: probably Cheney Bros., South Manchester, Connecticut[1]
Cotton (2 + 1 twill), discharge printed with silk embroidery (in stem, satin, and running stitches) plus couching of foil over paper-wrapped silk
L: 104 in. W: 50 in.
Marks: *AA* discharge printed within the design
Private Collection

Candace Wheeler (1827-1923) became an important voice in American design reform in her middle years. She taught at Cooper Union and other New York art schools and was a founder of the New York Society of Decorative Art and The Women's Exchange.[2] In 1879 she joined Louis Comfort Tiffany, Lockwood de Forest, and Samuel Coleman to found Associated Artists, an interior-decoration firm intended to

combine successful business practices with a collaboration of skilled artists, following the example of Morris and Company. The firm decorated the Hartford home of Samuel Clemens (Mark Twain), several rooms of the White House in Washington, D.C., and rooms in the Seventh-Regiment Armory in New York.

In 1883, the original Associated Artists disbanded, the interests of the founders having developed sufficiently that each felt compelled to pursue a separate career. Mrs. Wheeler claimed the name Associated Artists on the grounds that it had been her suggestion originally[3] and until 1907 she and her family ran the firm.

Portières, or curtains for a doorway, were part of the decoration of a room during the second half of the nineteenth century. Their use continued during the early years of the Arts and Crafts period and they were often the dominant fabric in a room that had few textiles. Because portières hung in open doorways and were viewed from both sides, it was necessary that there be a design on the back as well as on the front.

This curtain began with a very ordinary fabric, a sturdy blue cotton twill commonly known as jean or denim, which was being noticed by the artistic community.[4] The fabric was discharged printed, a technique that removes color, with a design that incorporates swirling fish and the signature "AA." Embellished with embroidery, including rust, yellow, and beige silk and metal, following the lines of the pattern, the resulting textile has strong Japanese overtones.

GM

1. Because the Wheelers and Cheneys were friends and because Candace Wheeler is known to have designed fabrics for the firm, the manufacture of this textile may be assigned to Cheney Brothers. There are, however, no manufacturer's marks on the fabric.

2. Candace Wheeler, *Yesterdays in a Busy Life* (New York: Harper and Brothers, 1918), p. 221. For other works by Wheeler, see *How to Make Rugs* (New York: Doubleday, Page, 1902), *The Principles of Home Decoration* (New York: Doubleday, Page, 1903), *The Annals of Onteora*, privately printed for the author (New York: Erle W. Whitfield, 1914), and *The Development of Embroidery in America* (New York: Harper & Bros., 1921).

3. Wheeler, 1918, p. 233.

4. Ibid., p. 417.

4

4

Pastoral Vase, 1876
Ott and Brewer, Trenton, New Jersey (1871-1892)
Designer and modeler: Isaac Broome (1835-1922)
Cast terracotta-colored porcelain
H: 17¾ in. W: 10¼ in.
Marks: incised in script 1876/*Broome. Sculp* (on side near base); OTT & BREWER (impressed below)
High Museum of Art, Atlanta
Collection of Virginia Carroll Crawford.
1981.1000.60

The belief that art should be applied to industrial processes in ceramics was not prevalent in the United States before the Centennial Exhibition in Philadelphia in 1876. Although porcelain in imitation of European factory products had been attempted (even with some commercial success in several instances), for the most part, American ceramics were made with only utilitarian objectives in mind. In a commentary of 1878 the ceramics historian Jennie Young summed up the situation succinctly: "Art grows slowly and, especially in a country so largely interested in commerce as America, is long in reaching its maturity."[1] She explained further that Americans did not seem to be interested in supporting the manufacture of fine ceramics at home, preferring imported goods instead because of their lower price and the *cachet* of foreign elegance.

John Hart Brewer took a giant step toward the maturity about which Miss Young wrote when he hired Isaac Broome to develop art ceramics of exhibition quality for Ott and Brewer's display at the Centennial Exhibition.[2] A Canadian by birth, Broome had studied and taught (1860-1863) at the Pennsylvania Academy of the Fine Arts in Philadelphia, worked on Thomas Crawford's statues for the pediment of the U.S. capitol (1855-1856), established a studio in Rome (1858), and ventured (unsuccessfully) to make architectural and garden terracotta in Pittsburgh and New York.[3]

Ott and Brewer's rival in American porcelain manufacturing, Thomas Smith of the Union Porcelain Works in Greenpoint, New York, also engaged an artist to produce exhibition pieces for the Centennial Exhibition – the German sculptor Karl Müller. The works created by both men were generally historical in nature: Müller's *Century Vase* alluded to settlement of the American wilderness; Broome's *Cleopatra* and the present piece employed figures reminiscent of the classical world.[4] Because of the combined references to classical mythology and rustic elements – goats' heads, grapevines, Chinese bamboo fretwork, and, near the bottom, a classical figure with tambourine dancing with goats to the tune of a flute played by a satyr – the latter was called the *Pastoral Vase*. Like all of Broome's exhibition pieces, it was slip cast in a plaster mold taken from an original model executed by the artist. The vase was fired in a kiln especially designed by Broome to accommodate the critical temperature range of his delicate ceramics.[5]

The public success of Broome's work for the Centennial Exhibition led to his appointment as Special Commissioner on Ceramics for the United States and New Jersey at the 1878 Paris Exposition, where his bust of Cleopatra also won awards. In addition to his duties as commissioner, Broome collected French and English books on the history of European ceramics for the State Library. They were to be used by students in Trenton's School of Industrial Design, which offered classes for young men in the pottery industry in 1879 and 1880.[6] The school was established by Trenton's pottery manufacturers so that "the future modeler should have a broad insight into the special studies of decorative design."[7]

Broome continued in the ceramics industry as a designer and consultant until his death, working for tile producers and porcelain manufacturers. He was also active in educational, political, and industrial reforms on which subjects he lectured extensively. He was a member of the Ruskin Co-operative Association and his book of 1902 recalled the final days of this organization.[8]

EPD and BRD

1. Jennie Young, *The Ceramic Art* (New York: Harper and Brothers, 1878), p. 445.

2. Brewer was an important figure in the history of American industrial ceramics in the late nineteenth century in terms of promoting both art in industry and the ceramic industry in U.S. political reform. See Harriet E. Brewer, "American Belleek," *Proceedings of the New Jersey Historical Society* 52 (April 1934), pp. 96-108; and James Mitchell, "Ott & Brewer: Etruria in America," *Winterthur Portfolio* 7 (1972), pp. 217-228.

3. *Who Was Who in America*, vol. 1, 1897-1942 (Chicago: A.N. Marquis, 1943), p. 144; and Barbara White Morse, "Tiles Made by Isaac Broome, Sculptor and Genius," *Spinning Wheel* 29 (January-February 1973), pp. 18-22. For information about the Dayton (Ohio) Porcelain Works operated by Broome and Matt Morgan in 1882, see Paul Evans, *Art Pottery of the United States* (New York: Charles Scribner's Sons, 1974), pp. 80-81.

4. Broome's best-known design of the period, however – the so-called Baseball Vases – celebrates a very contemporary subject rendered in an artistically conservative manner. For illustrations of *Cleopatra* and the *Century Vase*, see *19th Century America: Furniture and Other Decorative Arts* (New York: Metropolitan Museum of Art, 1970), numbers 198 and 200, respectively.

5. Like printmaking or bronze-casting, slip-casting is a process whereby any number of copies can be made from an original work of art. See Young 1878, p. 79, for illustration and discussion of this kiln.

6. *Crockery and Glass Journal*, August 14, 1879, p. 20. These books are now preserved in the State Library in Trenton.

7. *Crockery and Glass Journal*, August 21, 1879, p. 20.

8. Isaac Broome, *The Last Days of the Ruskin Co-operative Association* (Chicago: C.H. Kerr, 1902).

5

5

Vase, 1879
Chelsea Keramic Art Works (1872-1889), Chelsea, Massachusetts
Decorator: Isaac E. Scott (1845-1920)
Earthenware covered with glossy medium-green glaze; molded flask with applied modeled figure of dragon on "fractured-ice" ground
H: 8⅝ in. W: 6 in. D: 2½ in.
Marks: incised *Scott . . . / 79* (on front); impressed *CHELSEA KERAMIC ART WORKS / ROBERTSON & SONS* (on bottom)
The Glessner House, Chicago Architecture Foundation

"Mr. Scott was making pottery for us in Boston," Frances Glessner recorded in her journal for October 27, 1879.[1] This brief notation, the objects that survive from the event, and the web of persons and circumstances that surround them illuminate the aesthetic concerns of the decade in which the American Arts and Crafts movement was born. Mr. and Mrs. John Jacob Glessner were wealthy Chicagoans with

an interest in the fine and decorative arts and a sympathy for the writings of William Morris. Isaac Scott was a carver, designer, and architect who specialized in custom-made furniture.[2] The Boston pottery referred to came from the Chelsea Keramic Art Works, operated by James Robertson and his sons, British artisans who settled in East Boston in 1859 (see no. 31).

The Glessners are best known for the house designed for them by the Boston architect Henry Hobson Richardson (no. 16) in 1885, but the aesthetic interest that led them to him had its roots in the 1870s. They met Isaac E. Scott in 1875 during their early phase of discovery and learning; he would remain a close friend of the family. Later that same year they ordered the first of the many pieces of furniture and woodwork bought from him over time. The Glessners "began to make a collection of bric-à-brac in June 1876,"[3] and Scott helped again to furnish their home, this time with a set of four vases (including the present example) that he decorated in Chelsea.

The designation of the firm with which Scott was affiliated in 1879 – Chelsea Keramic Art Works – is evidence of the desire of Robertson & Sons to be known for something better than ornamental flower pots and rockingham pitchers.[4] Their work of the early 1870s was limited to classically shaped redware vases decorated in the manner of ancient Greek pottery. But the wealth of ceramic displays at the 1876 Centennial Exhibition in Philadelphia gave impetus to Hugh Robertson's desire to improve the nature of their output. In 1877, the firm developed a white clay body on which to display a variety of bright glossy glazes. At the time Scott decorated these vases, Robertson was making plaques and vases in the Aesthetic style, decorated primarily with flowers and birds.

The vase shown here – like its three mates – is in the form of a medieval pilgrim flask, a popular revival shape of the period. The primary decoration, a dragon on "fractured ice," is adapted from Chinese designs, while the secondary embellishments around the neck are reminiscent of the carving on Scott's furniture.

EPD and BRD

1. Quoted in David A. Hanks, *Isaac E. Scott: Reform Furniture in Chicago, John Jacob Glessner House* (Chicago: Chicago School of Architecture Foundation, 1974), p. 20. Information in this entry concerning the Glessners and Scott has been summarized from Hanks.

2. The nature of Scott's training as a carver is not known. He was raised near Philadelphia and worked

there in the late 1860s. By 1873 he was in Chicago and called himself a designer. His furniture for the Glessners shows that he was well educated in the new style of the English reform movement popularized by Charles Locke Eastlake.

3. Hanks 1974, p. 6.

4. For more about the Robertsons and their potteries, see Lloyd E. Hawes, *The Dedham Pottery and the Earlier Robertson's [sic] Chelsea Potteries* (Dedham, Mass.: Dedham Historical Society, 1968).

6

Vase, 1881
Rookwood Pottery Company (1880-1960), Cincinnati
Decorator: Maria Longworth Nichols [Storer] (1849-1932)
White earthenware, wheel-thrown; decorated with applied dragon and relief-modeled fish and waves covered in celadon-green and black glossy glazes
H: 25 in. Diam: 10½ in.
Cincinnati Art Museum. Gift of the Women's Art Museum Association. 1881.43

"The ladies of Cincinnati are slightly demented on the subject of art," noted a commentator for the *Crockery and Glass Journal* in 1879.[1] Compared with women in other cities at the time, they may well have seemed so to observers because in Cincinnati the arts were not just a luxury for the wealthy; they were a necessity. There, all forms of artistic expression were enthusiastically supported. Joseph Longworth, for example (the son of Nicholas, whose patronage helped Hiram Powers produce *The Greek Slave*), was no small contributor to artistic life in his home town. Instrumental in founding the Cincinnati Art Museum and the Art Academy of Cincinnati, he also supported the Rookwood Pottery established by his daughter, Maria Longworth Nichols, giving her an old schoolhouse as a studio in 1880.[2] A visit to Philadelphia's Centennial Exhibition in 1876 had sharpened Maria's awareness of the beauty and variety of ceramic decoration, and George Ward Nichols, her husband, was also keen on the decorative arts displayed there, especially those from China and Japan. In his treatise *Art Education Applied to Industry*, Nichols stated that the arts of the Orient were "more artistic, beautiful and attractive than those of any other nation" and that he expected these arts to "exert a wide and positive influence upon American art industries."[3]

With such encouragement on all sides, it is understandable that Mrs. Nichols could summon the personal dedication and financial resources needed to found one of America's first art industries. The historian E.A. Barber recorded in 1893 "that no ceramic establishment which has existed in the United States has come nearer fulfilling the requirements of a distinctively American institution than the Rookwood Pottery. . . . For this reason, and because of the additional fact that the founding of this factory was due to the intelligent and well directed efforts of a woman, the history of Rookwood, from its inception, cannot fail to have a peculiar interest for American collectors and patrons of art."[4]

While the concept of art was not entirely new to American ceramics, men like Isaac Broome and Karl Müller were artists who worked in the ceramic industry for commercial potteries that made useful wares primarily and artistic wares secondarily. During the same period Hugh Robertson worked alone to perfect his versions of Chinese glazes. But the Rookwood Pottery was conceived as an art industry, a place where Mrs. Nichols would have freedom to experiment in her own way without having to work around the shop practices of another's operation, where she could provide space for the training of others and where artists of like mind could flourish. Rookwood was not, in the opinion of Oscar Lovell Triggs, "merely a workshop"; it was "a school of handicraft, an industrial art museum, and a social center."[5] Furthermore, profit was not a major motivation in the beginning, nor was it a fact. Although wares from the first kiln were sold as far away as New York and Boston, money from the Longworth treasury continued to support the venture until 1883, when Mrs. Nichols's longtime friend William Watts Taylor brought a sense of business management to the enterprise.

This vase is an extraordinary example of the way Mrs. Nichols combined aesthetic sensibility in the Japanese taste with French decorative techniques. Here, a large relief-modeled dragon is entwined asymmetrically around a vessel of classical baluster form decorated on the surface with fish and waves rendered with impasto slip, the whole covered with a brilliant Oriental celadon-green glaze. Since the time it was made, the vase has been in the collection of the Cincinnati Art Museum as testimony to the work that the women of the city held in high regard. It was exhibited at the Tenth Cincinnati

Industrial Exposition in 1882 in a group of
pieces by Mrs. Nichols that included a Persian
coffee pot and decorative objects ornamented
in the Japanese manner.[6]

EPD and BRD

1. "Cincinnati," *Crockery and Glass Journal*, August 28,
1879, p. 19.

2. For more information about Mrs. Nichols and her
Rookwood Pottery, see Herbert Peck, *The Book of Rookwood Pottery* (New York: Crown Publishers, 1968); for
study of the personalities involved in the early art-
pottery movement in Cincinnati, see *The Ladies, God
Bless 'Em: The Women's Art Movement in Cincinnati in the
Nineteenth Century* (Cincinnati: Cincinnati Art Museum,
1976); for a study of the sources and artistic methods
used by various artists, see Kenneth R. Trapp, *Ode to
Nature: Flowers and Landscapes of the Rookwood Pottery, 1880-
1940* (New York: Jordan Volpe Gallery, 1980); and for a
study of the Japanese influence on Rookwood, see
Kenneth Trapp, "Rookwood and the Japanese Mania
in Cincinnati," *Cincinnati Historical Society Bulletin* 39
(Spring 1981), pp. 51-75.

3. George Ward Nichols, *Art Education Applied to Industry*
(New York: Harper & Bros., 1877), p. 176.

4. Edwin AtLee Barber, *The Pottery and Porcelain of the
United States* (New York: G.P. Putnam, 1893), pp. 284-
285.

5. Oscar Lovell Triggs, *Chapters in the History of the Arts and
Crafts Movement* (Chicago: Bohemian Guild of the Industrial Art League, 1902), p. 161.

6. *Illustrated Catalogue of the Art Department of the Cincinnati
Industrial Exposition*, 2nd edition (Cincinnati: Press of R.
Clark, 1882), p. 79.

7

Vase, 1880-1882
T.J. Wheatley & Company (1880-1882),
Cincinnati
Buff earthenware, molded with applied decora-
tion covered in glossy glazes of blue, green,
pink, and brown over white slip
H: 12⅞ in. W: (at widest point) 8½ in.
Marks: incised T J W Co / N 73 (on bottom)
Collection of Rosalie M. Berberian

The years immediately following the Centennial Exhibition of 1876 in Philadelphia were
important ones for the development of American art pottery. As a result of seeing the French
"Limoges faience" exhibited by Haviland &
Company, Auteuil (Paris), Mary Louise Mc-
Laughlin (see nos. 14 and 107) had been inspired to experiment with underglaze slip
painting at the Greenpoint Pottery in Long Island and the Cincinnati pottery of Patrick Coultry.[1] Thus began the revolutionary "Cincinnati

7

Faience," as more and more artists and decorators learned the techniques.

One of the converts to art pottery was a former Cincinnati School of Design student, Thomas Jerome Wheatley, who decorated wares and taught classes at the Coultry Pottery in 1879. That same year a reporter for the *Crockery and Glass Journal* explained: "I have before me now several pieces of faience made by T. J. Wheatley of Cincinnati, which in color, form, glaze and artistic merit will compare favorably with the best Limoges ware. Mr. Wheatley models his own vases, builds them up in bas-relief, and paints them on the wet clay. Then he bakes them with 3,300 [sic] degrees of heat, and glazes them as well as the best Haviland ware . . . . I believe in home art. When Mr. Wheatley takes five cents' worth of Ohio clay and out of it makes a beautiful vase, which will remain beautiful for a thousand years, he is a public benefactor, and when he makes this five cents' worth of clay worth $25 – thus keeping the $25 at home in our country – he is a valuable citizen."[2] Wheatley and Coultry worked in partnership for a short period until, in April 1880, T. J. Wheatley & Company was formed.[3]

The present example shows that Wheatley applied sculptural decoration in addition to his usual slip-painted designs. Haviland produced excellent pieces decorated in this style, but the true inspiration for the vase was the French Renaissance potter Bernard Palissy (ca. 1510-ca. 1589), whose enameled ceramic wares ranged from individual pieces ornamented with snakes, shells, frogs, and other flora and fauna to architectural conceits like a ceramic grotto. The publication of several popular biographies of Palissy and the reproduction of his pottery by French firms beginning in the early nineteenth century created a public awareness of his imaginative creations. The many sea creatures on the Wheatley vase, including crayfish, scallops, and snails all awash in seaweed and coral, probably molded from nature, echo French naturalistic applied decoration.

In 1882 Thomas Wheatley left the pottery to work independently; after 1897 he was involved briefly with the Weller Pottery in Zanesville, Ohio, returning to Cincinnati about 1900. The Wheatley Pottery Company, established in 1903 and continuing until Wheatley's death in 1917, produced artware in the Grueby style as well as architectural and garden pottery; art pottery was not made beyond 1910.[4]

BRD and EPD

1. Mary Louise McLaughlin, "Mary Louise McLaughlin," *American Ceramic Society Bulletin* 17 (May 1938), p. 218.

2. Eli Perkins, "American Faience," *Crockery and Glass Journal*, September 4, 1879, p. 12.

3. Paul Evans, *Art Pottery of the United States* (New York: Charles Scribner's Sons, 1974), p. 331; also see pp. 66-68 and 331-337 for additional history about Coultry and Wheatley.

4. Ibid., p. 335.

8

Covered vase, 1879
John Bennett's American Pottery (1877-1883), New York
Decorator: M.A.C.
White earthenware, molded and decorated under glaze with green leafy branches of pink prunus and yellow forsythia blossoms on mottled pale olive-green ground; cover and foot decorated with stylized pattern of yellow blossoms and green leaves
H: (including cover) 12 in. Diam: 6⅜ in.
Marks: painted in dark green JBENNETT / 42.E.24 / N.Y. / cipher MAC 79 (on bottom)
The Metropolitan Museum of Art, Friends of the American Wing Fund. 1985.168

According to an account written in 1879, a particularly successful vase from John Bennett's kiln, "with a glaze as beautiful as a soap-bubble in the air," was on view at Davis Collamore's fashionable china shop in New York City, where "a very distinguished foreigner" inquired about its origins. Surprised at its being American, he asked the price: " 'Forty dollars,' replied Mr. Collamore, who usually sells Limoges, Haviland, and Doulton vases of the same size for $15." Stunned by the stranger's rapid assent to the price, Collamore asked his name: " 'Haviland, sir: my brother and I own the Haviland faience establishment at Limoges. I have never seen such a beautiful piece of pottery as this vase. Such color, under glaze, has never been produced in Europe. I'm going to take this home and see if we can copy it.' "[1]

Although working in the United States with American materials, John Bennett (1840-1907) was not an American-born potter.[2] He arrived in 1877 from Lambeth, England, where he had been engaged at Doulton & Co., to develop and oversee the decoration of faience (colorfully painted earthenware).[3] Unlike French faience (made principally at Limoges), with slip applied thickly in an impasto technique, the English

8

type Bennett developed in 1873 appeared as luminous as a fine watercolor through the glaze. Both versions became popular in the mid-to late 1870s after being introduced at the Philadelphia Centennial Exhibition in 1876.

It was the French method that Mary Louise McLaughlin (see no. 107) emulated. Other potters worked briefly in the Limoges style in America, too – principally Charles Volkmar, Odell & Booth Brothers, T. J. Wheatley & Co. (see no. 7), and Matt Morgan Art Pottery Company, but Bennett and his shop of decorators in New York City were the only ones to practice the Lambeth style commercially in America. This covered vase, with colors applied thinly on a contrasting ground, is typical of the work of his studio, especially for the delicate rendering of flowers in a style identified with the Aesthetic movement.

Bennett retired in 1883 to his farm in West Orange, New Jersey, where he continued decorating faience for a short time.

EPD and BRD

1. "American Faience," *Crockery and Glass Journal*, September 4, 1879, p. 12.

2. For more information about John Bennett, see Alice Cooney Frelinghuysen, "Aesthetic Forms in Ceramics and Glass," in Doreeen Bolger Burke, et al., *In Pursuit of Beauty: Americans and the Aesthetic Movement* (New York: Metropolitan Museum of Art and Rizzoli International, 1986), pp. 198-251. Analysis of Bennett's work is on pp. 217-218; for a biography and full bibliography, see pp. 402-403.

3. In England, his fellow artists considered him "imperious and touchy"; Henry Doulton noted that "You can buy even gold too dear." See Desmond Eyles, *The Doulton Lambeth Wares* (London: Hutchinson & Co., 1975), p. 43.

9 (color plate, p. 5)
Tiles, 1881/83-1895
Low Art Tile Works (1878-1907), Chelsea, Massachusetts
White earthenware; pressed designs with glossy glazes
1971.545 (stylized lotus blossom, golden brown, 6¹⁄₁₆ x 6¹⁄₁₆ in.)
Marks: J. & J.G. LOW. / PATENT / ART TILE WORKS / CHELSEA / MASS. U.S.A. / COPYRIGHT 1881 by J. & J.G. LOW.
1971.456 (face of bearded man, deep blue, 6 x 6 in.)
1971.458 (overall pattern of octagons containing various geometric and floral patterns and cut with fan-shaped insert containing birds in flight, medium brown, 6⅛ x 6⅛ in.)
Marks: J.G. & J.F. LOW. / ART TILE WORKS. / CHELSEA, / MASS., U.S.A. / COPYRIGHT / BY J.G. & J.F. LOW / 1881
1971.534 (overall pattern of small flowers, golden olive-green glaze, 3¹¹⁄₁₆ x 3¹¹⁄₁₆ in.)
Marks: J. & J.G. LOW / PATENT ART TILE / WORKS, / CHELSEA, / MASS. / U.S.A. / COPYRIGHT 1883 by J.G. & J.F. LOW
1971.539 (overall fish-scale pattern, golden-yellow, 4⅜ x 4⅜ in.)
Marks: J. & J.G. LOW / PATENT ART TILE / WORKS / CHELSEA, / MASS. / U.S.A. / COPYRIGHT 1881 by J. & J.G. LOW
1971.515 (crowned Greek youth's head facing left, dark purple-brown, 4¼ x 4¼ in.)
Marks: J. & J.G. LOW / PATENT / ART TILE WORKS / CHELSEA, / MASS., U.S.A. / COPYRIGHT 1883 / by J.G. & J.F. LOW.

1971.517 (stylized flower on leafy background, dark green, 4⅜ x 4⅜ in.)
J. & J.G. LOW / PATENT ART TILE / WORKS / CHELSEA, / MASS. / U.S.A. / COPYRIGHT 1881 by J. & J.G. LOW

Museum of Fine Arts, Boston. Gift of Professor Emeritus F. H. Norton and the Department of Metallurgy and Materials Science at the Massachusetts Institute of Technology.

"Mr. Low, an absolutely unknown American, had bearded the British Lion in his den and carried away his laurels," wrote the American consul at Liverpool in recognition of John Gardner Low's accomplishment at the Royal Manchester, Liverpool, and North Lancashire Agricultural Society's 1880 exhibition at Crewe, near Stoke-on-Trent, in the heart of the English pottery district.[1] The Low Art Tile Works had won the Gold Medal for best art tiles over all British manufacturers, an achievement unheard of for an American company scarcely one and one-half years into production.

Art tiles had recently become popular with American buyers who desired to add to their homes a material at moderate cost that was both practical (i.e., easily cleaned) and artistic.[2] Until the late 1870s, Americans were dependent on English tile imports with pressed, relief-molded, and printed patterns and subjects. "Tile making is a new industry for this country," wrote the commentator for *Crockery and Glass Journal* in 1879, "and one which would give but small promise of success if an attempt was made to reproduce the styles which are turned out so cheaply and abundantly by the British manufacturers, and so largely exported to this country. But Mr. John Low had no idea of following the beaten paths of foreign manufacturers – least of all, of manufacturing printed tiles in black or color, which are so common and so generally unsatisfactory to lovers of art."[3] Instead, the Lows concentrated on the pressed relief-molded variety.

The features of John Low's enterprise that contributed to its success were his art training in Paris from 1858 to 1861 under both Thomas Couture and Constant Troyon, his ceramics training at the Robertson family's Chelsea Keramic Art Works (see nos. 5 and 31), expertise in chemistry furnished by George Robertson (who joined Low from the art pottery), adaptation of the well-known dry-clay process using damp clays and natural materials, artistic contributions of the English sculptor Arthur E. Os-

borne beginning in 1879, and financial backing of Low's father, the Honorable John Low.[4] Founded in 1878 as J. & J.G. Low Art Tile Works,[5] the firm enjoyed a prominent position in the American tile market during the late 1880s, even with competition from tile manufacturers such as the American Encaustic Tiling Company in Zanesville, Ohio, founded in 1875; the Trent and Providential Tile Companies in Trenton, New Jersey, founded in 1882 and 1886, respectively; and the Beaver Falls Art Tile Works founded in Beaver Falls, Pennsylvania, in 1886. But the taste for glossy relief-molded tiles like those shown here declined at the turn of the century in favor of matte-glazed tiles that emphasized surface patterns of color like those produced by the Grueby and Rookwood (see nos. 119 and 192) potteries. The Low Art Tile Works ceased tile production in 1902.

This group of tiles illustrates the variety of stylish products offered during the early years of the company. Egyptian motifs, classical heads, Aesthetic-style repeating patterns, and asymmetrical Japanese designs were stamped in relief or intaglio onto the clay. The colorful glossy glazes, similar to those used at the Chelsea Keramic Art Works because of the work of the chemist George Robertson at both, give the illusion of great depth to the patterns by pooling darkly in the recessed areas and turning pale where the clay is close to the finished surface.

The company was also well known for Arthur Osborne's "plastic sketches," tiles made with molds derived from Osborne's original models, and for Low's "natural process" by which designs were made from the imprint in damp clay of natural plant materials. Osborne's plastic sketches were available mounted singly in artistic frames in the manner of works of art.

EPD and BRD

1. Quoted in Irene Sargent, "Potters and Their Products," *Craftsman* 4 (June 1903), p. 158.

2. For more about the history of the American art tile industry, see Thomas P. Bruhn, *American Decorative Tiles 1870-1930* (Storrs: William Benton Museum of Art, University of Connecticut, 1979).

3. "American Tiles," *Crockery and Glass Journal*, July 31, 1879, p. 30.

4. For more about the Low Art Tile Works, see Frank D. Millet, "Some American Tiles," *Century Magazine* 23 (April 1882), pp. 896-904.

5. Low's father retired from the firm in 1883 when John G. Low's son, the chemist John F. Low, joined the enterprise.

10 (color plate, p. 6)
Pitcher, probably 1878
Tiffany & Co., New York (1837 to present)
Silver, with alloys of copper, silver, and gold
H: 8⅞ in. W: 6¾ in. Wt: (gross) 36 oz., 15 dwt.
Marks: struck incuse *TIFFANY & Co./ 5051 MAK-
ERS 632 / STERLING SILVER / -AND- / OTHER MET-
ALS / 144*
Private Collection

Japanese art, as it was embraced in the 1870s by
artists and tastemakers of the Aesthetic movement, was one of the most important influences underlying the Arts and Crafts. Following
Admiral Perry's historic visit to Japan in 1853,
the Western public got its first real viewing of
Japanese art at the 1862 International Exhibition
at South Kensington, London. Young artists and
designers of the William Morris circle were
inspired by the simplicity of Japanese wares and
drew on them for their increasingly influential
cult of beauty in everyday objects. The Gorham
Manufacturing Company introduced Japanese
motifs in holloware in 1869,[1] and Tiffany &
Company first employed them in flatware in
1871 in competition with other American silver
manufacturers.[2] Unlike Europe, America had
no great museums of decorative art for manufacturers to draw upon, and large firms like
Tiffany and Gorham began actively collecting
illustrated art books and art wares to instruct
their designers. In 1876 an English reform designer, Japanophile, and botanist, Christopher
Dresser, bought a shipment of Japanese objects
for Tiffany's.[3] In the same year a burgeoning of
the Japanese vogue followed Japan's elaborate
showing at the Philadelphia Centennial
Exposition.

This colorful pitcher is part of a group of
wares produced about 1880, marking the high
point of nineteenth-century *japonisme* in Western silver. A pitcher of the same design – with
iris, dragonfly, and fish – was part of the celebrated Tiffany & Company assemblage that created a sensation at the Paris Exposition of 1878.[4]
Prior to the Exposition the lamination of cast-
ings of various metals – a technique derived
from Japanese wares, particularly sword guards
– was a process unknown in the West. The
color and mottled effects of such laminations
were a novelty that aroused great interest. Also
greatly acclaimed in Tiffany's holloware group
were the random, gourd-like contours – less
apparent in this pitcher but readily seen in their
coffeepots and trays – and the silver's coarse,

hammer-faceted surface, an "invention," first
seen in Gorham and Tiffany silver of 1877.[5] The
combination of hammered and matte silver surfaces with colored metal mounts was a rare
American stylistic innovation swiftly emulated
in France and England.[6]

The color and textural effects of Japanese-
influenced metalwares, such as those produced
by Tiffany and Gorham, molded not only the
taste of Arts and Crafts metalsmiths but that of
collectors and connoisseurs of early American
silverware. After first forming and finishing
their *japonesque* silver, Tiffany and Gorham gave it
a hammered effect achieved by peening and
chasing. Retailers of the time claimed this treatment was the result of the silversmith's hammer
in raising (or forming) the work.[7] Both the
random effect and its association with handwork became emblematic of the art metalwares
of the handicraft revival, whose smiths of silver
and copper took care that final planishing did
not remove their telltale hammer-raising marks
from view. Arts and Crafts silversmiths also
adopted a soft gray finish in contrast to the
aggressive, brilliant, machine-processed surface. Dresser noted in 1882: ". . . to the Japanese
glitter is vulgar. They tell a tale of a servant
coming from the rural districts to Tokio, where
she entered the service of some distinguished
family. In her new abode she discovered a silver
teapot, which was beautifully oxydised and subdued in colour, which she at once proceeded
to brighten. To the Japanese this tale has a point
which is not so striking to us, for by this process
of polishing . . . what was a work worthy of high
appreciation had, by her labour, become an
object of absolute vulgarity."[8] The reverence for
surface effects evoking age was adopted by Westerners and has been important to Americana
and silver collectors from the turn of the century. Craftsmen were fascinated with achieving
such effects artificially both as an artistic expression and because historical association could
add commercial value to their wares.

WSB

1. Charles H. Carpenter, Jr., *Gorham Silver 1831-1981*
(New York: Dodd, Mead, 1982), p. 103.

2. Charles H. Carpenter, Jr., with Mary Grace Carpenter, *Tiffany Silver* (New York: Dodd, Mead, 1978), p. 186,
figs. 254, 255.

3. Tiffany, after studying the shipment, sold what they
did not care to retain and kept the remainder, which,
in Dresser's words at the time, was "doing its tutorial
work." See Carpenter 1978, p. 184. For an illustration

of Japanese metalwork imported by Dresser, see Shir-
ley Bury, "The Silver Designs of Dr. Christopher
Dresser," *Apollo* 72 (December 1962), p. 766, ill.

4. It was illustrated in Ludovic Baschet, ed., "Causerie:
Tiffany," *Les Chefs d'oeuvre a L'Exposition Universelle,* 1878
(Paris, 1878), p. 122, ill. Another edition of this pitcher
is in the collection of the Art Institute of Chicago
(1984.240). Gorham did not participate in the
Exposition.

5. See "Art Deco & Art Nouveau" (New York: Sotheby
Parke Bernet, November 24-25, 1978), lot 52, ill.; and
Carpenter 1982, p. 107.

6. An 1880 coffeepot by the French firm of Christofle
borrows heavily from one by Tiffany at the Exposition;
see Tony Bouilhet and Luc Lanel, "Le Modern Style,
L'Orfèvrerie Contemporaine (Paris, 1954), unpaged, ill. Unlike England, America was not hampered by hallmark-
ing laws meant to insure a metal standard based on
monetary value, which prohibited the employment of
base-metal mounts on silver.

7. Carpenter 1982, pp. 107-108 (as quoted from the
diary of a silversmith employed by Tiffany and
Gorham from 1876 to 1883). During the Arts and
Crafts period a large amount of silver from manufacturers, and even small shops, was formed by machine
and then hand-hammered to achieve a finish both
decorative and evincing handicraft.

8. Christopher Dresser, *Japan, Its Architecture, Art, and Art
Manufactures* (London: Longmans, Green, 1882), p. 429.

11
The Blessed Damozel, by Dante Gabriel Rossetti,
1886
Publisher: Dodd, Mead, New York (reproduc-
tions by the Forbes Company, letterpress by the
De Vinne Company, New York)
Designer and illustrator: Kenyon Cox (1856-
1919)
Brown and sepia ink on white paper
15 x 11 in.
Rare Book and Manuscript Library, Columbia
University, New York

During the second half of the nineteenth century, books became cheaper and more widely
available in the United States, owing to the
mechanization of the printing industry and to
the invention of papermaking processes utilizing inexpensive wood pulp instead of more
costly rags. At the same time, as education and
affluence increased, the middle class sought
more physically beautiful volumes and bibliophile societies were established across the nation. The Grolier Club, founded in New York
City in 1884, declared one of its objectives to be
"promotion of the arts pertaining to the pro-

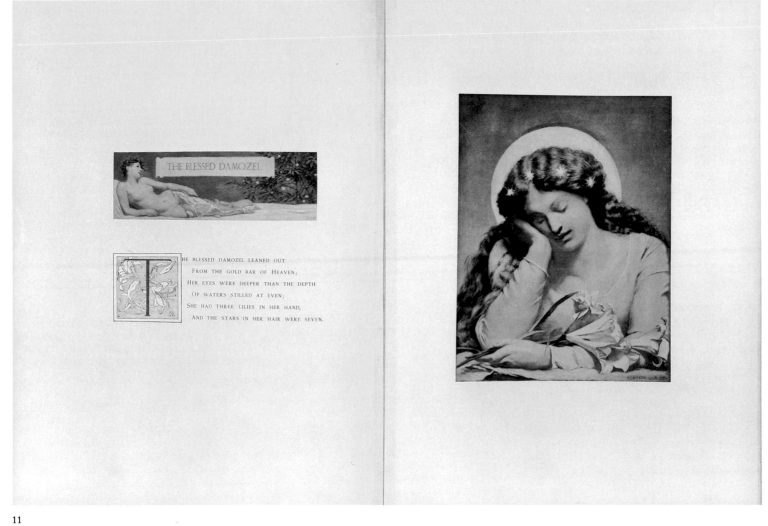

duction of books." In response, there appeared a number of lavish tomes designed by such well-known American artists as Elihu Vedder, Will H. Low, Howard Pyle, and Edwin Abbey. They produced not only illustrations but the entire pages of a book, sometimes hand-lettering the texts for photomechanical reproduction. These artists endeavored to make use of newly developed technology rather than to rebel against it. In their opposition to Victorian electicism, and in their efforts to alter the concept of a book as a product of various artists and artisans,[1] they were precursors of the Arts and Crafts movement of the nineties.

The Dodd, Mead version of Rossetti's *Blessed Damozel* exemplifies the eighties concept of the artistic unified book. The imposing size of the page is matched by the solemnity and gravity of the illustrations and decorations, photographically reproduced from brush drawings by Kenyon Cox. A scion of one of the leading families of Ohio, Cox studied art in Cincinnati, Philadelphia, and Paris. He settled in New York in 1883 and became known for portraits and landscapes, as well as for murals and other decorations in public buildings around the country, including the Library of Congress. His books of art criticism were written from a point of view more traditional than avant-garde.

The Blessed Damozel proved to be a landmark in Cox's career.[2] Criticism at the time of publication was favorable, on the whole, but with decided reservations.[3] Many writers, including Mrs. Schuyler Van Rensselaer, author of an appendix in the book itself, were disturbed by the overly literal copying of nude models. (To the modern viewer, the nudity that occurs in the purely decorative headpieces is an amusing combination of sentimentality and eroticism.) *The Magazine of Art* found the illustrations "almost too grand in style, too large in effect, for the purposes of book-illustration." And *The Christian Union* criticized the apparent use of more than one model, the Damozel's lover, for example, appearing both with and without a moustache.

ST

1. According to an anonymous writer who reviewed the present book in the *New York Critic* in May of 1886: "There is something very attractive . . . in the idea of a book illustrated by a single artist, for he naturally takes more interest than he would if others shared the work."

2. William A. Coffin wrote: "As a draftsman his illustrations for Rossetti's 'The Blessed Damozel'. . . have given him a wide renown." See "Kenyon Cox," *Century Magazine* 41, n.s. 19 (January 1891), p. 335.

3. Kenyon Cox papers, Fa 4371 (2d reel), Avery Library, Columbia University.

12 (color plate, p. 7)
Center table for the James J. Goodwin house, Hartford, ca. 1874-1878
Herter Brothers, New York (1865-1905)
Rosewood with inlaid woods
H: 29¾ in. W: 48 in. D: 29¾ in.
Mark: branded HERTER BROS.(under support for table top)
Wadsworth Atheneum, Hartford. Gift from the Estate of James J. Goodwin. 1939.662

Gustave Herter (1830-1989) immigrated to America in 1848, after studying in Paris and working with the German architect Christian Friedrich Liens to execute the interiors of the royal villa at Berg (outside of Stuttgart). After designing silver at Tiffany, Young, and Ellis (predecessor of Tiffany and Company) in New York for three years, he began designing and making furniture in partnership with others and then, in 1857, founded his own company. Gustave's half-brother Christian (1840-1883), a graduate of the Stuttgart Polytechnic and the Ecole des Beaux-Arts in Paris, joined the firm in 1860. Four years later he went back to Paris to study with the esteemed painter Pierre Victor Galland. In the early 1870s, Christian traveled abroad again to England, where he undoubtedly saw the "art furniture" of Bruce Talbert (1838-1881) and E.W. Godwin (1835-1886) that influenced the firm's work from this time on.[1] Herter Brothers became America's foremost furniture and decorating firm during the 1870s and 1880s, producing work in many styles, including Renaissance revival, Rococo, Louis XVI, modern Gothic, and English and Japanese reform.[2] Though the firm sold some stock furniture pieces from a showroom in New York, opened in the 1870s, its most prominent work was commissioned suites or entire interiors for a prosperous clientele that included Jay Gould, J. Pierpont Morgan, James J. Goodwin, William Henry Vanderbilt, and Collis Huntington. In the commissions the Herters received from McKim, Mead, and White, Richard Morris Hunt, and other castle builders of the day, they sometimes reused furniture forms, varying only the

decorative details.[3] A set of Anglo-Japanese chairs similar to ones made for the Goodwin house also appeared in the William Henry Vanderbilt mansion (1881-1882), for example, and the present table was executed with different marquetry designs for the home of Colonel Harold Elverson, owner of the *Philadelphia Inquirer*, and for several other estates.[4] Part of a larger commission of parlor, dining-room, and bedroom furniture,[5] the table is in the fashion of English art furniture popular in America in the 1870s and 1880s. The taste for ornate and precious objects is manifest in its fine carving, intricate marquetry, and exotic woods.

CZ

1. Talbert encouraged crisp carving and inlays of naturalistic details flattened into patterns on his neo-Gothic forms; Godwin introduced Japanese elements into his work to create elegant, attenuated furniture of minimalist structural design as early as 1867, just five years after the Japanese exhibited their work overseas for the first time at the London International Exhibition of 1862.

2. For more information about the Herter Brothers, see Marilynn Johnson, "Art Furniture: Wedding the Beautiful to the Useful," and Catherine Hoover Voorsanger, "Dictionary of Architects, Artisans, Artists and Manufacturers," in *The Pursuit of Beauty: Americans and the Aesthetic Movement* (New York: Metropolitan Museum of Art [Rizzoli], 1986); Derek Ostergard, "Herter Brothers Revival," *Art and Auction* 7 (February 1985), pp. 36-46; and David Hanks, "Christian Herter and the Aesthetic Movement in America" (exhibition brochure, Washburn Gallery, New York, May 7-31, 1980).

3. The size of the company's work force depended upon the commission. About 250 workers crafted the woodcarvings, furniture, carpets, mosaics, and marquetry for the William Henry Vanderbilt mansion in New York in 1881 and 1882. See Dianne H. Pilgrim, "Decorative Art: The Domestic Environment," *The American Renaissance 1876-1917* (Brooklyn: Brooklyn Museum [Pantheon Books], 1979), p. 121.

4. The table for the Colonel Harold Elverson estate was auctioned at Sotheby's (lot no. 131, sale no. 5486) on September 13, 1986. Marilynn Johnson recalls seeing several variations of this form.

5. According to Marilynn Johnson, the seating furniture for the parlor "featured the carved animal heads and deeply tufted upholstery or earlier work, the dining room displayed blond rectilinear furniture of the English reform taste against walls papered with Godwin's bamboo pattern; and the blond bedroom set, simple and functional, was adorned with inlays of the aesthetic sunflower." (See "The Herter Brothers," *House and Gardens* 157 [May 1985], p. 21.)

13

Armchair, ca. 1870
Designer: Frank Furness (1839-1912),
Philadelphia
Maker: Daniel Pabst (1826-1910), Philadelphia
Walnut, bird's-eye maple veneer, and leather
upholstery
H: 38¼ in. W: 26¾ in. D: 24⅝ in.
Private Collection

For the neoclassical townhouse of his brother,
Horace Howard Furness, a noted Shakespeare
scholar at the University of Pennsylvania, Frank
Furness did extensive remodeling and provided woodwork, lighting fixtures, and furniture for many of the rooms. The style of this
dining-room armchair was most influenced by
the English reformers Owen Jones and Christopher Dresser (see pp. 303-304).

Following Jones's dictum that ornament
must not be a three-dimensional addition to an
object,[1] Furness specified that the chair be decorated with shallow carving. Its rectilinearity, in
accord with the inherent character of wood,
derives also from Jones's principles of structural integrity.[2] The chamfered legs, scalloped
knee braces, and stylized flowers are all features
approved by the English reformers, the blossoms being very similar to abstract botanical
motifs illustrated in Christopher Dresser's *Principles of Decorative Design*.[3] Through the cameo technique of applying bird's-eye maple veneers
over darker stained walnut – a process popular
in Philadelphia furniture of the 1870s – Furness
created a polychromatic effect characteristic of
his buildings.

The chair is not solely the product of the
English reform movement. Furness, although
one of the most original designers of the nineteenth century, still employed the animal imagery standard in a Victorian dining room. A
stylized rabbit is carved on the back of the
armchair; herons, crabs, and other marshland
creatures decorate the dining room woodwork.

A note in Horace Howard Furness's hand
once attached to the back of the bookcase in his
library declared that they "were placed in position this day – February 18th, 1871. They were
designed by Capt. Frank Furness, and made by
Daniel Pabst."[4] A frequent collaborator with
Furness, Daniel Pabst was a prominent German
cabinetmaker who employed as many as fifty
craftsmen in his custom furniture shop.[5] The
similarity in style and craftsmanship among all
the furnishings substantiates the assumption

13

that Pabst executed all of Furness's designs for his brother's house.

WK

1. Jones declared: "Construction should be decorated. Decoration should never be purposely constructed." See *The Grammar of Ornament* (London: Day and Son, 1856), p. 5.
2. According to Jones, "The basis of all form is geometry." See ibid, p. 157.
3. Christopher Dresser, *Principles of Decorative Design* (London: Cassell, Petter and Galpin, 1873). See also idem, *The Art of Decorative Design* (London: Day and Son, 1862).
4. Quoted in David Hanks, et al., *The Quest for Unity: American Art BetweenWorld's Fairs, 1876-1893* (Detroit: Detroit Institute of Arts, 1983), p. 263. The most complete study of Furness remains James F. O'Gorman, *The Architecture of Frank Furness* (Philadelphia: Philadelphia Museum of Art, 1973).
5. David Hanks and Page Talbott, "Daniel Pabst – Philadelphia Cabinetmaker," *Philadelphia Museum of Art Bulletin* 73 (April 1977), p. 9.

14 (color plate, p. 8)
Standing desk, 1876
Designer and carver: Mary Louise McLaughlin, Cincinnati (1847-1939)[1]
Walnut and ebony
H: 60½ in. W: 35½ in. D: 15½ in.
Marks: *ANNO DOMINI 1876/L. MCL/1877*(on the sides)
Collection of Don and Rosemary Burke

(For biographical information about Miss McLaughlin, see no. 107.)

The works and writings of English reformers – Bruce Talbert, Christopher Dresser, and Charles Locke Eastlake – inspired the popularization of the modern Gothic style in America in the 1870s and 1880s. Cincinnati led the country in the production of this furniture. The aesthetic of rectilinear furniture forms and flat decorative designs, along with a strong interest in woodcarving, spread to Cincinnati in 1868, when Joseph Longworth commissioned the English woodcarver Henry Fry[2] and his son William Henry to decorate the interior of a house he had built for his daughter Maria (who was later to found the Rookwood pottery). During the next four years, William Henry Fry, along with several assistants, would carve his father's designs onto the cornice moldings, mantels, and built-in cupboards of the house. As the commission progressed, Longworth invited his

daughter and her friends to observe the work. The women persuaded the Frys to give them a class in woodcarving in 1872; many of them exhibited work at the Third Annual Cincinnati Industrial Exposition that same year.

Among others whose carving was shown at this fair were Benn Pitman, his wife Jane, and daughter Agnes, who had moved to Cincinnati from England in 1853.[3] Benn Pitman was teaching phonography – a system of phonetic shorthand developed by his brother, Sir Isaac Pitman – before he took up woodcarving professionally. In 1873, Pitman established a woodcarving department at the School of Design at the University of Cincinnati, enlisting 122 students, 94 of whom were female.[4] By 1878 nearly 2,000 separate pieces of work had been produced by pupils of the department.[5] Most literature of the day praised their work, making artistic woodcarving an appropriate activity for women. As a rule, they carved furniture to beautify their homes and fulfill their lives, rather than to help them earn a living.[6]

This standing desk was one of 200 pieces of furniture and decorative objects in the Gothic-revival style exhibited by Cincinnati women in the Women's Pavilion at the Centennial Exhibition.[7] It was shown there as a hanging cabinet; Henry Fry added the legs later. Where there are now copper plates there were once "hand painted tiles, with gold ground, representing ladies in costumes of 1776 and 1876."[8]

CZ

1. An unusually talented student, Miss McLaughlin was allowed to design this desk as well as to carve it under the guidance of the Frys.
2. Henry Fry had studied with A.W.N. Pugin and Sir George Gilbert Scott, champions of the Gothic style, before coming to America in 1851. See Anita Ellis, "Cincinnati Art Furniture," *Antiques* 21 (April 1982), p. 933.
3. Benn Pitman, once an aspiring architect, was a devotee of William Morris. For more information about Pitman, Fry, and this woodcarving movement, see Kenneth R. Trapp, "To Beautify the Useful: Benn Pitman and the Women's Woodcarving Movement in Cincinnati in the Late Nineteenth Century," in *Victorian Furniture* (Philadelphia: Victorian Society in America, 1983).
4. Trapp 1983, p. 177. Pitman later introduced a course in china painting to his woodcarving students with previous experience in drawing and painting, which prompted an interest in art pottery. Many of his students, among them Laura Fry and Clara Chipman Newton, would become decorators at the renowned Rookwood pottery.

5. "Fret-sawing and Wood Carving," *Harper's New Monthly Magazine* 56 (March 1878), p. 536.
6. See Ellis 1982, p. 938.
7. According to *Harper's New Monthly Magazine* (March 1878, p. 537), the School of Design at the University of Cincinnati exhibited 74 articles in the Women's Pavilion at the Centennial. The only other exhibitors there known to have presented furniture in the Eastlake style were A. Kimbel and J. Cabus of New York (see *The Pursuit of Beauty: Americans and the Aesthetic Movement* [New York: Metropolitan Museum of Art and Rizzoli, 1986], p. 153) and the Mitchell and Rammelsberg Furniture Company of Cincinnati (see Rodris Roth, "The Colonial Revival and Centennial Furniture," Art Quarterly 27 [1964], p. 58). See also Ellis 1982, p. 936.
8. *American Architect and Building News* 2 (March 31, 1877), p. 101.

15 (color plate, p. 9)
Armchair, ca. 1876
Maker: unknown, possibly from Gardner, Massachusetts
Oak and maple
H: 45½ in. W: 24½ in. D: 18⅜ in.
Marks: stenciled in black ink *Elder Brewster 1620* (on top of both rear posts)
Museum of Fine Arts, Boston. Arthur Mason Knapp Fund. 1978.386.

This chair is the product of a national movement that romanticized America's past in the late nineteenth century, prompting the study of genealogy, the collecting of antiques, and the formation of historical societies.[1]As early as 1864 the Brooklyn and Long Island Fair exhibited a "Colonial New England Kitchen" featuring a table that had belonged to Governor William Bradford and a chair that was 150 years old.[2] The present armchair is a reproduction of one belonging to William Brewster, a founder of the Plymouth colony.[3] It was presented to Samuel Francis Smith, author of the patriotic ballad *America* (*My Country, tis of Thee*), at the Centennial celebration in Boston of 1876. Lacking the top rail and bottom stretcher of the original, the chair imitates not only the form but the signs of wear.

CZ

1. The fervor for seventeenth-century forms in America continued strong into the 1920s and 1930s, when Wallace Nutting made and marketed "Brewster Chairs." In 1932, Stickley Brothers introduced a "Pilgrim" line of period reproductions "authentically designed from classic examples of the earliest known

furniture in this country, but adapted to modern usage" ("Stickley Brothers Bought by Firm's Executive," *Grand Rapids Herald*, January 11, 1932, p. 2).

2. Jonathan L. Fairbanks and Elizabeth Bidwell Bates, *American Furniture, 1620 to the Present* (New York: Richard Marek Publishers, 1981), p. 466.

3. The original is in the collection of Pilgrim Hall in Plymouth, Massachusetts. This museum, founded by the Pilgrim Society in 1824, is one of the oldest in the country.

16

Sidechair for Converse Memorial Library, Malden, Massachusetts (architect: Henry Hobson Richardson), ca. 1885-1886
Designer: Henry Hobson Richardson (1838-1886) or someone in his atelier, possibly Francis H. Bacon (1856-1940)[1]
Maker: A.H. Davenport and Company, Malden (1841-1973)
Oak
H: 37½ in. W: 17½ in. D: 17 in.
Converse Memorial Library, Malden

In the spirit of the Renaissance and the Arts and Crafts movement, Henry Hobson Richardson engaged some of the finest artists and craftsmen of his day – John La Farge, Louis Comfort Tiffany, and Augustus Saint Gaudens – to design and construct stained glass, sculpture, and decorative ornament.[2] A.H. Davenport and Company of Malden, Massachusetts, a major producer and supplier of fine furnishings, provided furniture for several of his later buildings, including the Billings Library in Burlington, Vermont (1883-1886),[3] the John J. Glessner house in Chicago (1885-1887), and the Converse Memorial Library (1883-1885).[4] One of several made for the Malden library, this chair is a hybrid of eighteenth-century Queen Anne and Windsor styles with late-nineteenth-century naturalistic carvings. The same fingered foliage that wraps its central splat is carved also on the balustrades and built-in benches and columns of the building.

CZ

1. The speculation that Francis H. Bacon may have designed furnishings for Richardson's interiors after 1885 has been suggested by Anne Farnam. (See "H.H. Richardson and A.H. Davenport: Architecture and Furniture as Big Business in America's Gilded Age," in Paul B. Kebabian and William C. Lipke eds., *Tools and Technologies: America's Wooden Age* [Burlington, Vermont: Robert Hull Fleming Museum, University of Vermont,

16

1979], p. 84.) Bacon had worked for Richardson in 1884 and 1885 before taking a position as A.H. Davenport's head designer; since Richardson was overextended with commissions during his last years, it is possible that he delegated some work to Bacon.

2. Richardson's studies at the Ecole des Beaux-Arts in Paris (between 1860 and 1865) would have encouraged these unified interiors. He was also influenced by William Morris and the Pre-Raphaelites; in 1882, he spent a half day with Morris at Merton Abbey.

See Henry-Russell Hitchcock, *The Architecture of H.H. Richardson and His Times* (Cambridge: M.I.T. Press, 1936, 1961), p. 245.

3. Many of the chairs and tables designed for the Converse Memorial and Billings libraries, concurrent commissions, are almost exactly alike. The Houghton Library at Harvard University has original sketches of many of these furniture designs.

4. Farnam 1979, p. 81.

I

Reform in Aesthetics:
The Search for
an American Identity

Arts and Crafts: Matters of Style

Robert Judson Clark and
Wendy Kaplan

"The revivalism of the present century . . . has done more to stamp out men's artistic common sense and understanding than any movement I know."[1] Thus, in 1893, the English architect C.F.A. Voysey denounced a plethora of imitative fashions, ranging from Louis XIV to the Rococo revival, that dominated the Victorian period: overstuffed furniture, ornament applied to every surface, an overabundance of ill-suited textiles, and pretentious styles that resulted in visual cacophony. A dining room designed for Leland Stanford in San Francisco (fig. 1) is an example of the High Victorian taste that Arts and Crafts designers in Europe and America set out to reform.

In contrast, the dining room designed by Frank Lloyd Wright for the Frederick C. Robie house in Chicago (fig. 2) is based on an interplay of linear, geometric forms; the undisciplined exuberance of the Stanford interior is replaced by consistency and order. Textiles are limited to a table scarf and an almost monochromatic carpet accented by carefully placed rectangles; only a thin leather slip-seat covers the severe, attenuated chairs. The moral aesthetics of the Arts and Crafts movement are embodied in the geometry of the Robie furniture, which conveys the forthrightness of American disciples of Morris, as though rectilinearity were "the language of rectitude."[2]

The Arts and Crafts was not, of course, the only reform impulse of the late nineteenth century in this country. The formal academic styles of the American Renaissance were the patrician urban alternative, best exemplified by the architecture of McKim, Mead and White. In the dining room of the Payne Whitney house in New York (fig. 3), the architects replaced the pastiche represented by the Stanford interior with a more historically correct Italian Renaissance style. Pilastered and paneled walls,

European tapestries, the coffered ceiling, and sculpture above the door all reveal a sophisticated understanding of the ways interiors could be arranged to produce a harmonious result without slapdash borrowing from a variety of sources.[3] Using either antique furnishings or copies so accurate that they were virtually indistinguishable from originals, American Renaissance designers achieved the unity of design sought by the Arts and Crafts but with a completely different vocabulary. Its solution, however, was almost as unacceptable to the Arts and Crafts as the untutored revivalism of the Stanford house. While drawing from many styles, Arts and Crafts reformers firmly rejected monumental and aristocratic precedents, which they believed to be unresponsive to human needs. They turned to the time-honored solutions of the vernacular, viewing it as more natural and as having evolved from a native climate and geography in direct contrast to classical styles, whose principles of symmetry and proportion were seen as artificial.

American reformers looked to their own heritage for inspiration, but they also looked abroad, especially to Great Britain. A case in point is the illustrator Will Bradley's design for a library (fig. 4), which shows clearly an indebtedness to British precedent. As part of the publisher Edward Bok's campaign to improve American domestic architecture, the Ladies' Home Journal had, from November 1901 to August 1902, carried a series of Bradley interiors incorporating much of the vocabulary of English design reform. Some of Bradley's design features – the exposed ceiling beams, leaded windows, and exposed mortise-and-tenon joinery – are endemic to the Arts and Crafts ideal of honest structure, while others derive from specific English architects. Bradley's elongated

Fig. 1. Samuel C. Bugbee and Son. Dining room of Leland Stanford house, San Francisco, 1874-1876. Stanford University Archives.

Fig. 3. McKim, Mead, and White. Dining room of Payne Whitney house, New York, 1902-1909. The McKim, Mead, and White Collection, Museum of the City of New York.

Fig. 4. Will Bradley. Drawing for library, watercolor on paper, mounted on linen, 1901. Henry E. Huntington Library and Art Gallery, San Marino, California.

Fig. 2. Frank Lloyd Wright. Dining room of Frederick C. Robie house, Chicago, 1909-1910. Collection of David R. Phillips.

metal hinges seem to be taken from the furniture of C.F.A. Voysey; the hooded fireplace, pictorial frieze, and stylized botanical motifs are very close to those found in M.H. Baillie Scott's interiors (see fig. 11). The rapid transmission of British and European design, either directly or through American interpreters such as Bradley, makes an understanding of events abroad critical to a comprehension of the American Arts and Crafts movement. Furthermore, the interrelationships among British, European, and American design of the period demonstrate that influences were reciprocal.

Vernacular Traditions in Great Britain

The adoption of vernacular traditions as the embodiment of an English national style evolved from the Gothic revival. As early as 1836 A.W.N. Pugin had stressed the importance of establishing "national types of architecture."[4] John Ruskin saw in Gothic buildings the ideal expression of utility in design: "It is one of the chief virtues of Gothic builders, that they never suffered ideas of outside symmetries and consistencies to interfere with the real use and value of what they did. If they wanted a window, they opened one; a room, they added one; a buttress, they built one; utterly regardless of any established conventionalities of external appearance. . . ."[5] William Morris echoed Ruskin's praise of the utility of a Gothic building, which "has walls that it is not ashamed of; and in those walls you may cut windows wherever you please; . . . you have no longer to make a lesson in logic in order not to sit in pitchy darkness in your own house."[6]

As was the case with the Gothic, vernacular styles were seen as being native to England and as having evolved from human needs rather than stylistic prescriptions. Providing a retreat from an impersonal urban present, they evoked a preindustrial past in their unembellished structure and natural materials. (For example, in the case of furniture, manipulated materials such as veneers, inlays, and laminations were rejected.) While Morris, Marshall, Faulkner and Co. (later Morris and Co.) preferred the medieval initially because of its potential to express the inherent qualities of materials (see fig. 5 as an example of leading forming an integral part of the design),[7] they soon moved away from Gothic historicism to a freer use of Pre-Raphaelite elements and an adaptation of seventeenth- and eighteenth-century forms. Gothic-inspired furniture such as their St. George cabinet (fig. 6) was executed as a special commission; far more common was a "Sussex" chair of eighteenth-century origin (fig. 7), which was first produced in 1865 and was for many years the firm's most successful line of furniture. "Copied with trifling improvement from an old chair of village manufacture picked up in Sussex,"[8] the rush-seated chair was produced in many variations, all of them inexpensive, lightweight, and informal.

The arts of Japan were another significant influence on the Arts and Crafts, especially in the 1870s and 1880s (fig. 8). The *japonesque* is most closely associated with the Aesthetic movement, whose credo that the artist's only duty was to beauty and his own self-expression would seem antithetical to the Arts and Crafts ideal of social responsibility. However, the asymmetrical and stylized surface decoration seen in the work of Edward Godwin was adapted by many designers (see nos. 12 and 33). The Japanese use of open screens and partitions to define space and the delicate balance achieved by careful positioning of furniture influenced architects from Paris to Pasadena.[9]

Although the impact of the Gothic

Fig. 5. Peter Paul Marshall. Design for stained glass, "St. Michael and the Dragon," early 1860s. Trustees of the Victoria and Albert Museum, London.

and the Oriental was significant, the domestic vernacular prevailed in the Arts and Crafts movement. Among the most important pioneers in developing a more informal English architecture were the architects William Butterfield (1814-1900), George Edmund Street (1824-1881), and George Devey (1820-1886). Devey, however, is the only one of the three who designed mostly country houses and not public buildings, a significant point in light of the domestic orientation of the Arts and Crafts movement.[10] His group of cottages for Penshurst Place in Kent (fig. 9) is one of the earliest examples of the "rural archaeology"[11] that would be embraced by Arts and Crafts architects toward the turn of the century. Devey drew upon the indigenous architecture of Kent; his use of half-timbering, rough-cast stucco, and tile hanging was inspired by local cottages.

C.F.A. Voysey (1857-1941), who worked in Devey's office in the early 1880s, often used the same basic vocabulary but abstracted and simplified the

Fig. 6. Philip Webb (designer), William Morris (painter). Cabinet, 1861, mahogany and pine, painted with scenes from the legend of St. George. Trustees of the Victoria and Albert Museum, London.

Fig. 7. "The Sussex Rush-Seated Chair." Page from the Morris and Company catalogue *Upholstered Furniture*. (London, ca. 1912). Collection of the William Morris Gallery, Walthamstow, London.

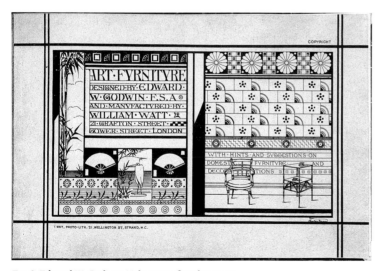

Fig. 8. Edward W. Godwin. Title page of catalogue *Art Furniture by Edward W. Godwin, F.S.A., and Manufactured by William Watt*, 1877. Kunstbibliothek, Stiftung Preussischer Kulturbesitz, Berlin.

Fig. 9. George Devey. Drawing for cottages at Penshurst, Kent, 1850. British Architectural Library/Royal Institute of British Architects, London.

Fig. 10. Charles F. A. Voysey. Furniture of the 1890s. Illustrated in *Dekorative Kunst*, March 1898.

forms as well as the materials of his buildings. His work is more horizontal than Devey's, his façades more consistent in their fenestration. Voysey was a consummate Arts and Crafts architect-designer who chose the simplicity of the vernacular not only for aesthetic reasons but because he believed it to be morally superior to complex ornamentation and classically derived styles. He deplored shoddy craftsmanship: "A mean man will inevitably tend to shabbiness in the hidden parts of his work; he will put deal bottoms to his satinwood casket, and fasten up his joinery with screws or nails to save the labour of dovetailing and mortising."[12] Extolling unity in design, he applied his principles to the manufacture of furniture, wallpaper, and carpets, as well as to the construction of buildings.

A group of furnishings illustrated in the German periodical *Dekorative Kunst* (fig. 10) is representative of Voysey in the early 1890s. His work is characterized by attenuation; the ladderback chair's rear posts extend beyond the crest rail and come almost to a point, exaggerating their height. Yet, the chair's rush seat echoes rural traditions; its crest rail is pierced by a heart, a folk image that Voysey was to use repeatedly on furniture and buildings. He believed that "simplicity in decoration is one of the most essential qualities without which no true richness is possible. To know where to stop and what not to do is a long way on the road to being a great decorator."[13] Accordingly, he preferred not to use finish on furniture (usually oak, the preference of many Arts and Crafts designers) and to leave his long strap hinges unpolished.

Voysey's work was often featured in publications on the Continent and in the United States. Furniture makers such as L. and J.G. Stickley and Stickley Brothers (nos. 53 and 105) found his

lines readily adaptable to factory production. At the turn of the century, Voysey's best-known designs were for wallpapers and carpets, which, unlike his furniture, were mass produced. Although the ideal house should need no wallpaper, its beauty coming from its proportions and from well-designed utilitarian objects, Voysey reasoned that wallpapers could enhance those rooms that did not live up to the highest standard. Wallpaper designs, Voysey explained in 1893, should be drawn from nature but rendered two-dimensionally, and, as Morris had shown, the pattern's repeat should be an integral part of the design. Voysey endorsed the analogy to stained glass, wherein "the artist makes the lead lines a prominent feature, instead of trying to ignore their presence"[14] (see fig. 5).

On the Continent and in America the work of M.H. Baillie Scott (1865-1945) was perhaps even better known than Voysey's. A prolific contributor to *Studio* magazine (his first architectural commissions resulted from the articles he published there), Baillie Scott was represented often in *Dekorative Kunst* and in American journals such as *House Beautiful* and *Indoors and Out*. In addition, he published two books of his designs and building philosophy, both entitled *Houses and Gardens* (1906 and 1933). Many American Arts and Crafts architects emulated aspects of his work (and of Voysey's) in their use of low gable roofs, simple massing, a strong emphasis on the horizontal, and integration of house and site. Interior details such as leaded casement windows, inglenooks, built-in furniture and broad, low doors owe a good deal to his influence (fig. 11).[15] Voysey and Baillie Scott were by no means the only English architects to incorporate these features into their architecture but, because their work was so widely known, they helped to disseminate these particular features of Arts and Crafts architecture.

Fig. 11. M.H. Baillie Scott. Dining room of Winscombe house, Crowborough, Sussex, 1899-1902. Illustrated in Charles Holme, ed., *Modern British Domestic Architecture and Decoration* (London, 1901).

Baillie Scott's furniture designs were influential as well. In 1901 he designed a line of eighty-one pieces of furniture to be manufactured by John P. White's Pyghtle Works in Bedford, England. Inspired either by the company catalogue or by photographs in magazines,[16] American furniture makers imitated several of the designs, for the most part undecorated pieces. Unadorned forms were better suited to machine production and American reformers were, if anything, even more vehement than their British counterparts about simplicity in design and economic expediency. Gustav Stickley copied Baillie Scott's adaptation of an English trestle table for his own house in Syracuse (fig. 12) and marketed the design about 1904. His brothers L. and J.G. Stickley made some minor changes and added the table to their own line of production about 1910 (see no. 104).

The architect Charles Rennie Mackintosh (1868-1928) offered a different variation after 1900. Upholding the Arts and Crafts view that a building should evolve

Dining Table 8 ft. by 3 ft. 6 in.

Price in Oak, £8 . 8 . 0
Price in Mahogany, £9 . 9 . 0

Fig. 12. M.H. Baillie Scott. Table illustrated in catalogue
*Furniture Made at the Pyghtle Works, Bedford, by John P. White,
designed by M.H. Baillie Scott* (London, 1901).

from specific geographic conditions, his
"Hill House" outside of Glasgow, built
of local sandstone and rough-cast
stucco, contains many references to
Scottish baronial architecture (for example, the corner stair tower). In the vernacular tradition, the outside of the
structure reflects the arrangement of interior spaces.[17] True to the ideal of building within a social context, Mackintosh
insisted that he know thoroughly the
family pattern of living before com-
mencing his design.[18] The hallway of the
Hill House (fig. 13) is a unified organic
whole, the woodwork, furniture, rugs,
and lighting fixtures all emphasizing the
motif of the square. Mackintosh's furniture designs were more abstract and
stylized than most adherents of the Arts
and Crafts movement would accept,
however, and he did not share their
devotion to craftsmanship. For Mackintosh considerations of execution were
secondary, and he had no compunction
about violating traditional methods of
construction.

Some critics objected to Mackintosh's
graphic designs (for example, the organic patterns stenciled on the wall of
the Hill House entrance hall), considering them too close to the Art Nouveau
style; his furniture was seen as man-
nered and severe. At the London Arts

Fig. 13. Charles Rennie Mackintosh. Entrance hall of
Walter W. Blackie house ("Hill House"), Helensburgh,
1903-1904. The Royal Commission on the Ancient and
Historical Monuments of Scotland, Edinburgh.

and Crafts Exhibition Society in 1896 "few could make sense of the dream-like designs of the beaten copper panels, the strange tangle of lines in the figural compositions, the stark forms of the furniture."[19] Mackintosh was highly acclaimed in Vienna, however, and his designs, widely published in *Dekorative Kunst* and *Studio* magazines, were also admired in America. Many furniture manufacturers were inspired by them, none more so than Charles Limbert, whose table of about 1905 (no. 51) is very similar to the one in the Hill House entrance hall.

Edwin Lutyens (1869-1944), another influential architect, began his practice fully committed to the vocabulary and ideals of the Arts and Crafts movement but adopted a sophisticated classicism. His "Little Thakeham" of 1902 (fig. 14) is still part of the tradition of late medieval indigenous architecture. However, he introduced classical detailing on the interior, especially in the hall, where moldings with keystones frame the fireplace and doorways, and the screen wall is rusticated. Although the exteriors of both Hill House and "Little Thakeham" are vernacular expressions, the architects imposed order on the interior in different ways – Mackintosh with a rectilinear grid, Lutyens with classicism. As Mackintosh sought greater abstraction and stylization, Lutyens moved toward the Georgian revival.

The effect produced by "Little Thakeham" is that of a house changing over time, as if eighteenth-century details had been inserted later into a sixteenth-century building. The house was one of Lutyens's last fully Arts and Crafts statements. His enthusiasm for classicism is expressed in a letter of 1903: "In architecture Palladio is the game! It is so big – few appreciate it now and it requires considerable training to value and realize it. The way Wren handled it

Fig. 14. Edwin Lutyens. Hall of Ernest Blackburn house ("Little Thakeham"), Thakeham, Sussex, 1902. Illustrated in Lawrence Weaver, *Houses and Gardens by E.L. Lutyens* (London, 1913).

was marvelous."[20] Although he was criticized for abandoning the vernacular (he wrote in 1906 that he had been "scolded for not being Yorkshire in Yorkshire"[21]), Lutyens became the most successful architect of country houses in England, his popularity sustained into the 1930s. The growing domination of classicism that was reflected in his career was taking place also on the Continent and in America, as well as in Britain.

On the Continent

It was a Continental European who produced the best analysis of British domestic architecture of the second half of the nineteenth century. In 1904 and 1905 Hermann Muthesius, the German architect who had served as cultural attaché in London from 1896 to 1903, published the three-volume study *Das englische Haus*.[22] He examined thoroughly the modern British house – its antecedents, construction, plans, familial and social uses, and interior furnishings. Recognizing the Anglo-Saxon roots from which it had developed, he lauded the new results: "It is most instructive to note . . . that a movement opposing the imitation of styles and seeking closer ties with simple rural buildings, which began over forty years ago, has had the most gratifying results. This same down-to-earth quality which we see in the design of the house is apparent too in its siting and in the way in which it relates to the country round it. The aim is to . . . make house and garden into a unified, closely-knit whole." He noted that the interiors could be extensive, but nevertheless "have simplicity, objectivity, plainness, and unobtrusive comfort as their aim."[23]

Muthesius saw the work of the British domestic revival as a model for Germany to follow, not by copying English styles of building but by adapting the philosophy of adherence to vernacular artistic traditions, climate, and geography of one's native land. This awareness of a regional, non-academic precedent was compatible with the growing sense of nationalism on the Continent; an architecture soon developed in Germany and other European countries that melded English ideas with local imagery.[24] For example, the Bernhard house (fig. 15), which was built in the Berlin garden suburb of Grunewald in 1905-1906, reveals Muthesius's own attempt to make an appropriate synthesis. Elements of English inspiration – the white rough-cast stucco, casement windows, and the large living hall with inglenook and adjacent stairway – are combined with Germanic ones – the gambrel roof with jerkin-head gable, a quasi-baroque stair tower, and a maze of halls and chambers on the second floor.[25]

As this house suggests, the Germanic world at the turn of the century was, despite its intense nationalism, rife with Anglophilism. The language of the imperial family was English, and an adaptation of an English country house was built for the crown prince, son of Emperor Wilhelm II.[26] British allegiance could also be seen, albeit to a lesser degree, in the activities of Wilhelm's cousin, the Grand Duke of Hesse, Ernst Ludwig, who founded an artists' colony in his capital city of Darmstadt in 1899. As in many instances of English-inspired reform, the emphasis was on architecture and the decorative arts; among the seven members invited, only one was originally an architect and none was principally an easel painter. With the hope of raising the level of taste among designers, manufacturers, and the Hessian public, Ernst Ludwig encouraged the artists to collaborate with local craftsmen and industries. The fully furnished houses and studios of the artists were opened to the public in 1901 for an exhibition called, quite optimistically, "A Document of German Art."[27]

The architect Joseph Maria Olbrich, who had come from Vienna, designed most of the buildings and many of the furnishings. His own house of 1900-1901 was, on the exterior, a spirited adaptation of the South German farmhouse, made modern by abstraction of the general form and by the addition of a stylish band of blue and white tiles. Inside, the two-story living hall featured a fireplace flanked by built-in seats (fig. 16). This very un-Germanic open hearth and its fittings owed something to what Baillie Scott had recently done for the Grand Duke's own palace. Yet the composition had lively contrasts of broad surfaces and small details, some curvilinear and some rectilinear, which were aspects of what soon came to be known as the "Darmstadt style." Now usually classified simply as *Jugendstil*, such work by Olbrich around 1900 can more properly be understood as a high point of the Arts and Crafts movement in Germany.

Peter Behrens was also an inaugural member of the Darmstadt colony. Arriving in 1899 as a minor painter and a major graphic artist, he soon became an architect and eventually the most important industrial designer of his generation. (Behrens's greatest contributions postdate his departure from Darmstadt in 1903, and, therefore, will be discussed later.) The third significant figure in the founding "Seven" was Hans Christiansen, a North German who designed posters, furniture, clothing, and ceramics. In 1899, prior to his move to Darmstadt, he had conceived a monumental leaded-glass window (fig. 17) that demonstrates the effective transmission of styles and techniques between continents, countries, and cities. Conceived in Paris, the window was inspired by the work of a New Yorker, Louis

Fig. 15. Hermann Muthesius (1861-1927), Bernhard
house, Berlin-Grunewald, 1905-1906.

Fig. 17. Hans Christiansen (1866-1945). Leaded-glass
window from the Kahn-Starré house, Mannheim,
1899. Hessisches Landesmuseum, Darmstadt.

Fig. 16. Joseph Maria Olbrich (1867-1908). Living hall
of Olbrich house, Darmstadt, 1900-1901. Illustrated in
J.M. Olbrich, *Architektur von Olbrich* (Berlin, 1901-1902).

Comfort Tiffany, which Christiansen had seen at the World's Columbian Exposition of 1893 in Chicago. Made in Hamburg, the window was installed in a fireplace niche in Mannheim.[28]

Darmstadt achieved an artistic importance far beyond the original intentions of the Grand Duke, and was a nexus of the creative exchanges that characterized the Arts and Crafts movement. For example, in 1902 Olbrich designed a series of wooden clocks that were executed in a Hessian workshop.[29] The following year, several similar, but larger clocks (fig. 18) designed by Ferdinand Morawe were made by the Vereinigte Werkstätten für Kunst im Handwerk, which had been founded in 1897 in Munich. (Morawe, who had visited Darmstadt, knew Olbrich's work well.)[30] Morawe's clocks were published in *Dekorative Kunst* in 1903; the tapered form and Voysey-like cornice of the clock on the right was, in turn, the model for a clock made at the end of the decade in the upstate New York factory of L. and J.G. Stickley (see no. 53).

The geometric decoration of the clocks by Morawe was unusual for Munich. More typical was the Arts and Crafts work of the prolific Richard Riemerschmid, which revealed a curious combination of the finely wrought curvilinearities of *Jugendstil* and more awkward forms suggesting a revived regional vernacular (fig. 19). Riemerschmid designed works in almost every medium, including architecture, and was a painter as well. To him, all of the arts contributed to a unity of life and thought. His influence seems not to have gone far beyond Germany until 1950, when Edward Wormley adapted a chair of 1898-1899 for the American firm of Dunbar.[31]

When Alexander Koch founded the magazine *Deutsche Kunst und Dekoration* in 1897, he proclaimed that it was time for

Fig. 18. Ferdinand Christian Morawe. Clocks, ca. 1902-1903. Illustrated in *Dekorative Kunst*, December 1903.

Fig. 19. Richard Riemerschmid (1868-1957). Buffet for Joseph Mayer, Munich, 1902. Illustrated in *Dekorative Kunst*, April 1904.

Fig. 20. Max Läuger (b. 1864). Detail of living room in German section, Varied Industries Building, Louisiana Purchase International Exposition, Saint Louis, 1904. Illustrated in *The Craftsman*, August 1904.

a German counterpart of *The Studio* and *Art et Décoration*, which would "promote a true and genuine German language of artistic forms" and "help Germany and German-speaking lands to victory in the competition with other nations" in the arena of the arts.[32] Catching up did not take long. When the Louisiana Purchase International Exposition was held in St. Louis in 1904, German designers and manufacturers won countless prizes. John Wanamaker purchased several of the interiors by Olbrich, Albin Müller, and others; to the chagrin of the Germans, however, he simply installed the furniture in various offices of his new department store in Philadelphia, rather than displaying it as merchandise, which might have led to additional commissions.[33]

Many Americans, including Frank Lloyd Wright, made pilgrimages to the German rooms in St. Louis and came away impressed by the sense of ensemble, quality of craftsmanship and materials, and novel color schemes. A writer in *House Beautiful* declared: "Not alone to decorators and furniture designers will the German section be of value, but to every house-builder and home-maker in the land. The rooms stand for thoroughness, stability, love of detail, and abhorrence of sham. These are German characteristics, and the exhibit is . . . a reflection of national traits."[34] Gustav Stickley's *Craftsman* magazine reproduced several photographs of the St. Louis interiors, and elements of the simple room by the Karlsruhe architect and ceramist Max Läuger (fig. 20) appeared the following year in a perspective drawing for a "Craftsman" living room (fig. 33). (The niches of the wainscoting and the large vase in the corner were literal borrowings.[35]) The Läuger interior, which the *Craftsman* had described as one that could be attributed to "some English decorative artist of the new

Fig. 21. Peter Behrens (1868-1940). Electric teakettle for the Allgemeine Electricitats-Gesellschaft, Berlin, 1909.

school," was now transformed into something appropriate for an American middle-class living room.

In 1907, the ideals of the Arts and Crafts movement and the growing concern in Germany for practical industrial production were joined and made programmatic by the founding of the Deutscher Werkbund. The intention was to bring together designers, architects, craftsmen, and manufacturers in a campaign to raise the standards of design and production throughout the German-speaking realm.[36] Thus, the hopes of various royal patrons (in Darmstadt, Weimar, etc.) and of the heads of workshops (such as in Berlin, Munich, and Dresden) were united with the resources of industry. The most impressive results of the alliance came after Peter Behrens arrived in Berlin in 1907 to design posters, letterheads, appliances, and buildings for the German

General Electric Company (A.E.G.). Classical forms were the hallmark of most of Behrens's mature work, but an electric teapot of 1909 (fig. 21), with its cast simulations of tooling, is a memento of his early attempts to imbue industrial objects with the lingering aura of the handworker.[37]

Behrens and Muthesius became leading spokesmen in the Werkbund for the idea of *Typesierung*, or standardization according to types for mass production. (This was in opposition to arguments for more individualistic designs championed by Henry van de Velde, who had been a major transmitter of English forms and ideas to the Continent and had helped to transform some of them into the vocabulary of Art Nouveau.) The establishment of abstract concepts of consistency and regularity was ultimately a classical idea. It is not surprising, therefore, that as early as 1905, and overwhelmingly by 1914 – when the Deutscher Werkbund staged its ambitious exhibition in Cologne – the German avant garde had developed a pronounced classicism. Sometimes it was in emulation of the Prussian classical tradition of around 1800; often it was a quite literal return to the simple and comfortable mode of the slightly later Biedermeier style (fig. 22).[38] In both instances, the intentions and results were analogous to the contemporaneous phase of the colonial revival in America: elegance and simplicity found in the nation's past were adapted and renewed for use in the present.

In Austria, avant-garde concerns in the arts at the turn of the century revolved principally around the Vienna Secession, which was founded in 1897 when a group of painters, sculptors, and architects had seceded from a gentleman-artist's club, the Künstlerhaus, in order to bring European "modernism" to their isolated capital.[39] From the begin-

Fig. 22. Friedrich Blume. Dining room in exhibition of the Deutscher Werkbund, Cologne, 1914. Illustrated in *Deutsche Form im Kriegsjahr, Die Ausstellung Köln 1914. Jahrbuch des Deutschen Werkbundes 1915* (Munich 1915).

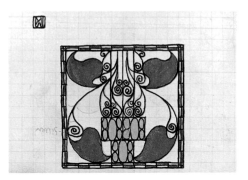

Fig. 24. Koloman Moser (1868-1918). Drawing for jewelry, ca. 1905. Österreichische Museum für angewandte Kunst, Vienna.

Fig. 23. Max Hegele (b. 1873). Lueger church at Central Cemetery in Vienna, 1907-1910. Bildarchiv der Österreichischen Nationalbibliothek, Vienna.

Fig. 25. Josef Hoffmann (1870-1956). Dining room of Adolphe Stoclet house, Brussels, 1905-1911. Illustrated in *Moderne Bauformen*, January 1914.

ning, the Secessionists had an Arts and Crafts concern for the decorative arts, which they exhibited alongside the fine arts in their new headquarters. Thus, their venture was similar to the founding in 1888 of the London Arts and Crafts Exhibition Society, whose members had objected to restrictions against the "lesser arts" that were imposed by the Royal Academy. The Secession Building, designed by Olbrich in 1897-1898 before his departure for Darmstadt, illustrates the Anglophilia shared by the young Secessionists. Ludwig Hevesi, the most astute critic of the arts in Vienna, was reminded of Voysey's "inexpensive houses" when he saw the stuccoed, whitewashed building. The dome and friezes of laurel leaves, as well as the clusters of sculpted owls of the exterior, were references to Voysey's wallpapers.[40] Although such details had symbolic associations, they were here almost purely decorative and reflected what was then being published in the *Studio* and in articles about English design that appeared in German periodicals throughout the late 1890s.

The Secessionists were encouraged (and in some cases actually taught) by the architect Otto Wagner, who had an unusual interest in materials and techniques. The freely composed classicism that evolved in his office during the transitional years of the 1890s was one aspect of what came to be known as the "Secession style." This inventive use of classical motifs, sometimes in almost brutal disjunctions, was popularized in Vienna and halfway around the world after 1900. It can be seen in the church of Vienna's Central Cemetery, a work of 1907-1910 by a lesser talent, Max Hegele (fig. 23). By this time, however, Wagner's own style had become much more elegant, with an emphasis on stone veneers and fine details.[41]

Wagner often collaborated with the

Fig. 26. Eugène Vallin (1856-1936). Dining room of J.B.E. Corbin house, Nancy (France), 1903-1906. Musée de l'Ecole de Nancy.

younger generation of artists, who supplied designs for windows and other decorative accoutrements of his buildings. The Viennese penchant for Arts and Crafts activity was best realized with the founding in 1903 of the Wiener Werkstätte, a group of designers and craftsmen who until the Great Depression produced exquisite objects of decorative arts.[42] In a drawing by Koloman Moser for a piece of jewelry (fig. 24), the synthesis of forms derived from England and passed through the Franco-Belgian world are seen in their Viennese transformation. Balancing decorative charm and discipline, the symmetrical stylized floral motifs are set in a rectilin-

ear grid that is expressed at the center and in the frame.

Josef Hoffmann, who, after Olbrich's departure from Vienna, was recognized as Wagner's best student and artistic heir, was the guiding light of the Wiener Werkstätte. It was through the firm's building department that the interiors of the Adolphe Stoclet house in Brussels – Hoffmann's finest house – were realized. Its most spectacular room (fig. 25) contrasts instructively with a slightly earlier French work, the J.B.E. Corbin dining room by Eugène Vallin (fig. 26). The latter is a heavy-handed display of the curvilinear forms of Art Nouveau, a robust offshoot of the design reform

Fig. 27. Adolf Loos (1870-1933). Dining room of Hugo Steiner house, Vienna, 1910. Published in Ludwig Münz and Gustav Künstler, *Der Architekt Adolf Loos* (Vienna 1964).

Fig. 28. H. Wouda (interior designer), William Dudok (architect) (1884-1974). Dining room of Van Erk house ("Villa Sevensteyn"), The Hague, 1920-1921. Illustrated in Heinrich de Fries, *Moderne Villen und Landhäuser* (Berlin 1924).

that grew out of the Gothic revival. By comparison, the Stoclet room, with its emphasis on rectilinearity and regularized detailing, is a culmination of Continental Arts and Crafts aspirations.[43]

As seen against the Stoclet example, the contemporaneous dining room in the Hugo Steiner house in Vienna by Adolf Loos (fig. 27) is almost American in its severity and in the use of dark-stained oak paneling and exposed timbers. Ornament is supplied by neo-Chippendale chairs that were made in Vienna, adapted from an English eighteenth-century example in the Austrian Museum of Applied Arts.[44] The arch-rival of Hoffmann, Loos objected to the creation of new ornamentation for its own sake; his devotion to Anglo-Saxon precedent (American and British) was at the heart of his severe interior style.

American designers had considerable influence in Europe after the turn of the century. This was especially true of Frank Lloyd Wright, whose work was published by Ernst Wasmuth of Berlin in 1910 and 1911 and in the Dutch *Wendingen* magazine in the 1920s.[45] The dining room of the Van Erk house in The Hague (fig. 28) surely owes something to its counterpart in the Robie house in Chicago (fig. 2). An even more obvious debt is revealed by a house in a Berlin suburb by W. Kühnert and K.J. Pfeiffer (fig. 29). Here the simple cubic forms of Wright's 1907 concrete house are translated into stuccoed masonry (no. 197; see also p. 122, fig. 25). At the time this Berlin house was built, the International Style was taking hold in Germany and elsewhere; thus, it looks curiously *retardataire*. It must be remembered that its prototype in the *Ladies' Home Journal*, almost twenty years earlier, was contemporaneous with Muthesius's Bernhard house in Grunewald (fig. 15). We are thus reminded of the striking novelty and the persistence of Wright's

Fig. 29. W. Kühnert and K.J. Pfeiffer. Suburban house, Berlin, 1925. Illustrated in J.G. Wattjes, *Moderne Architectuur* (Amsterdam, ca. 1927).

Fig. 30. Dard Hunter. "A Roycroft Dining Room" from the catalogue *Aurora Colonial Furniture* (East Aurora, N.Y., ca. 1905). Collection of Simeon Braunstein.

Fig. 31. Dard Hunter. "Reception Room of Roycroft Inn," illustrated in folio by Frances Holbrook Pfeiffer, *The Roycroft Inn* (East Aurora, N.Y., ca. 1910). Collection of Simeon Braunstein.

Fig. 32. Harvey Ellis. Entrance hall with view into living room, illustrated in *The Craftsman*, August 1903 and October 1905.

forms from his Arts and Crafts period, and of the constant cross-fertilization that was possible in this age of ambitious architectural publishing.

Some American Syntheses

While the artistic influence of America abroad was significant after the 1880s, its designers still looked to Europe as the major source of inspiration until the mid-twentieth century. The work of Dard Hunter, who spent several years in the Roycroft community (see nos. 168-171), demonstrates how quickly styles could be transmitted. In an illustration for the catalogue *Aurora Colonial Furniture*, published about 1905 (fig. 30), the pieces are ungainly and the wall details lack cohesion, especially the motifs of the frieze. Some three years later, after being inspired by Austrian and German periodicals (among them *Dekorative Kunst*

and *Deutsche Kunst und Dekoration*) that were available in the Roycroft library, Hunter went to Europe (principally Vienna) for several months; he returned to the Roycrofters with a new sense of line, color, and pattern. Hunter's drawing of the reception room of the Roycroft Inn (fig. 31) – with its panels of flat color and concentrations of geometric pattern combined with stylized plants and lettering inside a quadrate border – reveals the greater sophistication of his style. His mastery of the geometries of the Weiner Werkstätte influenced Roycroft production of leather and metalwork, as well as the books that he designed himself (nos. 54 and 171; see also no. 209).[46] The high style of Vienna was thus popular in America long before a showroom of the Wiener Werkstätte was opened in New York in 1922.

Two illustrations in the October 1905

Fig. 33. Artist unknown. Living room. Illustrated in *The Craftsman*, October 1905.

Fig. 34. Will Bradley at home in Concord, Massachusetts, after 1902. Collection of Robert Judson Clark.

issue of *The Craftsman* magazine further exemplify the wide variety of influences from abroad on American Arts and Crafts designers. The first was drawn in 1903 by Harvey Ellis (fig. 32; see also nos. 102 and 196). Almost every line (including the centrifugal rosebush and the abstracted botanical motif in the frieze) as well as the choice of colors (yellow, lavender, and ivory) reveals a familiarity with the work of Mackintosh and his fellow Glaswegians. In the contrasting drawing by an unknown artist (fig. 33), the exposed timber ceiling, the piano case, the trestle table, and the pattern of the rug show a more rustic Americanization of English ideas, along with some references to what had been seen in the German display in St. Louis (see fig. 20).

Will Bradley's drawing for the *Ladies' Home Journal* in 1902 (fig. 4) presents still another example of indebtedness to Great Britain. Its pictorial quality contrasts with Ellis's more abstract design and with the anonymous delineator's straightforward presentation of a "Craftsman" ensemble. Bradley, ironically, did not choose to execute such decorative designs for his own house in Concord, Massachusetts, whose interiors came closer to the "Craftsman" example. Instead, he ordered some furniture from Gustav Stickley and individualized it with green stain. A snapshot from the family album (fig. 34) shows him seated in the comfort of his Morris chair.[47]

Charles Rohlfs, on the other hand, lived in Buffalo amid furnishings of his own unusual production (fig. 35). He seems to have progressed from simple oak forms with exposed joinery to the curvilinearities of Art Nouveau (see nos. 98 and 99).[48] Yet he maintained a preference for slab-like members, which he reticulated and carved, then embellished with decorative pegs or brads.

Rohlfs was an idiosyncratic designer who, like the potter George Ohr (see no. 110), found his mature expression in complication rather than in simplicity. He was one of the few American Arts and Crafts figures to produce a convincingly personal version of the Art Nouveau, a style that was often resisted in this country as something exotic and overwhelming, uncorked from a "magic bottle of design . . . like a monster of the Arabian Nights."[49]

Such was the view of C. Matlack Price, who called the new houses of the midwest "Secessionistic" and praised them as a cleansing contribution from the Germanic world, a move toward simplification that was a purging of historicism as well as being opposed to Art Nouveau. Price described the three leaders of the Prairie School – Louis Sullivan, Frank Lloyd Wright, and Walter Burley Griffin – as "Secessionists at heart," for they had renounced the past, evolved a "peculiar and individual type of decorative design," and emphasized "the craftsmanship and appropriateness of furniture, fitments, rugs, curtains, lamps and even leaded windows."[50] In the spirit of the Arts and Crafts movement, these architects had indeed created an American regional style. And yet historical forms can be found in their work – even a latent classicism – as in the work of George Washington Maher. His house for E.L. King near Homer, Minnesota (fig. 36) has a completely symmetrical elevation and pendant side porches.[51] Classical references are also present in details such as the blocky units of the balustrade, which are like misplaced objects from the entablature of a primitive Doric temple. This unorthodox use of classical motifs can be described as Secessionist (see also fig. 23) and, in fact, Maher had a Germanic way of thinking in terms of "types." There hovers throughout his houses –

in the shapes of furniture and the patterns of the carpets – a certain awareness of Behrens and other Germans of that generation, and, like them, he stressed the ideal of a *Leitmotif*, or "motive rhythm," in each building (fig. 37; see also nos. 217-221).[52] In designs for the King house he repeated the lily in many places (see no. 219) and also echoed the curved pedimental form on the exterior and interior. This use of a persistent "signature" motif was seen elsewhere in America, as in the design for a house by John Hudson Thomas in Berkeley, which was a California version of a Prairie house with some "Secessionistic" details (see nos. 81 and 82).

The brothers Charles Sumner Greene and Henry Mather Greene were impor-

Fig. 35. Charles Rohlfs. Living room of Rohlfs house, Buffalo, ca. 1910-1912. Collection of Robert Judson Clark.

Fig. 36. George W. Maher. E.L. King house ("Rockledge"), Homer, Minnesota, ca. 1912. Illustrated in *Architectural Record*, October 1922.

Fig. 37. George W. Maher. Dining room of E.L. King house ("Rockledge"), Homer, Minnesota, ca. 1912. Illustrated in *Architectural Record*, October 1922.

tant in the establishment of a regional architecture in southern California during the first decade of the new century. Raised in the midwest and trained in Boston, the Greenes arrived in California in 1893 and designed houses in almost every revival style for a decade before they began to find their own synthesis. The Henry M. Robinson house in Pasadena (fig. 38), one of the most fascinating of their transitional works,[53] combines stuccoed piers, pergolas, half-timbering, and low rooflines. A writer for *The Craftsman* magazine tried unconvincingly to explain it all as "an echo of the Art Nouveau movement of western Germany."[54] The bewildering variety of forms enclosed a simple plan (fig. 39) that, because of its relationship of rooms to the two-storied entrance hall and the angle of the utility wing, derives from some early colonial revival (or "Shingle Style") houses in New England of the late 1870s and early 1880s.[55]

The dining room of the Robinson house (fig. 40) is also eclectic, including references to Oriental sources. Like the eighteenth-century cabinetmakers who created the Queen Anne and Chippendale styles, the Greenes adopted the curved splats and other details of Chinese furniture. The heavy structure of the table is softened by visual refinements also learned from Chinese objects, which Charles Greene collected. This combination of motifs resounds in the lighting fixture above (no. 37), which, with its counterweights and brackets, is one of the most audacious contraptions of the Arts and Crafts movement.

The houses of the Greene brothers (see nos. 68 and 69) were particularly suited to the western climate. Their work became a popular source for bungalows in southern California and elsewhere – sometimes in the crudest sorts of variations. For instance, a large bun-

Fig. 38. Charles Sumner Greene and Henry Mather Greene. Henry W. Robinson house, Pasadena, 1906. Architectural Documents Collection, College of Environmental Design, University of California, Berkeley.

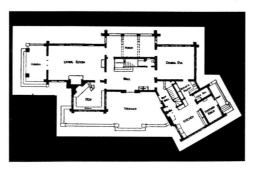

Fig. 39. Greene and Greene. Plan of Henry W. Robinson house, Pasadena, 1906. Illustrated in *The Craftsman*, August 1912.

Fig. 40. Greene and Greene. Dining room of Henry W. Robinson house, Pasadena, 1906. Architectural Documents Collection, College of Environmental Design, University of California, Berkeley.

galow by an unknown designer[56] was
the setting for one of the "colonial"
scenes marketed around 1915 by Wallace Nutting, the proselytizer for early
American crafts.[57] *A Southern Puritan* (fig.
41) featured a young woman in pseudo-
seventeenth century dress, with Holy
Writ in hand, on the steps of a heavily
timbered porch. The Japanese *Taru* containing yucca plants add to the incon-
gruity, as do the leaded glass panels influenced by the Prairie School, which
contrast with the double-hung sash windows on the body of the building. The
intended audience for such a curious
image is uncertain. But it reminds us of
the recurring presence of colonial
themes in much of Americana, and of
the fascinating global dialogue between
East and West – as well as between the
east and west coasts.

The amalgam of influences in the architecture of northern California at the
turn of the century is no less interesting.
Bernard Maybeck has received much attention in the recent past because of his
identification with the hills of Berkeley
and the unusual variety of his work.[58] He
moved with ease between quasi-medie-
val and classical modes. Although the
two drawings in this catalogue (nos. 75
and 76) recall his medievalistic
penchants, he was a product of the
Ecole des Beaux-Arts and did much to
establish classical architecture on the
edge of the Pacific. His James J. Fagen
house (fig. 42) was actually a group of
pavilions connected by pergolas around
a patio that was protected by giant oak
trees, a perfect embodiment, in a most
informal way, of the classical tradition.[59]
By the 1920s the best California architecture with historical analogies was, in
fact, Mediterranean: the Spanish colonial revival or, like the Fagan house,
something more Italianate.

The transformation of the Arts and
Crafts aesthetic into one that is classi-

Fig. 41. Wallace Nutting. *A Southern Puritan*. Photograph,
before 1915. Collection of D.J. Puffert.

cally inspired is seen in the painting
Youth by Arthur Mathews (fig. 43). Its
frame was carved and polychromed in
the shop owned by Mathews and his
wife Lucia, who were leaders of the Arts
and Crafts movement in San Francisco.[60]
Painters, furniture designers, carvers,
and civic reformers, the Mathews embodied the Arts and Crafts ideal of integrating all the arts with a commitment to
a better and more beautiful life. Their
work is set in the California landscape
(see nos. 79 and 80) but it recalls the
heritage of the Mediterranean world.
The ideals of the Arts and Crafts movement and the American Renaissance
were united in this canvas that came
into being at the time of the first World
War.

In the 1920s, the arts of America followed many paths, some continuing local or national traditions, others adopt-
ing newer modes from Europe. Classicism in architecture became more stub-
bornly entrenched as it was challenged
by the International Style. Increasing
concern with studied picturesqueness
or academic correctness, on the one
hand, and with standardization, univer-
sality, and machine imagery on the
other, replaced the Arts and Crafts devotion to individuality, honesty, and En-
glishness. "The Simple Life" had never
been truly simple, but it was fated to
become even less simple as the twentieth century unfolded.

Fig. 42. Bernard Maybeck. James J. Fagan house,
Woodside, California, 1920. Architectural Documents
Collection, College of Environmental Design, Univer-
sity of California, Berkeley.

Fig. 43. Arthur F. Mathews. *Youth*, ca. 1917, oil on
canvas; carved and painted wood frame. The Oakland
Museum, gift of Concours d'Antiques, Art Guild of
The Oakland Museum Association.

1. Quoted in "Some Recent Designs by Mr. C.F.A. Voysey," *Studio* 7 (May 1896), p. 215.

2. Carl Schorske, "Observations on Style and Society in the Arts and Crafts Movement," *Record of the Art Museum, Princeton University* 34, no. 2 (1975), p. 42.

3. Richard Guy Wilson, "The Decoration of Houses and Scientific Eclecticism," in Kenneth L. Ames, ed., *Victorian Furniture* (Philadelphia: Victorian Society in America, 1983), pp. 198-199. See also *The American Renaissance, 1876-1917* (New York: Brooklyn Museum, 1979).

4. A.W.N. Pugin, *Contrasts* (London, 1836), p. 18.

5. John Ruskin, "The Nature of Gothic," reprinted in John D. Rosenberg, ed., *The Genius of John Ruskin: Selections from his Writing* (Boston, London, and Henley: Routledge & Kegan Paul, 1980; first published in 1853), p. 189.

6. Quoted in Peter Davey, *Architecture of the Arts and Crafts Movement* (New York: Rizzoli, 1980), pp. 8-9.

7. "It was [Morris and Company's] glass which most clearly struck out a new line, achieving its effects not by elaboration or the pursuit of pictorial magnificence, but by treating the medium in terms of its own potential." See Ray Watkinson, *William Morris as Designer* (London: Studio Vista, 1967), p. 41.

8. "The Sussex Rush-Seated Chair," in Morris and Company catalogue *Upholstered Furniture* (London, ca. 1912), p. 63. The quote in the advertisement was taken from *Life of William Morris* by Prof. J.W. Mackail (London and New York: Longmans, Green & Co., 1899).

9. See Clay Lancaster, *The Japanese Influence in America* (New York: Walton W. Rawls), 1963. See also Roger Billcliffe, *Mackintosh Furniture* (Cambridge: Lutterworth Press, 1984), p. 9.

10. As the German architect Hermann Muthesius observed, "A revival of interest in the dwelling-house is absolutely essential if the applied arts are to persist in their renewed activity and to thrive. The house is their only possible home; the sole aim of any Arts and Crafts movement must be to furnish the dwelling-place and the house." See *The English House*, translated by Janet Seligman (London: Crosby Lockwood Staples, 1979; first published in German in 1904-1905), p. 10.

11. Mark Girouard, "George Devey in Kent – I," *Country Life* 149 (April 1971), p. 745.

12. Quoted in Duncan Simpson, *C.F.A. Voysey: An Architect of Individuality* (London: Lund Humphries, 1979), p. 109.

13. Quoted in "Some Recent Designs by Mr. C.F.A. Voysey," *Studio* 7 (May 1896), p. 216.

14. "An Interview with Mr. Charles F. Annesley Voysey," *Studio* 1 (September 1893), p. 233.

15. James D. Kornwolf, *M.H. Baillie Scott and the Arts and Crafts Movement* (Baltimore and London: Johns Hopkins Press, 1972), p. 392. See also Julius Meier-Graefe, "Baillie Scott," *Moderne Bauformen* 4 (January 1905), pp. 34-36.

16. See, for example, "A House in Vancouver that Shows English Tradition Blended with the Frank Expression of Western Life," *Craftsman* 13 (March 1908), pp. 675-688. The author states that the furniture in the central hall and drawing room was designed by M.H. Baillie Scott and made by John P. White in Bedford, England. A version of tea table no. 34 from the catalogue is seen in the photograph on p. 679. For a record of Baillie Scott's Pyghtle Works furniture, see *Furniture Made at the Pyghtle Works, Bedford by John P. White, Designed by M.H. Baillie Scott* (London: Bemrose & Sons, 1901).

17. "The idea, emanating from Ruskin and Morris ideologies, of the production of a building as a social process and not as a single creative act was with [Mackintosh] a firm principle." See Robert Macleod, *Charles Rennie Mackintosh, Architect and Artist* (London and Glasgow: Collins, 1983), p. 96.

18. Ibid., p. 90.

19. Muthesius 1979. For accounts of Mackintosh's influence in Vienna, see Eduard F. Sekler, "Mackintosh and Vienna," *Architectural Review* 44 (December 1968), pp. 455-456; and Roger Billcliffe and Peter Vergo, "Charles Rennie Mackintosh and the Austrian Art Revival," *Burlington Magazine* 119 (November 1977), pp. 739-744.

20. Quoted in Gavin Stamp and André Goulancourt, *The English House, 1860-1914* (London: Faber and Faber, 1986), p. 168. Major studies of Lutyens include Christopher Hussey, *The Life of Sir Edwin Lutyens* (London: Country Life, Ltd., 1950); Daniel O'Neill, *Lutyens' Country Houses* (London: Lund Humphries, 1980); and the exhibition catalogue *Lutyens: The Work of the English Architect Sir Edwin Lutyens (1869-1944)*, (London: Arts Council of Great Britain, 1981).

21. Quoted in Davey 1980, p. 160.

22. Hermann Muthesius, *Das englische Haus*, 3 vols. (Berlin: Ernst Wasmuth, 1904-1905).

23. Muthesius 1979, p. 10.

24. Hermann Muthesius, *Landhaus und Garten* (Munich: F. Bruckmann, 1910); and Stefan Muthesius, *Das englische Vorbild* (Munich: Prestel-Verlag, 1974). The latter emphasizes the English influences in Germany *before* 1900.

25. Hermann Muthesius, *Landhäuser von Hermann Muthesius* (Munich: F. Bruckmann, 1912), pp. 91-100. See also Julius Posener, et al., *Hermann Muthesius, 1861-1927* (Berlin: Akademie der Künste, 1977); "Die deutsche Gartenstadtbewegung," in Julius Posener, *Berlin auf dem Wege zu einer neuen Architektur: Das Zeitalter Wilhelms II* (Munich: Prestel-Verlag, 1979), pp. 264-288.

26. *Cecilienhof* was built in 1914-1915 near Potsdam, for Crown Prince Friedrich Wilhelm.

27. Alexander Koch, ed., *Grossherzog Ernst Ludwig und die Darmstädter Künstler-Kolonie* (Darmstadt: Alexander Koch, 1901); *Ein Dokument deutscher Kunst: Darmstadt 1901-1976* (Darmstadt: Mathildenhöhe Darmstadt, 1976), vols. 4 and 5.

28. Margaret Zimmermann-Degen, *Hans Christiansen: Leben und Werk eines Jugendstilkünstlers* (Königstein im Taunus: Hans Köster, 1981), pp. 12-13, 23, 29.

29. Joseph M. Olbrich, *Architektur von Olbrich*, vol. 1 (Berlin, 1901-1902), pl. 103.

30. Christian Ferdinand Morawe, "Darmstadt," *Das Interieur* 2 (September 1901), pp. 153-157. (Morawe's former wife married Olbrich in 1903.)

31. Winfried Nerdinger, ed., *Richard Riemerschmid, vom Jugendstil zum Werkbund: Werke und Dokumente* (Munich: Prestel-Verlag, 1982), pp. 532-533.

32. Alexander Koch, "An die deutschen Künstler und Kunstfreunde!" *Deutsche Kunst und Dekoration* 1 (October 1897), pp. i-ii.

33. "Korrespondenzen," *Dekorative Kunst* 8 (April 1905), pp. V-VI; and "Kleine Nachrichten," *Kunst und Handwerk* 55 (May 1905), pp. 227-228.

34. Jean Hamilton, "German Interiors as Seen at the St. Louis Fair," *House Beautiful* 16 (November 1904), p. 30. For an opposite view of German influence in the United States (after World War I), see Laura Shelby Lee, "German Kultur and American Art," *House Beautiful* 44 (December 1918), pp. 388-390. We thank Gordon Gray for finding these references.

35. *Craftsman* 7 (October 1904), pl. facing p. 56; and *Craftsman* 9 (October 1905), p. 67. See also Gustav Stickley, "The German Exhibit at the Louisiana Purchase Exposition," *Craftsman* 6 (August 1904), pp. 489-506; and Irving K. Pond, "German Arts and Crafts at St. Louis," *Architectural Record* 17 (February 1905), pp. 119-125.

36. Lucius Burckhardt, ed., *Der Werkbund in Deutschland, Österreich und der Schweiz: Form ohne Ornament* (Stuttgart: Deutsche Verlags-Anstalt, 1977); and Joan Campbell, *The German Werkbund: The Politics of Reform in the Applied Arts* (Princeton: Princeton University Press, 1978).

37. See also Gert Selle, *Jugendstil und Kunst-Industrie: Zur Ökonomie und Ästhetik des Kunstgewerbes um 1900* (Ravensburg: Otto Maier Verlag, 1974); and Tilmann Buddensieg, et al., *Industriekultur: Peter Behrens und die A.E.G., 1907-1914* (Berlin: Gebrüder Mann Verlag, 1979), pp. D 186 and D 191-194.

38. Robert Judson Clark, "The German Return to Classicism after Jugendstil," *Journal of the Society of Architectural Historians* 29 (October 1970), p. 273. Regarding Josef Hoffmann's classicism, see Eduard F. Sekler, *Josef Hoffmann: Das architektonische Werk* (Salzburg: Residenz, 1982), esp. pp. 101-164. There was a similar revival in France; see Nancy Troy, "Toward a Redefinition of Tradition in French Design," *Design Issues* 1 (Fall 1984), pp. 53-69.

39. Robert Judson Clark, "Joseph Maria Olbrich and Vienna" (unpublished Ph.D. dissertation, Princeton University, 1974), esp. chapter 2; Robert Waissenberger, *Die Wiener Secession: Eine Dokumentation* (Vienna: Jugend und Volk Verlagsgesellschaft, 1971).

40. The juxtaposition of these two motifs in Voysey's wallpapers can be seen in *Dekorative Kunst* 1 (March 1898), p. 273. It was in March 1898 that the revised working drawings for the Secession Building were prepared by Olbrich, with some details supplied in the following months.

41. Contrast especially Wagner's church at Steinhof (1902, 1905-1907), and the Postal Savings Bank (1903-1920) with the Stadtbahn stations of the 1890s; see Heinz Geretsegger and Max Peintner, *Otto Wagner, 1841-1918* (Salzburg: Residenz Verlag, 1964), pp. 53-84; 151-178; 211-246.

42. Wilhelm Mrazek, ed., *Die Wiener Werkstätte: Modernes Kunsthandwerk von 1903-1932* (Vienna: Österreichisches Museum für angewandte Kunst, 1967); Werner J. Schweiger, *Wiener Werkstätte: Design in Vienna, 1903-1932* (New York: Abbeville Press, 1984).

43. Eduard F. Sekler, "The Stoclet House by Josef Hoffmann," in Douglas Fraser, Howard Hibbard, and Hilton J. Lewine, eds., *Essays in the History of Architecture Presented to Rudolf Wittkower* (London: Phaidon Press, 1967), pp. 228-244; idem, *Josef Hoffmann: Das architektonische Werk* (Salzburg; Residenz Verlag, 1982), pp. 75-100.

44. Burkhard Rukschcio and Roland Schachel, *Adolf Loos: Leben und Werk* (Salzburg: Residenz Verlag, 1982), pp. 110-111.

45. See Nikolaus Pevsner, "Frank Lloyd Wright's Peaceful Penetration of Europe," *Architects' Journal* 89 (May 4, 1939), pp. 731-734; A.L.L.M. Asselbergs et al., *Nederlandse Architectuur, 1880-1930: Americana* (Otterlo: Rijksmuseum Kröller-Müller, 1975), esp. pp. 28-40.

46. Dard Hunter II, *The Life and Work of Dard Hunter*, vol. 1 (Chillicothe, Ohio: Mountain House Press, 1983), pp. 125-151.

47. Interview with Fern Bradley Dufner, August 31, 1971. Bradley later built two houses in Short Hills, New Jersey, which he furnished with English, American colonial, and colonial-revival pieces.

48. "Charles Rohlfs," in Robert Judson Clark, ed., *The Arts and Crafts Movement in America, 1876-1916* (Princeton: Princeton University Press), p. 28.

49. C. Matlack Price, "Secessionist Architecture in America: Departures from Academic Traditions of Design," *Arts and Decoration* 3 (December 1912), p. 53.

50. Ibid., pp. 51-53.

51. Thomas E. Tallmadge, "Country House Architecture in the Middle West," *Architectural Record* 53 (October 1922), pp. 294-296; Gary Hollander, "Rockledge: A Summer House Designed by George W. Maher," *Tiller* 1 (July-August 1983), pp. 10-16.

52. H. Allen Brooks, *The Prairie School: Frank Lloyd Wright and his Midwest Contemporaries* (Toronto: University of Toronto Press, 1972), see esp. p. 7.

53. Randell L. Makinson, *Greene & Greene: Architecture as a Fine Art* (Salt Lake City: Peregrine Smith, 1977), pp. 118-121; idem, *Greene & Greene: Furniture and Related Designs* (Salt Lake City: Peregrine Smith, 1979), pp. 36-43.

54. Una Nixon Hopkins, "The Development of Domestic Architecture on the Pacific Coast," *Craftsman* 13 (January 1908), pp. 452, 456.

55. Vincent J. Scully, Jr., *The Shingle Style: Architectural Theory and Design from Richardson to the Origins of Wright* (New Haven: Yale University Press, 1955).

56. Possibly the firm of Arthur Heineman or of G. Lawrence Stimson.

57. *Wallace Nutting Pictures: Expansive Catalog* (Framingham, Mass.: Wallace Nutting, 1915), p. 486, cat. no. C2122.

58. Kenneth H. Cardwell, *Bernard Maybeck: Artisan, Architect, Artist* (Salt Lake City: Peregrine Smith, 1977). For a study of Maybeck's context see Richard Longstreth, *On the Edge of the World: Four Architects in San Francisco at the Turn of the Century* (New York and Cambridge: Architectural History Foundation and M.I.T. Press; 1983).

59. Kevin Starr, *Americans and the California Dream* (New York: Oxford University Press, 1973), esp. chapter 12.

60. For more about Arthur and Lucia Mathews, see Harvey L. Jones, *Mathews, Masterpieces of the California Decorative Style* (Salt Lake City: Peregrine Smith), 1980.

American Arts and Crafts Architecture:
Radical though Dedicated to the Cause Conservative

Richard Guy Wilson

On a sunny and mild day in January 1909, the English Arts and Crafts designer Charles Robert Ashbee observed the Pasadena work of Charles and Henry Greene. Before his arrival in California, Ashbee had visited Chicago and the Rose Valley community, outside of Philadelphia; during an earlier trip he had met leading designers in Boston and many other parts of the country. He knew both Louis Sullivan and Frank Lloyd Wright and in 1911 he would write an introduction to the German publication of Wright's work. In Pasadena Ashbee observed a new sophistication in American Arts and Crafts design, and exclaimed on the "tenderness . . . subtlety [and] self effacement of the Greenes' designs." At the end of an auto tour Ashbee and Charles Greene retired to the latter's house on the Arroyo Seco and over tea they discussed Henry George's single-tax theory. Ashbee ran his fingers over the fine surfaces of the Greenes' furniture (nos. 70, 222-225) and recorded the view from the window: "As the afternoon wore on, a glorious sunset lit the snow on the mountains to rose red."[1]

Ashbee's experience provides a direct link with the origins of the Arts and Crafts movement in England; the themes he expressed – politics and reform, ornamental details and nature, and the mood of contemplation – were part of the essence of both. For Ashbee America offered a new arena for development, one that would be forged by the vision and self-conscious nationalism of a Walt Whitman and the attempt by American designers to create a new way of life through architecture.[2] Ashbee admired the work of Frank Lloyd Wright and he agreed that architecture must utilize the machine; yet he felt uncomfortable with Wright's machine-produced architectural ornament. Ashbee claimed that ornament should

have "a more living and tender detail."[3] Ultimately, he responded more favorably to the Greenes' work than to Wright's: "It is more refined and has more repose." He recognized that different regions called for different approaches, asserting: "perhaps it is California that speaks rather than Illinois. . . ."[4]

To identify an American Arts and Crafts architecture is to encompass diverse attitudes and contradictions toward style, image, history, the region, the machine, materials, nature, and how life should be lived. The individualism of Arts and Crafts designers and the wide geographical spread makes generalizations immediately subject to exceptions. In a sense Arts and Crafts represented not a true movement but a widespread group of very individualistic designers who had a sometimes kindred spirit and an allegiance to creating an organic art and architecture that owed its origins to William Morris. Within the geographical area of southern California, the architecture included the white cubed-concrete cottages of Irving Gill, the Spanish Mission hotels of Arthur Benton, and the elegant wood bungalows of the brothers Greene. Certainly no more different attitudes toward architectural form and details, the region, and the usage of the machine can be imagined, and yet they were all part of the same Arts and Crafts impulse.

From log cabins recalling mythical frontiersmen in Adirondacks resorts to Prairie School houses nestled in the broad landscape of the midwest and low-rising bungalows erected in every section of the country, many designers shared a common conviction: it was anathema to all of them to rely solely upon the traditions of other cultures. The Philadelphia architect Will Price summed up the sentiment in *The Craftsman* in 1912: "How long will Art be led

[sic] captive to education and be shackled to precedent?" Price could admire selective aspects of the past such as "the glorious, if barbaric Gothic age," but what "we call the Renascance [sic] was for Architecture no re-birth of art, but a grave-digging resurrection . . . . Better, a thousand times better, the rock-ribbed Gothic of a Whitman than all the curled darlings and simpering niceties of a borrowed culture."[5]

The use of the word "Gothic" for most of the Arts and Crafts designers did not mean a specific stylistic response – or the copying of the Gothic – but rather a freedom from academic travails. Bertram Grosvenor Goodhue, a founding member of the Boston Society of Arts and Crafts, summed up in a *Craftsman* magazine article the differences between those who called themselves Gothicists and the academic classicists: "We are all divided, broadly speaking, in two categories: Conservative and Radical; Reactionary and Revolutionist; the Satisfied and the Unsatisfied – if you like, Classicist and Gothicist – though Romanticist seems to me a better and more exact characterization than Gothicist."[6] Goodhue equated his Romanticist point of view with "Originality" and as accepting the new facts of modern construction such as steel and concrete. His partner, Ralph Adams Cram, once called Louis Sullivan "essentially the most Gothic of all," meaning not in style but in structural expression.[7] In a similar vein, Frank Lloyd Wright argued for "a revival of the Gothic spirit" not in forms or details but in an architecture that was "organic" and resulted from the conditions and life of the people.[8] To Wright "the Renaissance was inorganic" and unfit for America, which he claimed "presents a new architectural proposition." The sentiments of Wright, Cram, Goodhue, and Price expressing antagonism for aca-

demic design would be echoed by many others, but the path to a new American architecture was not altogether free of historical references. Reverberations of the past can be seen in a Price house that recalls English roughcast buildings of C.F.A. Voysey (fig. 1), half-timbered cottages on the Philadelphia Main Line (no. 26) and on Presidio Heights in San Francisco (no. 76), and in colonial revival detail – early American and Spanish – whether in southwestern buildings or along the eastern seaboard (no. 59). Most Arts and Crafts architects, however, sought an architecture rooted in the traditions of specific regions. Frank Lloyd Wright claimed a conservative stance, not a radical position, when he wrote that he had gone back to the beginnings of architecture, to nature, and not to "seeking inspiration in books and adhering slavishly to dead formulae."[9] For him and for others, there would be occasional references to history, but never to history by academics such as Vignola and Vitruvius. The acceptable imagery was the region, the vernacular, and nature, or, as Price wrote: "Architecture is creeping to our doors almost unnoticed, close to the soil, still finding its birth, as always, in the simple dwellings of the countryside."[10]

The word "nature" as a prime determinant for Arts and Crafts designers had many interpretations. They could range from ornamental motifs such as the vines and leaves of Louis Sullivan (nos. 83 and 84) to the entire building as a reflection of the landscape (as with Frank Lloyd Wright; no. 85). In writing about the bungalows of the Greene brothers, the critic A.C. David observed that the exterior of a house "should not be made to count very strongly in the landscape"; it should "tend to disappear in its natural background."[11] Materials were important in this organic relation-

ship for, as Gustav Stickley explained, they provided "roots": "A house that is built of stone where stones are in the fields, of concrete where the soil is sandy, of brick where brick can be had reasonably, or of wood if the house is in a mountainous wooded region, will from the beginning belong to the landscape. And the result is not only harmony but economy."[12]

In creating a relationship to nature distinctions between the house and the garden would often be blurred. Devices to extend the house such as piazzas, sleeping porches, terraces, patios, lattice work, planters, window boxes, and pergolas would bring nature and the occupants into close contact. A pergola was to Stickley like a fireplace in the living room, an attempt to focus activity.[13] Rectilinearity could be softened either by foundation plantings or by materials such as clinker brick, boulders, and fieldstone[14] (fig. 15). The brothers Greene offset the straight line by undulating patio walls. In the midwest considerable disagreement existed within the Prairie School between the outflung geometry prescribed by Frank Lloyd Wright and the curving or natural lines favored by Jens Jensen, who prescribed the use of local plant materials.[15] Gardens by Purcell and Elmslie, for example, combined both formal geometry and the more informal lines of nature in the same design (no. 91). As with the question of architectural style and history, individual taste ruled rather than general agreement.

Arts and Crafts architects walked a fine line between the sophisticated and the untutored, between the highly crafted – the wrought-iron hinge, the pegged joint – and a rustic sensibility. As a rule, their details came from nature or vernacular traditions and ultimately they became a fetish. Stylistic choices such as the log cabin or the farmhouse for modern housing were an almost "deliberate regression," a romantic escape into rusticity and even primitivism.[16] The use of heavy masonry or timbers that retained their bark, as if hewn by ax rather than cut by a saw, suggested to one writer that architects believed "that by keeping their houses uncouth and primitive, they are giving these buildings a much more genuinely natural character."[17] Primitivism was manifest also in the central feature of the Arts and Crafts living room (and frequently other rooms as well): the fireplace or hearth. Henry Saylor, the bungalow promoter, wrote in 1911: "A bungalow without a fireplace would be almost as much of an anomaly as a garden without flowers."[18] Frequently encased in its own special chamber or inglenook – which had origins in the medieval period – and surrounded by built-in seats, the fireplace became the high altar of the house (no. 212, fig. 9).[19] Although no longer necessary as the source of heat, the fireplace in the Arts and Crafts dwelling became the anthropological heart of the house: "Once more in our modern and materialistic souls . . . is kindled the spark bequeathed by our fire-worshipping ancestors; we glimpse again the halo of legend and romance that has ever encircled the altar of the open hearth. . . ."[20]

The dining room was the other major space of the Arts and Crafts interior that resounded with primitivism or – perhaps more properly – tribal rituals. Here the family would gather in a ceremonial environment, seated in tall chairs with appropriate emphasis on the patriarch and the matriarch, and break bread. The setting called for ancient chants, and indeed some Arts and Crafts songs were written for mealtimes.[21] In common with most nineteenth- and twentieth-century conservative reform movements, Arts and Crafts designers believed that industrialism had shattered

Fig. 1. William L. Price (1861-1916) and Martin Hawley McLanahan (1865-1929), McLanahan house, Rose Valley, Pennsylvania, 1906. Photograph in collection of George Thomas, Philadelphia.

the family, bringing rootlessness and a loss of tradition; hence, emphasis centered on the family and the hearth.

Of course custom-designed houses with furnishings were not available to the entire population, again an indication of some of the contradictions of the Arts and Crafts movement. Architects of the period did succeed in rehousing significant portions of the expanding middle and working classes in the new suburban residential areas of American cities; however, a wide economic gulf existed between the wealthy clients of the brothers Greene (nos. 68 and 69) and the more humble bungalow courts designed by Alfred Heineman a few blocks away in Pasadena (fig. 2). Arts and Crafts architecture for the home existed

on at least three levels: the wealthy elite, as exemplified by the exquisite jewels of Greene and Greene, Mellor and Meigs, and others; the upper middle class, represented by Forest Hills Gardens and the custom design of architects such as Wright; and then the middle- and working-class level of prefabricated bungalows by Aladdin Homes, Radford's Artistic Bungalows, and, to some extent, Stickley. While many railed at the impact of the machine, the pollution of the slums – at the fact that work had become labor and lost its joy – few architects or consumers had any desire to sacrifice the comforts of modern life, such as electricity and central heating. Irving Gill and Grosvenor Atterbury are representative of the architects who, in

Fig. 2. Heineman & Heineman, Architects. (Alfred
Heineman, designer), *Bowen Court*, Pasadena, 1912.
Greene and Greene Library, Gamble House, Pasadena.

fact, embraced modern technology as
an opportunity to create cheap and economical housing. Others such as Purcell
and Elmslie, midwestern Prairie School
architects, wrote about the possibilities
of steel-frame construction; for the Arts
and Crafts to reach a large majority, the
machine had to be accepted.[22] Yet only a
few designers shared Frank Lloyd
Wright's enthusiasm for the machine;
overall, the response was an ambiguous
caution.[23]

The problem of mechanization was –
as William Morris realized by the 1880s

– not the machine itself, but the way in
which it was used in modern society.[24]
Probably the clearest position was enun-
ciated by Oliver Lovell Triggs, a professor at the University of Chicago, a literary critic and biographer of Walt
Whitman, secretary of the William Morris Society of Chicago, and a founder of
the Chicago Arts and Crafts Society and
the Industrial Art League of Chicago. In
his *Chapters in the History of the Arts and
Crafts Movement*, Triggs wrote: "The function of the machine is clearly to do most
of the mechanical work of the world,

and all its drudgery. The ideal machine is
automatic; the better and more perfect
the machine, the more able is it to dis-
pense with an operator. For the present
at least the machine is calculated to do
the lower kind of work, and to render
serviceable to the world the less skillful
and less intelligent workmen. The
higher the work, the more of intelligent
design necessary for a product, the
greater is the need for skilled craftsmen
to initiate *and execute* a given design."[25]
Triggs's position was not that extreme;
many American designers recognized

the possibilities of mechanization and while exquisitely handcrafted objects and even architectural ornament were still possible and even desired, the machine was a necessity.[26] Otherwise, the Arts and Crafts would simply cater to an economic elite. Some reformers saw the real problem to be societal factors and a capitalist economic system that led to machine abuses.

Most American Arts and Crafts architects saw themselves as reformers, as trying to create settings removed from crass speculator housing filled with tasteless atrocities of "Grand Rapidism." Many, including Price and the Greenes, flirted with fads such as the single-tax theory and Stickley printed articles with a vaguely communitarian bias.[27] But in the majority of cases the architects proved inadequate in dealing with the scene of most reform in the United States at the turn of the century – the large metropolitan city. This was not for lack of trying; Louis Sullivan, Bernard Maybeck, and Wilson Eyre, for example, did do large commercial structures, but their overall impact was minimal. It seemed that only through the grand scale of the classical and Beaux-Arts-inspired American Renaissance could the problem of redesigning the American city be approached.[28] The architects associated with Progressive politicians were not the Arts and Crafters but their opponents: Daniel Burnham, Charles McKim, Arnold Brunner, John Carrère, and Thomas Hastings.[29] The alternative of the Arts and Crafts – the garden city – found application only in American suburbs such as the Berkeley hills, Mason City [Iowa], and Forest Hills Gardens. On the premise that a renewal of national architecture exemplifying the true American character could begin only with the design of the individual dwelling, designers such as Gustav Stickley argued that from the "honest expres-

sion" of the house the "progressive architect" would then understand the problems of larger buildings and the city.[30] In its garden cities and suburban enclaves, Arts and Crafts architects designed jewels of houses and filled them with exquisite details, as if the contemplation of an articulated joint, a smooth piece of redwood, or a flowered window would bring serenity and perhaps a new consciousness.

English Origins

Some of the contradictory impulses making up American Arts and Crafts architecture can be found in the call for design reform that was part of the English origins of the movement. Design reform in England stretched back to the 1830s and the initial writings and work of Augustus W.N. Pugin. Although he died in 1852, well before the founding in 1888 of the "Arts and Crafts Exhibition Society," Pugin's equation of morality and architecture and his assertion that England's highest achievements – social, economic, religious, and architectural – came prior to the sixteenth century would be a central theme of the Arts and Crafts movement. Pugin linked the fall from grace of English architecture with the introduction of alien classicism and industrialism. His writings called for an architecture along Gothic lines, with form dictated by construction; it should be indigenous to its place and soil or, in other words medieval or Gothic.[31]

Writing his major works at the mid-nineteenth century, John Ruskin picked up, elaborated, and made available to a wider audience many of Pugin's themes. Classical architecture, according to Ruskin, meant a mechanical perfection achieved by workmen with no individuality, following prescribed rules. Architecture was different from mere building, he claimed; it sought to sum up the

aspirations of a people or a nation, and it must be spontaneous, a product of designers and makers, each showing their talents. Equating architecture with morality, Ruskin's impact would be tremendous and his fixation on ornament would make it a prime concern of the later Arts and Crafts movement.[32]

The ideals of Ruskin and Pugin first became apparent in English church reform architecture of the Ecclesiologists. Basing their designs on medieval precedent, but never copying, architects such as William Butterfield and George Edmund Street created a robust and original style that utilized a great deal of handcrafted ornament and furnishings. Both Philip Webb and William Morris spent time in Street's office during the 1850s and out of this relationship came what is frequently identified as the first building of the Arts and Crafts movement: Webb's design of a house for Morris, which was erected at Bexley Heath in Kent (fig. 3).[33] The sources of Webb's *Red House* are complicated: the building owes much to the vicarages and village schools designed a few years earlier by Street and Butterfield; it also draws upon Pugin's examples of hierarchical massing. *Red House* has an L-shaped crank plan; the differentiation in massing between the front and the lower wing to the rear, as well as the jogs or cranks in the plan, was intended to make the house appear as if, over the years, it had grown, with wings being added as the family and functions changed. Separate high-pitched roofs, one with a French leaded lantern, windows of different sizes (placed with relation to the interior functions and not for external harmony), and the vestiges of pointed arches gave *Red House* an indigenous character, even though its location was suburban. Inside Morris, Webb, and their pre-Raphaelite artist friends Edward Burne-Jones and Dante Gabriel

Fig. 3. Philip Webb (1831-1915), *Red House* for William Morris, Bexley Heath, Kent, 1859.

Fig. 4. Richard Norman Shaw (1831-1912) *Leyes Wood*, Sussex, 1868. From *Architecture and Building News*, London 1871.

Rossetti created murals and built-in furniture such as a combination cupboard, settle, and minstrels gallery with plain semi-Gothic joinery, large iron pulls and hinges, and painted panels.[34]

Red House was not a revival in the sense of being a copy of a specific style; rather, it was an amalgam of various sources – a secular Gothic in the manner of the thirteenth century. Morris always claimed a primary allegiance to Gothic architecture as the most moral, "the outcome of corporate and social feeling, the work of not individual but collective genius . . . ," and adaptable to various conditions of society and climate.[35] The important sources for architecture lay with the unpretentious; he wrote that a "new and genuine architecture will spring [from them], rather than from our experiments in conscious style."[36] For Webb, good architecture should be both "barbaric" – possessed of primitive, rude strength – and also "commonplace," not overly artistic and posturing.[37] In 1864 he planned an addition to *Red House* that, while never built, provides an illuminating insight. The extension would enclose a cloistered courtyard around the well, and it would be tile-hung and timber-framed, following local Kentish traditions.

Morris and Webb's idea of creating a new architecture based upon the vernacular and not stylistic manipulation was a goal never entirely achieved. Style was too important to nineteenth-century architects to be so easily discarded. It was a central concern of the Aesthetic movement of the 1860s and 1870s, with which Morris, Webb, and others such as Richard Norman Shaw were associated. Architecturally, the Aesthetic movement had at least two sides: the "Queen Anne" – a loose, uncanonical classicism usually rigged out in red brick and white trim – and an "Old English" with hung tiles, half timbering, and long rambling

plans (fig. 4). Both expressions drew upon English vernacular examples as sources, buildings of the time of Queen Anne and Tudor manor houses. They were seen frequently by both English and Americans as answers to the question of finding an English national architectural style.[38]

In the '80s and '90s a progressive widening occurred in the possible sources for an indigenous architecture. Almost always filled with Morris and Company furnishings or those of some other "art furniture" maker such as Jackson and Graham or the Century Guild, the houses could be in a variety of idioms, including white roughcast stucco cottages by C.F.A. Voysey, rough fieldstone by Ernest Gibson, Scottish Baronial by Charles Rennie Mackintosh, and red brick by Edwin L. Lutyens. These were the houses of the mature phase of the English Arts and Crafts movement and they related very strongly to the site and the local materials, as well as the regional vernacular. Seeking to appear as if they had "roots," these Arts and Crafts houses did transcend their locality: Voysey built white roughcast houses all over England, from the Lake District to the London suburbs, while Lutyens could use images ranging from Tudor to Georgian within a few miles in Surrey.[39] In the same manner that Morris could revive the eighteenth-century Sussex chair, turn to medieval and Persian patterns for fabrics, and also claim inspiration from nature, architecture became ecumenical. For the American architect looking to England for inspiration, the Arts and Crafts movement seemed polymorphous, containing elements of a Gothic or medieval revival, vernacular sources, exotic free styles, and even aspects of a more formal Georgian. The relation to the past was ambiguous in England and so it would remain in America.

Continental and Oriental Inspirations

Compared with the impact of England upon American Arts and Crafts architecture, the role of other countries is minor; yet they helped to give a distinct cast to American design. From the 1860s onward American architecture – and the other arts – experienced a transformation as a great many young architects traveled to Paris to study at the Ecole des Beaux-Arts; by the 1890s numerous American architects subscribed to the Ecole system of education and the grand classical style for public buildings. This shift of allegiance away from England to France, which continued through the first World War, is complex, for Ecole-trained American architects stood in direct opposition to their English-oriented counterparts in the Arts and Crafts movement. At the same time several of the architects who introduced the Arts and Crafts aesthetic in America in the 1870s and 1880s, such as Henry Hobson Richardson and Charles Follen McKim, were Ecole trained. And a later generation represented by Bernard Maybeck, the brothers Greene, and Grosvenor Atterbury were educated either at the Ecole or its American derivatives. While the Ecole and its American counterparts were academic institutions (and as such stressed the books and lineage of classical architecture), they also advocated appropriate responses to design "problems." As an alternative to grand public buildings that would almost always dictate a classical solution, the schools gave "problems" for small residences in which classical styles were not the only answer. For those Americans who either had or would develop an Arts and Crafts sensibility the Ecole provided less a classical style than a system of architectural planning and composition.[40] The result for Americans was buildings with sequences of clearly defined spaces lacking the claustrophobia of many English interiors.[41]

Another French contribution to American Arts and Crafts architecture was the writing of Eugène Emmanuel Viollet-le-Duc. An outspoken opponent of classicism, Viollet-le-Duc argued – as did Pugin and Ruskin – for the Gothic and medieval, seeing them as the high point of French civilization. Yet the solution for the nineteenth century was not, for him, a straight revival of the Gothic or any medieval style, but to uncover the first principles and primitive sources that could lead to a new architecture. Among other beliefs, he held that iron offered the basis for a constructive architecture similar to the Gothic. Although Viollet-le-Duc's work is problematic today – he combined and confused the unrelated premises of historical and structural expression, identifying structure as a sign of high civilization or culture[42] – some of his cast-iron ornament with swirling organic foliage provided prototypes for the French Art Nouveau of the 1890s. More important for Americans, he stressed a principle of design beginning with interior spaces and progressing outward – not unlike that of the Ecole. Gustav Stickley, Frank Lloyd Wright, and others lauded Viollet-le-Duc as a spokesman for integrity of construction and an organic approach to architecture.[43]

The flowing sinuous curves of the Art Nouveau style, which emerged in the 1890s with Victor Horta in Brussels and Hector Guimard in Paris, was in many ways a continental reinterpretation of Morris's philosophy. By this time the American Arts and Crafts movement had assimilated the English background and the influence of Art Nouveau, especially of Paris, remained ancillary. The only real presence of the trend in America – and it was small – was in decorative arts.[44] Yet

the prime promoter and the person who coined the term Art Nouveau, Siegfried Bing of Paris, wrote extensively on American art. While Bing did not label any American architecture explicitly as Art Nouveau, he praised American country houses and especially the work of Henry Hobson Richardson. In Richardson's structures he found an "archaic" and "primitive" quality that he felt would lead to a new American art.[45]

Louis Sullivan and followers such as George Grant Elmslie have been linked with Art Nouveau because of similar stylistic motifs in the ornament, but the tie is tenuous.[46] Sullivan's development, which included some French as well as English ornamental motifs, proceeded independently.[47] Indeed, considerable confusion existed in America as to what was Art Nouveau, as exemplified by one scholar identifying it with English plaster houses and the work of George Maher.[48]

European movements such as the Vienna Secession, the German Jugendstil, and the Scandinavian National Romanticism of Eliel Saarinen in Helsinki, P.V.J. Klint in Copenhagen, and Ragnar Östberg in Stockholm were also known in the United States. What to call these offshoots remains problematic; some of them were tied to Bing in Paris, while others represented a rectilinear approach to design. They were animated both by Morris's call for an indigenous architecture free of academic trammels and by isolated nationalistic quests for identity. At the Saint Louis Exposition of 1904 both the German and the Austrian pavilions – done in the latest Secessionist styles – excited comment in the press and Frank Lloyd Wright, Walter Burley Griffin, and others made special trips to see them.[49] William Gray Purcell, a Prairie School architect, visited Hendrik Petrus Berlage in Amsterdam and Ferdinand Boberg in Stockholm in 1906

while in Europe studying vernacular architecture. Through a tour orchestrated by Purcell, Berlage visited America in 1911 and saw the work of Wright, Sullivan, and others.[50]

There was a small flurry of Secessionist or Jugendstil architectural designs in the United States, as can be seen in works by Claude Bragdon of Rochester, Milton Medary of Philadelphia, Louis Curtis of Kansas City, Thomas P. Barnett of St. Louis, and others. John Hudson Thomas of San Francisco did a number of houses with Secessionist elements (nos. 81 and 82), though one can detect American motifs – those of the Prairie School – as well. Significantly, a number of Secessionist and Jugendstil designers – Joseph Urban, Kem Weber, and later Wolfgang Hoffmann, the son of Josef Hoffmann – immigrated to the United States. Their impact would come in the 1920s with the development of the "Moderne" or "Art Deco" style. Several American critics identified a similarity of purpose in the Secessionists' "departures from academic traditions of design" (striving for a simplicity of decorative effects) and the work of Gill, Wright, Sullivan, and Griffin.[51]

European styles were not the only influence; Oriental and Middle Eastern design also had an impact on American Arts and Crafts architecture. Orientalism had been a current in European painting since the mid-nineteenth century, and Persian motifs appeared in some English Aesthetic movement design.[52] In America the grilles and screens used in Richardson's houses – the Paine house in Waltham or McKim, Mead and White's piazza screens in the Newport Casino – were direct reflections of the English interest; the work of other American architects appears to have been influenced by Middle Eastern abstractions of ornament and overall forms as well.[53]

Fig. 5. Japanese Pavilion at the Centennial, Philadelphia, 1876. From Thompson Westcott's *Centennial Portfolio: A Souvenir of the International Exhibition at Philadelphia,*1876.

Of more importance to many American Arts and Crafts designers was the Far East – Japan in particular. America had opened Japan to Western trade and Japanese pavilions were built at the 1876 Centennial Exposition in Philadelphia (fig. 5) and the 1893 World's Columbian Exposition in Chicago; during the 1890s substantial collections of Japanese art were being assembled in the United States. The first English language book on Japanese architecture was published in 1886 in Boston and the amount of writing in American Arts and Crafts literature devoted to Japanese subjects is overwhelming. Japanese motifs, from curved gable ends to nearly wholesale replication of pagodas and torri gates, appeared in Arts and Crafts houses and bungalows from coast to coast.[54] For American-oriented Arts and Crafts architects Japan offered the example of an indigenous culture that embodied the organic quality they found in the middle ages. Ralph Adams Cram, probably the most prominent Gothicist in America, felt that the "perfect simplicity" of a Japanese house caused the "chaos of Western houses" to become "an ugly dream."[55]

Frank Lloyd Wright drew upon Japanese architecture, but of more significance to him was the Japanese print. His large collection of prints – with which he paid employees when out of money – taught him a composition of simple, interlocking geometric elements. He spoke and wrote frequently about the lessons to be found: "those characteristic traits which the Japanese seize graphically and unerringly reduce to simple geometry; the graphic soul of the thing, as seen in the geometrical analysis of Hokusai."[56] Other writers found the simplicity of the Japanese and the Secessionists to be analogous – one of the major sources of the "originalia" of the midwest.[57] On the edge of the continent in California, the Oriental presence was more prevalent and, consequently, the influence more pronounced. Details such as cloud lift or scarf joints, *irimoya* roof tiles, porch posts resting upon rounded boulders half sunk in the ground, undulating patio walls, and trellises found in the work of the Greene brothers reflects a close inspection and adaptation of Japanese and Far Eastern details.[58] Such features stand far removed both temporally and spatially

from the rough barbarism of a Philip Webb or the half timbering and concrete of a Grosvenor Atterbury, yet they were all part of a search for an indigenous and organic culture and architecture.

The American Aesthetic Movement

As much as the American Arts and Crafts movement owed a debt to English and other foreign sources, it was also the product of a quest for a national style. Only after 1890 does the distinction between what was Arts and Crafts and what was academic, or the American Renaissance, become significant as two different approaches to creating an American architecture. The roots for both movements go back to the 1870s in designs such as the William Watts Sherman house in Newport by Henry Hobson Richardson and Stanford White (fig. 6 and no. 2). Based on Richard Norman Shaw's Old English manorial style, the Sherman house – a summer resort cottage – was smaller and its tall gabled roofs appeared more prominently as compositional planes holding the form together. The shingle covering of the second floor, used here to imitate Shaw's hung tiles, exemplifies an American method that dates to the earliest settlers.

Richardson died in 1886 at the age of 48; hence, one can only speculate as to whether he would have been a leading American Arts and Crafts architect. However, to many of those who would become identified with the Arts and Crafts – Sullivan, Wright, Cram, Bragdon, Eyre, Ellis, and others – Richardson was the individual who pointed the way to a new American architecture.[59] Taking a style of the past – the medievally based southern French Romanesque – Richardson made it uniquely American; while the basis of much of his planning and composition of form

Fig. 6. Henry Hobson Richardson (1838-1886) and Stanford White (1853-1906), William Watts Sherman house, Newport, Rhode Island, 1874-1876. Drawing attributed to Stanford White. From *The New York Sketch Book of Architecture*, May 1875.

Fig. 8. McKim, Mead and White (Charles F. McKim, William R. Mead, Stanford White), Samuel Tilton house, Newport, Rhode Island, 1880-1882, northwest view, ca. 1884.

Fig. 7. "Old House at Newport, R.I." Bishop Berkeley house in Middletown, Rhode Island. From *The New York Sketch Book of Architecture*, December 1874.

Fig. 9. Tilton house, north wall of living room. Historic American Building Survey, Library of Congress, Washington, D.C.

came from the Ecole des Beaux-Arts – which he had attended in the early 1860s – he frequently fitted out his buildings with fabrics, wallpapers, stained glass, and objects by William Morris and other Arts and Crafts designers. Tiles by the English art potter William De Morgan appeared in his own home. During a trip in 1882 Richardson arranged to be received by Morris. To his wife he described the event at Kelmscott House, Hammersmith: "Mr. Morris rec'd us very cordially & showed us upstair[s] into a large room about 35 [feet] long hung with his . . . blue bird tapestry . . . about 18 feet wide. I can't describe Mrs. Morris. Pre-Raphaelite to a degree . . . . I was more than pleased with Morris[,] his straight forward manner etc."[60]

Richardson was one of a number of American architects – among them Robert S. Peabody and William Ralph Emerson of Boston, Hudson Holly and Charles McKim of New York, and Frank Furness of Philadelphia – who discovered the English Aesthetic movement in the early and mid-1870s and began to use English "art" furnishings. At the same time merchants, notably Daniel Cottier in New York, sold both English- and American-designed Aesthetic objects. Between June 1875 and May 1877, Clarence Cook published in *Scribner's Monthly* eleven illustrated articles that promoted the Aesthetic movement approach along with American interpretations such as Charles McKim's "Old Colonial" work.[61]

The American Queen Anne was an amalgam of both the Old English tile-hung and half-timbered style and the red brick Queen Anne. Applied indiscriminately, the term referred to anything with shingles, red brick, sunflowers, half timbering, manipulated and distorted classical details, and perhaps a little oriental tossed in for spice. From the east coast resorts where it first appeared, the Queen Anne traveled inland to suburbs and city row houses, and then across the country to lake resorts and townhouses and finally came to rest on the west coast. The style was interpreted by most American architects and critics as an English nationalistic revival of their vernacular and, as such, it suggested looking closer to the American past for a native expression. Beginning in the mid-1870s the pages of American architectural journals were filled with polemics and drawings that illustrate the discovery by Americans of the seventeenth- and eighteenth-century heritage.[62]

Charles F. McKim emerges as the most important architect searching for an American expression based upon the native vernacular in the 1870s. While a student at the Ecole, McKim visited England in the summer of 1869 and saw the Aesthetic movement taking shape. He brought back news of it to Richardson's office, which he joined in 1870. Working partially on his own by the mid-1870s, McKim began investigating early American colonial. In 1874 he hired a Newport photographer, John Appleby Williams, to photograph the antiquities of the resort. Assembled as a book of twenty-nine photographs, McKim's choices provide a virtual panorama of future Arts and Crafts interests. The overall impression was a continuity of vision: furniture, buildings, and surrounding vegetation existed in an organic unity. The most famous of the series, "Old House at Newport, R.I.," which appeared in the *New York Sketch Book of Architecture* of December 4, 1874 (fig. 7), was the first published photograph of an early American building, the Bishop Berkeley house in Middletown, Rhode Island (1729).[63] Instead of the classically symmetrical front, McKim had the photographer capture the rear, a long sweeping roof pierced by two chimneys, and with a lean-to addition. In the accompanying text McKim complemented "the picturesque surroundings and architectural merit" of the old houses.

By the late 1870s and early 1880s, this examination of early American building resulted in a "modernized colonial," as one writer labeled it – a style that also incorporated elements of the Queen Anne and other exotic details such as the Japanese. The Samuel Tilton house (figs. 8, 9) by McKim and his partners – William Mead and Stanford White – indicates the new synthesis. A rectangular box dominated by a high gable, the building is taut and contained; windows are banked and placed where needed. The exterior covering is half timber and stucco on the north and west and shingled on the remainder, combining both Queen Anne and Colonial Revival. Semi-abstract mosaics of a sunburst and shield, composed of shells, pebbles, glass, and coal chips, worked in the stucco were inspired by Puritan examples.. The parlor, painted a dark English green with gold highlights, is a study in Aesthetic-movement eclecticism. The fireplace breast contains a variety of motifs such as Chinese Chippendale paneling, an Adamesque oval mirror and shell niches, all drawn from various periods of Newport's past. In front of the fireplace, creating an open inglenook, were built-in seats with sunflower rosettes.[64]

American architects had focused initially on the informal early American vernacular; however, by the mid-1880s interest was evident in the formal Georgian of the mid- and later eighteenth century. McKim, Mead, and White's Edgar house in Newport (fig. 10) of the mid-1880s displays an affinity to the work of Shaw and Webb in England, while bearing decidedly American features. A very free adaptation of Ameri-

Fig. 10. McKim, Mead and White, Commodore William G. Edgar house, Newport, Rhode Island, 1884-1886. Rendering attributed to Stanford White.

can images drawn from the south, Philadelphia, and Boston, the house has an Aesthetic movement refinement in details such as the long narrow buff-colored Roman brick. A critic describing the Edgar house in 1886 observed: "Although disclosing some affinity with the colonial style this house can scarcely be classed as colonial."[65]

The Edgar house begins to reveal the establishment of two conceptual ordering systems that occurred in American architecture and culture in the 1890s. Containing many features and details that would be identified with the Arts and Crafts, the Edgar house did not relate in any specific way to Newport or its surroundings; instead, it tended toward a grandiose statement of classical origins that McKim and his partners would promote as the true heritage of America. This attitude, which became known as the American Renaissance, saw the origins and aspirations of American architecture and culture as lying in the Greco-Roman classical tradition and various fifteenth-through eighteenth-century reincarnations; the result was a grand classical façade placed on most

American public and commercial buildings and many private residences. The resuscitation of forms, details, and motifs from the classical past became for many Americans the dominant image, and can be contrasted with the other trend that grew out of the experimentation of the 1870s and 1880s, out of the Americanized version of the Aesthetic movement: the Arts and Crafts.[66]

Both the Arts and Crafts and the American Renaissance mentalities were opposed to the extremes of the early High Victorian taste of the 1860s to the 1880s, and both were part of the great "clean-up" of cluttered Victorian interiors. In equal measure, they stood for good craftsmanship and for unification of the arts: the integration of painting, sculpture, and furnishings with the building. Both were highly didactic and viewed their work from a moralistic perspective as improving lives and as a vehicle for education. But there were pronounced differences. The American Renaissance, looking to academic models of European classicism or the Georgian of the American past, attempted to impose a single unified expression

upon America. The Arts and Crafts adopted the unacademic, and treated formal sources freely. Its exponents accepted diversity of image and expression and attempted to relate buildings to the site and locality, eschewing what they considered to be false and pretentious and embracing more organic forms that would reflect a truly American culture.

Anglo-American Imagery and Church Design

On one level the Arts and Crafts in America strove for the maturity to create a genuine American architecture, but on another level the ingrained cultural-inferiority complex toward England and Europe meant a strong reliance on imported imagery. As the fountainhead of the Arts and Crafts movement, England continued to exert a strong hold and consequently Old English, Queen Anne, and English-inspired plaster houses and churches were constructed across the country.[67]

Typically, this architecture seldom copied earlier buildings but contained a freedom of detail, as in the Fleur-de-Lys Studios in Providence, Rhode Island, of 1885 (fig. 11). Designed by Sidney R. Burleigh, an artist, and Edmund R. Willson, a Beaux-Arts-trained architect, the source was half-timbered stucco buildings such as those of Chester in England. The plaster decorations were by Burleigh, Charles Walter Stetson (a local artist), and John C. Aldrich (an industrialist-businessman for whom the Arts and Crafts were an avocation). Their work (see no. 27) displays a reverence for English sources; they later did a number of joint commissions under the banner of the "Art Workers Guild" in evident emulation of the English group of the same name. The facade of the Studios was conceived as a giant reredos on which symbols and signs could be placed. Growing in intensity from the

Fig. 11. Sidney R. Burleigh (1853-1928) and Edmund R. Willson (1856-1906) of Stone, Carpenter and Willson, Fleur de Lys Studios building, Providence, Rhode Island, 1885. Decorations by John G. Aldrich (1864-1952), Charles Walter Stetson (1858-1914), and Burleigh. Photograph in the collection of David Aldrich.

A medievally inspired communalism remained an ideal of the Arts and Crafts movement and helped provide a substructure of ideals for the many designers who were motivated by religious convictions.[69] Their church designs and fittings helped to maintain the English architectural connection and to spread the concept of the Arts and Crafts in America. The most influential examples came from Ralph Adams Cram and Bertram Grosvenor Goodhue. Together they succeeded in changing the entire face of American religious architecture, making the English medieval church the home of – as might be expected – Episcopalians, and also Presbyterians, Baptists, Swedenborgians, Catholics, and others. From Cram descended the Boston Gothicists, who held sway until the 1940s. Both Cram and Goodhue were part of a Boston arts community that, in the 1890s, expressed royalist sentiments, flirted with the "decadent" affectations inspired by Oscar Wilde, and belonged to the high Anglo-Catholic Episcopal church. As early as the mid-1880s Cram proclaimed: "Morris is without a doubt, the most wholly and roundly great man that the century can show." Both Cram and Goodhue helped found the Boston Society of Arts and Crafts in 1897 and showed their designs frequently in the annual exhibitions. Earlier, in 1892, Cram had edited *The Knight Errant*, a lavish arts magazine consciously modeled on the English *Hobby Horse* (fig. 12). Contributors included Bernard Berenson, Ernest Fenollosa, Walter Crane, F. Holland Day, and others on Japanese art, Renaissance painting, and the "Restoration of Idealism." Goodhue contributed the cover (fig. 12) and a number of articles, including a critical notice of William Lethaby's *Architecture, Mysticism and Myth*. Lethaby, an English disciple of Morris, proclaimed a mystical basis in nature as the origin of

Fig. 12. Bertram Grosvenor Goodhue, cover for *The Knight Errant*, Boston, 1891.

architectural form, while at the same time advocating the use of modern materials such as concrete. He would have an impact on some Americans seeking a new organic basis for architecture.[70]

Cram and Goodhue's church architecture of the 1890s derived from contemporary English practice, especially the work of George Frederick Bodley and his American disciple Henry Vaughan. Cram believed in "a medieval spirit vitalized by modern conditions," and these English architects had succeeded in banishing the aggressive crudity of the High Victorian and creating a new medievalism of fine details. According to Cram, he and Goodhue took up "English Gothic at the point when it was cut off during the reign of Henry VIII and go[ing] on from that point, develop[ed] the style England had made

bottom to the top, seagulls, flowers, and proto-Art-Nouveau swirls appear at the street level; heraldic shields, letters, and heads fill the middle section; and three large gowned pre-Raphaelite figures representing painting, sculpture, and architecture occupy the gable. The upper part of the gable was purposely misaligned with the lower section in an evident attempt to imitate the construction, over time, of earlier buildings. Inside, the studios appear relatively plain; Dutch tiles were arranged around Burleigh's fireplace and joinery and upright stair posts in the style of Philip Webb were used in the hall.[68]

her own . . . along what might be assumed to be logical lines . . . ." Their design for All Saints' in Ashmont (no. 22) follows this direction: the fifteenth-century Perpendicular was the beginning point, though modified and simplified. Decorated with extensive interior fittings – windows, altars, and liturgical vessels – the church illustrated a conservative source for much Arts and Crafts imagery.[71]

The later careers of Cram and Goodhue indicate the divergent paths of the American Arts and Crafts.[72] Cram went toward archaeology, or more accurate replication, while Goodhue was attracted by the modern, using traditional forms to create a native Art Deco. Cram claimed that this difference led to their separation in 1914; however, evidence indicates that the split came primarily from Goodhue's craving for recognition. Goodhue was a very talented designer and one of the great American ornamentalists and draftsmen; the Gothic could not offer enough stimulus, and he looked for increasingly exotic sensations.

English imagery played an important role in the work of many other American Arts and Crafts architects, ranging from nearly direct imitations to subtle replays. Harvey Ellis used both English examples and the Scottish Art Nouveau as a point of departure (fig. 14). Philadelphia architects such as Price, Eyre, and Mellor and Meigs turned English precedent into a regional expression (nos. 24, 25, and 26) and even in the work of Frank Lloyd Wright remnants of English half-timbering can be seen in Prairie School masterpieces such as the Ward Willits house (no. 85).

Stickley's Craftsman Homes and the Bungalow

Gustav Stickley's importance for the American Arts and Crafts cannot be

Fig. 13. Harvey Ellis for Gustav Stickley, color scheme for a dining room, published in *The Craftsman*, July 1903.

Fig. 14. Harvey Ellis for Gustav Stickley, perspective drawing for a house, published in *The Craftsman*, November 1903.

minimized – especially in the areas of decorative arts, furniture, and the dissemination of ideas – but his architectural contribution remains elusive. He lacked architectural training and, while he claimed responsibility for many architectural projects published under the "Craftsman" rubric, his role was more as a promoter and critic. His method of furniture design, talking and waving his hands at workmen, could not have produced much in the way of buildings. The work that Stickley promoted ranges from the very best – Irving Gill, the Greene brothers, and Louis Sullivan – to some of the most banal. His contribution lies in three areas: first, publishing ideas on regionalism and architecture along with the work of important architects; second, hiring designers to create inexpensive model bungalows (or "Craftsman Homes," as he called them), which he published; and third, overseeing the production of a small number of custom-designed houses that range from the mediocre to the important – such as the log cabin Craftsman Farms.[73] While Stickley claimed over twenty million dollars in construction in 1915 alone, the actual number is probably far less.[74]

The most inspired architecture published under the Craftsman label came from the pen of Harvey Ellis, whom Stickley employed between June 1903 and Ellis's death in January 1904. Ellis had absorbed the latest English and Continental Arts and Crafts design tendencies along with Japanese prints (see fig. 13); he brought a sophistication to Stickley, designing some furniture that helped to relieve Stickley's characteristic heaviness (no. 102) and also a series of house projects. Elements of Ellis's designs recall the stair towers of Mackintosh, the fenestration banks of Baillie Scott, and the gables and ornamental details of Olbrich and the Secession (fig.

Fig. 15. Gustav Stickley, perspective drawing for a "A Bungalow of Irregular Form . . .," published in *The Craftsman*, April 1907.

14). The death of Ellis deprived Stickley of the only genuinely talented architect he ever employed. Never again did his company generate houses of such artistic grace and poetry.[75]

The bungalow was a housing type popular with Stickley and other Arts and Crafts designers (fig. 15). While it has become almost synonymous with Stickley, he was but one of many promoters and if his contribution is measured against Henry Wilson and his *Bungalow Magazine*, and the bungalows sold by mail by the Aladdin Company or Sears and Roebuck, Stickley's position appears more modest.[76] The origin of the word "bungalow" goes back to the English settlement in India and the development of low-lying veranda-surrounded houses. In America the term "bungalow" came to mean an unpretentious single-story, or one-and-a-half story house with conspicuous roof and

a big porch, located at a resort, in suburbia, or in a semi-rural area.[77] Although the brothers Greene made some very costly bungalows, the genre became identified with inexpensive housing. By 1910 bungalows were ubiquitous and, while known at times as peculiarly southern Californian, they appeared in suburbs all across the country well into the 1920s. Henry Saylor emphasized that bungalows were not an architectural style but a housing type. He stressed that they were adaptable to different regions and styles, and showed examples covered in shingles, others that belonged to the Prairie School, and still others with colonial-revival details. To the basic prototype architectural imagery could be added.[78]

Stickley's "Craftsman Homes" and much of the architecture he published were part of the Arts and Crafts vogue for inexpensive middle-class, single-

Fig. 16. Aymar Embury, II (1880-1966), perspective drawing for a "Modern Colonial" house, published in *The Craftsman*, March 1912.

Fig. 18. Gustav Stickley, *The Log House* at Craftsman Farms, Morris Plains, New Jersey, 1908-1910. Northeast view, illustrated in *The Craftsman*, November 1911.

Fig. 17. Craftsman Architects for Gustav Stickley, perspective drawing for "A Craftsman House," published in *The Craftsman*, March 1904.

Fig. 19. *Log House*, living room, illustrated in *The Craftsman*, November 1911.

family housing that brought the occupants and nature together. His designs, sold by mail through the Craftsman Company, were intended as individualistic alternatives to the monotonous, poorly conceived builder's housing of the period. Craftsman houses were pictured in settings displaying landscape features such as foundation planting: "linking . . . a house to the ground on which it stands."[79] Styles included Mission, salt-box-shaped farmhouses, and "Modern Colonial cottages (figs. 15 and 16) constructed variously out of concrete, stucco, and logs. Illustrations showed interiors with the ritual of dining and the fireplace prominently displayed along with Craftsman furniture (fig. 13). Some of Stickley's enthusiasms defy stylistic categorization, such as the square box-shaped, hipped-roof dwelling that became omnipresent in every American town (fig. 17). In the accompanying text Stickley – or his ghost writer – stressed their adaptability to location.

The custom-designed houses produced by Stickley's firm exhibited a range of quality and price, from inexpensive homes to higher-priced models for the upper middle class. Of these, the log house at Craftsman Farms in Morris Plains, New Jersey (1910), is his most evocative contribution (figs. 18, 19). He originally intended it to serve as a centerpiece – the clubhouse – of a utopian community devoted, as he wrote, to "reviving practical and profitable handicrafts in connection with small farming carried out by modern methods of intensive agriculture."[80] Unfortunately, the community never materialized (perhaps because of overextended finances) and the log cabin clubhouse became his own dwelling. With its large-sized chestnut logs, it sums up perfectly the primitivistic, back-to-nature ethos of the American Arts and Crafts movement.

One reviewer in *The Craftsman* called it "nobly barbaric" and compared it to the poems of William Morris.[81] A large substantial structure, the living room measures fifty feet in length with huge ceiling beams spliced so that the center beam appears as one log. At either end massive rough-faced ashlar fireplaces contain copper hoods with mottoes in Gothic script such as "The lyf so short the craft so long to lerne."

The Resort

Resort and vacation architecture helped to give a special character to the American Arts and Crafts movement. The concept of annual vacations and the development of resorts and vacation homes began on a large scale in the 1870s and reached a peak in the first two decades of the twentieth century. By then, the idea of the "strenuous life" – a rustic escape from the false, overly mechanized, and commercialized urban world – paralleled very closely aspects of the Arts and Crafts ideology. Many of Stickley's Craftsman Homes and the bungalows of other builders were advertised as second homes fit for the lakes and the mountains.[82] These structures, incorporating rustic and natural imagery, provided Americans with a model for living. Dissatisfied with the tension existing between temporary and permanent conditions, many vacationers took the primitive and rustic back to suburban civilization and attempted to emulate a resort style of life year round.

Some architects made no clear distinction between designs intended for resorts and those suitable for other locations, such as suburbs. Gustav Stickley's "Bungalow of Irregular Form. . ." (fig. 15) actually derived from a vacation house on a mountain in New Hampshire.[83] Frank Lloyd Wright used virtually the same idiom for the suburbs of

Chicago as for vacation homes on midwestern lakes and the plains of Montana. Many of the commissions of the Greene brothers were vacation homes for easterners who came west for the winter months (nos. 68 and 69). And the bungalow court was intended initially as a temporary vacation home (fig. 2).

The log cabin comes closest to being a distinct resort idiom. An early American building type with roots in the structures of the German (Pennsylvania-Dutch) and Swedish settlers, it began to emerge in the mid-nineteenth century as an American symbol embodying traits of fortitude, hardiness, democracy, and the pioneer spirit. Romanticized, the log cabin became a national icon, the American equivalent to Abbé Laugier's "Primitive Hut" of antiquity.[84] At the Centennial Exposition of 1876 a "New England Kitchen of 1776" housed in a log cabin received favorable comment, even though it was historically fallacious. Shortly thereafter, the log cabin began to appear in a number of resorts, ubiquitous in certain localities such as the Adirondacks and the western national parks, while in others – such as the White Mountains of New Hampshire – it seldom appeared.

The Adirondack camp was the apotheosis of the family log cabin. From its inception there in the 1870s, its development closely follows national architectural trends: the earliest camps bear traces of the Aesthetic movement while at the turn of the century, the Arts and Crafts character becomes more prominent.[85] The William H. Read camp of 1905-1906 (fig. 20) exemplifies the rustic sophistication of the Adirondacks with its carefully designed features of standardized (10 inches in diameter) hewn logs "cut from the surrounding forest, each one selected with great care as to size, and more particularly to location, not more than one tree being taken

Fig. 20. Davis, McGrath, and Shepard, architects, Adirondack lodge for William A. Read, Little Simon Pond, New York, 1905-1906. Dining room, published in *American Architect and Building News*, July 14, 1906.

Fig. 21. Robert C. Reamer (1873-1938), Old Faithful Inn, Yellowstone National Park, 1902-1903. Northwest view by Cook Ely, 1905. Photograph in collection of Montana Historical Society.

from any one spot, so that its loss would not be noticed from the lake.''[86] Peeled logs used for the walls were stained a dark brown, while smaller braces were left in their "rustic" state. Ax marks were left on ceilings. A large complex of a main lodge with a living room measuring twenty-five by forty feet, there was also a dining and kitchen lodge and accessory buildings all located overlooking Little Simon Lake in the midst of a family forest preserve of 5,000 acres. Furnishings were in the appropriate Mission style.

The most impressive log cabin complex in existence is the Old Faithful Inn at Yellowstone National Park, designed by Robert C. Reamer in 1902 (figs. 21, 22). Shingle-covered outer pavilions containing guest rooms surround the main lodge, a six-story-high structure with small dormers on the roof. A two-story log portico leads into a log Gothic cathedral, a six-story covered atrium surrounded by balconies carried on fanciful twisted limbs and branches. Furniture is a mixture of Stickley, Limbert, and other Mission-style manufacturers. Anchoring the interior space is a giant rock fireplace and chimney, a permanent vertical feature of stasis counterpoised to the eruptions that took place scarcely a hundred yards from the Inn's front porch (fig. 22).[87]

Regionalism

What constitutes a regional response varied in Arts and Crafts architecture in America; it could be historically based and range from the early American colonial of the northeast to the Dutch colonial of the mid-Atlantic and the Spanish colonial or Mission style of the southwest. Less historical manifestations were determined by the landscape, as with the Prairie School of the midwest. Still another response – the work of the Greenes – took in the new lifestyle

Fig. 22. Old Faithful Inn, Yellowstone National Park.
Haynes Foundation Collection, Montana Historical
Society, Helena, Montana.

made possible by the salubrious climate of southern California. The architectural literature of the period recognized the importance of regional differences and, in addition to noting the usual "styles," such as "Colonial" or "Modern English Plaster," described "A Style of the Western Plains" and "the Northern Tradition."[88] Wilson Eyre claimed: "California has . . . its distinctive style to suit its climate and natural scenery; the Middle West is still experimental; and we here in the East are continuing to concentrate on a few styles, such as the English manor house and the smaller French chateaux, but especially the English."[89]

Philadelphia

The allegiance to English models was especially common to Philadelphia; however, Eyre and his compatriots mixed the foreign with local traditions to create a regional idiom. Responding to the historical situation of Philadelphia as the foremost English colony in the new world, Eyre claimed: "The people in England live more nearly the kind of life we lead, having made the most thorough study and having a greater knowledge of comfort and beauty combined in country living. We may not yet have developed a distinctive American style of our own, but we have so adapted and changed the existing forms of older countries to suit our own needs [as] to make them different from the originals."[90]

Together with William L. Price and Robert C. Kennedy, Eyre formed in 1883 the T-Square Club, which held exhibits and talks on decorative arts and provided an Arts and Crafts forum. Both the *T-Square Club Journal* and *House and Garden*, of which Eyre was a founder and editor from 1901 to 1905, promoted the Arts and Crafts. The group that developed around Eyre and the T-Square Club included Price, Walter Mellor, Arthur I.

Fig. 23. William Price (1861-1916) and Martin Hawley McLanahan (1865-1929), Alice Barber and Charles Stephens house, *Thunderbird Lodge*, Rose Valley, Pennsylvania, 1905. Photograph in collection of George Thomas, Philadelphia.

Meigs, Edmond Gilchrist, Robert R. McGoodwin, and Louis Duhring. Out of this rich background came magazines such as Edward Bok's *Ladies' Home Journal*, which also supported an Arts and Crafts viewpoint. And the tiles of Henry Chapman Mercer and the wrought iron of Harvey Yellin were part of the great variety of crafts activities in the region. Mercer's wide-ranging eclecticism, which appears in the diversity of his tiles, parallels the architectural sensibility (no. 212). Yellin shows the problem of assigning a specific stylistic label to any of the Philadelphia work, for his iron incorporates an assortment of historical styles reinterpreted with a wit and fluidity that was not specifically Gothic or

any other idiom (no. 21).

While England was the prime inspiration for Eyre, forms and details derived from French chateaus, Norman farmhouses, and rural Pennsylvania also played a role. The image was a pastoral idealism: fox hounds, horses, and riders might come through at any moment and the building should look as though it had grown over the years, an eccentric picturesque ramble of juxtaposed forms. Materials ranged from the ubiquitous red brick to Germantown schist and English rough-cast stucco (nos. 24, 26). Price's Stephans house (fig. 23) at Rose Valley included additions to an old barn, while Mellor and Meigs's Morris house on the Main Line (no. 26 and fig.

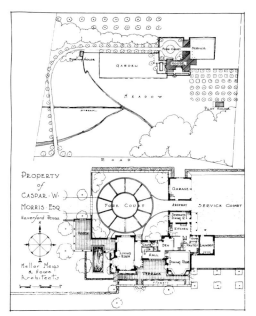

Fig. 24. Mellor, Meigs and Howe (Walter Mellor, Arthur Ingersoll Meigs, and George Howe), Caspar Wistar Morris house, Haverford, Pennsylvania, 1914-1916. Site and first-floor plans, published in *A Monograph of the Work of Mellor,Meigs and Howe* (New York, 1923).

24) stretched out looking like a series of additions, even though it had been designed and built as a unit. The Philadelphia awkwardness invaded even city work such as Eyre's double house for John Neil (no. 23), wherein the overall order of the form was undercut by differences in the bay windows.[91]

As a group the Philadelphians exemplified the individualism of the American Arts and Crafts movement, and in a sense they succeeded in creating a vernacular response that could look at home only in the area. The result was a series of environments that are perhaps unparalleled in the American Arts and Crafts and range from the thoroughly committed "Single Taxers" at Price's Rose Valley to the French Village development of Gilchrist and McGoodwin in Chestnut Hill and the high-class suburban houses of Eyre, Duhring, and Mellor and Meigs along the Main Line.

The Prairie School

The Prairie School was not the only architectural idiom in the midwest – there were houses in Old English, modern plaster, and farmhouse styles – however, even in the early twentieth century, it was recognized as a unique regional expression. One writer summed up "the so-called 'Chicago School' . . . as influenced by the character of the country itself, bringing to these homes of the West the long horizontal lines dictated by the vast reaches of the prairies."[92] While there was some question among the architects and critics as to what identifying term to use, the primary association with the landscape was noted by phrases such as "A Style of the Western Plains" and "thoroughly saturated with the spirit of the prairies."[93] Another writer stated: "The horizontal lines of the new expression appeal to the disciples of this school as echoing the spirit of the prairies of the great Middle West, which to them embodies the essence of democracy."[94] The connection with the midwestern landscape was an attempt to create an indigenous architectural expression that was suitable to all elements of a building, from its form to its furniture and leaded-glass windows, and one that would resonate with cultural and social meaning. This was an architecture that would embody the essence of America – truly original and truly democratic.[95]

Louis Sullivan acted as the ideological center of the midwestern Arts and Crafts group. Less a disciple of Morris than were his own followers, Sullivan called for an American architecture based upon democracy and nature, free of old-world stylistic traditions. Certainly much of his career before 1900 – when he was primarily a Chicago commercial building architect – lacks an Arts and Crafts orientation. Yet Sullivan gave vocal strength to the claim that the midwest was unique and not simply a colony of the east or Europe. Through Walt Whitman's poetry, which celebrated the possibilities of an American culture and art, and which pointed to the midwest as containing this promise, Sullivan began in the late 1880s to develop his ornamental system. Architecturally, the approach was strong simple overall forms and complexity of detail, a visual analogy to the broad simple forms of the landscape and to the enlivening features of flowers, grass, and seeds (nos. 83 and 84).

Frank Lloyd Wright worked for Sullivan between 1887 and 1893. He had been employed previously by a shingle-style suburban architect and his early work, such as his own house in Oak Park, betrays this heritage. Throughout the 1890s, Wright and a number of younger architects – George Washington Maher, Robert Spencer, Walter Burley Griffin, Myron Hunt, Dwight Perkins, Hugh Garden, and others – actively discussed the possibilities of a new midwestern idiom. Spurred by exhibits of work and visits by English Arts and Crafts reformers, Wright, Spencer, Perkins, Hunt, Triggs, and others founded the Chicago Society of Arts and Crafts at Jane Addams's Hull House in 1897.[96] By the early 1900s Wright and a number of Chicago-based architects had arrived at the mature Prairie School expression. As part of a series of middle-class home designs in *The Ladies' Home Journal*, Wright published two houses, one of which he labeled "A Home in a Prairie Town" (fig. 25). A few years later he published in the *Journal* an inexpensive concrete house to cost $5,000 (no. 197).[97] The work of Wright and other Prairie School architects, while oriented to the prairie, was seldom on it but

Fig. 25. Frank Lloyd Wright, "A Home in a Prairie Town,"published in *Ladies'Home Journal* (February 1901).

Fig. 26. Walter Burley Griffin, Rock Crest – Rock Glen development, Mason City, Iowa, 1912. Perspective rendering in gouache on green satin by Marion Mahony Griffin. Burnham Architectural Library, Art Institute of Chicago.

instead in the growing suburbs west, south, and north of Chicago. They captured the spirit of the landscape: broad and flat, with the houses having low proportions, sheltered overhangs, outflung walls, quiet skylines, and prominent chimneys. The buildings of Wright and the other Prairie School followers were family centered, or, as Wright claimed, "dedicated to the cause conservative in the best sense of the word."[98] They provided the traditional image of shelter and were oriented to certain primal symbols: the chimney and the hearth were always the center. For Wright, the idea of the open plan and total spatial integration – a fixation of the 1940s and 1950s and modernism – was seldom present. Rather, he oriented spaces for specific activities, the most highly ritualistic being the family sitting down at the table and breaking bread. Wright wanted an environmental totality that, while life-enhancing, demanded a tremendous commitment and ultimately a loss of individuality on the part of its occupants.[99]

In addition to the prairie landscape, Wright and other architects in his circle drew upon the ubiquitous vernacular of the midwest with origins in the midnineteenth century: the square boxy volumetric house built of a balloon frame and covered in clapboards or stucco (no. 197). Wright and others abstracted the form, banked the windows and trim, and reorganized the rooms surrounding the chimney into two interlocking spaces for living and dining. The larger houses they designed (such as those for Susan Dana and Ward Willits) have a source in spacious farmhouses with ells, additive compositions that are organized in one coherent expression (nos. 85 and 213). The Willits house, while entered through the side and essentially asymmetrical, has a Palladian balance.[100]

As noted earlier, Wright was one of the prime proponents of "The Art and Craft of the Machine." He and C.R. Ashbee carried on a spirited debate, with Wright claiming: "William Morris pleaded well for simplicity as the basis of all true art. Let us understand the significance to art of that word – SIMPLICITY – for it is vital to the Art of the Machine."[101] In a talk at Hull House in 1901, Wright claimed that Morris and Ruskin had misunderstood the possibilities: "The machine, by its wonderful cutting, shaping, smoothing, and repetitive capacity, has made it possible to so use it without waste that the poor as well as the rich may enjoy today beautiful surface treatments of clean strong forms . . . ." Wright's personal preference for pure design came from sources other than the machine, however; Japanese prints and Froebel blocks also played a role. Wright learned about Froebel's "gifts" when he was nine, but their impact came in the 1890s, when he gave the building blocks to his own children and saw the underlying geometrical order. Whereas Sullivan sought to create ornament based upon nature's line of growth, Wright's was a geometrical abstraction of nature.

The Prairie School architects, while committed to developing a regional idiom, were not entirely homogeneous. The work of Wright's chief associates – Walter Burley Griffin, Marion Mahony, and William Drummond – shows the influence of his geometry, yet it is often quite individualistic (fig. 26, no. 89). There were also Prairie School independents such as George Washington Maher (nos. 217-221) whose interpretation of the midwest displays the same geometry and reliance on nature for detail but in a very personal way. A third branch was more directly tied to Sullivan as the form-giver and included George Grant Elmslie, who had worked

for Sullivan for nearly twenty years, and William Gray Purcell, who had stayed for a shorter time. The successful firm of Purcell and Elmslie built banks and houses for small prairie towns in the midwest and in the east (nos. 90-94 and 198).[102]

California

California architects experienced, even more than midwesterners, an identity problem. A salubrious climate, new wealth, and the ethnic mix of easterners, Orientals, and Hispanics created a rich milieu in which rival regional architectural idioms emerged. Eastern, midwestern, and even foreign styles did appear but the claim of a regional identity remained strong.[103] Contemporary with the eastern discovery of the "old colonial" in the 1870s and 1880s, some transplanted easterners recognized the romance of the missions built under Spanish rule. In the writings of Helen Hunt Jackson and others, the crumbling bell towers, ruined sun-struck adobe walls, shady arcades, and red tile roofs struck a poignant note. Mission features began to appear in some architectural projects and by the 1893 World's Columbian Exposition in Chicago, California was represented by a full-scale Mission Revival building designed by A. Page Brown, A.C. Schweinfurth, and Bernard Maybeck.[104] Attention given the old missions led to interest in other examples of early adobe buildings such as ranch houses and native American structures. Charles Fletcher Lummis, editor of the Los Angeles magazine *Land of Sunshine*, enthused over massive walls, verandas, and patios found in early buildings.[105] By the early 1900s fascination with the Mission style had hit the east coast and Gustav Stickley ran an article that rhapsodized: "What would have been the result if the Franciscans of Spanish California and the Puritans of

Fig. 27. Arthur Burnett Benton (1857-1927), Mission Inn, Riverside, California, 1902-1909. View of courtyard by Avery Edwin Field, ca. 1909. Field Collection, University of California, Riverside.

Fig. 28. A. Page Brown (1859-1896), architect, with A. C. Schweinfurth (1864-1900) and Bernard Maybeck (1862-1957), Church of the New Jerusalem, San Francisco, 1894-1895. Sanctuary view with murals by William Keith (1838-1911). Photograph in collection of the Church of the New Jerusalem of San Francisco.

Plymouth Rock had exchanged continent-sides on coming to America? For one thing we should have missed the most superb and harmonious type of architecture known to the new continent – the architecture of the Old Missions. . . ."[106]

The result was a flood of Mission-styled buildings, not only in California and the southwest but across the country, and also the application of the term "Mission Style" to many of the other products of the Arts and Crafts movement.[107] Architecturally, the most impressive building was Arthur Benton's Mission Inn in Riverside, California – a gigantic project that occupied its owner, Frank Miller, from the 1880s well into the 1930s (no. 72; fig. 27). Miller's passion for the Hispanic heritage helped make Riverside into a wonderland of Mission-styled structures and street furniture even though the Spaniards had actually passed it by in the eighteenth century. A textbook example of various interpretations of the Spanish heritage over the years, the Inn was visited by Stickley and by Elbert Hubbard, both of whom found it enchanting and helped to publicize it.[108]

Interest in the indigenous mission led in two directions: one toward a stylistic confection – as with the Mission Inn – the other toward abstraction – as with the work of San Diego designers Irving Gill, Richard Requa, and Frank Mead, (nos. 72, 74, and 199). Taking elements such as the massive walls, the arch, and the tile roofs, they cast the simplified forms in concrete. The result contained a flavor of the Mediterranean and the Secession. Gill exemplified the contradictions of the sophisticated primitivism of the American Arts and Crafts, writing about a "simple cube house with creamy walls, sheer and plain, rising boldly into the sky unrelieved by cornices or overhang of roof, unornamented save for the vines."[109] For Gill "the straight line, the arch, the cube and the circle" represented, respectively, the horizon, the dome of the sky, completeness and power, justice, and firmness. Against this return to elemental sources, Gill sought to make his buildings contemporary in the sense of using advanced construction techniques of poured concrete and hollow tile. He was intensely interested in construction and efficiency and felt the home should be healthful and "perfectly sanitary." To this end, he tried to eliminate all dust-catching moldings.[110] Given the later development of the International Style, it is tempting to see Gill as a predecessor. He never put the machine first, however; his architecture was human centered and related to the past of the missions and the landscape.

Nothing could be more different from the stark cubes of Irving Gill than the intricate and shaggy shingle-covered buildings of Henry Mather Greene and Charles Summer Greene in Pasadena (nos. 68 and 69). They too cited the missions as a source, along with the California ranch house, but one can see also the influences of the Japanese, the East Coast shingle style, and the bungalow. Their interest in wood joinery was undoubtedly sparked by high-school shop courses in St. Louis. After MIT – where they trained in a curriculum oriented toward the Beaux Arts – and a short time in Boston offices, they arrived in Pasadena in 1893. Their work was undistinguished until about 1902, when they discovered oriental fine arts and Stickley's *Craftsman* magazine. Together, the fine craftsmanship of the Orient and the simple wooden structural elaboration of Stickley's furniture directed the Greenes toward their characteristic expression of complex details. They took simplicity and complicated it with an exquisite care: wooden details of cloud

lift and lapped joints, dowels, and pegs. In their hands the lowly bungalow became high art.[111]

The bungalow was almost synonymous with southern California – with Pasadena in particular. The extent of this identification can be seen in Sinclair Lewis's *Main Street* (1920), in which a character claims: "Mama and me are planning to go out to Pasadena and buy a bungalow and live there."[112] Henry Wilson's *Bungalow Magazine*, published in Los Angeles, popularized the idea of the area as "bungalowland." The bungalow court, originally designed as plush rental units for eastern wealth coming west for the winter months (fig. 2), quickly adopted populist overtones. Alfred and Arthur Heineman, Pasadena architects, helped to develop and design a number of such courts; with their low-slung wide-gabled roofs, projecting rafters, entrance gates of clinker brick and boulders, Batchelder tile fireplaces, and palm and eucalyptus trees, they became a popular image of southern California.[113]

In the heterogeneous climate of California works by or imitating the diversity of the Greenes, Benton, and Gill can be found in the northern Bay Area, side by side with the different architecture of Louis Christian Mullgardt (no. 77), John Hudson Thomas (nos. 81 and 82), and Bernard Maybeck (nos. 75 and 76). The most comprehensive attempt to create a regional Bay Area idiom can be seen in the work of Bernard Maybeck and his major sponsor, Charles Keeler. Maybeck's architecture encompassed a number of trends that reflected his many interests. In San Francisco in the 1890s Maybeck worked on several buildings, including the Swedenborgian Church of the New Jerusalem (1894-1895) high in the Pacific Heights section (fig. 28). The architect of record was A. Page Brown; however, the design was actually by the talented A.C. Schwein-

furth, assisted by Maybeck. The exterior had Mission and ranch house elements, while the interior evoked a primitivist sensibility with rough logs of madrone trees as braces; its sturdy plain maple chairs with woven tule rushes for seats became the prototypical "Mission" chairs (no. 71). William Keith, a local painter, contributed murals of the California countryside.[114]

The landscape and building as a unit would be developed by Maybeck and his friend Charles Keeler for the Hillside Club in the Berkeley Hills. Keeler, a naturalist, scientist, poet, journalist, and devotee of cosmic truths, gave Maybeck his first private commission for a house in 1895. Together, they developed an ideal of a "New Athens" in the Berkeley Hills and in 1904 Keeler wrote *The Simple Home* ("Dedicated to My Friend and Counselor Bernard M. Maybeck"), expressing a transcendentalist mystical communion with the California landscape in which "Home making [became] one of the sacred tasks of life . . . ." Reflecting Maybeck's eclectic philosophy and condemning buildings inappropriate for the Bay Area, such as the Mission Revival style, Keeler argued for half-timbering, shingles, and steep roofs; for the latter he cited examples of the Tlingit Indians of Alaska and the Maoris of New Zealand, as well as Hawaiian grass houses. Overall, wood, a natural material, was best for the interior and most of the exterior, and the machine was rigorously excluded. Classic temple and Mediterranean imagery could be used – and were – but Keeler preferred the pointed arch of the Gothic, which was "a means of expressing the ideal of aspiration."[115]

Maybeck's work for the Hillside Club perfectly embodies the message of Keeler's book. In addition to the clubhouse, covered in shingles with tall gables (no. 75), he designed numerous houses that included Swiss-style chalets, stucco-covered Mediterranean houses, Greek temples, and board-and-batten and shingled bungalows. He also helped to lay out winding streets, paths, and landscaping composed of native and exotic vegetation. While Keeler could accept a number of garden styles from Japanese to English, he admired most "the natural garden . . . the charm of the wilderness, tamed and diversified for convenience and accessibility."[116] A chiaroscuro effect was sought, a patch of grass, the brilliance of a flower bed, subdued and shadowed by tall woods.

The Arts and Crafts Community and Beyond

The contradictory impulses of American Arts and Crafts architecture were shown in the ambiguous nature of the community it sought to create. Attempts at communities were made by Wright in Oak Park, Griffin and Mahony in Mason City, the Greenes and Heinemans in Pasadena, Maybeck and Keeler in the Berkeley Hills, and Olmsted and Atterbury in Forest Hills Gardens on Long Island. Seeking to uplift, to improve taste and life, the architects succeeded in many notable ways, but the community they envisioned remained elusive and on the outskirts of the city, never central.

Funded by the philanthropic Russell Sage Foundation as a model town, Forest Hills Gardens (1909) was perhaps the most impressive attempt to lay out a community along Arts and Crafts lines. Planned to demonstrate the way in which business (i.e., revenue-producing) practices could be combined with "scientific" planning and artistic goals, Forest Hills Gardens reflects the impact of Ebenezer Howard's Garden Cities concept and its architecture in America. Howard argued that the large industrial city was no longer possible and that smaller "Garden Cities," each self-sup-

Fig. 29. Grosvenor Atterbury (1869-1956), architect, and Frederick Law Olmsted (1870-1957), landscape architect, Forest Hills Gardens, New York, 1909-1912. View of village green looking toward the inn, December 1914. National Park Service, Frederick Law Olmsted National Historic Site, Brookline, Massachusetts.

Fig. 30. Forest Hills Gardens, view along the arcade of the inn, December 1914. National Park Service, Frederick Law Olmsted National Historic Site, Brookline, Massachusetts.

porting with its own agriculture and industry, should be set up.[117] Lacking these essential features, Forest Hills Gardens acted as a commuter suburb located in Queens, about nine miles from downtown Manhattan and served by the Long Island Railroad. The landscape architect, Frederick Law Olmsted, Jr., laid out a 142-acre plan that defied the usual gridiron arrangement. His three principles of "Ample, Direct and Convenient Thoroughfares," "Cozy, Domestic Character of Local Streets," and "Playground and Public Open Spaces" translated into an arrangement of a major plaza at the railroad station, a few bordering through roads, and curving inner streets, landscaped to resemble a park (figs. 29 and 30).[118]

Grosvenor Atterbury, a Beaux-Arts-trained architect, acted as the architectural coordinator, approving all designs and designing himself some of the housing and the major buildings at the Square – the inn, shops, and station. Stylistically, Atterbury's work varied; he used Italian medieval, English half timber, and roughcast.[119] Other architects, such as Stickley, Wilson Eyre, Harrie Lindeberg, Aymar Embury II, and Eugene Schoen, used English models as well as expanded bungalows, American colonial, and other types for the row houses, duplexes, and single-family houses they built. Against the diversity of housing were consistent features such as wrought-iron street lamps and signs and stone and brick walls. Typical Arts and Crafts plantings were everywhere – "wisteria, trumpet vine, wild grape and ramble rose" – and, together with secluded garden enclaves, they helped create an ideal landscape. Forest Hills Gardens never looked new; by 1914 it already had a mellow air.[120]

Unfortunately, while Forest Hills Gardens was very successful, its example was only partially so. Some of the overall texture was captured in other suburbs – as were the house styles – but never with rigid controls, and Atterbury's system of economical concrete construction attracted little following. Mrs. Russell Sage and her primary adviser, the lawyer Robert De Forest, wanted to produce housing for "people of moderate income and good taste" and for the community to be "educational," but the emphasis upon a "business investment" meant that only upper-middle-class patrons could afford the prices, to say nothing of the railway fares to work and shopping.[121]

The triumph of the American Arts and Crafts movement can be seen in bungalows, half-timbered houses, stuccoed and shingled cottages, and horizontal Prairie School houses erected in suburban and resort areas from coast to coast. A housing revolution did take place as significant portions of the American middle classes were rehoused in these buildings, which continued to be designed and built into the 1920s and even the 1930s. In a sense, Arts and Crafts architects created their own academy – one based upon medieval cottages, Spanish Missions, and log cabins – but it was a system that remained open-ended, always expansive. The heart of the Arts and Crafts was not in its style but in its thought, in its details: the wrought-iron hinges, the geometric-patterned windows, the planter, the peg joints, and the overall feeling of care, from conception to design and the finished work.

1. Charles Robert Ashbee, "Memoirs" (typescript, vol. 3, pp. 106-107), Victoria and Albert Museum, London. I am indebted to Robert Winter for directing me to this source; see Robert W. Winter, "American Sheaves from 'C.R.A.' and Janet Ashbee," *Journal of the Society of Architectural Historians* 30 (December 1971), pp. 317-322; and Alan Crawford, *C.R. Ashbee: Architect, Designer and Romantic Socialist* (New Haven: Yale University Press, 1985), pp. 152-153.

2. Crawford 1985, pp. 66-67, 408.

3. C.R. Ashbee, "Frank Lloyd Wright, A Study and an Appreciation," in *The Early Work by Frank Lloyd Wright* (originally published as *Frank Lloyd Wright: Ausgeführte Bauten* [Berlin: Wasmuth, 1911]; reprinted, New York: Horizon Press, 1969), p. 8. See also C.R. Ashbee, "Man and the Machine," *House Beautiful* 28 (June-September, 1910), pp. 23-25, 53-56, 88-90, 109-111.

4. Ashbee 1911, p. 106

5. William L. Price, "Is American Art Captive to the Dead Past?" *Craftsman* 15 (February 1909), pp. 515-517.

6. Bertram Goodhue, "The Romanticist Point of View," *Craftsman* 8 (June 1905), p. 332.

7. Ralph Adams Cram, "Ecclesiastical Architecture" *Brickbuilder* 14 (August 1905), quoted in Montgomery Schuyler, "Gothic Revivals," *Architectural Record* 19 (January 1906), p. 67.

8. Frank Lloyd Wright, *Drawings and Plans of Frank Lloyd Wright, The Early Period (1893-1909)* (New York: Dover, 1983 [first published in German in 1910]), n.p.

9. Frank Lloyd Wright, "In the Cause of Architecture," *Architectural Record* 23 (March 1908), p. 158.

10. Price 1909, p. 518-519.

11. A[rthur] C. David, "An Architect of Bungalows in California" *Architectural Record* 20 (October 1906), p. 310.

12. Gustav Stickley, "A Word about Craftsman Architecture," in Gustav Stickley, *The Best of Craftsman Homes*, Barry Sanders, ed. (Salt Lake: Peregrine Smith, 1979 [originally published in 1909 and 1912]), p. 7.

13. Gustav Stickley, *More Craftsman Homes* (New York: Craftsman Publishing, 1912), p. 178.

14. Gustav Stickley, *Craftsman Homes* (New York: Craftsman Publishing, 1909), p. 11.

15. Leonard K. Eaton, *Landscape Artist in America, The Life and Work of Jens Jensen* (Chicago: University of Chicago, 1964); Wilhelm L. Miller, *The Prairie Spirit in Landscape Gardening* (Urbana: University of Illinois College of Agriculture, 1915).

16. Robert Harbison, *Deliberate Regression* (New York: Knopf, 1980).

17. David 1906, p. 312.

18. Henry H. Saylor, *Bungalows* (New York: McBride, Winston, 1911), p. 135.

19. For the history of inglenooks, see Edgar Kaufmann, Jr., "Precedent and Progress in the Work of Frank Lloyd Wright," *Journal of the Society of Architectural Historians* 39 (May 1980), pp. 145-149.

20. Gustav Stickley, "The Fire on the Hearth," *Craftsman* 25 (December 1913), p. 302. Stickley also wrote: "The big hospitable fireplace is almost a necessity, for the hearth-stone is always the center of the true home life, and the very spirit of home seems to be lacking when a register or radiator tries ineffectually to take the place of a glowing grate . . ." (Stickley 1909 [*Craftsman Homes*], p. 196).

21. Elbert Hubbard, *Music at Meals*; Frank A. Miller, *Songs of California's Mission Inn* (Riverside: Mission Inn, 1906); and *Songs of the Glenwood Mission Inn* (Riverside: Mission Inn), 1910) – all in the collection of Mission Inn Foundation, Riverside, California.

22. William Gray Purcell and George G. Elmslie, "The American Renaissance?," *Craftsman* 21 (January 1912), pp. 430-435.

23. Frank Lloyd Wright, "The Art and Craft of the Machine" (1901), in *Frank Lloyd Wright, Writings and Buildings*, Edgar Kaufmann, Jr., and Ben Raeburn, eds. (New York: Meridian Books, 1960); Ashbee 1910; Price 1909; and idem, "The Beautiful City," *Craftsman* 17 (October 1909), pp. 53-57. I am indebted to Deborah Fulton for assistance with the machine issue.

24. William Morris, "Art and Socialism," (1884), in *Architecture, Industry and Wealth* (London: Longmans Green, 1902), p. 123.

25. Oscar Lovell Triggs, *Chapters in the History of the Arts and Crafts Movement* (Chicago: Bohemian Guild, 1902), p. 193.

26. See Gustav Stickley, "The Use and Abuse of Machinery, and its Relation to the Arts and Crafts," *Craftsman* 11 (November 1906), pp. 201-207.

27. For Price see *A Poor Sort of Heaven/A Good Sort of Earth: The Rose Valley Arts and Crafts Experiment*, William Ayres, ed. (Chadds Ford: Brandywine River Museum, 1983); for the Greenes, see note 1 above and Robert W. Winter, "The Arroyo Culture," in *California Design 1910*, T.J. Anderson, E.M. Moore, and R.W. Winter, eds. (Pasadena: California Design Publications, 1974), pp. 11-28, especially pp. 25-26; for Stickley see the many articles reprinted in *The Craftsman: An Anthology*, Barry Saunders, ed. (Santa Barbara: Peregrine Smith, 1978), especially pp. 3-13, 18-24, 163-170, 171-179, 192-195.

28. Richard Guy Wilson, Dianne Pilgrim, and Richard Murray, *The American Renaissance, 1876-1917* (New York: Brooklyn Museum and Pantheon, 1979).

29. Ironically, some Arts and Crafts journals published articles supporting classically based civic art for metropolitan centers. Two examples are: Charles Mulford Robinson, "Handicraft Workers and Civic Beauty," *Craftsman* 5 (December 1903), pp. 235-239; and "Growth and Beauty of our American Cities: Practical Suggestions Offered by the Municipal Art League for Advancement in Art, Sanitation and General Comfort of Metropolitan Life," *Craftsman* 16 (July 1909), pp. 399-413.

30. Gustav Stickley, "The Value of Permanent Architecture as a Truthful Expression of National Character," *Craftsman* 16 (April 1909), p. 91.

31. A.W.N. Pugin, *The True Principles of Pointed or Christian Architecture* (London: Academy Editions, 1973 [originally published in 1841]), pp. 1-2.

32. John Ruskin, *The Seven Lamps of Architecture* (2d ed., New York: John B. Alden, 1885; first published in 1849), p. 15. See also Roger B. Stein, *John Ruskin and Aesthetic Thought in America, 1840-1900* (Cambridge: Harvard University Press, 1967).

33. The seminal position of *Red House* was first recognized by Hermann Muthesius, in *The English House* (New York: Rizzoli, 1980 [first published in German in 1904-1905]); subsequently by Nikolaus Pevsner, *Pioneers of the Modern Movement, from William Morris to Walter Gropius* (London: Faber and Faber, 1936).

34. The most thorough coverage is Peter Blundell Jones, "Red House," *Architect's Journal* 183 (January 15, 1986), pp. 36-56.

35. May Morris, *William Morris: Artist, Writer, Socialist* (Oxford: Oxford University Press, 1936), vol. 1, pp. 270-276.

36. William Morris, *The Collected Works of William Morris*, May Morris, ed. (London: Longmans, Green, 1910-1915), vol. 22, p. 429.

37. W.R. Lethaby, *Philip Webb and his Work* (Oxford: Oxford University Press, 1935), pp. 130, 136.

38. Elizabeth Aslin, *The Aesthetic Movement* (New York: Praeger, 1969); Mark Girouard, *Sweetness and Light, the 'Queen Anne' Movement, 1860-1900* (Oxford: Oxford University Press, 1977); and idem, "Creating the 'Old English' Style," *Country Life*, September 6, 1973, pp. 614-618.

39. The best survey of the English architecture is: Peter Davey, *Architecture of the Arts and Crafts Movement* (London: Architectural Press, 1980).

40. Wilson, Pilgrim, and Murray 1979, pp. 92-95; and Richard Chaffee, "The Teaching of Architecture at the Ecole des Beaux-Arts," in *The Architecture of the Ecole des Beaux-Arts* (New York: Museum of Modern Art, 1977), pp. 61-109.

41. H.W. Frohne, "Recent English Domestic Architecture," *Architectural Record* 25 (April 1909), pp. 259-270; and Francis S. Swales, "The Small English Home as a Place to Live In – Its Seamy Side," *Architectural Record* 25 (June 1909), pp. 400-403. See also David Gebhard, *Charles F.A. Voysey, Architect* (Los Angeles: Hennessy and Ingalls, 1975), pp. 29-30.

42. Eugène Emmanuel Viollet-le-Duc, *Discourses on Architecture*, Benjamin Bucknall, trans. (New York: Grove Press, 1959 [first published in 1889]).

43. For Viollet-le-Duc's impact in America see: Richard Guy Wilson, "American Architecture and the Search for a National Style in the 1870s," *Nineteenth Century* 3 (Autumn 1977), pp. 74-80; Donald Hoffman, "Frank Lloyd Wright and Viollet-le-Duc," *Journal of the Society of Architectural Historians* 28 (October 1969), pp. 173-183; "Viollet-le-Duc," *Craftsman* 3 (November 1902), p. 127; and Samuel Howe, "The Architectural Awakening," *Craftsman* 8 (June 1905), pp. 333-335.

44. Many articles on Art Nouveau, with which Gustav Stickley flirted for a time, were published in America; see, for example, the following: A.D.F. Hamlin, "L'Art Nouveau: Its Origin and Development," *Craftsman* 3 (December 1902), pp. 129-143; M. Jean Schopfer, "L'Art Nouveau: An Argument and Defense in Reply to Professor A.D.F. Hamlin of Columbia University," *Craftsman* 4 (June 1903), pp. 229-138; and S. Bing, "L'Art Nouveau," *Craftsman* 5 (October 1904), pp. 1-15.

45. S[iegfried] Bing, *La Culture artistique en amérique* (Paris, 1895), republished in S[iegfried] Bing, *Artistic America, Tiffany Glass, and Art Nouveau*, Robert Koch, ed. (Cambridge: MIT Press, 1970), pp. 83, 93.

46. See Diane Chalmers Johnson, "Louis Sullivan and American Art Nouveau," in *New Free Style*, Ian Latham, ed. (New York: Rizzoli, 1980), pp. 14-20; and idem, *American Art Nouveau* (New York: Abrams, 1979). See also A.D.F. Hamlin, "Style in Architecture," *Craftsman* 8 (June 1905), p. 331, as one example in which Sullivan is labeled Art Nouveau.

47. Theodore Turak, "French and English Sources of Sullivan's Ornament and Doctrine," *Prairie School Review* 11 (4th quarter, 1974), pp. 5-65; Paul Sprague, *The Drawings of Louis Sullivan* (Princeton: Princeton University Press, 1979); and idem, "The Architectural Ornament of Louis Sullivan" (Ph.D. dissertation, Princeton University, 1968).

48. Aymar Embury, II, *One Hundred Country Houses, Modern American Examples* (New York: Century Co., 1909), chapter 10.

49. Gustav Stickley, "The German Exhibit at the Louisiana Purchase Exposition," *Craftsman* 6 (August 1904), pp. 488-506; Irving K. Pond, "German Arts and Crafts at St. Louis," *Architectural Record* 17 (February 1905), pp. 118-125; Otto Teegen, "Joseph Urban," *Architecture* 69 (May 1934), p. 252; and H. Allen Brooks, *The Prairie School: Frank Lloyd Wright and His Midwest Contemporaries* (Toronto: University of Toronto Press, 1972), pp. 89, 91.

50. Leonard K. Eaton, *American Architecture Comes of Age* (Cambridge: MIT Press, 1972), pp. 208-216.

51. The critic Matlack Price labeled them "American Secessionist." See "Secessionist Architecture in America," *Arts and Decoration* 3 (December 1912), pp. 51-53; idem, "The Trend of Architectural Thought in America," *Century* 80 (September 1921), pp. 718-719. Price called Purcell and Elmslie and Steele's Woodbury County Courthouse (Sioux City, Iowa, 1915-1918) "Secessionist"; Irving Gill was labeled "secessionist" in Bertha H. Smith, "The Later Gospel of Simplicity," in *Architectural Styles for Country Houses*, Henry H. Saylor, ed. (New York: Robert M. McBride, 1919), p. 127.

52. Michael Darby, *The Islamic Perspective: An Aspect of British Architecture and Design in the 19th Century* (London: Leighton House Gallery, 1983).

53. David Gebhard argued that the Turkish Pavilion at the Chicago World's Fair affected Wright's Winslow and later buildings (see "A Note on the Chicago Fair of 1893 and Frank Lloyd Wright," *Journal of the Society of Architectural Historians* 18 [May 1959], pp. 63-65).

54. Edward S. Morse, *Japanese Homes and Their Surroundings* (Boston: Ticknor, 1886; reprinted New York: Dover, 1961); Morse's book was first published in Salem in 1885 by the University Press. See also Clay Lancaster, *The Japanese Influence in America* (New York: William T. Rawls, 1963). Lancaster (pp. 128-131) identified the example on the cover of *Bungalow Magazine* of January 1910 as actually built at Cedar Manor, Long Island. See idem, *The American Bungalow*, (New York: Abbeville Press, 1985), pp. 136-137; the author noted that a house identified as "Japanese" is probably more Middle Eastern in origin.

55. Ralph Adams Cram, *Impressions of Japanese Architecture and the Allied Arts* (Boston: Marshall Jones Company, 1930 [originally published in 1905]), p. 128. See also Stickley 1909 (*Craftsman*), p. 83.

56. Wright 1910, n.p. See also Margaret Williams Norton, "Japanese Themes and the Early Work of Frank Lloyd Wright," *Frank Lloyd Wright Newsletter* 4 (2d quarter, 1981), pp. 1-5.

57. See Price 1912, p. 52.

58. A.W. Alley, "House in Japanese style," *House Beautiful* 25 (March 1909), pp. 76-77; Henrietta P. Keith, "The Trial of Japan's Influence in our Modern Domestic Architecture," *Craftsman* 12 (July 1907), pp. 446-451. Ralph Adams Cram ("Preface," *American Country Houses of Today* [New York: Architectural Book Publishing Co., 1913], p. vi) wrote on the Greenes: "There are things in it Japanese; things that are Scandinavian; things that hint at Sikkim, Bhutan, and the vastness of Tibet, and yet it all hangs together, it is beautiful, it is contemporary, and for some reason or other it seems to fit California."

59. Ralph Adams Cram complained, however, that in the hands of followers the Richardson Romanesque became a "lurid atrocity." See *My Life in Architecture* (Boston: Little, Brown, 1936), p. 34. See also Wilson Eyre, "The Development of American Dwelling Architecture during the Last Thirty Years," *Architectural Review* (Boston) 5 (November 1917), p. 242; and Claude Bragdon, "Architecture in the United States," *Architectural Record* 25 (June 1909), p. 431.

60. Letter from H.H. Richardson to his wife (July 11, 1982) in the files of the firm of Shepley, Bulfinch, Richardson, and Abbott, Boston. See also "On Vacation with H.H. Richardson: Ten Letters from Europe, 1882," James F. O'Gorman, ed., *Journal of the Archives of American Art* 19 (1979), p. 4.

61. Clarence Cook's articles, all entitled "Beds and Tables, Stools and Candlesticks," published in *Scribner's Monthly* (1875-1877) were reprinted in book form as *The House Beautiful* (New York: Scribner, Armstrong, 1878). See also Girouard 1977, chapter 11; and Martha Crabill McClaugherty, "Household Art: Creating the Artistic Home," *Winterthur Portfolio* 18 (Spring 1983), pp. 1-26.

62. Scully 1971; Wilson 1977.

63. *Old Newport Houses*, 1875. One copy of this book exists at the Society for the Preservation of New En-

gland Antiquities, Boston. It was a gift of Charles McKim to William Dean Howells. Howells was then the editor of *Atlantic Monthly* and had McKim and his partners, William Bigelow and William R. Mead, design a summer house for him in Belmont, Massachusetts, in 1877 and 1878. Other copies of *Old Newport Houses* are in the Newport Historical Society. See *New York Sketch Book of Architecture* 3 (April 1876), p. 15 and opposite; and Richard Guy Wilson "Early Work of Charles F. McKim, Country House Commissions," *Winterthur Portfolio* 14 (Autumn 1979), pp. 235-267.

64. George W. Sheldon, *Artistic Country Seats* (New York: D. Appleton, 1886), vol. 1, p. 23. For an extended discussion of the Tilton and subsequent McKim, Mead and White houses, see Richard Guy Wilson, *McKim, Mead & White, Architects* (New York: Rizzoli, 1983).

65. Sheldon 1886, vol. 2, p. 25.

66. Wilson, Pilgrim, and Murray 1979; see also Richard Guy Wilson, "Architecture and the Reinterpretation of the Past in the American Renaissance," *Winterthur Portfolio* 18 (Spring 1983), pp. 69-87.

67. See Embury 1908 and Saylor 1919, both of which illustrate the continuing tendency to identify houses by styles.

68. Edgar Kaufmann, Jr., "Some American Architectural Ornament of the Arts and Crafts Era," *Journal of the Society of Architectural Historians* 24 (December 1965), pp. 285-291.

69. Mary Rankin Cranston, "The Socialized Church, What it is Doing for the Welfare, Comfort and Happiness of the People," *Craftsman* 12 (April 1907), pp. 51-58.

70. Ralph Adams Cram, letter to the editor, "William Morris: Poet, Artist, Socialist," from *Boston Evening Transcript*, undated (ca. 1883), in "Journal, 1881-1885," Cram Collection, Boston Public Library. See also Bertram Grosvenor Goodhue, review of William Lethaby, *Architecture, Mysticism and Myth* (New York: MacMillan, 1891), in *Knight Errant* 1 (April 1892), p. 31. For Cram see Richard Guy Wilson, "Ralph Adams Cram and the Idea of a Medieval Culture in America," in *Medievalism and American Culture*, B. Rosenthal and P. Szarmach, eds. (Binghamton: State University of New York, forthcoming, 1987).

71. Ralph Adams Cram, "Good and Bad Modern Gothic," *Architectural Review* (Boston) 6 (August 1899), p. 116; idem 1936, pp. 72-73; idem, "All Saints' Church, Dorchester (Boston), Mass., *Churchman* 79 (April 15, 1899), p. 560.

72. Cram 1936, pp. 78-79; Richard Oliver, *Bertram Grosvenor Goodhue* (Cambridge and New York: MIT Press and Architectural History Foundation, 1983), pp. 120-125.

73. See Mary Ann Smith, *Gustav Stickley, The Craftsman* (Syracuse: Syracuse University Press, 1983); and John Crosby Freeman, *The Forgotten Rebel, Gustav Stickley and His Craftsman Mission Furniture* (Watkins Glen: Century House, 1966).

74. Stickley 1979, p. vii (see note 12).

75. Harvey Ellis, "A Note of Color," *Craftsman* 5 (November 1903), pp. 152-163; Harvey Ellis, "Craftsman House," *Craftsman* 4 (July 1903), pp. 274-276. The dining room was frequently republished in *Craftsman* (see November 1905); see also Stickley 1909 (*Craftsman Homes*), p. 136, where it is published in color. Ellis's death was noted in *Craftsman* 5 (February 1904), p. 520.

76. Lancaster 1985; Robert Winter, *The California Bungalow* (Los Angeles: Hennessey & Ingalls, 1980); Gwendolyn Wright, *Building the Dream: A Social History of Housing in America* (New York: Pantheon Books, 1981), chapter 9.

77. "When you see a cosy one or one and a-half storied dwelling, with low pitched roof and very wide eaves, ample porches, lots of windows and an outside chimney of cobble or clinkerbrick half hidden by clinging vines – that is a bungalow whatever other houses may be." From Charles Saunders, "Bungalow Life, The Cost of Living It," *Sunset* 30 (January 1913), p. 33. See also Seymour E. Locke, "Bungalows, What They Really are," *House and Garden* 12 (August 1907), pp. 44-53.

78. See Saylor 1911, pp. 40-41, on the Prairie School connection; see also Robert C. Spencer, "Building a House of Moderate Cost, A Bungalow Suggestion," *Architectural Record* 32 (July 1912), pp. 37-45.

79. Stickley 1979, p. 14 (see note 12).

80. "The Craftsman House: A Practical Application of All the Theories of Home Building Advocated in This Magazine," *Craftsman* 15 (October 1908), p. 79.

81. Natalie Curtis, "The New Log House at Craftsman Farms: An Architectural Development of the Log Cabin," *Craftsman* 21 (November 1911), p. 201.

82. *Victorian Resorts and Hotels*, Richard Guy Wilson, ed. (Philadelphia: Victorian Society, 1982).

83. Stickley 1909, p. 62.

84. Marc-Antoine Laugier, *Essay on Architecture* (Los Angeles: Hennessey and Ingalls, 1977 [originally published in 1753]; Martin Perdue, "The Log Cabin in American Art and Architecture, 1840-1890" (master's thesis, University of Virginia, 1986); and "Architectural Development of the Log Cabin in America," in Stickley 1979, p. 88.

85. Craig Gilborn, *Durant, The Fortunes and Woodland Camps of a Family in the Adirondacks* (Sylvan Beach, N.Y.: North Country Books, 1981); and Harvey H. Kaiser, *Great Camps of the Adirondacks* (Boston: David R. Godine, 1982).

86. "An Adirondack Lodge," *House and Garden* 12 (December 1907), p. 203.

87. David Leavengood, "A Sense of Shelter: Robert C. Reamer in Yellowstone National Park," *Pacific Historical Review* 54 (November 1985), pp. 495-513.

88. See the various essays with titles in Saylor 1919.

89. Eyre 1917, p. 243.

90. Ibid. See also idem, "From Liverpool to London," *Architectural Review* (Boston) 4 (January 1896), pp. 3-5; idem, "The Surroundings of the Country House," *Brochure Series of Architectural Illustrations* 4 (1898), pp. 189-197; idem, "My Ideal for the Country House," *Country Life in America* 24 (May 1913), pp. 35-36; and Edward Teitelman, "Philadelphia Residential Regionalism," *Journal of Regional History* 2 (Fall/Winter 1982), pp. 23-36.

91. C. Matlack Price, "Sincerity in Architecture – Skillful Work in Pure Colonial," *Arts and Decoration* 3 (April 1913), pp. 194-197; and Edward Teitelman and Betsy Fahlman, "Wilson Eyre and the Colonial Revival in Philadelphia," in *The Colonial Revival in America*, A. Axelrod, ed. (New York: Norton, 1985), pp. 71-90.

92. Saylor 1919, p. 2.

93. Hugh Garden, "A Style of the Western Plains," in Saylor 1919, pp. 101-111; and "Letters, 1903-1906, by Charles E. White, Jr., from the Studio of Frank Lloyd Wright," Nancy K. Morris, ed., *Journal of Architectural Education* 25 (Fall 1971), p. 104.

94. Irving K. Pond, *The Meaning of Architecture: An Essay in Constructive Criticism* (Boston: Marshall Jones, 1918), p. 175. Pond, it should be noted, criticized this horizontality as "running counter to the laws of nature."

95. Discussion of the term "Prairie School" can be found in Brooks 1972, pp. 8-13; and idem, "Chicago School: Metamorphosis of a Term," *Journal of the Society of Architectural Historians* 25 (June 1966), pp. 115-118.

96. H. Allen Brooks, "Steinway Hall, Architects and Dreams," *Journal of the Society of Architectural Historians* 22 (September 1963), pp. 171-175; idem, "Chicago Architecture: Its Debt to the Arts and Crafts," *Journal of the Society of Architectural Historians* 30 (December 1971), pp. 312-317; and Brooks 1972, chapter 1 (see n. 49 above); the founding membership list and constitution of the Arts and Crafts Society were published in *Catalogue of the Eleventh Annual Exhibition by the Chicago Architectural Club* (Chicago: Art Institute of Chicago, 1898).

97. Wright's houses were published in "A Home in Prairie Town," *Ladies Home Journal* 18 (February 1901), p. 17; "A Small House with 'Lots of Room in It,'" *Ladies Home Journal* 18 (July 1901), p. 15; and "A Fireproof House for $5,000," *Ladies Home Journal* 24 (April 1907), p. 24.

98. Wright 1908, p. 155 (see note 9 above).

99. In addition to Wright's many writings explaining his work, see also Robert C. Twombly, *Frank Lloyd Wright: An Interpretive Biography* (New York: Harper and Row, 1971); and Norris Kelley Smith, *Frank Lloyd Wright: A Study in Architectural Content* (Englewood Cliffs: Prentice-Hall, 1966).

100. Richard Guy Wilson and Sidney K. Robinson, *The Prairie School in Iowa* (Ames: Iowa State University Press, 1977), pp. 6, 7; and H. Allen Brooks, "Percy Dwight Bentley at La Crosse," *Prairie School Review* 9, no. 3 (1972), pp. 6-8.

101. Wright 1901, pp. 55-73 (see note 22 above); "Ten Letters from Frank Lloyd Wright to Charles Robert Ashbee," Alan Crawford, ed., *Architectural History* 12 (1970), pp. 64-76. See also David Hanks, "Frank Lloyd Wright's 'The Art and Craft of the Machine,'" in *Victorian Furniture*, K. Ames, ed. (Philadelphia: Victorian Society, 1983), pp. 205-211.

102. The work of the Prairie School is covered in Brooks 1972; idem, *Prairie School Architecture, Studies from the Western Architect* (Toronto: University of Toronto Press, 1975); and *Prairie School Review*, 14 vols. (1964-1981).

103. Kevin Starr, *Americans and the California Dream, 1850-1915* (New York: Oxford University Press, 1973); and idem, *Inventing the Dream* (New York: Oxford University Press, 1984 (the best study of California culture in this period). See also Harold Clark Kirker, *California's Architectural Frontier; Style and Tradition in the Nineteenth Century* (San Marino: Huntington Library and Art Gallery, 1960); and Carey McWilliams, *Southern California Country* (New York: Duell, Sloan and Pearce, 1946), pp. 357-363.

104. See Karen J. Weitze, *California's Mission Revival* (Los Angeles: Hennessey and Ingalls, 1984); and David Gebhard, "The Spanish Colonial Revival in Southern California (1895-1930)," *Journal of the Society of Architectural Historians* 26 (May 1967), pp. 131-147. See also Richard Longstreth, *On the Edge of the World: Four Architects in San Francisco at the Turn of the Century* (New York and Cambridge: Architectural History Foundation and the MIT Press, 1983), pp. 263-266.

105. Lummis is quoted in Weitz 1984, p. 74.

106. See "Traces of the Franciscans in California," *Craftsman* 1 (February 1902), pp. 29-30; Harvey Ellis, "Sermons in Sun Dried Bricks. From Old Spanish Missions," *Craftsman* 5 (December 1903), pp. 212-216; "A Craftsman House," *Craftsman* 5 (January 1904), pp. 396-397 [this design by Ellis was republished in Stickley 1909 (*Craftsman Homes*), pp. 9-11. Another Mission-style structure is "A Craftsman House," published in *Craftsman* 5 (May 1904), pp. 170-176; and George Wharton James published a series of articles on the missions and Indians in *Craftsman*, 4-6 (1904-1905).

107. Embury 1909, p. 93; George C. Baum, "The Spanish Mission Type," in Saylor 1919, p. 67; Gustav Stickley, "How 'Mission' Furniture was Named," *Craftsman* 16 (May 1909), p. 225.

108. Gustav Stickley, "The Colorado Desert and California," *Craftsman* 6 (June 1904), p. 256; Esther Klotz, *The Mission Inn: Its History and Artifacts*, 2d ed. (Riverside: Rubidoux Printing, 1982), p. 16; George Wharton James, "The Influence of the 'Mission Style' upon the Civic and Domestic Architecture of Modern California," *Craftsman* 5 (February 1904), pp. 458-469.

109. Irving J. Gill, "The Home of the Future: The New Architecture of the West: Small Homes for a Great Country," *Craftsman* 30 (May 1916), pp. 149-151; reprinted in *Architect and Engineer* 45 (May 1916), pp. 77-86. For research help with Gill, I am indebted to Bruce Kamerling of the San Diego Historical Society.

110. Eloise Roorback, "A House of Individuality," *House Beautiful* 36 (August 1914), pp. 112-113; Irving Gill, "New Ideas about Concrete Floors," *Architect and Engineer* 44 (March 1916), pp. 81-83.

111. Randell Makinson, *Greene & Greene -- Architecture as a Fine Art* (Santa Barbara: Peregrine Smith, 1977); and idem, *Greene & Greene, Furniture and Related Designs* (Santa Barbara: Peregrine Smith, 1979).

112. Sinclair Lewis, *Main Street* (New York: Signet, New American Library, 1961 [originally published in 1920]), p. 139. See also Locke 1907; and "Some California Bungalows," *Architectural Record* 18 (September 1905), pp. 217-222. *Ladies Home Journal* seems especially to have popularized the bungalow as Californian in a long series of articles by Helen Lukens Gaut and W.H. Hill (vols. 23-27, 1906-1910).

113. Peter B. Wight, "Bungalow Courts in California, Illustrated by the Works of Arthur S. Heineman and Other Architects," *Western Architect* 28 (February 1919), pp. 16-18; idem, *Western Architect* 29 (March 1920), p. 6; see also Robert M. Winter, "Arroyo Culture" and "Alfred Heineman," in Anderson, Moore and Winter 1974, pp. 10-29 and 130. The Heinemans also used the mission idiom for bungalow courts.

114. Othma Tobisch, *The Garden Church of San Francisco* (San Francisco: Church of the New Jerusalem, 1982 [25th printing]); Kenneth Cardwell, *Bernard Maybeck: Artisan, Architect, Artist* (Santa Barbara: Peregrine Smith, 1977), pp. 32-34; Longstreth 1983, pp. 273-275; Leslie Mandelson Freudenheim and Elisabeth Sacks Sussman, *Building with Nature: Roots of the San Francisco Bay Tradition* (Santa Barbara: Peregrine Smith, 1974), chapter 1.

115. Charles Keeler, *The Simple Home* (Santa Barbara: Peregrine Smith, 1979 [originally published in 1904]), pp. 17, 25, 26.

116. Ibid., pp. 11-12; and Cardwell 1977, pp. 90-91.

117. Ebenezer Howard, *Garden Cities of Tomorrow* (Cambridge: MIT Press, 1965 [first published in 1898]). See Gustav Stickley, "Rapid Growth of the Garden City Movement, Which Promises to Re-Organize Social Conditions All over the World," *Craftsman* 17 (December 1909), pp. 296-310. Stickley also published a series of articles by Barry Parker, who with Raymond Unwin designed much of Letchworth Garden City in England. Parker's articles numbered twenty-nine and ran in *Craftsman* 18-23 (1910-1913).

118. Frederick Law Olmsted, Jr., "The Landscape Work," in *Forest Hills Gardens* (New York: Sage Foundation, Homes Company, ca. 1911), n.p. Other essays in this book include Robert W. DeForest, "Forest Hills Gardens"; Grosvenor Atterbury, "The Architectural Work"; William E. Harmon, "Scientific Methods of Handling and Distributing Suburban Land"; Alfred T. White, "The Development of A Harmonious Neighborhood"; and Edward H. Bouton, "Quality of Design." I am also indebted to Susan Holbrook Perdue, "Forest Hills Gardens, Architecture and Landscape Planning in a Model Garden Suburb, 1908-1915" (master's thesis, University of Virginia, 1985).

119. "The Theory of Grosvenor Atterbury, Who Bases all his Work Upon the Principle that Originality in Architecture Springs Only from the Direct Meeting of Material Conditions," *Craftsman* 16 (June 1909), pp. 300-313; Louis A. Graves, "A 'Model Village' Under Way," *Building Progress* 2 (January 1912), pp. 18-24; see also the entire issue of *Brickbuilder* 21 (December 1912).

120. Samuel Howe, "Town Planning on a Large Scale," *House Beautiful* 36 (October 1914), pp. 130-136.

121. De Forest in Olmsted 1911, n.p.

17

The Altar Book: Containing the Order for the Celebration of the Holy Eucharist According to the Use of the American Church, 1896
Printer: Merrymount Press, Boston (presswork by De Vinne Press, New York)
Illustrator: Robert Anning Bell (1863-1933)
Designer (of decorations): Bertram Grosvenor Goodhue (1869-1924)
Black and red ink on white paper
14¾ x 11⅛ in. (page)
Department of Rare Books and Special Collection, Princeton University Library

Daniel Berkeley Updike (1860-1941), one of the first Americans to show the influence of Morris's book design in his work,[1] began a publishing career in 1880 as an office boy for Houghton Mifflin & Co. in Boston, moving in 1891 to their printing house in Cambridge, the Riverside Press. He designed several books there before establishing his own Merrymount Press in 1893. During the early years Updike's establishment was aligned with the avant-garde group in Boston who published the periodicals *Knight Errant* and *Mahogany Tree*.[2] They also established several small publishing houses, following the example set in 1890 by William Morris.

Toward the end of his life, William Morris added printing to the long list of his accomplishments among the arts and crafts. Having written and illuminated manuscripts and designed books earlier in his career, he became concerned with the design of metal type in 1888, after attending a slide-lecture given by the typographer Emery Walker. Morris began designing his own typefaces, based on models from the fifteenth century, the earliest period of printing in the West. He soon set up a press of his own, named Kelmscott after his country and city homes. Workmen were hired, special paper was made by Joseph Batchelor in Kent, and the first book, *The Story of the Glittering Plain* (by Morris) appeared in 1891.

The book, printed in Morris's Golden type, contained his own floral borders and initials, and embodied his principles of book design. *The Story of the Glittering Plain* was characterized by two-page spreads of the open book regarded as one unit rather than two, lines closely spaced so as to give a solid, black appearance to the page, and headings set entirely in capital letters, flush left rather than centered. The result was a hand-made book with a proprietary (i.e., solely owned) typeface and specially designed deco-

rations. Produced in a limited edition, the book recalled the incunabula, or "cradle books," of fifteenth-century Europe, when the earliest printers attempted to copy Gothic manuscripts. Morris's loathing of the Renaissance and adoration of the Middle Ages were reflected in the books he made.

In 1896, the same year that saw the appearance of Morris's Kelmscott Press masterpiece *Chaucer*, Updike brought out the monument of American Arts and Crafts printing, *The Altar Book*. Composition and layout had begun in 1893 at Merrymount; the actual printing of 350 copies was done by the leading New York firm of Theodore Low De Vinne in a style very typical of Kelmscott.[3] Each section begins with a double spread within borders, illustrated on the verso and with text on the recto. There are running title shoulder notes in red and much other red rubrication. The margins are in Morrisian proportions and the numerous initials are totally Kelmscott-inspired, as are the borders. While the wood-engraved illustrations are the work of the British artist Robert Anning Bell, the chief design responsibility fell to the architect Bertram Grosvenor Goodhue[4] (see no. 22). He created the borders and initials, the binding, and the typeface. This proprietary type, called "Merrymount," is, like American Type Founders' "Jenson," based on Morris's "Golden," but is less spiky and Gothicized.[5]

The critical reception was enthusiastic, some calling *The Altar Book* "the most interesting piece of bookmaking yet produced in this country."[6] Ironically, while Updike became famous because of it, he later deplored the book's frank imitativeness. Likewise he had little interest in the ideals of the Arts and Crafts movement that produced it.[7] As Updike received more and more business from New York trade publishers and from private commissions, the style of Merrymount Press after 1900 became ever more conservative, moving away from that of the experimental publishing of the nineties. Decoration was left behind for classical simplicity and serenity, more in keeping with Renaissance and eighteenth-century printing.

ST

1. One of Updike's books of 1892, F. Hopkinson Smith's *A Day at Laguerre's and Other Days, Being Nine Sketches*, reveals an awareness of the format of the first Kelmscott book. For a longer discussion of Kelmscott influence in America, see Susan Otis Thompson, *American Book Design and William Morris* (New York: Bowker, 1977).

2. These were called "literary publishers" because their young owners were concerned more with getting new and classic literature into an artistic format than with making money. The Stone and Kimball firm moved on to Chicago, while those of Copeland and Day; Lamson, Wolffe; and Small, Maynard lived out their brief but productive lives in Boston.

3. De Vinne declared himself, however, to be "frankly out of sympathy with the style of the volume." See D.B. Updike, *Notes on the Merrymount Press and Its Work* (Cambridge: Harvard University Press, 1934), p.15.

4. For other comment on Goodhue and *The Altar Book*, see Nancy Finlay, *Artists of the Book in Boston, 1890-1910* (Cambridge: Houghton Library, 1985).

5. Updike wrote of it later that it was too dark for any but large pages. See *Printing Types* (2nd ed., Cambridge: Harvard University Press, 1951), vol. 2, pp. 217-218.

6. Joseph M. Bowles, "Mr. Updike's Altar Book," *Modern Art* 4 (Autumn 1896), p. 124.

7. According to Stanley Morison and Rudolph Ruzicka, "He had no respect for manual labor [. . . , nor for] machinery — to him both were means to an end merely . . . ." See *Recollections of Daniel Berkeley Updike* (Boston: Club of Odd Volumes, 1943), pp. 25-26.

18

Description of the Pastoral Staff Belonging to the Diocese of Albany New York, 1900
Printer: Merrymount Press, Boston (photogravure reproductions by A.W. Elson and Company, Boston)
Designer (of decorations): Bertram Grosvenor Goodhue (1869-1924)
Black and red ink on white paper
17¼ x 11¾ in. (page)
Rare Book and Manuscript Library, Columbia University, New York

The work of Bertram Grosvenor Goodhue evolved from a style influenced by contemporary English artists in the early and mid-nineties (see no. 17) to one explicitly medieval. *Description of the Pastoral Staff*, which may be called a late example of the Gothic revival, has a decorative exuberance that was more likely to occur in volumes commissioned privately from the Merrymount Press.[1] The borders represent subjects depicted on the staff itself: Christ and scenes from his life, the four Evangelists and their symbols, the Apostle Paul, the signs of the Zodiac, and the arms of the Diocese and city of Albany (the last including an Indian among other Americans). Enclosed within the borders is a solid black text block in Caslon type complemented by the equally black woodcut frontispiece, a realistic depiction of the interior of

17

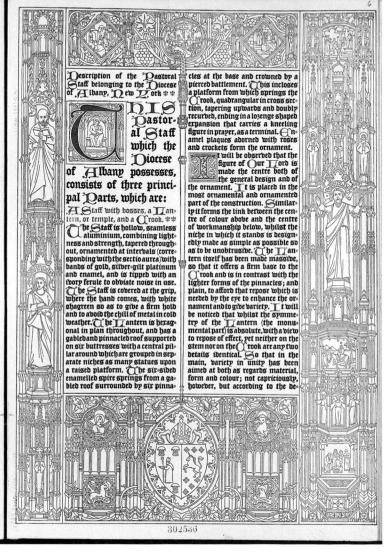

Description of the Pastoral Staff belonging to the Diocese of Albany, New York **

THIS Pastoral Staff which the Diocese of Albany possesses, consists of three principal Parts, which are:

A Staff with bosses, a Lantern, or temple, and a Crook. **

The Staff is hollow, seamless aluminium, combining lightness and strength, tapered throughout, ornamented at intervals (corresponding with the sectio aurea) with bands of gold, silver-gilt platinum and enamel, and is tipped with an ivory ferule to obviate noise in use. The Staff is covered at the grip, where the hand comes, with white shagreen so as to give a firm hold and to avoid the chill of metal in cold weather. The Lantern is hexagonal in plan throughout, and has a gabled and pinnacled roof supported on six buttresses with a central pillar around which are grouped in separate niches as many statues upon a raised platform. The six-sided enamelled spire springs from a gabled roof surrounded by six pinnacles at the base and crowned by a pierced battlement. This incloses a platform from which springs the Crook, quadrangular in cross section, tapering upwards and doubly recurved, ending in a lozenge shaped expansion that carries a kneeling figure in prayer, as a terminal. Enamel plaques adorned with roses and crockets form the ornament.

It will be observed that the figure of Our Lord is made the centre both of the general design and of the ornament. It is placed in the most ornamental and ornamented part of the construction. Similarly it forms the link between the centre of colour above and the centre of workmanship below, whilst the niche in which it stands is designedly made as simple as possible so as to be unobtrusive. The Lantern itself has been made massive, so that it offers a firm base to the Crook and is in contrast with the lighter forms of the pinnacles; and plain, to afford that repose which is needed by the eye to enhance the ornament and to give variety. It will be noticed that whilst the symmetry of the Lantern (the monumental part) is absolute, with a view to repose of effect, yet neither on the stem nor on the Crook are any two details identical. So that in the main, variety in unity has been aimed at both as regards material, form and colour; not capriciously, however, but according to the de-

302536

the choir of the Cathedral of All Saints in Albany. Goodhue's superb talents as an architectural draftsman as well as a fine artist are here richly displayed.

ST

1. For a survey of decoration, see *Book Decoration in America, 1890-1910*, a guide to an exhibition by Laurie W. Crichton, revised by Wayne G. Hammond and Robert L. Volz (Williamstown, Mass.: Chapin Library, Williams College, 1979).

19

Lock, 1904 or 1905-1911
Frank L. Koralewsky, Roxbury, Massachusetts (active ca. 1900-1930)
Iron with inlays of gold, silver, bronze, brass, and copper
H: 20 in. W: 20 in. D: 8 in.
Inscription: (in Gothic) *Schneewittchen*
Marks: engraved (in script) *F. KORALEWSKY/ 1911* and *F W*(inside shield on interior)
The Art Institute of Chicago, Gift of Richard T. Crane. 26.521

Throughout the nineteenth century casting was the primary technique used for iron grilles, fences, and architectural details; the revival of handwrought work in iron began about 1890 with the Arts and Crafts movement. On the European continent the craft was superbly wedded with Art Nouveau designs. Historic styles, however, dominated the revival of wrought iron in America, where it achieved great importance in the 1920s for domestic as well as public buildings.

"It was this lock that took me to see Mr. Koralewsky," explained Ralph Bergengren in the January 1915 issue of *House Beautiful*. He continued, "Mr. Koralewsky determined, many architects having denied that it could be done, to prove the intricate and beautiful metal work of the later Middle Ages and Renaissance could be produced if the craftsman gave himself the same freedom of time."[1] Koralewsky's proof was this lock, and indeed, it rivals the work of his German forebears, who often designed such locks with complicated devices mainly to show their skill in executing them.[2] Well acquainted with their work, Koralewsky even continued their practice of ornamenting the lock's interior surfaces. For some six or seven years, its fabrication provided him relaxation from the routine common to commercial enterprise. Representing countless hours of toil and exacting technical perfection, the lock is a

19

lexicon of ironworking methods. Frederick Krasser, Koralewsky's employer and associate, was devoted to preserving these methods, and both men would have valued the lock as a vehicle for this purpose rather than for merely recording personal skills. To one critic the lock brought to mind Longfellow's stanza:

> In the elder days of Art
>   Builders wrought with greatest care,
> Each minute and unseen part;
>   For the gods see everywhere.[3]

Upon its completion in 1911 Krasser featured the lock in a nostalgic essay on locksmithing and hardware extolling "olden times," which appeared in the Boston Society of Arts and Crafts' publication *Handicraft*.[4]

The theme of the lock, the popular German fairy tale "Snow White and the Seven Dwarfs" by Jacob and Wilhelm Grimm, appealed to turn-of-the-century taste for sentimental medievalism. *Schneewittchen* is inscribed above the lock's main plate, in which Snow White stirs a

pot over a wood fire in the underground home of the seven dwarfs. Three smaller panels, including highlights of the tale, are worked with contrasting metals. One with silver shows the queen consulting her looking glass. In another, with bronze, the queen, disguised as a witch, offers Snow White the poisoned apple. Gold highlights the third panel, where Snow White, in a deep sleep induced by the apple, is about to be found by the prince. Various duties occupy six dwarfs on the lock while the seventh has charge of the key. To find the keyhole a toadstool must be moved, but a dwarf guarding this action is asleep. A dragon forms a lever of the mechanism tended by three dwarfs. Two more dwarfs, one with a hare and the other with a carrot, bring dinner, and flora and fauna complete the ornamentation.

Koralewsky, who was probably born in the 1870s, served a traditional ironworker's apprenticeship in his native north-German town of Stralsund.[5] At eighteen he spent about a year studying ironwork in various German shops, after which he sailed for America, landed in Boston, and soon found employment at the Krasser Iron Company; by 1906 he was a craftsman member of the Boston Society of Arts and Crafts. A year later Koralewsky exhibited this lock – then unfinished – at the Society's decennial exhibition. When it was completed in 1911 it was exhibited first at the Society and later at the Museum of Fine Arts.[6] Greater acclaim followed: in 1914 the Society bestowed its Medalist award jointly in honor of Koralewsky for his individual work and in memory of Krasser (who had died the previous year), whose firm Koralewsky then directed.[7] This lock earned Koralewsky a gold medal at the 1915 Panama-Pacific Exposition, and, a decade later, was given to the Art Institute by one of Koralewsky's major private patrons, Richard T. Crane, Jr., of Chicago.

WSB

1. Ralph Bergengren, "An Adventure in the Medieval," *House Beautiful* 37 (January 1915), p. 47.

2. W.W. Watts, "Iron in Art: History," *The Encyclopaedia Britannica*, 14th edition (1929), vol. 12, facing p. 677, pl. 4, fig. 1.

3. E.L.C., "Arts and Crafts Department, The Boston Exhibition," *The Scrip* 2 (April 1907), p. 230.

4. Frederick Krasser, "Something About Locksmithing and Hardware in General," *Handicraft* 3 (March 1911), pp. 428-433, ill.

5. Katherine Gibson, "Mastersmith Frank Koralewsky," *The Goldsmith of Florence* (New York: Macmillan Company, 1929), p. 188.

6. *Exhibition of the Society of Arts & Crafts, Copley Hall* (Boston: Society of Arts and Crafts, 1907), p. 41, no. 684; "A Remarkable Iron Lock," *Art and Progress* 2 (April 1911), p. 181; F. Allen Whiting, "Arts and Crafts: At the Museum of Fine Arts, Boston," *Art and Progress* 2 (July 1911), p. 264.

7. The Krasser firm executed important commissions for eastern institutions such as Harvard University and the Cathedral of St. John the Divine in New York City. Koralewsky was also responsible for Italian-Renaissance-style ironwork at the Crane estate, "Castle Hill," near Ispwich, Massachusetts. Another important patron, George Booth, gave nineteen pieces of Koralewsky's ironwork, including screens, door hinges, knockers, locks, and latches to the Detroit Institute of Arts in 1919. See Ann Webb Karnaghan, "A Worker in Wrought Iron," *International Studio* 83 (August 1926), p. 30, ill.

20 (color plate, p. 10)
Alms basin, 1914
George Ernest Germer (1868-1936), Boston
Silver
H: 2½ in. Diam: 15¾ in. Wt: 48 ozs.
Inscription: *ALL THINGS COME TO THEE O LORD AND OF THINE OWN HAVE WE GIVEN THEE* (embossed and chased on rim)
Marks: inscribed *GEORGE E. GERMER / BOSTON, MASS. / 1914 / STERLING*
Cranbrook Academy of Art Museum, Bloomfield Hills, Michigan. 1944.114

The alms basin – sometimes called an alms dish or altar dish – is meant for collecting charitable donations to be laid upon the altar. Used originally in Catholic services, the form became common in Anglican church furnishings after the Reformation.

The imagery on this basin is wrought from metal of heavy gauge with exceptional definition and unusually high relief. A study of the iconography reveals a rich orchestration of Christian symbols and its style reflects a knowledge of Gothic art. Four undulating vines (grape, rose, pomegranate, and probably lily) radiate from the Agnus Dei (Lamb of God with victory banner) centered in a roundel. The Agnus Dei was a common feature on patens throughout the middle ages, and the vines were often a part of Gothic ornament. A circular motto, also in Gothic style, is subdivided clockwise by the Chi Rho (sacred monogram with alpha and omega), a laurel wreath, a grape cluster, and a crown of thorns.

The appropriateness of Gothic interpretations of liturgical objects was widely acknowledged by Arts and Crafts designers. Leading practitioners of the style – especially for churches, where Communion played an important part of the theology – were the noted architects Ralph Adams Cram and Bertram G. Goodhue (see no. 22). They were important policy makers in the Boston Society of Arts and Crafts, and their firm's commissions were a source of prestigious employment for the Society's member craftsmen.[1] The Gothic revival in churches was further energized by memorial commissions resulting from World War I, and the style predominated in liturgical metalwork into the Depression.

By the time he established his New Hampshire farmhouse-studio in 1917, Germer was the nation's foremost creator of ecclesiastical metalwork. The son of a Master Goldsmith,

Germer had apprenticed in his birthplace, Berlin, where in 1885 the city awarded him a medal at its annual apprentices' exhibition. His knowledge of art and design was expanded by visits to the important German art centers of Dresden, Hanau, and Cologne and by his employment at Berlin's Kunstgewerbe Museum.[2] He came to America in March of 1893, and for nearly twenty years worked as a designer, modeler, and chaser with major silver manufacturers in Boston, Providence, and New York. In 1912 Germer joined the Boston Society of Arts and Crafts, found bench space nearby, and began devoting his career to ecclesiastical silver.[3]

At the thirteenth Arts and Crafts annual at the Art Institute of Chicago in October 1914, Germer's single entry was this alms basin.[4] A year later it appeared in the American Federation of Arts First Exhibition of American Industrial Art in Washington and at the Boston Society of Arts and Crafts. When the basin was displayed at the Detroit Society of Arts and Crafts in 1916, George G. Booth purchased it and in 1919 gave it to the Detroit Institute of Arts.[5]

WSB

1. In the catalogue for the Society's 1907 decennial exhibition, the Department of Ecclesiastical Work – chaired by Cram – observed in its foreword: "In any movement towards a healthy reunion of Art and Craftsmanship, the Church, of all visible organizations, must be considered the power most interested." (See *Exhibition of the Society of Arts & Crafts, Copley Hall*, February 5-26, Boston 1907, p. 15.) For a silver-gilt bishop's staff, inlaid with ivory and with enameled coats of arms, designed by Cram and his partner F.W. Ferguson and executed by Germer, see Henry P. Macomber, "The Silversmiths of New England," *American Magazine of Art* 25 (October 1932), p. 214, ill.

2. Henriette J. Fuchs, "A Tribute to George Ernest Germer, Designer and Executor of Ecclasiastical Silver" (typescript, August 22, 1937), p. 1. The author is indebted to the late J. Herbert Gebelein for this reference.

3. Germer worked at 26 Lime Street, the site of George J. Hunt's Boston School of Metalry, founded in 1910, and Craftsman's Studios. More than a dozen handicraft metalsmiths or jewelers are known to have been there intermittently. It is undoubtedly where Germer fabricated the alms basin.

4. *Catalogue of the Thirteenth Annual Exhibition of Examples of Industrial Art and Original Designs for Decorations* (Chicago: Art Institute of Chicago, 1914), no. 369.

5. It was acquired by Cranbrook in 1944 through an exchange between the two museums.

21

Firescreen, ca. 1916
Samuel Yellin (1885-1940), Philadelphia
Wrought iron
H: 44 in. W: 34 in.
Collection of Mrs. Harvey Z. Yellin from the
Samuel Yellin Collection

Before the Depression and then military demands on metalworkers during World War II
brought the ornamental iron industry to an
end, hand-forged ironwork adorned many
structures built in the first third of the twentieth
century. Among the leading figures of the blacksmithing movement were Frank and Gustav
Koralewsky of Boston, Cyril Colnik of Milwaukee, and Samuel Yellin of Philadelphia.[1] Born
and raised in Poland, Yellin learned all aspects
of the blacksmithing process from making nails
to forging and decorating the most elaborate
gates. He worked in several shops in Germany,
Belgium, and England before immigrating to
Philadelphia in 1906.

Earning his living in the early years at odd
metalworking jobs and teaching blacksmithing
at the Philadelphia Museum School of Industrial Art, Yellin opened his first shop in 1909 on
5th Street. Two years later, in enlarged quarters,
he began to pursue commissions with architects like McKim, Mead, and White, whose
Beaux-Arts training made them more sympathetic to wrought iron than to the cast iron and
bronze so popular in America. The work he
executed for them and for other clients included grilles, gates, screens, lighting fixtures,
railings, and balconies, some of them large
commissions for universities, cathedrals, banks,
and libraries in addition to private homes.[2]
Within a short time, Yellin had so much business that a larger shop was necessary. His Arch
Street Metalworker's Studio, designed by Walter Mellor and Arthur Meigs and completed in
1915, included a showroom, library, museum
room, drafting room, and large open space to
accommodate sixty forges and over 200 workers. Yellin chose his craftsmen carefully to ensure the optimum standards. Recruiting highly
skilled immigrant artisans, he assigned them to
specific tasks such as chisel decoration, locksmithing, *repoussé,* and polishing.[3]

Yellin's training and exposure to the
wrought-iron revival in Europe endowed him
with a certain philosophy about design and
workmanship: "There is only one way to make
good decorative iron work and that is with the

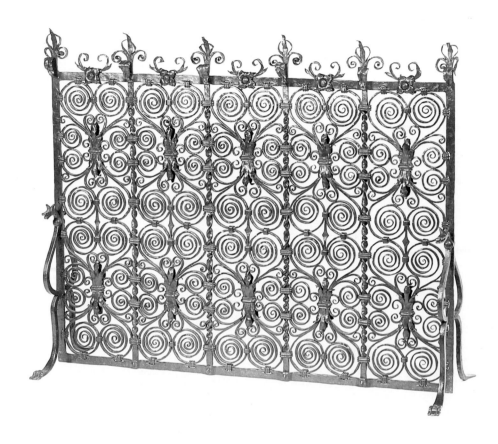

21

hammer at the anvil, for in the heat of creation
and under the spell of the hammer, the whole
conception of a composition is often transformed."[4] To develop the necessary aesthetic
judgment, Yellin believed it crucial to study the
best examples of the past. He lectured widely
on historical wrought iron, established a collection of historic examples (mounted in a museum room in his Arch Street studio) and
formed an invaluable reference library, including such varied works as *Pencil Points, International
Studio, Good Furniture,* and numerous illustrated
books on church architecture and interiors.
Such sources enabled Yellin to communicate
easily with architects and helped his workers to
adapt or find new uses for old traditional forms.
The present firescreen – made for the show-

room of his shop, a medieval-style room with
heavy ceiling beams, tapestries, and leaded windows – is based on a thirteenth-century choir
grille at Le Puy, which Yellin had seen either in
situ or in a book. The adaptation followed a
precedent established as early as the mid-nineteenth century in a firescreen based on the
great grille from Ourscamp.[5] Yellin himself
made a firescreen replica of the Ourscamp
grille in 1922 and substituted it for the present
screen. He then moved this example, which
was one of his favorite pieces of ironwork, to
his home.[6]

The inherent properties of wrought iron and
Yellin's techniques accorded well with Arts and
Crafts principles. Unlike cast iron, which had a
very consistent look, wrought iron acquired

attractive variations in color and texture at the moment of forging; the final result depended almost solely upon the skills of the blacksmith striking the red-hot metal. Yellin also emphasized appropriate techniques for assembling his work. While other wrought-iron craftsmen relied on the expeditious torch-welded and bolted joints typical of cast iron, he used the more traditional collared and pieced joints. Although Yellin clearly preferred the historic methods of forging iron, he did eliminate the most laborious and time-consuming parts of the craft. He made practical use of the new steel mills, which provided uniform-sized rods, bars, and plates and installed electronically controlled blowers to ensure steady optimal temperatures for each step of the process.[7]

ESC

1. For Frank Koralewsky, see the preceding entry. His brother Gustav made gates, grilles, and other iron work for the Isabella Stewart Gardner Museum in Boston. For Cyril Colnik, see Judith Simonsen, "Cyril Colnik," *Lore* 31 (summer 1981), pp. 21-27.

2. Among Yellin's many important commissions were Yale University, the National Cathedral in Washington, and *Vizcaya*, the Miami estate of James Deering. The best biographies are Jack Andrews, "Samuel Yellin, Craftsman in Iron," *Tiller* 2 (January-February 1984), pp. 9-25; and Richard Wattenmaker, *Samuel Yellin in Context* (Flint, Mich.: Flint Institute of Arts, 1985).

3. Jack Andrews, "Samuel Yellin, Metalworker," reprinted from *Anvil's Ring* (Summer 1982), pp. 2, 9-10; and Wattenmaker 1985.

4. Andrews 1982, p. 8.

5. Raymond Lecoq, *Fer Forgé et Serrurerie* (Paris, 1962), pp. 60-61; Wattenmaker 1985; Alphonse Didron, *Annales Archéologiques* 10 (May-June 1850), pp. 117-122. I am indebted to Richard Wattenmaker for pointing out the design source and the long tradition of adapting firescreens from grilles and gates.

6. Myra Tolmach Davis, *Sketches in Iron: Samuel Yellin, American Master of Wrought Iron, 1885-1940* (Washington, D.C.: Dimock Gallery, 1971), fig. 26; and conversation with Marian C. Yellin, April 1986.

7. Davis 1971; and George Geerlings, *Wrought Iron in Architecture*(New York: Scribner's Sons, 1929), pp. 5-24.

22
Presentation drawing: exterior perspective for All Saints' Church, Boston (Ashmont Square, Dorchester), 1891
Architect: Cram, Wentworth, and Goodhue (Ralph Adams Cram [1863-1942], Charles Francis Wentworth [1841-1897], Bertram Grosvenor Goodhue [1869-1924])

22

Renderer: Bertram Goodhue
Pen and ink on paper
15⅜ x 20 in. (image area)
Collection of John Rivers

All Saints' in Ashmont is perhaps the most important American church designed in the 1890s; it would influence American religious architecture for the next fifty years. The structure was the first of Ralph Adams Cram's high Anglo-Catholic, Episcopalian churches and would serve as an example for his very influential book *Church Building* (1901). An excellent illustration of the conservative impulse of the American Arts and Crafts movement, it shows his proclivities toward English fifteenth-century Perpendicular style. Explaining the use of precedent, Cram commented: "We have simply tried to preserve the spirit of the past, not its forms."[1]

The commission entered the Cram and Wentworth office in the late summer of 1891; Bertram Goodhue joined the firm in the fall.

Whereas Cram was chiefly responsible for the overall form and plan, it was Goodhue who contributed the details.[2] The rendering exemplifies his preference for large masses with closely observed features. Except for the parish house to the left, which was omitted, the church was built following substantially the rendering. The contrast in expression between the church and parish house in the drawing may have been meant to indicate the different functional purposes of the structures and to imply that the complex was built over a period of time. The construction of the church – with stone carving by John Evans, wood carving by Johannes Kirchmayer, and stained glass by Charles Connick – contributed to the development of a Boston-based crafts community.

RGW

1. Ralph Adams Cram, "All Saints' Church, Dorchester (Boston), Mass.," *Churchman* 79 (April 15, 1899), p. 563. See also Ralph Adams Cram, *Church Building: A Study of*

the *Principles of Architecture in Their Relation to the Church* (Boston: Small, Maynard, 1901), pp. 41-45; and Douglass Shand Tucci, *All Saints' Ashmont, A Centennial History* (Boston: All Saints' Church, 1975).

2. Ralph Adams Cram, *My Life in Architecture*(Boston: Little, Brown, 1936), pp. 47-49. See also Douglass Shand Tucci, *Ralph Adams Cram, American Medievalist* (Boston: Boston Public Library, 1975); Richard Oliver, *Bertram Grosvenor Goodhue* (New York: Architectural History Foundation, and Cambridge: MIT Press, 1983); and Richard Guy Wilson, "Ralph Adams Cram and the Idea of a Medieval Culture for America," in *Medievalism in American Culture*, B. Rosenthal and P. Szarmach, eds. (Binghamton: State University of New York, forthcoming [1987]).

23

Presentation perspective for John Neil and Frank Mauran double house, Philadelphia (315-317 South 22nd Street), 1891
Architect: Wilson Eyre (1858-1944)
Pen and watercolor on green paper
13 x 16½ in.
Inscription: *WE Jr./Neill & Mauran* (lower right); *Proposed Houses / to be built on 22nd / Street / Wilson Eyre Jr / Architect* (upper left)
The Architectural Archives of the University of Pennsylvania, Philadelphia

The architecture of Wilson Eyre follows an individualistic course, not easily classifiable. Born in Italy to American parents, he was schooled in Europe, Canada, and Newport, Rhode Island, and spent one year at the MIT School of Architecture in 1876. His work covers a number of idioms, from Queen Anne to shingle style, American colonial, English plaster, Georgian, and others that are not readily categorized. He was the architectural leader of the Philadelphia Arts and Crafts community.[1]

The double corner house Eyre designed for the land speculator John Neil in 1890-1891 is typical of his slightly eccentric individualism.[2] As renderings show, Eyre's work has a dreamy quality that is almost childlike. While the red brick and faint traces of colonial detail in the Neil house refer to Philadelphia's own eighteenth century, the form and materials are more evocative of the Queen Anne examples built by Richard Norman Shaw and others in the Chelsea and Kensington sections of London in the 1870s and 1880s. Against these mildly classical features, Eyre used a Gothic arch for the twin entrances, which are separated by an engaged buttress capped with a sculpture of a gowned

23

female figure. In the rendering, undercutting order with disorder, a gigantic gable encompasses the lower floors and asymmetry is introduced with the different bay windows. As built, the gable was transformed into a gigantic gambrel roof and the corner bay window reduced to a single story in height. Observing the seventeen different types of openings Eyre used on the two façades, a critic described the house as "hit-or-miss."[3]

RGW

1. Edward Teitelman entry on Wilson Eyre in *MacMillan Encyclopedia of Architects*, A. Placzek, ed. (New York: MacMillan Publishers, 1982), vol. 2, pp. 34-37.

2. Frank Mauran subsequently purchased half of the house.

3. Julian Millard, "The Work of Wilson Eyre," *Architectural Record* 14 (October 1903), p. 312.

24 and 25

Presentation drawing: front aerial perspective and elevations of living hall for Thomas Shields Clarke house, "Fernbrook," Lenox, Massachusetts (Route 7 and Route 20), 1902
Architect: Wilson Eyre (1858-1944)
Watercolor and gouache on brown paper
14 x 17¼ in.
Inscription: *Wilson Eyre Jr. / Architect* (upper left); *W Eyre Jr / 1901* (lower left); *T.S. Clarke* (lower right - not original); *WILSON EYRE, / ARCHITECT / 927 Chestnut St., Philadelphia* (stamped on verso)
The Architectural Archives of the University of Pennsylvania, Philadelphia

Presentation drawing: elevations of living hall for "Fernbrook"
Architect: Wilson Eyre (1858-1944)
Graphite and watercolor on paper
17¼ x 33 in.
Inscription: *Sketch for Living-Hall / Residence for Mr.*

Thomas Shields Clarke – at Lenox / Wilson Eyre, Architect / ½ inch scale – (lettering in pencil at center); *Elevation towards Dining Room* / (upper left); *Elevation towards Studio – Reception Room* / (upper right); *Ele-/vation towards Garden* / (lower left); *Elevation towards Entrance Porch* (lower right)
The Architectural Archives of the University of Pennsylvania, Philadelphia

The regional school of which Wilson Eyre was the leading member had an impact well beyond the locus of activity in Philadelphia; its architects designed numerous buildings for sites from Michigan and Ohio to Massachusetts and Long Island. For Thomas Shields Clarke, a prominent Philadelphia-based sculptor, Eyre designed a large summer house and studio at Lenox that was completed in 1905.[1] Stylistically the rough stucco covering of the Clarke house relates to English plaster houses; the prominent horizontal form may also reflect Voysey, but it has American roots as well.

In plan the house was U-shaped with a large living hall dominating the center, a studio in one wing, and service facilities in the other. One writer described Eyre's approach to design as follows: "As soon as rough sketch plans are made, he commences his birds-eye perspective. . . . Then perhaps the first suggestion of a garden scheme is evolved."[2] Leaving questions of style and materials to be developed later, Eyre treated the design of a country house as a total picture, "where no detail of local color, or detached light or shadow is allowed to interfere." He believed that country houses should not merge with nature or the landscape but they should contain references. For example, the building has a base and high chimneys of local fieldstone, and a critic noted that "the silhouette of the house is distinctly that of the mountain that rises behind it."[3]

In his numerous writings Eyre stressed that a house should be placed for "an extended view;" he added, however: ". . . we are beginning to realize that if we want beauty combined with privacy we must hedge ourselves in to a certain extent."[4] The Clarke house was placed well off the road on the edge of a broad green plateau. The woods were carved out to the rear and strong axes ran from the house to the garden. Pergolas from the porches on either side of the front also reinforced that outward movement, and extensive plantings and vines softened the form. Retaining the contrast between nature and the manmade, Eyre inte-

24

grated into his conception flowering rose bushes, red chimney pots, brown shingles on the roof, and green shutters with Voyseyesque hearts set against the white stucco.

While Eyre designed the interior decor, there is little evidence that he designed the furniture, either for the Clarke house or any other. Instead, he exerted influence through the delineation of wall surfaces and trim, such as with the Clarke house living hall, where heavy timber mandated a Craftsman style in furnishings. Period photographs of the Clarke house interiors show Mission-style furniture and Mercer tiled fireplaces.

RGW

1. Arthur Hoeber, "Thomas Shields Clarke," *Brush and Pencil* 5 (August 1900), pp. 193-199. The Clarke house was heavily illustrated at the time; in addition to citations below, see: "A House at Lenox," *House Beautiful* 25 (April 1909), p. 107; "A Design for an Artist's House," *House and Garden* 1 (November 1901), pp. 155-157 (reprinted in John C. Baker, ed., *American Country Homes and their Gardens* [Philadelphia: John H. Winston, Co., 1906], pp. 131-133); and illustrations published in *American Architect and Building News* 88 (September 23, 1905) p. 103.

2. Eyre liked to retain control of the entire project, from the house and its interior to the garden or, as one writer observed: "He has no sympathy with specialization." See Frederick Wallick, "The Rational Art of Wilson Eyre, an Architect Who Designs Houses to Meet the Needs and Express the Qualities of Today," *Craftsman* 17, no. 5 (February 1910), pp. 543-545.

3. Barr Ferree, "Homes of American Artists, 'Fernbrook': The Summer House of Thomas Shields Clarke," *American Homes and Gardens* 6 (May 1909), p. 177.

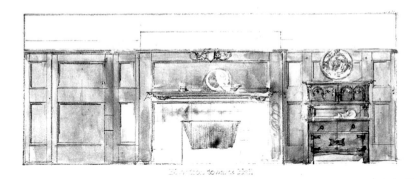

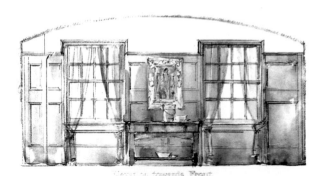

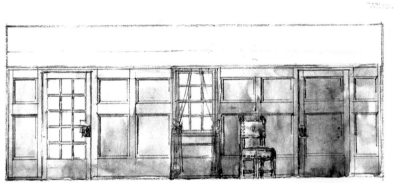

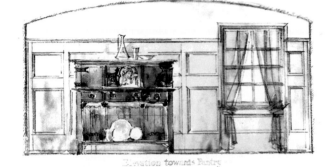

25

4. Wilson Eyre, "The Surroundings of the Country House," *Brochure Series of Architectural Illustration* 4 (1898), p. 195. See also Wilson Eyre, "The Planning of Country Houses," *American Architect and Building News* 93 (April 1 and 8, 1908), pp. 107-108, 115, 116.

26

Presentation drawing: side perspective for Caspar Wistar Morris house, Haverford, Pennsylvania (407 Rose Lane), 1914-1916
Architect: Mellor and Meigs (Walter Mellor [1880-1940] and Arthur Ingersoll Meigs [1882-1956])
Ink on brown card stock
15½ x 27¼ in.
Inscription: *Mellor & Meigs, Architects* (lower right); *House for C. W. Morris, Esq.* (lower center)
The Athenaeum of Philadelphia, Gift of the heirs of Mrs. Arthur I. Meigs

Walter Mellor and Arthur Meigs went into partnership in 1906 and almost immediately became leading suburban and country house architects, carrying on the regional tradition of Wilson Eyre. Walter Mellor, a Philadelphian, attended Haverford College and studied architecture at the University of Pennsylvania. He

then worked for a local architect, T. P. Chandler, before joining Meigs. Arthur Meigs's social prominence in Philadelphia assured the firm of a substantial clientèle, in spite of his having no formal architectural training. In 1916, just as the Morris house was reaching completion, Mellor and Meigs were joined by George Howe (1886-1955), who in the 1930s converted to modernism.[1]

The Caspar Morris house, on a site of ten acres, shows the type of historically based regionalism the firm excelled in creating.[2] Placed on top of a hill overlooking a stream, an imitation English manor house ranges along the hillside, its long fieldstone walls tying it to the site. One approaches first from below, then swings out and around to the entrance, which is a cobblestone court on the rear. A service wing with the garage limits movement at that point. Despite the appearance of an accretion of

HOUSE FOR C. W. MORRIS ESQ.

· MELLOR & MEIGS · ARCHITECTS ·

26

additive volumes (fig. 24), a geometrical order is evident in the house, as in the gardens. Along the south, overlooking the view, are arranged the principal entertainment spaces – the dining room, stair hall, and living room – while on the north are placed the den, entrance hall, and services. The attention to details of the house – with wrought-iron switch plates, grilles, and door handles by Samuel Yellin; pegs in the exposed timbering; and the exterior brick patterning – recalls, as does the inventive plan, the contemporary work of Edwin L. Lutyens in England.

RGW

1. George Thomas in *Philadelphia: Three Centuries of American Art* (Philadelphia: Philadelphia Museum of Art, 1976), pp. 499-501; and Robert A.M. Stern, *George Howe: Toward a Modern American Architecture* (New Haven: Yale University Press, 1975), pp. 30-33.

2. *A Monograph of the Work of Mellor, Meigs & Howe* (New York: Architectural Book Publishing Co., 1923), pp. 1-13.

27

Chest, ca. 1900
Designer: Sydney Burleigh (1853-1931)
Carver: Julia Lippit Mauran
Maker: Potter Company, Providence
Oak with carved and painted panels
H: 21¾ in. W: 40 in. D: 21⅞ in.
Museum of Art, Rhode Island School of Design.
13.429

The work of medieval craftsmen, epitomizing the union of art and labor,[1] often inspired motifs for Arts and Crafts designers. This chest serves as such an example, the hand-carved panels representing characters from the Arthurian legends.[2] While the theme and workmanship demonstrate an allegiance to the Arts and Crafts ethos, the chest does deviate in several respects. Both the hinges and the decorative moldings on the left and right sides of the panels are machine produced. Furthermore, the chest does not represent the unified work of a single craftsman.

Sydney Burleigh, designer of the piece, is best known for his paintings. Born in Little Compton, Rhode Island, Burleigh began his career as a painter in 1875 and traveled to Europe to study with Jean Paul Laurens. He returned in 1880 to Providence, where he es-

27

tablished himself as a leader of the local art community, active with the Rhode Island School of Design, the Providence Art Club, and the American Art Workers' Guild.[3] In addition to handcrafted objects,[4] the Guild members designed some of the City's finest buildings and interiors: Lyman Clapp's house on Hope Street, the Masonic Temple on Dorrance Street, the Fleur de Lys Studios,[5] and *The Rock* for Dr. C. Gardner in Little Compton were among their commissions.

JSB

1. John Ruskin described this union extolling the cooperative nature of the building of a Gothic cathedral. See "The Nature of Gothic," reprinted in John D. Rosenberg, ed., *The Genius of John Ruskin: Selections from his Writing* (Boston, London, and Henley: Routledge and Kegan Paul, 1980; first published in 1853).

2. On the front are carved Queen Guinevere, King Arthur, and a dragon, a symbol of the court. The left side panel carries symbols of Sir Lancelot of the Round Table, a banner, a coat of arms, and a helmet. Lancelot's son, Sir Galahad, who rediscovered the Holy Grail, is represented by the coat of arms on the

right side. The back panels display coats of arms, helmets, and banners to represent Sir Galahad, Sir Percival, and Sir Tristram, all knights of the Round Table.

3. Burleigh founded the Guild with painter Charles Stetson and the industrialist John Aldrich in about 1885.

4. The Guild apparently specialized in furniture decorated with panel paintings.

5. George L. Miner, *Angel's Lane, The History of a Little Street in Providence* (Providence: Akerman-Standard Press, 1948), p. 160.

28

28
Vase, 1900
Weller Pottery Company (1872-1949), Zanesville, Ohio
Decorator: Charles Babcock Upjohn (1866-1953)
Buff earthenware, molded with incised decoration of medieval figures moving through trees in brown, black, white, and green glazes
H: 17 in. Diam: 11 in.
Marks: incised *C. B. Upjohn / 1900* (on side); impressed *DICKENS WARE* in arch over *WELLER*, *x300 / 11* (on bottom)
Private Collection

In the 1890s Doulton & Company of Lambeth, England, produced a popular series of tableware and decorative accessories featuring characters and scenes taken from illustrations for the works of Charles Dickens. That one of Dickens's characters was named Samuel Weller suggested to the owner of the Weller Pottery Company (see no. 42) the idea of naming one of his

lines Dickens' Ware; his plan was partly a joke and partly a way to take advantage of the commercial possibilities. While the first examples were decorated only with floral designs under a glossy glaze, the second line of Dickens' Ware, designed by Charles Babcock Upjohn in 1900,[1] featured sgraffito decorations after the George Cruikshank illustrations to Dickens's stories.

Educated in the art schools of England, France, and Italy, Upjohn had joined the Weller Pottery in 1895, after the departure of William A. Long (see no. 56).[2] Other designs he used for the new line of Dickens' Ware included portraits of American Indians, animals and birds, monks, and historical scenes adapted from book illustrations of the period. The example shown here was decorated shortly before Upjohn left Weller to work for the new Cambridge Art Pottery in Cambridge, Ohio.[3] Its incised decoration – a procession of medieval characters, perhaps adapted from an illustration for Chaucer's *Canterbury Tales* – represents one aspect of the Gothic revival in the decorative arts and architecture within the Arts and Crafts movement. Weller's success depended in large part upon such ware – individually handcrafted – in combination with simple molded commercial goods. The variety they offered, in new styles of decoration and novel forms, kept the burgeoning market well supplied.

BRD and EPD

1. *Crockery and Glass Journal*, December 27, 1900, p. 17.
2. Ralph and Terry Kovel, *The Kovels' Collector's Guide to American Art Pottery* (New York: Crown Publishers, 1974), p. 295.
3. Paul Evans, *Art Pottery of the United States* (New York: Charles Scribner's Sons, 1974), p. 292. Upjohn designed the second Dickens' Ware line before he left for Cambridge, not after he returned to Weller.

29
Window, 1911
Charles Connick (1875-1945), Boston[1]
Leaded stained glass
H: 81½ in. W: 26¾ in. D: 1¾ in.
Inscription: *os homini sublime dedit coelumque tueri* (below upper panel); *astronomia docet astra* (below lower panel)
Marks: painted and glazed *CJ Connick Boston* (in lower right-hand corner)
Charles J. Connick Associates, Boston

Charles Connick Associates and the William Willet and Nicola D'Ascenzo studios in Philadelphia were the three major stained-glass studios working in the Gothic-revival tradition in America during the early decades of the twentieth century.[2] Connick founded his firm in 1912 with the financial support of an architect who may well have been Ralph Adams Cram.[3] The two men collaborated on several major commissions, among them All Saints' Church in Ashmont, Massachusetts (1923-1931; see no. 22), the Cathedral of St. John the Divine (1915-1931) in New York, the university chapel (1928-1939) and windows for Proctor Hall (1919-1922) at Princeton, and the American Church in Paris (1930-1931). The Connick studio also made windows for St. Patrick's Cathedral in New York (1941-1954) and the National Shrine of the Immaculate Conception in Washington, D.C. (1924-1971), designed by Charles D. Maginnis.[4]

Connick's shop functioned in the medieval tradition and was in many respects the Arts and Crafts ideal. At its height in the 1930s, forty to fifty men and women worked in the studio, which Connick noted at his death, was "only incidentally a business."[5] Promising young artists began as apprentices for four to six years, training in all aspects of the craft from designing to cutting glass to painting and glazing. With time and experience, he or she would become expert in a specific area and practice this aspect of stained-glass production in the studio. A reporter commented in 1931: "Attitude to his co-designers [is] that of one artist to another . . . . He [Connick] originates, supervises. They elaborate."[6] Connick believed that his greatest contribution to the craft was "rescuing it from the abysmal depth of opalescent picture windows"[7] of the sort popularized by John La Farge and hs followers. Using clear "antique" glass similar to that of the middle ages, Connick viewed it as "colored radiance, with the lustre, intensity, and baffling vibrant quality of dancing lights."[8] Among the artists, musicians, and poets who flocked to his studio were Robert Frost and Sherwood Anderson. Frost wrote of "Connick's stained glass wonder gift" and exchanged poems for medallions with Connick.

As craftsman, author, lecturer, and editor, Charles Connick played a leading role in the revitalization of stained glass in America. Serving as president of the Stained Glass Association from 1931 to 1939, he promoted its magazine, *Stained Glass*, and published a major work on the subject in 1937.[9] From 1934 to 1939 he was also president of the Boston Society of Arts and Crafts.

This window was one of three Connick designed and executed[10] and then exhibited in 1915 at the Panama-Pacific Exposition in San Francisco, where he won a gold medal for craftsmanship. According to a contemporary newspaper article, it had been displayed previously at the Boston Museum of Fine Arts;[11] it has since remained on view in the Connick studio. A virtuoso example of the Gothic-revival tradition in America, the window was designed and made just a year after Halley's comet passed by. It pictures a student with lantern, compass, and chart, sitting beside an astronomer observing the sky. A Latin inscription reads: "The Creator gave an upward-looking countenance to man and commanded him to look up to heaven" – a line from Ovid's *Metamorphoses* suggesting that astronomy has a divine sanction. Below is a full-rigged galleon of the Middle Ages and the inscription: "Astronomy teaches the stars."[12]

CZ

1. For assistance with this entry, I am indebted to Noreen O'Gara, who is completing her master's thesis at Tufts University ("Charles J. Connick: The Early Years [1910-1925]") and to Orin Skinner, president of Charles J. Connick Associates from 1945 to 1986.

2. The Boston stained-glass firms of Reynolds, Francis and Rohnstock (founded in 1920) and the Wilbur H. Burnham studio (founded in 1922) were also very important to the history of the Gothic-revival movement. The founders of the former studio had worked for Connick between 1913 and 1920.

3. Charles J. Connick, "The Education of an Artist in Brother Sun's Workshop," unpublished and undated manuscript; from the Connick Associates Collection, microfilm roll 985, frame 866, in the Archives of American Art, Smithsonian Institution. Connick wrote (pp. 27-28) that he got money not from a banker but "from a fellow struggler in the field of art – the Architect." Ralph Adams Cram became familiar with Connick and his work through Connick's first major commission at All Saints' Parish Church in Brookline (1910), a church that Cram designed. He encouraged Connick to travel to Europe to study windows of the old masters with the profits of this commission and then, upon his return, to execute glass work that would elicit other commissions. The present window was probably a result of this advice. See Archives of American Art, microfilm roll 985, frame 870.

4. Many thanks to Norene O'Gara for providing the dates of Connick's commissions.

29

5. "Orin E. Skinner: "An Autobiography," *Stained Glass* 72 (Winter 1977/1978), p. 234. According to Skinner, this was noted in Connick's will. The studio closed in 1986, when an aging workforce and a series of high-rise buildings blocking the studio's access to natural light prompted its demise.

6. "Gossip of the Town," *Boston Post*, May 21, 1931.

7. The quotation appeared in Connick's obituary: "Famed Stained Glass Expert is Dead at 70," *Boston Herald*, December 29, 1945.

8. "Lectures on Art of Stained Glass: Charles Connick Tells Its History and Possibilities at Currier Gallery," *Manchester Leader*, Manchester, N.H., November 7, 1930.

9. Charles J. Connick, *Adventures in Color and Light: An Introduction to the Stained Glass Craft* (New York: Random House, 1937).

10. Connick crafted the window in the Boston shop of Vaughan and O'Neill a year prior to the founding of his own studio. For the date of the window, see Connick 1937, p. 180. Although Connick did not move into his studio at 9 Harcourt Street or hire assistants until the spring of 1913, he began to number commissions as early as 1912. According to Norene O'Gara, there are several letters and files dating back to 1912 in the Connick Archives at the Boston Public Library.

11. "Award to Boston Man at Panama Exposition," *Boston Herald*, August 22, 1915.

12. I am indebted to R.J. and J. Tarrant for this translation and for identifying the line from Ovid's *Metamorphoses*, book 1, line 85.

30

Tea gown, ca. 1893
Dressmaker: Mrs. E.L. Mead, Auburn, New York
Twill-weave wool; machine-sewn seams, hand-sewn finishes
H: 56 in. in front; 8 in. train to 64 in. in back
American Costume Collection, Syracuse University. Gift of Mrs. Marion Walker Brodt. 84.165a,b

In the mid-1890s when Agnes Morton Walker planned the wardrobe for her journey to visit a sister in California, she probably expressed concern to her dressmaker for suitability and comfort, two important watchwords of the Arts and Crafts attitude toward apparel. She might also have asked – as any New Woman of the nineties might – that the costumes express her modernity, her individuality, her artistic inclinations, and her espousal of the principles of dress reform. Leading reformists in America and abroad were in favor of a return to antique

principles of apparel design, in particular the theory that costume drapery should originate at the shoulder region in the classic manner, to eliminate restrictions and weighted layers on the bodice and waistline. Writing on women's dress in 1884, Oscar Wilde noted that "the laws of Greek dress may be perfectly realised, even in a moderately tight gown with sleeves: I mean the principle of suspending all apparel from the shoulders, and of relying for beauty of effect not on . . . bows where there should be no bows, . . . but on the exquisite play of light and line that one gets from rich and rippling folds."[1] Princess-line house dresses, worn over a lightly boned corset, became popular tea-time wear; by the nineties they were so accepted that many women wore the ensemble with the addition of correct accessories for dinner at home, instead of changing into formal attire with its requisite lacing tight (hence the optional neck ruff for this costume).

Harmonious – if unlikely – collaborations could result from the union of haute couture Rococo Revival elements with those representing "Greek" principles and the Arts and Crafts attitude. The modified Watteau train, while at first glance reactionary, is an interpretation of the continuous princess line favored by dress-reform advocates such as architect-designer E. W. Godwin, who headed the Liberty and Company Costume Department at its inception in 1884. Influenced by the popularity of the soft Liberty silk fabrics, American manufacturers produced variations with names like "Kensington" (printed wild silk), "Satin Grec," "Athena" (also satin), and even "Liberty Satin"[2]; wool and wool-silk blends ("Crepe Diana"), often in imitation of Liberty silks, made a comfortable and affordable alternative for a young matron such as Mrs. Walker. The favored tertiary colors, which Wilde termed "a reaction against the crude primaries of a doubtless more respectable but certainly less cultivated age,"[3] are in the Rococo spirit and remind one of the Victorian fondness for dining; colors described by foods were especially in vogue: apricot, olive, curry, mustard, celery, almond, and salmon. Some are surprisingly "intense," lacking the saddened nuances associated with the William Morris circle.[4]

Agnes Walker was fortunate in her choice of dressmaker, for Mrs. Mead produced an elegant creation, demonstrating her mastery of the needle and knowledge of the popular fashion devices of the day. Smocking, a traditional skill of the English countryside, was enjoying a revival (especially on children's garments) and on this costume it lends a touch of the ingénue to an otherwise sophisticated presentation. Using only lavish spills of blond lace, Mrs. Mead showed the restraint of a professional designer in choosing not to combine an incongruous assortment of dress fabrics.[5] The words of W. R. Lethaby can well describe her artistic decision: "Efficiency, it will be said, is not all. . . . The next step is best thought of as still more beautiful finish, trimness, smartness, brightness. Then if the thing is in the hands of a real master designer, some little embroidery, as it were, on the plain garment, some little added fun of workmanship, may be permitted, and this is ornamentation."[6]

SK

1. Oscar Wilde, letter to the Pall Mall Gazette, October 14, 1884, published as an essay, "Woman's Dress," in Miscellanies, vol. 14 of The First Collected Edition of the Works of Oscar Wilde, 1908-1922, Robert Ross, ed. (15 vols.; reprinted, London: Methuen and Company, 1969), pp. 49-50.

2. James Chittick and E.A. Posselt, A Glossary of Silk Terms (New York: Cheney Brothers, 1915), pp. 56-63.

3. Oscar Wilde, letter to the Daily Chronicle, June 30, 1890, in Richard Ellman, ed., The Artist as Critic: Critical Writings of Oscar Wilde (New York: Random House, 1969), pp. 246-247.

4. In his later work Morris had tired of "art colors." A biographer related this anecdote: "Once when a customer, shocked by the brightness of the later Hammersmith carpets, remarked, 'But I thought your colors were subdued?' Morris dealt with him firmly: 'If you want dirt' he said, 'you can find that in the street.'" See A. Clutton-Brock, William Morris: His Work and Influence (London: Williams and Norgate, 1914; New York: Henry Holt, 1914), p. 104.

5. Bastien Lefarge, "Fashion and Fancy," Jenness Miller Quarterly Journal 1 (summer 1890), p. 229.

6. William Richard Lethaby, "Design and Industry," paper presented to the Design and Industries Association, 1915; in Lethaby: A Continuing Presence (Manchester: British Thornton Limited, 1982), p. 13.

31a and b (color plate, p. 11)
Two vases (The Twin Stars of Chelsea), ca. 1888
Chelsea Keramic Art Works (1872-1889), Chelsea, Massachusetts
Hugh C. Robertson (1845-1908)
Stoneware, wheel-thrown; red-blue reduction glazes with lustrous gold highlights
H: 6⅝ and 6¼ in. D: 2⅝ and 3 in.
Mark: impressed (on each) $K_W^C A$ (on bottom)
Museum of Fine Arts, Boston, Gift of Miss Eleanor M. Hearn. 65.1709 and 65.1710

While other American art potters in the 1880s were concerned about perfecting techniques that treated the surface of a piece like an artist's canvas, Hugh C. Robertson was struggling with his "rediscoveries" of the Chinese monochromatic glazes he had seen at the 1876 Centennial Exhibition in Philadelphia.[1] The stock-in-trade of the Chelsea Keramic Art Works had been Chelsea faience (see no. 5), a white- or buff-bodied ware modeled with Aesthetic motifs and covered with a brilliant glossy glaze in the English manner. After Robertson's brother Alexander left Chelsea for California in 1884, Hugh became more closely focused on the revival of Chinese glazes. For five years he worked painstakingly to achieve and perfect processes for several colors: deep sea- and apple-greens, a mustard yellow, turquoise, and a variation on the masterful Chinese red called ox-blood or *sang-de-boeuf*. It was the last of these glazes that was used for the present pair of vases and the potter's own term for it – "Robertson's blood" – refers to the source of inspiration as well as the amount of effort he had put into the project.[2] Robertson had developed something wholly his own, a "beauty of color, which is that of fresh arterial blood, possessing a golden lustre, which in the light glistens with all the varying hues of a sunset sky."[3] Because they embodied "the peak of his success" and had come from the same kiln, Robertson called these two vases the "Twin Stars of Chelsea." He referred to them also as his "life insurance," but he never needed to cash them in to survive.[4]

Although Robertson was forced to close the Chelsea Keramic Art Works in 1889 because of lack of funds, several collectors and connoisseurs of Asian ceramics in the Boston area pooled resources to reopen the pottery in 1891. The reorganized Chelsea Pottery U.S. was formed to provide capital for Robertson to perfect a glaze having an intentional crackled pattern overall: ". . . the enterprise was not in-

tended to be a money-making one; it is rather the luxurious amusement of a few wealthy men, who, familiar with the best products of China and Japan, believe that America can equal or even excel them."[5] In 1896 the pottery operation was moved to Dedham, Massachusetts, where it was renamed the Dedham Pottery (see no. 122).

EPD and BRD

1. For more about the Robertsons and their potteries, see Lloyd Hawes, *The Dedham Pottery and the Earlier Robertson's Chelsea Potteries* (Dedham, Mass.: Dedham Historical Society, 1968); and Edwin AtLee Barber, *The Pottery and Porcelain of the United States* (New York: G.P. Putnam, 1893), pp. 260-267.
2. Red is the most difficult color for a potter to achieve because it requires careful balance of glaze and clay chemistry and kiln atmosphere.
3. Barber 1893, p. 265. The classic Chinese *sang-de-boeuf* (ox-blood) glaze is a brilliant glossy red of relatively even color, while "Robertson's blood" usually exhibits strong lustrous or iridescent effects mingled with reds ranging in coloration from medium to dark.
4. Personal correspondence, J. Milton Robertson to Eleanor and Paul Hearn (September 14, 1964), on file in the Museum of Fine Arts, Boston. Mr. Robertson kept the "Twin Stars" after the close of the Dedham Pottery in 1943 and transferred them to the Museum of Fine Arts through Miss Hearn.
5. Nathan Haskell Dole, "The Best American Pottery," *House Beautiful* 2 (September 1897), p. 90.

32 (color plate, p. 12)
Vase, 1899
Rookwood Pottery Company (1880-1960), Cincinnati
Decorator: Kataro Shirayamadani (1865-1948)
Buff earthenware decorated under glossy glaze with white birds flying through green and brown cattails on black ground
H: 15 in. Diam: 9¼ in.
Marks: impressed with RP monogram surrounded by thirteen flames with 787B below (on bottom); incised artist's signature in Japanese (to left of company mark)
Collection of William and Marcia Goodman

"One large jar with flying storks and cattails against a black background is a masterpiece," wrote Marshall Fry, Jr., of his visit to the Paris Exposition in 1900. "The quality of the white of the birds and the treatment of edges is almost Whistleresque and I feel sure that this great master himself could find much to admire in this collection."[1] Fry, a well-known profes-

sional china painter in New York, was so taken by the beauty of this vase that he attempted to duplicate the design on a vase of American porcelain.[2]

The decoration is executed in one of several palettes labeled "Iris" because of the predominance of blues and grays on a pale ground in contrast to the mellow browns, yellows, and oranges of Rookwood's earlier "standard" palette. Pieces like this one in a darker color range were termed "Black Iris" to distinguish them from the regular production and denote the special quality of the decoration. It was the most prestigious of the lines developed in 1894 in the manner of Danish porcelains such as those made at Royal Copenhagen.

Although Maria Longworth Nichols (see no. 6) was never able to import an entire Japanese pottery as she wished, the services of Kataro Shirayamadani were obtained in 1887 through Louis Wertheimer, an Oriental art dealer in Boston. Shirayamadani had been one of the artists who toured with the "Japanese Village," a troupe of sixty to seventy Japanese who visited major American cities between 1885 and 1887 to demonstrate native trades and arts.[3] Except for a brief period when he worked in Japan, "Sherry," as he was called by his friends, continued at Rookwood as one of its best artists until his death in 1948.

The present vase demonstrates the predominance of conservative naturalistic painted decoration at Rookwood throughout much of the company's artistic history, in contrast to the emphasis at many other art potteries on such techniques as modeling, stylized design, or special glaze effects. Because it was founded on Mrs. Nichols's enthusiasm for china painting and because Rookwood's decorators consistently won major exposition awards during the 1890s and early 1900s, the company continued to embrace these techniques as their stock in trade.

EPD and BRD

1. Marshall Fry, Jr., "Notes from the Paris Exposition," *Keramic Studio* 2 (September 1900), p. 99.
2. Ironically Fry's vase, illustrated in the second edition of E.A. Barber's compendium of American potters, was perhaps better known than Shirayamadani's. Barber, probably unaware of the original artist's work, noted Fry's vase as "a striking example of his recent work" and stated that he generally had his vases made in Trenton of belleek china. Fry's vase was first published in *Keramic Studio* 2 (January 1901), p. 185. It was exhibited in 1900 at the New York Society of Keramic

Arts. See also Edwin AtLee Barber, *The Pottery and Porcelain of the United States*, 2nd ed. (New York: G.P. Putnam, 1901), pp. 515-516.

3. For more on Shirayamadani and the "Japanese Village," see Kenneth Trapp, "Rookwood and the Japanese Mania in Cincinnati," *Cincinnati Historical Society Bulletin* 39 (Spring 1981), pp. 64-68.

33

Two panels, ca. 1910-1915
Designer and maker: probably Elmer Livingston MacRae (1875-1953), New York and Cos Cob, Connecticut
Tulip poplar painted with metallic pigments in silver, bronze, and pale green
H: 60 in. W: 22 in. D: ¾ in.
The Connecticut Historical Society, Hartford. 1983-130-1A and 1B

These *japonesque* panels depicting a bed of irises and a draping branch of cherry blossoms, were part of a frieze that decorated the walls of the Holley boarding house in Cos Cob, Connecticut. The panels were probably carved and painted by Elmer Livingston MacRae, who began summering in Cos Cob in the early 1890s and lived there permanently after marrying Constant Holley, the daughter of the owner, in 1900. MacRae had been one of a community of artists who followed the American impressionists John Henry Twachtman and Julian Alden Weir to this coastal village to study, sketch, and paint.[1]

Japanese prints had fascinated painters on the Continent since the 1860s; Monet, Degas, Whistler, and others adopted their asymmetry, spatial organization, abstraction, and intimate subject matter. The interest in Japan subsequently spread to American artists: Theodore Robinson, for example, noted in his diaries of 1893-1894 that he had spent hours discussing Japanese art with Twachtman and Weir. Sometime between 1890 and 1902 the Japanese illustrator Gaingero Yeto visited Cos Cob to study with Twachtman. While there he conducted tea ceremonies for kimono-clad ladies and taught Constant Holley his native art of flower arranging.[2] MacRae was among those influenced by Japan; reviews of 1910 noted that his paintings were "suggestive of Japanese art."[3] Canvases of 1910-1915 exhibit the bold outlines, vigorous forms, and blocks of color of Japanese woodblock prints, qualities seen also in the Cos Cob panels.[4] Ten works from the period were exhib-

33

ited at the 1913 Armory Show, for which MacRae served as treasurer.[5] Although best known for pastels and oil paintings, MacRae did several woodcarvings as well, including free-standing panels and hinged screens.[6]

CZ

1. For more information regarding the artists' colony in Cos Cob, see Susan G. Larkin, "The Cos Cob Clapboard School," *Connecticut and American Impressionism* (Storrs: William Benton Museum of Art, University of Connecticut, 1980). The Holley House, now called the Bush-Holley House, is a museum owned and operated by the Greenwich Historical Society.

2. Ibid., p. 91.

3. Henry Tyrrell, "Mr. Macrae's Art During Past Year Shown at Cos Cob," *New York Evening World*, October 8, 1910; and "Elmer MacRae Exhibits," *Greenwich Press*, October 12, 1910, p. 6. Many thanks to Susan Larkin for these references.

4. I am grateful to Susan Larkin for bringing this to my attention. She points out two examples of MacRae's paintings of the period: *Japanese Iris* (1914) in the collection of the American Tradition Gallery, Greenwich, and *Still Life–Flowers* in the collection of the Colby College Museum of Art, Waterville, Maine.

5. The Milch Gallery in New York organized a posthumous retrospective in 1959: "Elmer Livingston MacRae: Forgotten Artist of the Armory Show" (see Larkin 1980, p. 167).

6. The information was provided by Lauren Kaminsky, former curator of the Bush-Holley House, to Robert Trent, curator of the Connecticut Historical Society (letter of December 28, 1983). There are other examples of MacRae's carvings on exhibition at the Bush-Holley House.

34

During the first decade of the twentieth century, garments for women evolved from the assemblage of bodice-and-skirt pieces typical of the nineteenth century to become single units. In the design of this day dress, the bodice and skirt are interrupted by a waistband; however, continuity between the upper and lower portion of the costume is provided by frets of blue bamboo leaves, expertly crafted with delicate satin stitches of silk on a cotton ground. Fretwork of this type could be purchased in the Orient, as Alice Motley Woodbury, the wearer of this dress, may have done, or at a domestic dry goods emporium. *The Craftsman* suggested for the young women sewing her own graduation frock: "At an embroidery shop, a Japanese design could be worked out, or she could achieve one herself with a little study and thought. And the delight of a gown so created is limitless. It is an object lesson in 'dress reform,' which no lectures nor sermons could equal."[1] It could be, as well, a lesson in various needle skills, as no. 34 suggests: in dressmaking, for the basic garment; in lacemaking, for the *torchon* lace and filigree inserts; in embroidery and appliqué for the fretwork; and in crochet for the ball fringe. Every decorative detail, every line of the garment, is exquisitely designed and constructed with the highest degee of virtuoso craftsmanship.

SK

1. "The Right to Beauty," *Craftsman* 12 (April 1907), p. 132.

34

Day dress, 1910-1913
Origin unknown
Cotton embroidery and linen lace, all by hand
H: 58⅝ in. W: across shoulder, 18⅛ in.
Margaret Woodbury Strong Museum, Rochester. 80.2515

Once the American public "discovered" it in 1876 at the Philadelphia Centennial, *japonisme* became an important and lasting enthusiasm. Its influence on dress was immediate and conspicuous. Gentlemen wore kimonos as smoking attire; women carried fans and included kimonos in their wardrobes, often as exotic wraps for reception wear over more conventional attire to convey an aesthetic attitude.

Into the twentieth century, domestic interiors featured Japanese nooks for the contemplation of carefully composed floral arrangements, and Oriental motifs were selected to ornament Arts and Crafts pottery and textiles. As kimono wrappers became popular *negligée* apparel, housedresses and bungalow aprons often revealed styling related to the kimono form, and dressmaking manuals included instructions for kimono bodices similar to this example. American dressmakers and designers looked beyond the elegance and novelty of the kimono into its possibilities for comfort, utility, and ease of movement: the "natural" waistline, gentle fullness, and wide sleeves were necessary features.

35 (color plate, p. 13)
Armchair, ca. 1894– ca. 1920s
Designer: David Wolcott Kendall (1851-1910)
Maker: Phoenix Furniture Company, Grand Rapids, Michigan (founded in 1870)
Oak with caned inserts
H: 34¼ in. W: 29¼ in. D: 22 in.
Mark: stenciled 443 (inside apron)[1]
Collection of Mr. and Mrs. Andrew B. Shapiro

David Kendall worked as a draftsman and designer at the Phoenix Furniture Company from 1879 until his death some thirty years later.[2] Kendall, who traveled widely, was interested in all furniture styles and ornamental history.[3] An active participant in the Grand Rapids Furniture Manufacturing Association, he was one of the first to revive period styles in that city and he helped to establish the importance of the designer to the trade.[4] Kendall also introduced finishes that made oak palatable to a public accustomed to walnut and other dark woods. As walnut became scarce in Grand Rapids in the 1880s and 1890s, he developed several stains, including an "antique oak" finish that brought out the grain of the wood. This armchair, in a form that was produced also as a rocker and a settee, was available in mahogany, natural birch, and oak with a variety of stains, including a dark green and a "Belgian" finish.

The longevity of this form – thirty years on the market – was exceptional in the rapidly changing industry.[5] But for its Gothic arches and greenish stain (popular on Arts and Crafts furniture of the turn of the century) it could easily be mistaken for a contemporary form today. The simple design with Chinese details and caning is distinct from Kendall's heavily carved furniture and demonstrates his work in a reform style. Kendall, who became manager, superintendent, and treasurer of the Phoenix Company,[6] perceived the machine as a liberator freeing his men from hard hand labor. As early as 1887, the company was purported to have "the most improved modern machinery of any factory of its kind in America."[7] In 1890 Kendall introduced plans to remodel his shops with the aim of making them "as convenient, clean, light and pleasant . . . [as can be found]. . . in the city."[8]

CZ

1. No. 443 corresponds with numbered photographs of chair styles in the library of the Kendall School of Design in Grand Rapids.

2. Jane Perkins Claney and Robert Edwards, "Progressive Design in Grand Rapids," Tiller 2 (September/October 1983), p. 33.

3. Claney and Edwards 1983, p. 39; Grand Rapids Furniture Record 20 [March 1910], p. 619. It is very likely that Kendall visited the Paris Exposition in 1900 (see Furniture Trade Review 20 [August 10, 1900], p. 14). Kendall noted that the Paris Exposition would create a greater revolution in furniture styles than the Centennial exhibition had. "The manufacturers of Berlin, Vienna, London, Glasgow, Florence and Milan have given up the conservatism that has governed their production in the past, and have brought out many new things which will combine with the furniture of the future."

4. Furniture Trade Review 20 (July 1900), p. 69. For information about the Grand Rapids furniture industry, see Frank E. Ransom, The City Built on Wood: A History of the Furniture Industry in Grand Rapids, Michigan, 1850-1950 (Ann Arbor, Mich.: Edwards Brothers, 1955). Mrs.

Kendall provided for the founding of the David Wolcott Kendall School of Art (now called the Kendall School of Design) as a memorial continuing her husband's contributions to the history of design.

5. This armchair, like other objects manufactured by the company, was retailed nationally through fine furniture stores.

6. The Phoenix Furniture company, with 590 employees in 1903, was among the largest manufacturers in Grand Rapids, the nation's major furniture center. See "An English View of American Furniture Factories," Furniture Trade Review 23 (May 10, 1903), p. 37.

7. Snaw L. Lloyd, Industries of Grand Rapids (Grand Rapids: J.M. Elstner, 1887), p. 40.

8. The Michigan Artisan, October 1890, p. 57; as cited by Claney and Edwards 1983, p. 35.

36 (color plate, p. 14)
Center table from the William Prindle house, Duluth, Minnesota, ca. 1905[1]
Designer: John Scott Bradstreet (1845-1914), Minneapolis
Maker: John S. Bradstreet and Co., Minneapolis
Cypress
H: 28⅜ in Diam: 30 in.
Minneapolis Institute of Arts. 82.43.11

John Scott Bradstreet was probably introduced to the Orient during his early years in eastern Massachusetts,[2] as Salem and Boston had been vital centers for the China trade since the eighteenth century. After working at Gorham Manufacturing Company in Providence in the late 1860s and early 1870s, Bradstreet moved to Minneapolis to establish John S. Bradstreet and Co., Manufacturers of Artistic and Domestic Furniture of Modern Gothic and Other Designs. In 1878 he took on a partner, Edmund Phelps, and enlarged his enterprise to six floors: "the largest and most elegant and complete furniture shop under one roof in America." When Phelps sold his shares to the Thurber family (owners of the Gorham Manufacturing Company) in 1883, the firm became Bradstreet, Thurber and Company and expanded its stock of decorative accessories of Moorish and Japanese design. Responding to a demand for the Japanese style, popular after the Centennial Exposition in Philadelphia, Bradstreet made biennial buying trips to Japan.[3] In the late 1890s, he began his own experiments with jin-di-sugi, the traditional Japanese practice of aging wood to raise its grain. Devel-

oping a technique to achieve the same effect by searing wood and scrubbing it with a wire brush, he went on to produce a line of Orientally inspired furniture, as exemplified by the present table.

Rather than espousing theory like Gustav Stickley or striving to produce "art for the masses," Bradstreet focused his energies on collecting, crafting, and selling goods of superior quality. After Bradstreet, Thurber and Company was destroyed by fire in 1893, he created a crafts center modeled very loosely on William Morris's precedent. Members of this community of Japanese and Scandinavian carvers, gilders, painters, and furniture makers processed cypress with the jin-di-sugi finish and carved its surface with clouds and flower motifs.[4] By 1899 the group (about thirty craftsmen) had opened a shop, which was later described as follows: "There are various arts and crafts movement enterprises throughout the country, but this Minneapolis Crafthouse is unusual in that it is both a workshop and a salesroom. It is as distinctive as the Kelmscott manor made famous by Morris in the output of its shop, and besides has for sale a vast number of curios and valuable objects brought from many distant lands."[5]

In 1904, Bradstreet moved his prospering company into an Italianate villa modified with Moorish and Japanese architectural features and Japanese gardens. Gustav Stickley visited Bradstreet there and reported on the gardens in The Craftsman. Another article, in House Beautiful, noted that "A crafthouse in which to house suitably the products of the art and craft movement is a necessity of the movement itself."[6]

CZ

1. Mina Merrill Prindle commissioned Bradstreet to decorate parts of the interior of her house and oversee some exterior details. The living room included several pieces of jin-di-sugi furniture, among them this table, a card table, several chairs, a piano, and a desk. All of them are now in the collection of the Minneapolis Institute of Arts. Bradstreet was advertising a table like this one as early as August 1903 in the Western Architect. At least one other is known to exist in an English private collection. For more information, see Michael P. Conforti, "Orientalism on the Upper Mississippi: The Work of John S. Bradstreet," Minneapolis Institute of Arts Bulletin 65 (1981-1982), pp. 2-35.

2. Bradstreet had grown up in Essex County and attended Putnam Academy in Newburyport, Massachusetts.

3. These trips were alternated with travel to Europe and to England, where Bradstreet established a reputation at Liberty and Company as "one of America's finest decorators."

4. This community of craftsmen also made period reproductions. The carving of furniture is characteristic of the Chinese, not of the Japanese tradition. The Japanese did carve architectural decoration such as interior ventilation panels and friezes and ornaments for shrines (see J.T. Coolidge, Jr., "A Few Considerations of Japanese Wood Carving," *Handicraft* 2 (June 1903), pp. 49-57).

5. "John S. Bradstreet and Co., Interior Furnishings and Decorations," 1905 (brochure on file at the Minneapolis Institute of Arts).

6. Keith Clark, "The Bradstreet Crafthouse," *House Beautiful* 16 (June 1904), p. 21; Gustav Stickley, "A Garden Fountain," *Craftsman* 7 (October 1904), pp. 69-75.

37 (color plate, p. 15)
Lighting fixture for H.M. Robinson house, Pasadena, 1906
Designers: Charles Greene (1868-1957) and Henry Greene (1870-1954)
Maker: Emil Lange, Los Angeles (wooden fixture made by Peter and John Hall)
Leaded stained glass, mahogany, cedar, ebony, and leather
H (extended): 72" W: 54 in. D: 54 in.
Private Collection

Henry and Charles Greene's commission for the design of a home and furnishings for H.M. Robinson of Pasadena offered them much opportunity for creative and experimental work. The Greenes used the house as a setting in which to experiment with new techniques in leaded stained-glass work, in particular as used in lighting fixtures. In so doing, they freed the fixtures from their strictly functional use to play an important role in the creation of an artistic interior.

The Greenes had earlier experimented with leading in stained glass, but were unable to achieve a result that could compare to the quality of their fine woodwork.[1] To ensure that the highest standards be met, the Greenes hired Emil Lange of the Sturdy-Lange firm to fabricate the glass. Lange had trained in Tiffany's Studios in New York before he began his Los Angeles firm with Harry Sturdy, and the firm had an extensive supply of Tiffany glass to work with. Pleased with Lange's work for the Robinson

house, the brothers continued to use him as their stained-glass craftsman.

This chandelier, made of mosaic leaded iridescent glass in a stylized cherry tree pattern, illustrates the Greenes' attraction to Japanese design. The simple geometric shapes and superb workmanship of its wooden elements are evidence of the close relationship they enjoyed with the cabinetmaking shop of Peter Hall, who designed the lamp to be raised and lowered by gently pulling on the lantern frame, which was suspended from the ceiling plate with leather straps. A large lateral center weight and two smaller square weights act to counterbalance the stained-glass fixture and frame, rising when the lamp is lowered, the entire load evenly distributed by screws driven into the ceiling, which are concealed beneath square ebony pegs in the plate. The chandelier was designed to hang low over a dining room table. It probably hung from about nine and a half feet in the Robinson dining room, low enough to prevent diners from looking into the open bottom of the lantern.

JSB

1. Randell Makinson, *Greene and Greene: Furniture and Related Designs* (Santa Barbara: Peregrine Smith, 1979), p. 35. For more information about the Greene brothers' work, see also Los Angeles County Art Museum, *Greene and Greene: The Architecture and Related Designs of Charles Sumner Greene and Henry Mather Greene, 1894-1934* (Alhambra, Calif: Cunningham Press, 1977).

38 (color plate, p. 16)
Three-panel screen, ca. 1900
Tiffany Studios, New York
Leaded opalescent glass; bronze frame
H: 70 3/8 in. W: 88 13/16 in.
Lillian Nassau, Ltd. New York

Louis Comfort Tiffany was known for his unique use of materials and for his mass-production of beautiful household objects that brought affordable art into the middle-class home. Born in 1848, the son of Charles Lewis Tiffany, New York's successful jeweler and silversmith, Louis studied painting in Paris with Leon Bailly in 1868 and 1869. Upon his return to America, he studied medieval glassmaking processes and techniques at Thill's glasshouse in Brooklyn and the glasshouse built by his own firm, Louis C. Tiffany and Company, as well as at Heidt's glasshouse (also in Brooklyn).[1] Out of

this period came experiments with new methods of glass manufacture to produce a wide variety of color and texture.

From 1879 to 1883, forming the prestigious firm of Associated Artists, Tiffany and Candace Wheeler, Samuel Colman, and Lockwood DeForest planned the interior decoration of many homes and buildings in New York. Three years later Louis C. Tiffany and Company reorganized as the Tiffany Glass Company, offering a wide array of services. They undertook decorative schemes for the homes of many prominent citizens, including the public rooms of the White House in 1883. The business was reorganized again in 1892 as the Tiffany Glass and Decorating Company.

Meanwhile, Tiffany continued to experiment with glassmaking techniques, striving to produce a great variety of textures and colors and to use the inherent qualities of the glass as a means to express his designs. He revived old methods and invented new ones to achieve unusual results: for example, he created "drapery glass" by pushing and twisting hot glass until it moved into rippled folds. Tiffany often recognized in "mistakes" a means of achieving interesting effects. He was able to produce an iridescent glass with a metallic luster by exposing the material to vapors and gases or by applying a film or by corroding the surface of the glass.

As the quality and strength of glass improved, less lead was required in the construction of windows and could function with greater freedom as a design element, to emphasize and affect the drawing, adding shadows and depth. Tiffany devised new methods of leading, making use of copper foil around the cames, using the latter as leaden strips, or using only solder. The choice depended upon the design of the piece and the quality of the glass.

Tiffany's own glassworks, the Stourbridge Glass Company, opened at Corona, Long Island, in 1893, providing a center for his experiments. Here he expanded into the production of glass objects as well as windows, making extensive use of the iridescent glass he called Favrile. The same year, at the encouragement of his friend Samuel Bing, a Parisian art dealer and collector, Tiffany installed a chapel at the World's Columbian Exhibition in Chicago and gained international renown for the design.

By 1898, the Tiffany Glass and Decorating Company was producing thousands of items each year, of great variety in type and style, and storing vast quantities and varieties of glass.[2] Since a single individual could not design and make each piece from start to finish and keep up such volume, Tiffany resolved the craftsman's dilemma by relying in part on the machine for cutting, grinding, and polishing. He pointed out that the production of a stained-glass window required the supervision of the artist himself, as each component of the design had to be chosen with respect to texture, color, thickness and shape, and arrangement. And in the production of blown glass, the constant addition of pieces of glass into the molten ball required the artist's presence in forming the desired design and colors.

After 1900, Tiffany was renowned primarily for art glass rather than for stained glass. His goal of bringing beauty into the home dictated the production of beautiful functional objects and Favrile glass was well suited for decorative household objects such as vases, paperweights, and lamps. With increased manufacture, Tiffany had less personal involvement in the firm, but he continued to direct craftsmen, solve problems, and control the studios. In 1902, his expanded business was reorganized as the Tiffany Studios, and his Stourbridge Glass Company at Corona reorganized as Tiffany Furnaces. Here craftsmen made metalwares, pottery, and enamels as well as glass. The same year, Charles Tiffany died and Louis began to design jewelry and enamels for his father's firm. He continued to take on special projects himself, such as a mosaic for Maxfield Parrish's painting *The Dream Garden* in 1915. Tiffany finally left the Furnaces in 1932. He continued to design windows and run Tiffany Studios until the firm was liquidated in 1938.

This unique three-panel screen was probably made as a showpiece for the 1900 Exposition Universelle in Paris.[3] It is the only one known of its size and type; Tiffany's other folding screens were small tabletop models of glass or silver.[4] (One that he designed in glass in 1881-1882 for the entrance hall of the White House was destroyed.) In this screen, Tiffany made use of a variety of glasses in brilliant colors. Bunches of grapes are formed with three-dimensional pieces in various hues; vari-textured opalescent glass appears both in the pictorial design and in the lower part of the screen. The three panels are linked by their botanical subjects and by the intrusion of elements from one panel into another.[5]

JSB

1. For more information about Tiffany's stained glass, see Robert Koch, *Louis C. Tiffany, Rebel in Glass* (New York: Crown Publishers, 1982).

2. Mario Amaya, *Tiffany Glass* (New York: Walker and Company, 1967), p. 75.

3. Michael Komanecky and Virginia Fabbri Butera, *The Folding Image: Screens by Western Artists of the 19th and 20th Centuries* (New Haven: Yale University Art Gallery, 1984), p. 100.

4. American interest in folding screens was apparently precipitated by the Philadelphia centennial exhibition in 1876, where several Chinese and Japanese screens and folding screens of London's Royal School of Art Needlework were featured. Toward the end of the nineteenth century, screens, particularly those of Oriental design, were increasingly popular as room dividers in middle-class American homes and were often featured in journals such as *House Beautiful*.

5. Komanecky and Butera 1984, p. 163.

39

Vase, 1905-1915
Tiffany Studios (1902-1919), Corona, New York
White earthenware covered with glossy medium olive-green glaze; molded and altered cylindrical form decorated with jack-in-the-pulpit plants
H: 11¼ in. W: 4¼ in.
Marks: incised cipher LCT / 7 (on bottom)
Collection of Martin Eidelberg

Pottery was one of many materials shaped by the aesthetic genius of Louis Comfort Tiffany (see no. 38), one of the foremost designers in America at the turn of the century. Tiffany's interest in pottery came long after his reputation as an interior decorator and glass designer was established. He had begun experimenting with an art pottery line at his Studios in Corona, New York, about 1898, but did not exhibit the new wares publicly until the 1904 Louisiana Purchase Exposition in St. Louis.[1] More pieces were shown the next year in the New York Keramic Society exhibition and offered for sale at his father's firm, Tiffany & Company, in New York. Like the family showroom, which had carried both American and European art pottery since the early days of the industry in the 1880s, Tiffany Studios also exhibited the work of foreign ceramists. For example, in 1901 pieces by Dalpayrat, Delaherche, Bigot, Doat (see no. 182), Jeanneny, and others were shown.[2]

Of the several American potteries that interpreted the energetic lines of the Belgian and

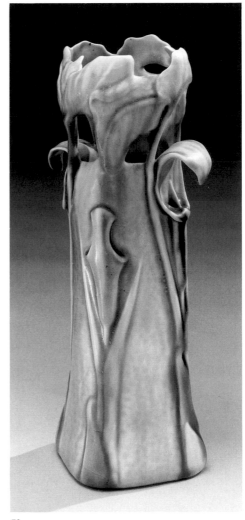

39

French Art Nouveau styles, Tiffany's is the most naturalistic and least derivative from European models. Indeed, some designs seem to have been molded directly from nature. His vase of Queen Anne's lace,[3] for example, appears to be based on an actual bouquet that has been frozen in plaster to produce the mold. In contrast, this jack-in-the-pulpit vase was worked from a cylinder. The outlines of the floral forms were transferred to the surface of the vase from the mold. Then the delicate hoods of two flowers were cut from the damp clay and gently curled downward to imitate the blossoms' natural shapes.

EPD and BRD

1. For more about Tiffany's work in clay, see Martin P. Eidelberg, "Tiffany Favrile Pottery: A New Study of a Few Known Facts," *Connoisseur* 169 (September 1968), pp. 57-61.

2. "Exhibition of French Pottery at the Tiffany Studios," *Keramic Studio* 3 (August 1901), pp. 82-83. L.C. Tiffany also designed shades for pottery lamp bases made by William Grueby's firm in Boston (see nos. 117-119) during the period when Tiffany was experimenting to produce his own ceramic art.

3. Paul Evans, *Art Pottery of the United States* (New York: Charles Scribner's Sons, 1974), pl. 1.

40

Vase (Lorelei), 1898
Artus Van Briggle (1869-1904), Cincinnati
Buff earthenware covered with semi-matte green glaze; molded with figure of long-haired woman draped around vase
H: 7½ in Diam: 4¼ in.
Marks: incised A·VAN BRIGGLE / 1898 (on bottom)
Label: (on printed paper) ROOKWOOD / POTTERY / CINCINNATI / UNIVERSAL / EXPOSITION / 1900
Collection of the Van Briggle Art Pottery Co., Colorado Springs. Courtesy of The Metropolitan Museum of Art, New York

Artus Van Briggle, a prominent artist for the Rookwood Pottery (nos. 6, 32, and 55), underwent an aesthetic transformation during his studies in Paris. He left Cincinnati in 1893 as a decorator who followed Rookwood's glossy standard painterly approach to surface decoration, but returned in 1896 as a ceramist who saw vases as small sculptures covered in textural matte glazes. Exposure to the Art Nouveau style in studios and galleries and to ancient Asian ceramics in public museums turned his attention to new avenues for artistic expression in clay. By 1903, he was described as one " . . . who is all the word craftsman implies in its new and deep significance. He unites in himself the designer and the maker. He is able equally to conceive and to execute: to produce form, calculate color, employ technical process and fashion by hand labor."[1]

Trained in Cincinnati's Academy of Art, Van Briggle had been a decorator at Rookwood since 1887, when he was chosen from the staff to study painting in Paris at the Académie Julian and the Ecole des Beaux-Arts.[2] Upon returning to Cincinnati, he assumed his old duties at Rookwood, continued painting in oils, worked

40

out new ceramic forms, and began experiments to develop a matte or "dead" glaze.[3] By 1898, his discoveries were being used at Rookwood.[4] The present vase with semi-matte glaze is a prototype for Van Briggle's "Lorelei" design no. 17 of 1903 (the later version is 10 inches high). A visible mold line suggests that he was already experimenting with the method of producing wares as multiple copies of an original work. ("Mr. Van Briggle's idea in this matter is that it is far more satisfactory to spend unlimited time and thought in carrying out an idea which may be worthy of repetition, each reproduction being different in color and glaze effect, than to attempt for every vase a new design which must of necessity often be careless and hasty in thought and execution."[5])

"Lorelei" was a legendary siren who lived on a cliff over the dangerous narrows of the Rhine and lured sailors to their deaths with her songs. Recorded in a poem by the nineteenth-century tragic romantic German writer Heinrich Heine, the legend also seems to portray Van Briggle's own seduction and death in the pursuit of art. The active agenda he had set for himself in

Cincinnati shattered his fragile health; tuberculosis interrupted his work in 1899 and took him to Colorado to recuperate. After several months, working with a small kiln in the office of William Streiby, professor of chemistry and metallurgy at Colorado College, Van Briggle began to develop body formulas using local clays and testing new glazes. By December 1901 he had 300 pieces ready to exhibit and in March 1902 a stock company was formed to provide capital for a greatly expanded operation, the Van Briggle Pottery Company (see no. 120). Investors included new Colorado acquaintances and an old supporter, Mrs. Bellamy Storer, the former Maria Longworth Nichols (see no. 6). Van Briggle's own work was short-lived, unfortunately; he died two and a half years later.

EPD and BRD

1. Irene Sargent "Chinese Pots and Modern Faïence," *Craftsman* 4 (September 1903), p. 422.

2. For more about Van Briggle and his pottery, see Barbara M. Arnest, ed., *Van Briggle Pottery: The Early Years* (Colorado Springs: Colorado Springs Fine Arts Center, 1975); and Scott H. Nelson, et al., *A Collector's Guide to Van Briggle Pottery* (published by the author in Harrisburg, 1986).

3. Although Rookwood had marketed successfully a dull finish in a pale palette called "Cameo" during the late 1880s along with its dark glossy standard glaze, Van Briggle's energies were directed toward a revival of a true matte glaze. For more about Rookwood's "Cameo" line, see Kenneth R. Trapp, *Ode to Nature: Flowers and Landscapes of the Rookwood Pottery, 1880-1940* (New York: Jordan-Volpe Gallery, 1980), p. 22. Three "Cameo" pieces, dating between 1886 and 1888, were included in the exhibition that this catalogue accompanies; one was a covered jar by Artus Van Briggle dated 1888.

4. Two matte-glazed vases by Sallie Toohey dated 1898 are in the Hermitage Museum, Leningrad (see Trapp 1980, p. 32). Although produced at the same time as Toohey's vases, the present example with artist's signature only and without the usual Rookwood impress was probably made privately (Rookwood allowed its senior decorators to use their pottery studios for personal work). However, the paper label shows that Rookwood later adopted the vase as its own work and showed it at the Paris Exposition of 1900. Either the vase remained at Rookwood when Van Briggle left Cincinnati in 1899 or Van Briggle chose to submit it for the Exposition under Rookwood's name. (Personal communication from Kenneth Trapp to Ellen Denker, August 13, 1986.)

5. "A Colorado Industry," *House Beautiful* 4 (October 1903), p. 168.

41

Vase, ca. 1911-1913
Valentien Pottery (ca. 1911-1913), San Diego
Maker: Anna Marie Valentien (1862-1947)
Earthenware with pale- to medium-green matte glaze; wheel-thrown with applied decoration of female figures
H: 16¾ in. Diam: 16½ in.
Marks: painted in blue *A.M.V.*, impressed *VP/Co* with stylized poppy in vertical rounded rectangle (on bottom)
Collection of Mr. and Mrs. A.A. Jaussaud

Anna Bookprinter, the daughter of a weaver, studied art in Cincinnati with Mary Keenan, Benn Pitman, Frank Duveneck, and Louis T. Rebizzo.[1] She worked first as a decorator for the Matt Morgan Art Pottery before joining Rookwood Pottery.[2] In 1887 she married Albert Valentien (1862-1925), who had also trained with Duveneck and worked in Cincinnati's early Coultry and T.J. Wheatley potteries before being hired in 1881 as the first decorator to be regularly employed at Rookwood. Accompanying her husband on assignments for Rookwood in Europe between 1899 and 1901, Mrs. Valentien studied sculpture at the Academy Colarossi and the Academy Rodin with Auguste Rodin. During these years when Art Nouveau was current in Paris, the idiom exerted influence on her work.

In 1905 the couple left Rookwood to pursue their own interests in Cincinnati; three years later they moved to San Diego, where Albert received a commission from Ellen Browning Scripps to paint California wildflowers, trees, grasses, and ferns – a project that consumed his attention during blooming seasons for ten years. Anna focused her talents on other media, including the design and execution of custom jewelry for J. Jessop & Sons.

In 1911, in buildings designed for them by Irving Gill near their home, the Valentiens opened a pottery staffed by Arthur Dovey.[3] Although short lived (production ceased late in 1913 because neighbors in this rapidly developing community complained about the smoke), the Valentien pottery represented the collective artistic genius of its two founders. With its energetic low-relief modeling, the present vase is an exceptional example of the work they produced.

After closing the pottery, Anna Valentien turned to teaching, which she continued until her retirement in 1938; her husband finished his wildflower commission.

EPD and BRD

41

1. Information in this entry is based on Bruce Kamerling's article "Albert and Anna Valentien: The Arts and Crafts Movement in San Diego," *Journal of San Diego History* 24 (Summer 1978), pp. 343-366.

2. Sculptural pieces she made for Rookwood in 1891 languished in the salesroom, but her life-size figure of Ariadne in the Beaux-Arts style received enthusiastic attention when shown in the Women's Department at the World's Columbian Exposition in Chicago in 1893.

3. The Valentiens knew Dovey as a turner at Rookwood in 1890; he subsequently worked at the Niloak Pottery (see no. 210).

42 (color plate, p. 17)
Vase, 1902-1907
Weller Pottery Company (1872-1949), Zanesville, Ohio
Decorator: Jacques Sicard (active in U.S 1902-1907; d. in France 1923)
Buff earthenware, molded and decorated with tulips in iridescent blue and pink glazes
H: 25¼ in. Diam: 9⅝ in.
Marks: painted in glaze *Weller Sicard* (on side); incised #6 (on bottom)
Private Collection

Samuel A. Weller learned the pottery business from the ground up as a young boy in Muskingum County, Ohio.[1] By the year 1872 he had opened a small pottery shop of his own in Fultonham, Ohio, where simple utilitarian ware, such as painted flower pots, was produced. Ten years later he established his factory at Zanesville, Ohio, home to so many potteries it was called the "clay city." Weller's first art pottery was made with William Long (see no. 56), who had been producing, at the Lonhuda Pottery, the underglaze- decorated ware popularized by Rookwood (see no. 55). This partnership, which lasted two years (1894-1895), provided Weller with basic technical knowledge. Soon new designs were required and the Weller Pottery, like many other American potteries, looked abroad for inspiration.

In 1901 Jacques Sicard and his assistant, Henri Gellie, came to Zanesville from France, where they had been making lusterware for the Clement Massier Pottery in Golfe Juan. A contemporary account of a visit to the Weller Pottery describes the experiments in Sicardo ware: "The metallic lusters require, not only the fine color sense of the artist, but the skill and knowledge of the chemist; these gifts M. Sicard happily possesses. Accustomed to the use of peat or dead brushwood to fire the kilns in France, M. Sicard could with difficulty be persuaded to use the natural gas in the kilns in which the luster ware was to be fired. In his first experiments, he insisted on firing the kilns with the wild growths found along the roadsides around Zanesville."[2]

The Sicardo line is one of the few examples of American art pottery made in the Art Nouveau style popular in Europe. Designs were painted in metallic glazes over predominantly molded forms, some unique to the line. Floral decoration was most frequently used, as seen on this example, and followed the French emphasis on sinuous natural designs. Sicard and Gellie worked in secret, perhaps to protect their technical expertise from Weller, but iridescent-glaze pottery was also produced at the Roseville Pottery (no. 123), the J.B. Owens Pottery, the Pewabic Pottery (see no. 114), and others. The inventory of Sicardo continued to be marketed through 1912, five years after Jacques Sicard returned to France.

BRD and EPD

1. Lucile Henzke, *American Art Pottery* (Camden, N.J.: Thomas Nelson, 1970), p. 33. The chapter on Weller Pottery (pp. 33-123) provides a good overview of this company's production.
2. May Elizabeth Cook, "Our American Potteries – Weller Ware," *Sketch Book* 5 (May 1906), pp. 340-346.

43

Ewer and stand, 1900-1904
Designer: probably William Christmas Codman (1839-1923)
Maker: Gorham Manufacturing Company, Providence (1831 to present); retailed by Spaulding & Co., Chicago
Silver
H: (assembled) 20½ in.
Ewer – Wt: 64 oz., 14 dwt.
Stand – Diam: 17⅛ in. Wt: 67 oz.
Inscription: engraved (in script) *HJG* and *JMMG*
Marks: (on each) struck incuse *Martelé* / spread eagle atop a shield (enclosing an anchor) and flanked octagons (enclosing a lion and *G*) / *950-000 FINE* / *SPAULDING & CO.* / *CHICAGO*
The Metropolitan Museum of Art. Gift of Mr. and Mrs. Hugh J. Grant. 1974.214.26ab

In the late 1890s the Gorham Manufacturing Company developed a line of art silver tablewares that came to be called "Martelé" after the French verb "to hammer."[1] Edward Holbrook, who in 1887 became the company's fourth president, had completed expanded production facilities in 1890, and on an annual visit to London and Paris persuaded the English artist W.C. Codman to become Gorham's new artistic director, a post he took up in 1891.[2] Combining their exceptional business and artistic talents, Holbrook and Codman set about bringing handicraft, based on ideals of the English Arts and Crafts movement, to a line of unique and costly wares, each individually overseen from start to finish and each meant to be a work of art in itself. The effort began in 1896 with a special school within the factory, where chosen men perfected manual skills for forming and ornamenting silver by hammer-wielded methods. This silverware was first shown publicly in New York City in late 1897; further experimentation and refinement followed before it was offered for sale in 1899 at Gorham's affiliate, Spaulding & Company in Chicago. In the following year Gorham won acclaim at the Paris Exposition and ensuing production, extravagantly conceived and marked "Martelé," was characterized by rich and fluid effects with a dull pearlescent hammered surface befitting handmade rather than machine-made metalwork.

This ewer and stand, an ensemble favored for Gorham's Martelé silver, constitute one of three closely related sets, the earliest of which appeared at the Paris Exposition of 1900.[3] Ornament is representative of the Art Nouveau style,

but it is also patterned after Mannerist silver of the late sixteenth and early seventeenth century. The ewer, with a top-heavy configuration common to Mannerist vessels, has a spout, high handle, and foot echoing those of a ewer-and-stand set of 1613 by Paulus van Vianen.[4] The Martelé stand, with swimming mermaids, sea-wave pattern, and swirling bosses, has its counterpart in a dish of 1635 made by Christiaen van Vianen, in which the dish's undulating rim – in the form of two dolphins – encloses a wavy sea and swimming fish.[5] Although Gorham Martelé silver typically exploited floral and naturalistic imagery for whiplash and curvilinear ornament in the French Art Nouveau style, a style traditionally considered as anti-historicist, it is also frequently based on Mannerist and other past silver examples.

The ewer bears the initials of Hugh J. Grant and Julia M. Murphy Grant. Hugh Grant, who made a large fortune in real estate, was mayor of New York from 1888 to 1892 and in 1895 married the daughter of Edward Murphy, U.S. Senator from New York.

WSB

1. For the best study of Gorham Martelé and its development see Charles H. Carpenter, Jr., *Gorham Silver, 1883-1981* (New York: Dodd, Mead, 1982), ch. 11-12, ill. When this ewer and stand was made, Martelé had a silver content of .950 fine silver; after 1904 Gorham used the .9584 "Britannia" standard. The alloy at .950 was two-and-one-half percent above the .925 fine "sterling" standard–slightly more costly as bullion than "sterling"–but, owing to its easier working properties, more economical to use in fabrication.
2. W[illiam] C[hristmas] Codman is often confused with his son William Codman, who preceded his father's arrival at Gorham and became the company's artistic director upon his father's retirement in 1914.
3. For the set at Paris, see the drawing in *American Art Annual 1900-1901*, Florence N. Levy, ed., vol. 3 (Boston: Noyes, Platt & Company, 1900), p. 34, ill. For the Grant set, see *International Studio* 26 (August 1905), p. AD. XVII, ill.
4. *Dutch Silver 1580-1830*, A.L. den Blaauwen, ed. (Amsterdam: Rijksmuseum, 1979), p. 45, ill. The spout of the Gorham ewer, now bent downward, was originally the vessel's highest point.
5. Possibly known to Codman, it is in the collection of the Victoria and Albert Museum, London (see *Dutch Silver 1979*, p. 77, ill.).

43

44

Spoon, probably 1905-1907
Horace E. Potter (1873-1948), Cleveland
Silver and *basse-taille* enamel
L: 6 ⅛ in. W: 2 ⅜ in. Wt: (gross) 1 oz., 5 dwt.
Marks: struck incuse *H. E. POTTER / STERLING*
Collection of Gary Breitweiser

In the late nineteenth century Liberty & Company was a leading purveyor of Continental pewter, furniture, and ceramics in the emerging Art Nouveau. Sensing the retail potential for metalwares in the increasingly popular style, Liberty joined with the Birmingham silversmiths W.H. Haseler & Company to produce a new line of silver called "Cymric"—a name chosen to underscore the Celtic source of the ornament. The silver was introduced at the Arts and Crafts Exhibition Society's sixth exhibition in December of 1899.[1]

"Cymric" designs were subsequently illustrated in Liberty catalogues and were widely disseminated through illustrations in periodicals such as *The International Studio*; Horace Potter may have known them from these sources, from their occasional inclusion in Arts and Crafts exhibitions, or from a trip to England. Like "Cymric" examples, Potter's artistic spoon employs a combination of Celtic and Art Nouveau ornamental motifs, especially the stemmed spade shape and interlacing. If the linear patterns in "Cymric" silver are tamer than the asymmetrical churning motifs found in Continental Art Nouveau wares, Potter's spoon is even more subdued and regularized. The handle and bowl subtly echo each other, and the handle has a suggestion of interlacing that makes a pleasing frame for an enameled iris blossom.

Potter graduated from the Cleveland School of Art in 1898 and continued teaching design and historic ornament there while he established himself as a designer and craftsman. He studied in Boston (exhibiting textile and wallpaper motifs in 1899 at the Society of Arts and Crafts) and abroad at C.R. Ashbee's Guild of Handicraft, probably from 1903 to 1904; Cleveland city directories of 1900-1905 list him as a designer located in the Rose Building. Soon after his return to Cleveland, Potter established a workshop at his family's farm and collaborated with Cleveland artist and craftswoman Wilhelmina Stephan.[2] Potter and Stephan had seven silver spoons with enameled handles among their large showing at the Art Institute of

44

Chicago in 1905, and one critic observed a Celtic motif in their work displayed at the Institute the following year.[3] When the two showed at the Boston Society of Arts and Crafts' historic decennial exhibition in 1907, their work included silver spoons that were pierced, carved, and adorned with enameled floral motifs suggestive of the example shown here. About 1908 Potter and a group of assistants moved to a house that became a mecca for Cleveland artists and craftsmen. Eventually called the Potter Studio, it was the forerunner of the prestigious Cleveland firm of Potter and Mellen that continues today.

WSB

1. See Glennys Wild and Alan Crawford, "Metalwork: By Hammer and Hand," in *The Arts and Crafts Movement in Birmingham*, Alan Crawford, ed. (Birmingham, England: Birmingham Museums and Art Gallery, 1984), pp. 110-112, ill.

2. Also a pupil at the Cleveland School of Art, Stephan studied under the renowned English enamelist Alexander Fisher and the noted Chicago jeweler and teacher James H. Winn.

3. Maude L.G. Oliver, "The Exhibition of Arts-Crafts at the Art Institute of Chicago," *International Studio* 30 (February 1907), p. cvii.

45

Necklace, ca. 1905
Brainerd Bliss Thresher (1870-1950), Dayton, Ohio
Amethysts, carved horn, and gold
L: 13½ in.
Marks: incised triangle enclosing a pellet
Private Collection

The practice of mounting costly gems merely to underscore their size and brilliance, spawned by the boom in South African diamond mining that began in 1867, was renounced during the 1890s by European jewelers who reaffirmed artistic expression in their craft with new materials, colors, designs, and symbolism. The pre-eminent source of reform influence was René Lalique, whose jewels, attuned to careful color harmonies, often gave common stones prominence among costly subordinate ones to emphasize aesthetics over the inherent worth of materials. His innovative jewelry of 1896 introduced horn, a material of no intrinsic value but attractively light in weight and one that, when carved or tinted, yielded a broad range of effects.

In the manner of contemporary French and

Belgian artist-jewelers, Brainerd Thresher turned to nature rather than historical designs for inspiration, as is evident in the Art Nouveau mode of this necklace. Its subtle composition of horn fluidly carved in rhythmic curls is embellished with modestly faceted amethysts and is accented softly by wrought-gold settings and chain links. Thresher, who shared the contemporary view (fostered by the Aesthetic movement) that dazzling, costly gems were vulgar and ostentatious, was greatly influenced by the reverence for nature found in Japanese art. In 1903, lecturing in New York at the National Arts Club, he touched on the merits of the baroque pearl: "Does it not inspire design more readily than its opulent fellow? Can we refrain from echoing in the line of its settings the swish and swirl of waters, or the sinuous, current-swayed grasses which once lay about it?"[1]

Although a number of American craftsmen embraced the Art Nouveau style at the turn of the century, few, like Thresher, produced examples easily mistaken for superior French or Belgian work, and none shared his special awareness of the style's development by Edward Colonna (1862-1948), one of its leading exponents.[2] Indeed, Colonna's three-year Dayton sojourn was the significant influence guiding the later development of Thresher's sophisticated Art Nouveau style.[3] From 1885 to 1888 Colonna designed train car interiors for a Dayton company allied with Thresher family interests, supplied decorations and furnishings for the Thresher home, and published his vanguard ideas on design.[4] Although the connection was brief, Colonna's impact on Thresher is readily seen when their work is compared. The jewelry of both is less fantastic than many of the jewels-for-show examples of Lalique and his followers.[5]

Thresher, for whom handicraft was a "recreation and pastime" from commercial and financial pursuits, exemplifies the aesthetically inclined, cultured upper class who responded to William Morris's philosophy not so much by returning art to work as by bringing it to leisure.[6] Thresher's activities as a craftsman were complemented by his patronage of the arts through collecting and organizational support. He was instrumental in founding both the Dayton Society of Arts and Crafts and the Dayton Art Institute; to the latter he gave, among other things, a ring collection he began as a youth. In the early 1920s, he introduced the idea of an art museum circulating paintings and sculpture in

45

the manner of a library, a practice that has been emulated widely here and abroad.

WSB

1. Irene Sargent, "The Work of an Amateur Goldsmith, Brainerd B. Thresher," *Keystone* 26 (September 1905), pp. 1417-1420, ill.; Henry W. Belknap, "Jewelry and Enamels," *Craftsman* 4 (June 1903), pp. 178-180, ill. For Thresher's jewelry at the National Arts Club's November 1903 "Exhibition of Jewelry and Precious Stones, Modern, Old and Oriental," see "Jewelry - Modern and Antique," *Art Interchange* 52 (January 1904), p. 31.

2. Colonna was associated with Louis C. Tiffany and later S. Bing's L'Art Nouveau store. For his life and an account of his Dayton sojourn, see Martin Eidelberg, *E. Colonna* (Dayton, Ohio: Dayton Art Institute, 1983).

3. At the Art Institute of Chicago's first Arts and Crafts exhibition Thresher's thirty-nine entries constituted one of the largest showings of jewelry and metalwork. See *Catalogue of the First Annual Exhibition of Original Designs for Decorations and Examples of Art Crafts Having Distinct Artistic Merit* (Chicago: Art Institute of Chicago, 1902), pp. 34-35, nos. 317-355.

4. The Threshers maintained contact with Colonna after 1888 and his influence was probably transmitted to Brainerd in additional ways: via a youthful kinship; via his mother, Sara Bliss Thresher, an accomplished craftswoman whose work was influenced by Colonna; and through contemporary publications illustrating Colonna's work. See Eidelberg 1983, p. 78 n. 133.

5. Gabriel Mourey, "French Jewellery and Fans," in *Modern Designs in Jewellery and Fans*, Charles Holme, ed. (London, Paris, New York: Studio, 1902), p. 3, pls. 25, 26.

6. The quoted words were Thresher's response to a biographical questionnaire circulated by the Boston Society of Arts and Crafts in 1906. In the 1920s Thresher executed furniture, screens, and pictorial wood panels with carved ivory (see "Notes on Current Art," *International Studio* 84 [June 1926], p. 86, ill.).

46

War is Kind, by Stephen Crane, 1899
Publisher: Frederick A. Stokes, New York
(printed at University Press, Cambridge)
Designer and illustrator: Will H. Bradley (1868-1962)
Black ink on gray paper
8¼ x 5 in. (page)
Department of Rare Books and Special Collections, Princeton University Library

Employed in his youth in various capacities in printing establishments, Will Bradley became well known as a freelance designer in the mid-nineties.[1] In 1895 he set up his own Wayside Press in Springfield, Massachusetts, and continued with the operation following its merger three years later with the University Press of Cambridge. Both his limited editions and the books he designed for trade publishers had followings; after 1900 he was an independent designer without equal in the field[2] and he was described as "the highest paid commercial artist in the United States."[3]

Sometimes called "the American Beardsley" for his flat, two-dimensional massings of black and white and his swirling curvilinear lines, Bradley was indeed profoundly influenced by Aubrey Beardsley, as well as William Morris and his Kelmscott Press books. His work also reflected a knowledge of other leading artists: Walter Crane, Howard Pyle, Eugene Grasset, Charles Ricketts, and Laurence Housman.[4] Embracing all three of the major art movements of the time – Arts and Crafts, Aestheticism, and Art Nouveau – Bradley was in turn widely influential. His foreman at the Wayside Press credited him with the principal responsibility for the colonial revival in America.[5]

In addition to creating the illustrations for the first edition of *War is Kind*, published in 1899, Bradley designed the layout. At the time critics did not understand either the unusual poems or the illustrations.[6] With hindsight, the volume stands as Bradley's most powerful contribution to graphic art. Accomplished during the period when his Wayside Press had proved financially unsuccessful, it marks his place in the literature of despair, in which the grotesque element seems uncannily appropriate.

ST

1. Bradley gained public attention especially through his covers and posters for Stone and Kimball's *Chap-Book* and *The Inland Printer*.

2. For a time, Bradley held the post of art diretor for William Randolph Hearst's motion pictures and publications.

3. Robert Koch, "Will Bradley," *Art in America* 50 (Fall 1962), p. 82.

4. H.A Adams, "Bradley's Influence on Printing," *Printer and Bookmaker* 24 (June 1897), p. 142.

5. Fred T. Singleton, "Will Bradley: Turn of the Century Renovator of American Typography and Decorative Art," *American Printer* 103 (August 1936), p. 13. Bradley himself told of reviving the use of Caslon types and studying colonial typography – "the most direct, honest, vigorous and imaginative America has ever known" – in the Boston Public Library. (See "The Gay Nineties" in *Will Bradley, His Work, An Exhibition* [San Marino: Huntington Library, 1951], p. 8.)

6. *The Nation* said that "Mr. Bradley's share in the book is perhaps worse than Mr. Crane's, being purely imitative . . ."; *The Bookman* agreed that "The less said of Mr. Bradley's drawings the better"; *The Criterion* called Bradley a "drearily deliberate saltimbanque of an artist." Only *The New York Times* found merit in the drawings, which "add, in no small degree, to the beauty and worth of the volume." See R.M. Weatherford, *Stephen Crane: The Critical Heritage* (London: Routledge & Kegan Paul, 1973), pp. 230-238.

WAR IS KIND

Do not weep, maiden, for war is kind.
    Because your lover threw wild hands
        toward the sky
And the affrighted steed ran on alone,
Do not weep.
War is kind.

    Hoarse, booming drums of the regi-
        ment,
    Little souls who thirst for fight,
    These men were born to drill and die.
    The unexplained glory flies above
        them,
    Great is the battle-god, great, and his
        kingdom --
    A field where a thousand corpses lie.

9

47

47
Dish, ca. 1902-1917
Marcus & Company, New York (1878 to present)
Silver and turquoise
H: 3 in. W: 12⅞ in. Diam: (of rim) 4¼ in.
Wt: (gross) 7 oz., 5 dwt.
Inscription: engraved *M·A·C*
Marks: struck incuse *MARCUS & CO / STERLING*
The Metropolitan Museum of Art. Friends of the American Wing Fund. 1985.92

This Marcus & Company two-handled footed dish was inspired by examples executed about 1900-1905 at C.R. Ashbee's Guild of Handicraft.[1] The dishes, which date from the Guild's peak years at Essex House in London and, after 1902, its rural location at Chipping Campden, Gloucestershire, derive from Greek drinking bowls. Ancient kylix and kantharos forms suggested the exaggerated handles, trumpet-shape foot, and even the punched-bead ornamentation.[2]

Ashbee's greatest influence on the American Arts and Crafts movement was the model his Guild's shop practices provided metalworkers and their organizations, particularly the adoption of hammered surfaces as a metal finish (see

nos. 134, 135, and 141). There was also significant development via the effect of its designs on metalwork of the Wiener Werkstätte and the silver of Georg Jensen – innovations that eventually directed a change in American silver. Although the Guild's progressive style was widely emulated, the only other close imitations of its silver known among American pieces are two two-handled dishes bearing the mark of the Boston firm Shreve, Crump, and Low and a pair of triple-handled salts with amethysts by Marcus and Company.[3] Compared with Guild dishes, however, the wing-like handles of the Marcus examples are more assured and more in the spirit of their Greek prototypes, which emphasize the horizontal silhouette of the bowl. It is assumed that the wire handles are preserved in the shape originally intended.[4]

Best known through the jewelry designs of George E. Marcus (1859-1917), which were shown in the Boston Society of Arts and Crafts initial exhibitions of 1897 and 1899, the Marcus & Company firm continued to figure prominently among American jewelers up to World War II.[5] The present piece may be as late as 1917, when the company exhibited as an Amer-

ican manufacturer in both the jewelry and silver categories at the Metropolitan Museum of Art's first industrial art annual.[6]

WSB

1. Guild prototypes include two basic models – one-handled unfooted and two-handled footed dishes. Unlike the Marcus example, handles of footed Guild dishes usually spring from the bowl's rim and return to the foot. Known dishes are with or without ornamental cabochons, beaded rims, enameled covers, pierced-foot ornamentation, and vine-leaf-handle terminals. They were called jam or butter dishes by the Guild and some survive with accompanying glass liners. See Alan Crawford, *C. R. Ashbee* (New Haven and London: Yale University Press, 1985), pp. 334-337, ill.; C.R. Ashbee, *Modern English Silverwork* (London: B. T. Batsford, 1909), pl. 17.

2. The Marcus dish is very close in dimension and configuration to a kantharos of silver and applied gold from Rhodes in the Louvre, possibly known to Ashbee. See D.E. Strong, *Greek and Roman Gold and Silver Plate* (London: Methuen, 1966), p. 58, pl. 8B; and Crawford 1985, p. 348.

3. The salts are in a private collection. For one Shreve, Crump & Low example at the Art Institute of Chicago, see Crawford 1985, p. 409, ill. Shreve, Crump, & Low sold the dishes; however, it seems certain that they did not fabricate them. Although the Shreve, Crump &

Low dishes and the Marcus dish relate closely to Guild of Handicraft dishes in fabrication, dimensions, and weight, all bear engraved initials; the Guild's inscriptions are routinely pricked – a technique requiring far less skill than engraving.

4. Ashbee's ingenious employment of extruded wire is astonishing for the rich effect achieved with elementary bending and soldering techniques. It is also an excellent example of his interest in providing the Guild silversmiths with designs requiring modest fabrication skills and affording a broad range of individual interpretation.

5. In 1942 Marcus & Company relocated from 679 Fifth Avenue to the Gimbel Brothers department store; see *New York Times* (November 14, 1942), p. 16. (Harold Schlackman to author, Marcus & Company executive vice-president, telephone interview, May 29, 1986.) Upon the demise of Gimbels the Marcus Galleries moved to B. Altman & Company in September 1986.

6. *American Industrial Art: Annual Exhibition of Current Manufactures Designed and Made in the United States* (New York: Metropolitan Museum of Art, 1917-1940), unpaged.

48

Teapot, ca. 1915
Designer and maker: probably Emery W. Todd (active ca. 1909-1930) at the T.C. Shop, Chicago (1910-1923)
Silver and wood
H: 5½ in. W: 10⅜ in. Diam: 6¼ in. Wt: (gross) 20 oz.
Inscription: RDS in a circle (applied)
Marks: struck incuse TC conjoined / *CHICAGO* / *HAND WROUGHT* / *STERLING*
Collection of Gary Breitweiser

There can be little doubt that this design derives from one of the well-known electric kettles developed by the German architect and industrial designer Peter Behrens (1868-1940) for the large Berlin-based manufacturer AEG (Allgemeine Elektricitäts-Gesellschaft), which first produced them in 1909. Offered in some thirty variations, the Behrens kettle series comprised three basic forms–round, oval, and octagonal, each set on a molded foot–the round form being the only kettle shape also supplied without the electric element as a teapot.[1] The T.C. Shop example has the onion-shaped body and molded circular foot of the round-form Behrens kettle as well as a similar spout and domed lid with tapering knob finial. Although the comparatively subtle hammer-faceted surface of the T.C. Shop pot was a direct result of hand-raising, it recalls the ornamental hammer-faceted surface of the AEG kettles.

48

The present piece is an example of the influence of progressive German design on the work of American craftsmen. After spending six years in Britain reporting on British architecture and design developments for the Prussian Board of Trade, Hermann Muthesius (1861-1927) returned to Germany in 1903 to spread and implement the reform ideals of the English Arts and Crafts movement. A colleague, Peter Behrens, resigned his post as head of Dusseldorf's School of Applied Arts to assume artistic control of AEG in 1907. The year took on great importance to the history of twentieth-century design when Muthesius simultaneously founded the German Werkbund, an association that brought together Germany's major manufacturers and its leading architects, artists, designers, and craftsmen. Werkbund members translated nineteenth-century design-reform ideas into mass-produced designs, focused on functional rather than decorative considerations, for the middle class. Americans studied these developments at first hand in 1912, when Charles Dana took the Werkbund's products on national tour. Nickel and brass teapots designed by Behrens for AEG were among the 1,300 exhibits,[2] and it seems probable that they

included a round-form teapot from the kettle series that inspired this T.C. Shop teapot when the tour came to the Art Institute of Chicago in 1912.

Established in 1910, the T.C. Shop derives its name from its co-owners, Emery Todd and Clemencia Cosio, who for thirteen years designed, produced, and occasionally exhibited handwrought jewelry, silverware, and monogram designs for stationery.[3] The Shop was in Chicago's Fine Arts Building, a haven for the city's Art and Crafts workers. Simple forms, unadorned except for applied monograms, dominate Chicago handicraft silverware, such as the T.C. Shop pitchers featuring paneled designs that Todd would have known earlier as a Kalo Shop silversmith (see no. 142).[4] In 1917 Todd showed unfooted onion-shaped vessels with skillfully composed handle and spout appendages that were further modifications of the Behrens-based teapot.[5]

WSB

1. See Tilmann Buddenseig, in collaboration with Henning Rogge, *Industriekultur: Peter Behrens and the AEG, 1907-1914*, Iain Boyd Whyte, trans. (Cambridge: MIT Press, 1984), p. 426, ill. For a standard reference discussing Behrens and another view of his round-body

AEG kettle, see Nikolaus Pevsner, *Pioneers of Modern Design* (rev. ed., Baltimore: Penguin Books, 1974), pp. 201-207, fig. 135.

2. *Deutsches Kunst-Gewerbe* (Newark: Newark Museum, 1912), p. 84, nos. 1095-1096. See also "Modern German Applied Arts," *Art and Progress* 3 (May 1912), pp. 583-587.

3. Todd exhibited at the Art Institute of Chicago's eighth Arts and Crafts annual in 1909 and the Shop exhibited at later annuals in 1910, 1913, and 1916. He later taught jewelry at the Institute, but during the Depression he was occupied mainly with candy manufacture. Cosio married Nixon A. Hall and became a sales representative for other Chicago silversmiths. See also Sharon Darling, *Chicago Metalsmiths* (Chicago: Chicago Historical Society, 1977), p. 65, ill.

4. *The Artists Guild, An Illustrated Annual of Works by American Artists and Craft Workers, 1915-1916* (Chicago: Artist Guild Galleries), p. 80.

5. *The Artists Guild, An Illustrated Annual of Works by American Artists and Craft Workers, 1917* (Chicago: Artist Guild Galleries), p. 63.

49
Wallpaper frieze, 1910-1920
W.H.M. and Company (origin unknown)
Roller-printed paper
L: 19½ in. W: 88 in. W: (of repeat) 18 in.
Marks: *W.H.M. & Co* and 1897 (style number)
Cooper-Hewitt Museum, the Smithsonian Institution's National Museum of Design; Gift of Victorian Collectibles. 1979-91-36

In the early twentieth century horizontally patterned friezes – often the only wallpaper used in a room – were pasted to the top of a wall, just below the ceiling line. While this practice reflected the Arts and Crafts concern for restraint in room decoration, it was not in the best interest of the marketplace. Manufacturers naturally wanted the frieze to be used in conjunction with other papers, following the custom that prevailed in the second half of the nineteenth century, when a frieze, a dado, a filling and two or three borders, all in different patterns, were used at the same time. Thus, they created friezes on which a bold pattern stood out against a subtly figured background. Paper with the less intrusive pattern was made to cover the entire wall surface of a room.

This wallpaper, with abstracted flower-and-leaf forms repeated on a striated background, was undoubtedly sold with a coordinate paper roller printed with the fainter background pattern only. The design is a response to the popular emphasis given to the square, a shape char-

acteristic of so much of the work of this period. Here the edges have been softened so that there are no sharp corners, yet the essence of a square remains. The restraint in design and color, the quality of the paper, and the roller-printed execution all indicate that this paper was prepared for the popular rather than the trend-setting market. A smaller example of the same frieze, in shades of brown, in the Cooper-Hewitt Museum reveal that the manufacturer offered the customer color choices as well.

GM

50
Side chair, ca. 1904
Designer: probably Walter J.H. Dudley
Maker: Joseph P. McHugh and Company, New York (1884-ca. 1920s)
Oak; linen seat cover (not original)
H: 52½ in. W: 19 in. D: 17 in.
Collection of Mr. and Mrs. Daniel Dietrich

Somewhat overlooked in today's literature on the Arts and Crafts movement, Joseph P. McHugh (1854-1916) received widespread publicity for his work during his lifetime. In May of 1900 the *Ladies Home Journal* published his progressive designs along with those of William Martin Johnson and the renowned English art furniture manufacturer Heal and Company.[1] McHugh's furnishings in the New York State Building at the Pan-American Exposition in 1901 won him not only a silver medal but recognition from abroad; both the *London Furniture Record* and the *International Studio* noted his innovative work.[2] The South Carolina Interstate and West Indian Exposition in 1902 bestowed two gold medals upon McHugh: one for the Mission furniture he exhibited and another for the color scheme and decorations in the New York State Building there.[3]

A child prodigy who grew up in his father's dry-goods store,[4] McHugh established his first shop of upholstery and draperies in 1880. Four years later he had settled into New York's residential district on West 42nd Street,[5] stocking his store with the latest wallpapers, fabrics, and household furnishings and offering complete decorating services. By 1892, "The Popular Shop" (McHugh's trademark registered in 1894) was highly influential; McHugh made annual buying trips to England, France, Belgium, and Holland to gather pottery and other decorative objects in the latest styles.[6] Among the

goods imported were Liberty and Company pottery, metalwork and quaint furniture, William Morris chintzes, grass cloths specially colored from Japan, and wallpapers designed by Walter Crane, Charles Knowles and Company, and Shand Kydd.[7]

Having found a ready market for imported Chinese wicker, McHugh decided to produce his own in 1893.[8] He introduced Mission furniture (see no. 71) the next year, in the same colors as the wicker. By the turn of the century, the company was offering a large variety of furniture in the Mission style; this elegant chair with branch-like slats was one of them.[9] Exhibiting the delicate lines of the English reformer C.F.A. Voysey's work and the stump feet of A.H. Mackmurdo's, the chair was advertised in McHugh's catalogue of about 1904. It was probably designed by the company's leading designer from 1896 on, Walter J.H. Dudley, who joined McHugh after studying at the Art Students League in New York and the Brooklyn Institute of Arts and Sciences and spending several years drawing in the architectural office of one H. Edwards-Ficken.[10]

CZ

1. William Martin Johnson, "In the Ways of Chairs and Tables," *Ladies Home Journal* 17 (May 1900), p. 23.

2. *London Furniture Record* (November 29, 1901), as cited in "Admired in England," *American Cabinetmaker and Upholsterer* 65 (December 21, 1901), p. 10; "American Studio Talk," *International Studio* 12 (February 1901), pp. xxiv-xxvi.

3. "More Honors," *Upholstery Dealer and Decorative Furnisher* 2 (June 1902), p. 59.

4. McHugh entered Holy Cross College in Worcester when he was only eleven years old with the intention of pursuing a learned profession, but family reverses forced him to work in his father's store. See "Obituary," *Upholstery Dealer and Decorative Furnisher* 30 (July 1916), p. 62.

5. "Joseph P. McHugh – His Shop," *Upholstery Dealer and Decorative Furnisher* 29 (October 1915), p. 47.

6. Ibid., p. 48.

7. Ibid.

8. Ibid., p. 53.

9. An innovator, McHugh illustrated furniture with Mackintosh-like inlays of abstracted floral motifs in his 1898 catalogue, along with Mission designs and a "Colonial Collection."

10. Matlack Price, "Practicality, Imagination and the Designer: A Study of the Work of Walter J.H. Dudley," *Arts and Decoration* 15 (July 1921), p. 167.

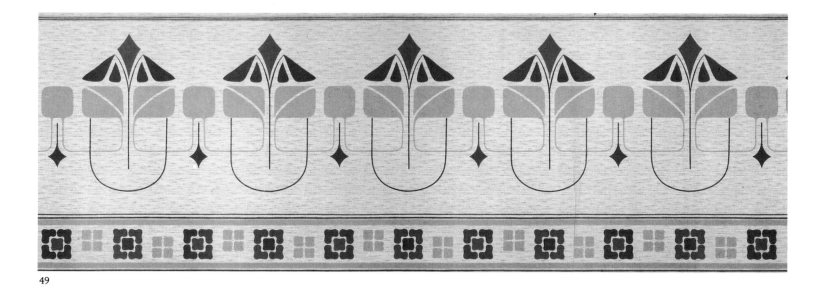

49

50

51

Table, ca. 1905
Charles P. Limbert Company, Grand Rapids and
Holland, Michigan (1902-1944)
Oak
H: 29¼ in. W: 47½ in. D: 36¹⁄₁₆ in.
Marks: Limbert brand (depicting a man planing
wood) and 158 stamped in blue ink on wood
(both under shelf)
Private Collection

52

Secretary bookcase, ca. 1905[1]
Charles P. Limbert Company, Grand Rapids and
Holland, Michigan (1902-1944)
Oak
H: 54½ in. W: 38 in. D: 13½ in.
Private Collection

Charles Limbert helped to popularize progressive British and European designs in America in the early 1900s by mass-producing variations of them at his Holland Dutch Arts and Crafts furniture factory. Inspired by the acclaim Gustav Stickley's Mission furniture received at the Grand Rapids trade show in July 1900,[2] Limbert and many other manufacturers began to offer similar rectilinear pieces. Unlike Stickley, however, who developed his own "structural style," Limbert manufactured forms that were, for the most part, derivative of proven work. The Dutch label he applied to both his furniture and his workers was a romantic marketing ploy;[3] his most successful work was imitative of the "quaint" furniture of British designers – C.R. Mackintosh, C.F.A. Voysey and M.H. Baillie Scott.[4] The present oval table with square cutouts resembles one in the entrance of Mackintosh's 1903 Hill House (see fig. 13, p. 84); the secretary-bookcase with spade-shaped cutouts derives from Voysey and Baillie Scott designs.[5]

Limbert established himself as a manufacturer of Arts and Crafts furniture in 1902. That spring he published a catalogue of "the ideal furnishings for country and suburban homes and library and den use."[6] According to various trade journals, his furniture was so popular that a work force of 200 men was required[7] and the company had to convert its showroom into a shipping room to send out orders.[8] Though it was not the handmade furniture that its promotion and trademark advertised it to be, most of it was well designed and well constructed of good materials. It was made entirely of solid white oak without veneer and held together with mortise-and-tenon joints, pins, dowels, splines, and screws. "Spanish Morocco" leather, made in the Limbert tannery from goat skins imported from Germany and Russia, was used to upholster cushions "of double-deck crucible springs."[9]

Although Mission furniture was beginning to disappear from the lines of many manufactur-

51

ers by 1915, Charles Limbert continued to produce it to the exclusion of other styles (except for a few designs with Austrian or Swiss motifs).[10] By 1916, while Limbert was still offering "the largest line of Arts and Crafts furniture on the market," he had expanded his production to include pieces in Chinese, Italian, Queen Anne, William and Mary, and Federal styles, in another year he had discontinued everything except colonial-revival furnishings. The firm, which Limbert sold in 1922, marketed furniture under his name until 1944.[11]

CZ

1. A bookcase very similar to this object is illustrated in Limbert's catalogue of 1905.

2. *Furniture Trade Review* (20 [August 10, 1900], p. 14) noted that Stickley's exhibit of plain furniture attracted great attention.

3. Bearing out his claim that "Holland Dutch Arts and Craftsmen . . . live in the proper environment and love their work, use their heads, hearts and hands, and impart an individuality and superiority to every piece," Limbert ran a factory that came closer to the Arts and Crafts ideal of a happy workplace than most manufacturers promoting this furniture style (see advertisement in *House Beautiful* 24 [August 1908]).

4. Limbert referred in his fall catalogue of 1905 to Arts and Crafts furniture being "cultivated by European artists." While he never referred specifically to Mackintosh or the Glasgow School as a source, he did suggest that the Arts and Crafts style was "an outgrowth of the early German and Austrian Secessionistic School," adding that the essential characteristics of the style were grounded in the fourteenth and fifteenth centuries, perhaps in the Netherlands. See Charles P. Limbert, "The Arts & Crafts Furniture," *Furniture* 1 (October 1909), p. 31.

5. Limbert introduced furniture with spade-like cutouts as early as 1902 and the more grid-like cutout designs by 1905. In his catalogue of 1905, he illustrated a line of chairs and bookcases decorated with abstracted inlaid designs of copper, brass, and pewter sheet metal. Again, this decoration was prompted either by Mackintosh's own work or by Mackintosh via Harvey Ellis's inlaid line of Craftsman furniture.

6. "Catalogues," *American Cabinet Maker and Upholsterer* 65 (March 15, 1902), p. 5.

7. "Arts and Crafts Summer Furniture," *Grand Rapids Furniture Record* 5 (March 1902), p. 118.

8. *American Cabinet Maker and Upholsterer* 65 (April 12, 1902), p. 8.

9. "Charles P. Limbert Company, Cabinet Makers," booklet no. 100, reprinted by the American Life Federation, Watkins Glen, New York, 1982. According to Robert Edwards, Limbert later used brocade on his Mission furniture (personal communication, November 1986).

52

10. *Grand Rapids Furniture Record* 31 (August 1915), p. 118.

11. For the history of the Charles P. Limbert Company, see Deborah DeVall Dorsey Norberg, "Charles P. Limbert: Maker of Michigan Arts & Crafts Furniture," *Herald*, Henry Ford Museum, October 1976, pp. 38-39.

53

53

Shelf clock, ca. 1913[1]
Designer: Peter Heinrich Hansen (1880-1947)
Maker: L. and J.G. Stickley, Fayetteville, New York (1902-present)
Oak with copper-plated face and Seth Thomas or Waterbury works[2]; glass insert
H: 22 in. W: 16 in. D: 8 in.
Marks: L. and J.G. Stickley logo of broken cube at center of clock face and also at 12, 3, 6 and 9 o'clock
Label: (handwritten) *This Clock was built/at Factory of/ L. & J.G. Stickley, Inc./Fayetteville, N.Y./Peter Hansen Designer./Purchased about 1913./C.M. Kessler/Dec. 1941/Written*[3] (adhered to back of clock works)
Collection of Mr. and Mrs. Peter M. Brandt

Peter Hansen was born in Germany and apprenticed as a cabinetmaker there before immi-

grating to America around the turn of the century. He was employed as a draftsman and designer for Gustav Stickley in New York City prior to moving to Fayetteville in about 1909 to work for Leopold and John George Stickley as a designer and mill foreman.[4]

The design for this shelf clock may have been inspired by one of Ferdinand Christian Morawe's illustrated in *Dekorative Kunst*, a popular German periodical of the decorative arts (see p. 88, fig. 18).[5] Gustav Stickley and Adelaide Alsop Robineau are known to have subscribed to the magazine and it is likely that Peter Hansen and the other Sticklleys also read it to stay informed of the latest design trends. It is also possible that Hansen saw the work of Joseph Olbrich, Josef Hoffmann, and other Secessionist designers in Germany prior to moving to America. The clock has some very English features as well as German ones; its verticality and cornice suggest C.F.A. Voysey's work. Voysey was influenced by the Secessionists' designs and was particularly interested in Joseph Olbrich's work.

CZ

1. This clock was available by about 1910 as it was illustrated at that time in the L. and J.G. Stickley catalogue. According to the handwritten label adhered to its back, it was purchased in about 1913, and thus was probably manufactured around then.

2. The works had been attributed to Seth Thomas. Another identical clock is known to have Waterbury works.

3. Charles M. Kessler and Leopold and John George Stickley incorporated the firm of L. and J.G. Stickley in 1904. According to Olive and William Hansen, Kessler was the comptroller or bookkeeper for the company in about 1941 (personal communication, October 23, 1986, and letter from Olive Hansen, October 27, 1986).

4. Louise Stickley noted in an interview with David Cathers that Leopold Stickley would rough out the basic designs while Hansen refined them. See David M. Cathers, *Furniture of the American Arts and Crafts Movement: Stickley and Roycroft Mission Oak* (New York: New American Library, 1981), p. 84, note 1. According to Olive and William Hansen, Peter Hansen also did many detailed drawings for L. and J.G. Stickley's "Cherry Valley" line of colonial reproductions.

5. *Dekorative Kunst*, December 1903. Thanks to Robert Judson Clark for this connection and reference. The clock may also have been inspired by a Gustav Stickley design for a similar example (see *What Is Wrought in the Craftsman Workshops* [Syracuse, N.Y.: Gustav Stickley, 1904]).

54

Hanging lantern, ca. 1906-1908
Designer: Dard Hunter, 1883-1966
Roycroft, East Aurora, New York
Copper, German silver, and stained glass
H: 30 in. W: 16 in. D: 6 in.
Museum of Fine Arts, Boston. Harriet Otis Cruft Fund. 1980.279-280

While Dard Hunter is best known as a book designer and maker (see no. 171), he worked in other media as well. The bold and simple geometric design of this lantern reflects his familiarity with the work of the Vienna Secessionists and the Wiener Werkstätte. His interest in modern design was kindled by German magazines such as *Dekorative Kunst* and *Deutsche Kunst und Dekoration*, which Hunter read at Roycroft. In his own words: "these magazines were a monthly inspiration, and many of the commercial designs I made during my early years at the shop show this influence".[1] The German publications also inspired Hunter's first trip to Vienna in 1908.[2]

During Hunter's first year at the Roycroft community in 1903 he expressed an interest in learning the techniques of leaded-glass construction. Elbert Hubbard sent him to the New York architectural firm of J. and R. Lamb, known for their designs of church interiors, to learn the craft.[3] Shortly thereafter, Hunter returned to East Aurora, and by 1906 he was making windows, lampshades, and lighting fixtures of leaded glass for the Roycroft Inn and Shops.[4] This three-light lantern is one of twelve identical fixtures he designed for the main dining hall at the Inn; a photograph in Roycroft's 1912 catalogue shows the lanterns in place. They were probably made before Hunter's trip to Vienna, and are known to have been offered for sale by 1910.[5]

Using glass from the Opalescent Glass Works in Kokomo, Indiana, Hunter made several types of lighting fixtures: hanging chandeliers, wall lamps, freestanding lamps, and floor lamps. Karl Kipp, master artisan in the Roycroft copper shop, designed the bases and frames for several of Hunter's leaded-glass shades. The lampshades ranged from elaborate to simple in design: some were pictorial or utilized natural motifs such as the dragonfly, others incorporated the leaf and rose motifs found in his dining-room windows, and many were based on simple geometric patterns. Several designs were illustrated in Hunter's "Things You Can

Make," published for a leaded-glass correspondence course available through Roycrofters.[6]

Dard Hunter pursued the practice of leaded
glass beyond his East Aurora days; he continued
to design and construct stained-glass windows
at each of his studios in Marlboro (New York),
Lime Rock (Connecticut), and Chillicothe
(Ohio).

JSB

1. Dard Hunter, *My Life With Paper: An Autobiography* (New
York: Alfred A. Knopf, 1958), pp. 43-44.

2. The designs from Hunter's Vienna period are
among his best, and some were made into windows
and panels by Geiling and Sohn, an important Viennese leaded-glass firm. Hunter's visit took place during the flowering of the Vienna movement, led by the
artists of the Wiener Werkstätte. Founded by designers
Josef Hoffmann and Kolomon Moser in 1905, the
Werkstätte was a result of the Vienna Secession, artists
revolting against the increasing commercialization of
art and the historic revival styles of the late nineteenth
century. In their rejection of historicism, the Secessionist artists often emphasized geometric forms –
squares, circles, checkerboards, and other geometric
shapes–stated boldly and simply. (Ibid., p. 44.)

3. In his autobiography Hunter cites June 1903 as the
date of his arrival at East Aurora (ibid., p. 30). Dard
Hunter, Jr., claims, however, that his father arrived at
Roycroft first in July of 1904, returning there from his
stay at Lamb's studio in November and taking charge
of the stained-glass work at Roycroft then (see *The Life
Work of Dard Hunter*, vol. 1 [Chillicothe, Ohio: Mountain
House Press, 1981], pp. 11 and 167). According to this
source, Hunter was "well into the making of lampshades and windows for the Roycroft Inn and Shops"
by early 1906.

4. The Inn opened in 1903 to house tourists visiting
the Roycroft community of craftsmen; it became also
a place for the exhibition of furniture, stained glass,
hardware, and fixtures designed and made by the
Roycrofters.

5. *Roycroft Shop Catalogue*, 1910 (East Aurora, N.Y.:
Roycrofters, 1910), p. 97.

6. See Hunter 1958, p. 178.

55

55

Vase, 1898
Rookwood Pottery Company (1880-1960), Cincinnati
Decorator: Frederick Sturgis Laurence (active as decorator 1895-1903)
Buff earthenware, molded in "pillow" shape and decorated in underglaze slips of browns, yellows, and greens with head of American Indian in full feathered headdress
H: 16 in. W: 15 in. D: 6½ in.
Marks: incised *CHIEF "GOES-TO-WAR," SIOUX / STURGIS LAURENCE* (on front); impressed RP monogram surrounded by twelve flames with 707xx below (on bottom)
Michael Bernstein, Pieces of Tyme Antiques, Bala Cynwyd, Pennsylvania

By the late nineteenth century, America's first inhabitants had been pushed from their original homes. With their numbers greatly diminished by war and disease and their independent spirit virtually broken, the tribes were compressed and contained by the U.S. government on generally poor western lands. Only then did many Euro-Americans begin to romanticize the glorious days when Indians lived in close harmony with nature. Images of noble warriors, gentle potters, weavers, and basketmakers in academic-style paintings by artists such as Henry Farny, Joseph Henry Sharp, Edward Curtis, and Frank A. Rinehart reflected this nostalgia. Accordingly, portraits of Indians, both bust length and standing, took their places next to

studies of dogs, children, and flowers as Rookwood's "standard" decorative style and color palette evolved under the direction of William Watts Taylor during the mid-1880s.

The Rookwood Pottery underwent significant changes beginning in 1883, when Taylor took over its management from Maria Longworth Nichols.[1] Taylor proposed to turn it into a profit-making venture by standardizing the general appearance of the wares and marketing them through fashionable stores. On the premise that Rookwood could not become a recognizable commodity if anyone could decorate a Rookwood blank, the School for Pottery Decoration, begun by Mrs. Nichols as an adjunct to the Pottery, was discontinued in favor of standardization. Experiments were increased to determine the most consistently successful colors and shapes from a technical standpoint, thereby reducing the high percentage of loss in the kilns. A survey of what had sold and what had not led to conclusions about the marketability of certain types of decoration. At the same time, the decorator Laura Fry developed the use of an atomizer to create evenly shaded colored grounds on which to paint. This technique, in combination with the other changes, produced the Rookwood "standard": backgrounds shading from dark to light with painterly decoration rendered in mellow browns, yellows, greens, and oranges. The "standard" glaze persisted until well after new palettes were developed and introduced in 1894.

As another marketing maneuver, Taylor promoted the concept of collecting Rookwood as an art form. Each piece was uniquely decorated and each was fully marked with the Rookwood monogram (adopted in 1886), the year of manufacture, the shape number, and the artist's cipher. Lists of artists were published from time to time and buyers were encouraged to become collectors, even patrons, of the fine art of Rookwood Pottery. As a result of Taylor's changes, the year 1886 was the first in which a profit was recorded for all twelve months.

This was also the year that Taylor met the ceramics historian Edwin AtLee Barber, director of the Pennsylvania Museum and School of Industrial Arts, the ancestor institution of the current Philadelphia Museum of Art. To make certain that Rookwood pottery was well represented in Barber's history of the American ceramics industry, Taylor sent him more than twenty pieces over the years. Among them was this portrait vase of Sioux Chief Goes-to-War,

which is illustrated in the 1901 edition of Barber's book.[2] F. Sturgis Laurence's rendering of the Sioux chief in Rookwood's "standard" technique may have been based on a photograph of about 1898 by Jesse Hastings Bratley.[3] It is painted on a shape first introduced in 1893 to provide a broad expanse for ambitious decoration.[4] Laurence signed his portrait on the front to legitimize it as a work of art. The condition of the vase undoubtedly recommended it for disposal by gift to Barber.

EPD and BRD

1. For information about the history of the Rookwood Pottery, see Herbert Peck, *The Book of Rookwood Pottery* (New York: Crown Publishers, 1968).

2. Edwin AtLee Barber, *The Pottery and Porcelain of the United States*, 3rd ed. (New York: G.P. Putnam, 1901), p. 480. Although it suffered from firing defects, the damage was on the reverse and did not intrude on the portrait. The vase was later sold from the Museum's collection along with other pieces of commercial and art ceramics of this period that Barber had collected for his books.

3. Laurence was a decorator at Rookwood from 1895 to 1903, when he went to New York to manage the architectural faience office for Rookwood. He remained with the company in New York until 1923 with time off for military service during World War I.

4. Information about the Bratley photograph was kindly supplied by Paula Fleming, National Anthropological Archives, National Museum of Natural History; for the shape, see Herbert Peck, *The Second Book of Rookwood Pottery* (published by the author in Tucson, 1985), p. 81.

56

Vase, 1906-1911
Clifton Art Pottery (1905-1914), Newark, New Jersey
Red earthenware, molded with intaglio geometric designs in the manner of American Indian motifs delineated in black and white semi-matte glazes; black-glazed interior
H: 12 in. Diam: 9¾ in.
Marks: impressed *MIDDLE MISSISSIPPI / VALLEY / CLIFTON / 227* (on bottom); and incised *MISSISSIPPI A* (at bottom edge)
Museum of Fine Arts, Boston. Gift of Charles Devens. 1985.360

William A. Long, a chemist and pharmacist from Steubenville, Ohio, began the Clifton Art Pottery in Newark with Fred Tschirner, also a chemist and a graduate of the University of Berlin. Clifton was the last of several small in-

56

dustrial art potteries of which Long had been the chief founder, and its production was the most diverse in form and decoration.[1] The earliest wares produced, wholly new in conception, were called "Crystal Patina" for their flowing glaze with pale-green muted crystallization similar to bronze oxidation. Yet another contribution to the growing lexicon of American industrial art ceramics was the distinctive Clifton Indian Ware, in the style of American Indian pottery.[2] Undoubtedly inspired during his tenure in Colorado (see note 1 below), Long saw the advantage of capitalizing on the new popular awareness of native crafts. American museums of natural history had been collecting ethnographica for many years and after 1900 art and history museums increasingly became repositories for native American arts as well. By that time, many Americans had advanced from the sentimentality of earlier decades to an appreciation of Indian material culture. Accordingly, Long's Indian Ware is markedly different from the native portraits on Rookwood pottery (see no. 55), derived from romantic images in the style of Edward Curtis's photographs.

Clifton Indian Ware included both decorative and useful forms molded of New Jersey red earthenware. While the table wares were gener-

ally in Euro-American shapes, Long limited the decorative pieces to close adaptations of Indian pottery in museum collections. Each was identified by a mark specifying the model's place of origin. The vase shown here is based on a bottle form associated with the Middle Mississippi Valley at the time, but today assigned to Caddoan groups in Arkansas.

EPD and BRD

1. Long had been the first to put the Cincinnati faience technique into large-scale industrial production. He had perfected the adaptation of the method to industrial processes through his earlier Lonhuda Pottery, which attracted the interest of Samuel A. Weller (see no. 28) and resulted in collaborative work after 1894. In 1901 Long founded the Denver China and Pottery Company in the hope of furnishing the western market with wares in this decorative technique. Using local materials, his pottery offered utilitarian wares as well as two art lines: the old faience ware and a new line molded with energetic low-relief designs and covered with monochromatic glazes to compete with the wares made at the new Van Briggle Pottery (no. 120) in Colorado Springs. Low-relief designs and an unglazed faience line were produced at Clifton in addition to the "Crystal Patina" and Indian Ware. Long's rapid succession of ventures illustrates how one potter of this period attempted to stay ahead of the competition by developing industrial methods to reproduce the costlier hand processes of others' artwares. For more information about Long, see Paul Evans, *The Art Pottery of the United States* (New York: Charles Scribner's Sons, 1974), pp. 59-62, 88-90, and 141-144.

2. Both Weller's and J.B. Owens's potteries copied Long's Indian Ware, but the effect was of cheap imitation rather than close adaptation.

57
Basket, ca. 1903
Harriet Blanche Thayer (b. 1869)
Society of Arts and Crafts, Hingham, Massachusetts
Coiled raffia
H: 4 ½ in. Diam: 8 in.
Label: printed paper pasted on bottom; circle with bucket and *HINGHAM SOCIETY ARTS AND CRAFTS.* (at center) *APPROVED* (below circle)
Hingham Historical Society, Hingham, Massachusetts

The Hingham Society of Arts and Crafts, founded in 1901, was often linked with the renowned village industries of Deerfield, Mas-

sachusetts, in contemporary reviews,[1] indicating the stature the society achieved. Rug weaving (see no. 63), whitework embroidery, metalwork, and toymaking were crafts Society members practiced in addition to basketmaking. (They were noted for dyeing basketry fibers, as well as making the baskets themselves.) Because local woodworkers had been in the bucket-making business from the eighteenth century on, the Society used an illustration of a bucket as its trademark.

Indian baskets or, like this example, baskets made in the Indian style, were used in Arts and Crafts interiors as waste containers, letter trays, and sewing baskets. Often they had no specific function within a room but were placed on tabletops or mantelpieces simply because of their association with techniques and the use of natural materials: reeds, wood splints, and plant components. This example is made of raffia, a palm fiber imported from tropical countries. The process of coiling involves using a needle threaded with a length of raffia to sew around a bundle of raffia fibers. Each "stitch" wraps the raffia core and passes through the top of a stitch on the previous row, thus creating a tight structure with stitches closely spaced. Shape is achieved by controlling the material with the hand and by the placement of stitches. Design and pattern are determined by the color of the raffia on the threaded needle. Here three colors – yellow, dark blue, and red (now faded to a pink-orange) – were used to create a repeating pattern of birds; hence, the name "oriole"[2] designated by the maker of the basket, Harriet Blanche Thayer.[3]

GM

1. Sylvester Baxter, "The Movement for Village Industries," *Handicraft* 1 (October 1902), pp. 157-158; and Mary L. Riley, "Arts and Crafts Societies in Massachusetts," *House Beautiful* 17 (October 1905), pp. 31-33.

2. The basket is illustrated in C. Chester Lane, "Hingham Arts and Crafts, Their Aims and Objects," *Craftsman* 3 (December 1903), pp. 276-281.

3. Miss Thayer is also known to have designed and made netted doilies. See *Exhibition of the Society of Arts & Crafts, Copley Hall,* Boston, February 5-26, 1907, p. 78.

57

58

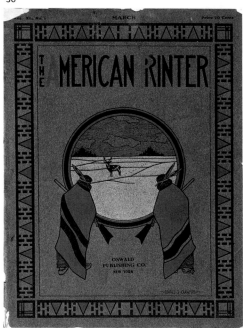

58
The American Printer, March 1905
Publisher: John Clyde Oswald Publishing Company, New York
Designer: Edward S. Crawford
Black and red ink on gray paper
11¾ x 9 in. (page)
Private Collection

The American Printer, which was published until 1958 (having begun in 1885 as *The American Bookmaker*), was one of the industry's most widely read journals, disseminating the development of the typographic revolution fostered by William Morris's Kelmscott Press. In fact, articles of June and July 1890 referred to Morris even before the existence of his press and described the mood of bibliophily that paved the way for his impact.[1]

The cover of this issue, reminiscent of Will Bradley and Maxfield Parrish, shows two Indian braves with rifles peering through a central roundel at a deer. Typical of Arts and Crafts design is the border of native American motifs, which would figure prominently in what came to be called Art Deco. Also characteristic is the convention of changing the cover design of a periodical with each issue, which had been introduced some ten years earlier.[2] The same designs were often used for posters to advertise the new issues, and they rarely had anything to do with the content of the magazine. For example, nothing in the March issue of *The American Printer* can be connected with American Indians.

ST

1. "Art Designing," *American Bookmaker* 10 (June 1890), p. 153; "American Bookmaking," *American Bookmaker* 11 (July 1890), p. 2. Evidence of Morris's ideas, anticipating his approach to type, had appeared in the issue of November 1887 (p. 185): an advertisement for the type-founding firm of Farmer, Little & Co. showed "Primitive" type, a very black old-style face with a Gothic upper case and a Venetian slanting crossbar on the lower case "e."

2. Will Bradley, *Will Bradley: His Chap-Book* (Mount Vernon: Peter Pauper Press, 1955), p. 36.

59

Presentation perspective for W.F. Etherington cottage, Fortunes Rocks, Biddeford, Maine, 1909
Architects: John Calvin Stevens (1855-1940) and John Howard Stevens (1879-1958)
Renderer: John Howard Stevens
Medium: watercolor on paper mounted on board
Inscription: *John Calvin Stevens, John Howard Stevens. Arch 'ts* with monogram and date '09
5½ x 12¼ in.
The Avery Architectural Library, Columbia University, New York

59

John Calvin Stevens was the leading Maine architect from the 1880s into the 1930s. His work well illustrates the changing forms and focuses of the Arts and Crafts in New England and continuous reinterpretations of the colonial style.[1] Born in Boston, Stevens grew up in Portland, Maine, and trained with a local High Victorian architect, Frances H. Fassett (1823-1909). During a few years in which he operated a branch office for Fassett in Boston, he came into contact with the advanced Aesthetic movement architecture of William Ralph Emerson (1833-1917).[2] Stevens returned to Portland and set up his own practice in 1888; he was joined in partnership for three years with Albert Winslow Cobb (1858-1941), an alumni of the Emerson office. The chief product of this brief association was a book entitled *Examples of American Domestic Architecture* (1889). Cobb contributed the text and Stevens produced the renderings for this extraordinary volume, one of the few publications of the period in which specific social goals were linked to architectural form. The book argued for an American architectural style independent of European forms, which represented the "days of greatest moral corruption." The philosophy combined William Morris's utopian socialism, determinist sociology, democratic idealism, and Christian brotherhood. Cobb wrote that "the good or the bad character of the homes where people eat, drink, [and] sleep may be said to practically determine the life-weal or life-woe of their occupants."[3] Calling for an architecture sympathetic to the environment, he pointed to early American buildings, both those of the "Old Colonial" or Georgian style and those with less formal – hence more vernacular – characteristics.

Stevens's architecture with Cobb and afterward alternated between formal Georgian and an informal modernized colonial, or what Vin-

cent Scully has dubbed "The Shingle Style."[4] The gambrel roof became in his hands a compositional device – a broad, spreading, quiet form that gave a feeling of repose and order to buildings made up of disparate elements. Frequently identified as Dutch in origin,[5] the gambrel form appeared in New England as early as the mid-seventeenth century, as can be seen in the 1641 and 1654 wings added to the Fairbanks-Morse house in Dedham, Massachusetts, and in early-eighteenth-century houses along Newport's waterfront. By the early 1880s Emerson and McKim, Mead, and White were exploiting the gambrel roof and Stevens used one in 1884 on his own house in Portland.

The Etherington summer cottage in Maine, designed by Stevens in conjunction with his son – who joined him in partnership in 1906 – illustrates how the varying spaces of a house, arranged on a diagonal axis, are united by the gambrel roof. As shown in the rendering, fenestration and chimneys are placed asymmetrically for functional purposes and a deep void of a porch invades one end, balanced by a single-story extrusion at the other end. With a modicum of colonial-revival detail – a small Chinese Chippendale railing over the extension, shutters, and some trim around the door – the house is covered with shingles, which would weather to a sea gray and help to tie the house to the site. Evoking the New England seacoast tradition while avoiding too literal an interpre-

tation of the past, the cottage is fully as regional in its forms, materials, and colors as any midwestern Prairie School dwelling.

RGW

1. I am indebted to Earle G. Shettleworth, Jr., director of the Maine Historic Preservation Commission, for information about the work of Stevens. See Earle G. Shettleworth, Jr., and William David Barry, "new introduction" in John Calvin Stevens and Albert Winslow Cobb, *American Domestic Architecture* (Watkins Glen, N.Y.: American Life Foundation and Study Institute, 1978; reprint of *Examples of American Domestic Architecture* [New York: William T. Comstock, 1889]); and Earle Shettleworth, "Turn-of-the-Century Architecture: From about 1880 to 1920," in Deborah Thompson, *Maine Forms of American Architecture* (Camden: Down East, 1976), pp. 184-212.

2. Cynthia Zaitzevsky, *The Architecture of William Ralph Emerson, 1833-1917* (Cambridge: Fogg Art Museum, Harvard University, 1969); and Vincent J. Scully, Jr., *The Shingle Style and the Stick Style*, rev. ed. (New Haven: Yale University Press, 1971), pp. 82-88, 108-112.

3. Stevens and Cobb 1978, pp. 10,18,24,38.

4. Scully 1971, pp. 113-120.

5. For examples of the gambrel roof as Dutch, see C. Matlack Price, " 'Old Colonial' – A Native Style of Country House Architecture," *Arts and Decoration* 3 (February 1913), pp. 118-119; and Aymar Embury, II, "The Dutch Colonial House," in Henry Saylor, ed., *Architectural Styles for Country Houses*, enlarged ed. (New York: Robert McBride, 1919), pp. 89-97.

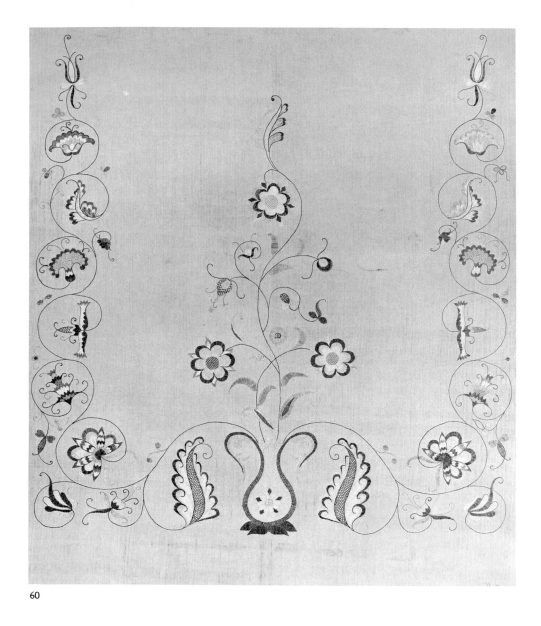

60

60
Embroidered door curtain, 1899
Designer: Margaret Whiting (1860-1946) after
antique patterns
Maker: members of the Society of Blue and
White Needlework, Deerfield, Massachusetts
(1896-1926)
Linen embroidery (running, chain, Roumanian,
satin, herringbone, buttonhole, lattice, and
looping stitches) on plain weave (linen warp
and cotton weft)
L: 93 in. W: 80 in.
Marks: embroidered D within spinning wheel;
A.D. in faded red linen cross-stitch (in one of
the corners)
Pocumtuck Valley Memorial Association, Me-
morial Hall Museum, Deerfield, Massachusetts.
NBW-72

61
Embroidered table cover, ca. 1899-1910
Designer: Margaret Whiting (1860-1946)
Maker: members of the Society of Blue and
White Needlework, Deerfield, Massachusetts
(1896-1926)
Linen and cotton embroidery (including her-
ringbone, Roumanian, stem, and surface satin
stitches) on plain-weave linen
L: 26 in. W: 27 in.
Marks: embroidered D within a spinning wheel
Label: *Not for Sale* on paper (attached to back)
Pocumtuck Valley Memorial Association, Me-
morial Hall Museum, Deerfield, Massachusetts.
NBW-95

The Society of Blue and White Needlework was
founded in 1896 by Ellen Miller and Margaret
Whiting, artists and friends, who had become
interested in the eighteenth-century embroidery housed in their local historical society. In
an effort to preserve the designs, they made
adaptations of the embroidery and traveled up
and down the Connecticut River Valley studying other patterns. Most of the early work of the
Society – bed curtains, tea cloths, table centers,
doilies, and bureau and table covers – was done
with blue and white linen yarns on linen or
cotton foundation cloth,[1] but within a year,
greens, browns, and pinks were being used.[2] As
their colonial predecessors had done, the Society colored yarns and fabrics with various natural substances – including indigo, madder, and
butternut – believing that the natural dyes
would last longer than modern man-made ani-
line ones. Moving beyond colonial pattern

61

sources for their work, Miss Miller and Miss Whiting also created door curtains, cushions, screens, and wall panels with innovative designs, among them colorful birds, sheep, and landscape scenes.[3] The table cover with embroidered poppies is a product of this later phase.

Since Miss Miller and Miss Whiting perceived embroidery as an art form requiring training and discipline, they designed all of the Society's work. Both women had studied at the New York Academy and Miss Miller had taught art for several years in the public schools. Instead of offering classes in embroidery or selling designs and materials to the general public, they focused their energies on teaching a limited number of local women to execute the stitchery with the aim of producing "embroiderers of the highest excellence."[4] All work was reviewed before receiving the Society's trademark – the D within a spinning wheel – setting a standard for craft.[5] The pay structure reflected a respect for the design, organization, and embroidering aspects of the industry. Half of an object's cost went to its maker, one-fifth went to its designer, and the rest went toward materials and the cost of running the Society.[6] Mrs. Whiting's experience had taught her to be skeptical of both the do-gooder who started village industries to help the "old decayed village" and the avid follower of Ruskin and Morris. In 1911 she wrote: "After some years of grinding, even my convictions are few, and chiefly discoverable by comparison with the more numerous

theories of the enthusiasts for whom Morris and Ruskin yet live . . . . It is not charity but art that founds and maintains a craft."[7]

The Society received invitations to exhibit from cities across the country and won prizes at both the Pan-American Exposition of 1901 and the Panama-Pacific exhibition of 1915.[8] Members' embroideries were sold to summer tourists, at Arts and Crafts exhibitions, and through correspondence; many of their projects were custom orders for country houses and mansions. It was their success that prompted the founding of the Deerfield Society of Arts and Crafts, makers of baskets, rugs, furniture, and jewelry (see no. 63).

CZ and GM

1. Max West noted in "The Revival of Handicrafts in America" (*Bulletin of the Bureau of Labor* 9 [November 1904], p. 1613) that many of these were purchased from Berea College in Kentucky and from weavers in Georgia and Vermont and that some of the finer grades were imported from abroad.

2. "Women and Their Work: The Deerfield Society of Blue and White Needlework: Craft of Colonial Women Revived – Unique Organization," *Evening Post*, August 11, 1897, p. 5.

3. "Arts and Crafts at Deerfield," *Springfield Daily Republican*, September 5, 1899.

4. Mary Emily Curtis, "The Crafts of Deerfield," *New Ideas Women's Magazine*, n.d. (Pocumtuck Valley Memorial Association, Deerfield Town Papers, Box 5-VII). There were thirty-one makers listed in the business papers of the Society for 1901.

5. The Society closed in 1926, when Miss Miller's failing health and Miss Whiting's failing eyesight would no longer permit them to review the work satisfactorily and confer this insignia of fine craftsmanship. See Margery Burnham Howe, *Deerfield Embroidery* (New York: Charles Scribner's Sons, 1976, p. 35).

6. Ibid. p. 23.

7. Margery Howe, speech at Essex (Pocumtuck Valley Memorial Association, Deerfield Town Papers, Box 5-VII).

8. The Society received a silver medal for color and design in 1901 and a gold medal in 1915. See Howe 1976, p. 23.

62

Joined chest, ca. 1901
Makers: Dr. Edwin C. Thorn (1874-1920) and Caleb Allen (1861-1927), both from Deerfield, Massachusetts
Carver: Dr. Edwin C. Thorn
Blacksmith: Cornelius Kelly (1874-1954), Deerfield, Massachusetts
Oak and pine with wrought-iron hinges, zinc lining
H: 36 in. W: 47 in. D: 20 in.
Historic Deerfield, Inc., Deerfield, Massachusetts. Gift of Dr. Preston Bassett

A prosperous Connecticut River Valley farming community settled in the late seventeenth century, and site of the famed French and Indian Massacre of 1704, Deerfield inspired a sense of historical consciousness in its residents from an early date. In 1870 George Sheldon organized there one of the nation's first historical societies – the Pocumtuck Valley Memorial Association – which opened one of the first museums in the country ten years later. In the 1880s, "believing in a more intimate acquaintance with our ancestors as men and women, realizing and protesting against the intensely material tendencies of American life . . .,"[1] the town hosted the Deerfield Summer School of History and Romance.

The three men who made this chest – Edwin Thorn (a doctor), Caleb Allen (a farmer),[2] and Cornelius Kelly (a blacksmith) – were all active members of the Deerfield Society of Arts and Crafts, organized in 1899 and later known as the Deerfield Industries.[3] Its amateur members made weavings, photographs, rugs, baskets, wrought iron, jewelry, and furniture. Unlike the Society of Blue and White Needlework (see nos. 60 and 61), in which two women designed and oversaw the majority of work executed by a limited group, the Deerfield Industries encouraged independent activity by a broader membership.[4]

The stylized tulips, leaves, diamonds, and central "knurled wheel" carved on this object resemble those on chests made in Hadley and Hatfield, Massachusetts, between 1690 and 1720. Except for its drawer, hardware, lack of initials, and zinc lining, the chest is very close to an early-eighteenth-century example attributed to Ichabod Allis (1647-1747) of Hatfield on view at the Memorial Hall Museum in Deerfield.[5] Thought to have been completed in 1901, it occupied the place of honor in front of the

62

63
Rag rug, 1905-1910
Arts and Crafts Society, Hingham,
Massachusetts
Plain weave (cotton warp, cut-fabric weft)
L: (of warp) 130 in. W: (of weft; three loom
widths sewn together) 9 ft.
Hingham Historical Society, Hingham,
Massachusetts

Distinctive for their weft – cut strips of fabric –
woven rag rugs were among the practical articles produced when handweaving was revived
and became a popular craft. Although worn-out
fabric was historically used as weft, Arts and
Crafts weavers often cut up new material in
order to control the pattern and avoid a hit-or-
miss look; the warp was almost invariably commercially produced cotton. Bypassing the original intention of re-using every scrap of old
fabric, the rag rug became typical of the Arts
and Crafts romanticizing of the past.

One of the first crafts undertaken by members of the Hingham society[1] (see no. 57), rag
rugs were intended, as a rule, not for the living
room or dining room but instead for the bedroom, piazza, and bathroom.[2] They were usually about five feet in length and one loom
width (about three feet), and were used as
occasional or accent rugs. This example – a
room-sized rug with separate loom widths
sewn together – is uncommonly large. It is remarkable also for the skill evident in the weaving: the red, white, blue, and brown bands
repeat at such regular intervals that it was possible to sew lengths together side by side and
have the bands of color run across the width of
the finished rug. The secondary pattern of the
warp – alternate stripes of brown and cream
cotton yarn – is overpowered visually by the
"rags" of the weft.

GM

1. Susan Willard, "The Hingham Society of Arts and
Crafts" in *Hingham* (Hingham: Old Colony Chapter,
Daughters of the American Revolution, 1911), pp. 120-
121.

2. Mabel Tuke Priestman pointed out that rag rugs
could withstand hard wear and could be washed
many times. See "Weaving as an Occupation for Women," *American Homes and Gardens* 2 (April 1906), p. 250.

chimney at the Deerfield Industries exhibition
that summer and was heralded by the local
press as "a beautiful specimen of true craft."[6]
The chest was sold as soon as it was exhibited
and prompted several other orders, one of
them from Great Britain.[7]

CZ

1. "The Deerfield Summer School of History and
Romance," 1886-1891 (brochures in the Pocumtuck
Valley Memorial Association Library, Deerfield).

2. Dr. Thorn and Caleb Allen made a number of other
furnishings. Thorn exhibited a splint-bottomed chair
and small square stand at the Deerfield Industries
exhibition in 1901 and a dressing table at the exhibition in 1905; Allen exhibited a hanging smoker's cabinet at the 1901 exhibition. See "In Deerfield's Home
Week: The Home Arts of the Old Street," *Springfield
Daily Republican* July 30, 1901; "Arts and Crafts at Deerfield: Yearly Show of Industries," *Springfield Daily Republican,* July 11, 1905.

3. Thorn and Kelly served on the board of directors of
the Society in 1901 and 1902 and Thorn was the
"Director of Furniture" in 1903.

4. Many women and a few men were involved in the
Deerfield Industries. Between 1902 and 1917 there
were 106 members and 33 associate members, the
average number of members at any time being from
45 to 50. In contrast, the Blue and White Needlework
Society grew from four members at its founding in
1896, to 25 members in 1899 and 31 to 34 members in
1901; it probably never grew any larger.

5. Pocumtuck Valley Memorial Association no.
MR216. The eighteenth-century chest is illustrated in
Madeline Yale Wynne, "Brides and Bridal Chests,"
House Beautiful 6 (September 1899), p. 163; the Thorn,
Allen, and Kelly chest appears in Sylvester Baxter,
"The Movement for Village Industries," *Handicraft* 1
(October 1902), p. 145.

6. *Springfield Daily Republican,* July 30, 1901.

7. Baxter 1902, p. 154.

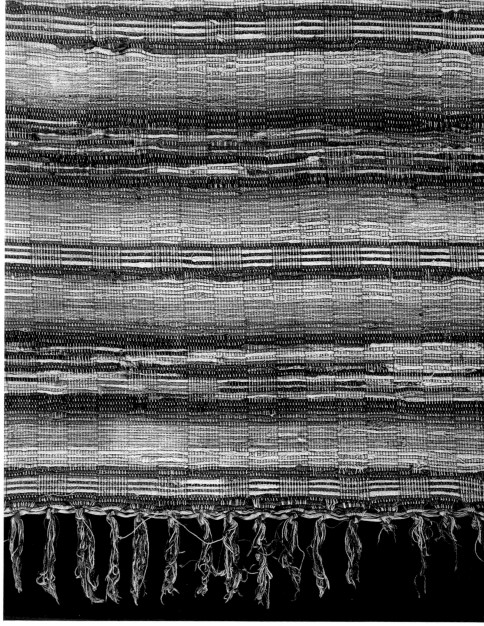

63

64

Settee, 1927
Designer: Wallace Nutting (1861-1941)
Maker: Wallace Nutting Period Furniture,
Framingham, Massachusetts (1917-ca. 1941)
Maple, oak, and white pine
H: 42¾ in. W: 49½ in. D: 17¾ in.
Marks: branded *Wallace Nutting* (under seat)
Labels: *No. 565 Date: 927; John A.V. Davies, M.D.,
Farmington, Conn.* (under seat)
Museum of Fine Arts, Boston. Gift of Mr. and
Mrs. Frederick C. Dumaine and Mr. James G.
Hinkle. 1985.47

Wallace Nutting was a leading figure of the
colonial revival in the 1920s. Once a minister in
the Congregational Church, he became an avid
lecturer, writer, collector, and producer of colonial objects. In addition to many articles, he
wrote more than twenty books in his lifetime,
including *Antique Treasury, Furniture of the Pilgrim
Century*, and *Windsor Handbook*. He also owned
and operated the Wallace Nutting Chain of Colonial Houses, his own restorations furnished
with antiques and open to the public for an
admission fee of twenty-five cents. Some of the
rooms in these houses were sets for sentimental photographs depicting colonial interiors and
the New England landscape. According to Nutting, it was this photography business that supported his furniture reproduction industry.

Claiming that "no style has been evolved that
can bear comparison side by side, for a moment, with the old styles," Nutting began reproducing and "improving upon" period furniture in the late teens.[1] Over the course of the
next twenty or more years, he oversaw the
construction of more than 1,000 furniture
forms, based on his own collection.[2] Nutting's
workshop of some twenty-five "men of character" produced block-fronts, court cupboards,
and windsor chairs, made with the intention of
reforming twentieth-century taste. All forms
were crafted following Nutting's own Ten Shop
Commandments, based on the truisms of John
Ruskin and William Morris. Among them were:
"If the work can be better done by hand do it
that way," and "Let nothing leave your hands till
you are proud of the work."[3] Nutting also
wrote: "We love the earliest American forms
because they embody the strength and beauty
in the character of the leaders of the American
settlement . . . . We carry on their spirit by
imitating their work."[4]

Nutting's early reproductions were of oak

64

furniture of the seventeenth century, country pieces from the eighteenth, and windsor chairs, which he thought to be a colonial form and preferred for their pure structure and lack of superfluous ornament. In a catalogue of 1918, Nutting boasted that his examination of hundreds of windsors and ownership of more than one hundred of the finest examples, had qualified him to produce them.[5] This example, called "The Supreme Windsor Double Chair," [6] has bulbous turned legs and arm supports and finely carved knuckle-molded handholds and scrolls on the comb. Its varnished finish is unusual; as a rule, eighteenth- and early-nineteenth-century windsors were painted (com-

monly in green and also in black, red, and yellow, and other colors) in order to disguise the variety of woods underneath. The settee has an oak crest, a white pine seat, and maple legs, arms, and spindles (traditionally the spindles would have been made of hickory or ash).

CZ

1. Other companies were producing copies or "improvements" on colonial furniture forms before Nutting. The *Cabinetmaker and Upholsterer* reported in March of 1884, that "The manufacture of antiques has become a modern industry .... The popular taste is supplied and the craze continues." The Stickleys and many others made these "antiques" before turning to the Mission style. Nutting is significant for his crusade

to put good furniture back into the American home in the 1920s and 1930s and for the fine quality of his reproductions.

2. For more information about Nutting, see William L. Dulaney, "Wallace Nutting: Collector and Entrepreneur," *Winterthur Portfolio* 13 (1979), pp. 47-60.

3. Introduction by John Crosbee Freeman in *Wallace Nutting Period Furniture* (n.d.), republished by the American Life Foundation & Study Institute, Watkins Glen, New York, 1969.

4. Ibid.

5. *Wallace Nutting Windsors: Correct Windsor Furniture,* (Saugus, Mass.: Wallace Nutting, 1918).

6. This is the designation given in *Wallace Nutting Period Furniture. Wallace Nutting Windsors: Correct Windsor Furniture* (1918) noted that form no. 565 is the same as no. 503 – "the comb-back courting chair" – but has six legs.

65

Tea set, 1920 and 1927
Designer: George Christian Gebelein (1878-1945) after Paul Revere II (1735-1818)
Maker: Gebelein Silversmiths, Boston (1909 to present)[1]
Silver and ebony
Teapot – H: 6 in. W: 12 in. D: 3¾ in. Wt: (gross) 21 oz., 13 dwt.
Teapot tray – H: 15/16 in. W: 6⅜ in. D: 5¾ in. Wt: 9 oz., 3 dwt.
Sugar bowl – H: 3⅝ in. W: 7½ in. D: 3 in. Wt: 8 oz., 5 dwt.
Cream pitcher – H: 3½ in. W: 7 in. D: 2⅝ in. Wt: 8 oz., 16 dwt.
Waste bowl – H: 3¼ in. W: 4⅛ in. D: 2 ¾ in. Wt: 6 oz., 6 dwt.
Marks: struck incuse *GEBELEIN* (in cut-corner rectangle) / *STERLING* / *Boston*
Gebelein Silversmiths, East Arlington, Vermont

The production of handcrafted silver in the colonial-revival style came about as a result of late-nineteenth-century patriotic sentiment combined with the Arts and Crafts movement's interest in pre-industrial craft methods and indigenous styles. The Boston Society of Arts and Crafts 1899 exhibition included a dual display of contemporary and old arts and crafts, an early indication of its conservative practice of judging new designs with standards set by past examples. Indeed, the Fogg Art Museum's director, Charles H. Moore, declared in 1902: "If he [the craftsman] thinks too much of design, and strives for novelty, he will surely go wrong.

There is little need for original design in the forms of most objects of use. The best shapes for utensils and household furniture were evolved long ago. . . . For the form of a spoon, a bowl, or a pitcher, better models already exist than any others that the most clever designer can invent."[2] The case for using historical objects to instruct designers would be championed repeatedly by American design schools and museums for the next generation.

No craftsman of the handicraft era surpassed George C. Gebelein in knowlege and love for America's early silver. In 1893, at age fourteen, Gebelein began a three-year apprenticeship with the prestigious Boston silver manufacturers Goodnow & Jenks. Well versed in both hand- and machine-production methods, he gained further journeyman experience at Tiffany & Company and William B. Durgin and Company. In 1903, embracing the reform movement, he joined the Handicraft Shop (see nos. 135 and 136), where he soon distinguished himself with prizes, commissions, pupils, and more technically difficult assignments. In 1909, with the aid of his pupil David Mason Little, Gebelein opened his own shop.

This tea service is one of Gebelein's numerous reproductions and interpretations of silver by Paul Revere, the most venerated silversmith of America's colonial past. Both craftsman and patriot, Revere symbolized the ideals – integrity, hard work, and individual achievement – that characterized the colonial revival's romantic view of the American past. Therefore, when the first display of early American crafts in an art museum took place in 1906 (the Museum of Fine Arts exhibition "Early American Silver") 65 of the 330 examples were works by Revere, among them his "Sons of Liberty" bowl.

Gebelein shop records reveal that the teapot of the present set was made to order in 1920 after "a Paul Revere original"; seven years later the same client ordered the sugar bowl, cream pitcher, waste bowl, and teapot tray. Although the form of the accessories derives from the teapot rather than from Revere's own shapes for these pieces, the waste bowl does recall an actual Revere fluted tea caddy.[3] The set is identical to or may be the one illustrated in Scribner's Magazine in 1927, bearing the caption "George C. Gebelein, a master craftsman in silver work, received permission from the Boston Museum to make an exact reproduction of a teapot by Paul Revere, and from it construct an entire service."[4] It is possible that the text refers to a

65

coffeepot made for Jonathan Hunnewell in 1796;[5] the two are very close in size and weight with the most significant difference being the proportion of their bodies. The Gebelin teapot is three-eighths of an inch greater in length, which increases the volume and makes the flutes fatter. Differences are also evident in the engraving. Whereas in the original, hanging tassels were looped realistically over pendant cords, the tassels in the 1920 version merely butt against the cords. Revere's cord-and-tassel engraving is clumsy when it continues over contours of the spout and handle socket; Gebelein wisely omitted it in these areas. Although still lacking the life and dynamism of the original, the 1927 accessories capture better the rhythm of Revere's flutes and reveal in their engraving greater understanding of the tassel ornament.

WSB

1. Shop records reveal that the 1927 pieces (all but the teapot) were fabricated by Paul Logel, William Edmund Lawrie, George Fairburn, Frank Parsons, and Arthur Gebelein; cast handles were obtained from Goodnow & Jenks, where they were made by P. Charles Machon.

2. Charles H. Moore, "Modern Artistic Handicraft," *Atlantic Monthly* 90 (November 1902), pp. 674-679.

3. See Martha Gandy Fales, *Early American Silver for the Cautious Collector* (New York: Funk & Wagnalls, 1970), p. 30.

4. "The Fifth Avenue Section of Scribner's," *Scribner's Magazine* 81 (January 1927), advertising supplement p. 21, ill.

5. Although the two are not identical, such duplication would have been well within Gebelein's technical expertise. See Kathryn C. Buhler, *American Silver 1655-1825, in the Museum of Fine Arts Boston* (Boston: Museum of Fine Arts, 1972), vol. 2, p. 456, ill.

66

Boston Society of Arts and Crafts: "Her silver is costly for it takes her somewhat longer to do her work than for a man and she is inclined to make a greater charge than do others."[4]

The present bowl, which was probably meant for salad or fruit, was adapted from two-handled paneled brandy bowls made in New York in the early eighteenth century. The colonial bowls usually had six panels rather than the eight seen here, and featured S-curve opposing handles often ornamented with caryatids. Whereas panels on the early bowls tend to be apple-shaped and echo the scrolled handles, Miss Pratt employed concentric panels with straight tops and sides that trace the bowl's contours. Possibly in response to colonial examples she used one of the panels to frame a monogram. Also reminiscent of early silver are the ornamental bosses, grouped in threes, that appear in the interstices between the rounded bottom and the circular foot.

WSB

1. See, for example, the Little Gallery's advertisement in *Town & Country* 83 (December 15, 1928), p. 85.

2. Obituary, *Santa Barbara News Press* (September 22, 1978).

3. After she retired Miss Pratt reflected, "...I think the long, long, apprenticeship is discouraging....Most women sign up for about 20 lessons and give it up." See Jenny Perry, "Woman Silversmith Continues to Learn," *Santa Barbara News Press* (July 4, 1967).

4. "Photos of Various Crafts, with comments and Notices from other organizations" (ca. 1939 bound scrapbook in the archives of the Society of Arts and Crafts, Boston). The report was based on field notes by Robert Hurley for an economic study of handicrafts for the American Handicrafts Council.

66
Bowl, ca. 1930
Katherine Pratt (1891-1978), Boston
Silver
H: 3⅜ in. Diam: 8⁹⁄₁₆ in. Wt: 25 oz., 16 dwt.
Inscription: engraved *A.L.W.*(on exterior)
Marks: struck incuse *PRATT / STERLING*
The Museum of Fine Arts, Houston. Museum purchase with funds provided by the Museum Collectors. 82.64

For bringing superb craftsmanship to a large body of work produced over a lifetime, Katherine Pratt was America's foremost woman silversmith. After graduating in 1914 from the Boston Museum School, she apprenticed under George C. Gebelein (see no. 65). Miss Pratt was an elder member of Boston's second generation of handicraft silversmiths that included Alfred Swanson and K. Edwin Leinonen (nos. 67 and 135). The group received their training following the first World War, prior to the advent of modernistic decorative styles in the late

1920s, and continued the conservative design of the previous generation; after 1925 they supplemented their styles with designs based on those of the Danish silversmith Georg Jensen. From about 1917 Miss Pratt shared bench space at the Handicraft Shop, where she combined her design skills with technical mastery learned under rigorous Gebelein tutelage. By the late 1920s she was competing with the older, all-male generation whose work dominated the silver retailed by the Boston Society of Arts and Crafts and the Little Gallery of New York City.[1] In 1931 the Society elected her a Medalist craftsman, and six years later her work received a gold medal at the Paris Exposition.[2]

The physical stamina needed to forge silver holloware of substantial size, coupled with the long – usually seven-year – apprenticeship, discouraged most women from silversmithing.[3] That Miss Pratt's extraordinary achievement did not come easily is suggested further by the report of Humphrey J. Emery, Secretary of the

67
Sandwich tray, 1929
Frans J.R. Gyllenberg (b. 1883) and Alfred Henry Swanson (b. 1899), Boston
Silver
H: 1⅝ in. W: (including handles) 14¼ in. Diam: 8⅜ in. Wt: 14 oz., 12 dwt.
Inscription: engraved P^B C / 1929
Marks: struck incuse cipher *F.J.R.G. / A.H.S. / STERLING/ 592*
Museum of Fine Arts, Boston. Gift of Mrs. Irvin Taube in memory of Ann Murphy Holmes. 1985.56

Colonial was the most popular of the revival styles that dominated interior decoration in

America after World War I. Exact reproductions abounded, but equally common were forms adapted from past styles to new functions. The handles of this sandwich tray derive from the "keyhole" handles on porringers made in America between 1740 and 1800.[1] Their open-work design provided insulation from the heat of the contents. Gyllenberg and Swanson, however, incorporated only the style and not the insulating function when they adapted them to sandwich trays, a popular form at the time. And whereas early porringer handles were cast, those of the present example were sawed and saw-pierced from stacks of sheet silver. They are larger and more grandly ornamental than is typical on other contemporary examples.

The Gyllenberg and Swanson partnership at the Handicraft Shop (see no. 136) was formed about 1926. In the late 1920s their reproductions of a Revere tankard and bowl in the Boston Museum of Fine Arts were commended by the city's Society of Arts and Crafts and were widely publicized through articles and advertisements as well as exhibitions;[2] their well-crafted silver, in alternately simple, fluted, or colonial-revival style, contributed significantly to the Society's sales. Although Gyllenberg and Swanson, like other silversmiths, suffered disruptions from the economic conditions of the 1930s,[3] they were still producing silver actively as late as 1946.

WSB

1. The term "keyhole" refers–not very aptly–to the handle's central tear-shape piercing. Colonial porringers usually had single rather than paired handles.

2. "Exhibitions," *Bulletin of the Society of Arts & Crafts* (Boston) 10 (October 1926), unpaged, ill.; "The Society of Arts and Crafts, Boston," *American Magazine of Art* 17 (October 1926), pp. 543-544, ill.; "Silversmiths," *Boston Transcript* (October 22, 1926), p. 28, col. 4; *Tricentennial Exhibition of the Society of Arts & Crafts* (Boston: Museum of Fine Arts, 1927), p. 8; advertisement, Society of Arts & Crafts (Boston), *House Beautiful* 64 (August 1928), p. 117, ill.; "Silver Shown at Little Gallery," *Art News* 26 (April 21, 1928), p. 12.

3. According to annotations made in 1935 to the records of consigners organized by craft type in the archives of the Boston Society of Arts and Crafts, "Since the depression they have both been working in a garage in Dedham [a Boston suburb] . . . [they] are anxious to get back to [their] silver work but [there is] no demand for it and they are too much stock ahead . . . ."

67

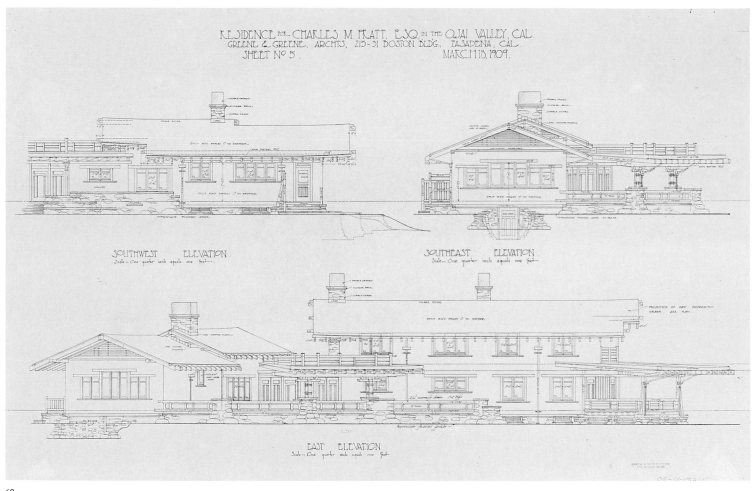

68

68 and 69

Elevation and first-floor plans for Charles M. Pratt house, "Casa Barranca," Ojai, California (1330 North Foothill), 1909
Architects: Greene & Greene (Charles Sumner Greene [1868-1957] and Henry Mather Greene [1870-1954])
Ink on linen
24 x 38 in.
Greene and Greene Library, The Gamble House, University of Southern California

(For biographical information about Greene and Greene, see introduction to nos. 222-225.)

Greene and Greene's Charles M. Pratt house in the Ojai Valley illustrates the rustic origins of

some portions of the American Arts and Crafts. Ojai Valley was a farming community that became popular as a winter home for wealthy easterners such as Pratt. A shareholder in a local land company that owned the Foothills Hotel, he and his wife used the resort for formal entertaining.[1] Consequently, their home could be more informal and, indeed, the house the brothers Greene designed perfectly expresses a casual lifestyle; rooms are loosely organized around a series of interlocking diagonals. Sited at the head of a valley with a view of the foothills, the house has terraces, pergolas, and sleeping porches opening off all major rooms. From a distance, the house appears to be com-

posed of three different structures built over time. The unpretentious bungalow is one obvious source, but given the Greenes's penchant for looking at the local vernacular, one might suspect that they took their inspiration from ranch cabins and extended them.[2]

On the entrance elevation a low terrace of boulders and bricks creates an organic, undulating form. A tremendous pile of stream-rounded boulders containing a chimney and fireplace pushes up one corner and through the thin roof. The building crouches low in the landscape, presenting a shaggy image with its cedar shakes and protruding rafters; yet, up close is revealed an intricacy of finely wrought

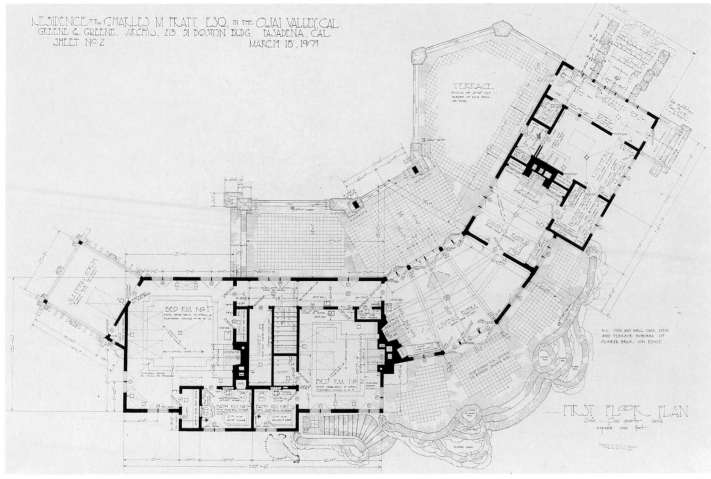

69

details, such as rounded beam ends sheathed in copper. Entry is at the lowest point in the building's mass, and the front doors open immediately into the low-ceilinged living room. The rear wall of this room is a bank of doors that opens onto a terrace and porch. The diagonal feature of the plan creates a splayed or radiating form, which becomes one of the organizing ornamental motifs. Large ceiling beams in the living room converge on the patio, and brickwork and wood trim have a splayed motif. Against the informal entrance and the rambling plan, the dining room – the highest space in the house and nearly a perfect twelve-foot-square cube – is very formal. The

elevations are divided almost equally between a lower section of openings – fireplace, built-in cabinets, doors to the exterior and to other rooms, all done in white cedar paneling – and the upper area of large redwood panels, framed in linear strips with cloud-lift undulations across the top. A large wood-and-glass chandelier with insets of jade by Tiffany, suspended from a molded wooden bracket at the center of the ceiling, unites the two areas.

The detailed work of the Greenes obviously depended upon highly skilled and committed workmen. This they had in Peter Hall, a Swedish-born craftsman and builder whose carpenters executed most of the Greenes's

houses and furniture. The intricate nature of the work meant that a considerable part of the design was done on the job and Charles Greene, in particular, was known to work along with the builders, selecting stones, carving a prototypical detail, or changing the plans. The brothers' drawings, while highly detailed, are remarkable for what was left to be developed on the site. Since only one watercolor presentation drawing exists (for another project), it is assumed that the Greenes depended upon their prior work to persuade prospective clients.

RGW

1. Basic information about the Pratt house – which seems not to have been published in the magazines –

can be found in Randell L. Makinson, *Greene & Greene, Architecture as a Fine Art* (Salt Lake City: Peregrine Smith, 1977), pp. 168-173. For furniture, see idem, *Greene and Greene, Furniture and Related Designs* (Salt Lake City: Peregrine Smith, 1979), pp. 94-98.

2. Charles Sumner Greene, "Bungalows," *Western Architect* 12 (July 1908), pp. 3-5, pls. 1-9. See also "California's Contribution to a National Architecture: Its Significance and Beauty as Shown in the Work of Greene and Greene, Architects," *Craftsman* 22 (August 1912), p. 2534.

70

Desk for Adelaide Tichenor house, Long Beach, California, 1904
Designers: Charles Sumner Greene (1868-1957) and Henry Mather Greene (1870-1954)
Ash
H: 50 in. W: 31 in. D: 16 in.
Private Collection

When the California architects Charles and Henry Greene (see nos. 222-225) began in 1901 to follow the designs of Gustav Stickley (see nos. 101-103), they limited themselves initially to the house structure only. For the furnishings of these moderate-sized bungalows, the Greenes relied upon the client's existing possessions and upon commercially available items that were aesthetically compatible with their Craftsman interiors. Within a few years, however, they were inspired by the idea of integrated domestic environments – structure, furnishings, and landscapes designed by the same hand – a philosophy engendered by *The Craftsman* and by a series of articles by Will Bradley published in *Ladies' Home Journal*.[1]

The Greenes's first attempts to design an entire house inside and out were two commissions in Long Beach in 1904, one for Jennie Reeve and the other for Adelaide Tichenor. The latter featured a large, very sophisticated U plan, open interior, and explicitly expressed joinery. Adelaide Tichenor played an important role in the Greenes's design maturity. She was an active client who encouraged the brothers to complete everything to their satisfaction and was willing to pay for such services. Sympathetic to her architects' needs to absorb other ongoing developments, she recommended that Charles Greene visit the Louisiana Purchase Exposition in 1904 to see the varied types of wood used for furniture and interior finish and to acquaint himself with east coast Arts and Crafts ceramics and glass. The leaded glass and light-

70

ing fixtures of the Tichenor house demonstrate the influence of this trip; other designs reveal motifs of Oriental art, an interest the Greenes shared with Mrs. Tichenor.[2]

The desk from the Tichenor house illustrates well the Greenes's mature Craftsman style and hints at the future direction of their work. Its conception – two strong vertical sides with a fall-front writing surface over a doored cabinet – is borrowed directly from an example illustrated in the first issue of *The Craftsman*. The slightly raised decorative butterfly splines are also adapted from Stickley and the applied battens on the cabinet doors and on the front of the writing surface suggest his influence.[3] The Greenes transformed the Stickley prototype slightly by executing it in ash rather than oak, by using a sawed profile (a Craftsman decorative technique) to create the Oriental lift motif in the drawer pull and along the front face of the sides, by using brass-headed screws to express construction (even though they are mainly decorative, applied to the decorative battens to provide visual rhythm to the façade), and by adding a false back to the desk compartment – opened by pushing the panel through open mortises concealed by the rearmost vertical strip along the side.

ESC

1. They furnished their first true Arts and Crafts bungalow, the James A Culbertson house (1902) in Pasadena, with Gustav Stickley furniture. See Randall Makinson, *Greene & Greene: Architecture as a Fine Art* (Santa Barbara: Peregrine Smith, 1977), pp. 60-69; and idem, *Greene & Greene: Furniture and Related Designs* (Santa Barbara: Peregrine Smith, 1979), pp. 15-19.

2. Makinson 1977, pp. 82-85, 94-99; and Makinson 1979, pp. 22-33.

3. Examples of the desk form, butterfly splines, and large strap hardware can be seen on the furniture illustrated in the early issues of *The Craftsman*. For reproductions of these illustrations, see Robert Edwards and Stephen Gray, eds., *Collected Works of Gustav Stickley* (New York: Turn of the Century Editions, 1981), pp. 22, 28, 33, and 38.

71

Side chair, 1894- ca. 1920s
Joseph P. McHugh and Co., New York (1884 -ca. 1920s)
Oak with rush seat
H: 36 in. W: 17 in. D: 17¾ in.
Collection of Robert Edwards

71

"Mission" furniture was first introduced to large audiences at the Pan-American Exposition of 1901.[1] While Joseph McHugh, Gustav Stickley, and George Clingman of the Tobey Furniture Company all claimed to have introduced the style,[2] the best evidence indicates that it was McHugh who first marketed it in 1894. Soon after one A. Page Brown, a prominent San Francisco architect, sent McHugh a chair replicating the simple lines of those in the old Spanish missions of California, McHugh made a few chairs and a settee.[3] Following their quick sale at his "Popular Shop," he manufactured a wide variety of furniture of the same substantial construction.[4]

McHugh's furniture was praised in 1901 as epitomizing an effort to capture the simplicity and harmony preached by William Morris and his followers. Instead of looking to European sources, however, "McHugh . . . , as befits an American craftsman, has sought inspiration from the old Spanish missionaries whose courage and self-sacrifice form so distinguished a chapter in the history of American coloniza-

tion." The handcrafted furniture of native ash and oak and stained with natural colorings was commended "because any attempt to develop a taste for simplicity in life is to be commended, especially in a society like the new Americas, where enormous wealth makes for a luxurious and complicated social existence."[5]

The name "Mission" came to connote a cause as well: to upgrade public taste. Contemporary opinion held that "Furniture of the mission type is a lesson in the value of form apart from added ornament and it is the first lesson in the philosophy of good furniture. It is a furniture with a mission, and that mission is to teach that the first laws of furniture making should be good material, true proportion and honest workmanship."[6]

CZ

1. At least one contemporary historian has argued that there was no distinctive Mission style in furniture as there could be said to be in architecture. George Wharton James (see *In and Out of the Old Missions* [New York: Grosset and Dunlap, 1905], pp. 342-343) maintained that the furniture of the missions – pulpits, confessionals, lecterns, and candelabra – consisted of whatever objects were most easily obtainable and were not homogeneous in style.

2. McHugh argued that he introduced the style as early as 1894; Gustav Stickley, in 1898; and George Clingman at Tobey, by 1900. Clingman noted in a letter to Leopold Stickley on May 26, 1911, that he had first designed and executed Mission furniture in 1885 while working for John A. Colby and Sons. (This letter is in the Stickley Collection, Archives and Library, Henry Ford Museum & Greenfield Village, Dearborn, Michigan.)

3. Brown used replicas of the Mission chair at the Swedenborgian church in San Francisco.

4. Joseph Adams, "Mission Furniture," *Truth*, May 1902, p. 96. There are several accounts regarding the way in which McHugh first began selling and producing this furniture. See also *American Cabinetmaker and Upholsterer*, June 19, 1915; "More About Mission Furniture," *Upholstery Dealer and Decorative Furnisher* 30 (July 1915), p. 50; *Arts and Decoration* 15 (July 1921), pp. 167-168.

5. "American Studio Talk," *International Studio* 12 (February 1901), pp. xxiv - xxv.

6. "The Mission Furniture: Its Design and Execution," *Upholstery Dealer and Decorative Furnisher* 1 (October 1901), p. 53.

72 (color plate, p. 18)
*Presentation drawing: aerial perspective for expansion of
Glenwood Mission Inn, Riverside California (between
Main and Orange and 6th and 7th Streets [undergoing
restoration currently]), 1908*
Architect: Arthur Burnett Benton (1857-1927)
Renderer: William A. Sharp (1864-1944)
Ink and watercolor on paper
16 x 44 in.
"The Mission Inn" National Historic Landmark
Hotel, Riverside, California

William Benton, the architect of the Mission
Inn, concluded his lengthy article of 1911 on
the California Missions and their modern-day
impact upon architecture with the following:
"The commercial value of the Missions is
nearly as great as their architectural and historic
worth. They advertise the State as nothing else
can. They give a touch of that romantic and
historical atmosphere . . . . Our railroads, [in]
whom we have no better advertisers, have their
Mission folders, Mission stations and now their
Mission Cars. Our Mission hotels are proving
how great the demand by tourists for something 'different.' "[1]
The Mission Inn was primarily a resort hotel,
an architectural attraction for easterners seeking California's winter sun and climate. As an
image of California's past, it succeeded so well
that many visitors thought it was the real thing
and not a fantasy re-creation – a reconstruction
of a romantic past that never existed – by its
owner, Frank A. Miller (1857-1935) and his
architects, principally Arthur Benton. It stands
as a testament to the Arts and Crafts search for
native roots.
The Glenwood Mission Inn – its formal
name – dates back to a two-story adobe room-
ing house that Frank Miller's parents built in
1875. Additions were made to the house almost
immediately and Frank Miller became the
owner in 1880. By the 1890s southern California
had acquired a reputation as a winter resort and
Miller sought funds – unsuccessfully at first – to
increase the size of his hotel. By 1902 he had
the financing and Arthur Benton began to design a new complex that would occupy him, off
and on, for the remainder of his life. Having
begun as a railroad architect, Benton came in
contact with Charles Fletcher Lummis in the
1890s and developed an interest in the old
Missions. He was a noted spokesman for the
preservation and restoration of the Missions
and used Mission motifs in his work.[2]

The rendering of 1908 by William Sharp, an
English-born artist who worked for Benton,
was probably a publicity piece, illustrating the
hotel as taking up about half a city block. In
time Miller's hotel would encompass the entire
block and a portion of an adjoining block,
which was linked by an arched bridge. Benton's
expansion, shown in the 1908 rendering, was
for a U-shaped four-story hotel with an arcade
across one end. Bell-laden towers and pedi-
ments broke the skyline of the structure while
palm trees, the original "Old Adobe" section,
and a low campanile occupied the courtyard.
The interior was furnished with "Mission"-
styled furniture produced by Stickley and by
the Mission Inn.[3] Miller, a compulsive collector, frequently traveled abroad, bringing back
Spanish, Italian, Aztec, and other artifacts with
which he encrusted the building. He also
brought in other architects: Myron Hunt (1868-
1952) and Elmer Grey (1871-1962) – former
midwestern Arts and Crafts designers – and G.
Stanley Wilson (1879-1958), an English-born
Riverside architect, extended the structure
from 1913 into the early 1930s. From the Mission courtyard the inn grew to include a Spanish cloister, a Romanesque tower, a court of the
bells, and even a rooftop Japanese garden.
Much of the construction was of poured-in-
place concrete and in several of the 1910s and
1920s additions, marks on the concrete from
wood forms used in pouring the walls were left
exposed to add texture.

RGW

1. Arthur Burnett Benton, "The California Mission and
its Influence upon Pacific Coast Architecture," *Architect
and Engineer* 24 (February 1911), p. 75. See also idem,
"Architecture for the Southwest," *Land of Sunshine* 4
(February 1896), pp. 126-130.

2. Basic background can be found in Esther Klotz, *The
Mission Inn: Its History and Artifacts* (2nd ed., Riverside:
Rubidoux Printing, 1982).

3. Some of the furniture is stamped "Mission Inn."

73
*Presentation drawing: elevations, perspective, and plans
for George Kautz house, La Jolla, California (7753
Draper Avenue), 1913*
Architect: Irving John Gill (1870-1936)
Ink on linen
23 x 19 in.
Architectural Drawing Collection, University of
California, Santa Barbara

Irving Gill worked first for a local architect in
Syracuse, New York, where he was born, and
then, between 1890 and 1938, in Chicago for
Dankmar Adler and Louis Sullivan. (A fellow
employee at that time was Frank Lloyd Wright.)
For health reasons, Gill went to San Diego at the
age of twenty-three and set up architectural
practice. His work during the next thirteen
years explored a number of directions, including English cottage, Beaux Arts classicism, Prairie School, bungalow, and Mission styles.[1]
Around 1907 Gill – during a brief partnership
with Frank Mead, with whom he had worked
earlier – created what is known as his mature
style.[2] Drawing on the Missions, the Prairie
School, and the idea of the Mediterranean, Gill
evolved a simple, austere idiom of white cubic
forms. The anti-ornamental architectural image
was related to Gill's passionate interest in construction. In his concrete buildings, all extrane-
ous features – interior moldings, exterior trim,
and ornament – were eliminated.
The flat two-dimensional treatment of forms
in the rendering shows similarities to Japanese
prints and also to the office style of Frank Lloyd
Wright. (The foliage, in particular, resembles
that of Marion Mahony [see nos. 85, 197]).
While Wright and Gill had known each other
and Gill had used some elements of the Prairie
style in his earlier work, the connection may be
even more direct, since Wright's eldest son,
Frank Lloyd Wright, Jr. (known as Lloyd Wright
[1890-1978]), was in Gill's office in 1912 and
1913.[3]

RGW

1. Essential background information about Gill is in
Esther McCoy, *Five California Architects* (New York: Rein-
hold Book Co., 1960), pp. 59-101; idem, *Irving Gill* (Los
Angeles: Los Angeles County Museum, 1958); Helen
McElfresh Ferris, "Irving John Gill: San Diego Archi-
tect," *Journal of San Diego History* 17 (Fall 1979), pp. 1-19;
Bruce Kamerling, "Irving Gill: The Artist as Architect,"
Journal of San Diego History 25 (Spring 1979), pp. 151-200.

2. I am indebted to Bruce Kamerling for help with the
Mead connection.

3. David Gebhard, *Lloyd Wright* (Santa Barbara: Art Galleries, University of California, 1971), pp. 18-19. Because of their mutually competitive natures, the relationship of Gill and the senior Frank Lloyd Wright was
strained. Wright's willingness to allow his son to come
under another architect's influence, however, indicates a measure of respect. See also Frank Lloyd
Wright, *An Autobiography* (New York: Horizon Press,
1977), p. 249.

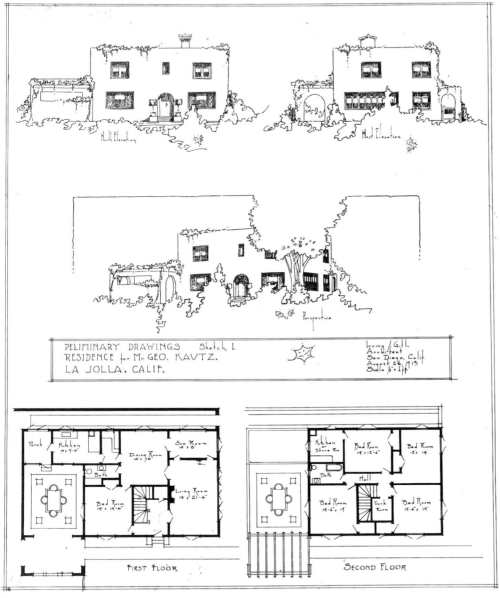

PELIMINARY DRAWINGS   Sketch. I.
RESIDENCE for Mr GEO. KAUTZ.
LA JOLLA, CALIF.

Irving J. Gill.
Architect
San Diego, Calif.
August 26, 1913
Scale ¼"=1ft.

FIRST FLOOR   SECOND FLOOR

73

74

Presentation drawing for A.H. Sweet house, San Diego (435 West Spruce Street), 1913-1914
Architect: Mead and Requa (Frank Mead [1865-1940]; Richard Requa [1881-1941])
Renderer: C. C. Mesick (signed C. C.)
Ink over pencil on tracing paper
15⅜ x 28 in.
Inscription: 1913 (lower right)
San Diego Historical Society, San Diego. Bequest of Elaine Sweet, 1985

The architecture situation in San Diego at the turn of the century bore similarities to musical chairs, with architects frequently changing offices and partners. Both Frank Mead and Richard Requa had worked in the office of Gill and Hebbard, perhaps as early as 1903. In 1907 Irving Gill and W.S. Hebbard had a falling out and Mead became Gill's partner for about seven months. During this brief partnership, several of the seminal "anti-ornament" houses that became Gill's trademark were designed.[1]

Frank Mead undoubtedly helped to push Gill toward the simple cubic idiom, yet his own architecture remains more romantic and historically based. Born in New Jersey, Mead had some training as an architect and worked in Philadelphia with an Arts and Crafts architect, Bart Keane, before traveling to North Africa to photograph Bedouin villages. On the same trip he also toured the Mediterranean, studying the native architecture. Mead was in San Diego by 1903 and his interest in vernacular structures was transferred to American Indian buildings. In 1908 his concern over the government's treatment of Indians led to his becoming their advocate and then to the position of superintendent of several reservations. When he returned to San Diego around 1912, he established with Requa a partnership that lasted until 1923 and resulted in a number of important structures such as the second Baily house in La Jolla in the Pueblo style (Gill and Mead had done the first in 1907) and a new town center for Ojai in the Spanish Mission style.[2]

About Richard Requa less is known; he was apparently very interested in construction and in the partnership with Mead his concern was structural, while Mead acted as the chief designer. Requa's interest in concrete construction, because of its perceived similarity to adobe, was essential to the developing San Diego idiom and he tried – as did Gill – to promote concrete as the appropriate material. A book of his from 1926, filled with photographs

74

of Spanish and Mediterranean architecture to be rendered in concrete, claimed that it was "a logical and appropriate style of architecture for California and the Pacific Southwest."[3]

The A.H. Sweet house is a softened and more exotic version of the idiom Gill had developed. The concrete structure was actually two separate buildings linked by a terrace, arcades, and a passageway. Placed on top of a hill with a view of the bay and the Pacific beyond, the site and forms were exploited to create a massing similar to both Mediterranean villages and Pueblos; detailing is minimal on both exterior and interior.[4] Beneath the simple red tile roofs – Mission or Spanish in origin – greater complexity takes shape; Mead, in contrast to the understatement of Gill, exploited diversity: rooms, bay windows, and different chimneys emerge from the mass. A high street wall provides a barrier to the outside world, similar to the houses of the Mediterranean, and at the same time creates a rich spatial sequence of steps and turns to bring the visitor to the main house. The pen-and-ink rendering was by C.C. Mesick, who did drawings for a number of San Diego architects during this period.

RGW

1. I am indebted to Bruce Kamerling, Curator of the San Diego Historical Society, for information about Mead, Requa, and Gill.

2. See "Frank Mead" in Timothy J. Anderson, Eudorah M. Moore, and Robert W. Winter, *California Design 90* (Pasadena: California Design Publications, 1974), p. 133.

3. Richard S. Requa, *Architectural Details: Spain and the Mediterranean* (Los Angeles: Monolith Portland Cement [1926]).

4. The Sweet house is pictured in an advertisement by the Bay State Brick and Concrete Company, *House Beautiful* 50 (September 1924), p. 273.

75
Architectural drawing for Hillside Clubhouse, Berkeley, California [destroyed in 1923], 1906
Presentation sketch
Architect: Bernard Maybeck (1862-1957)
Pencil and pastel on Kraft paper
31 x 24½ in.
College of Environmental Design, Documents Collection, University of California, Berkeley

Bernard Maybeck's diverse architecture reflects both his interests and background. The son of a cabinetmaker who had immigrated from Germany to New York City, Maybeck attended the Ecole des Beaux-Arts in Paris from 1881 to 1886. He returned to New York and worked for Carrère and Hastings on the Ponce de Leon Hotel in St. Augustine, which, while Beaux Arts in concept, is related stylistically to the indigenous Spanish culture of Florida. After a brief attempt at a practice in Kansas City, Maybeck arrived in the Bay area in the mid-1890s and worked for A. Page Brown on the Swedenborgian Church in San Francisco (fig. 28, p. 124). His mature architectural expression encompassed a number of idioms, from using Gothic, Swiss, and Japanese in a totally unconventional manner for the First Church of Christ, Scientist, in Berkeley (1910) to a personalized classicism for the Palace of Fine Arts at the Panama-Pacific International Exposition (1915). He was an individualist both in architecture and in personal demeanor, wearing artistic clothing – smocks and sashes – and affecting a flowing beard.[1]

In 1902 his friend Charles Keeler had formed the Hillside Club with the purpose – as the minutes read – of fostering "civic patriotism among the residents of Berkeley, to encourage parks, playgrounds, planting of trees, beautifying streets and gardens," in order to make Berkeley "an educational, art and home center."[2] Maybeck acted as the architectural conscience for the club, preparing in 1907 a small leaflet on hillside residential architecture and serving as the club's president two years later. When the members decided to erect a clubhouse for meetings, lectures, and musical and theatrical events, Maybeck became the architect.[3]

The clubhouse had its origins in the small resort and suburban casinos erected in the late 1870s and 1880s by eastern architects such as McKim, Mead, and White.[4] Maybeck, however, departed from the Queen Anne and colonial revival of the east and created his own regional expression. An innovative system of columns, trusses, girders, and joists created the framework for an open and luminous space in which voices seemed to float. Redwood was used exclusively as shingle and shake covering and as structural members on both the inside and the outside. Some of the covering was placed on top of skeletal structure and at places inside, creating a dynamic interplay of planes. The exterior with the tall roof had the appearance of

76

75

a small Gothic church, and, in fact, Maybeck's plans show a nave, an aisle or gallery, a transept, and, in place of the pulpit, a large fireplace.

RGW

1. Jacomena Maybeck, *Maybeck, The Family View* (Berkeley: Berkeley Architectural Heritage Association, 1980).

2. Hillside Club, "Minutes of Meeting," August 23, 1902, Bancroft Library, University of California, Berkeley.

3. Photographs of the club are rare; basic background and plans are in Kenneth Cardwell, *Bernard Maybeck: Artisan, Architect, Artist* (Santa Barbara: Peregrine Smith, 1977), pp. 90-91. See also Dimitri Shipounoff, "Introduction" in Charles Keeler, *The Simple Home* (Santa Barbara: Peregrine Smith, 1979 [first published in 1904]), p. xxxix.

4. Richard Guy Wilson, "From Informality to Pomposity: The Resort Casino in the Later 19th Century," *Victorian Resorts and Hotels* (Philadelphia: Victorian Society, 1982), pp. 109-116.

76

Presentation drawing: Locust Street elevation for Leon L. Roos house, San Francisco (3500 Jackson Street [extended by Maybeck in 1926]), 1909
Architect: Bernard Maybeck (1862-1957)
Pencil and colored pencil on illustration board
26 x 36⅛ in.
College of Environmental Design, Documents Collection, University of California, Berkeley

The townhouse Maybeck designed for the San Francisco department store owner Leon L. Roos in the Presidio Heights section illustrates his extraordinary ability to synthesize complex and difficult images. The building has a variety of parts, each of which is expressed in the complicated elevation. Exterior volumes mirror different interior space: a vertical living room in the high-roofed rear structure and the piling up of horizontal layers in the front. Maybeck preferred not to bring visitors directly into the house but to lead them along the side at least halfway. In the Roos dwelling, the entry is in between the two major volumes. Covered by a

77

grid of timbers on the exterior, the house has little relation to the Anglophiliac Tudoresque style; instead, the variety of beams and forms recalls European townscapes, an effect Maybeck would have thought appropriate for a hillside in San Francisco.[1]

RGW

1. Kenneth Cardwell, *Bernard Maybeck, Artisan, Architect, Artist* (Santa Barbara: Peregrine Smith, 1977), pp. 108-111; and Esther McCoy, *Five California Architects* (New York: Reinhold Book Company, 1960), pp. 15-17. Concerning Maybeck and the European townscape analogy, see Richard Longstreth, *On the Edge of the World, Four Architects in San Francisco at the Turn of the Century* (New York and Cambridge: Architectural History Foundation and MIT Press, 1983), pp. 331-332 and passim.

77

Presentation perspective for Henry W. Taylor house, Berkeley, 1908-1910 (destroyed)
Architect: Louis Christian Mullgardt (1866-1942)
Tempera on illustration board
13¾ x 26⅛ in.
Inscription: L.C. *Mullgardt '08* (lower right in pencil)
Collection of Mr. and Mrs. Robert Judson Clark

Born into a German immigrant family in Missouri, Louis Christian Mullgardt worked in Saint Louis, in Boston with Shepley, Rutan and Coolidge, and (after a brief period at Harvard) in Chicago, where he participated in the World's Columbian Exposition. He then formed a partnership in Saint Louis and worked in London for two years before arriving in San Francisco in 1905. His Bay Area houses of the period 1905-1910 were unlike anything he had done before or would do later; they demonstrate an Oriental-Occidental confrontation mixed with references to the Secession and the Prairie School. The Taylor house reflected a knowledge of Voysey and English rough-cast houses, the California missions, and Mediterranean architecture. Its hilltop perch and spreading mass along with extensive terracing recalled to some a Tibetan monastery. Standing apart from the landscape, the building complemented it in a manner similar to Frank Lloyd Wright's Los Angeles work of the 1920s. The light-colored rough-cast stucco walls and the red mosaic tile roof united what would have been a disparate composition. Mullgardt's work has a strange eclectic quality, suggesting that Californians could adopt almost any image and transform it into a regional idiom.[1]

RGW

1. Robert Judson Clark, *Louis Christian Mullgardt, 1866-1942* (Santa Barbara: Art Galleries, University of California, 1966); and idem, in *California Design 1910*, Timothy Anderson, Eudorah M. Moore, and Robert W. Winter, eds. (Pasadena: California Design, 1974), pp. 134-135.

78

78
Bowl, 1928-1932
Clemens Friedell (1872-1963), Pasadena
Silver
H: 3¾ in. Diam: (of rim) 9³⁄₁₆ in. Wt: 13 oz., 13 dwt.
Inscription: embossed *ATJ*
Marks: FRIEDELL / PASADENA STERLING
Collection of Francis E. Condit Ballard, M.D.

Soon after his birth in New Orleans, Clemens Friedell was taken by his parents to their native Vienna, where he grew up and underwent a traditional seven-year apprenticeship under a Viennese silversmith.[1] Friedell returned to America in 1892 and worked for a San Antonio jeweler. In 1901 he found a position with Gorham (see no. 43) and stayed for several years – ornamenting their Martelé wares and executing a lavish dinner service for the industrialist Charles M. Schwab – until the financial panic of 1907, when Gorham was forced to lay off many silversmiths. Following an unsuccessful year operating a shop with two other silversmiths in Providence, Friedell returned briefly to San Antonio before moving to California in 1909 and establishing a workshop in Pasadena the following year. In the decades prior to World War I, Pasadena was California's unrivaled inland winter retreat for rich midwestern

and eastern families. Their annual visits nurtured Friedell's growing handicraft business. Among his important clients were Adolphus Busch, Mrs. Phoebe Hearst (mother of William Randolph Hearst), and the David B. Gamble family of Cincinnati. Friedell's greatest pride was the 107-piece handwrought sterling silver dinner set chased with orange blossoms that he made in 1912 for the Los Angeles brewer R.E. Maier. At the California Pacific Exposition in 1915, he is said to have shown a huge punch bowl, several portraits in silver, a coffee set, and other pieces for which he won a gold medal. A year later Friedell's advertisement in *Out West Magazine* proclaimed him as a silver craftsman of handwrought tableware, trophies from special designs, and portrait reliefs.[2] For many years he designed and made trophies awarded at Pasadena's annual Tournament of Roses, and in 1928 he was shown in *The Pasadena Spectator* holding a huge example with an announcement of his new location at 626 East Colorado Street.[3]

Floral ornament and forms frequently characterize Friedell's silverware. They show his familiarity with Gorham designs and may even stem from his Austrian training, but it is notably Pasadena's abundant flowers that inspired the designs and ornament in his work, such as this bowl depicting a California poppy.[4] Clemens Friedell, Jr., recalled that the design was introduced about 1930 and for some customers was made with a gilt interior whose color underscored the poppy theme.[5] A silver goblet in the form of a stemmed poppy was made for the Gamble family, and other flowers found in Pasadena's lush gardens – such as roses, hibiscus, fuchsias, and orchids – were also design sources for bowls, boxes, and stemmed flower-petal tazzas and compotes. Assisted by one man who hand-fabricated the shop's silver holloware, Friedell had close to a thousand chasing tools for ornamenting it. Whereas monograms are usually engraved or applied on Arts and Crafts movement silver, embossed ones – such as the modest example on this bowl's supporting foot – were a Friedell specialty.

WSB

1. See Leonard Kreidt, "A Life Lined with Silver," *Pasadena Star News* (February 12, 1960); obituary in *Pasadena Star News* (October 22, 1963). The author is indebted to Milo M. Naeve for these sources.
2. *Out West Magazine* 43 (February 1916), p. 111.
3. *Pasadena Spectator* 1 (April 1928), p. 10, ill.

4. A coffee service, doubtless one of Friedell's earlier Pasadena works (on loan from June and Robert A. Berliner at the Los Angeles County Museum of Art, L.84.10.1-3), follows the design of a coffee set for Charles M. Schwab and is lavishly embellished with floral ornamentation characteristic of Gorham's Martelé silver. The Schwab set is shown in *Country Life in America* 52 (May 1927), p 32.
5. Clemens Friedell, Jr., to author, telephone interview, June 5, 1986. Interestingly, a small dish produced by Gorham in 1927 also took the form of a poppy; see, for example, one in the Art Institute of Chicago (1980.204).

79
Desk, ca. 1910-1915
Designer: Arthur (1860-1945) and Lucia Kleinhans (1870-1955) Mathews
Maker: The Furniture Shop, San Francisco (1906-1920)
Painted wood
H: 59 in. W: 48 in. D: 20 in.
Collection of The Oakland Museum (72.15). Gift of Mrs. Margaret R. Kleinhans

80 (colorplate, p. 20)
Rectangular box with lid,[1] 1929
Designer: Lucia Kleinhans Mathews (1870-1955)
Painted wood
H: 5 in. W: 16 in. D: 12 in.
Marks: signed *Lucia Mathews* 1929 (on lid, bottom center)
Collection of The Oakland Museum (66.196.42a). Gift of Concours d'Antiques, Art Guild, The Oakland Museum Association

Arthur Mathews trained in the classical tradition at the Académie Julian in Paris, where he studied in 1885 and 1886 with Gustave Boulanger and Jules Lefebvre. He returned to San Francisco, his home since boyhood, to paint murals and standard canvases of classical studies set in the local landscape; he also taught at the Art League and the California School of Design, where he became director in 1890.

With his wife Lucia, Mathews founded The Furniture Shop in 1906.[2] He and his assistant, Thomas A. McGlynn, designed most of its furniture and decorative accessories: entire suites and individual objects for wealthy homes and commercial establishments in the San Francisco Bay area.[3] Lucia Mathews assisted with designing and supervised color choices and carving. She also decorated richly painted and gilded acces-

sories, including boxes, candlesticks, lamps, and frames. Maintaining a work force of twenty to fifty craftsmen, The Furniture Shop carried out major commissions for the interior of the Savings Union Bank in 1911 and for the Masonic Temple in 1913.

Active members of their community, Arthur and Lucia Mathews helped to launch a small magazine, *Philopolis*, devoted to the ethical and artistic aspects of rebuilding California after the earthquake; from 1906 to 1916 they provided illustrations and stories for it. Mathews and his managerial assistant and financier, John Zeile, also founded the Philopolis Press to publish limited editions of collections of essays and poems and works on art or California subjects.

CZ

1. The box, decorated with California poppies and scenic landscapes, was probably a commissioned piece.

2. For more information about the Mathewses and The Furniture Shop, see Harvey L. Jones, *Masterpieces of the California Decorative Style* (2nd ed., Layton, Utah: Gibbs M. Smith, 1985).

3. The shop produced high-quality furniture in a variety of styles, including pieces demonstrating Chinese and Vienna Secessionist influence.

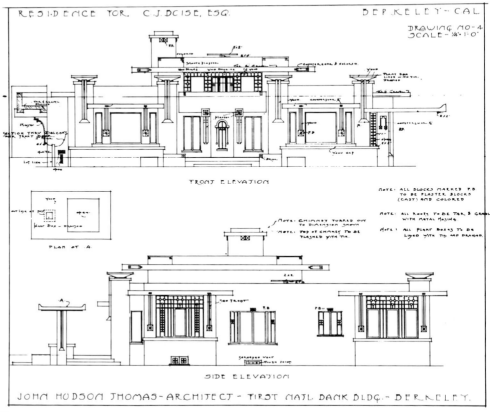

81

81 and 82

Working drawings: front and side elevation and plan for C.J. Boise house, Berkeley, ca. 1912 (destroyed)
Architect: John Hudson Thomas (1875-1945)
Ink on linen
15½ x 19 in.
Architectural Drawing Collection, University of California, Santa Barbara

Bay Area architects seemed compelled to adopt disparate imagery in order to create a unique regional idiom. One excellent example is John Hudson Thomas, who designed in a number of modes reflecting such styles as the California bungalow, the Mission, the southwestern pueblos, the Swiss cottage, the Prairie School, outrageously tall gabled Gothic cottages reminiscent of the cookie house in Hansel and Gretel, and the Vienna Secession. Thomas had been an undergraduate at Yale University and then studied architecture at the University of California, Berkeley. His architectural practice was almost totally devoted to residential design.

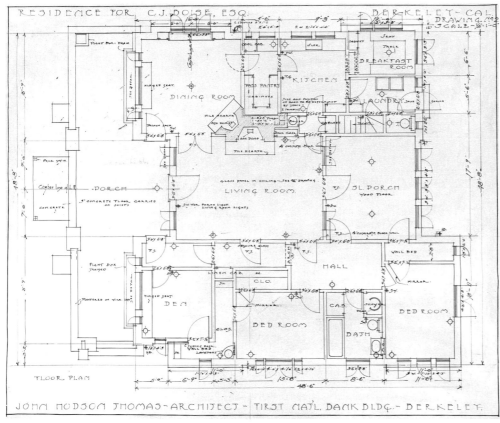

82

83

Door panel, for Samuel Stern House, Chicago, 1885
Designer: Louis H. Sullivan (1856-1924)
Carved butternut
H: 27¾ in. W: 28 in. D: 2¼ in.
Louis H. Sullivan Architectural Ornament Collection, Southern Illinois University at Edwardsville. 66.69

Louis Sullivan, an associate and, from 1880 until 1895, partner of the architect Dankmar Adler, subsequently headed his own firm and became recognized as the dean of the influential Chicago school of architecture. As the midwestern city strove to recover from the great fire of 1871, its architects sought to establish aesthetically and theoretically viable alternatives to the eastern neoclassical academic tradition. In the last two decades of the nineteenth century, these Chicago designers formed several organizations to facilitate the interchange of ideas and to protest the stronghold of the architectural establishments, especially the American Institute of Architects. The fresh energy of Sullivan's projects and the principles of his writings inspired and guided their efforts to redefine American architecture along simpler lines that did not rely on historicism.[1]

Sullivan was much more than an architect concerned with correct styles and the historic implications of ornament and orders. Well versed in Ralph Waldo Emerson and Walt Whitman, captivated by Richard Wagner, and always eager to discuss ideas and abstractions, Sullivan was a late-nineteenth-century romantic who searched for the meaning of art in architecture. To him, an artful structure was achieved by using technology and materials to draw beauty from an inherent inner spirit, transcending the inorganic. At first, Sullivan borrowed from Owen Jones's principles of abstraction and from the Romanesque massing and conventionalized Gothicism of Henry Hobson Richardson and Frank Furness,[2] but he soon grew dissatisfied with abstraction and began to explore more naturalistic motifs. He transformed the compositional ideas of Furness and Richardson by energizing them with his own personal interest in botany, particularly the principles of plant morphology set forth by Asa Gray in the *School and Field Book of Botany*.[3]

By the early 1890s, Sullivan sought another way to express his interest in organic ornament and inorganic structure by combining luxurious foliage with striking geometric patterns

Around 1910 Thomas became aware of the Secessionists, probably through the *International Studio* periodical; consequently, their ornament and some forms appeared in his work for several years. His Boise house – markedly horizontal, its substantial piers capped by broad planters combined with elaborate vertical ornament – merges the Prairie School with mid-European and Secessionist detail. The house was one story in height – very much in the bungalow vogue – and compactly planned with zones for sleeping, study, living, and eating. The living-room space located at the center was raised and lighted by clerestory windows. Thomas had a unique talent for overscaling certain elements, such as the violently exaggerated piers that served to unite his composition.[1]

RGW

1. Thomas Gordon Smith, "John Hudson Thomas and the Progressive Spirit in Architecture, 1910-1920" (master's thesis, University of California, Berkeley, 1975). See also Sally Woodbridge, ed., *Bay Area Houses* (New York: Oxford University Press, 1976).

83

(see no. 84). This carved panel, originally a part of the front door for the Samuel Stern house, demonstrates his emphasis upon natural representation in ornament. The organic qualities of the blossoming buds, sinuous fern-like tendrils, and crisp leaves distinguish the panel from the more stylized decoration designed by Frank Furness and executed by Daniel Pabst.[4] The quality of the woodworking is attributable to the skills of craftsmen in Chicago at this time. Many furniture-making firms employed Europeans, especially Germans, who had acquired a solid foundation in traditional joinery and carving techniques prior to immigrating. In fact, much of the flowering of both architecture and decorative arts in Chicago can be traced to the close interaction between progressive designers and skilled immigrant craftsmen.[5]

ESC

1. For the Chicago school, see H. Allen Brooks, *The Prairie School: Frank Lloyd Wright and His Midwest Contemporaries* (New York: W. W. Norton, 1976), pp. 3-44; and Brian Spencer, ed., *The Prairie School Tradition* (Milwaukee: Prairie Archives of the Milwaukee Art Center, 1979), pp. 8-11.

2. While studying architecture at the Massachusetts Institute of Technology for a year, Sullivan was awed by Richardson's buildings; he worked in Furness's office for several months in 1873.

3. Sullivan demonstrated his philosophical approach to art and discussed his early influences in *Autobiography of an Idea* (New York, 1924; reprinted, New York: Dover Publications, 1956). I am indebted to Tim Samuelson of the Commission on Chicago Landmarks for

sharing his views on Sullivan. Published works that chart Sullivan's stylistic development include Linda L. Chapman, Joyce Jackson, and David C. Huntley, *Louis H. Sullivan Architectural Ornament Collection* (Edwardsville: Southern Illinois University, 1981); and Paul Sprague, *The Drawings of Louis Henry Sullivan* (Princeton: Princeton University Press, 1979).

4. The work of Furness and Pabst is discussed by David Hanks and Page Talbott in "Daniel Pabst–Philadelphia Cabinetmaker," *Philadelphia Museum of Art Bulletin* 73, no. 316 (April 1977), pp. 5-24.

5. Sharon Darling, *Chicago Furniture: Art, Craft, & Industry, 1833-1983* (New York: W. W. Norton, 1984), pp. 53, 197-205. Studies that demonstrate the importance of designer-craftsman collaboration include Darling 1984; idem, *Chicago Ceramics & Glass: An Illustrated History from 1871 to 1933* (Chicago Historical Society, 1979), especially pp. 97-204; and Cheryl Robertson et al., *George M. Niedecken, Interior Architect* (Milwaukee: Milwaukee Art Museum, 1981).

84 (color plate, p. 19)
Architectural ornament for the Henry Babson residence, Riverside, Illinois, 1908-1909 (destroyed)
Designers: Louis H. Sullivan (1856-1924) and George G. Elmslie (1871-1952)
Modeler: probably Kristian Schneider
Maker: Northwestern Terra Cotta Company (1884-1956), Chicago
Molded and modeled terra-cotta with yellow, green, blue, and purple glazes
H: 25½ in. W: 23 in. D: 8¾ in.
Collection of David Norris

This architectural ornament demonstrates the continuing development of Louis Sullivan's design career in the early 1890s. His new emphasis upon combining naturalistic foliage with geometric elements, a synthesis of his earlier explorations, coincided with a shift in production. Beginning at about this time, Sullivan concentrated more upon larger business buildings and designed fewer residences. He also pursued a career as an architectural theoretician, presenting major talks for the Chicago Architectural Club and the Architectural League of America and publishing a collection of architectural essays entitled *Kindergarten Chats*. Although many designers took his principles in different directions, Sullivan's early projects and writings influenced both his contemporaries and the next generation of Chicago architects.[1]

Irascible, fond of alcohol, and perhaps a manic-depressive, Sullivan experienced considerable difficulty in establishing his own practice

after Dankmar Adler (1844-1900) dissolved their partnership in 1895.[2] Sullivan's brusque behavior alienated prospective clients; thus, he devoted less time to design and more to philosophical discussion and debate on architecture. For the actual projects his office received, he worked closely with two chief draftsmen: George Grant Elmslie (his main assistant from 1893 until 1909) and Parker Berry (who held that position from 1909 until 1917). On projects such as the Henry Babson House, the National Farmer's Bank in Owatonna, Minnesota (1906-1908), and the People's Savings and Loan Association Bank in Sydney, Ohio (1916-1918), these younger men developed and gave form to Sullivan's ideas and initial drawings.[3]

The Henry Babson house was one of the finest residential designs produced by the Sullivan office. Sited broadside to the road, the long structure featured maroon tapestry brick walls, cantilevered balconies and porches opening off the second floor, and a low, broad roof. Inset polychrome terra-cotta panels, used as accent marks upon the façade of the dark mass, provided color. The Babson ornament reveals the work of two distinct hands. Whereas Sullivan sought to interweave the natural and geometric and to represent the floral motifs in flowing S-curves that radiate from the center, the detailing of this panel manifests Elmslie's contribution.[4] His crisp leafage is quite distinct from the geometric banding, the background is more crowded than in other Sullivan examples, and the basic organizational framework is a neoclassical lyre. An abstracted oval seed pod within the lyre provides the vertical axis of symmetry over which foliate designs were reflected.[5] Located as punctuation points beneath a bank of stained-glass windows that lie in the shadow of an overhanging second-story room (a typical Sullivan convention), this ornament and its mate illustrate Sullivan's polychromy theory. To simulate the highlights of direct light he painted the high areas of the relief with yellow-gold tones. Against the contrasting red hues of the brick surrounding the ornaments are the varied greens of the foliage and the purple and blue background, evoking the effect of the sky. The way the colors play off one another creates a sense of glimmering natural light.[6]

For a number of reasons, terra-cotta was the perfect material of choice for Sullivan. It possessed significant cost and weight advantage over iron and stone; its hollow mass allowed foundations and walls to be lighter, thereby facilitating construction and reducing costs, especially for tall buildings; its manufacture in models permitted efficient production; its durability ensured the retention of details longer than other materials; and its plastic qualities allowed a more naturalistic appearance. This ornament was made by the Northwestern Terra Cotta Company, which Sullivan patronized almost exclusively from about 1880 to 1918.

At Northwestern, Sullivan enjoyed a particularly close artistic relationship with the modeler Kristian Schneider, a Norwegian-born sculptor, whom he trained to interpret and execute his drawings exactly. Sullivan's faith in Schneider's work was so complete that when the sculptor left Northwestern in 1906, Sullivan continued to hire him for the next twelve years to provide architectural models for Sullivan designs in iron, plaster, and terra-cotta. It was probably Schneider who made the models for the Babson terra-cottas and submitted them to the Northwestern firm for manufacture. When Schneider began work for the American Terra Cotta and Ceramic Company in 1918, Sullivan switched his allegiance also. From then on, Sullivan, as well as Elmslie, used the American Terra Cotta and Ceramic Company. Their shared reliance on Schneider helps to explain the difficulty of separating ornaments designed by Sullivan from that by Elmslie while working for Sullivan.[7]

ESC

1. Linda L. Chapman, Joyce Jackson, and David C. Huntley, *Louis H. Sullivan Architectural Ornament Collection* (Edwardsville: Southern Illinois University, 1981), pp. 17-18; H. Allen Brooks, *The Prairie School: Frank Lloyd Wright and His Midwest Contemporaries* (New York: W. W. Norton, 1976), pp. 7, 22-23, and 47-58.

2. Robert Twombly, *Louis Sullivan, His Life and Work* (New York: Viking, 1986).

3. Chapman, Jackson, and Huntley 1981, p. 19; Brooks 1976, pp. 57-58, 140-141, 143-144, and 309-312; and Paul Sprague, "The National Farmer's Bank, Owatonna, Minnesota," *Prairie School Review* 4, no. 2 (1967), pp. 7-10.

4. W. R. Hasbrouck, review of *Drawings for Architectural Ornament by George Grant Elmslie, 1902-1936*, in *Prairie School Review* 6, no. 3 (1969), p. 27; and *Prairie School Architecture in Minnesota, Iowa, Wisconsin* (St. Paul: Minnesota Museum of Art, 1982), pp. 69-79.

5. See Sullivan's diagram in *A System of Architectural Ornament* (New York: Press of the American Institute of Architects, 1924), pl. 2.

6. Sullivan 1924 and Lauren S. Weingarden, "The Colors of Nature: Louis Sullivan's Architectural Poly-

chromy and Nineteenth-Century Color Theory," *Winterthur Portfolio* 20, no. 4 (Winter 1985), pp. 243-260.

7. Sharon Darling, *Chicago Ceramics & Glass: An Illustrated History from 1871 to 1933* (Chicago: Chicago Historical Society, 1979), pp. 163, 168-169, 172-185; Larry Millet, *The Curve of the Arch: The Story of Louis Sullivan's Owatonna Bank* (St. Paul: Minnesota Historical Society Press, 1985); Hasbrouck 1969, p. 27; and conversation with Tim Samuelson, May 1986.

85 (color plate, p. 18)
Presentation rendering: front perspective for Ward W. Willits house, Highland Park, Illinois (1445 Sheridan Road), 1902-1903
Architect: Frank Lloyd Wright (1867-1959)
Ink and watercolor with white tempera on brown paper
8¾ x 32½ in.
The Frank Lloyd Wright Memorial Foundation, *Taliesin West*, Scottsdale, Arizona

(For biographical information about Wright, see introduction to nos. 213-216.)

Biographers have seen in Wright's Prairie houses several consistent themes revolving around shelter, the family, and the landscape.[1] The Ward Willits house is an acknowledged masterpiece of the Prairie period.[2] Broad extended eaves and low-pitched roofs provide a sense of shelter and relate the long form to the landscape; the massive chimney and hearth pin it to the ground. Raised up on a podium, its long horizontal lines, interrupted by short verticals, are stressed. Windows are placed in banks and the glass is leaded. As a form the house is hierarchical with a prominent central block and subsidiary wings that could relate to the tripartite massing of Palladio. However, Wright undercut the usual classical balance with unequal and transparent wings composed of a porch and *porte-cochère*. The overall broad and simple geometry of the house is highlighted and then broken down by its wood trim into complex details.

Spatially the Willits house is protective, with a recessed entry halfway along the side and a complex series of reception spaces and level changes. The living room and dining spaces overlap and interpenetrate at the corners; however, a screen provides a barrier and emphasizes the particulate nature of the different activities. Typically, in a Wright house from this period, a large living-room fireplace provides one focus and the dining room's specially designed table and high-backed chairs provides

another. The family is the center and rituals are emphasized.

Ward Winfield Willits (1859-1949), a prosperous businessman, commissioned the house from Frank Lloyd Wright in late 1901 or early 1902. Working drawings were ready by June 1902 and construction began in late summer. Some interior details were not designed until 1903 and the house, complete with Wright-designed furnishings, was occupied in May 1903. The young Walter Burley Griffin (1876-1937) was in Wright's office during this period and served as intermediary between the client and architect (no. 89). In spite of some problems, Wright and Willits did become friends and toured Japan together with their wives in 1905. However Wright's later unconventional behavior apparently soured their relationship.

There exists a preliminary rendering in Wright's hand that shows the house from approximately the same perspective as the present drawing. This early rendering shows the indebtedness of the Willits design to one of Wright's *Ladies' Home Journal* houses of 1901. While many of his eye-level perspective renderings were done after construction, the presence of the early perspective view may indicate that this presentation rendering came earlier. It is assumed that Wright may have done some aspects of the drawing; however, there are details in foliage that indicate also the hand of Marion Mahony (1897-1962), who was in Wright's office (see no. 197). The same rendering with slightly changed vegetation and trees was published in a German portfolio of 1910.[3] Typically Arts and Crafts are several affectations of the rendering such as the vines spilling from planters and the scarf draped from the second-floor window.

RGW

1. Robert C. Twombly, *Frank Lloyd Wright: An Interpretive Biography* (New York: Harper & Row, 1973); Norris Kelley Smith, *Frank Lloyd Wright: A Study in Architectural Context* (Englewood Cliffs: Prentice-Hall, 1966)

2. For most of the information about the Willits house I am indebted to Mark David Linch's three-part article in *The Frank Lloyd Wright Newsletter* 2, nos. 2 (pp. 12-17) and 3 (pp. 1-5) (1979); and vol. 3, no. 1 (1980), pp. 7-11; see also Grant Carpenter Manson, *Frank Lloyd Wright to 1910, The First Golden Age* (New York: Reinhold, 1958), passim.

3. *Ausgeführte Bauten und Entwürfe von Frank Lloyd Wright* (Berlin: Ernst Wasmuth, 1910), pl. 25; see also H. Allen Brooks, "Frank Lloyd Wright and the Wasmuth Drawings," *Art Bulletin* 48 (June 1966), pp. 193-202.

86

86

Presentation drawing: perspective view for Unity Temple, Oak Park, Illinois (Lake Street at Kenilworth Avenue), 1905-1906
Architect: Frank Lloyd Wright (1867-1959)
Renderer: Marion Mahony (1871-1962)
Watercolor and sepia ink on paper
12 x 25⅛ in.
The Frank Lloyd Wright Memorial Foundation, *Taliesin West*, Scottsdale, Arizona

Perhaps the most non-traditional design associated with the American Arts and Crafts movement, Unity Temple, a Universalist church, illustrates the progressive tendencies of Frank Lloyd Wright. In contrast to the conservative Arts and Crafts designs by architects such as Cram and Goodhue (see no. 22), Wright disavowed not only the traditional forms of the church but also the spirit of handicraft and ornament. Most if not all of Unity Temple's detail was machine-made or, as C.R. Ashbee wrote: "In this building anything that savored of hand detail imitated by machinery has been rigidly excluded."[1]

The main portions of the building are of concrete – chosen because, in Wright's words,

"Concrete was cheap." He described the relation of concrete to the final form: "Why not make the wooden boxes or forms so the concrete could be cast in them as separate blocks and masses, these separate blocks and masses grouped . . . in some such way as to preserve . . . [the] desired sense of the interior space."[2]

Stylistically, Unity Temple follows Wright's Prairie School philosophy; he defended its flat roof as truthful to the purpose of worship, explaining to the church building committee that steeples were "a perversion of sentiment – sentimentality."[3]

RGW

1. C.R. Ashbee, "Man and the Machine," *House Beautiful* 28 (July 1910), p. 56.

2. Frank Lloyd Wright, *An Autobiography* (New York: Horizon Press, 1977), p. 178.

3. Ibid.

87

The House Beautiful, by William C. Gannett, 1897
Printer: Auvergne Press, River Forest, Illinois
Designer: Frank Lloyd Wright (1867-1959)
Black and red ink on white paper
13½ x 11 in. (page)
Chicago Historical Society

Frank Lloyd Wright set up an architectural office in 1893 (see nos. 213-216). His first independent commission after leaving the firm of Sullivan and Adler was for the home of a manufacturer of ornamental iron and bronze, William Herman Winslow (1857-1934), on Auvergne Place in River Forest. The golden Roman brick structure still stands today, its decorative plaster frieze emphasizing the house's horizontal lines. A River Forest neighbor of Winslow's was Chauncey L. Williams (1872-1924), partner with Irving Way in the "literary" publishing firm of Way and Williams in Chicago, who lived in a house also designed by Wright in 1895. In February of 1896 Winslow and Williams joined in the purchase of some type and a Washington press to establish the Auvergne Press. Business was conducted "first in the attic of Williams's house and, when warm

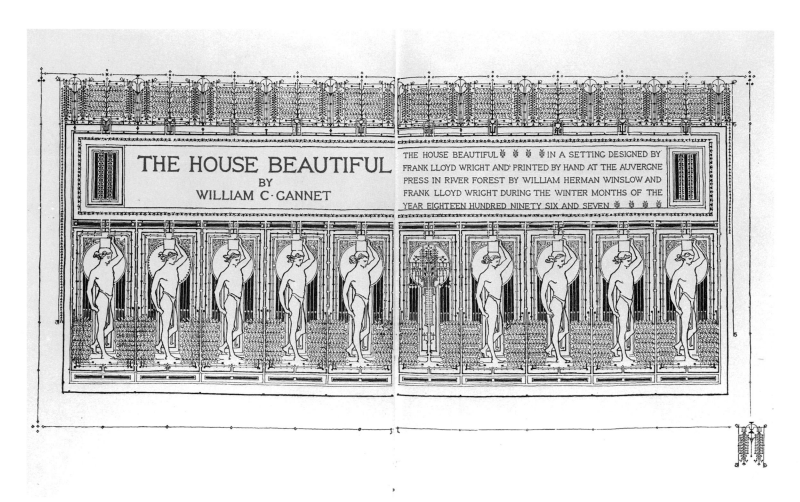

87

weather made the attic unbearable, in the basement of the Winslow house."[1] John Keats's *Eve of St. Agnes*, in an edition of 65 copies, was finished in December of 1896, with the help of Wright in presswork and design of the title page. The only other title issued by Auvergne – *The House Beautiful* by William C. Gannett – came off the press in 1897 in a much larger format and with more extensive designs.

The text itself expresses an Arts and Crafts philosophy, calling for simplicity, truthfulness, and the influence of nature, literature, and art in ornament. Wright's stylized repetitive forms reflect the music he loved and the Oriental rugs he collected;[2] being "geometric products of the

architect's T-square, triangle, and compass," they also echo his architectural background.[3] The work of William Morris is recalled in the marginal proportions, in the lavish title page, and in the double spreads of solid ornament with no text; instead of Kelmscott's medievalism, however, there are reminders of concurrent developments in British Art Nouveau. Wright's work continues to appear fresh and innovative, despite his own later condescending description of it: "an amateur feeling for a decorative pattern to harmonize with the type of the text – looking for it in the seed pods of weeds growing all about. The dried weeds were photographed and the photographs added to

the fly-leaf of the book in a little brochure. Winslow and I did the printing ourselves in the basement of the house I designed for him."[4]

The House Beautiful, printed in a limited edition, gives no feeling of publicity-seeking, despite its lavishness. The mood is of youthful idealism, exemplified by Winslow's verse on an early page:

And so we fashion the printer's serious art
And newly wed the thought with vision'd text.
A dainty trend for book and a page and pen;
And merged in strength a more completed whole.

ST

1. Joe W. Kraus, *A History of Way & Williams* (Philadelphia: Geo. S. McManus, 1984), p. 8.

2. Letter to Samuel R. Merrill, September 27, 1949, quoted in *The Turn of a Century 1885-1910* (Cambridge: Department of Printing and Graphic Arts, Houghton Library, Harvard University, 1970), p. 112.

3. Ibid., p. 112.

4. David A. Hanks, *The Decorative Designs of Frank Lloyd Wright* (New York: Dutton, 1979), pp. 175-176.

88
Rug from F. C. Bogk house, Milwaukee, 1917-1918
Designer: Frank Lloyd Wright (1867-1959)
Machine-woven cotton warp and wool (chenille) weft
L: (of warp) 142¾ in. W: (of weft) 76½ in.
Private Collection

Frank Lloyd Wright shared the Arts and Crafts conviction that a building and all the objects within it should have a unified appearance.[1] Thus, the design of each piece of furniture intended for the Bogk house, as well as the rugs, curtains, lamps, and decorative objects, contained similar motifs that, in turn, related to the building. Much of the furniture was designed and executed by George Niedecken and his brother-in-law, John Wallbridge. Their firm (founded in 1907) often collaborated on the interiors of Wright houses, and, in this case, used squares, rectangles, and long straight lines to echo the forms of the structure. While much of the Niedecken furniture had long lines of "stringing" inlay, a reference to the elongated horizontal bands of mortar in the interior, this rug – designed by Frank Lloyd Wright himself – is decorated with squares and rectangles only.

The rug was made for a short flight of three stairs between the living room and the dining room. The small squares that rose vertically when the rug was in place created a satisfying geometric pattern. Notes on the original rendering indicate a color choice of "warm gray," a description not too far from the color of the completed piece.[3]

Contrary to previous reports,[4] the rug is not hand-knotted but machine-woven with a wool chenille weft. It was executed by a commercial carpet company working on commission.

GM

1. In fact, Wright designed dresses for his wife and for Mrs. Avery Coonley and may also have designed dresses for Susan Lawrence Dana and Mrs. Frederic C.

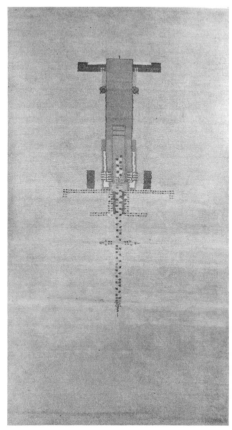

88

Robie. See David A. Hanks, *The Decorative Designs of Frank Lloyd Wright* (New York: E.P. Dutton, 1979), p. 25.

2. Communication from Terry Marvel, Prairie Archives, Milwaukee Art Museum.

3. Design published in Hanks 1979, fig. 131. The rendering is now owned by Centre Canadien d'Architecture in Montreal.

4. Hanks 1979, p. 126.

89
Presentation drawing: perspective and plans for Joshua G. Melson house, Mason City, Iowa (56 River Heights Drive), 1912-1914
Architect: Walter Burley Griffin (1876-1937)
Renderer: Marion Mahony Griffin (1871-1962)
Pen and black ink on drafting cloth
37 x 21¼ in.

Inscription: signed *Walter Burley Griffin* at lower right
Mary and Leigh Block Gallery, Northwestern University, Evanston, Illinois

Walter Burley Griffin was educated at Oak Park High School and then studied landscape gardening and architecture at the University of Illinois under Nathan C. Ricker (1843-1924). He graduated in 1899, came to Chicago, and from 1901 to 1905 worked for Frank Lloyd Wright. After a disagreement over pay, he left and set up his own practice. In 1912 Griffin won the international competition for a new capital city in Canberra, Australia, and thereafter spent most of his time abroad.[1]

While in Wright's studio, Griffin met his future wife, Marion Mahony. She was a graduate of the MIT program in architecture and became the first woman registered as an architect in the state of Illinois. Miss Mahony had worked intermittently for Wright since 1895 and was responsible for many of the beautiful and distinctive renderings that came from his office. She was in charge of Wright's commissions after he left for Europe in 1909, and she also designed several houses on her own. The exact division of the Griffins' work after their marriage in 1911 is unclear, since all of the work appears under Griffin's name alone with his signature. However, as in the case of the Melson house and Rock Crest–Rock Glen, she is known to have drawn all the renderings.[2]

The Mason City development of Rock Crest–Rock Glen in which the Melson house is located provides one of the few examples of Prairie School planning. The story is complicated, involving at least nine architects and stretching over ten years (1908-1917). In 1908 Frank Lloyd Wright obtained commissions for a bank, a hotel, and two houses – including one for Joshua Melson – in Mason City; all were built except for the Melson house. When Wright left for Europe, Melson, still seeking a house, approached Miss Mahony, who called in Griffin. They developed a scheme for a site, close to downtown, covering about eighteen acres bordering a creek with steep limestone cliffs on one side and a low rising grade on the other. A former quarry, it was used as a trash dump. The design called for roads and houses used as a boundary around a central space – a large community green – or, more properly, a prairie river landscape. Limestone ashlar, laid up rough-faced, would be a unifying element for the foundations of the houses and as terrace walls and gateposts. Seduced by Miss Mahony's enchanting oriental-style rendering with vegetation as flat planes of color (fig. 26), Melson and three other businessmen purchased the site and signed an agreement to clean it up and use it for residential purposes.[3]

Of the sixteen houses projected in the Mahony rendering eight were built. The most significant is the Melson house, which seems to have grown out of the limestone cliffs. Based on Wright's $5,000 scheme (see no. 197), although the overhanging roof is eliminated, the house was treated as an extrusion of the cliffs. Order was provided through the massive concrete mullions, voussoirs, and keystones that articulated the fenestration and openings; their form is analogous to crystalline prisms, as though the rock were exfoliating upward. The interior of the Melson house is typical of the Prairie School in a number of respects: there is a central fireplace and built-in bookcases and cabinets are located in the substantial corner piers on the main floor. Several pieces of decorative arts designed by Marion Mahony (including a library table and table scarf) repeat the triangular forms of the keystone. A spatial flow is achieved by the L-shaped living-dining room configuration and cove lighting helps to maintain continuity. But overall, the thick walls convey an oppressive air, a feeling of being closed in.

RGW

1. For Griffin see Mark L. Peisch, *The Chicago School of Architecture: Early Followers of Sullivan and Wright* (New York: Random House, 1964), chiefly devoted to Griffin despite its title; David Van Zanten, *Walter Burley Griffin: Selected Designs* (Palos Park, Ill.: Prairie School Press, 1970); James Birrell, *Walter Burley Griffin* (Brisbane, Australia: University of Queensland Press, 1964); H. Allen Brooks, *The Prairie School* (Toronto: University of Toronto Press, 1972), p. 30 and passim; and Donald Leslie Johnson, *The Architecture of Walter Burley Griffin* (Melbourne: Macmillan, 1977).

2. For Marion Mahony see David Van Zanten, "The Early Work of Marion Mahony Griffin," *Prairie School Review* 3, no. 2 (1966), pp. 5-24; Brooks 1972, p. 79 and passim.

3. Longer considerations of the Mason City development and the Melson house can be found in Richard Guy Wilson and Sidney K. Robinson, *The Prairie School in Iowa* (Ames: Iowa State University Press, 1977), pp. 10-16; Robert E. McCoy, "Rock Crest–Rock Glen: Prairie School Planning in Iowa," *Prairie School Review* 5, no. 3 (1968), pp. 5-39; and Brooks 1972, passim.

J.G.MELSON
DWELLING
MASON CITY IOWA
SCALE

90

*Presentation drawing for Harold C. Bradley bungalow,
Charles Crane estate, Woods Hole, Massachusetts, 1911-
1912*
Architects: Purcell, Feick and Elmslie (William
Gray Purcell [1880-1965], George Feick, Jr.
[1881-1945], George Grant Elmslie [1871-1952])
Renderer: William Gray Purcell
Ink on linen
32 x 48 in.
Inscription: *Purcell April 11, 1913*
Northwest Architectural Archives, University of
Minnesota, Minneapolis

Among Prairie School architects after Frank
Lloyd Wright, the Minneapolis-Chicago-based
firm of Purcell and Feick (1907-1909); later Purcell, Feick, and Elmslie (1910-1913) and then
Purcell and Elmslie (1913-1922) was the most
successful. While influenced by Wright, their
primary allegiance was to Sullivan, for whom
both Purcell and Elmslie had worked.[1]

William Gray Purcell was raised in Oak Park
and thus saw as a youth the new architecture
taking shape. He attended the Cornell University School of Architecture and then, in 1903,
spent about five months in the office of Sullivan, where he met his future partner, George
Grant Elmslie. For the next four years Purcell
traveled extensively, working with Arts and
Crafts designers in California and Seattle and
then meeting Art Nouveau designers and studying the local vernacular in Europe and Asia
Minor. George Feick, a Cornell classmate and
engineer who accompanied him, became his
partner in Minneapolis in 1907. With a facility
for public relations and the stance of a provo-
cateur in his writings, Purcell made a reputation
and saw his firm, especially with the addition of
Elmslie, become the largest Prairie School office; they oversaw more than seventy executed
commissions and innumerable unexecuted
projects.[2]

George Grant Elmslie was born in Scotland
and came to the United States in 1884. He
learned architecture first in the office of J.L.
Silsbee, where he met Wright and Maher, and
then, after 1889, in the office of Adler and
Sullivan. During Elmslie's twenty-year stay with
Sullivan, he became, in a sense, his alter ego, or
at least a pen in Sullivan's hand. Many of the
projects and buildings from the Sullivan office
after 1899 were rendered by Elmslie and in
some cases it appears that he was the major
designer. At the same time, he acted as a con-

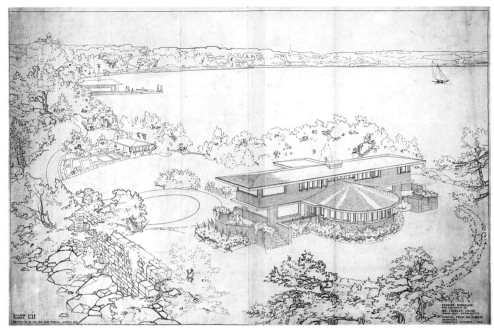

90

sultant to Purcell on occasion and when Sullivan's alcoholism made working conditions
difficult Elmslie joined Purcell and Feick in
partnership, opening a branch office in
Chicago.[3]

The Bradley house at Woods Hole is one of
several projects demonstrating the position of
Purcell and Elmslie as the successor of Louis
Sullivan's firm. So unsuccessful was a Sullivan
house built in Madison, Wisconsin, in 1910 for
Harold C. Bradley that four years later Bradley
commissioned a new house from Purcell and
Elmslie. In 1911 his father-in-law, Charles Crane,
a Chicago industrialist who had also experienced problems with buildings designed for
him by Sullivan, asked Purcell to advise on a
portable bungalow the Bradleys were considering erecting on the Crane property in Woods
Hole. Instead, Purcell proposed remodeling an
older house on the property and constructing a
large main bungalow and outbuildings consisting of a gardener's cottage, ice house, and tool
shed. The costs rose from a $600 portable bun-
galow to a new complex in excess of $30,000; as
Purcell reported: "Everyone was happy and sat-

isfied." The house was designed and built
within an amazingly short period of five
months, with Purcell and Feick on the site
for most of the summer of 1911.[4]

The open plan and the use of the term "bungalow" make it clear that the Bradley house was
intended for summer living. Sited on a spit of
land, the house was placed so that the semicircular living room – which has analogies to the
stern of a large sailing ship – commanded a
panorama of sea and shore. Certainly both in
plan and in basic form the Bradley bungalow is
Prairie School, its fireplace pinning the house to
the ground; however, the extended second
floor and voids of the porches beneath give it a
light, almost hovering appearance, and the exterior shingle covering indicates that Purcell
tried to relate it to the seaside structures (both
indigenous and of later construction) that had
so inspired architects in the area. Perhaps in no
other Prairie School work is a respect for other
regional idioms so apparent.

The rendering by Purcell was done after the
building was completed and was probably
sketched from photographs. This was a custom

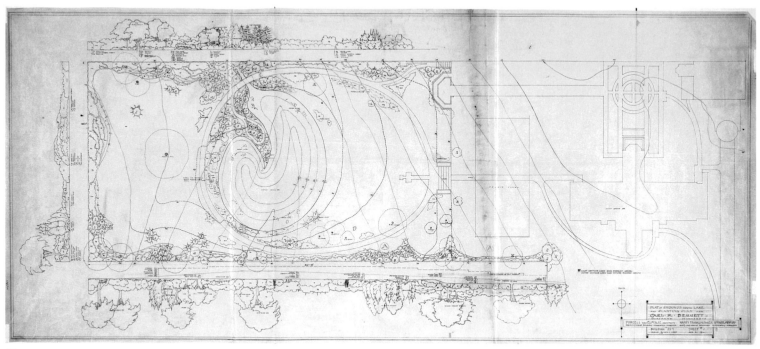

91

common in Wright's studio, wherein the drawing was useful for future sales as well as for exhibitions and publications.[5]

RGW

1. David Gebhard, "William Gray Purcell and George Grant Elmslie and the Early Progressive Movement in American Architecture from 1900 to 1920" (Ph.D. dissertation, University of Minnesota, 1957). See also reprints of Purcell and Elmslie's work from 1913 and 1915 in H. Allen Brooks, ed., *Prairie School Architecture: Studies from "The Western Architect"* (Toronto: University of Toronto Press, 1975), pp. 46-162, and the discussion in idem, *The Prairie School* (Toronto: University of Toronto Press, 1972), passim.

2. See Brooks 1975, p. xiii, for an account of Purcell's activities.

3. Letter from Elmslie to Carl Bennett, December 7, 1909 (copy in possession of Elmslie family descendants).

4. William Gray Purcell, *Parabiography* (1911), quoted in Gebhard 1957, p. 185. See also Brooks 1975, pp. 58-60.

5. H. Allen Brooks, "Frank Lloyd Wright and the Wasmuth Drawings," *Art Bulletin* 48 (June 1965), p. 193.

91

Presentation drawing: plan and planting plan for Carl K. Bennett house, Owatonna, Minnesota, 1914 (destroyed)
Architects: Purcell and Elmslie (William Gray Purcell [1880-1965] and George Grant Elmslie [1871-1952]), and Harry Franklin Baker (1872-1961)
Renderer: Laurence A. Fournier (1878-1944)
Ink on linen
27½ x 65 in.
Northwest Architectural Archives, University of Minnesota, Minneapolis

Carl K. Bennett (1868-1941) was so inspired by an article by Louis Sullivan in *The Craftsman* magazine that he commissioned the architect to design a new building for his National Farmers' Bank in Owatonna, Minnesota. The result, completed between 1906 and 1908, was Sullivan's finest building of his late career and one in which George Grant Elmslie played a major role.[1] Bennett remained in close contact with Elmslie after he formed a partnership with William Gray Purcell. Bringing to the firm at least ten commissions for houses and banks, Bennett

must rank as one of the most important promoters of the Prairie School.

A house Purcell and Elmslie designed for Bennett was never realized owing to the banker's financial reverses after World War I.[2] The landscape plan was, however; it utilized the outline of a blueprint by Sullivan executed in 1912,[3] with a garage of their own design. Purcell explained: ". . . we were especially interested in the mechanics of creative movement within bounded areas, a person's entrance to and exit from units of a plan . . . ."[4] On a generous lot measuring 44 by 135 feet a series of separate incidents were developed: a long side entrance to the house, a formal rear terrace laid out in the form of a large piece of Sullivanesque geometric ornament, a tennis court, a more informal garden with a pond, a meandering path, and a glade. Plans for the informal garden have a rough outline that also resembles a piece of Sullivan ornament. The midwestern plant types specified were probably the contribution of Harry Baker, a landscape gardener consultant.

RGW

1. When Sullivan dismissed him, Elmslie claimed in a letter to Bennett: "He did none of the work you see on your building, none whatever." (Letter dated December 7, 1909; copy in possession of Elmslie family descendants.)

2. Larry Millett, *The Curve of the Arch: The Story of Louis Sullivan's Owatonna Bank* (St. Paul: Minnesota Historical Society Press, 1985), pp. 100-111, 124-152; and Robert R. Warn, "Part II: Louis H. Sullivan, '... an air of finality,'" *Prairie School Review* 10, no. 4 (1973), pp. 7-13.

3. Bennett had commissioned a house on which Sullivan worked intermittently between 1911 and 1914. Sullivan's design was extravagantly expensive – three times the budget – but Bennett planned to erect it. Ultimately he abandoned the Sullivan design and commissioned one from Purcell and Elmslie.

4. Warn 1973, p. 12.

92

Armchair, from Merchants Bank, Winona, Minnesota, 1912
Designers: William Gray Purcell (1880-1964), George Grant Elmslie (1871-1952), and George Feick, Jr. (1881-1945)
Oak; leather, jute webbing, steel spring, and cotton upholstery
H: 36¾ in. W: 25¼ D: 25¾ in.
Collection of Tazio Nuvolari

The architects of the Prairie School received critical attention not only for their low, horizontal houses but also for their bank buildings. Although located in small, rather parochial towns throughout the upper midwest, the banks they built were not conservative in style. Architects like Louis Sullivan and Purcell, Elmslie, and Feick provided innovative designs that were quite different from the imitative Greek and Roman forms embraced elsewhere in America.[1]

The Minneapolis firm of Purcell, Elmslie, and Feick, in particular, denounced the uninspired look of neoclassical and neo-Georgian banks. Following the lead of Louis Sullivan, for whom Elmsie worked as chief draftsman and Purcell as temporary help (see nos. 84 and 93), they created a number of designs in a new American style. These box-like structures were distinguished by steel frames, brick façades, stylized terra-cotta ornament, arched entries, taut pier-and-lintel façades, and integrated interiors. One of the most successful examples by Purcell, Elmslie, and Feick was the Merchants Bank in Winona, a growing city in southwestern Minnesota. The firm provided designs for all aspects

92

of the building: the ornament of the exterior, the stained glass along the walls and in the ceiling, the grilles for the tellers, the lighting fixtures, and even the furniture.

Whereas the pierced splats of the other chairs designed by the Minneapolis firm (see no. 93) manifest a close affinity with the stylized decoration of Sullivan, the modular, geometric proportions of the Winona bank chairs follow designs of the Austrian Koloman Moser.[3] The influence probably comes from Purcell's travels abroad, which exposed him to the modular style in Austria during its heyday. An engineer interested in geometric design,[4] he transformed the Austrian cube chair into a distinctive American form by following Frank Lloyd Wright's theory of designing for the machine. Although Purcell's wood for the present example – millworked oak – lacks the rich veneered and inlaid surfaces of the more expensive Austrian version, the relationship of the vertical spindles with horizontal spacers and the thick framing members results in a surface geometry that is equally pleasing.

ESC

1. Alan K. Lathrop, "The Prairie School Bank: Patron and Architect," in *Prairie School Architecture in Minnesota, Iowa, Wisconsin* (Saint Paul: Minnesota Museum of Art, 1982), pp. 54-67.

2. H. Allen Brooks, ed., *Prairie School Architecture: Studies from "The Western Architect"* (New York: Van Nostrand Reinhold Company, 1983), pp. 46-106; and idem, *The Prairie School: Frank Lloyd Wright and His Midwest Contemporaries* (New York: W.W. Norton, 1976), pp. 201-205.

3. Both types of chairs were used in the Edna Purcell house in Minneapolis. The armchairs, like the Winona example, seem to serve as easy chairs; the tall-backed versions are desk and dining chairs. Most other interior views of Purcell and Elmslie houses illustrate the taller-backed type. (See Brooks 1983, pp. 93-94.) For examples of Moser's designs, see Kirk Varnedoe, *Vienna 1900: Art, Architecture & Design* (New York: Museum of Modern Art, 1986), pp. 78-79 and 82-83.

4. Brooks 1983, p. xvi.

93

93

Side chair,[1] *from Harold C. Bradley House, Madison, Wisconsin, 1910-1912*
Designer: George Grant Elmslie (1871-1952)
Maker: Jean B. Hassewer Co., Chicago
Oak, laminated wood; leather, jute webbing, and horsehair upholstery (not original)
H: 50 in. W: 20⅜ in. D: 21¼ in.
Marks: branded *Made & Guaranteed / By / Jean B. Hassewer Co. / Chicago* (on inside of rear seat rail)
Collection of Sigma Phi Society, Alpha, of Wisconsin

Among the few residential designs by the office of Louis Sullivan were the Babson house in Riverside, Illinois (see no. 84), and the Harold C. Bradley house in Madison, Wisconsin. Conceived in 1909, the Bradley house was the last commission on which George Elmslie worked in the Sullivan studio. As was the practice there, Elmslie took Sullivan's basic composition and gave it actual form. His hand is particularly

evident in the leaded glass – which resembles the geometric pattern in no. 94 – and the original furnishings such as lamps, tables, and chairs. The Bradleys' continued patronage of Elmslie when he formed a new partnership with William Purcell testifies to the significance of his role in the 1909 Bradley commission. Purcell and Elmslie created two more houses for the Bradley family over the next five years (see no. 90).[2]

In all of his designs, Elmslie sought to construct a very geometric presence that could be achieved efficiently. For stained glass, he relied upon commercially available glass and simple techniques; for furniture, he followed existing practices of the industry. In one decade, 1910 to 1920, Purcell and Elmslie executed over seventy commissions (many of which included interior furnishings),[3] attesting to an ability to satisfy clients' aesthetic and financial expectations.

The present chair is a tall-backed rectilinear type favored by such prominent designers as Josef Hoffmann, Charles Rennie Mackintosh, and Frank Lloyd Wright. Used with slight variations in the back splat for many of Elmslie's other commissions, it illustrates two characteristic features: a strong sense of graphic composition and a dependence on machine production, its straight lines permitting easy sawing and surfacing. For the most part, however, the techniques used to provide the aesthetic have compromised the chair's functional stability.[4] The front rail and side seat rails were fastened at the front corner with a splined miter joint set upon a shouldered tenon that extended from the top of the front leg; such a joint depends for strength upon the corner block, screwed into the seat rails behind it. The tenons at the rear of the side seat rails do not fit snugly into their mortises, which, having been chopped out with a mortising machine, are too large to function effectively. Finally, the rear seat rail is supported only by bridle joints (rather than tenons) on the splats and by corner blocks. The overall effect of these technical shortcomings is a weak chair prone to loose joints. One exception is the rear splat, which is a laminated board strong enough to prevent any shortgrain breakage as a result of the fine lines of the cutout pierced design.

ESC

1. The date range of the chairs is determined by the years in which the Jean B. Hassewer Company operated and by the first published photograph of the chairs in the Bradley house. The Hassewer Company existed only from 1910 to 1914; the chairs were illustrated in the January 1913 issue of *The Western Architect*. Olivia Mahoney, Assistant Curator of Decorative Arts at the Chicago Historical Society, found the dates of Hassewer in the Chicago City Directories.

2. H. Allen Brooks, *The Prairie School: Frank Lloyd Wright and His Midwest Contemporaries* (New York: W.W. Norton, 1976), pp. 139-146.

3. Ibid., p. 131.

4. For a discussion of the relative strengths of different joints, see Tage Frid, *Tage Frid Teaches Woodworking – Joinery: Tools and Techniques* (Newtown, Conn.: Taunton Press, 1979).

94

Stained glass window, from Edna S. Purcell house, Minneapolis, ca. 1913
Designers: William Gray Purcell (1880-1965) and George Grant Elmslie (1871-1952)
Maker: E.L. Sharretts of the Mosaic Art Glass Company, Minneapolis
Stained glass and zinc
H: 89 in. W: 19 in.
Minneapolis Institute of Arts, Gift of Anson B. Cutts

Many of the Prairie School architects used "curtains of glass" to diffuse natural light in their interiors. William Grant Purcell, for example, was drawn to the effects of daylight coming through windows of clear, opalescent, and colored glass into rooms with high ceilings.[1] Thus, it is no surprise that he included seventy-two windows filled with stained glass in the house he built for his family in 1913, several of them long windows that provided light for the split levels of the rooms. This particular example was located originally on a small staircase that led from the stairway hall to the maid's room. In contrast to the more traditional English style – with curving cames and colored panes – it is made up of predominantly clear fields with color accents composed in rectangles, triangles, and diamonds.

Probably derived from Frank Lloyd Wright, who began to design such glass in 1902, the new geometric style was inextricably connected to technological changes as steam-powered rolling machinery permitted the efficient manufacture

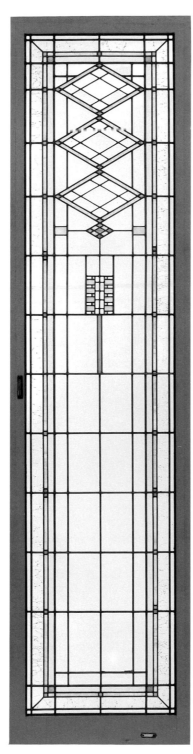

94

of larger panes. Opalescent glass, a machine-rolled milky type introduced in the 1870s, could be set within stiff zinc cames – a method that reduced the danger of buckling, eliminated the need for bracing, and allowed thinner windows. The ease of cutting and preassembling straight-sided panes and cames, rather than custom fitting thick small irregular shapes, contributed to the widespread use of Wright's geometric style. In fact, it was about half as expensive as traditional glass of the type made by George Washington Maher, whose windows probably required more time to execute and therefore cost considerably more.[2]

Purcell and Elmslie were among the most successful designers of geometric-patterned glass. They used commercially available Pittsburgh Plate Glass, cut and assembled by E.L. Sharretts, who worked closely with them on all their Minnesota projects.[3] Such consistent collaboration allowed the architects to ensure standards of composition, color, and control of pattern.

ESC

1. William Gray Purcell, "Own House Notes" (manuscript on file at the Minneapolis Institute of Arts), p. 7; and drawings of the house in the Purcell papers, Northwest Architectural Archives, University of Minnesota Libraries, Minneapolis.

2. Sharon Darling, *Chicago Ceramics & Glass: An Illustrated History from 1871 to 1933* (Chicago: Chicago Historical Society, 1979), pp. 101-103, 119-127.

3. Technical information about the construction of the Edna S. Purcell house is provided in a "parabiography" in the Northwest Architectural Archives, University of Minnesota Libraries, Minneapolis. I am indebted to Cheryl Robertson for these references.

95

Dining chair, ca. 1910
Majestic Furniture Company, Mexico, New
York (1909-1916)
Oak with linen (not original) upholstery
H: 47½ in. W: 17¼ in. D: 16¾ in.
Private Collection

The Majestic Furniture Company advertised
"High Grade Mission Furniture in Suites Complete for Dining Room, Library, Den and Chamber."[1] While most of its designs do appear to be
in the Mission style inspired by the work of
Gustav and L. and J.G. Stickley, there were exceptions: the present chair resembles a design
by Frank Lloyd Wright for the B. Harley Bradley
house in Kanakee, Illinois (1900).[2]

CZ

1. This chair is illustrated in an advertisement in the
Grand Rapids Furniture Record 20 (February 1910), p. 405.
According to the ad, the Majestic Furniture Company
exhibited its work at the Grand Rapids trade fairs.

2. Robert Edwards pointed out this comparison. The
chair differs in that it lacks the applied moldings on
the seat rail and has a shaped stretcher and varied post
construction. For an illustration of the Bradley house
chairs, see David Hanks, *The Decorative Designs of Frank
Lloyd Wright* (New York: E.P. Dutton, 1979), p. 76.

95

II

Reform in Craftsmanship

"Dreams of Brotherhood and Beauty": The Social Ideas of the Arts and Crafts Movement

Eileen Boris

How could a college-educated woman with training in the fine arts and a passion for social justice aid the laboring classes of late nineteenth-century America? Vida Dutton Scudder – the Wellesley College professor of literature, Christian Socialist activist, and writer – posed one answer in her 1903 semi-autobiographical novel *A Listener in Babel*: "Be a servant of beauty, but beauty the creating of which shall bring life to many and which when created shall bring life to many more," proclaimed her heroine, Hilda Lathrop. As an artist and an individual who "must monkey . . . with production," Hilda planned to disappear into a factory, not for a few weeks to expose working conditions as her class commonly did, but for years to learn all the trades where art has played a part (such as bookmaking, pottery, and textiles) as preparation for her own cooperative workshop. Without dismissing the machine, as did many arts and crafts proponents, she envisioned adjusting the processes of labor so as to make industry educational and delightful, capable of fostering worker creativity. "And there is a song I shall sing at my weaving," Hilda concluded, "'Life without industry is guilt; industry without art is brutality.'" Thus quoting the English art and social critic John Ruskin, whose Oxford lectures in the 1870s had converted Vida Scudder to socialism, Hilda left her residence in a social settlement house to begin reuniting art and labor – for her salvation's sake, if not for those who labor with their hands out of necessity and not from desire.[1]

Like her fictional alter-ego, Vida Scudder belonged to a generation of artists, intellectuals, and social reformers who criticized modern civilization for destroying art in the process of degrading labor. Dreaming of "brotherhood and beauty,"[2] they looked to the examples of John Ruskin and William Morris to forge

a "new industrialism" that offered an alternative to the factory system and its products. In their call for honesty and truth to materials, attacks on commercialism, and praise of nature, the natural, and the simple life, they shared in a generalized vocabulary of reform. As a group, however, they were diverse, including traditionalists and primitivists who longed for a medieval or preindustrial past, modernists who would adapt the ideal of craftsmanship to the machine age, socialists who envisioned the "cooperative commonwealth," and promoters who popularized the ideas of the others even as they turned these ideas into objects of consumption.

The great majority of arts and crafts enthusiasts were searching not for a new order but for an alternative within the existing one, based on the cultivation of art in everyday life. Influenced by a growing coterie of tastemakers and domestic shelter magazines, they sought to express their personalities through decoration, especially the design and furnishings of the home. Like the social reformers, this group also turned to arts and crafts as a reaction to social change, to the industrialization, urbanization, and immigration that despoiled the environment and, in the process, debased the look of daily life.

The history of the Arts and Crafts movement, from its origins in the midnineteenth century, is part of the history of the middle class – encapsulating its fear and hatred of class conflict, its own loss and redefinition of autonomy and independence, its creating of rebels within its own midst. The idealistic, optimistic spirit of the crafts movement reflects the class that turned to arts and crafts as solution and escape from the industrial world it did so much to forge. Functional and symbolic, modern and traditional, individualistic and communal, nationalist and universal – the Arts and Crafts movement contained contradictory tendencies; if its leaders and publicists often seemed confused, they reflected the more generalized bewilderment of a generation that looked back to the past – to the medieval, the colonial, the folk – in the process of creating a very different future. Assuming the tone of a moral crusade in the writings of proponents as different as the Brahmin leather worker Mary Ware Dennett and the Roycroft "Fra" Elbert Hubbard, Arts and Crafts represented idealism with a material face, with the goal to rebeautify daily life and labor. That much of the pottery thrown, rugs woven, and metal hammered was amateurish meant less than the engagement of so many in the process of making. In its own way, the handicraft revival was a democratic movement: every man, woman, or child could be creative. Unlike the decorative arts revival of the 1870s and '80s, initiated by upper-class Anglophiles and local elites in major urban centers (Boston, New York, Philadelphia, Chicago, Cincinnati, and Detroit), art became, thirty years later, firmly part of the middle-class scheme of things.

For American followers of Ruskin and Morris, the majority of whom were educated women and men cut off from either manual or paid labor, the craftsman ideal provided a way to step outside of their position within the developing corporate order and find individual autonomy within a renewed secular (rather than religious) community. While the artistic reinterpretation of pre-industrial forms provided a vocabulary for this community, its terms, like the individualism of the craftsman ideal itself, were part of the language of the larger culture – even as they were used to critique that culture. Crafts proponents spoke of "honesty," "sincerity," "masculinity," "fellowship," and "the simple life"; they promoted the work ethic, the

cult of domesticity, and ultimately the espousal of art above other human activities. But because its values remained tied to the old order, it could never generate a truly oppositional culture – a culture that offered a new set of core values within a different economic and political structure. What began as a critique of art and labor under industrial capitalism turned into a style of art, leisure activities, and personal and social therapy.

America in 1900

Uneven and unequal development characterized the United States during the last quarter of the nineteenth century and the first years of the twentieth. Coexisting with the rise of industrial America stood the sharecrop system of virtual peonage for southern blacks and the reservation system of near extinction for native Americans. Although mining, farm homesteading, and cattle ranching were opening up the west, the structure of production had shifted overall from agriculture to manufacturing, from the local and regional to the national market, and from the small to the large firm. A centralized urban and industrial nation, made even more heterogeneous by millions of southern and eastern European immigrants, supplanted the society of small workshops, small towns, and small farms. Victorian Americans – white, propertied, Anglo-Saxon, and Protestant – were witnessing the birth of a disconcertingly new world.[3]

As the nature and location of work shifted, so did the constituent classes of society. The definition of the middle class changed as both the autonomous artisan and the self-employed businessman became eclipsed by the salaried employee.[4] Between 1860 and 1900, the number of white-collar, managerial, and professional workers tripled; the corpo-

ration, by its very nature, generated the need for lawyers, salesmen, and office workers who facilitated the transfer of products rather than making them. Even the professional – the writer, minister, architect, or artist – felt loss of autonomy as he or she became dependent on corporate beneficence for salaries, patronage, or employment in universities and museums, themselves creatures of the new wealth. Similarly, by 1900, the number of industrial wage earners swelled to nearly equal the number of farmers, farm renters, and farm laborers. Wage labor, increasingly for women as well as for men, had come to dominate the American economic landscape.

The arts and crafts, no less than heavy industry, suffered from the general mechanization and reorganization of labor. In a host of crafts, including glassmaking, pottery, furniture and cabinetmaking, iron molding, bookbinding, printing, and jewelry, labor became divided and subdivided, planning separated from making, as machines replaced handicraft artisans and managers set up a hierarchical division of labor. Meanwhile, a growing professionalization more strictly differentiated the architect from the builder and subdivided the drafting room of the architectural office, transforming the master craftsman into a foreman and the architect into a businessman. While the decorative arts suffered from machine competition, painting found its "Grand Rapids" (named after the center of mass-produced furniture) in cheap lithographic reproduction. "Artist" and "artisan" seemed totally different species in an America where few pockets of craftswork remained between the fine arts and mass production.[5]

The last third of the nineteenth century also marked the emergence of a consumer culture. By the mid-eighties, Marshall Field in Chicago, John Wanamaker's in Philadelphia, Macy's in New York, and Jordan Marsh in Boston had expanded from small retail firms to huge multi-product stores. Montgomery Ward published its first mail-order catalogue in 1872; Sears, Roebuck and Co. outpaced Montgomery Ward in the late nineties by offering mass-produced household furnishings and clothing to the rural market. The user had turned into a consumer, a faceless purse for the "art" of advertising to persuade, no longer one's neighbor for sellers to satisfy out of mutual respect and shared culture.[6] Furthermore, the growth of mass marketing and the department store transformed distribution; whereas local variation once provided customers with a certain degree of choice, product standardization now began to restrict consumer options.

While "Captains of Industry" grew rich, while Andrew Carnegie preached "the gospel of wealth" and John D. Rockefeller the survival of the fittest, children labored in mines and mills and families crowded into tenement slums. The genteel press worried about "the labor problem" as well as "the problem of the trusts," while its middle-class readership feared revolution from below even more than reaction from above. Just as all industry appeared to move toward one big trust, so the webs of society seemed to diminish the individual. In this context, where work increasingly became divided, where individuals lacked control over the environments of their lives, a broad stratum of the middle class embraced a wide variety of reform movements to share more equitably the fruits of industrial progress and to restore America to the values of her past.

"The Age of Reform," as historian Richard Hoftstader named the period, presented a mixture of panaceas and proposals.[7] Ranging from the single tax on unearned land values of Henry George to the ballot-box politics of German socialists, from the centralized utopian state of Edward Bellamy to the grain cooperatives of the Populists or "farmer's revolt," from the efficiency and fair play in government of municipal reformers to the child-welfare programs of women social-settlement leaders, the period witnessed much popular questioning of the results of unbridled competition and unrestrained industrial progress. Urbanization, immigration, and the factory system seemed responsible to many for destroying community, undermining the work ethic, destabilizing the family, and replacing the purity and godliness of the past with greed and commercialism. The rise of giant corporations and the nationalization of business and intellectual life also seemed destined to crush the individual, leaving him or her a cog in the machine of progress. In the face of such barbarities, Progressivism appeared as a crusade against the forces of evil as much as a legislative agenda to promote labor standards and clean government, Americanize immigrants, and rationalize business.

Those who embraced the craftsman ideal shared in the Progressive rhetoric of antimonopolism. Like others of their class, they sought to alleviate the injustices of industrialism, not least because slums and child labor destroyed beauty. Embracing the language of efficiency in their visions of both home and workplace, they belonged to the organizational revolution of these years even as they sought to escape it into a simple life filled with bungalow aprons and floral cretonnes. Despite its inadequacies, the craftsman ideal of more satisfying labor and a holistic environment closer to nature uplifted individual reformers, providing them with an aesthetics compatible with their social impulses.[8]

Preindustrial Motifs

Medievalists and primitivists looked to past societies in which craftsmanship stood interwoven with the rest of life. Re-created portraits of fourteenth-century England or seventeenth-century New Mexico provided them with alternatives to those of the existing order from which they hoped to forge a new society reuniting art and labor. For the architect Ralph Adams Cram, progress had stopped when Renaissance individualism shattered the organic unity of the medieval world. He looked back to the Gothic past not to copy its forms but to revive its spirit, to develop the potential aborted by the Reformation. For in the process of fracturing the medieval world, the forces of modernism – individualism, materialism, and lawless democracy – also destroyed the potential for art. Thus, Cram argued that "the Gothic principle is the very principle of progress, and faithfully applied to modern conditions would result in an architecture . . . unlike in form [but] . . . kindred in spirit to the medieval building in which thus far it has found its most triumphant expression."[9] Movement backward, with a firm adherence to the principles of simplicity, utility, functionalism, and honesty, would then lead toward a new American architecture.

Cram would become the leading Gothicist in twentieth-century America, but in the 1890s in Boston he propounded a version of fin-de-siècle aestheticism that was labeled by a future architectural partner, Bertram Grosvenor Goodhue, as "Pre-Raphaelite in its tradition . . . and decadent."[10] The late romantic emphasis on color, texture, and line represented for Cram and his circle "the final flowering of age-end art."[11] These young artists and designers revolted against commercial America, fashioning an alternative ethos out of Christianity, Gothicism, monarchism, anti-capitalism, craftsmanship, and hatred of modern democracy. In Morris, Edward Burne-Jones, Walter Crane, and A.H. Mackmurdo they found role models and artistic inspiration; the Kelmscott Press and the Century Guild's *Hobby Horse* inspired their short-lived journal *Knight Errant*, which displayed an idealistic medievalism similar to the hazy romanticism of Morris's pre-socialist writings and even more elitist in its deference to aristocratic virtues.

Cram never fully abandoned playing at medievalism. In 1916 he created a fully costumed medieval pageant for the opening of the Cambridge campus of the Massachusetts Institute of Technology, for which he served as head of the architecture department. He was one of the leaders in the Boston Society of Arts and Crafts (BSAC) who promoted the establishment of guilds to revive the crafts and to break down the impersonality that developed with the growth of the Boston crafts society. Cram lamented "that the idea of team work has so utterly died out of a hyper-individualized generation that a communal spirit could not be built up." He went on to encourage collaboration in the arts, the coming together in workshops of all the craftsmen necessary for church building, even if "individualism or commercialism or division of labour or the trade unions stand in the way."[12] In works ranging from All Saints' of Ashmont (no. 22) to St. John the Divine Cathedral in New York City, he carried out this ideal – the unification of architect and artisan – developing, in the process, the art of stained-glass makers, wood and stone carvers, embroiderers, and metalworkers.

In *Walled Towns*, a 1919 tract against liberal capitalist society, Cram laid out his vision of a new order based on the hierarchies of the guilds.[13] Like his own estate *Whitehall*, with its gardens and per-sonal chapel, and the New Hampshire farm of his "Squire" uncle, the walled town evoked the small-scale, self-sufficient unit of the middle ages; it was the urban counterpart to the medieval manor. Common religion, artistic pageantry, and the rule of fathers would bond together these decentralized living units in which cooperatives and guilds would supplement the family, church, and school. Here traditionalism would merge with spirituality to offer a new paradigm for a reformed world.

While Cram dreamed of life before the ungodliness and ugliness of the Renaissance, Charles F. Lummis turned toward Indian cultures in the hope of recapturing the naturalness and beauty lost to modern America. A graduate of Harvard University, Lummis set out in September 1884 to "tramp across the continent" and report his observations for the *Los Angeles Times*.[14] Along the way he discovered the Spanish, Mexican, and Indian cultures of the southwest, cultures that he spent his life recording, preserving, and promoting as more natural than eastern urban society. Thus, in the 1890s he transformed the real estate promotion sheet *Land of Sunshine* into the literary journal *Out West*, which spearheaded campaigns to save the missions and reproduce the "primitive" culture of old-time California, of the golden days before the greed of massive Anglo settlement. As "the man of culture in a corduroy suit," Lummis would not merely struggle for the civil rights of Indians; he would collect their pottery, photograph their ceremonials, and record their songs – turning them into objects of study even as he helped "save" them from a hostile society. In so doing, he resembled other folklorists and preservationists whose collections of indigenous artifacts ironically transformed such cultures into phenomena romanticized by urban elites.

Like the self-taught architect and former Hubbard associate George Harris,[15] another transplanted easterner, Lummis embraced the naturalness of California. In forging his own lifestyle and an environment suitable for it, he epitomized California living: close to nature, romantic, generous, simple, content. Certainly his house *El Alisal* in the Arroyo Seco of Pasadena captured the spirit of what has been named "the Arroyo culture."[16] Built with stones from the canyon and eight-by-twelve-foot beams hewn with an adze by Lummis himself (aided by men from the Isleta Pueblo), full of cedar logs that were burned, charred, and rubbed for a satiny finish, here was the pueblo, hacienda, and mission transformed into luxurious simplicity – the primitivism of the sophisticated, the proper scene for literary bohemianism, for the artistic life. Lummis, in what after Morris became an Arts and Crafts trademark, developed his own monogram and, not surprisingly, derived its form from the sacred serpent of the Inca ruins of Tiahuanaco. The building of his house reflected not only the recombination of local materials that Harris would elevate into the philosophy of architecture "fashioned by nature"; it also embodied the cult of masculinity so central to the craftsman ideal. As Lummis commented: "Any fool can write a book but it takes a man to dovetail a door."[17]

"The New Industrialism"

Radical proponents of the arts and crafts, like their English mentors Ruskin and Morris, deplored the ways that the pursuit of profit crushed beauty from both the makers of everyday goods and the products that resulted from their deadening labor. Even as they rejected aestheticism or "art for art's sake," the concept of art – as a symbol of pleasure, spontaneity, freedom, and joy – provided the criterion against which they judged the labor of the world. Beauty as "the outcome of a free person's pleasure in creation"[18] was impossible for the wage laborer who controlled neither the nature of his work nor its reward. Nothing less than reform in society would develop art.

Because Morris never meant for art to disappear during the struggle for a new society, social reformers sought to fashion a "new industrialism" wherein labor would be both artistic and educative and the product of labor useful and beautiful. This new system would combine production in workshops with industrial education, merging studio, school, and factory into one organic whole. Joining handicraft with farming, it would also connect city with country, ending the major divisions of social life that had developed since the advent of industrialization. The Victorian work ethic would shed its gray and ponderous covering; joy would return to labor.[19]

At the center of this vision lay a critique of factory work and the commercialism so central to capitalistic social relations. Adherents sought "to destroy the present factory system, surrounded with its filth, bad ventilation, and unwholesome influences, and to transform disease breeding lairs into studios and pleasant workrooms."[20] As Edward Pearson Pressey, the founder of the New Clairvaux handicraft community, explained: "The Arts and Crafts [movement] is a soul-reaction from under the feet of corporations and the wheels of machines."[21] Radical adherents of the arts and crafts thus rejected an industrial system geared toward making commodities in which "the artist will usually become an affected idler and the artizan [sic] an unartistic 'hand.'"[22] Proposals to educate consumers to know beauty and fine workmanship were bound to prove

Fig. 1. Oscar Lovell Triggs in the quarters of the Industrial Art League and Bohemian Guild of Arts and Crafts, Chicago, 1902. Illustrated in *The New Industrialism* (Chicago, 1902).

inadequate unless craftsmen inhabited an environment that encouraged such making.

In a series of essays for *The Craftsman*, a leading journal of the Arts and Crafts movement, and in an expanded study published in 1902, University of Chicago professor Oscar Lovell Triggs (fig. 1) set forth the major tenets of the new industrialism.[23] The hierarchical "old workshop" was inhumane, ranking goods before people, neglecting both the social good and individual happiness. But the self-determination of the artist, his or her freedom in labor, could extend to all workers. With machinery taking over the routine, deadening work of the world, handicraft workshops would encourage the individuality blocked by

factory organization and restore artistic results. Freedom in the workshop – along with good fellowship or the spirit of cooperation – would facilitate unity of design through a democratically derived, limited division of labor. Under this new industrialism, the making of actual products would coexist with experiment and study to improve product use and beauty. Combining mental and manual, art and labor, work and play, education and life, Triggs's workshop substituted organic unity for the dualisms characteristic of Western industrial thought.[24]

Like other critics of industrial civilization, Triggs envisioned this ideal workshop as part of nature: "It will betoken the love which the natural unperverted man has for the sky and for trees and for gardens." Placed in an attractive setting, the workshop would fulfill Ruskin's prerequisite for beautiful goods. This led Triggs to praise those art manufactories (like Rookwood Pottery in Cincinnati or nearby Pickard China in Ravenswood, Illinois) that housed their work in pleasant and artistic buildings more like studios than factories.[25] Such decentralized environments, merging country and city, resembled many of the utopian visions influenced by Morris's *News from Nowhere*, including Leonard Abbott's Arts and Crafts tract "The Society of the Future" and William Dean Howells's novel *A Traveller from Alturia*. But they also paralleled real workplaces then being established by welfare capitalists as a beneficent strategy to control workers.[26]

The new workshop offered one solution to renewing craftsmanship; arts and crafts societies provided actual environments. Modeled upon the English Arts and Crafts Exhibition Society, these groups brought crafts workers, amateurs, and enthusiasts together for talks, exhibitions, and the sale of crafts. They were important factors in improving taste and in encouraging artistic design; more radical members hoped that they would help transform conditions of labor. Thus, Mary Ware Dennett of the Society of Arts and Crafts in Boston counseled that "the greatest service that was possible for such a society, was to work, first of all, for the industrial independence of [the] craftsman, and to do this with unerring persistency, even though it meant discarding for the time being, all thought of aesthetic excellence."[27] Since "*all* special privilege is the craftsman's enemy," including monopolies and trusts, corrupt legislatures, and a "weighty" military establishment, the craftsman and his friends should fight for industrial democracy as a first step toward transforming the look of daily life. Given the larger economic and social forces of the period – that it was possible for the factory to imitate art and that it was nearly impossible for the craftsman to make an adequate living without exploiting the labor of others – the crafts societies could never act seriously on her pleas.

Over the years, Mrs. Ware Dennett advocated the combination of craftswork with agriculture (especially scientific farming as presented by the Russian anarchist Prince Peter Kropotkin), the cooperative salesroom, and various educational and information bureaus. After 1905, when she left the governing council of the BSAC protesting the crafts group's preference for art objects over conditions of craftsmanship, she continued to fight for industrial democracy through a wide range of reform groups – the Single Tax League, the Free Trade League, the Anti-Imperialist League, and the Consumers' League – and, later, the women's suffrage and birth control movements, a mixture of causes that suggest the unsystematic, catholic quality of Progressive reform.[28]

Looking Forward: Modernism and Socialism

Socialists like Morris and Walter Crane were important figures in the crafts revival in England.[29] In America, however, where immigrant workmen were unaware of the English crafts example, the two movements stood further apart. Here the socialist faith in the machine as a precondition for greater abundance predominated over the artisan heritage. Combining positivism and religious zeal, the socialist creed extolled progress in such a way as to appear hostile to any return to an outmoded form of production. Nonetheless, a small but significant group of socialist intellectuals, most of whom combined non-Marxian and Christian socialism, connected craftsmanship explicitly with the end of exploitation and promoted the arts and crafts. Native-born or English in origin, they embraced the culture of English socialism as their own, founding *The Comrade* in 1901 as a socialist magazine of art and culture (fig. 2).

The party leader Algie Simons predicted that in the future "we shall see that capitalism lays an even heavier curse upon the worker when it deprives him of the joy of creative craftsmanship than it does when it steals away the lion's share of his product."[30] While working-class unions fought to do less work for higher wages, Arts and Crafts reformers called for redesigning work rather than eliminating it, making work more like art. Thus Ellen Gates Starr, cofounder of the Hull House social settlement in Chicago, chose "to go out from among [the mass of men] and live a rational life, working 'in the spirit of the future' – that future which shall make common the privilege now exclusive of doing the work one loves to do and expressing one's self through it, which, as Morris so often said, is art."[31]

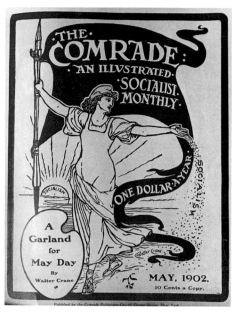

Fig. 2. Walter Crane (1845-1915). Cover for *The Comrade: An Illustrated Socialist Monthly*, May 1902.

For Starr, who became a socialist out of Christian convictions, the settlement house had to fight for the soul of the worker as well as the life; like art and labor, each depended on the other. Modeled on the Ruskinian Toynbee Hall, where college men went to live among London's poor, Hull House, founded in 1889 with Jane Addams, became the country's foremost social settlement.[32] Starr influenced its early programs by conducting art and literature classes and attempting to beautify the neighborhood. In less than a decade, however, she became convinced of the necessity to unite mental and manual labor in her own life; with funds from a benefactress, she apprenticed herself in 1897 to the English Arts and Crafts bookbinder T.J. Cobden-Sanderson. After a fifteen-month stay, she returned to set up the Hull House bookbindery.

With a cell-like apartment glowing from Morris papers and leaves from the

Kelmscott Chaucer and Doves Press, with photographs of Ruskin and Morris as icons hung on the bookbindery wall, Ellen Starr exemplified living "the future in the present." But such a course hardly came easy. Apart from despairing over her inability to make a living and her lack of apprentices, she began questioning the class nature of her products. Years later she admitted to her niece: "If I had thought it through, I would have realized that I would be using my hands to create books that only the rich could buy."[33] Still, Starr emerged as one of the militant middle-class allies of the labor movement, arrested on picket lines, collecting food and money for strikes, and serving as treasurer of the local branch of the Women's Trade Union League. Ultimately, medievalism would characterize a lifelong quest for religious certainty; in the 1920s she converted to Roman Catholicism and retired to a convent.

Vida Scudder shared with Starr a belief in Ruskinian moral aesthetics, religious longings, and political commitment to aid the working class. She too incorporated the lives of the saints and the forms of the medieval world into the devotions of her daily life. Her political program, however, looked forward to the socialist future rather than backward to a medieval past.[34] Scudder grew up among the well-connected, educated elite of Boston. A graduate of one of the early classes of Smith College (1884), she joined the faculty of Wellesley a few years later as a teacher of English literature. She was also a founder of the College Settlements Association and Denison House in Boston's South End, an organizer of the Women's Trade Union League, and a member of the Socialist Party. Scudder argued that "the beautiful only exists as found in use, as it springs from the common life of all and ministers to the common life of all."[35.] She

explained the way in which class position shaped work experience as follows: "In the days of handicraft, work was its own reward; it is so no longer. The professional classes possibly work as hard as manual laborers. But their work is life . . . they employ, cultivate, delight, the higher faculties. But to iron two thousand linen collars a day . . . to carry on any one of the minute occupations introduced by the division of labor, leaves people where it found them, only a little more stupefied. The real life of the modern wage-earner must lie without, not within his trade; and he has freedom for it only in the weary evening hours after work is done, on Sundays and holidays."[36] It was this separation of work and play, art and life, that the crafts enthusiasts attacked; if their organic vision reflected their own relation to production – a "professional" class situation with autonomy and creativity over their labor – it also reflected their anxiety over possible loss of control in an America where they were becoming the employees of corporations and bystanders to class conflict.

This class anxiety expressed itself for men in a longing for fellowship, a brotherhood of art that would provide them with a homosocial community that the white female middle class already possessed through their "women's culture" and through enclaves created by feminist reformers like Starr and Scudder.[37] Crafts groups elevated the concepts of brotherhood, fellowship, and masculinity, reflecting the domination of men in leadership positions, as in England, even though the majority of members were women. Among the heroes in the crafts movement were figures such as the American poet Walt Whitman, the British homosexual philosopher Edward Carpenter, and the noble William Morris.[38]

For Will Price, an architect and

founder of the crafts community of Rose Valley, brotherhood became the basis for "a fit society."[39] Such a brotherhood turned metaphysical with the Boston journalist Sylvester Baxter, a supporter of Edward Bellamy's Nationalist movement and a founder of the BSAC, celebrating "a group of artists working as one . . . and all acting to a common end" so that "his associates are extensions of his own hands and enlargements of his own mind and soul, – One with himself and he one with them."[40] Another utopian view was expressed by the non-Marxian socialist Triggs as "voluntary co-operative individualism"; he described it as "the goal toward which . . . industrial work is now tending."[41] Identifying "industrial liberty" with "the return of manhood to common work," Triggs revealed the gendered meaning of crafts brotherhood.

As his picture (fig. 1) in the workshop of the Industrial Art League in downtown Chicago suggests, Triggs took pride in his masculinity. The painted fireplace wall of the workshop celebrated the free man in all his glory; so too Triggs's writings called for the cooperation of comrades in a reconstructed workshop along the lines drawn up by the British craft exponent C.R. Ashbee, wherein friends and shopmates merge as citizen, apprentice, and worker. Comradeship encouraged individuality within the protectiveness of community, setting up an alternative to the hostility of professional competition as well as the harshness of the industrial system. Here was essentially a modern, vitalistic viewpoint that projected the affection of comrades within the crafts workshop as the basis for society.[42]

Triggs developed his ideas as part of the larger ferment at the University of Chicago.[43] Founded as a Baptist college, Chicago's premier educational institution grew from the generous financial contributions of John D. Rockefeller. Under the leadership of William Rainey Harper, the faculty became one of the most distinguished in the nation. As a center of practical sociology, of the application of social science to the problems of the industrial city (particularly the conditions of immigrants), and the seat of the science of political economy, the University reinforced the sociological orientation of Triggs, one of its own Ph.D. recipients in literature who had studied abroad in Germany. Like many other reformers, Triggs came to the city from the small-town midwest and, like others of his class, brought a secularized religiosity to his quest for a renewed community. In his enthusiastic championship of individual expression amid democratic fellowship, in his choice of life and pleasure over narrow restraint, Triggs proved a worthy disciple of Walt Whitman, the poet whose works he annotated. From his colleague Thorstein Veblen, the iconoclastic economist who condemned conspicuous consumption (and, in the process, attacked the unreadable typography and unusable pots of handicraft enthusiasts), Triggs learned to distinguish real labor from false and to consider the "instinct of workmanship" as another name for the artistic.[44] From Chicago's Lab School director John Dewey, the philosopher, he absorbed the idea of learning by doing, a new educational philosophy that elevated industrial training in its attempt to end the separation of education and living. At nearby Hull House, he observed the Labor Museum that the head resident Jane Addams had established to preserve immigrant arts and crafts while showing the preindustrial peoples of southern and eastern Europe how their knowledge fitted into industrial evolution. Meanwhile, Chicago's vigorous socialist movement protested actual conditions at factories and workshops, and

out of this social context, Triggs's ideas on the new industrialism took shape.[45]

Like Dewey and Addams, Triggs was a doer as well as a thinker. A tireless lecturer and publicist, he served as secretary to the Industrial Art League (1899-1905) and also to the Morris Society (1903-1904), two of the various groups promoting the arts and crafts that sprang up in Chicago.[46] Like the Chicago Society of Arts and Crafts, the League drew together intellectuals and practicing craftsmen, held lectures (though of a more sociological cast), and conducted a salesroom. Under Triggs's guidance, the League spawned a number of crafts workshops, most prominent among them the Bohemia Guild. The leaders – the sculptor Julia Bracken, the bookbinder Gertrude Stiles, and the handprinter Frederick W. Goudy – ran its School of Industrial Art and Handicraft. Other workshops were oriented to a more amateur membership of suburban residents and university students and faculty. The South Park Association, for one, catered to University of Chicago families by providing an educational hobby center, classes in bookbinding and woodworking, and discussions of the life and work of William Morris. Members of the League planned an experimental center for the industrial arts and attempted to establish a workshop training course with the Art Institute of Chicago, but these efforts foundered when Triggs was dismissed from the University and major trustees of the League died or became incapacitated. Although the League never fulfilled its goal of ushering in the new industrialism, its focus on "the dignifying of Labor," as one member explained its objective, provided a radical alternative to the usual crafts society.[47]

Veblen praised the Industrial Art League for recognizing the "historical necessity" of machine production. One

of its trustees, the architect Frank Lloyd Wright, defended, more forcefully than others within the Arts and Crafts milieu, the artistic integrity of the machine. Although a few regarded machines as acceptable tools for the "thinking man," most American craftspeople promoted handicraft – alone capable of artistic perfection – as intrinsically superior to machine work. In a talk to the Chicago Society of Arts and Crafts in 1901 Wright offered an alternative interpretation of the craftsman ideal.[48] Machine technology made "obsolete and unnatural" the old handicraft tradition of "laboriously joined" structural parts; it compelled the artist to become "the leader of an orchestra, where once he was a star performer." With mechanical processes in mind, the artist would design for the manufacturer and his employees. In such a world, the arts and crafts society would not hold exhibitions but rather run "an experimental station that would represent in miniature the elements of this great pulsating web of the machine where each . . . of [the] significant tools in printing, lithography, galvano-electro processes, wood and steel working machinery, muffles and kilns would have a place." The scientist would collaborate with the artist while members would go into factories to study the actual operation of machines. Only when artists and manufacturers united could craftsmanship flourish and "Man [gain] . . . a true sense of his importance as a factor in society, though he does tend a machine."

Wright's modernism shared the socialists' faith in progress; he too peered into the future rather than merely backward. Through the machine, he would end the distinction between art and life, a central goal of the crafts revival. The critic Carlton Noyes best expressed this basic sentiment when he wrote in 1903 to Horace Traubel, editor of *The Artsman*, the "parrish record" of Rose Valley: "I recognize the difference in essence between art and life; one is simply the expression of the other; there is no break in the continuity. All the mischief and confusion about art comes from divorcing art from life, from regarding art as a cult, a thing apart."[49] Art was, in other words, the spirit in which something was done and not necessarily a specialized activity. Thus, any form of labor could be artistic and even the humblest product deserved to be made "a thing of beauty."

Promoters as Popularizers: Gustav Stickley and Elbert Hubbard

Though significant as shapers of ideas, the radical crafts proponents reached only a small audience; Gustav Stickley and Elbert Hubbard, on the other hand, popularized the craftsman ideal to the broad middle class. In the process, and in their own ways, both Stickley – furniture maker and publisher-editor of *The Craftsman* – and Hubbard – writer, advertiser, businessman, printer, and creator of the Roycroft craft enterprises – reinterpreted the new industrialism.[50] Each, however, removed the challenge to capitalism initially central to its vision. While Stickley came to reflect the somewhat contradictory strains of Progressive reform, including its enthusiasm for scientific management and hostility to organized labor, Hubbard became an outright apologist for big business. Nonetheless, each man spread the practice of handicraft and reformed the design of daily objects. They democratized, even as they diminished, the legacy of Ruskin and Morris.

On first glance, Stickley seems to repeat many of the key tenets of the new industrialism. He advocated the workshop, industrial education, and the combination of handicrafts with farming. Claiming that man cannot be happy at work unless some element of art is in his labor, Stickley often reiterated Morris's definition of art as "the expression of man's joy in his work." Like other upholders of the craftsman ideal, he emphasized "not the work itself, so much as the making of the man; the soul-stuff of a man is the product of work, and it is good, indifferent or bad, as is his work." But here work appeared "bad" if it was "careless or dishonest" rather than because division of labor or the profit motive placed any barriers in the craftsman's way.[51]

With a focus on individual crafts-workers, Stickley could neglect larger economic and structural conditions, even if he often railed against commercialism and greed. Thus, "if the chair is to be valued as an individual piece of work, the man who makes it must have known the joy and enthusiasm of carrying out an idea that is his own, or with which he is in such perfect sympathy that the work becomes a delight." He also needs "the sympathy and appreciation of the man who will own and use it." The producer and consumer thus stood in a symbiotic relationship. Not surprisingly then, use joined with beauty in Stickley's definition of "the joy of the craftsman" as "putting all his inventive genius, all his technical skill, into the production of something that shall supply a want that is felt, and that shall be as perfect as he can make it."[52] By 1905 he had shifted the movement's terms of analysis somewhat from the structures of labor that interfere with such processes to the techniques used for true, rather than, false art.

Born in rural Wisconsin in 1857, the eldest in a large and poor family, Stickley first learned his true craft from his uncle, a Pennsylvania manufacturer of wooden and cane-seated chairs. Within a few years he was retailing these chairs in Binghamton, New York, but success came to him only in the mid-1880s, when he began manufacturing his own mixture of Shaker, Queen Anne, and colonial types. Even after he moved to Syracuse, New York, in 1891, he continued to produce reproductions of historic styles. But within a decade he was arguing against furnishing American homes with the styles of Europe, advocating a truly American art, and by the turn of the century he had exhibited his version of oaken mission furniture, that solid and bulky straight-lined style associated with the California missions and later identified with Stickley's own Craftsman line.[53]

Stickley transformed himself from an entrepreneur into a master craftsman under the influence of Irene Sargent, a teacher of Romance Literature at Syracuse University and a follower of Ruskin and Morris. The initial October 1901 issue of *The Craftsman*, devoted to the life and work of Morris, appeared as a booklet with Gothic lettering and a border of swirling foliage, with Morris's "Daisy" wallpaper for its cover. The foreword stated: "The United Crafts [Stickley's firm] endeavor to promote and to extend the principles established by Morris, in both the artistic and the socialistic sense. In the interest of art, they seek to substitute the luxury of taste for the luxury of costliness; to teach that beauty does not imply elaboration or ornament; to employ only those forms and materials which make for simplicity, individuality and dignity of effect."[54] Stickley's guild of cabinetmakers and metal and leather workers – as he called his business, now reorganized as a profit-sharing company in which employees received stock options – repeated Morris's conception of worthy work: ". . . which shall be worth doing, and be pleasant to do; and which should be done under such conditions as would make it neither over-wearisome, nor over-anxious." Thus, the United Crafts would attempt to unite the designer and workman in the same individual, increasing the workman's knowledge of drawing and raising his "general intelligence, by the increase of his leisure and the multiplication of his means of culture and pleasure." Such a philosophy, along with Stickley's economic control, suggested an incomplete understanding of "constructive Socialism." But, after all, Morris was himself an employer even as he became one of Britain's major socialist agitators and thinkers.

Within a few years, shaky finances and a quadrupling of the work force ended the United Crafts as a venture in profit-sharing; in 1903 The Craftsman's direct imitation of the English movement changed when Stickley took full editorial charge and switched to a standard size and modern print format. The journal continued to promote art, arts and crafts, labor, and social reform, switching its subtitle from "In the Interests of Arts Allied to Labor" to "For the Simplification of Life," and finally in 1906 to "Better art, better work, and a better and more reasonable way of living."[55] By then Stickley was linking handicrafts "to the actual doing of good and useful work," a concern that led him to promote manual training and vocational education, especially as a way to teach immigrants the equal dignity of all labor and the importance of aiming at efficient standards. Such a philosophy of labor began to justify not only better working conditions, however, but the segmentation of labor and the tracking of specific groups of children into industrial wage work.[56] Meanwhile, The Craftsman presented designs and plans for bungalow-type "Craftsman homes" and lessons in making Craftsman furniture and embroideries; from the start, Stickley had advertised his own wares in the journal.

As even the initial statement of the United Crafts suggests, The Craftsman would emphasize "simplicity, individuality and dignity of effort." Stickley constructed his language of virtue out of a number of often-used terms that together set the contours of the good life: "content," "simple," "comfortable," "useful," "just," "individual," "personal," "standard," "honest," "sincere," "unselfish."[57] "Simplicity" took two interrelated forms. One referred to functional Craftsman designs and room arrangements accompanying them; the other meant the life lived within those rooms. "The few articles necessary for the maintenance of comfort, habitual occupation and the healthful enjoyment of the senses, are the only ones to be admitted into living, bed, or dining rooms," declared one early advertisement for Stickley's products. Such furnishings solved "the servant problem" because they eliminated the stuffy, crowded, and overdecorated interiors of the Victorian parlor, replacing dust collectors with geometric lines and uncluttered surfaces so that the housewife could do her own work. In Stickley's mind, beauty became the "returning to the old frankness of expression, the primitive emphasis upon structure, the natural adaptation of ornament to material."[58] This return to past virtues reflected one significant strand of thought shared by antimodernists like Ralph Adams Cram and Charles Lummis.

"Simplicity" turned into a call for "the simple life," a return to nature and a strenuous masculine existence.[59] As one letter to The Craftsman noted, it taught "a more restful, quiet life, and the getting away from overcivilization and its burdens." The archetypical Arts and Crafts room, as presented by Stickley, combined motifs from the medieval, folk, and colonial American traditions to evoke simplicity and stand as a counterpoint to the overcivilized stuffed urban dwelling. Stickley recommended Indian rugs and Navajo blankets to turn any porch into a peaceful outdoor living room. The Craftsman advertising department listed "hand-wrought" metal, "genuine" Navajo blankets from New Mexico, antiques and "hand-braided" rugs from Ipswich, Massachusetts, and "handwoven" Pequot rugs from Norwich Town, Connecticut. Meanwhile, Stickley argued the virtues of the colonial forefathers who, having less change in their lives, "had consequently greater affection for their surroundings. They did not acquire an object one day to grow weary of it on the morrow."

Like Charles Lummis, Craftsman writers praised the art, work, and lives of preindustrial peoples. Irene Sargent, for one, noted the lessons in decoration to be learned from baskets of "women of the red race of America."[60] Others called the work of Indian women "the only real handicraft this country knows."[61] Still others celebrated the patchwork quilts of Appalachian mountain folk, the embroidery of Russian peasants, and the linen weaving of Irish cottagers.[62] All offered an alternative to the industrialized urban milieu surrounding most Craftsman readers; by owning a Swedish tapestry, a Hopi jar, or an eighteenth-century crewel-stitch bedspread (or its reinterpretation by the Deerfield [Massachusetts] Blue and White Needlework Society [nos. 60 and 61]), modern Americans could simplify their lives. Folk artifacts could replace brocaded curtains and mass-produced bric-a-brac as marks of good taste, suggesting the identification of their owner, however vicariously, with "the people."

Stickley's message was populist, that is, he appointed himself the spokesman of "the great middle classes, possessed of moderate culture and moderate material resources, modest in schemes and action, average in all but in virtue."

Echoing the "republican" heritage of Thomas Jefferson, he called for an art conducive "to plain living and high thinking, to the development of the sense of order, symmetry and proportion."[63] After Ruskin, he argued that handicraft could flourish only when it was of and by the people, adapted to their way of life and reflective of their spirit. In article after article, he suggested that buyers of his style could join a family tree whose lineage included medieval burghers, the peasants of Germany and Tyrol, English Puritans, yeoman farmers, and the log cabin frontiersman. True American democrats, possessors of Craftsman designs would uphold manliness and family togetherness, values best represented by Theodore Roosevelt, Stickley's political idol. Their hard work and virtue promised to restore the pristine goodness of the republic, a goodness that existed before the rise of the "unscrupulous rich" and the equally "unscrupulous poor."[64]

In rejecting class conflict, in calling for cooperation between employers and employees, in blaming "the social unrest" on "separating The People into Two factions, Capital and Labor," Stickley reflected the views of his class. He offered handicraft as a solution; like Triggs, he believed that the workshop – in the form of individual or small cooperative industries – would create far better social conditions than those generated by the giant industries.[65] But not by means of organized labor; Stickley was hostile to that system for thwarting individual initiative, ambition, and energy. "... In return for the increased pay and lessened time which they have exacted from employers, unions have given no more competent work; rather, the standard of efficiency has been lowered to the level of the least competent, thereby taking away from the individual workman all incentive to increase his own

efficiency as a means of obtaining steady employment or advancing to a higher grade of work," he charged. Reverence for the individual, so central to the general Arts and Crafts love of handicraft, here combined with a particular interpretation of work – one that equated efficiency with craftsmanship. Pointing to preindustrial forms as symbols of a self-reliant past, he counseled labor to "combine [forces] for greater efficiency" and thus become "more in accord with the old American spirit . . . of independence, self-confidence and of ambition to rise in life by force of ability, intelligence and honesty."[66]

In upholding organization and efficiency, including the scientific management principles of Frederick Winslow Taylor, while simultaneously calling for small-scale units of manufacturing tied to subsistence agriculture, Stickley expressed two conflicting strands within reform thought: the regulatory faith in centralization and efficiency, associated with the New Nationalism of Theodore Roosevelt, and the anti-monopoly credo of decentralization, associated with the New Freedom of Woodrow Wilson. In fact, he printed articles praising both Roosevelt and Wilson a few years before the election of 1912.[67] Ultimately, Stickley limited his notions to consumer, rather than producer, cooperatives.[68] The individual and his expression took precedence and any arrangement that disrupted this basis for pure craftsmanship, whether it be factories, commercialism, or labor unions, became a target for reform.

Like Stickley, Elbert Hubbard shared much with the crafts radicals. "Work is for the worker," he declared in his *Little Journeys*, arguing, "it's not so much what a man gets in money wages, but it's what he gets in terms of life and living that counts."[69] His own dissatisfaction with mere business success led Hubbard, a

self-made man and pioneer in mass-marketing techniques, to retire in 1893 to devote himself to literature and the arts. Drawing upon his boyhood experiences (in rural Illinois as the village doctor's son) to romanticize manual labor, farming, and country life, he set up a crafts colony that spread both the affectations and the functionalism of the arts and crafts through mail-order gift catalogues. Roy- croft (in East Aurora, New York, outside of Buffalo) differed from the ventures of reformers and missionaries like Will Price and Edward Pearson Pressey, not only by bringing "culture" to the larger public but also by commercializing the craftsman ideal and ultimately appropriating it for big business.

According to the official Roycroft story, after visiting Morris's Merton Abbey, "where they made just a few beautiful things, [Hubbard's] business brains clicked and he realized that in America an institution built along similar lines was sure to prosper. Thenceforth his motto was to be, 'Not how cheap but how good.'"[70] In 1895 with the help of a few friends and his wife, Hubbard set up a handprinting operation after the example of the Kelmscott Press and published his first book, a heavy-set imitation of Pre-Raphaelite design. He also began *The Philistine*, a monthly booklet that captured the boastful individualism of the time, full of distilled aphorisms on work and beauty, new poetry, and self-promotion. With a circulation of over a hundred thousand a month, *The Philistine* opened up new worlds of thought to young people in small towns across America. Hubbard ran a series of articles under the name "Clavigera," presumably from Ruskin (who wrote a series of books called *Fors Clavigera*), announcing Clavigera-Ruskin's membership in the Society of Philistines (a club open to all subscribers to the journal);[71]

he also legitimized his own patchwork ideas by combining phrases from Ruskin's writings with sentences close enough to the master's style to fool the less educated.

Hubbard later confessed, "The Roycroft began as a joke, but did not stay one; it soon resolved itself into a commercial institution." Named after a pair of sixteenth-century printers, it meant "the king's craft" or "the king's country place."[72] With its English Tudor central workshop made of local stone, its half-timbered and stone cottages for various crafts, workrooms with extended halls under beamed ceilings, Hubbard's place evoked a monastery, school, or squire's estate more than a factory. One venture led to another: the print shop to a bindery and then to leather and copper shops. Cabinetmaking began with furnishing the Roycroft Inn, a hotel built to accommodate the rush of curious visitors, and expanded to produce duplicates for them to take home. By 1909, portable souvenir items like hammered copper trays and inkwells, leather bookends, stained-glass lamps, and even maple-sugar candy were available through the elaborate Roycroft catalogues. In these models of self-advertisement,[73] symbolic medievalism, communitarianism, and benevolent capitalism all joined together to sell consumers the simple life of the Arts and Crafts home.

Though Hubbard claimed his venture to be "a social and industrial experiment"[74] that provided work for village people and kept them from moving to the city, Roycroft more closely resembled the welfare capitalism of the day than any utopian colony. With excellent working conditions, playgrounds and libraries for leisure and study, and some flexibility in work despite divided labor processes and mechanization, Roycroft was a school and factory combined. Hubbard actually organized a school to teach crafts, farming, nature appreciation, and the work ethic. Even with talented artists like the designer Dard Hunter, the illustrator Samuel Warner, and the coppersmith Karl Kipp, however, Roycroft fell short of Triggs's new workshop because Hubbard retained economic and social control. To the end, he remained a paternalistic employer, paying beginner's wages to the youth and keeping the more skilled at a minimum, supplementing money with gifts, like the proverbial Christmas ham.[75]

"A Message to Garcia," printed in *The Philistine* in 1899, thrust Hubbard forward as a major spokesman for corporate capital.[76] Hubbard saw the ordinary worker as incompetent and lazy, reserving praise for those who loyally fulfill the orders of their bosses. Such persons would be rewarded; they would never fear layoff or need to strike. A lesson in initiative and thoroughness, "Garcia" assumed a community of interest between employer and employee. Thus, George H. Daniels of the New York Central reprinted the essay, eventually distributing two million copies. So did other corporations, including People's Drug Stores, Wanamaker's, and Westinghouse of England. Hubbard began to write articles calculated to attract corporate purchasers, devoting a new series of his *Little Journeys* to businessmen. Meat packers bought a million copies of his account of a visit to the home of Phillip Armour, which ridiculed Upton Sinclair's muckraking attack in *The Jungle*. Hubbard reserved his highest praise for enlightened capitalists like National Cash Register's John H. Patterson, the type of self-made man with whom he identified.[77] He also wrote advertisements for business, associating clients with craftsman virtues; a "testimony" for one hotel declared, "'Art,' says William Morris, 'is not a thing, it is a way.'

Art is the beautiful way. It stands for reciprocity, mutuality, beauty, order – Human Service."[78] In such conflations art and business became one.

The Moral Environmental Imperative

What distinguished the Arts and Crafts movement from other aspects of social reform was, after all, its emphasis on art. Even the most enthusiastic supporter of "simplicity of life" who argued that "the Arts and Crafts aim, first, . . . to rescue the individual" could declare that it also strives "to make beautiful things – graphic, plastic, decorative."[79] Tastemakers within the movement sought to remake the look of objects rather than to restructure the nature of work; they shared the moralism of social reformers but not their emphasis on transforming industrial relations. As George Twose, president of the Chicago Society of Arts and Crafts, explained in his 1898 review of the Society's first exhibition, "Cups and platters, pots and pans, tables and chairs, though insignificant in their humble ministering, are important articles when considered in the light of the sensitiveness of man's character and the persistency of their effect."[80] Or, to put it another way, everyday articles set a standard for good or evil; they both reflected personality and made character. A table, thus, could suggest "hospitality" and defy "time." Such moral environmentalist premises – that good art not only revealed the spirit of its maker but also affected its users – represented more than a legacy from Ruskin; they became a way to elevate beauty without the decadence associated with aestheticism. Further, they suggested a way to reconcile the evangelical's distrust of art, still a part of the heritage of the American middle class, with a desire for beauty.[81]

Tastemakers like H. Langford Warren

and Frederic Allen Whiting of the BSAC upheld the hand over the machine, the workshop over the factory, as means to improve artistic ends and beautify daily life. Seeking to raise the standard of taste of both craftsman and consumer, they associated craftsmanship with superior aesthetic qualities, the combination of the useful and beautiful, the finely wrought and unique. Through the museum, school, and crafts society, the Arts and Crafts aesthetic would be spread to prompt "an awakening interest in things artistic and . . . [a] growing appreciation of the supreme importance of beauty to the welfare and happiness of mankind," as the catalogue of the second exhibition of the Boston Society of Arts and Crafts proclaimed.[82] And, as one writer put it in *The House Beautiful*, the major home decorating magazine, "It is not enough to satisfy the demands of utility, the debt owing to good taste and culture must also be discharged, and in the solution of this will be found the whole mystery of the domestic decorative arts."[83] Moral environmentalist principles, thus, crept into such articles that recommended Oriental over Western rugs and faience over bronze because mere utilitarianism was not enough to make a joyful and restful home.

Certainly domestic values lay at the center of the tastemaking discourse. "The home is the center of life, and if we can take art into the homes and then through the homes into the neighborhood, and then from one neighborhood into another, we shall soon make our whole city beautiful," explained the president of the Chicago Women's Club in 1910.[84] One member of the Detroit Society of Arts and Crafts recommended: "Esthetics being a necessity in the full development of a people it would seem important that the study of interior decoration be seriously considered as a means of civilization."[85] Be-cause people spent so much time at home, she claimed, the arts and crafts society should teach home decoration. A New York City home decorator stated the overall position more bluntly in a newspaper interview: "Inartistic homes ruin our manners and morals and wreck our nervous systems."[86]

The functional designs, natural woods, and nature motifs of the Arts and Crafts home were a fitting response to the call for a simple life so central to the crafts reformers' critique of commercial civilization and the factory system. An ideal crafts bungalow invited rest, comfort, and family togetherness, all values thought lacking in the competitive divisiveness of modern urban and industrial life. As the California poet-naturalist Charles Keeler asserted in *The Simple Home*: "No home is truly beautiful which is not fitted to the needs of those who dwell within its walls."[87] So he counseled elimination of all factory-made accessories "in order that your dwelling may not be typical of American commercial supremacy, but rather of your own fondness for things that have been created as a response to your love of that which is good and simple and fit for daily companionship." Despite Keeler's exhortation, the simple home became available in mail-order copies for those unable to purchase custom work. Thus, furnishings were offered in a wide variety of forms – from the hand-made to the mass-produced –and the American middle class was provided with a new artistic self-definition.

The components of the craftsman ideal – skilled workmanship, organic unity of thought and labor, individuality of expression – appealed to those cut off from such experiences but capable of purchasing them. Either through membership in a crafts society or leisure-time engagement in crafts work, through decorating with Arts and Crafts designs, intellectual men and housewives could become part of a historic tradition of craftsmanship that linked the medieval guildsman with the colonial American forebear, the European peasant, and the native American craftsman. In a world where new corporate forms – the trust and bureaucracy – were undermining even the autonomy of the bourgeois, arts and crafts allowed a broad middle-class public to reclaim beauty, if not the dream of brotherhood.

1. Vida Scudder, *A Listener in Babel* (Boston: Houghton Mifflin, 1903), pp. 314-321; idem, *On Journey* (New York: E.P. Dutton, 1937), pp. 78-84.

2. For the phrase "dreams of brotherhood and beauty," see Leonard Abbott, *The Society of the Future* (Chicago: Charles Kerr, 1898), n.p.; for an extension of this analysis, see Eileen Boris, *Art and Labor: Ruskin, Morris, and the Craftsman Ideal in America* (Philadelphia: Temple University Press, 1986).

3. The most useful general discussions of the social and economic forces of this period remain Robert Wiebe, *The Search for Order, 1877-1920* (New York: Hill and Wang, 1967); and Alfred D. Chandler, *The Visible Hand: The Managerial Revolution in American Business* (Cambridge: Harvard University Press, 1977). See also David M. Gordon, Richard Edwards, and Michael Reich, *Segmented Work, Divided Workers: The Historical Transformation of Labor in the United States* (New York: Cambridge University Press, 1982).

4. For the term "middle class," see Stuart M. Blumin, "The Hypothesis of Middle-Class Formation in Nineteenth-Century America: A Critique and Some Proposals," *American Historical Review* 90 (April 1985), pp. 299-338.

5. For the process of deskilling, see Harry Braverman, *Labor and Monopoly Capitalism: The Degradation of Work in the Twentieth Century* (New York: Monthly Review Press, 1974); for specific crafts, see Walter E. Weyl and A.M. Sakolski, "Conditions of Entrance to the Principal Trades," Bureau of Labor, Bulletin 67 (November 1906), pp. 691-780; for the subject of architecture, see Bernard Michael Boyle, "Architectural Practice in America, 1865-1955," in *The Architect: Chapters in the History of the Profession*, Spiro Kostof, ed. (New York: Oxford University Press, 1977), pp. 309-344; and Gwendolyn Wright, *Moralism and the Model Home: Domestic Architecture and Cultural Conflict in Chicago, 1873-1913* (Chicago: University of Chicago Press, 1980), pp. 46-97; see also John A. Kouwenhoven, *The Arts in Modern American Civilization*

(New York: Norton, 1948); and Raymond Williams, *Culture* (London: Fontana Paperbacks, 1981), pp. 33-56.

6. Chandler 1977, pp. 209-239; John William Ferry, *A History of the Department Store* (New York: Macmillan, 1960); and Susan Porter Benson, "Palace of Consumption and Machine for Selling: The American Department Store, 1880-1940," *Radical History Review* 21 (Fall 1979), pp. 199-221.

7. Richard Hofstadter, *The Age of Reform* (New York: Random House, 1955); Wiebe 1967, passim.

8. Daniel Rodgers, "In Search of Progressivism," *Reviews in American History: The Promise of American History, Progress and Prospects* 10 (December 1982), pp. 113-132.

9. Cram is quoted in Douglass Shand Tucci, *Ralph Adams Cram: American Medievalist* (Boston: Boston Public Library, 1975), pp. 15-16; idem, "The Gothic Ascendency," *The Gothic Quest* (Garden City, N.Y.: Doubleday, Page, 1917), pp. 53-75. For a full discussion of his thought, see Robert Muccigrosso, *American Gothic: The Mind and Art of Ralph Adams Cram* (Washington, D.C.: University Press of America, 1979).

10. Bertram Grosvenor Goodhue, "The Final Flowering of Age-End Art," *Knight Errant* 1 (1892), pp. 108-110.

11. Ralph Adams Cram, "Concerning the Restoration of Idealism and the Raising to Honour Once More of the Imagination," *Knight Errant* 1 (1892), pp. 12-13; see idem, *My Life in Architecture* (Boston: Little, Brown, 1936) for a record of his own perception of this period.

12. Ralph Adams Cram, "The Craftsman and The Architect," *The Ministry of Art* (Boston: Houghton Mifflin Co., 1914), pp. 143-166, esp. pp. 164-165.

13. Idem, *Walled Towns* (Cambridge: Marshall Jones Company, 1919).

14. For a general study, see *Chas. F. Lummis – The Centennial Exhibition*, Daniel P. Moneta, ed. (Los Angeles: Southwest Museum, 1985), quote from p. 17.

15. Esther McCoy, "George Harris," in *California Design1910*, Timothy J. Andersen, Eudorah M. Moore, and Robert W. Winter, eds. (Pasadena: California Design Publication, 1974), pp. 110-111.

16. Robert Winter, "The Arroyo Culture," in Andersen, Moore, and Winter 1974, pp. 10-17; see also Kevin Starr, *Inventing the Dream: California through the Progressive Era* (New York: Oxford University Press, 1985), pp. 107-124.

17. Lummis is quoted in Moneta 1985, p. 49.

18. Mrs. Hartley Dennett, "Aesthetics and Ethics," *Handicraft* 1 (May 1902), pp. 33, 38.

19. Oscar Lovell Triggs, "The Workshop and School, *Craftsman* 3 (October 1902), pp. 20-32; idem, "A School of Industrial Art," *Craftsman* 3 (January 1903), pp. 218-219; idem, *Chapters in the History of the Arts and Crafts Movement* (Chicago: Bohemian Guild of Arts and Crafts, 1902), pp. 148, 160-161; Leonard D. Abbott, "Edward Markham: Laureate of Labor," *Comrade* 1 (1904), no. 4, p. 75.

20. L.M. Turner, "The Little Shop, its Wares and Influence," *Artifact* 3 (April 1904), p. 145.

21. [Edward Pearson Pressey], "Editorial," *Country Time and Tide* 4 (September 1903), p. 168.

22. Leonard Abbott, "Art and Social Reform," in *Encyclopedia of Social Reform*, W.D.B. Bliss, ed. (New York: Funk and Wagnall's, 1908), p. 67.

23. See note 19 above and Oscar Lovell Triggs, "The Play Principle," *Craftsman* 6 (June 1904), pp. 290-291; idem, in 1902 Report of the Secretary of the Industrial Art League (Chicago, n.p.), p. 10.

24. Oscar Lovell Triggs, "The New Workshop," *Triggs Magazine* 1 (September 1905), pp. 14, 21-22; idem, "Industrial Feudalism – and After," in *The Changing Order* (Chicago: Oscar L. Triggs Publishing Company, 1905), p. 232.

25. Triggs 1905 ("New Workshop,"), pp. 17-18; see advertisement in *Triggs Magazine* 1 (September 1905), "Pickard," inside front cover; for Rookwood, see Triggs 1902, pp. 157-162.

26. William Morris, *The Collected Works of William Morris*, May Morris, ed., vol. 24 (London: Longman's, 1910-1915); Abbott 1898; William Dean Howells, *A Traveller from Alturia: A Romance* (New York: Harper and Brothers, 1894).

27. Letter from Mary Ware Dennett to the chairman of the Council, January 27, 1905, Papers of the Society of Arts and Crafts, Boston (BSAC Papers), Archives of American Art, Smithsonian Institution, Roll 300, pp. 446-449.

28. Mary Ware Dennett, "The Arts and Crafts: An Outlook," *Handicraft* 2 (April 1903), pp. 3-27, esp. pp. 16-17; idem, letter to Frederic Allen Whiting, February 7, 1905, BASC Papers, Roll 300, pp. 455-456.

29. For the complex relationship between socialists among the Arts and Crafts leadership in England and the larger movement there, see Peter Stansky, *Redesigning the World: William Morris, the 1880s, and the Arts and Crafts* (Princeton: Princeton University Press, 1985); for the American scene, see Boris 1986, pp. 169-188.

30. Algie M. Simons, "Chicago Arts and Crafts Exhibition," *International Socialist Review* 2 (January 1902), pp. 511-512; idem, *Wasting Human Life* (Chicago: Socialist Party), pp. 90-91.

31. Ellen Gates Starr, "The Renaissance of Handicraft," *International Socialist Review* 2 (February 1902), p. 574.

32. Ellen Gates Starr, "Art and Labor," *Hull House Maps and Papers* (New York: T.Y. Crowell, 1895), pp. 165-179; idem, "Why I am a Socialist," clipping of 1917, Box 1, Ellen Gates Starr Papers, Sophia Smith Collection, Smith College, Northampton, Massachusetts. For her biography, see Allen F. Davis, "Ellen Gates Starr," *Notable American Women*, Edward James and Janet W. James, eds. (Cambridge: Harvard University Press, 1971), vol. 3, pp. 351-353.

33. "Notes by Josephine Starr on Ellen Gates Starr, April 1960," Starr Papers, Box 1; see also catalogue for "Exhibition of a Collection of Bookbindings by Ellen Gates Starr, including Some Work by Associates, Assistants, and Pupils," Hull House Bindery, March 18-25, ca. 1906, Starr Papers, Box 1.

34. Vida Scudder's life is sketched by the author in "Vida Dutton Scudder," *Dictionary of American Biography* (New York: Charles Scribner's, 1977), supplement 5, pp. 616-617.

35. Scudder 1903, pp. 38-39.

36. Idem, *Social Ideals in English Letters* (New York: Chautauquan Press, 1898), p. 167.

37. The term "women's culture" is meant to encompass the activities, knowledge, skills, and values shared among women and passed on to the next generation. For a discussion of this term, see Ellen DuBois, Mari Jo Buhle, Temma Kaplan, Gerda Lerner, and Carroll Smith-Rosenberg, "Politics and Culture in Women's History: A Symposium," *Feminist Studies* 6 (Spring 1980), pp. 26-64; for its presence among women reformers, see Kathryn Kish Sklar, "Hull House in the 1890s: A Community of Women Reformers," *Signs: Journal of Women in Culture and Society* 10 (Summer 1985), pp. 658-677.

38. For a discussion of gender divisions in the crafts movement, see Boris 1986, pp. 99-121; on homosocial bonding, see Anthea Callen, *Women Artists of the Arts and Crafts Movement, 1870-1914* (New York: Pantheon, 1979), pp. 10-17, 218-221; and Lionel Lambourne, *Utopian Craftsmen: The Arts and Crafts Movement from the Cotswolds to Chicago* (Salt Lake City: Peregrine Smith, 1980), p. 146.

39. William Price, "Several More Answers for Charles Cantor," *Artsman* 2 (May 1905), p. 270.

40. Sylvester Baxter, "The Artist as Craftsman," *Handicraft* 1 (August 1902), pp. 113-114.

41. Triggs 1902, pp. 187, 147-157.

42. Triggs 1905 (*The Changing Order*), "A Type of Transition: William Morris," p. 147; idem, "The Meaning of Industrial Art," *House Beautiful* 15 (May 1904), p. 357; idem, "The Democracy of Art," *International Socialist Review* 2 (January 1902), p. 481.

43. For background on the University of Chicago, see Richard J. Storr, *Harper's University: The Beginnings: A History of the University of Chicago* (Chicago: University of Chicago Press, 1966); Triggs is discussed in "Oscar Lovell Triggs," William R. Harper Papers, Box 64, Folder 16, in President's Papers, University Archives, University of Chicago. See also "Triggs Folder," Wallace Rice Papers, Newberry Library, Chicago.

44. Thorstein Veblen, *The Theory of the Leisure Class* (reprint ed., New York: New American Library, 1953), pp. 190-218; for his influence on Triggs, see "Announcement," *Triggs Magazine* 2 (April 1906), p. 2.

45. For Dewey, Addams, and the Chicago crafts environment, see Boris 1986, pp. 45-51, 92-98, 131-133.

46. Triggs 1902, pp. 195-198; see also Max West, "The Revival of Handicraft in America," U.S. Bureau of Labor, *Bulletin* 55 (November 1904), pp. 1601-1603.

47. "Industrial Art League," Harper Papers, Box 40, Folder 1.

48. "The Arts and Crafts of the Machine," in *Frank Lloyd Wright, Writings and Buildings*, Edgar Kaufmann and Ben Raeburn, eds. (New York: New American Library, 1960), pp. 55-73; for Wright and the crafts movement, see H. Allen Brooks, "Chicago Architecture: Its Debt to the Arts and Crafts," *Journal of the Society of Architectural Historians* 30 (December 1971), pp. 312-316.

49. Carlton Noyes to Horace Traubel, October 25, 1903, Box 8, Horace Traubel Papers, Library of Congress.

50. By 1905 *The Craftsman* had a circulation of around 25,000, considered large for such a specialized periodical (figures from N.W. Ayer and Sons, *American News Annual*, 1895-1915); Hubbard's *Philistine* circulated to 52,000 in 1900 and 110,000 two years later, according to Freeman Champney, *Art and Glory: The Story of Elbert Hubbard* (New York: Crown Publishers, 1968), pp. 58, 92.

51. Gustav Stickley, "Als Ik Kan: Art True and False," *Craftsman* 8 (August 1905), pp. 684-686.

52. "Als Ik Kan," *Craftsman* 8 (September 1905), pp. 835-836.

53. For Stickley, see Mary Ann Smith, *Gustav Stickley: The Craftsman* (Syracuse: Syracuse University Press, 1982); Barry Sanders, "Introduction," in *The Craftsman: An Anthology* (Santa Barbara: Peregrine Smith, 1978), pp. vii-xv; and John Crosby Freeman, *The Forgotten Rebel: Gustav Stickley and His Craftsman Mission Furniture* (Watkins Glen, N.Y.: Century House, 1966). Stickley recounted his own life in "Thoughts Occasioned by an Anniversary: A Plea for a Democratic Art," *Craftsman* 7 (October 1904), pp. 42-57; see also "Gustav Stickley," *New York Times*, April 22, 1942, p. 24.

54. "Titlepage" and "Foreward," *Craftsman* 1 (October 1901), pp. i-ii; for Irene Sargent, see Freeman 1966, pp. 15-16.

55. See *Craftsman*, volumes 1-11, passim; for shift in perspective, see [Stickley] "Als Ik Kan," *Craftsman* 11 (October 1906), pp. 128-130.

56. For manual training, see Stickley, "Manual Training and Citizenship," *Craftsman* 5 (January 1904), pp. 410-411; for Americanization of immigrants through the work ethic, see also "Als Ik Kan," *Craftsman* 12 (September 1907), p. 705.

57. See *Craftsman*, volumes 1-20, passim.

58. "Utility – Simplicity – Beauty," *Craftsman* 1 (November 1901), pp. v-vi; "Als Ik Kan," *Craftsman* 10 (June 1906), pp. 396-399; Gustav Stickley, "From Ugliness to Beauty," *Craftsman* 7 (December 1904), p. 310.

59. For more about the association of *The Craftsman* with masculinity, see Boris 1986, pp. 76-77. For the simple life, see "Als Ik Kan," *Craftsman* 12 (May 1907), p. 348; Stickley 1909, p. 97; "Craftsman Advertising Department," *Craftsman* 18 (May 1910), n.p.; Stickley 1904 ("From Ugliness to Beauty"), p. 315.

60. Irene Sargent, "Decoration," *Craftsman* 7 (December 1904), p. 321.

61. "Indian Blankets, Baskets and Bowls: The Product of the Original Craftworkers of This Continent," *Craftsman* 17 (February 1910), p. 588.

62. Elizabeth Daingerfield, "Patch Quilts and Philosophy," *Craftsman* 14 (August 1908), pp. 523-527; "A Russian Peasant Industry," *Craftsman* 4 (July 1903), pp. 291-294.

63. Stickley 1904 ("Thoughts Occasioned by an Anniversary"), p. 53.

64. Stickley 1910, pp. 194-205; "Some Examples of the Craftsman Wall Hangings," *Craftsman* 4 (July 1903), pp. 289-290; Stickley, "Social Unrest: A Condition Brought about by Separating the People into Two Factions, Capital and Labor," *Craftsman* 13 (November 1907), pp. 183-191.

65. Stickley 1907 ("Social Unrest"), p. 186.

66. Gustav Stickley, "The Guild Stamp and Union Label," *Craftsman* 13 (January 1908), pp. 375-384; idem, "Als Ik Kan," *Craftsman* 13 (March 1908), pp. 724-725; idem, "Waste: Our Heaviest National Liability," *Craftsman* 20 (July 1911), pp. 343-348.

67. Gustav Stickley, " A New Political Party Founded on Conservation and The Square Deal," *Craftsman* 18 (August 1910), pp. 515-520; idem, "Woodrow Wilson: One of the Men Needed by the People," *Craftsman* 19 (November 1910), pp. 117-123.

68. Examples of articles on cooperatives included Gustav Stickley, "Cooperative Stores in England: A System of Economical Distribution that Has Solved the Problem of High Prices," *Craftsman* 18 (May 1910), pp. 187-193; "The Future of Garden Cities in America: Democratic Town Planning To Be Accomplished by Cooperation," *Craftsman* 22 (May 1912), pp. 117-122.

69. Elbert Hubbard, *Little Journeys*, Anniversary Edition (New York: Wm. H. Wise and Co., 1916), pp. 24-25; for his life and a critical popular appraisal, see Champney 1968. See also Robert Beisner, " 'Commune' in East Aurora," *American Heritage* 21 (February 1971), pp. 72-77, 106-109; David Balch, *Elbert Hubbard: Genius of Roycroft* (New York: Frederick A. Stokes, 1940).

70. Felix Shay, *Elbert Hubbard of East Aurora* (New York: Wm. T. Wise & Sons, 1926), pp. 31-32.

71. Clavigera, "A Protest and A Prayer," *Philistine* 2 (January 1896), pp. 41-50; "Some Things America Needs," *Philistine* 3 (June 1896), pp. 1-16. For the influence of Hubbard's magazine on young "provincials," see letter from Will Ransom to Henry Taber, July 21, 1930, Hubbard File, Wing Collection, Newberry Library, Chicago.

72. Elbert Hubbard to Lyman Chandler, March 4, 1903, as quoted in Robert Judson Clark, ed., *The Arts and Crafts Movement in America, 1876-1916* (Princeton: Princeton University Press, 1972), p. 47, caption 52.

73. For descriptions of Roycroft and its work, see Robert Koch, "Elbert Hubbard's Roycrofters as Artist-Craftsmen," *Winterthur Portfolio* 3 (Charlottesville: University Press of Virginia, 1967), pp. 67-82; Albert Lane, *Elbert Hubbard and His Work* (Worcester, Mass.: Blanchard Press, 1901).

74. Elbert Hubbard, "A Social and Industrial Experiment," from *Cosmopolitan*, reprint ed. in 1902 Roycroft Catalogue, p. 13, in Hubbard File.

75. Shay 1926, pp. 124-129; Francis and Abigail Farrar, "A Little Journey to East Aurora," in Hubbard File; and Champney 1968, pp. 135-177.

76. Hubbard, " A Message to Garcia," *Philistine* 8 (March 1899), pp. 109-116.

77. Beisner 1971, p. 109; and Champney 1968, pp. 88-89.

78. "Story and Testimony for Sherman Hotel, Chicago," *Philistine* 34 (March 1912), p. xvi.

79. William Sloane Kennedy, "Simplicity of Life in Arts and Crafts," *Artsman* 1 (April 1904), p. 237.

80. George Twose, "The Chicago Arts and Crafts Society's Exhibition," *Brush and Pencil* 5 (May 1898), p. 74.

81. For examples of such reasoning, see Anne McD. Powers, "The Quisisana Furniture," *House Beautiful* 11 (February 1902), p. 197.

82. "Society of Arts and Crafts," *Exhibition of The Society of Arts and Crafts, Together With a Loan Collection of Applied Art*, Copley and Allston Halls, Boston, Mass., April 4-15, 1899 (Boston: Heintzlemann Press, 1899), p. 7.

83. Caryl Coleman, "Bric-A-Brac, Or What You Will," *House Beautiful* 2 (January 1899), pp. 80-81.

84. Mrs. John O'Connor, quoted in "Report on the Chicago Society of Arts and Crafts, May 27, 1910, Chicago Society of Arts and Crafts," *Handicraft* 3 (August 1910), p. 184.

85. Clara Dyar, "A Suggestion to Arts and Crafts Societies," *Handicraft* 4 (September 1911), p. 221.

86. "Ugly Homes and Bad Morals," interview with Mrs. Herbert Nelson Curtis, reprinted from the *New York Sun*, in *Artsman* 3 (December 1905), pp. 73-78.

87. Charles Keeler, *The Simple Home* (1904, reprint ed., Santa Barbara: Peregrine Smith, 1979), pp. 1-55.

The Art of Work

Robert Edwards

At the core of Arts and Crafts philosophy lay the concept that work should be the creative and joyful essence of daily life rather than a mere act of sustenance. To actualize this ideal, spokesmen from William Morris to William Price devised all the multifarious, often doctrinaire, programs of the movement, promulgating them with crusading intensity. Price, who termed work "the art that is life," and the wealthy amateur craftsman Ralph Radcliffe Whitehead advocated working in communities located where closeness to nature would enhance workers' lives. There the making of domestic furnishings was a way to make daily living art.[1] Others, without eschewing pastoral utopias, addressed the reality of industrialization by attempting to find ways to improve the worker's lot within a factory context. Gustav Stickley and Charles P. Limbert, factory owners who experimented with profit sharing and improved working conditions, exemplify this group. Still others, such as Elbert Hubbard of Roycroft and David Wolcott Kendall, chief designer for the Phoenix Furniture Company, were associated with Arts and Crafts products for pragmatic reasons. Arts and Crafts was a burgeoning market.

At one extreme of the idealism-pragmatism spectrum was Julius Augustus Wayland. His choices of environment, worker, and product evidence a fanatic idealism. Wayland chose a barren, sandy site in Tennessee to establish "Ruskin," a community inspired by political socialism.[2] Whitehead, visiting the Ruskin community found the concept (not to mention the sight) too dreary and restrictive. He could afford the luxury of scouring the entire country to discover the spot most nearly matching his preconceived vision of ideal natural beauty. He founded Byrdcliffe on a sylvan mountainside near Woodstock, New York. Will Price, founder of the

Arts and Crafts community at Rose Valley, allowed practical considerations to temper his utopian zeal, situating his experiment within commuting distance of Philadelphia, where he maintained his architectural practice and where most of the original Valley residents worked. At the other end of the spectrum, the social reformers Ellen Gates Starr and Jane Addams established their settlement house, Hull House, in the middle of Chicago close to the immigrants they helped, and large factories such as Limbert's were sensibly located near both a sizable labor force and suppliers of raw materials.

The ideological relevance of handwork versus use of the machine and the degree to which both were practiced were other issues on which Arts and Crafts movement participants differed widely. The role of machinery in the Arts and Crafts workplace depended on what was produced, as well as on philosophies of production. "Ruskin's" products were chewing gum, suspenders, and commercial printing, so arguments about the relative merits of machinery or handwork were of decidedly minor import.[3] Whitehead, a purist, had hoped to power his woodworking machinery with water, following the precepts of his teacher John Ruskin. However, the mountain streams did not provide strong or constant enough water power for the elaborate equipment installed at Byrdcliffe (fig. 1). (Whitehead does not document his compromise solution, which was probably gasoline.) Before Price arrived, Ridley Creek had provided power to mills at Rose Valley for decades, but, even though Ruskin approved of water power, Rose Valley furniture was made almost entirely with hand tools. Existing photographs of the woodworking shop show no use of the readily available water power. Elsewhere the use of ma-

1

2

3

Fig. 1. Woodworking shop of Byrdcliffe, Woodstock, New York, ca. 1904. Collection of Mr. and Mrs. Mark Willcox, Jr.

Fig. 2. A Craftsman workshop, Syracuse, New York. Illustrated in *House Beautiful*, October 1899.

Fig. 3. Rose Valley furniture shop, Moylan, Pennsylvania, 1903. Illustrated in *House and Garden*, October 1906.

Large factories like Craftsman, Phoenix, and Roycroft had far more powered machines than were to be found even in the elaborately equipped Byrdcliffe wood shop. The difference in size among shops relying on handwork, such as Rose Valley, was apparent in the number of woodworking benches. Will Price (seen at the drawing board in the background) installed several benches where each craftsman worked on separate parts of the same table.

chinery was assumed and power for it was not considered an ideological issue. Although most photographs of Gustav Stickley's Craftsman workshops in Syracuse and Elbert Hubbard's Roycroft Shops in East Aurora, New York, show craftsmen working without power tools, much machinery was, in fact, used (see figs. 1, 2, and 3).

Skills demanded of the labor pools in Arts and Crafts workplaces varied widely. The paid workers at "Ruskin" and Roycroft were not necessarily skilled craftsmen and their labor rotated between farm work and craft work. Will Price thought Americans had already lost their craft skills to machinery so, rather than train young men as did John Scott Bradstreet at the Minneapolis Crafthouse, he hired immigrant woodcarvers. Limbert took advantage of the local pool of Dutch workers for his factories in Grand Rapids and New Holland, Michigan, while Whitehead used a newly available labor source: professionally trained artists and craftsmen.

With the spread of industrialization, it had become uncommon for young Americans to undergo long apprenticeships. In 1907 a writer for a builder's journal observed that "Our factories and our trades are filled with boys in their teens. Where do we expect them to be educated? At the bench or at the machine from the age of 12 years."[4] Some thought they could, indeed, be taught in factories, although the lesson to be learned was what machines were capable of doing rather than one of craftsmanship. Men like Kendall and Stickley knew how moldings were "run up" by machines as well as how the particular charcteristics of materials would govern their uses. But where would ideas about beauty be taught?[5] The many design schools that were established across America toward the end of the nineteenth century created a new generation

Fig. 4. Parke Edwards (center) at work in the Pennsylvania Museum School of Industrial Art forge, from Parke Edwards's scrapbook. The Athenaeum of Philadelphia.

of craftsmen and a new profession, the industrial designer. The Rhode Island School of Design, the Pennsylvania Museum and School of Industrial Art (now the Philadelphia College of Art), Pratt Institute, Cooper Union, and Cranbrook began with the specific mandate to train designers for industry. Such professionals, educated to simplify designs to best utilize the machine's potential, contributed to the development of a recognizable Arts and Crafts style.

One such designer was Parke Edwards (1872-1975), significant both because he represents the first generation of school-trained craftsmen and because his career reveals Arts and Crafts practices reaching well into mid-century.[6] While at the Pennsylvania Museum School of Industrial Art (he graduated in 1913), Edwards studied under the renowned blacksmith Samuel Yellin and was exposed to the art education theories of Howard Fremont Stratton, then director (fig. 4). An extant school portfolio of Edwards's shows experiments in a wide variety of media, most dependent on designs conventionalized from plant forms (figs. 5-8). School notebooks became a manual from which the mature Edwards drew inspiration for the infinitely varied designs of copper bosses, bolt heads, lighting fixtures, stone capitals, hinges, handles, and railings for his major work, the Swedenborgian Church at Bryn Athyn, Pennsylvania. To build the cathedral and later, *Glencairn*, the residence of Raymond Pitcairn, the financial backer of the community, a guild was set up in which craftsmen in

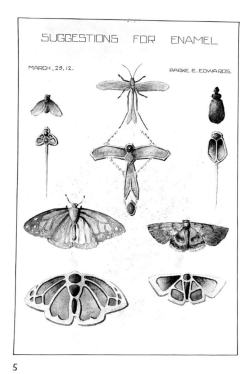

5

7

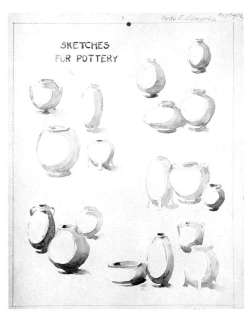

8

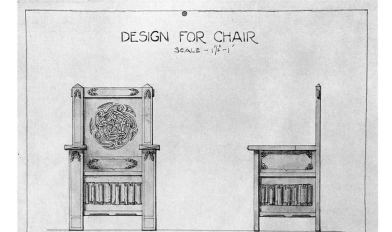

6

Figs. 5-8. Sketches from the Parke Edwards design portfolio. Collection of Robert Edwards.

Parke Edwards's portfolio for his senior year at art school in 1912 included designs for objects made from traditional materials like clay, silver, and silk as well as for new materials such as linoleum.

all the traditional trades worked. Glass was made on the site for stained glass and mosaics; carvers worked in oak and teak; stonecutters fitted local granite, while Edwards headed the metal shop, where a new alloy called monel was wrought in historical styles as well as in Edwards's own style.

Although style developments associated with the Arts and Crafts movement appeared in metalwares as much as in other media, the movement's most obvious influence showed in the surface finish of silver, copper, and iron. For centuries silver had been finished to remove any evidence of handwork. During, and as a result of, the Arts and Crafts movement, the marks of craftsmen's tools appeared alike on simply designed pieces from shops such as the Kalo (for example, no. 141) and on lavish, elaborate confections such as those made by the Gorham Company (see no. 43).[7] Elsewhere, marks sometimes became mere symbols of handcraftsmanship analogous to the false tenons on wooden furniture. A meretricious hammered surface was added to some of Roycroft's copper giftwares; "hammer marks" appeared incongruously on Fulper ceramics, and Gustav Stickley used "hammered glass" in his lighting fixtures. The elaborate iron chandeliers and andirons handmade at Roycroft incorporated the twists and turns of wrought iron in a pedestrian way, but wrought iron as art was not within Hubbard's scope. For iron as art, one must turn to the work of master smiths such as Frank Koralewsky of Boston (no. 19), Cyril Colnik of Milwaukee, or Samuel Yellin of Philadelphia (no. 21). Koralewsky and Colnik would have agreed with Yellin's claim that "the perfection of mechanical means of production . . . has blinded many to the simplicity of the means which produced the great works of the past."[8]

Fig. 9. Frost Factory Workrooms, from *The Frost Arts and Crafts Workshop, Catalogue Number Fifty-Two* (Dayton, Ohio, 1910). Collection of Robert Edwards.

Techniques used at the Frost factory required no more than basic skill and equipment. Its setup could easily be duplicated in a home, and by offering metalworking supplies to their customers the company encouraged home craft.

While Yellin's shop depended on masterful skill to establish its reputation and win commissions, several metalworking factories capitalized on an apparent lack of skill in order to suggest handwork. The Frost Arts and Crafts Workshop of Dayton, Ohio, is an example (fig. 9). This small shop was well versed in Arts and Crafts rhetoric. It proudly asserted that "the workshop is conducted on the profit-sharing plan, and twice each year the various craftsmen receive a dividend which usually amounts to from 12 to 15 percent of their regular wages for the six-month period. Best of all, our workmen have plenty of fresh air and sunshine."[9] Frost's catalogue offerings "wrought up by hand" certainly looked handmade and, if unmarked, their jewelry could be mistaken for homemade.

The cult of the handmade extended across media to ceramics, sometimes with odd results emanating from factories offering wares that appeared to be made by unlikely factory methods such as coil building. The Fulper Pottery produced such wares, for example. Other routes brought the work of potters such as Mary Chase Perry, Hugh Robertson, and Adelaide Alsop Robineau into close association with the Arts and Crafts movement. These potters were fascinated by Oriental glaze effects dependent upon drips, cratering or crazing caused by firing rather than artistic underglaze painting. Thus, their interests closely paralleled the Arts and Crafts philosophy of truth to materials.

Numerous potters made a philosophical connection to the Arts and Crafts movement. Perry was a founder of the Detroit Society of Arts and Crafts, Robineau propounded the movement's tenets in the pages of *Keramic Studio*, of which she was editor, and the Rookwood Pottery was singled out as the model for historian Oscar Lovell Triggs's ideal workshop.[10] When Triggs defined this ideal in 1902, Rookwood had already given some twenty years to the development of its characteristic style: pots decorated primarily with naturalistic underglaze painting. The pottery's promotions encouraged collecting of Rookwood wares as if each example were a unique work of fine art. Such implication of creative individuality was important to Triggs, who thought Rookwood's production methods ensured "design unity." Surely this was a romantic notion when one considers that the wares were thrown or molded in one shop, decorated with flowers, dogs, or

Fig. 10. Gates Pottery workroom, Terra Cotta, Illinois, ca. 1905. Collection of the family of William Day Gates.

gremlins (not studied from nature) in another, and glazed and fired in still others. The intensive handwork involved may have fitted the Arts and Crafts requirement that workers be given back the creativity taken away by machines, but considering the product as fine art certainly excluded the expensive decorative vases from the equally important precept that good design be accessible to all consumers regardless of financial status.

William Day Gates, a manufacturer who built and situated his pottery in accord with Arts and Crafts standards of ideal working conditions, came closer to the democratic concept with his Teco line of pottery (fig. 10). He took advantage of the molding process's guarantee of technical predictability, quality control, and reduced costs. A well-designed inexpensive product could be had through the elimination of artistic hand-

work applied individually to each piece and through mass production of identical objects – the chief virtue of molding.

While some metalwork and ceramics show that process may have no more than a symbolic reference to handwork, and some molded ceramics stand as an illustration of mass production, which does not violate Arts and Crafts principles, furniture making offers the widest range of applications of Arts and Crafts process to industry. The furniture-making industry was changed so thoroughly by the introduction of powered machinery that a survey of factories, from small to large, may serve to illustrate how manufacturers in all media – ceramics, metalwares, and textiles as well as wooden objects – hoped to implement ideal methods of production. Studios and small workshops, while most limited in production, were the least restricted in potential realization of

Arts and Crafts philosophy. Biltmore Industries was established in the self-sustaining village on George W. Vanderbilt's Asheville, North Carolina, estate. The woodcarving department was concerned mainly with fulfilling special commissions, but an inventory of ornamental woodwork was kept on hand for sale to visiting tourists. The wood used there – carefully seasoned native black walnut and oak – was "gotten out with special reference to the production of strong, durable furniture. Machine tools are used in roughing out . . . but all of the carving and joining is done by hand."[11]

Although set up with the most modern machinery, Byrdcliffe produced fewer than fifty pieces of furniture. One reason the founders had chosen Woodstock was its proximity to rail service to New York City, where they planned to sell furniture through the McCreary retail store. But as soon as the first ponderous cabinets were built, it became obvious that cartage over ten miles to the depot was damaging to the furniture and that the custom nature of Byrdcliffe's offerings could not meet the inventory demands of a large urban retail outlet. Whitehead was disappointed by this practical failure but persisted with his experiment. He used his inherited fortune to support the colony for twenty-five years until his death in 1926. Free from financial constraints, the artists he backed were able to design to the letter of Ruskin's law. Dawson Watson, a Canadian recruited from the Boston Society of Arts and Crafts, and Zulma Steele and Edna Walker, both Pratt graduates, provided surface decoration for Whitehead's furniture designs that were adapted from examples published in *Studio*, among other sources, primarily British.[12] Steele's and Walker's designs were stylizations of their delicately drawn, tinted nature studies of plant life

Fig. 11. Byrdcliffe cabinet, carving by Ernest Troccoli, ca. 1904. Collection of Mr. and Mrs. Mark Willcox, Jr.

indigenous to the Woodstock area (see no. 165). Watson's designs, while also based on plant forms, were more abstract. The designs were usually planned as modular inserts for doors or sides of the monolithic case pieces (the hallmark of Byrdcliffe). Joinery, which had become the primary decorative device at some factories under Arts and Crafts influence, was of minor concern in Byrdcliffe designs. Dovetails, where used, were hand cut, but machines may well have aided the precise execution of other, usually hidden joinery. Even the carved two-level relief decoration could have been accomplished by machine without diminishing the effect, which was reliant upon color. One cabinet did incorporate virtuoso bas-relief carving by the Boston Society of Arts and Crafts member Ernest Troccoli, but it may have been an anomaly (fig. 11). The Troccoli piece owes its beauty to the iridescent surface of the unfinished quartered oak

as much as to the carving. Since many pieces were to be colored with transparent stains to the specification of the client, it cannot be determined if Troccoli's cabinet was left unfinished intentionally.

By contrast, handcarving and exposed joinery were an intrinsic part of Will Price's designs for Rose Valley furniture (see no. 166). In some instances three-dimensional figures formed the fully functional mortise pins of the tables and chairs that were the mainstay of Rose Valley production. Comparatively few case pieces were made, and all of the known examples of the five hundred pieces estimated to have been made are of quartered oak finished with a dark Cabot's stain.[13] One piece shows evidence of polychromy on the background of relief decorations but, as used, it merely serves to enhance the carved Gothic motifs and is not painterly as is the shaded Byrdcliffe work.

The Rose Valley experiment wrestled with the compromise reality forces upon the ideal. Woodworkers had no creative control over the product's design nor were they accepted as peers by residents of the community (where most workers did not reside). These same woodworkers had worked for Price's architectural firm making woodwork and furniture indistinguishable from the Rose Valley product long before Price described his ideal craftsman: "the Artsman . . . [a] lover of men who thru his work has learned the worth of life and is filled with a yearning and a pity for those whose work and environment are not so happy as his own."[14] Workers were content neither with pity nor with the damp stone mill in which they worked. After five years, the woodworking shop closed amid complaints about poor working conditions.

Charles Rohlfs included himself as an

Arts and Crafts practitioner, yet there is little in his method of manufacture or the style of his furniture that relates particularly to the prevailing Arts and Crafts ideal. Quality of wood and joinery were little consequence to Rohlfs; elaborate exaggerations of pinned mortises and tenons had nothing to do with structural integrity. While no reliable study has revealed the size of Rohlfs's shop, contemporary documents suggest that hundreds more pieces were built there than at Rose Valley or Byrdcliffe. Rohlfs, like Price, designed his workshop's output, which ranged from simple Mission-style pieces to the bizarre, intricate works for which he is today best known (see nos. 98 and 99). Rohlfs was not wedded through either process or product to Arts and Crafts. In fact, the Moorish flourishes that typify his work show him to be closer in sensibility to the exotic Italian furniture designer Carlo Bugatti than to reform theorists.

Elbert Hubbard's Roycroft and Gustav Stickley's Craftsman Workshops were, however, very sensitive to Arts and Crafts rhetoric. Both were large operations and must be considered mass producers.[15] Hubbard claimed that his furniture was custom made and sold only by catalogue from East Aurora, yet thousands of pieces were made over approximately twenty years. Roycroft catalogues stated that each piece was made by a single craftsman, but the presence of machines described in a contemporary furniture-making journal suggest otherwise. "Here is a disk sander, a band saw, a tenoner, shaper, a rip-saw, a mortiser built by the L. Houston Co. of Montgomery, Pa. and a jointer made by Frank L. Clements Co. of Rochester, N.Y. Most of the machines bear the familiar stamps of the American Wood Working Machinery Co., Ltd. of Williamsport, Pa. The cut-off and two planes are at the opposite end of the room . . . these planers are manufactured by the Williamsport Machine Co. of Williamsport, Pa. The second floor of the factory . . . has bench accommodation for a dozen men. The benches are all of the same make and came from the Vanmanen Buys Co., Ltd. of Grand Rapids. At the south end of the room is the glue room equipped with a good array of clamps and a 6-pot glue kettle, the latter of the Taggart type. . . . Three men are employed in this branch of the department."[16]

Set up in a similar way, Stickley's factory also offered furniture through catalogues, but supplied retail outlets across the country as well. Business records suggest that only a small proportion of Stickley's work was made to order. Since there is not enough information on the inventories, one cannot estimate the factory's total production.[17] The thousands of pieces of furniture extant do, however, provide an idea of the factory's fifteen-year output. The amount of handwork possible in so large an operation then becomes problematic. Arts and Crafts theorists in America did not, on the whole, denounce the use of machines so their use at either factory fits within Arts and Crafts ideology. Nevertheless, Stickley's and Hubbard's rhetoric, laden with concepts of honesty, integrity, and other moral issues, denied the use of machines in order to imply total handwork.

A dichotomy between image created in print and the actual method of production would be less apparent in the smaller factories like Byrdcliffe, which did not pursue a national market, or in the larger companies like Phoenix, which usually sold wholesale and needed no public image. For Stickley, Hubbard, Joseph P. McHugh, and Limbert public image was important. Each attempted to distinguish his company's offerings from his competitors' through claims couched in Arts and Crafts terms. When analyzed, these terms reveal more a mastery of advertising copywriting than a commitment to movement principles. Elbert Hubbard became the recognized master of that equivocating craft, hiring his skills out to companies like Colgate and Gillette. His primary interest was business, and he was willing to make any associations to sell Roycroft furniture, calling it "East Aurora Colonial" or stating that it resembled furniture made by the "old Mission Monks of California" in appearance and quality of workmanship.

Terminology was important to mass producers; McHugh claimed to be the first to offer Mission furniture, while Gustav Stickley sought to dissociate his product from the term, which was fast becoming a generic name for the American version of Arts and Crafts furniture. Limbert attempted to cover all bases by calling his furniture "Limbert's Holland Dutch Arts and Crafts." He went blatantly further than his competitors, re-writing decorative-arts history to make Holland the birthplace of Arts and Crafts, even though some of his own products were interpretations of the Glaswegian Charles Rennie Mackintosh's designs (see no. 51).[18] The only apparent Dutch influence was in a table lamp shaped like a windmill, though there were several hidden associations in the Dutch connection. Long associated with cleanliness, the Dutch now became an advertising symbol for the hygiene-conscious American consumer. Dutch Boy white lead paint and Dutch cleanser were but two among many products to make the connection. Limbert and Stickley took pains to point out the hygienic qualities of their oak beds, trying to compete with metal beds so popular with a public newly aware that germs and vermin might lurk in wood.

Charles Limbert can be called an enlightened capitalist, since he did provide better working conditions for his machine operators. Limbert moved his factory from the city to New Holland, which was near a lake, not only to escape the negative image then being attached to Grand Rapids furniture products but also to provide a healthful environment. Moreover, he elevated the self-image of his workers by calling them a guild of cabinetmakers and giving them social rooms at the plant.

The simple, straight-cut lines of Limbert furniture were highly suited to machine production. Except for processes like complicated decorative carving, still better done by hand, workers (having lost the skill for or never having been trained in handwork, as Price noted) needed to be skilled only in the use of power tools such as the jointer, glue machines, and planers. Yet in their published utterances Stickley, Limbert, and Hubbard still chose to equate simplicity of design with handcraftmanship and to ignore its source in mechanical expediency.

Most larger manufacturers like Tobey in Chicago or Phoenix in Grand Rapids were unconcerned with Arts and Crafts rhetoric: Phoenix because they were wholesalers who never had to appeal philosophically to the consumer and Tobey because they used the same advertising copy for each line, be it rococo or "Russmore (fig. 12)." They both carried a line of Arts and Crafts goods as one among many other styles in demand from retailers (see nos. 35 and 100). Their techniques, however, were often in keeping with Arts and Crafts thought. Both companies realized that elaborately embellished designs could not be done well by machinery and turned to handcarving. Neither made a moral issue of it. Stickley made much of the patriotic nature of the use of Ameri-

Fig. 12. Advertisement for the Tobey Furniture Company, from *House Beautiful*, April 1907.

Although the Tobey Company was a leader in promoting the domestic decorations of William Morris in America, they were not committed to his ideals beyond advertising copy.

can white oak and extolled design inherent in materials, allowing only the quarter grain to decorate his furniture. Actually the rayed-grain pattern produced by quartering oak logs characterized the overwhelming percentage of turn-of-the-century furniture, regardless of quality or style. Oak was plentiful and quarter cutting provided a stable surface on which to apply veneers or carving.[19] Gustav Stickley, then, was following standard factory practice when he applied veneers to make laminated legs and pieced desk lids look solid.

It was David Kendall who did the most to make oak the wood of choice. Hitherto, the coarse grain of oak and the harsh yellow it acquired after varnishing had kept it from fitting well into popular decorating schemes. The dark colored finishes Kendall developed made oak more compatible with the current taste for walnut, a wood in short supply during the late nineteenth century. Oak was processed through Grand Rapids factories in such large amounts that it too soon became scarce. By the early 1920s fashion changed in favor of a new crop of walnut.

Marketing methods also forced designers to keep turning out new lines of exotic finishes. Every six months furniture exhibitions were staged for the wholesalers to capture the buyers' attention.[20] This scramble for novelty resulted in a plethora of names for designs that often differed only in hardware or wood color. "Quaint," "New Art," "Craftsman," "Modern," "Mission," "German," "Russmore," "Hand Craft," and "Arts and Crafts" were among the many lines of furniture (figs. 13 and 14). The best of these designs, such as some of Limbert's Mackintosh interpretations or Stickley Brothers' (the Grand Rapids branch of Gustav Stickley's family) versions of high-style British design, are admirable for their sophistication (see no. 105), while the worst had fake tenons and pins glued to improbable parts in the hope that consumers would accept symbol for substance. While some Phoenix designs respond to the Arts and Crafts aesthetic, the company, perhaps because its product was not marketed under its own name (leaving promotion to retailers like Paine's in Boston), did not specify such connections. Its lines ran the gamut from Chippendale-style rockers to Morrisian barrel chairs and simple Mission benches (figs. 15 to 18). Some of the latter were decorated with Art Nouveau carving unusual in American furniture.

Kendall's idea that "furniture is made to sell" is in direct opposition to the movement ideal of beauty before commerce. He was frustrated by public taste and envisioned "designs for a line of goods that it would not do for me to try. The goods would not take with the buyers and yet, to my mind, it would be as artistic as any work I've ever attempted."[21] Still, his experiments in technology brought results very much in line with Arts and Crafts ideology, as a 1909 article suggests. In "Merits of Arts and Crafts,"

13

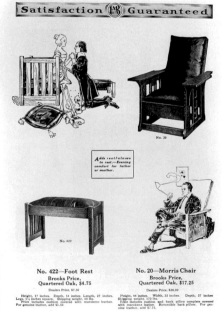

14

Fig. 13. Advertisement for the Grand Rapids Furniture Manufacturing Company from *House Beautiful*, January 1911.

The Arts and Crafts do-it-yourself ideology made possible the marketing of everything from houses to furniture in kit form. Although this "knock-down" furniture is not ideologically related to Arts and Crafts design, clever advertising copy assured homemakers of its Arts and Crafts construction and finish.

Fig. 14. Page from Catalog No. 18, October 1915, "Brooks 'Master Built' Furniture." Collection of Ralph and Terry Kovel.

The Brooks Manufacturing Company also featured "honest furniture" shipped ready for home assembly, "no skill or special knowledge required" and so simple that "it can be done by any woman."

Figs. 15-18. Phoenix Company, Grand Rapids, Michigan. Models 2953, 31 N, 2531, and 887. The Kendall School of Design, Grand Rapids, Michigan.

Factories operating at the turn of the century like Tobey, Phoenix, and Gorham had design lines intended to appeal to many tastes. Figure 15 is a Phoenix interpretation of a Chippendale chair (with the incongruous addition of rockers), while figure 16 is a version of H.H. Richardson's Romanesque style. Figures 17 and 18 relate more to Arts and Crafts style, 17 being a medieval form found also in Morris and Company tapestries and 18 a Mission "wagon seat" settee.

15

16

17

18

Albert Stickley (of Stickley Brothers) wrote: "A chair ought to be well built and its structural qualities should be exemplified in two ways: first, the greatest possible amount of structural strength and dignity should be obtained with the smallest amount of wood; next, the wood must be handled expertly as wood, and not made to simulate the properties of any other material."[22]

None of Stickley's products exemplifies this ideal as well as a chair patented by Kendall in 1897 (no. 35). Kendall's chair is joined with dowels, a method then considered to be the best for mechanized mass production. The chair was widely used and remained popular for over thirty years, a remarkable span when one remembers the six-month marketing cycle. Furthermore, it well represented the Arts and Crafts concept of a democratic style. There was no elaborate handwork, bringing the cost of the chair well within the means of a broad segment of the population, and it was used in simple farmhouses, sophisticated Prairie School houses, and even in Elsie de Wolfe's elegant Trellis Room at the top of the Colony Club in New York City. Such a successful blend of the ideal with the materialism of commerce was seldom realized.[23]

An editor for *Good Furniture*, a trade magazine that proselytized all aspects of Arts and Crafts thought, noted that "idealism and materialism are [in America] the dominant powers that fight each other and put the fatal stamp of their senseless struggle upon our lives and hearts."[24] Joseph Leiser wrote in *Furniture, A Magazine of Education for the Home*: "The arts and crafts cannot wholly change the industrial regime. It is a protest against subordination of the individual to the machine, since the machine is a tool of commerce wherein the aim is to create a value and profit, and not to realize an ideal."[25] Significantly, such

Fig. 19. Colonial dames with Mission table, from *Good Housekeeping*, May 1912.

Colonial associations were popular at the turn of the century. This illustration shows a woman in eighteenth-century dress, ironing with a nineteenth-century "sad" iron on a varnished and decidedly twentieth-century library table.

thinking did influence the way some factories were designed and operated; Limbert's lakeside location, improved working conditions instigated by Kendall at the Phoenix factory, and Craftsman profit sharing are examples. However, succumbing to the rhetoric that equated handwork with "good" and machine work with "evil," furniture manufacturers sometimes responded to market demands by faking a handmade appearance on machine-made products, just as some ceramics and metalwork manufacturers did. In one case (a Gustav Stickley bench), when the machine cut a tenon too short to extend beyond the mortise on a standardized design, a little piece was nailed on. Thus is revealed the irony of a craftsman stepping in to make a machine-made joint look like handwork. In an address given to the Architectural League of New York entitled "How Good Furniture is Built,"

John P. Adams, president of the Kensington Manufacturing Company said: "Only the best and most cleanly made of mortise and tenon joints will hold like a dowel joint, for the reason that the dowels are made to fit properly in holes made by standard size bits and the dowels are grooved to take the proper amount of glue . . . ."[26] Adams was speaking of mass-produced furniture primarily and a mortise and tenon could, of course, be made cleanly over and over again by machine. But for Gustav Stickley and Elbert Hubbard, the exposed mortise-and-tenon joint was such a potent symbol of honest handcraftsmanship that they used it on their mass-produced furniture whether it was required structurally or not.

Although powered machinery may have threatened the skilled handcraftsman's place in industry by allowing leisure time for all but the poorest workers, machines gave birth to a completely new kind of craft worker – the home craftsman. Home was where handicraft was to flourish. Magazines like *Godey's Lady's Book* had contained instructions for making beaded penwipes and macramé flyrests, but this was woman's work. *The Craftsman* magazine, *Keramic Studio*, the *Popular Mechanics* series on making furniture and lighting fixtures, and *Our Wonder Book* set men, women, and children to work stenciling curtains, hammering sheet-metal bookends, creating Mission dining tables out of packing boxes, decorating china teapots, tooling leather penwipes, or weaving baskets. Office work, be it in the administration of a large factory or the supervision of an increasingly mechanized household, was thought to deprive many of the moral uplift handwork provided; therefore, creativity was exercised at home with the same quasi-religious fervor that accompanied other self-improvement activities such as

Bernarr MacFadden's physical culture. Step-by-step instructions or craft kits ironically removed responsiblity for aesthetics from the maker by dictating the design of what was to be made. Thread companies offered table scarves with patterns and colors stamped on coarse linen that looked handwoven. China blanks printed with patterns for coloring could be had and furniture, even houses, could be shipped in pieces (see fig.13). Everything one needed to build the "Arden" bungalow, from a keg of just the right number of nails to the bathroom fixtures, could be delivered to one's yard by boxcar.[27]

Gustav Stickley and the Frost Arts and Crafts Workshop provided tools, materials, and guidelines for the amateur craftsman. While such home crafts might be written off as merely the beginning of the hobby mentality, the transformation of handicraft from an essential skill for earning a living to a nonessential enrichment of leisure time was arguably the most pervasive and long-lasting Arts and Crafts legacy. The quest to ennoble handwork was too idealistic to change the direction of industry, but the concept of an individual making something "by hand" gained and still retains a mystical respect. The piecework and mass production of machine-dominated factories could not satisfy the need to create, so home became the place where one learned and practiced craft skills.

In retrospect, the ideals of the Arts and Crafts movement could be met by objects made in almost any style, since the movement was concerned with the way an object was made, of what materials, and how it was used in the home. If homemakers were to make their own furnishings, a simple style suited to limited crafts skills would have to be made fashionable.

A writer in a 1910 issue of *Wood Craft*, a

magazine published for commercial woodworkers, suggested colonial as the best style for American homes, although "go-ahead" trade journals saw "a hopeful tendency of today in decoration, [which was] the movement toward the creation of a 'home' style. In America this is the only style that will appeal to the vast number of well-to-do when once created. The avidity with which the Mission and Arts and Crafts styles have been taken up shows that our people want a 'home' style and are ready for it now"[28] (see fig. 19). One might doubt that the "well-to-do" would want a plain style but the most luxurious house ever built from Gustav Stickley's plans was partially furnished with the product of the owner's home workshop, and Daniel Guggenheim's "Firenze Cottage" had Craftsman furniture on the porch among grand fluted columns. Stickley furniture was also to be found in the library arrayed before silk damask walls, Circassian walnut woodwork, and a gray marble fireplace.[29] The *Wood Craft* writer continued: "We Americans desire a real home life and prefer cheaper comfort to the most expensive furnishings of alien sources."[30] For him, "alien sources" were the French "palace styles" appropriate only in the houses of American multimillionaires (suggesting that millionaires were somehow un-American). A British journalist, discussing in 1906 the art of cabinetmaking and the machine, wrote: "Speaking of the possibility of developing a typically American style . . . most writers on the subject make one serious mistake. They look for the style to be some sort of handicraft style. Never, my masters! The most typical American feature is the use of machinery. America is the greatest machine-using nation, and the American style will be one adapted to machine manufacture."[31] It would be machines, therefore, not handicraft, that affected the style of objects used in homes.

Beauty could be brought into the daily lives of the average American by both machine-made objects that had the appearance of being handmade and by the objects the householder made for his own use. Joseph Leiser, who equated the Arts and Crafts movement with the industrial-arts movement, proclaimed: "There is not a home in this country that is not influenced, in some measure, by the industrial art movement. The introduction of the simple and useful to displace the gaudy, the tawdry, the garish and merely ornamental, has been almost universal."[32] This claim was too optimistic, but a democratic style did evolve. Appreciation of simplicity carried with it no indication of social or financial status, although it did require a certain aesthetic sophistication not at all universal. The movement missed the top and bottom socioeconomic levels of the American population, since "the poor taste of the rich" (to use the pejorative terminology of a series published in *House Beautiful*)[33] was not usually inclined toward inexpensive, homely comforts and the poor, finding ornate furnishing styles best suited to their material values, rejected attempts by middle-class reformers to impose Arts and Crafts simplicity on them.[34] The style had its greatest effect on "the vast field of intelligent, well meaning people between the poor and the wealthy" or Charles Limbert's "great average class of home builders."[35] The ideals of the Arts and Crafts movement reached most of the American public wrapped in the visible trappings of style as distilled by manufacturers who were not always philosphers.

1. "The art that is life" was the subtitle of Will Price's journal *The Artsman* (Philadelphia: Rose Valley Press), 1903-1907. The same sentiment was expressed by many other Arts and Crafts theorists, including William Morris and Ralph Whitehead. The latter wrote: ". . . of all the arts, the art of life is the greatest." See "A Plea for Manual Work," *Handicraft* 2 (June 1903), p. 67.

2. Charles H. Kegel, "Ruskin's St. George in America," *American Quarterly* 9 (Winter 1957), pp. 412-420.

3. Described by Ralph Whitehead in a letter to his wife, Jane Byrd McCall, dated June 1901; material used with the permission of the Whitehead heirs.

4. Frank G. O'Dell, "Modern Residence Construction – I," *Carpentry and Building* 29 (January 1917), p. 6.

5. Stickley learned the mechanics of the furniture industry at his uncle's chair-making factory, where chair spindles were turned on power lathes. Kendall was trained at Bromley, Hunn & Smith, a furniture factory, where he apprenticed in the design department. He also attended art classes at night.

6. I am indebted to Lita Solis-Cohen, who made me aware of Bryn Athyn's importance as a utopian experiment and so led me to acquire the Parke Edwards material.

7. A detailed discussion of Gorham's manufacturing techniques may be found in Charles Carpenter's *Gorham Silver* (New York: Dodd, Mead, 1982).

8. C. Matlack Price, "The Modern Craftsman in Wrought Iron," *Craftsman* 22 (September 1912), pp. 627-634.

9. *The Frost Arts and Crafts Workshop*, catalogue number 52 (Dayton, Ohio: "The Western," 1910).

10. Oscar Lovell Triggs, *Chapters in the History of the Arts and Crafts Movement* (New York: Benjamin Blom, 1971; first published in 1902), p. 160.

11. "Examples of Wood-carving and Furniture Design," *Woodcraft* 14 (February 1912), pp. 136-137.

12. For comparisons see Edgar Wood's designs in "Studio Talk," *Studio* 14 (September 1898), pp. 284-285; and "Home Arts and Industries," *Studio* 8 (July 1896), p. 93. These and other *Studio* magazines in Whitehead's library carry his penciled notations.

13. William Ayres, ed., *A Poor Sort of Heaven, A Good Sort of Earth: The Rose Valley Arts and Crafts Experiment* (Chadds Ford: Brandywine Conservancy, 1983), p. 54.

14. Will Price, "The Artsman" (typescript play in the collection of the late Eleanore Price Mather).

15. The number of employees at Roycroft in 1905 was "some 350 people," with no specific figure given for the woodworking shop. See "Roycroft Ideals and Cabinetmaking," *Wood Craft* 4 (October 1905), p. 11. "A couple of hundred workmen" were at Stickley's shops in 1906, again with no specific number given to the furniture shops. (See "The Craftsman Shops," *Wood Craft* 5 [June 1906], p. 69.) The Phoenix Furniture Company, which made only furniture, had 300 workers in 1911, according to *Furniture Manufacturers and Artisan* 1 (May 1911), p. 215.

16. "Roycroft Ideals and Cabinetmaking," *Wood Craft* 4 (October 1905), pp. 13-14.

17. The incomplete Craftsman factory archives now at the Winterthur Museum indicate that Gustav Stickley drew a salary of $500 per month. (See John Paschetto, "The Politics of Gustav Stickley, in Theory and in Practice" [Philadelphia: Philadelphia Museum of Art; forthcoming], p. 17.) A 1915 survey made by Scott Nearing states that the average American worker received less than that annually. (See Percy Stickney Grant, *Fair Play for the Workers* [New York: Moffat, Yard, 1918], p. 35.)

18. *Limbert's Arts and Crafts Furniture* (Grand Rapids; Fall 1905), n.p.

19. John T. Strahan, superintendent of the Phoenix factory, stated that "common sawn lumber would shrink so as to leave a crack, whereas quarter sawed oak would not. For instance, take a board of quarter sawed oak six inches wide and an inch thick. The board would not shrink the wide way, but in the inch thickness. This makes it especially desirable for furniture and for surfaces on which to glue fine and delicate carvings. See *The Michigan Artisan*, April 1890, p. 5.

20. A.S. White, "Correctness of Design Everything, Observations on European Methods of Designing and Manufacturing Furniture, Made by the Late D.W. Kendall, Twenty Years Ago," *Furniture Manufacturer and Artisan* 3 (February 1912), p. 70.

21. White 1912, p. 70.

22. Albert Stickley, "The Marriage of Arts and Crafts," *Furniture, a Magazine of Education for the Home* 1 (April 1909), p. 30.

23. For a complete discussion of Kendall's importance to the Grand Rapids furniture industry, see Jane Perkins Claney and Robert Edwards, "Progressive Design in Grand Rapids," *Tiller* 1 (September/October 1983), pp. 33-52; and Frank E. Ransom, *The City Built of Wood: A History of the Furniture Industry in Grand Rapids, Michigan 1850-1950* (Ann Arbor: Edwards Brothers, 1955).

24. "Current News and Comment," *Good Furniture* 8 (June 1917), p. 313.

25. Joseph Leiser, "The Arts and Crafts Movement," *Furniture* 1 (January 1910), p. 31.

26. John P. Adams, "How Good Furniture is Built" [address given to Architectural League of New York], *Good Furniture* 12 (May 1919), p. 209.

27. *Homes of Character* (Bay City, Mich.: Lewis Manufacturing Company, 1920), pp. 71-72. The price for the "Arden" was $2,093. "Arden" was also the name of the single-tax community Will Price helped to establish near Wilmington, Delaware.

28. "English and American Cabinetmaking," *Wood Craft* 4 (February 1906), p. 201.

29. "Dumblane, a Southern Craftsman Home," *Craftsman* 23 (February 1913), pp. 522-534. The house was built in Washington, D.C., in 1912 for Mr. and Mrs. S. Hazen Bond. The Guggenheim house was illustrated in Barr Ferree, "Notable American Homes," *American Homes and Gardens* 6 (September 1909), pp. 337-340. The style of the "Firenze Cottage" interiors was characterized as Pompeian.

30. "English and American Cabinetmaking" 1906, p. 200.

31. Ibid.

32. Leiser 1910, p. 31.

33. During the years 1904 and 1905, *House Beautiful* published several essays under the general title "The Poor Taste of the Rich: A Series of Articles Which Show That Wealth Is Not Essential to the Decoration of a House, and That the Homes of Many of Our Richest Citizens Are Furnished in Execrable Taste."

34. See Lizabeth A. Cohen, "Embellishing a Life of Labor: An Interpretation of the Material Culture of American Working Class Homes, 1885-1915," in Thomas J. Schlereth, ed., *Material Culture Studies in America* (Nashville: American Association for State and Local History, 1982), pp. 289-305.

35. *Limbert's Arts and Crafts Furniture* 1905.

96

Dresser for Mrs. Lawrence Demmer house, Milwaukee,
ca. 1904
Designer: George Mann Niedecken (1878-1945)
Maker: probably F.H. Bresler Company,
Milwaukee
H: 66⅝ in. W: 65 in. D: 22 in.
Oak, birch, brass, and pressed glass
Private Collection

97

Bedstead for Mrs. Lawrence Demmer house, Milwaukee,
ca. 1904
Designer: George Mann Niedecken (1878-1945)
Maker: probably F.H. Bresler Company,
Milwaukee
H: 48½ in. W: 60⅝ in. D: 84¾ in.
Oak and birch
Private Collection

George Niedecken received his training in the
highly charged reform movement that sought
to develop and refine America's cultural awareness and taste. He attended the Wisconsin Art
Institute, studied decorative design with Louis
Millet at the School of the Art Institute in Chicago, and traveled through Europe, stopping to
study in Berlin and Paris. Upon arrival back in
the United States in 1902, Niedecken began to
offer decorator's services and to teach design
classes at the Milwaukee Art Students League.
Shortly thereafter he began to collaborate with
Frank Lloyd Wright, providing furnishings for
several Wright homes based upon the architect's rough sketches. In 1907, he established
Niedecken-Walbridge, a larger firm that
reupholstered goods, refinished furniture, retailed local or imported items, painted murals,
and drew up designs for custom-ordered furniture, glass, and lighting fixtures.[1] Working both
for architectural firms and for individual clients,
Niedecken was one of the first to give definition
to a new profession: that of the interior
architect.[2]

For a new house designed by the architectural firm of Buemming and Dick for Mrs. Lawrence Demmer, a supporting member of the
Wisconsin School of Art, Niedecken provided
murals, art glass, light fixtures, textiles, and furniture.[3] Since the present bedroom suite shares
certain similarities with such built-in features as
the radiator covers and stair banisters and since
it resembles the furniture Niedecken designed
for the Bresler Art Gallery, also completed in

1904, it was probably made in that year. The
most likely manufacturer of the set is F.H. Bresler, upon whom Niedecken relied prior to establishing his own furniture shop in early 1909.[4]

This bedstead and dresser (the latter lacking
its original light fixtures, which were set into
the holes on either side of the mirror) manifest
the various components of Niedecken's education. The sawed-out stylized floral decoration
on the dresser's upper doors and on the head-
board and footboard of the bedstead reflect the
abstractions from nature taught in design
schools. The constructivism of the dresser –
evident in the slab components, the strong
framing pieces, and the enclosure of the drawers separately from the legs (thereby isolating
the storage function from the structural one) –
can be attributed to his familiarity with German
and Austrian work, particularly the Secessionists. The influence of Frank Lloyd Wright, for
whom Niedecken began to work at this time,
can also be discerned. Horizontal moldings of
the bedstead and crisp beveled edges of the
dresser's upper compartments and grooved
molding resemble similar features on Wright's
work.[5]

In spite of the sophisticated design, the bedstead and dresser have been constructed in a
rather expedient manner characteristic of
millwork. Each of the side rails of the bedstead
consists of a single piece of oak with grain
parallel to the floor. A series of oak veneers
with grain oriented vertically is applied to these
rails. The decoration on the frame consists entirely of the sawed-out slats and applied moldings and panels. The dresser is a more complex
piece of furniture, yet the joints remain simple.
Mortises were cut on a table saw, splined miter
joints connected parts of the carcass, the
dovetailed joints along the front edges of the
drawer fronts were cut uniformly with a rotary
dovetailing machine, and the rear corners were
fastened by using a machine to cut dowels on
the end section of the drawer backs and corresponding holes in the drawer sides.

ESC

1. Cheryl Robertson et al., *The Domestic Scene (1897-
1927); George M. Niedecken, Interior Architect* (Milwaukee:
Milwaukee Art Museum, 1981), pp. 15-32.

2. The new professionals also served as contractors
who selected and coordinated craftsmen and manufacturers known for quality work and aesthetically
appropriate objects. As mediators between architect

and craftsman or between craftsman and client, they
thus served an important role in the spread of styles.
See Robertson 1981, esp. pp. 9-12.

3. Mrs. Demmer moved into this house in the fall of
1904, about a year after her husband had died. See
ibid., p. 20; and Demmer files, Prairie Archives, Milwaukee Art Museum. H.W. Buemming, like Mrs. Demmer and Niedecken, was a second-generation German
immigrant. Many of Niedecken's clients and associates
belonged to this Germanic community of Milwaukee.

4. Like the dresser and the bedstead, the radiator
covers and banisters have a slight green stain on them.
This coloring helped to link the different parts of the
interior together. See Niedecken-Walbridge Account
Books (1907-1923) and Niedecken-Walbridge Journal
(1907-1909), Prairie Archives, Milwaukee Art Museum.
I am indebted to Cheryl Robertson, Mrs. William
Teweles, and Terrance Marvel for their assistance in
dating this set.

5. Niedecken was a transmitter of Prairie designs in
Wisconsin when working for Wright, Dwight Perkins,
and Robert Spencer, but he did not work exclusively
in that style. With individual clients, Niedecken
demonstrated a number of different styles. See Robertson 1981, pp. 11, 41-47, 69-91; and Sharon Darling,
Chicago Furniture: Art, Craft, & Industry 1833-1983 (New
York: W.W. Norton, 1984), pp. 181-183.

98

Chair, 1900
Designer: Charles Rohlfs, Buffalo (1853-1936)
Maker: Charles Rohlfs Workshop, Buffalo,
(1898-1928)
Oak
H: 35⅛ in. W: 19 in. D: 21½ in.
Marks: branded R within bow saw and 1900 on
back of seat rail
Collection of John H. Nally

99

Bench, ca. 1900
Designer: Charles Rohlfs, Buffalo (1853-1936)
Maker: Charles Rohlfs Workshop, Buffalo (1853-
1928)
Oak with iron loops on side and copper hinges
and latch; interior stained green
H: 45½ in. W: 35⅛ in. D: 21½ in.
Marks: branded R within bow saw (at top right,
inside bench)
Museum of Fine Arts, Boston. Gift of a Friend of
the Department and Arthur Mason Knapp Fund.
1983.14

Charles Rohlfs studied art at the Cooper Union in New York, designed cast-iron stoves and furnaces, and won recognition as a Shakespearean actor and scholar before he tried his hand at woodworking in the late 1880s. Unable to afford the antiques he coveted for his home, Rohlfs began making furniture in an attic workshop[1] and was soon producing furniture for neighbors, friends, and outside clients as well. Around 1898, Rohlfs moved his workshop into a commercial space in downtown Buffalo. Two years later, Marshall Field and Company in Chicago hosted an exhibition of his work and *House Beautiful* devoted an article to him.[2]

Rohlfs won acclaim for his work at the Pan-American Exposition of 1901, the Turin Exposition of 1902, and the Louisiana Purchase Exposition of 1904.[3] Following the Turin showing, he was made a member of the Royal Society of Artists in London and was commissioned to make a set of chairs for Buckingham Palace. The *Buffalo Times* reported in 1905 that: "The home of Marshall Field in Chicago has room after room furnished with pieces from the Rohlfs workshop, the Cleveland home of one of America's wealthiest citizens has a Rohlfs room, palatial mansions in Chicago, Paris, London, Bremen, New York, Philadelphia and Buffalo, as well as smaller towns, both here and abroad, have handsome pieces designed and executed by the Buffalonian."[4] Rohlfs made furniture for some large camps in the Adirondacks and several office suites, including one for a piano manufacturer in Detroit and the Taber Pump Company in Buffalo.[5] He also designed numerous complete interiors – including woodwork, lighting fixtures, and furnishings.[6] These accounts suggest that the Rohlfs Workshop's production was substantial, yet others make it clear that the staff was relatively small.[7]

Rohlfs looked to a variety of sources for inspiration. This chair with intricate pierced splat, legs, and seat rail is an original design derived from medieval, Moorish, and early Norwegian furniture illustrated in art journals of the period.[8] The bench exhibits the sinuous lines and spirit of Art Nouveau.[9] Though Rohlfs refused to categorize his style and bristled at its being labeled "Mission," he promoted many of the ideals of the Arts and Crafts movement,[10] for example, the precept that art "should be expressive of workmanship that is a pleasure rather than a toil."[11] According to at least one visitor, his shop demonstrated this spirit: "One feels that there can be no drudgery, no ennui; that

the endless and delightful possibilities of all this raw material are ever revealing themselves and that the most painstaking application in working them out is Rohlfs's chiefest pleasure."[12]

Also in the spirit of the Arts and Crafts movement, Rohlfs had a deep respect for his material: wood and nature. Using ash, oak, and mahogany woods and solid brass, iron, or copper with a Japanese "bronze" finish as hardware, he professed to "treat my wood well, caress it perhaps and that desire led to the idea that I must embellish it to evidence my profound regard for a beautiful thing in nature. This embellishment consisted of line, proportion and carving."[13] Examination of the furniture, however, reveals that Rohlfs's talents were in design rather than construction. Although passionately enthusiastic about his craft and gifted as a designer, Rohlfs had no formal training in cabinetry. Like much Arts and Crafts furniture, both this chair and bench have screws (concealed by plugs) rather than mortise-and-tenon joints.[14] The screws are often within a half inch of the edge of the boards, giving little structural support and making the wood vulnerable to splitting as it expands and contracts.

CZ

1. *Literary Digest* 50 (May 29, 1915), p. 1291. An oak settee with subtle carved ornament, made by Rohlfs for his wife (the novelist Anna Katharine Green), was illustrated in *Decorator and Furnisher* 12 (June 1888), p. 78.

2. Charlotte Moffitt, "The Rohlfs Furniture," *House Beautiful* 7 (January 1900), p. 81.

3. The Austrian and German press gave him special praise and featured his work in articles in *Kunst und Kunsthandwerk* and *Dekorative Kunst*.

4. *Times* (Buffalo, N.Y.), February 17, 1905.

5. "An Attractive Camp in the Adirondacks," *International Studio* 38 (July 1909), p. xxv; and *Arts Journal* 7 (November 1925), p. 57. Michael James learned about Rohlfs's work for the Taber Piano Company from discussion with a former employee of the company. (A member of the Taber family was once a foreman in the Rohlfs shop.)

6. According to a brochure Rohlfs published in about 1904, he designed chafing dishes – manufactured in Belgium – as early as 1896, and was designing metalwork, writing sets, candlesticks, and anniversary gifts "of a unique character," in addition to his other work.

7. Michael James, who is writing a biography, has identified twelve of the craftsmen (ten with German names) who worked for Rohlfs. Many of these artisans, possibly untrained in cabinetmaking, continued in careers as architects, sculptors, and artists. According to Roland Rohlfs (son of Charles Rohlfs), who provided this information in an interview with Robert Judson Clark on

August 1, 1971, no more than about eight men worked at any one time in the shop. See also *Upholstery Dealer and Decorative Furnisher* 2 (May 1902), p. 55; Moffit 1900, p. 82; and *Literary Digest* 50 (May 29, 1915), p. 1291.

8. According to Robert Judson Clark, this chair, or one just like it, is pictured in a photograph of Rohlfs's living room. The same chair (or duplicate) is also illustrated in Moffitt 1900, p. 85.

9. Rohlfs was one of very few American furniture makers to produce work influenced by Art Nouveau. Gustav Stickley introduced a line of organically inspired furniture after his trip to the Continent in 1898, but this style was shortlived for him. He quickly moved to a clean line devoid of superfluous ornament.

10. Rohlfs referred to his work as "strangely suggestive of the days when the world was young, but in spite of that, distinctive of this progressive twentieth century, and strictly American. It has the spirit of today blended with the poetry of the medieval ages." (He also noted that he would make furniture of any style, to suit the customer's taste.) The text appears on the title page of a packet of illustrations of Rohlfs's furniture printed in November of 1907 (copy in the Department of Prints and Drawings at the Metropolitan Museum of Art, New York).

11. "Arts and Crafts Conference," *Chautauqua Assembly Herald*, July 15, 1902, p. 3.

12. Moffitt 1900, p. 81.

13. Charles Rohlfs, "The Grain of Wood," *House Beautiful* 9 (February 1901), p. 147; and Charles Rohlfs, "My Adventures in Woodcarving," *Arts Journal* (September 1925), pp. 21-22. Thanks to Michael James for the latter citation.

14. I am indebted to Robert Walker, furniture conservator at the Boston Museum of Fine Arts, for his insights concerning construction.

99

100

Card table, ca. 1901-1920s[1]
Tobey Furniture Company, Chicago (1856-1954)
Mahogany
Label: round metal tag *Tobey / Established / 1856 / Chicago / Hand-Made Furniture* (affixed to underside of tabletop)
H: 29¾ in. W: 36 in. D: 18¼ in.
Museum of Fine Arts, Boston. Anonymous Gift and Helen and Alice Colburn Fund. 1985.3

As the rhetoric of William Morris and his followers spread to America in the late 1890s, the Tobey Furniture Company, one of the leading manufacturers of fine commercial and residential furniture in Chicago, responded by introducing a "Hand-Made" line advertised as having "no veneers, no machine-carving or stamped ornament."[2] Although it was not custom work, Tobey furniture was expensive, being made of mahogany, curly birch, and bird's-eye maple, much of it finished by hand.[3]

In 1896 the company hired an Englishman, Joseph Twyman (born 1842), as head of the decorating department. Twyman designed much of the company's furniture until his death in 1904. A trendsetter, Twyman introduced Arts and Crafts social and aesthetic theories by marketing William Morris's textiles and wallpapers and lecturing on his ideas. In 1902, he established a "William Morris Room" at Tobey; the following year he helped to found the William Morris Society in Chicago. Twyman advocated "a vigorous effort after originality based on the best things that have been done in the past" and believed that colonial furniture answered "every requirement of the Morris and Ruskin school."[4] It is entirely possible that Twyman designed this card table, an updated old form in the Empire style with Art Nouveau flourishes, since it was produced during Twyman's tenure at Tobey.

CZ

1. This popular form was still being marketed in 1924. See advertisement in *Town and Country* 18 (June 1, 1924), p. 95. I am indebted to Scott Braznell for the reference.

2. See advertisement in *Harper's Monthly Magazine* 101 (October 1900), p. 58; cited by Sharon Darling, *Chicago Furniture* (New York: W.W. Norton, 1984), p. 233. Tobey was also selling Mission furniture – "an unconventional style for unconventional people, admirably suited to rest and sunshine" – by the spring of 1900. See *Chicago Tribune*, April 19, 1900, p. 14. The company sold Gustav Stickley's "New Furniture" in the fall of 1900 and marketed its own brand of Arts and Crafts furnishings: the "New Furniture in Weathered Oak" in 1901 and "Russmore" furniture in 1902. George Clingman (1857-1933), head designer for Tobey from 1888 to 1894, and general manager until at least 1929, was instrumental in the introduction of these lines. (See Darling 1984, pp. 234-240.)

3. Many large furniture houses began in the late nineteenth century to apply spray lacquer, rather than to finish by hand. This table appears to have been finished by the former method.

4. George B. Davis, "The Future of House Decoration," *House Beautiful* 5 (May 1899), pp. 260-261; and "The Victorian Age in Furniture," *Furniture Worker* 37 (May 10, 1901), p. 18 [cited in Darling 1984], pp. 192-193).

100

Gustav Stickley and the Craftsman Workshops

Catherine Zusy

In the summer of 1900, Gustav Stickley (1858-1942) exhibited his "New Furniture" for the first time to a large audience at the Grand Rapids Furniture fair.[1] The display received great attention, as did his exhibition at the Pan-American Exposition the next year, prompting the production of similar lines of furniture by dozens of manufacturers in Grand Rapids, Chicago, Indianapolis, Cincinnati, and New York state.

Stickley drew on the rhetoric of William Morris and the furniture styles of designers such as M.H. Baillie Scott to create his own line, which he saw as the embodiment of simplicity, honesty, and strength. His company, first called the "United Crafts" and soon thereafter the "Craftsman Workshops," was "a guild of cabinetmakers, metal and leather workers, formed for the production of household furnishings." Stickley wrote in 1901 that this guild was intended to parallel Morris and Company; he envisioned himself as the master craftsman, overseeing the production of objects in his shop and endorsing each one with his signature.[2] Like Baillie Scott, whose furniture designs were illustrated extensively in art journals of the 1890s and 1900s, Stickley advocated simple furniture in a structural style.[3] Several of his designs (see, for example, no. 103) are adapted from the Englishman's work. Similarly, many of the renderings for room settings published in *The Craftsman* were inspired by Baillie Scott's illustrations. Distilling the ideas and work of his English mentors, Stickley created a furnishing aesthetic that appealed "strongly to the directness and common sense of the American people."[4]

After his "debut" in Grand Rapids, Stickley sold furniture not at the major fairs but, instead, at Arts and Crafts exhibitions, at the factory and Craftsman stores in Boston and Washington, and through some fifty major retailers lo-

cated throughout the country. As his furniture became popular, Stickley began manufacturing and importing metalwork and textiles to complement it. In 1904, he founded the Craftsman Home-Builders Club, offering complete sets of Arts and Crafts house plans to his subscribers. Four years later, he purchased land on which he hoped to build a cooperative community – the Craftsman Farms – near Morris Plains, New Jersey.[5] In 1913, Stickley moved all aspects of his business, except for the manufacturing division, into a new building in New York City. The twelve-story structure housed not only furniture showrooms but a permanent exhibition of the Craftsman Home-Builders Workshops, editorial offices for the magazine and offices for architectural services, a library, clubrooms, a lecture hall, and a restaurant.[6] Stickley justified the expansion of the Craftsman enterprises in his magazine that year; what he had founded as a furniture manufacturing company had become a religion to him and he felt compelled to nurture its development.[7]

Overextended, Stickley filed for bankruptcy in 1915, when the taste for Mission furniture was ebbing and attention shifted from domestic concerns to the war in Europe. He attempted to revitalize his industry by introducing new lines, including "Chromewald" period furnishings, but the sale of this colonially inspired furniture was not enough to salvage the company, already in great debt. When *The Craftsman* magazine ceased publication after the December 1916 issue, Gustav Stickley and his brothers Leopold, John George, and Albert tried to begin a new concern. This venture – the Stickley Associated Cabinetmakers – was not successful, and Leopold and John George Stickley absorbed the Craftsman Workshops factory in Syracuse in 1918.

1. "Observations," *Furniture Trade Review* 20 (August 10, 1900), p. 14.

2. Foreword in *Craftsman* 1 (October 1901), p. i. In reality, Stickley's signature was a decal and his "guild" a modern factory of some 200 workers in 1904. See *What is Wrought in the Craftsman Workshops*, (Syracuse: Gustav Stickley, 1904).

3. See M.H. Baillie Scott, "On the Choice of Simple Furniture," *International Studio* 1 (1897), pp. 152-157 (reprinted in *House Beautiful* 6 [November 1901], pp. 372-377). See also Gustav Stickley, "The Structural Style in Cabinet-Making," *House Beautiful* 15 (December 1903), pp. 19-23.

4. *Catalogue of Craftsman Furniture*, (Syracuse: Gustav Stickley, 1910), p. 4. Stickley promoted his furniture as being made of "American" white oak.

5. Stickley wrote in 1908 that he hoped to revive "practical and profitable handicrafts in connection with small farming carried out by modern methods of intensive agriculture" at the Craftsman Farms. See "The Craftsman House: A Practical Application of All the Theories of Home Building Advocated in This Magazine," *Craftsman* 15 (October 1908), p. 79.

6. For more information about Gustav Stickley and the Craftsman Workshops, see Coy L. Ludwig, *The Arts and Crafts Movement in New York State, 1890s-1920s* (Hamilton, N.Y.: Gallery Association of New York State, 1983), pp. 62-67; Robert Judson Clark, ed. *The Arts and Crafts Movement in America, 1876-1916* (Princeton: Princeton University Press, 1972); Mary Ann Smith, *Gustav Stickley: The Craftsman* (Syracuse: Syracuse University Press, 1983); John Crosby Freeman, *The Forgotten Rebel* (Watkins Glen, N.Y.: Century House, 1966); David Cathers, *Furniture of the American Arts and Crafts Movement* (New York: New American Library, 1981); and Stephen Gray and Robert Edwards, eds., *The Collected Works of Gustav Stickley* (New York: Turn of the Century Editions, 1981).

7. Gustav Stickley, "The Craftsman Movement: Its Origins and Growth," *Craftsman* 25 (October 1913), pp. 17-18, 23-26.

101

Corner cupboard, ca. 1902
Craftsman Workshops, Eastwood (Syracuse),
New York (1899-1916)
Oak with wrought-iron hardware
H: 72 in. W: 42 in. D: 29½ in.
Marks: large red decal depicting joiner's compass with *Stickley* outlined below (on back, top right corner)
Private Collection

According to his own account, Gustav Stickley grew discontent with factory-made furniture designed only for ease of production in the 1890s. Believing that the new work had lost the "subtleties of modeling that had marked handmade furniture of the old cabinet-makers," he turned his attention to "reproducing by hand some of the simple and best models of old Colonial, windsor and other plain chairs" and to studying this period as a foundation for original work along the same lines.[1] In 1898 Stickley traveled to England and to Europe. Impressed with the "New Art" there, he came home determined to "cast aside my traditions, forget the formulas which I used previously, and begin to study structural principles."[2] Though most of the furniture Stickley marketed before World War I was ahistorical in nature, he continued to produce some colonial forms,[3] including this corner cupboard;[4] made for his own use, it was exhibited at the Craftsman Building in the spring of 1903.[5]

CZ

1. *Chips From the Craftsman Workshops* (Syracuse: Gustav Stickley, 1906).

2. Gustav Stickley, "A Plea for a Democratic Art," *Craftsman* 7 (October 1904), pp. 42-64.

3. In fact, Stickley's first furniture catalogue, *New Furniture From the Workshops of Gustave Stickley, Cabinetmaker, Syracuse, New York, U.S.A.* (ca. 1900), included colonially inspired stools and stands with sausage turnings, etc.

4. Though this form does not appear in Stickley's catalogues, plans for a corner cabinet were published in the *Craftsman* in April of 1906 (pp. 114-115). A pair of large corner cupboards was made in about 1908 for the main house at the Craftsman farms. Stickley did not include the cupboard form in his general line until about 1916, when he began again to market colonially inspired furnishings.

5. According to Robert Judson Clark, the cupboard was made for Gustav Stickley's dining room after the interior of his house was destroyed by fire in 1901. It was later owned by his daughter, Barbara Stickley

Wiles. This object, along with a matching sideboard and server, are illustrated in Irene Sargent, "A Recent Arts and Crafts Exhibition," *Craftsman* 4 (May 1903), pp. 68-83.

102

Music cabinet, ca. 1903
Designer: Harvey Ellis (1852-1904)
Maker: Craftsman Workshops, Eastwood (Syracuse), New York
Oak with copper and pewter inlays
H: 64⅞ in. W: 23¾ in. D: 14⅜ in.
Marks: red decal depicting joiner's compass with *Stickley* underneath, all enclosed within a rectangle (on back, top center)
Collection of Morton Abromson and Joan Nissman

Between June 1903 and January 1904, Harvey Ellis (see no. 196) provided designs for houses, furniture, and wall decorations in Gustav Stickley's magazine. Included in his first room settings published in *The Craftsman*[1] was a side chair with the inlaid decoration for which he would become known at the Stickley factory. The inlays of abstracted floral forms were based on details by Charles Rennie Mackintosh and Margaret MacDonald published in art journals of the period.[2]

During his eight-month tenure at the Craftsman Workshops, Ellis also introduced lighter, more vertical forms with overhanging tops (reminiscent of C.F.A. Voysey's work) and arched aprons. The Craftsman Workshops continued to produce work influenced by Ellis's designs after his death in 1904. Stickley took pains to explain how this decorated furniture, a seeming violation of his severe structural style, fitted within its scheme.[3] The inlay emphasized the structural lines of the furniture, he argued, and "accented the vertical elements . . . giving a certain slenderness of effect to a whole. . . otherwise too heavy." Like ornamentation of the Greeks, it "appears to proceed from within outward," bearing no trace of having been applied.

CZ

1. "A Child's Bedroom," *Craftsman* 4 (July 1903), p. 284.
2. The Craftsman Workshops was not the first or the only furniture manufacturer to market an inlaid line of furniture in the English tradition. Joseph P. McHugh and Co. was advertising "The Lady Teazle" chair, elbow chair, and settee with delicate inlays in 1898 and the Stickley Brothers Company was making furniture with inlays of fancy woods, metals, and mother-

102

of-pearl by 1900. In his fall 1905 catalogue, Charles P. Limbert advertised both chairs and bookcases with inlaid decoration.

3. "Structure and Ornament in the Craftsman Work shops," *Craftsman* 5 (January 1904), p. 396. Only a year before, Stickley had written: "Again, the structural lines should not be subjected to the indignity of applied ornament, which, in its nature as a parasite, never fails to absorb the strength of the organism on which it feeds . . ." (see "The Structural Style in Cabinet-Making," *House Beautiful* 15 [December 1903], p. 21).

103

104

103

Bookcase, ca. 1902
Craftsman Workshops, Eastwood (Syracuse),
New York (1899-1916)
Oak with copper door pull
H: 56 in. W: 31⅜ in. D: 12⅜ in.
Marks: large red decal depicting joiner's compass with *Stickley* outlined below (on back, top
center)
Collection of Stephen Gray

This bookcase – an example of Gustav Stickley's
"structural style"[1] – was produced with few
modifications from about 1902 to about 1915.
Ornamented with a self-consciously hand-
hammered copper door pull,[2] the piece resembles an M.H. Baillie Scott design for a china
cabinet published in the Pyghtle Works catalogue of 1901. Stickley would have been familiar
with the work from numerous articles in art
magazines of the late 1890s.[3] He could also have
seen Baillie Scott's furniture on one of his many
trips to England. Inspired by British contemporaries, Stickley developed entire interior

schemes for furnishings with textiles, metalwork, and often wall decoration.

CZ

1. See Gustav Stickley, "The Structural Style in Cabinet-
Making," *House Beautiful* 15 (December 1903), pp. 19-
23.

2. Stickley had opened a metalworks by 1904 to make
hardware for his furniture. See *What is Wrought in the
Craftsman Workshops* (Syracuse: Gustav Stickley, 1904).

3. Between 1894 and 1902, *The Studio* alone published
over ten articles illustrating Baillie Scott's furniture
and interiors.

104

Table, ca. 1910
L. and J.G. Stickley,[1] Fayetteville, New York
(1902- present)
Oak
H: 30 in. W: 72 in. D: 36 in.
Mark: red "Handcraft" decal depicting wooden
screw clamp (inside top of one of the legs)
Private Collection

The Stickley brothers – Gustav, Leopold, John
George, Albert, and Charles – all worked in the
furniture industry as boys, making cane-seated
wooden chairs at their uncle's chair factory in
Brandt, Pennsylvania. In the 1880s, Gustav,
Charles, and Albert moved to Binghamton,
New York, to establish their own wholesale and
retail store. As "Stickley Brothers," they sold
such popular items as Brandt chairs and black
walnut parlor furniture, plush rockers, and rattan and bamboo chairs; they were soon manufacturing their own furniture as well. In the
following years, the brothers worked separately
and together. Leopold (1869-1957) and John
George (1871-1921) each worked with Gustav in
Binghamton (and Leopold for the Gustav Stickley Company in Syracuse) before founding
their own firm in Fayetteville, New York, in
1902;[2] their business success owed much to
Gustav's example. They borrowed not only
their brother's furniture designs but his promotional materials and marketing techniques as
well. The mark they used, a wooden screw

clamp, could easily be mistaken for Gustav's joiner's compass and their earliest catalogue, *Some Sketches of Furniture Made at the Onondaga Shops* (ca. 1904), consisted of illustrations and rhetoric reminiscent of their brother's publications. While they also promoted furniture as personal expression, they were concerned primarily with supplying a market.[3]

Unperturbed by the fact that their "Handcraft" furniture was made by machine, L. and J.G. Stickley proudly announced in their catalogue of about 1910: "The Work of L. and J.G. Stickley, built in a scientific manner, does not attempt to follow the traditions of a by-gone day. . . ." The "Handcraft" line, unlike Craftsman furniture, was advertised in major trade journals, including the *Upholstery Dealer and Decorative Furnisher*, the *American Cabinetmaker and Upholstery Dealer*, and *Good Furniture* magazine, and was offered at the Grand Rapids trade fairs.

Like much of L. and J.G. Stickley's production, the present table is a copy of a design manufactured earlier by the Craftsman Workshops. This version was first published in a catalogue of about 1910, whereas Gustav Stickley had advertised it in about 1904.[4] The piece is based on a Baillie Scott design, which was inspired by a medieval trestle table (see p. 84, fig. 12).

CZ

1. The early history of Leopold and John George remains unsorted. Fragments are recounted in Leopold Stickley's biography by Kenneth L. Duprey, Sr. (attendant to Leopold Stickley), in the Stickley Collection, Archives and Library, Henry Ford Museum and Greenfield Village, Dearborn, Michigan. See also John Crosby Freeman, *The Forgotten Rebel: Gustav Stickley and His Craftsman Mission Furniture* (Watkins Glen, N.Y.: Century House, 1966); Mary Ann Clegg Smith, "History," in Stephen Gray, ed., *The Mission Furniture of L. & J.G. Stickley* (New York: Turn of the Century Editions, 1983), p. 7.; and Mary Ann Smith, *Gustav Stickley: The Craftsman* (Syracuse: Syracuse University Press, 1983).

2. Leopold worked as the foreman in Stickley's factory from 1899 to 1901. See Smith, *Mission Furniture of L. and J.G. Stickley* (see note 1 above), p. 7. The L. and J.G. Stickley Company began in 1902 (see *American Cabinetmaker and Upholsterer* 64 [February 1, 1902], p. 5); it was incorporated in 1904 (see *American Cabinetmaker and Upholsterer* 69 [January 30, 1904], p. 18).

By January of 1904, L. and J.G. Stickley had introduced their "Simple Furniture and Leather Work" as well as "a line of framed posters, plate and pipe racks in the Arts and Crafts" at the Grand Rapids furniture market. They soon diversified their product line, selling textiles and metalwork to complement "Handcraft" furniture. See advertisements in *Upholstery Dealer*

and Decorative Furnisher, issues of January 1904 (p. 14) and September 1904 (p. 92).

3. Commercial motives gave the Stickleys the flexibility to adapt to a market tired of Mission furniture and desiring colonial reproductions in the late nineteenteens. In 1917 they began marketing furniture with a Chromewald finish (see advertisement in *Good Furniture* 8 [May 1917], p. 17), and six years later they replaced their Arts and Crafts line with "period designs in popular finishes." The company continues to market this "Cherry Valley" line of colonial reproductions today.

4. Though Gustav's table is illustrated in *Craftsman* by November 1902 (facing page 76), it was first advertised in about 1904 in his *Cabinet Work from the Craftsman Workshops* (Catalogue "D"; as no. 631).

105

Drop-front desk, ca. 1904
Stickley Brothers Company, Grand Rapids[1]
(1891–ca. 1932)
Oak with copper pulls and brass hinges
H: 41½ in. W: 32 in. D: 14 in.
Museum of Fine Arts, Boston. H.E. Bolles Fund. 1986.35

Albert and John George Stickley incorporated the Stickley Brothers Company in 1891 (see no. 104). By July 1900 they were marketing a line of furniture[1] derived from what Albert Stickley considered two distinctive types: the Mission style, from the Spanish missions of California and Mexico, and a style that he attributed variously to Hungary, France, and England.[2] "Quaint furniture" was an amalgam of the best elements of the two.

The "Quaint" forms were modeled after Gustav Stickley's work (some, in turn, inspired by M.H. Baillie Scott's furniture) and after that of C.R. Ashbee, C.F.A. Voysey, and Liberty and Company.[3] This drop-front desk with elongated lines and decorative cutout hinges, recalling Voysey's work, was probably designed by Arthur E. Teal, who had studied in Scotland before beginning to work for the Stickleys in about 1904.[4] Although the desk has earmarks of the progressive design in which the Stickley Brothers took pride, it is not well made. Put together with dowels, it has an oak veneered back and plywood drawer bottoms and is made up of unmatched narrow pieces of oak board.

CZ

1. For information about the Arts and Crafts furniture made in Grand Rapids, see Don Marek, *Arts and Crafts*

Furniture Design: The Grand Rapids Contribution 1895-1915 (Grand Rapids: Grand Rapids Art Museum, 1987). According to Marek, the *Grand Rapids Furniture Record* published an ad illustrating an Arts and Crafts oak chair in its July 1900 issue. Two years later, this Mission line was so popular that the company – with 275 workers in 1901 – was having a difficult time supplying all of its orders. See *American Cabinetmaker and Upholsterer* 65 (April 12, 1902), p. 8; and *White's Directory of Manufacturers of Furniture and Kindred Goods of the U.S., British Provinces and Mexico* (Grand Rapids: White Printing Company, 1901.)

2. According to Albert Stickley, "The leading architects and artists in Hungary recognized the merits of the Arts and Crafts style more than thirty years ago, and did much work in it. Indeed, it grew in popularity to such an extent that the Hungarian government established Arts and Crafts schools at public expense." He claimed that the movement was later taken up in France as "New Art" and subsequently traveled to England. See "Merits of the Arts and Crafts," *Furniture* (April 1909), p. 30.

3. The Stickley Brothers Company was extremely proud of the British character of its work. The term "Quaint furniture" was, in fact, borrowed from the English name for furniture of Arts and Crafts design. See *Quaint Furniture in the Arts and Crafts* (Grand Rapids, Michigan: Stickley Brothers Company, ca. 1904), with afterword by one "J. Taylor, Glasgow, Scotland, Leading Designer and Critic of Great Britain." Taylor noted that upon seeing the Stickley Brothers' work, he "felt instinctively that if some British influence was not at work here, the designer was working in such similar lines as to be strongly in sympathy with the modern British school."

In keeping with the company's interest in English design, Stickley Brothers advertised a very Victorian inlaid wing chair in the *Grand Rapids Furniture Record* in the issue of December 15, 1900, and an inlaid highback settee of Arts and Crafts design in the same source in January of 1901 (p. 222). The inlay was done by Timothy A. Conti, who, in 1903, established his own plant separate from Stickley Brothers but continued to do work for the firm. See *American Cabinetmaker and Upholsterer* 65 (April 12, 1902), p. 8; *Grand Rapids Furniture Record* (February 1903), p. 243; and Dwight Goss, *History of Grand Rapids and Its Industries*, 2 vols. (Chicago: C.F. Cooper, 1906).

Additional evidence of English influence appears in "Gone to Europe," *American Cabinetmaker and Upholsterer* 61 (January 20, 1900), p. 32. The Stickley Brothers, who had a London showroom, did substantial business abroad in fancy chairs, tables, and rockers. See *American Cabinetmaker and Upholsterer* 65 (February 1, 1902); and *Grand Rapids Herald*, December 27, 1927, p. 38.

4. Like his European contemporaries, Teal designed not only furniture but whole room settings, including wall decoration. See "High Art in Furniture: A.E. Teal – Whose Life is Bound Up in His Work," *Daily News* (Grand Rapids) January 11, 1908.

105

106 (color plate, p. 21)
China cabinet, ca. 1906
The Shop of the Crafters, Cincinnati (1904-1920)
Oak; inlaid woods and copper hardware
H: 63⅛ in. W: 42 in. D: 15¾ in.
Marks: paper label with lantern trademark (adhered to top center back)
Private Collection

Inspired by the popularity of Gustav Stickley's Craftsman forms and the acclaim that the Austrian exhibits had won at the recent Louisiana Purchase Exposition, Oscar Onken (1858-1948) introduced his own line of "Furniture of Austrian Design" in Cincinnati in the fall of 1904. Also as a result of having viewed the fair, Onken hired the Budapest designer Paul Horti (1865-1907), who had exhibited a dining room there and overseen the installation of the Hungarian sections[1] in the Palace of Fine Arts, Manufacturers, and Mines and Metallurgy buildings.[2] Horti had taught at the School of Arts and Crafts in Budapest for fifteen years and won prizes in international expositions in London, Paris, Turin, and America.

The Shop of the Crafters made furniture decorated with inlays, applied carving, tiles, painted designs, and hardware and stained with a variety of dull finishes of Onken's own invention.[3] It was marketed through trade journals and popular upper-middle-class periodicals (including *The Saturday Evening Post*, *Scribner's*, *McClure's*, *Munsey's Magazine*, *Everybody's Magazine*, *Country Life in America*, *Harper's Bazaar*, and *Literary Digest*) as well as through dealers and by catalogue.

CZ

1. Budapest was then part of the Austro-Hungarian empire.
2. According to Robert Judson Clark, a contemporary Hungarian journal noted that Horti had also helped to design furniture for Charles P. Limbert's exhibit at the fair.
3. Kenneth R. Trapp, introduction in Stephen Gray, ed., *Arts and Crafts Furniture: Shop of the Crafters at Cincinnati* (New York: Turn of the Century Editions, 1983; first published in 1906). For more information, see Kenneth R. Trapp, "The Shop of the Crafters at Cincinnati, 1904-1920," *Tiller* (May-June 1984), pp. 8-25.

Mary Louise McLaughlin

Ellen Paul Denker
and
Bert Randall Denker

Mary Louise McLaughlin was the consummate amateur of American Arts and Crafts.[1] Born into a prosperous family in Cincinnati, she began her artistic education there, taking classes in drawing at a private art academy. At the School of Design of the University of Cincinnati, she studied drawing, woodcarving, and china painting from 1873 to 1877. She then received training at the Art Academy from Frank Duveneck, whom she described as "the only teacher who had any influence on my artistic development."[2] Miss McLaughlin's work in ceramics began in 1874 as a member of a china-painting class at the School of Design. At the Centennial Exhibition of 1876 in Philadelphia (see no. 14), where she exhibited examples of woodcarving and china painting, Miss McLaughlin examined the French *barbotine* wares displayed by Haviland and Company of Limoges. This experience, combined with her work in underglaze blue decoration on porcelain, led to experiments with underglaze colored slips on unfired earthenware. Although the technique differed from Haviland's, the effect was similar.[3]

First exhibited in Cincinnati, Paris, and New York in 1878, McLaughlin faience attracted the attention of professional and amateur decorators. In 1879 she organized the Cincinnati Pottery Club, which used facilities at the Dallas Pottery until 1881 and those of the Rookwood Pottery until 1883. Miss McLaughlin's technique, which she described in *Pottery Decoration under the Glaze*,[4] became the basis for the decorative process at Rookwood (see no. 6), as well as several other art potteries. Thus, the presence of the Club members at Rookwood was both competitive and distracting: "It may well be imagined with what abandon the women of that time, whose efforts had been directed to the making of antimacassars or woolen af-

ghans, threw themselves into the fascinating occupation of working in wet clay. The potters imparted to them various tricks of the trade and some fearful and wonderful things were produced."[5]

Following her dismissal from Rookwood's facilities, Miss McLaughlin worked sporadically in ceramics. In 1894 she patented an inlay technique in which slip was painted inside a mold prior to casting in a contrasting color. Four years later she was pursuing porcelain manufacture in a kiln specially constructed in her backyard. Her "Losanti" ware (see no. 107) was first shown in Cincinnati in 1899 and subsequently in Paris, Buffalo, New York, and Turin.

Although she is renowned today for her contributions to American ceramics, Mary Louise McLaughlin's *oeuvre* included carved woodwork, decorative metalwork (for which she won a silver medal at the Paris Exposition of 1889), stained glass, needlework, drawings, paintings, and sculpture. She was also the author of seven books on ceramic processes, oil painting, and various aspects of European history.

1. For details of her life and career in ceramics, see "Mary Louise McLaughlin," *American Ceramic Society Bulletin* 17 (May 1938), pp. 217-225 (chiefly autobiographical); *The Ladies, God Bless 'Em: The Women's Art Movement in the Nineteenth Century* (Cincinnati: Cincinnati Art Museum, 1976), pp. 63-64; and Kimberly Dunn, "The Losanti Ware of Mary Louise McLaughlin" (master's thesis, University of Cincinnati, 1983).

2. *American Ceramic Society Bulletin* 17 (1938), p. 217.

3. Mary Louise McLaughlin adapted an old and long-used process: colored slips (clay mixed with water to the consistency of cream) applied to the surface of the damp, unfired clay body. At Haviland glazes were made from fritted colored clays (fired and ground) and applied to bisque-fired ware. Charles Volkmar, an art potter of New York and New Jersey, experimented with the French process at the same time. Miss McLaughlin's first successful piece of faience was fired in January 1878 and is preserved in the Cincinnati Art Museum. Much has been made of the fact that T.J. Wheatley patented the process she "invented," although even she believed that it was not different enough from ancient techniques to be patentable. For

more about this controversy, see *American Ceramic Society Bulletin* 17 (1938), pp. 219 and 222-225.

4. Mary Louise McLaughlin, *Pottery Decoration under the Glaze* (Cincinnati: Robert Clarke, 1880).

5. *American Ceramic Society Bulletin* 17 (1938), p. 219.

107

107

Vase, 1901-1904
Mary Louise McLaughlin (1847-1939), Cincinnati
Porcelain, molded with tulips and leaves; gray and red-green transmutational glazes
H: 5¾ in. Diam: 4½ in.
Marks: incised cipher *MCL* and 166; painted in blue vertically *LOSANTI* (on bottom)
The Ross C. Purdy Museum of Ceramics, Columbus, Ohio

Mary Louise McLaughlin's development of the underglaze slip technique on earthenware in 1877-1878 founded a decorating industry; her experiments twenty years later with a line of porcelain called "Losanti" reflected a growing desire among decorators to participate in the total process of ceramic production.[1] Although art porcelain in the conventional English manner was made by several American commercial manufacturers by 1899, independent china

painters had not ventured into this difficult realm.[2]

The obstacles for Miss McLaughlin seemed overwhelming at times: no published technical instruction to follow, the necessity of adapting foreign formulas to American materials, complaints from neighbors about the burning of coal in a backyard kiln (coke was later used), consultation with experts who insisted on doing things their own way.[3] But she succeeded and, once the kiln was constructed and fired satisfactorily, began a long series of experiments involving numerous combinations of eighteen formulas for clay bodies and forty-five for glazes of her own preparation. Finally, she produced the "one-fire porcelain," body and glaze fired at the same time, in emulation of the Chinese method.[4] With Miss McLaughlin directing the operation, designing the molds, and determining the schedule of experiments, her assistant, Margaret Hickey (whose "interest and aid . . . contributed so much to the success of Losanti Ware") cast the ware and watched over the kiln.[5] By 1904 Miss McLaughlin had laid porcelain experiments aside to pursue metalwork again.[6] "I would give up much to indulge in [ceramic's] excitements and have done so," she wrote in 1938, "but I stopped short of putting my furniture in the kiln."[7]

"Losanti" designs are among the best examples of work by the few American potters inspired by French and Belgian Art Nouveau decoration. Miss McLaughlin's nephew by marriage, the designer Edward Colonna, may have been the catalyst for this style. She was cautious in her adaptation, explaining, "The movement known as 'L'Art Nouveau' will and must have influence, but it cannot be followed without reason or moderation, except to the detriment and degradation of the Beautiful."[8] The most important source for her porcelain was Chinese; she cited once-fired Chinese porcelains as her inspiration to experiment in the first place. In fact, the colors achieved in this vase echo the difficult transmutational glaze known as "peach bloom."[9]

EPD and BRD

1. Among these decorators were Susan Frackelton (no. 176) and Marshall Fry; others who turned to pottery at the same time included the geologist Linna Irelan of the Roblin Pottery and Henry Chapman Mercer (no. 212), an anthropologist, historian, and collector. For more about McLaughlin, see "Mary Louise McLaughlin," *American Ceramic Society Bulletin* 17 (May 1938), pp. 219-220.

2. These American porcelain manufacturers include Ott and Brewer (1871-1892), Willets Manufacturing Company (1879-1910), Ceramic Art Company (1889-present, Lenox), Columbian Art Pottery (1893-1905), and Knowles, Taylor and Knowles (1870-1928, "Lotus Ware" after 1889). Adelaide Alsop Robineau did not begin working in porcelain until about 1902.

3. Mary Louise McLaughlin, "The History of Porcelain Making: The Losanti Ware," typed manuscript, n.d., excerpted for *American Ceramic Society Bulletin* 17 (1938). Archives of the American Ceramic Society, Columbus, Ohio.

4. Louise M. McLaughlin [sic], "Losanti Ware," *Craftsman* 3 (December 1902), p. 186.

5. See McLaughlin manuscript cited in note 3 above, p. 12.

6. "Louisiana Purchase Exposition Ceramics," *Keramic Studio* 6 (March 1905), p. 252; the present vase is illustrated on page 251.

7. *American Ceramic Society Bulletin* 17 (1938), p. 222. This image is in reference to a well-known event in the life of Bernard Palissy, a sixteenth-century French potter whose trials and tribulations were often cited in the nineteenth century as evidence of the ultimate devotion of a potter to his craft.

8. Martin Eidelberg, "Art Pottery," in Robert Judson Clark, ed., *The Arts and Crafts Movement in America, 1876-1916* (Princeton: Princeton University Press, 1972), p. 164; for illustrations of Colonna's work, see Martin Eidelberg, *E. Colonna* (Dayton, Ohio: Dayton Art Institute, 1983). See also McLaughlin 1902, p. 187.

9. Although the Chinese method of fusing glaze and clay together in a single firing was developed originally for economic reasons, beautiful wares were achieved by this practice. Mary Louise McLaughlin's desire to emulate the method came from her admiration of Chinese ceramics. For more about the influence of Chinese ceramics on American art ceramics, see Ellen Paul Denker, *After the Chinese Taste: China's Influence in America, 1730-1930* (Salem, Mass: Peabody Museum, 1985), pp. 43-46.

108 (color plate, p. 22)
Vase, 1908
Adelaide Alsop Robineau (1865-1929), Syracuse
Porcelain, wheel-thrown with brown and tan flowing matte glazes and aqua, blue, and orange crystalline glazes; decorated with incised crabs; stand perforated with matching crab decoration
H: (of vase and vase with stand) 7⅜ in. Diam: (of vase) 3 in.
Marks: vase – excised conjoined *AR* in circle and incised *571* (on bottom); stand – incised conjoined *AR* (on inner ring)
Everson Museum of Art, Syracuse. Museum Purchase. 16.4.2a,b

Few individuals working in ceramics during the Arts and Crafts movement had more influence on contemporary craftsmanship or design reform than Adelaide Alsop Robineau. Born in Middletown, Connecticut, she demonstrated an early interest and talent in china decorating, which she taught at St. Mary's Hall, her alma mater in Faribault, Minnesota.[1] Shortly thereafter, she moved to New York and studied painting with William Merritt Chase, exhibited her watercolors at the National Academy, and continued to teach china painting.

With Samuel Edouard Robineau, a collector of antique English and Oriental ceramics, whom she married in 1899, Mrs. Robineau founded the Keramic Studio Publishing Company.[2] Despite widespread popular interest in china decoration, and several existing manuals for practitioners, no quality periodical existed to serve them until *Keramic Studio* was published in Syracuse in May 1899. Benefiting from articles by such accomplished ceramists, decorators, and art historians as Edwin AtLee Barber, Charles F. Binns (no. 177), Frederick H. Rhead (nos. 183 and 191), Kathryn Cherry (no. 184), Mary Chase Perry (no. 114), and Taxile Doat (no. 182), *Keramic Studio* (*Design* beginning in 1924) quickly became a financial and artistic success. Reports of arts and crafts exhibitions and societies, technical articles, and especially china-painting designs gave this slim periodical vast influence over craft and design practice in the United States.

Within a few years of founding *Keramic Studio* Mrs. Robineau's personal artistic ambitions transcended design and decorating and she began to create her own porcelain works. A key element in this transition was the translation by Samuel Robineau and publication in *Keramic Studio* of the treatise *Grand Feu Ceramics* by the well-known Sèvres ceramist Taxile Doat. His technical information on porcelain clay bodies and formulas for matte and crystalline glazes provided Mrs. Robineau with the basis for her experiments. She exhibited porcelains made and fired at home at the Syracuse Arts and Crafts exhibition in 1903 and the St. Louis World's Fair in 1904.

In an article in the December 1907 *Keramic Studio* the present vase and stand are shown after being carved and bisquit fired but prior to glazing and final firing.[3] The consequences of working in so fragile a medium are mentioned in the same article: "It is a curious fact that when the editor had misfortune with one design she continued to have misfortune with it, or if she had luck the luck repeated itself. The vase carved in relief with crabs and seaweed, and which has an openwork ring of the same motif to prevent tipping is the fourth of this design . . . the first two were broken."[4] The "Crab vase" illustrates Mrs. Robineau's early emphasis on carved decoration and her complex, flowing crystalline glaze. Shortly after her death in 1929, it was shown in the memorial exhibition of her ceramics at the Metropolitan Museum of Art.[5]

BRD and EPD

1. For more information about this artist, see Peg Weiss, ed., *Adelaide Alsop Robineau: Glory in Porcelain* (Syracuse: Syracuse University Press in association with Everson Museum of Art, 1981).

2. Edwin AtLee Barber's *Anglo-American Pottery* (Philadelphia: Patteson & White Co., 1901) includes a "Directory of Collectors" at the end. On page 198 is the following listing: "Robineau, Samuel E. Syracuse, N.Y. (Editor of 'Old China') Anglo-American pottery. Collection of 100 pieces. Correspond, purchase or exchange."

3. The piece was designated as the "Crab vase" by its maker. See Adelaide Alsop Robineau, "Porcelains," *Keramic Studio* 9 (December 1907), pp. 178-180.

4. Ibid., p. 178.

5. Joseph Breck, *A Memorial Exhibition of Porcelain and Stoneware by Adelaide Alsop Robineau 1865-1929* (New York: Metropolitan Museum of Art, 1929); the exhibition was held from November 18, 1929, to January 19, 1930.

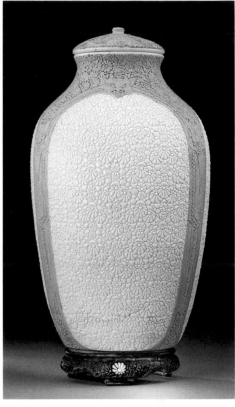

109

109

Vase, 1910
Adelaide Alsop Robineau (1865-1929), University City, Missouri
Porcelain, wheel-thrown with excised decoration of daisies and satyrs' mask; glazed in gray and white
H: (with cover and stand) 9¼ in. Diam: 4½ in.
Marks: excised cipher of conjoined *AR* in circle; incised 2 above and 1910 below cipher, with U and C flanking cipher; PASTORAL (on bottom)
National Museum of American History, Division of Ceramics and Glass. Gift of Priscilla R. Kelly. 1979.0104.01a,b

Stand, 1910
Porcelain, excised floral decoration, three carved feet; white, brown, black, and gray glazes
H: ⅞ in. Diam: 3⅜ in.

Mark: excised cipher of conjoined *AR* in circle (on bottom)
Everson Museum of Art, Museum Purchase, 1930 30.4.88

In November 1909, Adelaide Robineau noted in *Keramic Studio* that her mail should be sent to University City, Missouri, where a new and important school of ceramic art was soon to open under the auspices of Edward G. Lewis's American Woman's League.[1] Mrs. Robineau was associated in this enterprise with the famous French ceramist Taxile Doat (no. 182), the English potter and teacher Frederick H. Rhead (nos. 183 and 191), and the popular china painter Kathryn E. Cherry (no. 184). It was a distinguished assemblage of talent, but financial difficulties in the League forced closure in 1911.

During this brief period, however, Mrs. Robineau created some of her most ambitious pieces, including the tour-de-force "Scarab" vase,[2] which required over 1,000 hours to carve and glaze, and this "Pastoral" vase featuring the elaborate layered glaze technique of *pâte-sur-pâte*. Both pieces reflect the strong influence of Doat in precision carving and a soft color palette.[3] Another powerful inspiration for the Robineau style and technique was that of Royal Copenhagen and Bing and Grondahl, especially their porcelains with modeled, carved, or pierced decoration. The work of both companies was praised in early issues of *Keramic Studio*, along with Mary Louise McLaughlin's "Losanti" carved porcelains (no. 107).

After the failure of the University City experiment, Mrs. Robineau went home to Syracuse and worked there until her death in 1929. She continued to experiment in porcelain, ran a six-week arts and crafts summer school at her Syracuse studio, and was appointed to the faculty of Syracuse University. In addition to her active career, she raised a family and maintained a household, but not without sacrifice: "And now what are we going to do about the domestic problem, those of us who have homes and children and husband and still feel called to follow the lure of art? It is because of the children and the home that we cannot and will not give up, that the woman can never hope to become as great in any line as man. Art is a jealous mistress and allows no consideration whatever to interfere with her supremacy."[4]

The products of Mrs. Robineau's small pottery on the hill overlooking Onondaga Park in Syracuse continued to attract the admiration of her fellow ceramics enthusiasts and the general public through exhibitions and magazine articles, but hers was a highly personal art that would never become self-supporting.[5] Mrs. Robineau's work could be purchased for as little as five or ten dollars (although the most expensive could cost $1,500), but even with mail-order sales, only about 600 pieces were sold in her lifetime.[6] As part of her Grand-Prize-winning exhibit at the 1915 Panama-Pacific International Exhibition in San Francisco, the "Pastoral" vase was offered at $500. Unsold, it was finally left to one of her daughters, while the base became separated and was later sold in a lot to the Syracuse Museum of Fine Arts.[7]

BRD and EPD

1. *Keramic Studio* 11 (November 1909).

2. Peg Weiss, ed., *Adelaide Alsop Robineau: Glory in Porcelain* (Syracuse: Syracuse University Press in association with Everson Museum of Art, 1981), opposite p. 32.

3. Porcelains by Mrs. Robineau exhibited with the American Woman's League at the 1911 International Exposition in Turin (Italy) won the Grand Prize in Ceramics; see illustration in *Keramic Studio* 13 (August 1911), p. 83.

4. *Keramic Studio* 15 (May 1913), p. 1.

5. Revenue from the publication of *Keramic Studio* and the constant encouragement and aid of her husband meant that Mrs. Robineau could be free to pursue her experiments in high-fired porcelain.

6. S.E. Robineau, "Adelaide Alsop-Robineau," *Design* 30 (April 1929), p. 206.

7. Weiss 1981, p. 215.

110 (color plate, p. 22)
Vase, ca. 1900
Biloxi Art Pottery (ca. 1880 - ca. 1909) of George E. Ohr (1857-1918), Biloxi, Mississippi
Red earthenware with glazes of matte blue-gray and pink and glossy mottled green and blue; wheel-thrown and altered with applied handles and "snake" inside rim
H: 7 in. W: (including handles) 7 in.
Marks: impressed twice GEO. E. OHR / BILOXI, MISS. (on bottom)
The Shack Collection

Virtually all potters and decorators included in this study worked in the mainstream of American art ceramics. They knew each other, moved between potteries, shared similar sources of inspiration, showed their work in many of the same international expositions and local Arts and Crafts exhibitions, read and wrote about each other in art and trade journals and enjoyed the attention and appreciation of their peers. George Ohr did not. Indeed, a comment of F.H. Rhead (see nos. 183 and 191) that he was "entirely without art training and altogether lacking in taste"[1] says as much about the art-pottery world at the time as it does about Ohr himself. But Ohr represents the tenets of the Art and Crafts Movement in several very basic ways. He worked with local materials that he gathered himself and found joy in labor and beauty in the products of his hands. Also, like some other independent art potters, he supported his artistic work and his family by producing wares that found a ready market: "If it were not for the housewives of Biloxi who have a constant need of flower pots, water coolers, and flues, the family of Ohr would often go hungry," he stated.[2]

The sources Ohr drew upon were familiar to art potters at the time, but in the context of his work were not recognizable to critics and are just becoming understood by students of his pottery today. He boasted that he was the greatest potter on earth, referring to himself as the "Second Palissy."[3] In fact, the asymmetrical bravado of Ohr's work and character is rooted in the popular nineteenth-century conception of the sixteenth-century potter as interpreted by the rustic American imagination. Ohr was probably looking also at Victorian commercial art wares for inspiration. The frilly edges and ribboned handles of his most exaggerated pieces recall colorful crimped glass and elaborate molded and modeled porcelain of the period. Ohr, however, translated those shapes into clay that was formed by hand to exquisite thinness on the potter's wheel and then, just as expertly, deformed.

Despite his lack of formal training, Ohr was undoubtedly aware of contemporary European, English, and American art ceramics, which he would have seen as he "sized up every potter and pottery in 16 states, and never missed a shop window, illustration or literary dab on ceramics...."[4] He represented himself as a crazy country bumpkin, but he was probably well-read, visually literate, and quite familiar with the avant-garde work of such clay artists as the Martin brothers, the sophisticated London stoneware potters who also worked with rustic themes, and the English designer Christopher Dresser, who produced some tortured clay designs for the Linthorpe Pottery that were shown at the New Orleans Cotton Centennial Exposition in 1884.

Although he seems to have made his living as a potter from about 1880 to 1909, Ohr's mature style as represented by the vase shown here did not emerge until about 1895.[5] This vase illustrates many of his characteristics to good advantage in the eccentric handles, altered rim, and extraordinary delicacy of the walls. The glazes are also typically unconventional. Ohr divided the vase in half by putting a dull gray glaze with maroon spots on one side and a glossy brown mottled glaze with blue spots on the other. The differentiation of the two halves by color accentuates the dissimilarity of the handles. The small snake inside the rim is a device borrowed from country potters of the period.

EPD and BRD

1. Quoted in Paul Evans, "Reflections of Frederick Hurten Rhead," *Pottery Collectors Newsletter* 9 (September/October 1980), p. 45.

2. *Crockery and Glass Journal*, December 30, 1909, p. 50, quoted in Paul Evans, *Art Pottery of the United States* (New York: Charles Scribner's Sons, 1974), p. 30.

3. The reference is to Bernard Palissy, the sixteenth-century French potter who was appointed "inventor of the King's rustic pottery" in 1562 and received popular acclaim in the nineteenth century as the epitome of Protestant and artistic determination. For more about Palissy, his work, and his nineteenth-century imitators, see Malcolm Haslam, "Bernard Palissy," *Connoisseur* 190 (September 1975), pp. 12-17. For a consideration of the work of American country potters in terms of the Palissy revival, see Ellen Paul Denker, *The Kirkpatricks' Pottery at Anna, Illinois* (Champaign: Krannert Art Museum, University of Illinois, 1986).

4. George E. Ohr, "Some Facts in the History of a Unique Personality," *Crockery and Glass Journal*, December 15, 1901, quoted in Garth Clark, "George E. Ohr: Avant-Garde Volumes," *Studio Potter* 12 (December 1983), p. 11.

5. Ohr, the son of a blacksmith, learned the art of pottery about 1880 from Joseph F. Meyer, who later worked as the thrower for many years at the Newcomb Pottery (see nos. 178 and 179). For more biographical information, see Robert W. Blasberg, *George E. Ohr and His Biloxi Art Pottery* (Port Jervis, N.Y.: J.W. Carpenter, 1973); and Clark 1983, pp. 10-19.

111

111

Vase, ca. 1915
Overbeck Pottery (1911-1955), Cambridge City, Indiana
Elizabeth Gray Overbeck (1875-1936), Mary Frances Overbeck (1878-1955), and Hannah Borger Overbeck (1870-1931)
Earthenware, wheel-thrown; matte glaze in medium brown, slate gray, and dark brown; incised decoration
H: 15¼ in. Diam: 7¾ in.
Marks: incised OBK conjoined, E and F (on bottom)
The Kathleen and Arthur Postle Collection, Public Library, Cambridge City, Indiana

The art pottery established as a family enterprise in the Overbeck Cambridge City home was probably inspired by a fourth sister, Margaret (1863-1911), who had worked as a decorator in the Zanesville Art Pottery just prior to her death.[1] While all four sisters had been actively involved in china painting, only Elizabeth had

had any practical training.[2] Hannah graduated from Indiana State Normal School in 1894 and taught for a year in Clinton, Indiana, but ill health brought her back to the family home, where she continued to practice drawing, watercolor, and design. Elizabeth studied art with Margaret and ceramics with Charles Fergus Binns at the New York State School for Clayworking and Ceramics in Alfred (1909-1910). The youngest sister, Mary Frances, also studied with Margaret and, later, with Arthur Dow and Marshall Fry at Columbia University; she taught briefly in Colorado and Indiana.[3] Once the pottery was begun, none of the sisters was allied any longer as a teacher with a formal educational institution. However, they opened their home to art and home economics classes and clubs from the area and Elizabeth often lectured on pottery to women's clubs. The necessity of keeping the operation inexpensive – they used it to support themselves – meant that all but the heaviest work was performed by

Elizabeth and Mary Frances, using only the most essential potter's equipment.

This vase, which was exhibited at the Panama-Pacific Exposition in San Francisco in 1915, was the product of the creative efforts of Elizabeth, Hannah, and Mary Frances. Based on a design of nasturtiums by Hannah,[4] the vase was thrown by Elizabeth and decorated by Mary Frances. The somber color palette and strong rectilinear quality of the decoration illustrate how the sisters had absorbed early-twentieth-century design and given it their own impress. Although their work continued to emphasize abstract patterning throughout the years the subjects, treatments, and colors reflected contemporary preferences. Unlike the production of larger commercial art potteries – such as Rookwood, Grueby, and Newcomb – that often exhibited a uniformity calculated to appeal to a large market, the ceramics of the Overbecks were always fresh.

EPD and BRD

1. After study at the Cincinnati Art Academy (1892-1893 and 1898-1899), Margaret was an art instructor at several colleges, including DePauw University (1899-1910), where she taught china painting, drawing, and watercolor.

2. For a complete study of the Overbeck sisters, see Kathleen R. Postle, *The Chronicle of the Overbeck Pottery* (Indianapolis: Indiana Historical Society, 1978).

3. After Elizabeth and Hannah died in the 1930s, Mary Frances continued to make pottery, specializing in lively robust figurines, until her death in 1955.

4. Published in *Keramic Studio* 15 (September 1913), p. 106. All the Overbecks made substantial contributions to *Keramic Studio* between 1904 and 1916. After that the nature of the magazine changed from one concerned with educating china painters to a publication for studio artists.

112

Vase, 1913-1921
Markham Pottery (1905-1921), Ann Arbor, Michigan, and National City, California
Red earthenware, molded; textured, mottled matte finish in buff, brown, and orange
H: 8 in. Diam: 3¾ in.
Marks: incised MARKHAM and 7211 (on bottom)
San Diego Museum of Art. Gift of Mrs. Robert Cameron Stone. 37.43

"The story of the Markham Pottery is not one of a large establishment, complete equipment and many workmen turning out hundreds of pieces

112

of ware each day. It is rather the story of one man, his love of nature and the beautiful in everything, his delight in his labor, the years of investigation and experiment based, not on technical skill, but upon the necessity of working out what was within himself – his failures and successes."[1]

Herman C. Markham, an employee of the Archaeology Department of the University of Michigan, began making vases to display the roses from his garden. Porous earthenware answered the need for vases that would keep water cool by surface evaporation. After a long period of trial and error, his ware, made of clay from his own yard was put into commercial production in 1905. Joined by his son Kenneth in that year, Markham cast vases of creamy slip in molds made from his own wheel-thrown or hand-built models. The use of molds enabled him to produce a marketable quantity of ware

and, as a result of the time saved, to concentrate on decoration. Fired once at a fairly low temperature, the wares had unusual surface effects achieved through the interaction of fire and glaze in Markham's own finishing process. Two types of finish were used: *reseau*, having a finely textured surface of delicate traceries only slightly raised, and *arabesque*, with a maze-like surface texture in coarser relief. The classical forms, textured surfaces, and restrained color palette gave the ware an "appearance of age – as if the vases had been excavated from some long-buried ancient atelier. . . .The colors are always soft, pastel-like, and so harmoniously blended and distributed that it seems to be the work of nature rather than man. . . . Not entirely beyond the potter's influence, the character of these surface designs is quite beyond his control."[2] Thus, no two pieces were identical and Markham emphasized their individuality by incising a consecutive number on the base of each piece.[3] The four digits on the present vase (an example of the *arabesque* finish) indicate that it was made after 1913, when the pottery moved from Michigan to California.

When Markham's pottery was displayed in the exhibition of the New York Society of Keramic Arts in 1907, the reviewer for *Keramic Studio* was critical of it from a technical standpoint, insisting that despite its "simple and good" shapes and "vaguely mysterious and suggestive" surface, "to one at all versed in the mechanical process of pottery making, this ware does not ring true . . . it reminded us of a refined edition of the scrapings of our palette."[4] In spite of such criticisms, the pottery achieved considerable popular success. The same article conceded that it "attracted more favorable comment from the general public than any other pottery," and in 1915, Markham's ware won a Gold Medal at the Panama-Pacific Exposition.

EPD and BRD

1. *The Markham Pottery Book* (Ann Arbor: Pottery, n.d. [ca. 1906]), taken from Lillian Gray Jarvie, "Our American Potteries: The Markham Pottery," *Sketch Book* 5 (November 1905), pp. 123-129.

2. Ibid., pp. 4, 6, and 7.

3. Paul Evans, *Art Pottery of the United States* (New York: Charles Scribner's Sons, 1974), p. 163. Numbers above 6,000 are identified with the National City period after Markham's move to California in the fall of 1913; those below 6,000 are assigned to Ann Arbor.

4. "Exhibition of the New York Society of Keramic Arts," *Keramic Studio* 9 (June 1907), p. 41.

113
Bowl, ca. 1913
Attributed to Willets Manufacturing Company (1879-1910), Trenton
Decorator: Dorothea Warren O'Hara (1875-1963), New York
Belleek porcelain, molded; decorated with conventional floral pattern of thick overglaze enamels in lilac, violet, green, and yellow on dark blue ground
H: 6⅝ in. Diam: 10⁵⁄₁₆ in.
Marks: *Dorothea Warren O'Hara* in overglaze black enamel; small overglaze blue bird obscuring manufacturer's mark (on bottom)
Collection of Rosalie M. Berberian

Like Adelaide Robineau, Susan Frackelton, Mary Louise McLaughlin, and Mary Chase Perry, Dorothea Warren O'Hara grew as an independent artist from china painter to ceramist during her long career.[1] Born and raised in Malta Bend, Missouri, she studied art first in Kansas City and subsequently at the Herr von Debschitz School of Design in Munich, London's Royal College of Art, and in the museums of Paris. In America she tutored with three leading New York instructors in china painting: Adelaide Robineau, Franz Bischoff, and Marshall Fry.

Shortly after 1900 Dorothea Warren settled in New York City, where she advertised her skills in porcelain design and decoration and offered enamels and instruction to china painters. For sixteen years she contributed to the china painters' journal *Keramic Studio* as a correspondent and artist. During seven of those years *Ladies' Home Journal* published her work as well. Late in 1912 her slim volume, *The Art of Enameling on Porcelain*, joined the legion of earlier manuals for the amateur and expert.[2] As a result of these activities, Mrs. O'Hara was hailed in 1913 as the "pioneer of enamel decoration of the kind and character in vogue today. [She] began experimenting twenty years ago, and during that time perfected by actual tests the ready-for-use enamels now so successfully used by keramic teachers and students."[3] In 1915, she won gold medals at the Panama-Pacific Exposition in San Francisco, where two of her vases were bought by the Japanese government.

Mrs. O'Hara was an outstanding practitioner of china painting on American belleek,[4] a variety of porcelain characterized by a fine translucent cream-colored body perfected by manufacturers in Trenton during the early 1880s. The

113

Willets Manufacturing Company and the Ceramic Art Company, in particular, courted china painters as customers. From the time that china painting captured the imagination of amateur and professional alike, debates raged over which country made the best porcelain blanks for practicing the art – France, Germany or America. In 1899, Charles F. Binns recommended that Americans patronize American belleek manufacturers out of patriotic duty and because the shapes did not determine what the decoration should be: "no style is so uncompromising as the French."[5] Mrs. O'Hara must have heeded such advice because much of her work in the early 1900s is painted on belleek blanks made in Trenton.

Although this bowl may seem daring today for its abstract design at so early a date, the style was shared by other prominent china painters at the time and derives from several influences.

By the turn of the century, two basic modes were current in American china painting, as in other media: the naturalistic and the stylized. For those artists attracted to the latter, German, Austrian, and French sources offered numerous models, including adaptations from ancient patterns. When this bowl was shown in the New York exhibition of the National Society of Craftsmen in 1914, a reporter noted that O'Hara designs "show the influence of Persia, though one lovely jar is French in inspiration."[6] The broad decorative use of colors rather thickly applied is in contrast to the thinner washes that characterize most other artists' methods of application when they executed stylized designs.

In 1920, Mrs. O'Hara left her prominent position in New York craft and china-painting circles to found her own Apple Tree Lane Pottery in an abandoned barn on the ten-acre farm she and her husband had purchased in Connecti-

cut. Indeed, she tends to be identified among American ceramists today as a clayworker rather than as a china painter. In her ceramics she translated the cheerful rhythms of a flat style on belleek to objects of earthenware, many carved or modeled in relief, on which a monochromatic engobe formed the ground for designs in brilliant colorful glazes.

EPD and BRD

1. Biographical information about Mrs. O'Hara was compiled from Adelaide Alsop Robineau, "Mrs. Dorothea Warren O'Hara," *Keramic Studio* 18 (January 1917), p. 143; Amy Bonner, "Mrs. Dorothea Warren O'Hara, Great American Ceramist, Finds Work Greatest Joy," *Christian Science Monitor*, June 10, 1941, p. 10c; and Beatrice Colgate, "Dorothea O'Hara," *Darien Review*, November 22, 1955, pp. 89-91.

2. Dorothea Warren O'Hara, *The Art of Enameling on Porcelain* (New York: Madison Square Press, 1912), 32 pp.

3. "Some Recent Work of Dorothea Warren O'Hara," *International Studio* 50 (July-October 1913), p. 77.

4. Belleek was first produced in Ireland in the mid-nineteenth century.

5. Charles F. Binns, "The Use of American Wares by American Ceramic Decorators," *Keramic Studio* 1 (August 1899), pp. 81-82.

6. "Exhibition of the National Society of Craftsmen, New York," *Keramic Studio* 15 (March 1914), pp. 180-181. Miss O'Hara applied her conventional style also to American Indian motifs: "The designs and colors of her exhibit at the Natural History Museum [with the Keramic Society of New York] are based on native American inspiration, such as the gorgeous beadwork of the Micmacs or Ojibways and the more formal patterns used by tawny and mysterious Incas and Montezumas before the discovery of this continent. . . ." (See "What Talent and Skill Can Do in the Pottery Industry," *Good Furniture* 8 [June 1917], p. 322.)

114 (color plate, p. 23)
Vase, ca. 1929
Pewabic Pottery (1903-1961), Detroit
Decorator: Mary Chase Perry [Stratton] (1867-1961)
Earthenware, wheel-thrown and covered with reduction luster glaze in pale lavender, tan, black, turquoise, and medium blue
H: 9⅝ in. Diam: 6¾ in.
Mark: impressed in circle PEWABIC / DETROIT (on bottom)
Cranbrook Academy of Art Museum. Gift of George G. Booth. 1932.13

For many young women in the late nineteenth century, china painting was more than a pastime; it was one of the few acceptable ways in which a genteel woman with artistic proclivities could make money for her family. In addition, success as a china painter sometimes opened new avenues of achievement for these women. Adelaide Robineau (nos. 108 and 109) parlayed her talents as a china painter into publishing a national magazine as a method to support her art work; Mary Chase Perry founded an architectural tile company and continued throughout her life to experiment with the chemistry of lustrous glazes.[1]

Like many of her contemporaries, Miss Perry chose the ceramic art of the Orient as a source for inspiration, concentrating on Near Eastern lustrous surfaces. Examples in the collection of the Detroit industrialist Charles Lang Freer, now housed in the Smithsonian's Freer Gallery, offered ready inspiration. One of her earliest patrons, Freer thoroughly appreciated her achievement, as did George G. Booth, founder of the Cranbrook Academy. Miss Perry's work was included in the architecture of the Academy's buildings, designed by Eliel Saarinen, as well as in Booth's private collection.

But patronage by nationally prominent collectors and architects came only after years of experimentation and struggle. Miss Perry's most loyal patron was also her partner, Horace J. Caulkins, who owned a flourishing dental-supply company. Employed by him initially as a demonstrator and salesman of his Revelation Kiln, designed for preparing dental work, she used it for firing decorated ceramics and sold models to china painters throughout the country. As Miss Perry's interest in glaze chemistry grew so, too, did Caulkins's personal and financial involvement with her experiments. Their collaboration led eventually to the establishment of the Pewabic Pottery in 1903 and the construction in 1907 of a quaint English half-timbered style building designed by William Buck Stratton, whom Miss Perry later married. It was Caulkins who sat up with the kiln at night to provide the critical change in atmosphere needed to produce lustrous glazes and it was Caulkins (and later his wife and son) who provided the extra capital year after year to keep the Pewabic Pottery financially solvent.[2]

Mary Chase Perry's goals in founding the pottery were to produce commercial artwork that used local materials and to maintain a small operation that allowed her to monitor the process and product closely. While expansion would increase profits, it would preclude the

control she wanted to maintain. Pewabic Pottery is best known for brilliant iridescent tiles installed in public and private buildings. The most successful of Miss Perry's vases illustrate the depth and range of the lusters she developed for the tiles. Unlike Binns or Robineau, she did not consider form to be as critical as surface. Therefore, she never learned to use the potter's wheel, but had vases made for her while she concentrated on the glazes that would dazzle the surface of otherwise pedestrian forms. The complexity of the many colors that break and develop down the sides of this vase and the exquisite timing of the brilliant streak of turquoise luster have turned the plain cylindrical shape into a classic statement of the art of glaze chemistry.

EPD and BRD

1. For further information about Miss Perry and the Pewabic Pottery, see Lillian Myers Pear, *The Pewabic Pottery: A History of Its Products and Its People* (Des Moines: Wallace-Homestead Book Co., 1976).

2. The ceramics teacher and critic Charles F. Binns (see no. 177) noted this "happy combination of genius and finance" in 1916. In his opinion the Pewabic Pottery straddled the fine line between studio and factory "without any depreciation in quality . . . . To Miss Mary Chase Perry is due the superb quality of the product, but the results would have been impossible without the kindly and substantial aid of Mr. H.J. Caulkins. See "Pottery in America," *American Magazine of Art* 7 (February 1916), pp. 133-135.

115

Vase , ca. 1909
Marblehead Pottery (1904-1936), Marblehead, Massachusetts
Earthenware, wheel-thrown and decorated with band of haystacks in landscape painted in brown, dark green, blue, light green, and yellow on medium mustard ground
H: 8⅞ in. Diam: 7¼ in.
Mark: impressed outline of sailing ship from front, flanked by M and P and enclosed in circle (on bottom)
Private Collection

The Marblehead Pottery was founded by Herbert J. Hall in 1904 as part of a group of therapeutic crafts enterprises known as the Handcraft Shops. The various crafts – including handweaving, woodcarving, metalwork, and pottery – were intended to rehabilitate "nervously worn out patients for the blessing and

115

privilege of quiet manual work, where as apprentices they could learn again gradually and without haste to use their hand and brain in a normal, wholesome way."[1] Arthur E. Baggs, a young student of Charles F. Binns (see no. 177) at the New York School of Clayworking and Ceramics at Alfred, went to Marblehead to assist Dr. Hall with the pottery,[2] and by 1908 standardized production was achieved with a small staff.

In addition to serving as supervisor, Baggs was a designer, along with Arthur Hennessey and others. A mixture of New Jersey stoneware and Massachusetts brick clays was used for the pottery, which with few exceptions was thrown on the wheel by a talented English potter, John Swallow. Mrs. E.D. (Hannah) Tutt served as the primary decorator, while Baggs and Mrs. Swallow also decorated some wares.[3] The products included vases, lamp bases, tiles, and tea and cider sets, many of them undecorated except for the use of single-color matte glazes. Those pieces with designs, such as the present example, were incised and/or painted with flowers, ships, animals, and landscapes in a conventional style with several harmonizing shades of colored matte glazes. Successful designs were offered for sale by number from a catalogue; customers chose the background color while the decorators worked out the rest of the palette.[4] A muted color range and decoration abstracted from nature were the attributes that especially recommended the wares to consumers: "The Marblehead Pottery stands for simplicity – all that is bizarre and freakish have been avoided. It stands for quiet, subdued colors, for severe conventionalization in design, and for careful and thorough workmanship in all details."[5] This vase may be dated about 1909 by comparison with a similar example exhibited that year at the New York Society of Keramic Arts.[6]

EPD and BRD

1. Herbert J. Hall, M.D., "Marblehead Pottery," *Keramic Studio* 10 (June 1908), p. 31.

2. After the first year, when the technical requirements of production proved too demanding, the pottery was separated from the sanitorium. The concept was later tried more successfully at the Arequipa Pottery (see no. 163).

3. For Mrs. Tutt, see Hall 1908, p. 31; for Mrs. Swallow and others, see Gertrude Emerson, "Distinctively American Pottery: Marblehead Pottery," *Craftsman* 29 (March 1916), p. 672.

4. *Marblehead Pottery* (Marblehead, Mass.: Marblehead Pottery, 1919).

5. Jonathan A. Rawson, Jr., "Recent American Pottery," *House Beautiful* 31 (April 1912), p. 149.

6. The nearly identical example is illustrated in *Keramic Studio* 11 (June 1909), p. 40.

116

116

Bowl, 1916
Marblehead Pottery (1904-1936), Marblehead, Massachusetts
Attributed to Arthur Eugene Baggs (1886-1947)
Earthenware, wheel-thrown with red and black striped glaze on gray ground on outside of bowl and inside rim; mottled gray-beige interior
H: 2¾ in. Diam: 5⅝ in.
Marks: impressed outline of sailing ship from front, flanked by M and P and enclosed in circle; incised 60 (on bottom)
Label:(on paper) MARBLEHEAD / POTTERY
Museum of Fine Arts, Boston. Gift of Arthur E. Baggs. 1942.3

The standard line of art pottery developed at the Marblehead Pottery by Arthur E. Baggs established a formula for maintaining the pottery as a favorite among critics and consumers alike. However, the technical and artistic ceramist in Baggs demanded more. In 1912 he introduced a new faience line that permitted more free-painted decoration to be used.[1] Further glaze experiments were carried out and the color range of Marblehead's usual matte earth tones was expanded to include lusters and Chinese blues and reds.[2]

Baggs assumed ownership of the pottery in 1915, and in that year the firm received the J. Ogden Armour prize at the annual exhibition of applied arts at the Art Institute of Chicago. Other significant recognition came from the Boston Society of Arts and Crafts (1925) and the Syracuse Museum of Fine Arts (1933).[3] Baggs maintained a close association with the Marblehead Pottery until it closed in 1936.[4]

This bowl, which heralds the studio-pottery movement of the coming decades, shows Baggs's commitment to expanding the horizons of Marblehead Pottery's more chaste production (see no. 115).[5] An abstract linear pattern rendered in an unusual glaze of red and black is the only decoration. Shortly after it was made, Baggs loaned it to the Museum of Fine Arts as an example of his development.

BRD and EPD

1. Jonathan A. Rawson, Jr., "Recent American Pottery," *House Beautiful* 31 (April 1912), pp. 148-149.

2. Paul Evans, *Art Pottery of the United States* (New York: Charles Scribner's Sons, 1974), p. 158.

3. Marblehead won the first prize for pottery at the Robineau Memorial Exhibition in Syracuse in 1933.

4. Baggs was also a professor of ceramic arts at Ohio State University in Columbus from 1928 to 1947, having taught earlier at the New York School of Design and Liberal Arts and the Cleveland School of Art.

5. In the 1919 Marblehead catalogue Baggs announced: "SPECIAL WORK - Constant experiments are being made in the laboratory and kilns and many beautiful and interesting pieces are produced which it is impossible to catalog."

117 (color plate, p. 24)
Vase, 1899-1912
Grueby Faience Company (1897-1909) or
Grueby Pottery Company (1907-1913), Boston
Designer: attributed to George Prentiss Kendrick (active with Grueby 1897-1901)
Decorator: Gertrude Stanwood
Buff stoneware, wheel-thrown with applied
decoration of daffodils and leaves in yellow and
green matte glazes
H: 10¼ in. Diam: 9⅛ in.
Marks: impressed in circle with centered lotus
blossom *GRUEBY·POTTERY / BOSTON·U·S·A·* with
181 below; incised cipher *GS* (on bottom)
Collection of Betty and Robert A. Hut

118
Vase, 1899-1912
Grueby Faience Company (1897-1909) or
Grueby Pottery Company (1907-1913), Boston
Designer: attributed to George Prentiss Kendrick (active with Grueby 1897-1901)
Buff stoneware, wheel-thrown with applied
decoration of leaves and buds covered with
ocher matte glazes accented with white
H: 12 in. Diam: 5½ in.
Marks: impressed in circle with centered lotus
blossom (at center) *GRUEBY·POTTERY / BOSTON
U·S·A·* (on bottom)
Collection of Frederick R. Innes

The philosophy underlying William Grueby's
art pottery was summarized in a company pamphlet: "With the advent of machinery the intimate relation of the potter to his ware disappeared. Here it has been resumed. Instead of
the mechanical formality which has so often
been mistaken for precision, every surface and
line of this ware evinces the appreciative touch
of the artist's hand. As in the old wares [ancient
Oriental ceramics], there are no two pieces that
are exactly alike, for while the general form may
be maintained, every detail is a matter of individual regard . . . . Both in conception and
design, in glaze and color, each piece of the
Grueby ware is individual and of unusual merit,
and deserves to take a prominent place
amongst the best known wares."[1]
   Noteworthy art potteries had subscribed to
this philosophy for over twenty years, but Grueby was the first to put design in the hands of
architects and the execution of the prescribed
patterns in the hands of women trained in art
schools.[2] At other firms, such as the Rookwood
Pottery, the uniqueness of the wares depended

118

on the ideas of individual decorators, who
painted their own designs. Although Grueby's
decorators did not enjoy such freedom, their
methods did insure some distinctiveness. Because molds were not used, each piece was
shaped on the potter's wheel and then, while
damp, decorated by laying small ropes of clay
against the body in one of the patterns prescribed for that particular shape. Clay from the
vase was worked up along the outside of the
applied design and smoothed along the inside
of the clay fillets. After a bisquit firing the wares
were glazed.
   Apart from its handmade qualities Grueby
pottery appealed to buyers who furnished their
living spaces in the Arts and Crafts mode for its
design references to ancient art and to nature.
The color green was extremely popular in most

media at the turn of the century[3] and the taste
for matte glazes was growing in America as a
result of exposure to French art pottery during
the 1890s. The characteristic appearance of
Grueby wares is attributable to the glazes developed by William Grueby and to the conventionalized designs of George Prentiss Kendrick,
an architect. Trained in the pottery business at
the Low Art Tile Works, William Grueby (1867-1925) worked in architectural terra-cotta and at
the age of twenty-five was a partner in Atwood
& Grueby, a short-lived division of Fiske, Coleman & Company in Boston.[4] He represented
the latter firm at the 1893 World's Columbian
Exposition in Chicago, where he was inspired
to pursue the development of flowing matte
glazes after seeing the work of French potters
Ernest Chaplet and Auguste Delaherche. Experiments were begun shortly thereafter under the
auspices of the Grueby Faience Company, organized in 1894 for the production of glazed
bricks, tile, and terra-cotta executed in the variety of Beaux-Arts styles then current. Art wares
were exhibited in the 1895 annual exhibition of
the Architectural League of New York, but these
vases still showed adherence to fashionable
historical modes. The year 1897 was pivotal for
the fact that the Grueby Faience Company was
reorganized and incorporated to include Kendrick and another architect, William H. Graves,
who was in charge of accounting, publicity,
organization of exhibitions, and consignment
to retail outlets. It was also in 1897 that the new
art pottery was first shown in the annual exhibition of the Boston Society of Arts and Crafts.
Grueby's award-winning displays at major international expositions between 1900 and 1904
served to encourage buyers. In addition, the
inclusion of its pottery with Gustav Stickley's
furniture in promotional displays and Arts and
Crafts exhibitions enhanced the reputation of
both makers.
   Modern ceramics historians have pointed to
the large number of imitators of Grueby pottery
as the reason for the product's decline after
1910. Indeed, the popular success of the wares
encouraged production potteries to market
similar goods in the same way, for example, that
Rookwood's underglaze technique spawned
many copyists. However, these mimics had not
put Rookwood out of business. It is more likely
that Grueby's short tenure in art pottery was the
result of poor business management and the
stale nature of the product's design in later
years. Kendrick left the firm in 1901 to be

succeeded by Addison LeBoutillier, also an architect. Although LeBoutillier introduced some stunning designs in tiles (see no. 119), the three-dimensional work of the company stagnated; art wares continued to be derived from Kendrick's work of the late 1890s. By 1910 the market for Grueby pottery had probably been satiated. *Keramic Studio* noted with regard to the wares in 1900 that "No collection would be perfect without a piece of this ware," but also pointed out that "seeing so many pieces together gives a sense rather of monotony."[5] Consumers may well have felt that once the perfect piece of Grueby pottery had been chosen for a collection, there was little reason to acquire additional work. Although offered in yellow-ocher, mauve, blue, and medium-brown as well as the basic green, color variation might not have been enough to encourage repeat business and new patterns were not forthcoming. Finally, after several company failures and reorganizations a disastrous fire in 1913 at the Grueby Pottery (organized in 1907 specifically to produce the art wares) put an end to what small production there was by that time.

The vases shown here are good examples of work in two colors produced at the Grueby Pottery: the forms are classically Oriental, the major thrust of the designs is vertical, and the decorations are based on real plants, identifiable though rendered abstractly. A vase similar to no. 117 was used on promotional literature and in photographs provided by the firm to domestic and foreign publications.

EPD and BRD

1. C. Howard Walker, *The Grueby Pottery* ([Boston: Grueby Faience Company, ca. 1900]), n. p.; also published as C. Howard Walker, "The Grueby Pottery," *Keramic Studio* 1 (March 1900), p. 237.

2. Their method of organization – men as designers and women as decorators – was typical of industrial potteries and can probably be attributed to Grueby's development from an architectural terra-cotta company.

3. Diana Stradling, "Teco Pottery and the Green Phenomenon," *Tiller* 1 (March-April 1983), pp. 8-36.

4. Factual data included in this entry is summarized from Martin Eidelberg, "The Ceramic Art of William H. Grueby," *Connoisseur* 184 (September 1973), pp. 47-54.

5. *Keramic Studio* 1 (February 1900), p. 212.

119 (color plate, p. 25)
Tile, 1906-1920
Grueby Faience Company (1897-1909), Grueby Pottery Company (1907-1913), or Grueby Faience and Tile Company (1909-1920), Boston
Designer: Addison B. LeBoutillier (1872-1951)
Buff terra-cotta, press-molded with stylized pines in landscape; covered in green, blue, lavender, ocher, and brown matte glazes
H: 12 3/16 in. W: 12 in. D: 3/4 in.
Museum of Fine Arts, Boston. Anonymous Gift in Memory of John G. Pierce. 65.215

William Grueby was in the architectural tile and terra-cotta business throughout his career. Prior to the emergence of the reorganized Grueby Faience Company in 1897, the output of his firms was in several Beaux-Arts modes popular in contemporary architecture: for example, the Italian Renaissance style used for the Reading Railroad Terminal in Philadelphia (ca. 1892) by Atwood & Grueby and the fashionable Moorish style of the hall illustrated in the company's 1893 brochure.[1] Grueby's apprenticeship at the Low Art Tile Works in Chelsea, Massachusetts, had given him thorough knowledge of standard practices in the tile business in the 1880s, but by the turn of the century his Grueby Faience Company would introduce a new way of decorating tiles. Rather than the glossy monochromatic intaglio and relief work of the late 1800s, tiles of the early 1900s emphasized two-dimensional design, visual surface texture, and a matte finish.[2] Such attributes recommended tiles for interiors conceived to be natural; here the tiles' nonreflective finish and broad conventional motifs provided subtle decorative accents among the dark woods and patinated base metals of the architecture. "Landscape and figures should be reduced to ornament," declared Addison LeBoutillier in 1906.[3]

From 1904 until about 1907, Addison LeBoutillier worked as a designer for Grueby's pottery in the place of George P. Kendrick, who had left in 1901. Born in Utica, New York, LeBoutillier trained as an architect with a Rochester firm from the age of sixteen and worked in Chicago during the 1890s before moving to Boston. Many years later his son remembered that "architects in Boston were not very busy . . . so Dad was making a thin living designing jewelry and newspaper advertisements for Bigelow, Kennard & Company. This brought him a reputation as a designer, particularly for his lettering."[4] Since Bigelow, Kennard & Company carried Grueby's art pottery it is likely that LeBoutillier met Grueby through the retailer.

Although LeBoutillier did little to alter the characteristic style of the holloware developed by Kendrick, his tiles were innovative. LeBoutillier's ability with two-dimensional design combined with Grueby's flowing matte glazes offered a new product for other American companies to admire and emulate. This tile from *The Pines* frieze designed by LeBoutillier in 1906 shows his technique and style exceptionally well.[5] Like Grueby's holloware, motifs were outlined with ridges of clay, but unlike the art pottery, the tiles were made by pressing damp clay into molds. When taken from the mold the ridges were ready made to hold the glazes and prevent their flowing together during firing. *The Pines* is particularly effective because its conventionalized design is based on natural models and rendered in the full palette of colors perfected by Grueby.

The demise of Grueby's art pottery operation after 1910 did not affect the continued production of architectural terra-cotta and tile work. In 1919, however, the operation was sold to the C. Pardee Works, a tile company based in Perth Amboy, New Jersey, and in 1920, when the physical assets were transferred, William Grueby moved to New York.

EPD and BRD

1. See Martin Eidelberg, "The Ceramic Art of William H. Grueby," *Connoisseur* 184 (September 1973), pp. 50-51, for discussion and illustrations of early work.

2. For more about the history of decorative tiles in America, see Thomas P. Bruhn, *American Decorative Tiles 1870-1930* (Storrs: William Benton Museum of Art, University of Connecticut, 1979).

3. Addison LeBoutillier, "Modern Tiles," *Architectural Review*, September 13, 1906, pp. 117-121.

4. Neville Thompson, "Addison B. LeBoutillier: Developer of Grueby Tiles," *Tiller* 1 (November-December 1982), p 22.

5. The work is illustrated and identified as Le Boutillier's in *Brickbuilder* 15 (May 1906), p. 107.

120
Vase, 1903
Van Briggle Pottery Company (1902-1910), Colorado Springs
Designer: Artus Van Briggle (1869-1904)
Buff earthenware, molded in handled bulbous form with elongated neck, relief iris blossoms at top; covered in matte glaze shading from

deep gray-green at bottom to medium green at top
H: 13½ in. W: (including handles) 7 in.
Marks: incised cipher of conjoined *As* in rectangle / *VAN BRIGGLE* / 1903 / III; impressed 167 (on bottom)
Collection of Scott H. Nelson

The approach to form and glaze that identified the avant-garde American potteries at the turn of the century was an exciting change from the emphasis on descriptively decorated surfaces that had characterized earlier production. "The Van Briggle pottery is perhaps the most important of the new work," reported *Keramic Studio* in 1903. "The pottery has been running for a little over two years, and already has gained quite a reputation among lovers of ceramic art."[1] Like the wares produced at the potteries of William Grueby (nos. 117-119) and William Gates (nos. 121 and 211), Artus Van Briggle's designs concentrated on form as decoration and in much of his own work form seems to grow from within the clay itself. His special contributions were translations of the eccentric organic line of the European Art Nouveau style to a calmer version that featured American flora as a principal design source. Glaze treatment did not describe the form; rather, it enhanced the final effect.

According to Van Briggle's method, a master mold was created from the original work and casting molds were made subsequently. The present vase was then covered first in a gray-green glaze and dipped in a second green color at the top – a subtle touch that emphasizes the upward movement. Likewise the strong vertical orientation, in which the handles seem to flow from the base, focuses attention on the irises at the top.

A great variety of glazes was developed for Van Briggle by Frank Riddle, the chemist for his pottery. Most of the new glazes had a semi-matte finish and although some were firm and even against the body, many were intended to give texture to the surface, breaking and sliding down over it. Although the effect is similar to Grueby's glazes, the combination of colors gives greater depth and visual interest to Van Briggle's work than Grueby was able to achieve using a single color.

Anne Gregory Van Briggle, whom Artus had met in Paris and married in 1902, carried on the pottery for several years after Artus's death, building a new facility in 1908. But the company

120

was reorganized in 1910 and passed into other hands in 1912. Subsequent owners have retained the Van Briggle name and continue to use many of the designs developed during the early years of the operation.[2]

EPD and BRD

1. "Pottery at the Arts and Crafts Exhibit, Craftsman Building, Syracuse," *Keramic Studio* 5 (June 1903), p. 36.
2. For more about Van Briggle and his pottery, see Barbara M. Arnest, ed., *Van Briggle Pottery: The Early Years* (Colorado Springs: Colorado Springs Fine Arts Center, 1975); and Scott H. Nelson, et al., *A Collector's Guide to Van Briggle Pottery* (published by the author in Harrisburg, 1986).

121
Vase, ca. 1904
Gates Potteries (ca. 1885- ca. 1922), Terra Cotta, Illinois
Designer: Fernand Moreau (1853-1919)
Buff earthenware, molded and covered overall in matte medium-green crystalline glaze
H: 12½ in. W: 6½ in. (at base), 7½ in. (at top)
Marks: vertical *TECO* and 405 (each impressed twice on bottom)
Collection of William and Mary Hersh

"In Teco Art Pottery the constant aim has been to produce an art pottery having originality and true artistic merit, at a comparatively slight cost, and thus make it possible for every lover of art pottery to number among his treasures one or more pieces of this exquisite ware."[1] It was owing to the success of the American Terra Cotta and Ceramic Company, the parent of the Gates Potteries, that William Day Gates was able to offer such a product. While the original company, founded in 1881, was a major manufacturer of architectural terra-cotta, the Gates Potteries subsidiary, beginning about 1885, made garden ornaments and terra-cotta vases for amateur decoration.[2] By the late 1880s Gates had decided to develop an art pottery and subsequently spent nearly a dozen years in these experiments. The hallmark glaze of Teco ware, a soft silvery matte green, was first exhibited in 1900 and offered for sale two years later. Critics also approved of such methods; Gate's ceramics joined those of Van Briggle, Rookwood, and Grueby as winners of the highest honors at the 1904 Louisiana Purchase Exposition in St. Louis.

Some modern commentators have suggested that Gates was one of many potters who borrowed a matte green glaze from Grueby (see no. 117) in the hope of sharing in its commercial popularity, but these two glazes have little in common visually.[3] Grueby's is generally a cucumber-green, while Gates's is softer and paler; whereas the one breaks and slides down the body, the other is firm and even. Both men shared the general enthusiasm for matte glazes that was current in European and American art communities in the late 1890s, and both were attracted to the new matte finish displayed on French ceramics at the 1893 World's Columbian Exposition in Chicago.

Gates's close association with the architectural community of Chicago gave him access to some of the best designers of the day. William B. Mundie (no. 211), Howard Van Doren Shaw,

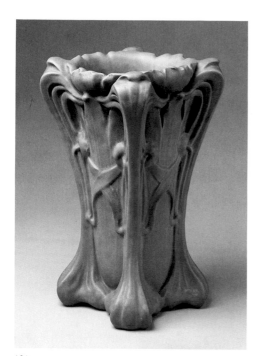

121

Hugh M.G. Gardner, Max Dunning, and Frank Lloyd Wright (nos. 213 and 216) were among the many architects who contributed stylish forms intended to harmonize with Prairie School architecture. Gates himself was responsible for about half of Teco's forms, and two modelers from his terra-cotta company, Fritz Albert and Fernand Moreau, also designed for him. Both were sculptors – Albert a German trained in Berlin and Moreau a Frenchman trained in Paris – and both had come to Chicago to participate in the 1893 World's Columbian Exposition. In the 1870s and 1880s Moreau, who conceived the present vase, had a studio in Washington, D.C., and was teaching clay modeling at the Chicago Art Institute when he joined Gates's staff in 1904.[4] His designs tended to follow the Art Nouveau style in their organic compositions and emphasis on sinuous lines.

Like the vases of Van Briggle (see no. 120), Teco wares were produced with molds taken from an original piece by an artist. In defense of multiple production, Elmer C. Mitchell noted in 1905 that the use of molds for art pottery was "more expeditious, and besides permits of the exact duplication of pieces, an obvious advantage from the standpoint of trade. In these days

it must be recognized that an art product that becomes a manufacture, as pottery must, has to have a commercial side to be a success."[5] There was also an advantage to the consumer. For only a few dollars anyone could purchase the work of an accomplished designer, artist, or architect and Gates's goal, to produce an object of "originality and true merit, at a comparatively slight cost," had been met. Critics also approved of such methods; Gates ceramics joined those of Van Briggle, Rookwood, and Grueby as winners of the highest honors at the 1904 Louisiana Purchase Exposition in St. Louis.

EPD and BRD

1. Teco Art Pottery (Terra Cotta, Ill.: Gates Potteries, 1904), pp. 9 and 11.

2. For more about Gates and his Teco ware, see Sharon Darling, Chicago Ceramics and Glass (Chicago: Chicago Historical Society, 1979), pp. 54-67; and Diana Stradling, "Teco Pottery and the Green Phenomenon," Tiller 1 (March-April 1983), pp. 8-36.

3. For these modern comparisons, see Paul Evans, Art Pottery of the United States (New York: Charles Scribner's Sons, 1974), p. 120; and Kirsten Keen, American Art Pottery 1875-1930 (Wilmington: Delaware Art Museum, 1978), p. 32. According to Darling 1979 (p. 55), Gates denied that his product was intended to be imitative.

4. Information about Moreau's earlier career was given by personal communication from Mary Claire Hersh, granddaughter of Fernand Moreau, October 1985. Mrs. Hersh also supplied the artist's life dates. For more about Moreau's work for Gates, see Darling 1979, p. 62.

5. Elmer C. Mitchell, "The Art Industries of America – II: The Making of Pottery," Brush and Pencil 15 (April 1905), p. 74.

122

Plate, 1910-1929
Dedham Pottery (1896-1943), Dedham, Massachusetts
Stoneware, jigger-molded and covered with white-crackled glaze, decorated in cobalt blue with polar bears on rim (icebergs are in low relief)
Diam: 8½ in.
Marks: impressed foreshortened rabbit and blue stamp of rabbit below DEDHAM / POTTERY in rounded rectangle (on bottom)
Museum of Fine Arts, Boston. Gift of the Misses Aimée and Rosamond Lamb. 67.1059

The attraction of Westerners to blue-and-white ceramics goes back several hundred years to the time when costly Chinese porcelain first

122

appeared in small quantities in European royal collections. By 1700 wealthy Europeans and Englishmen had access to blue-and-white delft – earthenwares made in imitation of the porcelain – and the market never waned. When the Chinese products came within the means of middle-class households in the early 1800s Western blue-and-white earthenwares and porcelains were made in increasingly larger quantities.

Hugh Robertson and his Dedham Pottery stepped into this popular market in the late 1890s. One of several Chinese-revival glazes that Robertson drew from his experimental kilns of the previous decade was a gray-white crackle.[1] With the backing of wealthy Boston-area patrons, he perfected the glaze for production with blue decoration in 1891. After producing a limited number of shapes during the early years, he added a wide range of tablewares and decorative objects. While many of the earliest patterns were derived from Oriental motifs, the standard work from Dedham's kilns was characterized by stylish, conventionalized designs.

Dedham's border decorations were designed by a number of individuals, most associated with the firm.[2] Joseph Lindon Smith, a director of the company, and Alice Morse, a student at the School of the Museum of Fine Arts, conceived the rabbit border, always the most popular. Denman W. Ross, a Harvard design professor, contributed the tapestry lion. The elephant, dog, cat, and chick borders came from Charles Davenport, a Dedham decorator for many years. Polar bears, dolphins, butterflies, crabs, grapes, mushrooms, strawberries, turtles, and a large variety of flowers and birds were some of the many patterns Dedham offered over the years. Maud Davenport, the painter of this polar-bear plate, was a decorator who also concerned herself with sales and other aspects of the daily operation of the plant.[3]

The Dedham Pottery finally succumbed to economic pressures in 1943, but a recent revival of the wares by another company speaks of the continued attraction of New Englanders to the delightful aspect of sitting down to a table full of charming rabbits ever-marching clockwise.

EPD and BRD

1. For more about this pottery, see Lloyd E. Hawes, *The Dedham Pottery and the Earlier Robertson's [sic] Chelsea Potteries* (Dedham, Mass.: Dedham Historical Society, 1968).

2. Ibid., p. 32.

3. According to Electa Tritsch, director of the Dedham Historical Society, Maud Davenport worked from 1910 to 1929 as an aide to William Robertson (son of Hugh Robertson, who had died in 1908). William, a practical potter, suffered from severe injuries as the result of a kiln explosion in 1904. After his death in 1929, he was succeeded by his son J. Milton Robertson.

123 (color plate, p. 23)
Vase, ca. 1905
Roseville Pottery Company (1892-1954), Zanesville and Roseville, Ohio
Designer: Gazo Fudji (also Fujiyama, Foudji) (active ca. 1905)
Buff earthenware; incised floral and leaf design glazed in glossy brown and mauve against airbrushed matte-glazed background of browns shading to russet and sandy lemon
H: 17⅝ in. Diam: 4⅞ in.
Mark: *Fujiyama* (stamped in black in arc on bottom)
"Elizabeth's Olden Days," Atlanta

In contrast to the many small art potteries and studio potters operating within the Arts and Crafts movement in America, a number of large commercial firms offered art pottery in addition to utilitarian crockery and industrial ceramics. One of the largest and most successful was the Roseville Pottery, which produced the best of its art pottery at the Linden Avenue plant in Zanesville. Their early products consisted of imitations of Rookwood "standard" ware (see no. 6), called "Rozane," and equally derivative lines to capitalize on successful designs produced at other companies.

In order to stay ahead of the competition, designers were hired occasionally to introduce novel effects. Gazo Fudji, a Japanese artist who had worked as a decorator for the French firm of M.H. Boulanger at Choisy-le-Roi, developed two lines for Roseville.[1] "Woodland" or "Fujiyama" ware seems to be his first design; he probably decorated these pieces as well. The present example, a standard shape used also for "Rozane" and "Della Robbia" lines, features incised and enameled parrot tulips and leaves against a matte-glaze shaded ground. According to the Roseville catalogue of 1905: "While Woodland is not an attempt at imitation of the Old Chinese Celadon, familiarity with the latter, and with its exquisite qualities, was inspiration to the artist who created the idea of Rozane Woodland."[2]

The "Rozane Fudgi" line was Gazo Fudgi's other contribution to Roseville's production. Like "Woodland," it presented enameled floral designs on a neutral matte-glaze ground, but exploited the popular stylized European mode of decoration rather than the naturalistic.[3] After his short tenure at Roseville, Fudji worked as a porcelain decorator and published Japanese-style designs for popular magazines.[4]

BRD and EPD

1. Gisela Reineking von Bock and Carl-Wolfgang Schümann, *Sammlung Gertrud und Dr. Karl Funke-Kaiser Keramik vom Historismus bis zur Gegenwart* (Cologne: Kunstgewerbemuseum der Stadt Köln, 1975), p. 196, catalogue no. 101.

2. *Rozane Ware* (Zanesville, Ohio: Roseville Pottery, 1905). Chinese celadons are characterized by monochromatic glazes in various shades of green with designs sometimes carved or molded beneath the glaze. The catalogue misinterprets these wares as a design source; there is actually no resemblance to the Roseville Pottery product.

3. In 1905 this ware was advertised as "Woodland," but the 1906 catalogue designates it separately as "Fudgi." See Roseville Pottery Company advertisement, *Ladies' Home Journal* (June 1905), p. 28; *Rozane Ware* (Zanesville, Ohio: Roseville Pottery Company, 1906), p. F1.

4. "Gazo Foudji," *Ladies' Home Journal* (September 1907), p. 41.

124
Lamp, ca. 1918
Fulper Pottery Company (1860-ca. 1935), Flemington, New Jersey
Stoneware, molded with cucumber-green crystalline glaze overall; shade holds red and green stained glass mounted with copper foil
H: (of lamp) 17 in. Diam: (of shade) 16½ in.
Mark: vertical ink stamp FULPER in rounded rectangle and 6 (on base)
Collection of Gordon William Gray

Established by Samuel Hill about 1815, the predecessor to the Fulper Pottery Company manufactured utilitarian earthenware and stoneware for local customers. Abraham Fulper began working for Hill during the 1820s and by 1860 had taken over the operation. In the late nineteenth century, when glass and tin containers and commercially preserved foods pushed heavy salt-glazed stoneware out of the market, many traditional potteries folded. Although utilitarian wares continued to be produced, Abraham's grandson, William Hill Fulper, rose to the challenge of new market conditions and used the standard stoneware body for decorative wares in shapes and glazes to suit contemporary tastes. "The art pieces are made from the same clay, in the same factory, and in some cases by the same workmen that are working on the more common articles. The art pieces again are burned in the same large commercial kilns, and are packed in the same department by the same packers who pack the regular line of stoneware, such as pots, jugs, etc. There is therefore, coming out of this particular pottery, almost the most common that is made, with the most artistic that is made in the world."[1] The influential pottery teacher Charles Fergus Binns noted that Fulper represented "the praiseworthy attempt of a manufactory of severely utilitarian wares to produce pieces of artistic quality."[2]

Fulper experimented with a wide variety of glazes beginning in 1900.[3] For the "Vasekraft" line introduced in 1909, flambé and crystalline art glazes were applied to classical and Oriental shapes that were hand-thrown or molded. J. Martin Stangl, a German potter, was hired in 1910 to continue glaze development and design new shapes, and may well have contributed this lamp form to Fulper's repertoire.[4] When lamps were included in the "Vasekraft" offerings for the Christmas market in 1910,[5] writers for art and decorating journals admired the unity of base and shade in the same material, the utility of the lamp for reading, and the harmony of the glazes and forms within "the general scheme of artistic home furnishing."[6] The base and shade were wheel-thrown or molded, depending on the particular shape being produced. Openings to accommodate stained-glass inserts were cut out by hand and the glass mounted using copper foil.[7]

Offered through home furnishing magazines and shops, company catalogues, and at Fulper's showrooms in New York City, electric "luminaries" ranged in price from $8.50 (for small boudoir lamps) to $40 in 1911. By 1918 the range was $24 to $75. The lamp with crystalline glaze shown here was priced at $35 in 1913 and $75 in 1918, making it one of the most expensive of Fulper's offerings, although these were moderate prices for a lamp during the period.[8] (Tiffany's table lamps sold for more than $100 each in the early 1900s.[9]) The Fulper Pottery also marketed shades of leather and parchment (some jeweled and fringed) at higher prices. The present lamp cost $73.50 when sold in 1914 with a shade of leather and parchment rather than pottery.

EPD and BRD

1. "Making Pottery at the Fulper Vase Kraft Shop," *Pottery and Glass* 9 (December 1912), p. 41.

2. Charles F. Binns, "Pottery in America," *American Magazine of Art* 7 (February 1916), p. 137.

3. For a discussion of the variety of Fulper glazes, see Robert W. Blasberg, *Fulper Art Pottery: An Aesthetic Appreciation 1909-1929* (New York: Jordan-Volpe Gallery, 1979).

4. Except for a brief period from 1915 to 1918, when Stangl worked for Haeger Pottery in Ohio, he remained with the company until his death in 1971, acquiring control from the Fulper family in 1930.

5. In the difficult economic conditions brought on by World War I, the Fulper Pottery ceased to manufacture lamps as such about 1918. In the following year, the company developed an economical method of electrifying vases so that a piece could be produced as either vase or lamp.

6. Mary W. Mount, "The Artistic Unity of Lamp Shades and Bases," *Arts and Decoration* 2 (December 1911), p. 83; see also "Lamps, Lighting Fixtures, Shades and Art Metal," *Pottery and Glass* 7 (September 1911), pp. 17-18; and "Art Pottery Put to Practical Uses," *Pottery and Glass* 6 (April 1911), pp. 8 and 16-18.

7. In 1912, W.H. Fulper patented his pottery lamp with "vase-like base" and cover/shade combination electrified with a minimum of equipment exposed. The wires and sockets were mounted in the reservoir at the top of the base; the cover for the reservoir was

124

extended downward to provide also a shade of the same pottery material. Patent 1,045,965 for "Lamp" was granted to Fulper on December 3, 1912, according to U.S. Patent Office records.

8. Prices were compiled from Fulper Pottery Company trade catalogues from about 1911 to 1913 (Hagley Museum and Library), 1914 (Newark Museum), and 1918 (Gordon Gray Collection). Fulper lamps also appear in the catalogue of the Emma Louise Art Shop, Belmar, New Jersey (fifth edition, 1915), which specialized in art needlework (John and Nancy Glick Collection). Gustav Stickley offered Fulper bases with fabric-lined wicker shades. Stickley Glass Negatives 429, 443, and 445 in the Winterthur Museum and Library (Decorative Arts Photographic Collection) show such lamps.

9. Robert Koch, *Louis C. Tiffany, Rebel in Glass* (New York: Crown Publishers, 1966), p. 134.

125 a and b
Watch fob and belt clasp, ca. 1900
Madeline Yale Wynne (1847-1918) Deerfield,
Massachusetts
Fob – silver and rock crystal L: 5 1/16 in.
Clasp – copper and pebbles H: 2 9/16 in. W:
(assembled) 3 1/16 in.
Private Collection

Handwork in metal, enamels, and jewelry was
Madeline Yale Wynne's specialty, but this
widely talented woman was a writer, painter,
and watercolorist whose interest in the crafts
also included furniture, leather, needlework,
pyrography, and basketry. Her pursuit of the
crafts predates America's handicraft revival and
resulted from an interest fostered by her parents. In 1906 she recalled her early years, noting, "Being the daughter of Linus Yale, Jr., the
inventor of the Yale Lock, I had a training in
mechanics and access to shop and machinery–
. . . thus naturally became interested in Arts and
Crafts – [and] developed my own line in metalwork and enamels without instruction."[1]

With a sparkling personality and energy to
match her skills, Mrs. Wynne inspired legions
through her teaching, her work, and her leadership roles in Arts and Crafts organizations.[2] She
studied painting in 1877 at the recently founded
School of the Museum of Fine Arts in Boston
and taught drawing there for several years,
maintaining a studio in Boston; she also studied
at the Art Students League in New York. Sometime in the 1870s, with her widowed mother,
Catherine Brooks Yale, Mrs. Wynne bought
"The Manse," one of the historic homes in
Deerfield, Massachusetts, and began a seasonal
pattern that brought her there in the summer
from Boston or Chicago and later from her
North Carolina home at Tryon. In a barn adjoining the house, she forged jewelry and metalwork; elsewhere in the town she established a
painting studio.[3]

Mrs. Wynne's early role in merging artistic,
antiquarian, and craft interests generated the
Deerfield Society of Blue-and-White Needlework in 1896 and the Deerfield Society of Arts
and Crafts in 1899. When business interests of
her younger brother Julian called him to Chicago in 1893, she and her mother joined him
and soon their lakeview home became a mecca
for figures in artistic, literary, and musical circles. By 1896 Mrs. Wynne had established a
studio in Chicago's Tree Building and a year
later she was a founder of the Chicago Arts and
Crafts Society. Her brother exhibited silverware

125a

and she showed various metalwares and jewelry at the Society's first exhibition in 1898.

The deliberately unrefined hammered and
enameled metalware and jewelry Mrs. Wynne
submitted to the Chicago Arts and Crafts Society's 1899 exhibition aroused keen critical interest and conveyed, in the opinion of one
reviewer, the "vital force of the artist's orginal-
ity and purpose."[4] These aspects are found in
the present fob and clasp, whose silver and
copper are exploited for their inherent handwork properties contrasted with the color and
textures of stones in their natural state. The
means are simple, but the effect is big and
direct. Mrs. Wynne, who believed that jewelry's
proper use was for artistic adornment and not
for displaying wealth, demonstrated that beautiful pieces were possible with common materials. Clasps like this one, for women, were sewn
through their small drilled holes onto grosgrain
ribbon sashes and worn at the waist. The fob
would have been hooked to a watch placed in a
small pocket just below the waistband of a
man's trousers and the rock crystal ornament
hung outside to extract the watch. George
Twose, a young English metalworker and secre-

125b

tary of the Chicago Arts and Crafts Society, championed the work of Mrs. Wynne and her pupil, Mrs. Homer Taylor, at the 1898 exhibition and its departure from commercial production. He proposed that their work was not "barbaric" but was better called "protestant" because it protested "that art, as imaginative production, has other methods of expression than oils and canvas."[5] In 1906, Mrs. Wynne wrote: "I have made jewelry and silver tableware – each article is designed and made by myself – and I never repeat the design. Therefore, I consider each effort by itself as regards color and form much as I would paint a picture."[6]

WSB

1. From Mrs. Wynne's response to a biographical questionnaire circulated by the Boston Society of Arts and Crafts in 1906 (in the archives of The Society of Arts and Crafts, Boston). For more about her upbringing, see "A Gifted Chicago Woman: Versatile Madeline Yale Wynne," Chicago Tribune (January 26, 1896), p. 41; and Sharon Darling, Chicago Metalsmiths (Chicago: Chicago Historical Society, 1977), pp. 63, 67.

2. See "Madeline Yale Wynne" (printed pamphlet containing a biographical sketch and tributes, ca. 1918, 44 pp.), in the collection of the Pocumtuck Valley Memorial Association, Deerfield, Massachusetts. For instances cited by a close friend, see Annie C. Putnam (of Boston), "Necrology. Madeline Yale Wynne," in "Annual Meeting–1918," History and Proceedings of the Pocumtuck Valley Memorial Association 9 (1912-1920), pp. 420-424.

3. A brass bowl – remaining at Deerfield – that Mrs. Wynne decorated with etched chrysanthemums in 1880 appears in Mary E. Allen, "Handicrafts in Old Deerfield," Outlook 69 (November 2, 1901), p. 594, ill.

4. Mabel Key, "A Review of the Recent Exhibition of The Chicago Arts and Crafts Society," House Beautiful 6 (June 1899), p. 6. Other Wynne jewelry appears in Mary Adams, "The Chicago Arts and Crafts Society," House Beautiful 9 (January 1901), p. 98; and Isabel McDougall, "Some Recent Arts and Crafts Work," House Beautiful 14 (July 1903), p. 71. A record of Mrs. Wynne's craft work by Deerfield photographers (the sisters Mary and Frances Allen), which includes a large amount of her later and more technically ambitious jewelry, is in the collection of the Pocumtuck Valley Memorial Association, Deerfield, Massachusetts.

5. George M.R. Twose, "The Chicago Arts and Crafts Society's Exhibition," Brush and Pencil 2 (May 1898), pp. 74-79.

6. From Mrs. Wynne's response to a biographical questionnaire circulated by the Boston Society of Arts and Crafts in 1906 (in the archives of The Society of Arts and Crafts, Boston).

126 (color plate, p. 26)
Brooch, 1904-1905
A. Fogliata (active ca. 1903-1907), Hull-House Shops (ca. 1898-ca. 1940), Chicago
Opals and gold
H: 2¾ in.
Chicago Historical Society, Gift of Mrs. Charles F. Batchelder. 1983.131.3

This opal and gold brooch was given to the Chicago Historical Society by a granddaughter of Frances M. Glessner, for whom it was said to have been made at Hull House[1] by one A. Fogliata. Little is known about the Hull House master craftsman outside of his exhibition activities in the years 1903-1905 and his association with Mrs. Glessner. Fogliata's role in making a bronze and enamel triptych shown in London in 1903 indicates that he was trained in England.[2] A selection of his work – after designs of Hull House resident Frank Hazenplug, except for a silver cup designed and made by Fogliata – was exhibited in December 1904 at the Art Institute of Chicago and the Detroit Museum of Art (now The Detroit Institute of Arts).[3] Fogliata was then providing at-home instruction in silversmithing to Mrs. Glessner, who is thought to have begun lessons in metalwork with Madeline Yale Wynne a few months earlier.

Arts and Crafts jewelers preferred modest jewels, close to or in their natural state, such as cabochons and blister pearls and materials such as unground enamels and even butterfly wings and pebbles (see no. 125b);[5] opals, because of their superb intrinsic fire, were especially favored. Fogliata enhanced the random shape and contour of the large example featured in this brooch with a skillfully composed cast floral frame that recalls Continental Art Nouveau easel frames. Drops suspended on chains are a jewel effect that may have been inspired by Madeline Yale Wynne, who exhibited a pendant with seven round and rectangular cabochons suspended on individual chains at the Chicago Arts and Craft Society's exhibition in 1902. C.R. Ashbee had introduced the device in the 1890s, not only in jewelry but in overhead electric light fixtures as well.[6]

WSB

1. The Chicago Arts and Crafts Society was founded at Hull House in 1897 and crafts instruction promoted by the Society members soon spawned the Hull House Shops. Wares exhibited and offered for sale included metalwork, jewelry, bookbinding (see no. 159), carving, pottery, lacemaking, spinning, weaving, and basketry.

2. "The Arts and Crafts Exhibition at The New Gallery: Fourth Notice," International Studio 20 (July 1903), p. 30, ill.

3. By 1904, under the guidance of Fogliata and Isadore V. Friedman, both Hull House master metalsmiths, a large group of Hull House jewelry, brass, and copper wares was exhibited for sale at the Cincinnati Museum. See Catalogue of the Handicraft Exhibition (Cincinnati: Mercantile Library Building, May 11-18, 1904), p. 12, nos. 371-384.

4. See Sharon Darling's quotations from Glessner's diary and observations about Glessner and Fogliata in Chicago Metalsmiths (Chicago: Chicago Historical Society, 1977), pp. 67-68. Darling wrote: "[Glessner] also commissioned Fogliati [sic] to make silver platters and other distinctive pieces for wedding gifts and gestures of appreciation."

5. See "The Personality of Jewels: How the Arts and Crafts Workers Gain Inspiration From the Color and Shape of the Stones," Town & Country 64 (July 3, 1909), pp. 14-15, ill.

6. Alan Crawford, C.R. Ashbee (New Haven and London: Yale University Press, 1985), pp. 73, 355, 366, ill.

127
Jewelry ensemble, ca. 1905
Florence D. Koehler (1861-1944), Chicago and New York
Gold, painted enamel, pearls, emeralds, sapphires, and tortoise shell
Pendant – H: 2¾ in. W: 2½ in.
Necklace – L: 14 in.
Comb – W: 4¾ in.
Inscription: (on pendant) enameled leaf-and-berry spray flanked by E and C
Marks: (on pendant) enameled F·K and painted 27.640; (on necklace catch) inscribed 1737; (on comb) painted 27.642
The Metropolitan Museum of Art, New York, Gift of Emily Crane Chadbourne. 52.43.1-3

In a succession of careers – first designing domestic interiors and continuing as a china decorator, jeweler, and painter – Florence Koehler embraced the progressive focus of the Aesthetic, Arts and Crafts, and modern art movements. Her pottery was shown at Chicago's

127

World's Fair in 1893, a year in which she may have been on the Rookwood Pottery's large staff of china painters whose work was there on view.[1] Mrs. Koehler probably studied enameling under Alexander Fisher in 1897.[2] From 1898 she was engaged by Chicago's Atlan Club and for about six years guided its members in painted porcelain decoration. Simultaneously, she gained recognition for leading American handicraft interest in jewelry, enamels, and metalwork.[3] By the end of the decade Mrs. Koehler had settled abroad, first in London, then – about 1912 – in Paris; there, because of the arduousness and expense it entailed, she abandoned making jewelry and turned to painting.

Like other important American Arts and Crafts jewelers, Mrs. Koehler traveled abroad to study historical examples of jewelry in museum collections. A woman used to mixing with and influencing those with power and position, she made this ensemble for a daughter of the Chicago industrialist Richard T. Crane, Emily Crane Chadbourne, who shared the decorative arts interest of her brothers Richard, Jr. (see no. 19), and Charles.[4] The pendant, which was designed to be worn also as a brooch, suggests the jewelry of Hans Holbein,[5] possibly from a specific design in the British Museum.[6] Both pieces – enameled gold pendants – frame an oval cabochon with four rectangular gems and alternate pearl clusters amid leaves. The composition of the Koehler example is marked by the lively contrast in the sizes and shapes of the four square emeralds, the ovals of the center star sapphire and surrounding eight sapphires, and

the pearl spheres. Its massiveness is relieved by the random pearl clusters, green enameled leaves, and tapering emerald drop. Mrs. Koehler deplored glitter and faceted effects; she preferred – as can be seen here – to work in twenty-two-carat dull gold, often muted with enamel, to harmonize with the deep liquid glow from gems chosen for color harmony and velvety sheen rather than for intrinsic preciousness.

Florence Koehler's virtuoso achievement received rare acclaim when the eminent critic Roger Fry devoted an article to her, stating: "The jeweller plays with the richest, the most noble palette that the material world affords . . . [which] needs . . . a real creative effort . . . of the same order as those which the 'Fine Artist,' the creator of great figurative design, displays. It is in the imaginative and definitely poetic quality that Mrs. Koehler's jewellery marks such an important moment in the modern revival of craftsmanship."[7]

WSB

1. See A. Clinton Landsberg's tribute in *Portrait of An Artist, The Paintings and Jewelry of Florence Koehler* (1861-1944), Laurie Eglinton Kaldis, ed. (Providence: Museum of Art, Rhode Island School of Design, 1947), unpaged. Mrs. Koehler's Rookwood marks are recorded in Edwin A. Barber, *Marks of American Potters* (Philadelphia: Patterson & White Company, 1904), pp. 122, 124, ill. Her (unfilmed) papers are at the Archives of American Art, Washington, D.C.

2. Fisher taught enameling at London's Central School of Arts and Crafts from 1896 to 1898 and set up his own school in 1904.

3. Mabel Key, "A Review of the Recent Exhibition of the Chicago Arts and Crafts Society," *House Beautiful* 6 (June 1899), pp. 6-7, ill. See also Rho Fisk Zueblin, "The Production of Industrial Art in America II," *Chautauquan* 37 (April 1903), p. 60, ill.; "The Education of the Producer and the Consumer," *Chautauquan* 37 (May 1903), p. 175, ill.; and Isabel McDougall, "Some Recent Arts and Crafts Work," *House Beautiful* 13 (July 1903), p. 71, ill.

4. Mrs. Koehler accompanied Mrs. Chadbourne on a trip through the Orient and probably enlivened the entertainments Mrs. Chadbourne gave international society at a large house she leased in London.

5. Compare also the pearl necklace with pendant in Agnolo Bronzino's portrait of about 1540 depicting Lucrezia Panchiatichi at the Uffizi in Florence; illustrated in Guido Gregorietti, *Jewelry through the Ages* (New York: American Heritage Press, 1969), p. 180, ill. At the turn of the century women wore their hair piled high; back-combs, like that seen here, were used to adorn the hair as well as hold it in place.

6. Joan Evans, *English Jewellery* (London: Methuen, 1921), pl. XVI, especially nos. 5 and 2. Jewelers had been drawing on Holbein's jewelry compositions from the mid-nineteenth century.

7. Roger Fry, "A Modern Jeweler," *Burlington Magazine* 17 (June 1910), p. 174.

128

Necklace, ca. 1915
Josephine Hartwell Shaw (active ca. 1900-1935),
Duxbury, Massachusetts
Gold, jade, and glass
L: 20 in. W: 3⅝ in.
Marks: struck incuse J. H. *SHAW* (on applied tab)
Museum of Fine Arts, Boston. Gift of Mrs. Atherton Loring. 1984.947

Josephine Hartwell Shaw's jewelry attracted considerable awards and patronage. Following training in the late 1890s at Massachusetts Normal Art School and Pratt Institute, Mrs. Shaw taught drawing courses in Providence and near Philadelphia. She began her handicraft career as a metalworker[1] and in 1905 was elected a Craftsman member of the Boston Society of Arts and Crafts. Her jewelry came to public notice in 1906 (about the time she married Frederick A. Shaw, a silversmith and sculptor), appearing in *Good Housekeeping* magazine and the historic decennial exhibition of the Boston Society of Arts and Crafts.[2] The Boston Museum of Fine Arts exhibition of the Society's selections in 1913 included a brooch and ring that was purchased by the Museum for its collections, an unusual instance of contemporary handicrafts being acquired by a major art museum; a year later Mrs. Shaw was among the early recipients of the Society's Medalist award. Indicating her popularity at the time, a journalist for *House Beautiful* observed, "rings, brooches, necklaces, – and with them photographs of yet other jewels, the names of whose present owners would make my modest article take on the semblance of a Society Column."[3] Mrs. Shaw was widowed by 1914, when she left Boston for nearby Duxbury; there her neighbor, Atherton Loring, a life member of the Boston Society of Arts and Crafts, purchased this superbly crafted necklace for his wife.

Lively contrasts in colors and textures account for the success of the necklace design, with emerald-hued glass used as a foil to white

128

jade and green-toned gold: the flat polished glass rectangles are complemented by the pierced irregular surface of the jade and the chain with its alternating rods, round wire loops, and balls. The pattern of the supporting chain and glass links is skillfully contoured to drape gracefully on the neck and bust and permit free movement of the pendant drops. Mrs. Shaw featured sensuous color combinations in her jewelry and, in the manner of Arts and Crafts jewelers, probably considered their suitability for each client. The necklace – which, like the jades, is worked both front and back – reveals Mrs. Shaw's great technical skill and extraordinary sense for composing color, form, and texture, which she also passed on to her apprentice, the well-known Arts and Crafts jeweler, Edward E. Oakes.

The carved jade plaques of the Shaw necklace are typical of eighteenth-century work from western China, which were being collected in Boston at about this time; after 1895 they could have been purchased at the Boston branch of Yamanaka and Company, importers of Oriental goods.[4] The pendant jades, which may originally have formed the sides of a pomander, depict birds in an acanthus-like scroll; the jade catch depicts bats, which symbolize blessing, and orchids and chrysanthemums, symbolizing nobility of spirit.[5] The Shaw necklace demonstrates the importance of Oriental art and culture as a source of inspiration for the handicraft jeweler.

WSB

1. A copper tea set with silver and carnelian handles is listed in *Arts and Crafts Exhibition* (New York: National Arts Club in collaboration with National Society of Craftsmen, 1907), p. 7. Beginning in 1908 Shaw exhibited eleven times at the Art Institute of Chicago's arts and crafts annuals, where her jewelry received highest awards in 1911 and 1918.

2. Claire M. Coburn, "Specimens of Craftsman Jewelry," *Good Housekeeping* 43 (November 1906), p. 507, ill.; *Exhibition of the Society of Arts & Crafts, Copley Hall* (Boston: Society of Arts and Crafts, 1907), p. 28.

3. Ralph Bergengren, "Some Jewels and a Landscape," *House Beautiful* 37 (January 1915), p. 148.

4. Bostonians, under the guidance of Ernest F. Fenollosa, Edward S. Morse, and Arthur W. Dow, one of Mrs. Shaw's instructors at Pratt Institute, had begun studying and collecting Oriental art at the turn of the century.

5. I owe this description to the kindness of James Watt, formerly Curator of Asiatic Art at the Museum of Fine Arts, Boston.

129 (color plate, p. 26)
Box, 1922
Elizabeth E. Copeland (1866-1957), Boston
Silver, parcel gilt, enamels painted and *cloisonné*
H: 5 in. W: 6¹⁵⁄₁₆ in. D: 5⅛ in.
Marks: EC / 1922 (applied wire)
Collection of Henry Scripps Booth

The enamelist, silversmith, and jeweler Elizabeth Copeland was about thirty years old before taking her first art class. Problems assigned by her teacher, the noted designer and illustrator Amy M. Sacker, were tacked above Miss Copeland's kitchen ironing board, to be solved while "no doubt the garments suffered."[1] In 1900 during her last year at Cowles Art School in Boston, she took a supplementary course in metalwork from Laurin H. Martin, a Cowles graduate recently returned from distinguished student accomplishment in England.[2] Also attending Martin's class was Sarah Choate Sears, a founding member of the Society of Arts and Crafts and a leader in Boston cultural affairs. Impressed with Miss Copeland's abilities, she became her adviser and patron, and in 1908 sent her on a tour of European museums and study in London, presumably under Alexander Fisher, the foremost enamelist of the era.[3]

By 1903 Miss Copeland began exhibiting actively in major Arts and Crafts exhibitions such as the recently begun annual at the Art Institute of Chicago. The following year, after a brief period at the Handicraft Shop (see nos. 134 and 135), she established a studio on Boylston Street in Boston, where she continued to work until retiring in 1937.[4] Her designs won significant recognition: a bronze medal at the 1915 Panama-Pacific Exposition and, a year later, the Medalist award from the Boston Society of Arts and Crafts.

Henry Scripps Booth, a son of the Cranbrook Academy founder George C. Booth, purchased this box in 1924 from the Detroit Society of Arts and Crafts, where Miss Copeland had been consigning her work since 1907.[5] The box reveals the passion for vibrant color shared by other early-twentieth-century artists and the distinctive vision and techniques Miss Copeland had refined in boxes produced over two decades. Jewelry formed a large part of her early work as did *repoussé* ornament on enameled boxes. Although she continued to embellish with semiprecious stones, *repoussé* ornament was generally abandoned for a richer effect of bright wire strips and balls as a foil to

an oxidized silver background. Copeland boxes, consciously suggestive of the jeweled and enameled reliquaries of the middle ages, reflect a revival of interest in this earlier period. The perched-bird motif, rendered here with vegetation in blue, green, puce, purple, and yellow translucent and opaque enamels, may have been inspired by the 1922 Tutankhamen tomb discoveries. The box was used to carry the wedding ring during the ceremony of Booth's marriage to Carolyn E. Farr on September 17, 1924.[6]

WSB

1. Dora M. Morrell, "The Arts and Crafts – Beauty in Common Things," *Brush and Pencil* 5 (February 1900), pp. 222-232.

2. Hazel H. Adler, "American Craftsmen," *Century Magazine* 91 (October 1916), pp. 891-892.

3. Consigner and member records, Society of Arts and Crafts, Boston.

4. Irene Sargent, "The Worker in Enamel with Special Reference to Miss Elizabeth Copeland," *Keystone* 27 (February 1906), p. 193.

5. *Papers of the Detroit Society of Arts and Crafts* in the Archives of American Art, roll 281, frame 955.

6. Letter to author, October 4, 1984.

130
Chalice, ca. 1920
Janet Payne Bowles (1876-1948), Indianapolis and New York
Silver, gold, and trace of copper
H: 9¹³⁄₁₆ in. Wt: 17 oz. 5 dwt.
Indianapolis Museum of Art, Gift of Mira and Jan Bowles. 68.21.2

After a series of events that directed her from an initial career in music to handicrafts, philosophy, and writing, Janet Payne Bowles achieved unusual distinction as a metalworker and jeweler.[1] In 1899 she married and moved from Indianapolis to Boston, where her husband, Joseph M. Bowles, had transferred publication of *Modern Art*, the lavish vanguard quarterly he had founded in Indianapolis in 1893. Undertaking new pursuits there, she studied psychology with William James at Radcliffe, executed illuminations published by her husband, and participated in local activities of the Society of Arts and Crafts. About 1901 she encountered a Russian immigrant's metalsmithing shop, where she absorbed the rudimentary techniques of

the craft; six years later, after relocating in Manhattan, she set up a metalworking and jewelry studio on 28th Street, the site of her husband's press.[2] There Mrs. Bowles refined her skills on prestigious commissions, won top exhibition prizes, and established an international reputation as a jeweler and metalsmith.[3] Upon her return to Indianapolis in 1914 (separated from her husband) she began teaching metalsmithing courses and actively produced metalwares and jewelry into the 1930s, after which time she focused on teaching until her retirement in 1942.[4]

While Mrs. Bowles's career was shaped by the Arts and Crafts movement and its departure from machine methods, her work was unconventional, both artistically and technically, for letting natural forces and the properties inherent in her materials determine form. She explored metalsmithing on her own and arrived at a visceral approach – an attitude developed in later art movements – in her amuletic jewelry and ceremonial chalices, reliquaries, and spoons. The archaistic and runic aspects of the work may derive from ancient Greek, Celtic, and Norse art, which were said to be chief sources of inspiration.[5] Although Mrs. Bowles employed vague worm or animal forms in her designs, they are essentially non-pictorial. This chalice is made of silver in molten, cast, sheet, and extruded states, alternately hammered, bent, snipped, curled, soldered, or raised. Snips and lengths of wire were soldered on the interior, while the base is composed of hammered sheet, extruded rods, and soldered lumps. The gold "halo" thumb-ring, which aids in bringing the cup to the lips, introduces color symbolically.[6]

WSB

1. See Rena Tucker Kohlman, "Her Metalcraft Spiritual: Janet Payne Bowles seeks to express the universal and eternal in rhythmic modeling of gold and silver," *International Studio* 51 (October 1923), pp. 54-57, ill.; and Jerome Sikorski, "Out of Indianapolis: Janet Payne Bowles, Goldsmith" (master's thesis, Wayne State University, Detroit, 1974). The Indianapolis Museum of Art holds the major collection of studies and finished works by Mrs. Bowles and includes pieces that won her exhibition prizes.

2. She spent the intervening years writing while occupied with raising children in a succession of New York City area households that included Upton Sinclair's communal living experiment at Helicon Hall.

3. In 1909 Mrs. Bowles won an award for carved jewelry given by Spencer Trask, president of the National Society of Craftsmen. In 1910 she published

"A Situation in Craft Jewelry" in *Handicraft*, and made jeweled ornaments worn on the stage by Maude Adams. About 1911 she executed work commissioned by Sir Caspar P. Clark, director of the Metropolitan Museum of Art; he introduced her to J.P. Morgan, who commissioned her to make gold spoons and plates. In 1912 she won first prize in the London-Paris International Jeweler's Competition, and in 1913 the Paris International Goldsmith's prize.

4. Mrs. Bowles won a bronze medal at the Panama-Pacific Exposition in 1915. She is said to have made ecclesiastical metalwares for St. Patrick's Cathedral and the Cathedral of St. John the Divine; as a result of her achieving first prize in the London-Paris International Jewelers Competition of 1920, she received from I. Bossellini, a Florentine patron, commissions for metal vessels now in Italian churches. Showings of her work at the Art Center in New York included a large solo exhibition in 1929.

5. Kohlman 1924, p. 55.

6. Mrs. Bowles's inventory description of the object in 1931 was "one large silver chalice gold halo." See curatorial files, Indianapolis Museum of Art.

131

131

Box, ca. 1912
Mildred G. Watkins (1883-1968), Cleveland
Silver, amethyst, and *champlevé* and *plique-à-jour* enamel
H: 1⅜ in. W: 2⁹⁄₁₆ in. D: 2⅝ in. Wt: (gross) 3 oz., 10 dwt.
Marks: struck incuse MILDRED WATKINS / STERLING / sailboat
Collection of Barbara V. Wamelink

Among the nation's earliest practitioners of handicraft enamels, jewelry, and metalwork was a group of artists in Cleveland that included Mildred Watkins, Horace Potter, Carolyn Hadlow (Vinson), Ruth Smedley, Mary Blakeslee, Anna Wyers (Hill), Jane Carson (Barron), and Frances Barnum (Smith). Miss Watkins, a graduate of the Cleveland School of Art (now called the Cleveland Institute of Art) was first associated with Jane Carson (Barron) and Frances Barnum (Smith). A collaborative metalwares and jewelry exhibit from the three women appeared at the 1904 Louisiana Purchase Exposition and won Miss Barnum a silver medal; about this time, Miss Watkins studied in Boston with Laurin H. Martin and at the Handicraft Shop with George Gebelein. In 1907 she exhibited works at the decennial exhibition of the Boston Society of Arts and Crafts and was

awarded Master Craftsman standing by the Society.[1] Miss Watkins continued collaborating with Cleveland women craftsmen for another decade, but from 1907 she also produced and exhibited on her own works such as the jewelry, boxes, small tablewares, and serving pieces that appeared at the Art Institute of Chicago annual exhibitions through 1923.[2] In 1917 she was elected president of the Cleveland Women's Art Club and the following year began teaching at the Cleveland School of Art, a post she held until 1953. Cleveland has been the nation's foremost center for enameling since the 1930s and Mildred Watkins was the senior member in a group of artists preeminent in the field; she won important prizes for enameled metalwork and jewelry at the "May Shows" of the Cleveland Museum of Art from their inception in 1919 to 1948.

In 1912 Miss Watkins exhibited a box at the Art Institute that was described as "silver, plique-à-jour, enamel and amethysts"; it may well be the one shown here.[3] Combining the skills of enameling, silversmithing, and jewelry-making at the small scale appealing to women craftsmen, the box provides an ideal vehicle for detailed embellishment. Although the ornamentation calls for exacting skills and patience for drilling and sawing the many pierced openings, the fabrication of the box is technically simple, especially because of its overhanging lid and base, and requires little physical strength. Enclosed by a chased line bordering a convex-

sided triangle, the center of the lid design is a six-petaled hexagon with three cabochon amethysts set to let the light play through. Their color is echoed by the purple hues of the stylized tulip blossoms in *plique-à-jour* enamel and played off against the blue-green leaves and stems in *champlevé*.

WSB

1. *Exhibition of the Society of Arts & Crafts, Copley Hall,* Boston, February 5-26, 1907, pp. 28, 46, nos. 46, 808. In 1940 the Society elected Miss Watkins a Medalist Craftsman and in 1962 awarded her a life membership.

2. Examples of her accomplishments were shown in "National Society of Craftsmen Exhibition," *Palette and Bench* 1 (February 1909), p. 121, ill.

3. *Catalogue of the Eleventh Annual Exhibition of Examples of Art Crafts and Original Designs for Decorations* (Chicago: Art Institute of Chicago, 1912), no. 1062.

132

Bowl, ca. 1922
Marie Zimmermann (1878-1972), New York
Patinated copper and paint
H: 3¾ in. W: 15⅛ in. D: 7 in.
Marks: struck incuse M Z cipher encircled by *MARIE ZIMMERMANN -MAKER - /* 92 and 318
Marie Zimmermann Archives

In 1910, following the opening of a decorative arts wing (later called the Pierpont Morgan Wing), the Metropolitan Museum of Art implemented a policy to educate designers, craftsmen, and manufacturers in the use of its collections for creating contemporary products; annual exhibitions of American industrial art began a few years later with the requirement (eliminated in 1924) that objects must be based on designs in the Museum's collections.[1] Also in 1910 "antiques loaned for the purpose of inspiring the craft workers to a higher effort" were included in the National Society of Craftsmen's annual exhibition, held at their headquarters in the National Arts Club on Gramercy Park.[2] Marie Zimmermann, who maintained a studio and residence at the club, and who often visited the Egyptian, Far Eastern, and Greek rooms of the Metropolitan Museum,[3] was among many craftsmen visibly influenced by the practice of drawing upon historical decorative arts in creating modern works.

This hammered bowl, based on Chinese

132

polylobed beaten silver dishes of oval or pointed oval shape popular during the T'ang Dynasty, is one of Miss Zimmermann's many patinated variations of petal bowls.[4] Rapidly induced "antique" patinas fascinated metalworkers and few could approximate the broad range of color and textural effects Miss Zimmermann achieved. Aided by assistants, she worked with iron, copper, bronze, silver, gold, and occasionally brass, upon which she practiced endlessly varied chemical treatments, gilding, and plating. Remarkable testimony to Miss Zimmermann's interest in exploring color is her application of paint to chemically patinated metal, to achieve the blue surface on the bowl shown here.

Miss Zimmermann designed and practiced various handicrafts, painting, and sculpture, but it was metalwork and jewelry that gained her national renown. After completing courses at the Art Students League, and exhibiting work at the Art Institute of Chicago in 1903, important recognition came in 1915 and 1916, when she began exhibiting work at Manhattan's Ehrich Galleries. In 1922, through articles acclaiming

her work in *The International Studio*, *Arts & Decoration*, *House & Garden*, and *Vogue*, and through purchase by the Metropolitan Museum of Art of one of her jeweled silver boxes,[5] she became one of the nation's best-known metalworkers and jewelers. Miss Zimmermann's active production throughout the 1920s – encompassing fan holders, candlesticks, tableware, and furniture – also included prestigious architectural metalwork commissions in the east and midwest. In 1924 the Art Institute of Chicago awarded her the Logan prize for silver and metalwork and by the end of the decade her silver tablewares – often rhodium plated – were recognized among the era's early modernistic designs.

WSB

1. Richard F. Bach, "Museum Service to the Art Industries: An Historical Statement to 1927," *Industrial Arts Monograph No. 3* (New York: Metropolitan Museum of Art, 1927), pp. 5-6.

2. "Art Notes," *Town & Country* 64 (December 24, 1910), p. 8.

3. Gay Zimmermann, comp., "Metal Works by Marie Zimmermann" (unpublished exhibition catalogue, Colby College Museum of Art, Waterville, Maine, 1982), p. 1.

4. Bo Gyllensvärd, *T'ang Gold and Silver* (Göteborg, Sweden: Elanders Boktryckeri Aktiebolag, 1958), pp. 58, 202, fig. 20m. In 1922 a similar Zimmermann bowl was described as "bronze [sic], with a rich antique blue patina"; see Mary Fanton Roberts, "Art," *Vogue* 59 (April 15, 1922), pp. 64, 78, ill.

5. Metropolitan Museum of Art acc. no. 22.186. See Hanna Tachau, "On the Decorative Arts," *International Studio* 74 (January 1922), pp. ccxxxvii- ccxxxviii, ill.; Matlack Price, "Industrial Art and the Craftsman: Who Are Our Designers?" *Arts & Decoration* 16 (January 1922), pp. 185-187, ill.; Giles Edgerton, "An American Worker in the Crafts," *House & Garden* 41 (February 1922), pp. 28-29, 78, ill.; Roberts 1922.

133 (color plate, p. 27)
Tea and coffee set, ca. 1910
Designer: Louis Rorimer (1872-1940)
Maker: The Rokesley Shop, at Rorimer-Brooks
Studios Co., Cleveland (ca. 1907-ca. 1916)
Silver, moonstones, and ebony
Coffeepot – H: 11⅛ in. W:9¾ in. Wt: (gross) 29
oz., 5 dwt.
Teapot – H: 7⅛ in. W: 10⅞ in. Wt: (gross) 24
oz., 5 dwt.
Waste bowl – H: 3⅝ in. Diam: 5⅞ in. Wt:
(gross) 10 oz.
Cream pitcher – H: 3½ in. W: 7½ in. Wt:
(gross) 10 oz., 15 dwt.
Sugar bowl – H: 3¾ in. W: 8 13/16 in. Wt: (gross)
13 oz., 3 dwt.
Sugar tongs – L: 5 11/16 in. Wt: (gross) 2 oz., 5
dwt.
Marks: (on each) struck embossed in rectangle
ROKESLEY / STERLING
Private Collection

This tea and coffee set, made for use in the
family of Louis Rorimer, is the only known
silver tableware to survive from the Rokesley
Shop of Cleveland. Documentary information
from eight exhibitions suggests that the set was
the exception to Rokesley's usual output of
jewelry and minor metal items. The shop probably began in 1907, when it participated in the
second annual arts and crafts exhibition of the
National Society of Craftsmen in New York City.
It was then located at the Rorheimer Studios, an
interior decorating firm at 285 Erie Street,
where the shop's principals, Carolyn Hadlow
(Vinson), Mary Blakeslee, and Ruth Smedley are
known to have been working and exhibiting
since 1904. "Rokesley" combines letters of the
names [Ro]rheimer, Bla[kes]lee, and Smed[ley].
According to city directories, the decorating
firm became the Rorheimer-Brooks Studios Co.
in 1910; it housed the Rokesley Shop until 1916,
when the studios assumed their long-known
Euclid Avenue address. The Rorheimer name
was modified to Rorimer during World War I.
    Louis Rorimer received decorative arts train-
ing at the Kunstgewerbeschule in Munich and
the Académie Julien in Paris. His keenness for a
wide range of decorative styles is attested by his
later work, which reflects historic models but
on occasion reveals the influence of modern
French and British decorative design. At the
first annual exhibition of Cleveland artists and
craftsmen at the Cleveland Museum of Art in
1919, Rorimer won recognition as a designer of

furniture and interiors.[1] A dedicated supporter
of the museum, he was also on the faculty of
the Cleveland School of Art for eighteen years.
    The fabrication of this service, with its jew-
eled embellishment and embossed and chased
ornament, shows superior technical skill. It
could have been the work of Mary Blakeslee,
who had taught metalwork classes in 1908 at the
Art Students League in Buffalo and who left the
shop sometime after 1909. Or it might have
been executed by Wilhelmina Stephan, who
had a distinguished career as a Cleveland silversmith and craftsman from 1906 to the late
1930s, and was also associated with the shop. A
distinctive formal aspect of Rorimer's design is
the ebony handles of the cream pitcher and
sugar bowl, which pierce an extended brim – a
configuration that derives ultimately from ancient Greek cups.[2] Moonstones embellish the
brim as well as the sugar tongs and the domed
covers of the two pots; they suggest fruit in the
arboreal band encircling each of the vessels.
This running-tree pattern, which probably
originated in English work such as Walter
Crane's "May Tree Frieze" wallpaper of 1896,[3]
was a decorative device widely in use by 1910;[4]
dragonflies were frequently substituted for the
trees.[5] Certainly the tree motif would have been
known to Rorimer through the monthly appearance – from May 1894 onward – of R. Anning Bell's cover for *The Studio*. There, sheltering
the male and female figures who represent the
arts and crafts, is the compacted band of leaves,
fruits, and flowers. The pierced bowls of the
sugar tongs are distinguished by the eye-of-the-
peacock's-tail shape common to decoration of
the Glasgow School at the turn of the twentieth
century.
    Although evidence suggests that jeweled tea
and coffee services were produced in the American Arts and Crafts movement, surviving examples are rare. This set, when added to the work
of Cleveland's Potter Studio (no. 44) and the
collaborative efforts of Frances Barnum
(Smith), Jane Carson (Barron), and Mildred
Watkins (no. 131), attests to the city's vigorous
and early reception of silver as a handicraft.
Ohio was in the vanguard in metalwork, jewelry, and enamels as well as in ceramics.

WSB

1. "In Memoriam – Louis Rorimer," *Bulletin of the Cleveland Museum of Art* (February 1940), p. 16.

2. Henry Stuart Jones, "Greek Plates of the Bronze
Age," *Encyclopaedia Britannica*, 11th ed. (1911), vol. 21,
facing p. 792, pl. 1, fig. 21. The handles of the pots are
molded, while those of the cream pitcher and sugar
bowl are not.

3. The Crane wallpaper appears in Catherine Lynn,
Wallpaper in America (New York: W. W. Norton, 1980),
pp. 460-461.

4. See "The Dining Room of the Poplar Frieze," *Craftsman* 6 (June 1904), pp. 308-309, ill. I am indebted to
Robert Judson Clark for this reference.

5. A local source for information about such current
European artistic developments was the shop of the
Cleveland book dealer M. A. Vinson, who advertised
in 1908 as "the only place west of New York City
where you can examine and purchase interesting
books from England, France and Germany, on the
various Arts and Crafts." Half of the books in his
advertisement were German titles on jewelry and
metalwork. See *Arts and Crafts Exhibition, Cleveland School of
Art* (Cleveland Decorative Arts Club, n.d.), unpaged.
The exhibition was held from March 26 to April 5,
1908.

134
Sauce set, 1902-1908
Designer: Mary Catherine Knight (b. 1876)
Maker: enameled and tooled by Mary Cathe-
rine Knight at The Handicraft Shop, Boston
(1901-1903, 1907-ca. 1940); Wellesley Hills, Mas-
sachusetts (1903-1907)
Silver and *champlevé* enamel
Bowl – H: 2 in. Diam: 4 ⅛ in. Wt: (gross) 4 oz.,
10 dwt.
Plate – H: ½ in. Diam: 5 ½ in. Wt: (gross) 5 oz.,
5 dwt.
Ladle – L: 4 ½ in. Wt: (gross) 1 oz.
Inscription: engraved D·T (on underside of
bowl and plate)
Marks: struck incuse *STERLING* / struck shield
enclosing relief K and knight on horseback
The Art Institute of Chicago, Americana Fund.
1982.205a-c

This sauce or mayonnaise set is from a series
produced between about 1902 and 1908 at the
Handicraft Shop.[1] An outgrowth of Boston's
Society of Arts and Crafts, the shop was established in 1901 by the Society's president, Arthur
Astor Carey, who provided the financial backing; by the secretary Frederick Allen Whiting;
and by the Society's leading spokesman for
craftsmen, Mary Ware Dennett, a gilt-leather
worker. Mary Catherine Knight, a designer
from Gorham and a former pupil of Mrs. Den-

134

nett's four-year design course at the Drexel Institute in Philadelphia, was engaged early on in a supervisory capacity at the shop. Miss Knight's designs were executed variously by her alone and collaboratively with other craftsmen in the shop. Work in wood, leather, and metal was produced initially, but by 1906 the output was exclusively handwrought silver, copper, brass, and enamel.

At the Handicraft Shop objects were made in a spirit of artistic cooperation. Given an escape from the specialized mass-production processes found in factories, silversmiths had the opportunity to collaborate with others in the the fabrication of objects from start to finish. In 1906, working alongside Mary Catherine Knight,[2] there were five foreign-born male silversmiths; their supervisor was Karl F. Leinonen (no. 135), who had apprenticed for ten years with Finland's largest silver firm before immigrating to America in 1893. The skillful finish of this sauce set shows the hand of one of the male silversmiths and its distinctive tooled ornamentation reveals Miss Knight's use of Mrs. Dennett's leatherworking equipment.[3]

Silver from America's colonial past inspired work produced by the Handicraft Shop. The shop not only utilized hand-production methods of the earlier era; it adapted its ornament as well. The strapwork and floral band on this bowl and plate derive from those used on beakers by the seventeenth-century Boston silversmiths John Hull and Robert Sanderson.[4]

WSB

1. For other Knight examples, see the bowl with tooled and enameled interior in Isabel McDougall, "Some Recent Arts and Crafts Work," *House Beautiful* 14 (July 1903), p. 75, ill.; and Eva Lovett, "Second Annual Exhibition of the National Society of Craftsmen," *International Studio* 33 (January 1908), p. XCII, ill. A closely related bowl and plate in the collection of the Houston Museum of Fine Arts, featuring the white and blue-green enamels she used here, was probably fabricated by Miss Knight herself. Her work is not known to bear the Handicraft Shop mark.

2. Files of the Boston Society of Arts and Crafts contain correspondence of the Handicraft Shop from 1906 and their stationery bears the names K.F. Leinonen, Seth Ek, F.J.R. Gyllenberg, Mary C. Knight, C.G. Forssen, and G.C. Gebelein.

3. For a description of these fabrication processes and the shop, see "Idealism at 'The Handicraft Shop,'" *Providence Sunday Journal* (June 5, 1905), p. 30, ill.

4. A Hull and Sanderson beaker is illustrated in John H. Buck, *Old Plate* (New York: Gorham Manufacturing Company, 1903), p. 258 (attributed to Jacob Hurd) and ill. opposite p. 257, lower right. Buck was a Gorham employee and Miss Knight could have known the colonial work from this and other sources.

135

Chocolate set, 1906
Karl F. Leinonen (1866-1957) at The Handicraft Shop, Wellesley Hills, Massachusetts (1903-1907)
Silver and ivory
Pot – H: 8¹/₁₆ in. Wt: (gross) 13 oz., 17 dwt.
Pitcher – H: 4¾ in. Wt: 5 oz., 12 dwt.
Covered sugar bowl – H: 3⅜ in. Wt: 10 oz., 2 dwt.
Bowl – H: 2⅜ in. Wt: 6 oz., 5 dwt.
Inscription: engraved (in script) *L.G.D. / from / A.A.C. / and the children / July 1905* (on underside of each)
Marks: (on each) struck incuse 1906 (except pot and pitcher) / STERLING / embossed shop mark H anvil S / incuse L
Yale University Art Gallery, New Haven. Gift of Mrs. Alfred E. Bissell and Mrs. Edward Leisenring in memory of Alfred Elliott Bissell, B.A. 1925. 1978.64

This chocolate set, completed during the time the Handicraft Shop was in Wellesley Hills, bears the mark of Karl F. Leinonen. The engraved inscription documents its presentation by Arthur Astor Carey, the shop's financial backer, to Louise Gordon Dietrick, the governess of the Mt. Prospect School in Waltham,

Massachusetts.[1] Its use for hot chocolate is suggested by the pot's insulated handle and traditional configuration – elongated and lacking straining holes – and the companion pieces for milk, sugar, and whipped cream. The set is an important document of America's Arts and Crafts movement, both as a record of the Handicraft Shop's communal artistic production and as a response to Carey's call for "the necessity of sobriety and restraint, of ordered arrangement, of due regard for the relation between the form of an object and its use, and of harmony and fitness in the decoration put upon it."[2]

The Handicraft Shop's move to Wellesley Hills, influenced by the relocation of C.R. Ashbee's Guild of Handicraft to Chipping Campden, was expected to bring wholesome benefits denied to craftsmen by city living.[3] It was a time of ideological conflict within the Society that encompassed many disagreements and led to Carey's resignation as president in November 1903.[4]

After the Handicraft Shop returned to Boston,[5] its stalwarts, Leinonen and his associate F.J.R. Gyllenberg, maintained it and provided bench space for silversmiths such as Katherine Pratt and instruction for others.[6] Leinonen won the Boston Society of Arts and Crafts Medalist award in 1918, and in the mid-1920s formed a partnership with his son K. Edwin Leinonen; their output continued into the 1950s, relying greatly on the silver designs of the Handicraft Shop's earliest years.[7] The Leinonens' sober workmanlike production, often fluted but seldom ornamented, was supplemented, after 1930, by designs adapted from those by the Danish silversmith Georg Jensen.

WSB

1. Ms. Dietrick was an associate member of the Boston Society of Arts and Crafts from 1902 to 1904, residing at the same address as Mrs. A.A. Carey.

2. Arthur Astor Carey, "The Past Year and Its Lessons" (an address delivered to the Boston Society of Arts and Crafts, November 22, 1901), *Handicraft* 1 (April 1902), p. 4.

3. Also the building in which the shop had been housed since its founding in 1901 was about to be razed.

4. For a discussion of these events, see Beverly Kay Brandt, *"Mutually Helpful Relations": Architects, Craftsmen and the Society of Arts and Crafts, Boston 1897-1917* (Ann Arbor: University Microfilms International, 1985), pp. 191-202.

135

5. Why the shop returned to Boston is unclear; however, most of its craftsmen lived in Boston and may have tired of commuting.

6. Gyllenberg, Leinonen, and George C. Gebelein were the three Handicraft Shop craftsmen from the Carey years to have long and distinguished careers.

7. Many of these designs were by Mary C. Knight.

136
Bowl, ca. 1921
Frans J.R. Gyllenberg (b. 1883), Boston
Copper
H: 3½ in. Diam: 10⅜ in.
Marks: struck incuse cipher F.J.R.G. / 177; inscribed in black ink 6 - 2244 / 20-
Private Collection

By tradition copper objects had been utilitarian in nature, used primarily in the kitchen. In the later decades of the nineteenth century, however, the metal also appeared in the parlor for smoking and coffee sets, reflecting the taste for exotic Near Eastern designs. Copper became a popular handicraft metal of the Arts and Crafts movement because its working properties–ductility and malleability–come closest to those of precious metals, but at a fraction of their cost, and because it has a greater capacity to be colored and patinated than any other metal. Thus, copper served the needs of the amateur (see no. 138) or the most skilled professional (see no. 144) for useful and artistic wares.

In 1906, when Augustus Foster Rose (1873-1946), a teacher at Providence Technical High School and the Rhode Island School of Design, introduced his text *Copper Work*, copper was the favorite material of student and amateur metalworkers as well as commercial producers of art metalwares. By 1931 his manual was in its eighth edition and the many surviving anonymous copper desk and smoking accessories, buckles, fobs, sconces, lanterns, nut bowls, and spoons come mainly from manual arts classes and those in occupational therapy that followed World War I.

An identical copper bowl by Frans Gyllenberg appeared in 1921 in an advertisement placed by the Boston Society of Arts and Crafts, an early instance of its policy of advertising in a national periodical.[1] The design had been introduced in the form of a fluted silver punchbowl displayed by Karl F. Leinonen at the Society's

136

1907 decennial exhibition.[2] Fabrication of these fluted bowls in either silver or copper usually meant raising – by the crimping method – from a disc, truing the cyma curve profile, and planishing.[3] Concave flutes, located by pencil, were then beaten down into a form (fluting block) held in a vise and the metal was annealed as needed. Here the craftsman exploited a feature of fluting, which tends to incurve the rim, by reversing the bowl's edge outward into petals.

Gyllenberg was born in Sweden, where he probably served his apprenticeship. Little is known of his career prior to 1905, when, as an early member of the Handicraft Shop, he executed designs by Mary Catherine Knight that were exhibited at the Art Institute of Chicago.[4] The Boston Society of Arts and Crafts admitted him as a Craftsman member in 1906. By 1926 Gyllenberg had formed a partnership at the Handicraft Shop with his younger assistant Alfred Swanson (no. 67), and in 1929 the Society of Arts and Crafts elected him a Medalist craftsmen, its highest honor.

WSB

1. *Arts & Decoration* 14 (January 1921), p. 259, ill. The text reads: "The fluted Copper Bowl, hand hammered, 10 ½" diameter, 3 ½" high, $20"; it suggests that the annotation "20-" on this example was its price.

2. *Exhibition of the Society of Arts and Crafts, Copley Hall* (Boston: Society of Arts and Crafts, 1907), frontispiece.

3. Raising by the angle method was usual in the schoolroom; skilled metalsmiths employed the more difficult but faster crimping method.

4. *Catalogue of the Fourth Annual Exhibition of Original Designs for Decorations and Examples of Art Crafts Having Distinct Artistic Merit* (Chicago: Art Institute of Chicago, 1905), p. 25. Gyllenberg exhibited at these annuals consecutively from 1907 to 1914.

137 (color plate, p. 28)
Table lamp, probably 1911-1915
Dirk Van Erp (1859-1933), probably after a design by Eleanor D'Arcy Gaw (active ca. 1900-1920) at Dirk Van Erp Studio, San Francisco (1910-ca. 1950)
Copper and isinglass
H: 26 in. Diam: (of shade) 23 in.
Marks: struck incuse windmill / disconnected rectangle enclosing DIRK VAN ERP
Collection of James and Janeen Marrin

"An inheritor, not an imitator of pre-industrial craftsmanship,"[1] Dirk Van Erp was born in Leeuwarden, The Netherlands, and trained in his family's hardware business, producing handwrought milk cans and cooking utensils. At the age of twenty-six he emigrated to America and settled in California, where he was employed eventually as a coppersmith in San Francisco's shipyards. In middle age Van Erp drew upon his handicraft skills for making art metalwares, adapting machine-made brass shell casings into vases. By 1906 he was consigning metalwares to the prestigious San Francisco art dealers Vickery, Atkins and Torrey; two years later, at age forty-nine, he opened a metalwork shop in Oakland, where his daughter Agatha and Harry Dixon (see no. 138) were apprentices.

The turning point in Van Erp's career was his brief partnership with the designer, weaver, and metalworker D'Arcy Gaw, a native of Montreal. Miss Gaw, who had studied decorative design at the Art Institute of Chicago in 1900 and trained at C.R. Ashbee's Guild of Handicraft, probably in 1904, was designing and making electric light fixtures as early as 1902.[2] By 1905 she was in San Jose, California, and in 1907 her residence was listed as 1825 California Street, San Francisco, an address that is known to have been shared by other metalworkers and craftsmen.[3] In 1910 Van Erp established a shop with Miss Gaw at 1104 Sutter Street and for about a year collaborated with her in designing and producing hammered copperwares. Their skills were complementary; Gaw had formal design training and Van Erp was an accomplished coppersmith. Wares from the partnership are marked with their names below a windmill – emblematic of Van Erp's birthplace. A copper lamp designed by Miss Gaw and made by both of them was exhibited at the Art Institute of Chicago in 1910[4] and may have been the catalyst for the shop's notable lamp designs. When Miss Gaw resumed interior design work in Chicago, Van Erp, often working from designs contributed by others, continued at the Sutter Street location until he retired in 1929.[5]

The Dirk Van Erp shop produced a variety of metal accessories, but its copper electric table lamps are distinctive among the metalwares of the Arts and Crafts movement. Substantial and functional, this lamp exemplifies inspired coppersmithing skills, particularly in the use of copper for both the base and the shade to create a unified composition. When illuminated, the isinglass panels, coated with colored shellac, give warm tones harmonizing with the softly reflective patinated copper base. The contours of the shade recall the wide overhanging roofs of California bungalows, while its ribs and panels echo the contrast of their wood-trimmed plaster interiors. In the early 1920s Van Erp lamps were offered with a variety of bases and their characteristic robust shape was repeated in vases the shop produced into the Depression.[6]

WSB

1. See Bonnie Mattison, "Metalwork," in *California Design 1910*, exhibition catalogue (Pasadena: California Design Publications, 1974), pp. 78-81, 87. See also *American Art Annual 1932*, vol. 29 (Washington, D.C.: American Federation of Arts, 1933), p. 516.

2. *Catalogue of the First Annual Exhibition of Original Designs for Decorations and Examples of Art Crafts Having Distinct Artistic Merit* (Chicago: Art Institute of Chicago, 1902), p. 19, no. 112. For Miss Gaw's background and activities, see *The Artists Guild, An Illustrated Annual of Works by American Artists and Craft Workers, 1917* (Chicago: Artists Guild Galleries), p. 82.

3. See National Society of Craftsmen directories for 1907-1908 (pp. 57-61) and 1909-1910 (pp. 60-65).

4. *Catalogue of the Ninth Annual Exhibition of Original Designs for Decorations and Examples of Art Crafts Having Distinct Artistic Merit* (Chicago: Art Institute of Chicago, 1910), no. 492.

5. Other designers of Dirk Van Erp wares were Thomas McGlynn and Edna Hall; see Robert Judson Clark, "The Pacific Coast," in *The Arts and Crafts Movement in America, 1876-1916*, exhibition catalogue (Princeton: Art Museum, Princeton University, 1972), p. 91, ill; and Edgar W. Morse, "California Twentieth Century Metalwork, Part One: San Francisco Bay Area" (typescript at Argentum Antiques, San Francisco, 1978), p. 1. Although the shop's location changed sometime after 1932, Van Erp's son William continued it, offering various metalwares from 1929 until at least 1944, when it was called the Dirk Van Erp Studio (see *Mastai's Classified Directory of American Art & Antique Dealers*, 2nd ed., 1944-1945 [New York: Boleslaw Mastai, 1944], p. 48).

6. *The School Arts Magazine* 22 (January 1923), pp. 286, 315, ill.; "California Develops Handicrafts," *California Arts & Architecture* 42 (November 1932), pp. 17, 30, ill.

137

138

Desk set, ca. 1915
Harry St. John Dixon (1890-1967), San Francisco
Patinated copper and painted and encrusted enamels
Pair of bookends – H: 5 11/16 in. W: 5 1/8 in. D: 4 1/2 in.
Pen tray – H: 5/8 in. W: 13 1/4 in. D: 3 13/16 in.
Paper knife – L: 8 1/16 in. W: 1 9/16 in. D: 1/4 in.
Marks: (on each) inscribed HDIXON / San Francisco
P.G. Pugsley & Son Antiques, San Francisco

It seems certain that the motif of this desk set was appropriated from an illustration of a *repoussé* finger plate (or push plate for a door) in copper and enamel by the English craftsman C.E. Thompson, published by *The International Studio* in 1902.[1] *The Studio*, which was founded in England by Charles Holme in 1893 and introduced its edition *The International Studio* four years later, influenced craftsmen and followers of the Arts and Crafts movement all over the world.

Harry Dixon, the younger brother of the well-known painter Maynard Dixon, found his lifetime craft as a metalsmith by age eighteen. In 1908 he was a pupil of the coppersmith Dirk Van Erp (see no. 137). He continued to train in other San Francisco shops and during World Wars I and II worked in the city's shipyards. It is likely that Dixon opened his own shop in 1921 or 1922 after he began teaching; his practice of signing metalwares with the punch mark designed by his brother Maynard (depicting a man forging a bowl) probably dates from that time.[3] In 1923 he wrote an article entitled

C.E. Thompson. Fingerplates in *repoussé* copper and enamel, illustrated in *International Studio*, January 1902.

1. "The First International Studio Exhibition, Part I," *International Studio* 15 (January 1902), pp. 172-187, ill. A pair of long rectangular lead and enamel Dixon candle sconces from the same collection as the desk set copied Thompson's finger plate even more closely.

2. See *American Art Annual 1930*, vol. 27 (Washington, D.C.: American Federation of Arts, 1931), p. 522; *Who's Who in American Art 1940-1941*, vol. 3 (Washington, D.C.: American Federation of Arts, 1941), p. 182; Bonnie Mattison, "Metalwork," in *California Design 1910*, exhibition catalogue (Pasadena: *California Design Publications*, 1974), pp. 82, 86, 141, ill.; and Edgar W. Morse, "California Twentieth Century Metalwork, Part One: San Francisco Bay Area" (typescript at Argentum Antiques, Ltd., San Francisco, 1978), p. 1.

3. *A Book of American Trade-Marks & Devices*, Joseph Sinel, comp. (New York: Alfred A. Knopf, 1924), pp. 32, 63, ill. An example of Dixon metalwork inscribed "HDixon / 1920" is known.

4. Harry Dixon, "Combining Design and Craftsmanship," *The School Arts Magazine* 22 (January 1923), pp. 278-283, ill.; *The Art Institute of Chicago Twenty-First Annual Exhibition of Applied Arts* (Chicago: Art Institute of Chicago, 1923), no. 114.

5. This point was made in a panel discussion in which Dixon was a participant: "Theories of Design in Relation to Metals," in *Asilomar: First Annual Conference of American Craftsmen sponsored by the American Craftsmen's Council*, June 1957 (Asilomar, Calif.: American Craftsmen's Council, 1957), p. 85.

"Combining Design and Craftsmanship" for *The School Arts Magazine*, presenting his thoughts on teaching metalcraft to beginners. Metalwork by Dixon and his wife, Florence Dixon, appeared in the article, and the same year a patinated jar designed by the couple and made by Dixon was shown at the Art Institute of Chicago.[4] Like his teacher, Dirk Van Erp, Dixon participated in the forty-eighth annual exhibition of the San Francisco Art Association, held about 1928, and showed metalwares and jewelry. Elevator doors that Dixon made about 1930 for the tenth floor of the San Francisco Stock Exchange were cited repeatedly in biographical directories, suggesting that the artist considered them his major work. He maintained an active interest in metalware design until his death, often adapting forms in nature.[5] This desk set bears out Dixon's directive that the nature of the material should be considered and proper choice be made among the metals appropriate to the design: the copper is wondrously exploited to yield a soft iridescent patination supplementing the peacock-feather motif.

WSB

139
Candlestick with bobêches (one of a pair), possibly 1902
Robert Riddle Jarvie (1865-1941), Chicago
Patinated bronze
H: 13½ in. Diam: (of base) 6¹⁄₁₆ in.
Collection of Robert F. Cohn

The transformation of Robert Jarvie from home-hobbyist and amateur to professional craftsman demonstrates the inspiring force of the Arts and Crafts movement, whereby a man might abandon a successful conventional occupation in order to devote his life to handicraft. Born of Scottish parents in Schenectady, New York, Jarvie was a clerk in Chicago's city government by 1893;[1] he began his metalsmith career with an antique-style horn-and-iron lantern, designed and executed for a Chicago antiquarian friend at about this time. The project directed his attention to interior illumination, which he researched thoroughly; he even developed a collection of early American lamps. Encouraged by the success of a candlestick he

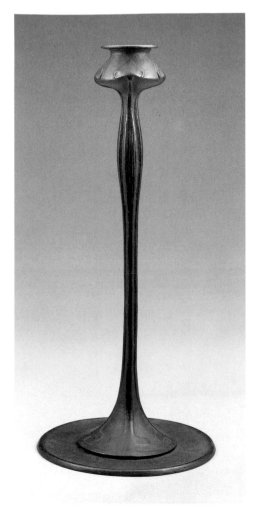

139

made for his own house, Jarvie soon began producing others. He first came to public notice as a designer and craftsman through lanterns and candlesticks in the Chicago Arts and Crafts Society's third annual exhibition in December of 1900.[2] From October 1901 onward, Jarvie advertisements illustrating candlesticks and lanterns appeared frequently in *House Beautiful* and listed him at 608 West Congress Street, a workshop location he maintained while advancing in his city career.[3]

Jarvie, who soon proclaimed himself "The Candlestick Maker," announced in October of 1903 that his designs were being reproduced by others and thereafter would bear his signature.[4]

At the year's end *The Craftsman* profiled Jarvie and acclaimed his work, observing, "Nearly all of this work is of cast brass or copper, brush polished, a process which leaves the metal with a dull glow. Some pieces are cast in bronze and their unpolished surfaces are treated with acids which produce an exquisite antique green finish."[5] The *International Studio* soon followed with a similar article and such recognition probably encouraged Jarvie to abandon his city position and establish "The Jarvie Shop."[6]

By 1906 Jarvie had outlets for candlesticks in more than ten states. Locations included the Boston Society of Arts and Crafts, The Handicraft Guild of Minneapolis, and Paul Elder & Company of San Francisco. Jarvie Shop craftsmen produced the candlesticks in sixteen or more brass, copper, or "verdegrene" (patinated bronze) designs, each coded by a Greek letter, and advertised at $2.50 to $15. At the end of the decade Jarvie was executing major Chicago presentation and trophy commissions and was an officer in local arts organizations.[8]

Artificial electric light had recently become available for the home, and Jarvie shared the preoccupation of many turn-of-the century craftsmen with designing fixtures to serve it. He was undoubtedly influenced by the form and green bronze patination of Tiffany Studios candlesticks and light fixtures published in *House Beautiful* in 1899, or seen for sale at Marshall Field & Company.[9] Indeed, the candlestick illustrated here is in the sweeping plant-tendril mode that Tiffany's work popularized.[10] Jarvie preferred unshaded candles, "feeling the shade to be, as a rule, out of harmony with the tapering suggestiveness which candlestick and candle ought to combine."[11] A tall, sleek, vertically attenuated configuration – evocative of long-stemmed flower buds – distinguishes the major group of Jarvie's candlestick designs.

WSB

1. David A. Hanks, "Robert R. Jarvie, Chicago Silversmith," *Antiques* 110 (September 1976), pp. 522-577, ill.

2. At the same time *House Beautiful* illustrated four of his candlestick designs in brass and pewter. See Margaret Edgewood, "Holiday Gifts," *House Beautiful* 9 (December 1900), pp. 2-8, ill.

3. *House Beautiful* 9 (October 1901), p. 322. It is one of Jarvie's earliest illustrated advertisements and features his "Beta" model candlestick at $5.

4. *House Beautiful* 14 (October 1903), p. xvi.

5. "An Appreciation of the Work of Robert Jarvie," *Craftsman* 5 (December 1903), pp. 271-276, ill.

6. "Notes on the Crafts," *International Studio* 23 (September 1904), pp. CCCLXIV, CCCLXVI, ill. The Jarvie Shop advertised in *Craftsman* 6 (May 1904), unpaged.

7. For Jarvie outlets, see *House Beautiful* 19 (March 1906), p. 42. Jarvie candlestick designs are illustrated in *Country Life in America* 11 (November 1906), p. 6; other Jarvie metalwares appear in *Country Life in America* 9 (September 1906), p. 488.

8. Jarvie is listed as secretary of the Chicago Arts and Crafts Society in *American Art Annual, 1910-1911*, vol. 8, Florence N. Levy, ed. (New York: American Art Annual, 1911), p. 308. He was also a member of The Artists' Guild (Chicago) and in 1914 chairman of its committee for selection of Arts and Crafts (see *American Art Annual, 1914*, vol. 11, Florence N. Levy, ed. [New York: American Art Annual, 1914], p. 92).

9. See "Illumination in the Home," *House Beautiful* 5 (March 1899), pp. 174-179.

10. A candlestick identical to the design illustrated here appeared among Jarvie's entries in the third public exhibition of the Society of Arts and Crafts of Minneapolis in January 1903. See Katherine Louise Smith, "An Arts and Crafts Exhibition at Minneapolis," *Craftsman* 3 (March 1903), pp. 373-377, unpaged ill.

11. Ellen Judith Gould, "Candlestick Novelties," *House Beautiful* 28 (November 1910), p. 175.

140

140

Pitcher, 1911
Robert Riddle Jarvie (1865-1941), Chicago
Silver
H: 10¼ in. W: 8¼ in. D: 6½ in. Wt: 42 oz., 5 dwt.
Inscription: engraved PRESENTED TO / CHARLOTTE AILEEN HENRY / ON HER WEDDING DAY / OCTOBER THE TENTH / NINETEEN HUNDRED AND ELEVEN / BY / ALBERT AND MARY GRAY / ROBERT AND LILLIAN JARVIE / SAMUEL AND WINIFRED GRACIE / JAMES WILBUR GRAY and Made by the Shop of Robert Jarvie Chicago / Sterling (on underside)
Marks: struck incuse Jarvie / STERLING
The Art Institute of Chicago, Gift of Raymond W. Sheets. 1973.357

From about 1910 Robert Jarvie shifted significantly from "the candlestick maker" who produced metalwares in an organic, naturalistic mode (see no. 139) to become a major silversmith of trophies and presentation commissions in a geometric, architectonic style.[1] The change coincided with Jarvie's association with members of the Cliff Dwellers, an organization of painters, writers, musicians, craftsmen, and artists founded in 1909 and located in the midst of Chicago's lakefront cultural hub, across the avenue from the Art Institute. Among its charter members were Jarvie, the noted Prairie School architect George Grant Elmslie, and the president of the Art Institute, Charles L. Hutchison. Hutchison commissioned a silver punchbowl for Jarvie to design and execute for the Cliff Dwellers; Elmslie (whose wife, Bonnie, worked in the Jarvie Shop) designed certain commissions that Jarvie executed.[2] In the latter commissions, Elmslie masterfully joined two architect-originated ornamental styles – the geometric arabesque ornament of Louis Sullivan (nos. 83 and 84) and the linear right-angle fret ornament of Charles Rennie Mackintosh. After executing this work for Elmslie, Jarvie's silver designs became more geometric and usually featured abstract *repoussé* ornament as an integral part of the composition. The vanguard styles of Glasgow came naturally to Jarvie; both his parents and Elmslie were Scottish immigrants.[3]

This superb pitcher of 1911 exemplifies Jarvie's tendencies to create silver designs unifying form and ornament and to respond to Glasgow School styles. The initials C.A.H., in the characteristically Chicago tradition of embellishing presentation pieces with ornamental monograms and elaborate inscriptions, are artfully composed of embossed, Celtic-style interlaced ornament on a stippled ground. Both the monogram and the sweeping curves of the pitcher's handle, spout, and base echo the spade shape common – like the Celtic interlacing – in Mackintosh ornament. The lettering of the engraved inscription is in an architectural draftsman's style possibly transmuted to Jarvie from Elmslie. Included among Jarvie's 1912 exhibits at the Art Institute, the pitcher was loaned by Charlotte Henry Sheets, whose husband gave it in 1973.

WSB

1. Ornamental letters of the inscription on Jarvie's Pillsbury golf trophy of 1907 echo organic contours of a vessel configurated to serve as a tablet for the inscription. For this and other Jarvie works, see Sharon Darling, *Chicago Metalsmiths* (Chicago: Chicago Historical Society, 1977), p. 42, ill.

2. The completed bowl and ladle ornamented with an Amerind-based motif became the subject of an elaborate theatrical presentation (see "Among the Shops," *Handicraft* 4 [May 1911], pp. 72-75, ill.). In 1909 Jarvie executed silver memorials – a loving cup and testimonial book – designed by Elmslie, honoring the retiring president of the University of Michigan (see Edward J. Vaughn, "Sullivan & Elmslie at Michigan," *Prairie School Review* 6, no. 2 [1969], pp. 22-23).

3. This tendency and Jarvie's powerful and confident design response to Elmslie's cue are seen in his 1912 Aero and Hydro Trophy. Its spindle verticals and chamfered rectangular base recall Mackintosh designs and are in the mode – by way of Vienna – of Karl Kipp's "Princess" candlesticks (no. 209).

141

Cream pitcher and sugar bowl, ca. 1908
Designer: Clara Pauline Barck Welles (1868-1965)
Maker: The Kalo Shop(s) (1900-1970), Chicago and Park Ridge, Illinois (1905-1914), and New York (1914-1918)
Silver and jade
Cream pitcher – H: 2⅛ in. W: 4⅞ in. Wt: (gross) 5 oz., 10 dwt.
Sugar bowl – H: 2⁵/₁₆ in. W: 4¹³/₁₆ in. Wt: (gross) 4 oz., 15 dwt.
Inscription: (on each) applied cipher ASM
Marks: (on each) struck incuse STERLING / KALO
Chicago Historical Society. 1975.218a,b

The Kalo Shop, founded by Clara Pauline Barck in 1900, thrived as Chicago's leading producer

141

of handicraft silver for more than three generations.[1] At age thirty-two, Miss Barck, the daughter of Swiss and Finnish emigrants, left her Oregon home to attend design classes at the Art Institute of Chicago. Following her graduation a year later, she founded the shop and named it "Kalo," the Greek word for "beautiful." During the shop's early years, production focused on burnt-leather wares, supplemented increasingly by technically simple jewelry, usually made by women. Upon Miss Barck's marriage in 1905 to George S. Welles, a coal businessman and self-taught amateur metalworker, they established the Kalo Art-Craft Community at their home in suburban Park Ridge. Doubtless inspired by C.R. Ashbee's rural-based Guild of Handicraft, the community served an important purpose in Chicago since the Art Institute had recently abandoned the metalwork and jewelry class it began in 1903. The Kalo Shops were both workshop and school, "where designers, weavers,

jewelers, silversmiths and basket makers, experts and apprentices worked together in harmony" and produced goods sold at their Chicago salesroom.[2]

Early Kalo metalwork was made in copper and brass, but Mrs. Welles soon found trained silversmiths, mostly of Scandinavian heritage, to execute her designs for holloware and flatware and to instruct others.[3] A renaissance of silversmithing resulted in Chicago, and many of the craftsmen went on to establish or serve in competing shops that emulated Mrs. Welles's designs. In 1914, Mrs. Welles had left her husband, and the shops, producing metalwork and jewelry exclusively, were consolidated in Chicago. The same year saw the establishment of a retail outlet in New York City that was maintained until 1918. Mrs. Welles retired in 1940, but the firm operated for another thirty years.

Although the term "Arts and Crafts movement" is employed frequently as a style label for wares of the late-nineteenth and early-twentieth century, the long success of the Kalo production is a reminder that the "movement," as a philosophy directing craft and design, continued far into the modern era. In the spirit of the shop's motto, "Beautiful, Useful, and Enduring," its substantial handwrought hammer-textured silverware designed by Mrs. Welles in plain, paneled, and fluted shapes, infrequently ornamented with chasing, was consistently expressive of the metal and revealed subtle shifts in styles and taste.

The overall simplicity and hammer-textured surfaces of this cream pitcher and sugar bowl are typical of the shop's production. They are known by their marks–"KALO" and "STERLING"–to be among the earliest Kalo silver holloware. The green cabochons, recalling C.R. Ashbee's innovative silver designs, are also associated with Kalo's early production.[4] Likewise, the seamed bodies of the vessels are indicative of practices in the early years of the shop, when fabrication techniques were being taught. In this case the metalworker was afforded an opportunity to exercise difficult seaming and soldering skills, as opposed to the more expeditious hand-raising process. The monograms on these pieces are a superb synthesis of object and ornament. The swelling contours of the S derive from the bulbous-shaped vessels, the A's straight and curved legs derive from the handles, and the M is designed to complete the composition. Single and multi-letter monograms are an important feature of

Chicago art silverware, and it is rare to find the letters so successfully composed.

WSB

1. See Sharon Darling, *Chicago Metalsmiths* (Chicago: Chicago Historical Society, 1977), pp. 44-53, 70, 80, ill.

2. See Bessie Bennett, "Crafts at the Art Institute of Chicago," *The World To-Day* 5 (August 1903), pp. 1008-1010, ill.; W.M.R. French, "Report of the Director," The Art Institute of Chicago, Twenty-Seventh Annual Report, June 1, 1905 - June 1, 1906 (Chicago: Art Institute of Chicago, 1905), p. 43. The shop's early crafts were recalled in "Handicrafts for the Disabled," *American Magazine of Art* 9 (May 1918), pp. 297-298.

3. Copper and brass candlesticks are listed in *Catalogue: Second Annual Exhibition of Applied Arts* (Detroit: Detroit Museum of Art, 1905), p. 2. Mrs Welles hired the immigrant silversmiths Heinrich A. Eicher and Julius O. Randahl in 1907.

4. Welles may have been influenced by English metalsmiths following the style of Ashbee, whose work was on exhibition at the Art Institute in 1907. See "Special Exhibition of English Handicrafts. Brought to America by the Society of Arts and Crafts of Detroit, Michigan," *Catalogue of the Sixth Annual Exhibition of Original Designs for Decorations and Examples of Art Crafts Having Distinct Artistic Merit*(Chicago: Art Institute of Chicago, 1907), pp. 59-67.

142

142
Pitcher, probably 1914
Designer: Clara Pauline Barck Welles (1868-1965)
Maker: The Kalo Shop(s) (1900-1970), Chicago and Park Ridge, Illinois (1905-1914) and New York (1914-1918)
Silver
H: 8 13/16 in. W: 7 5/8 in. D: 5 5/8 in. Wt: 25 oz., 19 dwt.
Inscription: applied initial T
Marks: struck incuse STERLING / HAND WROUGHT (forming an arch) / AT / THE KALO SHOPS / CHICAGO / 9944
Collection of Robert Edwards

A salient characteristic of Chicago handicraft silver evinced by this seamed pitcher is a pronounced hammer-textured surface, an appearance derived from silverwares produced by C.R. Ashbee's Guild of Handicraft. Ashbee was attracted to the effect, familiar in the Japanese-taste metalwares of the 1880s (see no. 10), for its telltale sign of human endeavor and as a protest against the impersonal perfection of machine-produced wares. Adopted as a shop practice by the Guild silversmiths (others in England soon

did likewise), the finish widely became a style in itself, defining handicraft metalwares.[1] Americans visited Ashbee's Guild, wrote about it, and even attended its school (see nos. 44 and 137). His greatest influence in America, however, was in Chicago, where in 1898 Ashbee's jewelry and silver was on view at the Art Institute in the Arts and Crafts Society's first exhibition.[2] Two years later his visit and lecture at the Institute aroused great interest furthered by international coverage of the Guild's activities in periodicals available in the Institute's library.[3]

Clara Barck Welles, founder of the Kalo Shop(s), was among the Chicago artists influenced by Ashbee, for example in paneled designs,[4] which Ashbee may have derived from early-eighteenth-century chocolate pots.[5] Paneled holloware is a feature of Chicago art silver production and on this example the T monogram echoes the arched contours of the vessel and its handle. The earliest Kalo silver holloware was marked only "KALO" and "STERLING," but by 1910 the words "HAND BEATEN" were added, underscoring the importance of hammer-textured finish. Following the lead of other Chicago makers, the Kalo

Shops adopted the mark "HAND WROUGHT" in 1914. This pitcher's date is established by the marks "HAND WROUGHT," "THE KALO SHOPS," and "CHICAGO," which replaced "HAND BEATEN," "KALO SHOPS," and "PARK RIDGE" in 1914, when the Kalo shops were consolidated in Chicago.[6]

After 1910 Chicago patronage exceeded other American cities for substantial handwrought silver tablewares in plain, curved, lobed, or paneled forms, unornamented except for monograms applied to muted hammered surfaces. The suburban home of Harry Rubens, Esq., designed by the architect George W. Maher, documents local demand for such silver: its dining-room sideboard was photographed with an elaborate assortment of large trays, dome-covered platters, and other tablewares.[7]

W.S.B.

1. Fred Miller, "Some Gold, Silver and Coppersmith," *Art Journal* 58 (1896), pp. 435-439, ill.

2. *First Exhibition of the Chicago Arts and Crafts Society*, in conjunction with the Architectural Club (Chicago: Art Institute of Chicago, 1898), p. 133, nos. 271-275.

3. Significant coverage of the Guild appeared in *The Art Journal, Magazine of Art, International Studio,* and *House Beautiful.* For Ashbee's 1900 Chicago visit, see Alan Crawford, *C.R. Ashbee* (New Haven and London: Yale University Press, 1985), pp. 96-98.

4. Designs by Mrs. Welles appear in a section illustrating techniques of paneled metalwares in Arthur F. Payne, *Art Metalwork with Inexpensive Equipment* (Peoria: Manual Arts Press, 1914), figs. 105, 108, 120, and 121.

5. See the coffee service in David Whipple, "A Silver Kettle By Charles Ashbee," *Bulletin of The Cleveland Museum of Art* 63 (October 1976), p. 250, fig. 1.

6. Silver marked "CHICAGO AND NEW YORK" identifies the New York shop operating between 1914 and 1918, after which time the marks "THE KALO SHOP" (singular), with and without "CHICAGO," were used. See also Sharon Darling, *Chicago Metalsmiths* (Chicago: Chicago Historical Society, 1977), p. 48, ill.

7. George W. Maher, "An Architecture of Ideas," *Arts and Decoration* 1 (June 1911), p. 328, ill.

143
Fruit tazza, ca. 1901
Arthur J. Stone (1847-1938), Gardner, Massachusetts
Silver with gold details
H: 4¾ in. W: 9 in. D: 6 in. Wt: 14 oz., 7 dwt.
Marks: struck incuse STERLING and hammer; chased *Stone* (conjoining hammer)[1]
Private Collection

143

Arthur Stone was a senior practitioner of America's handicraft revival who found his calling before many of its familiar figures were born. The production of his shop, perhaps more than that of any other, developed the ideals of the Arts and Crafts movement and carried them into the modern era. Stone's training began in 1862 under the Sheffield master-silversmith Edwin Eagle, with whom he devoted fifty-nine hours a week to manual labor. Three evenings a week he attended the Sheffield National School of Design and the other evenings worked overtime to pay tuition fees. Following his apprenticeship Stone worked as a designer and chaser in Edinburgh and Sheffield before emigrating in 1884 and joining the William B. Durgin Company in Concord, New Hampshire. An offer to establish a holloware department at F.W. Smith and Company brought him in 1887 to Gardner, where (following a one-year sojourn in New York City in 1895-1896 as a partner in J.P. Howard Co.) he married and remained for the rest of his life.

Stone's unusually long career spans seventy-six years, fifty-six of which were as an active designer and craftsman. Shortly after establish-

ing his shop, Stone was rivaling the most acclaimed American work in silver (see no. 144). From 1906 he was aided by assistants (see no. 145) who shared recognition from silverware that increasingly attracted coveted commissions and awards. The business acumen of Stone's wife and the sale and widespread promotion of the shop's wares by the Boston Society of Arts and Crafts insured the shop's success and contributed to its endurance long after the Arts and Crafts movement lost its popular interest. Greatly admired and respected personally and for the model his shop represented, Stone was the acknowledged "dean" of American silversmiths during his lifetime.

As a designer of silverware, Stone always took care in anticipating how the configuration of an object would complement its use, where it would be placed, and the sight line of its beholder. This fruit tazza is a masterful resolution of his concerns. Fruit arrangements are displayed to visual advantage and with care to their fragility in an elevated oval dish, rather than, as was typical, in a deep round bowl. Stone's use of ornament is characteristically discreet and occasionally humorous; the tazza, with its mis-

chievous gold-eyed serpent, is a bewitching reminder of the fruit-laden tree of knowledge from the Garden of Eden.

WSB

1. The mark appears in Elenita C. Chickering, *Arthur J. Stone: Handwrought Silver, 1901-1937* (Boston: Boston Athenaeum, 1981), p. 22, fig. d. Also by Chickering: "Arthur J. Stone, Silversmith," *Antiques* 129 (January 1986), pp. 274-283, ill.; and "Arthur J. Stone's Silver Flatware 1901-1937," *Silver* 19 (January-February 1986), pp. 10-19, ill.

144 (color plate, p. 29)
Jardinière, ca. 1902
Arthur J. Stone (1847-1938), Gardner, Massachusetts
Copper with silver details
H: 5 in. Diam: (of rim) 7½ in.
Marks: struck incuse hammer conjoining chased *Stone*
Private Collection

This jardinière was part of a small group of Stone metalwares awarded a silver medal at the 1904 Louisiana Purchase Exposition.[1] An important showcase for the Arts and Crafts movement, the event was America's first international exposition in which the applied arts were deemed worthy of display with painting, sculpture, and architecture – not, as had been the case previously, with manufactures. The Exposition established a long-sought nationwide standard for arts and crafts wares, achieved through an exacting selection process coordinated by regional juries. The treasurer and secretary of the Boston Society of Arts and Crafts, Frederick A. Whiting, was appointed Superintendent of the Division of Applied Arts for the Exposition, and its craftsman members from coast to coast responded enthusiastically to the call for exhibits and garnered over half the awards. The only awards higher than Stone's for American metalwork were gold medals for "artistic rendering of design" won by Paulding Farnum of Tiffany & Company and by William C. Codman of the Gorham Manufacturing Company.[2]

Whiting's comment on Farnum and Stone at the Exposition gives helpful insight into their work and Stone's measure as an artist: "The case of work designed by Paulding Farnum shows the extent of mechanical perfection to which such expert specialists as those employed by Tiffany & Company can go, and, in contrast with other silver work exhibited by individual workers (such as that by Mr. Stone), gives an excellent illustration of the loss which must result where work is passed through the hands of a number of workers, no matter how experienced. What is gained in mechanical perfection is lost in the artistic 'feeling,'– that quality which cannot be described, but which is the most important element in a real work of art to those who value things from other than the commercial standard."[3]

The Exposition heralded a period of intense and mutually beneficial activity for Stone and the Boston Society of Arts and Crafts. The Society's monumental commissions repeatedly went to Stone, who expertly gave substance and glory to the designs created by the Society's member architects. With a comprehensive library to draw upon, Stone refined the designs given him and adapted them to the requirements of the metal; he simultaneously executed other commissions. In 1913 the Society instituted the custom of awarding a medal for excellence in craftsmanship and service to no more than three craftsmen in a single year. Stone was among the first to be honored.

This jardinière reveals virtuoso skills in chasing and *repoussé* combined with passion and tenderness for the craft and for nature. The oak leaf and acorn wreath accent the restful contours and texture of the bowl; the leaves are superbly rendered through deeply undercut chasing in a metal artfully exploited for its autumnal color; and the silver acorns, inlaid not in halves but in their entirety, give a subtle jewel-like contrast. One feels Stone's presence in the way he, mindful of nature, chose to render one acorn having shed its nut. Among his large output this early work especially reveals the compelling magic whereby Stone could impart to a modest object a life of its own.

WSB

1. Irene Sargent, "The Work of Arthur J. Stone Silversmith," *Keystone* 27 (January 1906), p. 36, ill.; *Official Catalogue of Exhibits, Universal Exposition, St. Louis, U.S.A., Department B, Art* (rev. ed., St. Louis: Official Catalogue Company, 1904), p. 87, no. 752. Stone's other three pieces were in chased and *repoussé* silver, two of which featured gold inlay. The jardinière was probably one exhibited previously. See *Catalogue of the First Annual Exhibition of Original Designs for Decorations and Examples of Art Crafts Having Distinct Artistic Merit* (Chicago: Art Institute of Chicago, 1902), p. 33, no. 302.

2. This jardinière and the Codman-Gorham pieces – a silver-mounted table and chair and a silver desk set – are the Exposition's only known surviving American metalwork. See Charles H. Carpenter, Jr., *Gorham Silver 1831-1981* (New York: Dodd, Mead & Company, 1982), fig. 219. For the Exposition's awards, see *American Art Annual 1905-1906*, Florence Levy, ed., vol. 5 (New York: American Art Annual, 1905), p. 264.

3. Frederic Allen Whiting, "The Arts and Crafts At the Louisiana Purchase Exposition," *International Studio* 23 (October 1904), p. CCCLXXXVIII. For several Farnum designs at the Exposition see "Recent Works in Objets d'Art and Artistic Jewellery By Paulding Farnum," *International Studio* 29 (October 1906), pp. XCIII-XCIX, ill.

145

Vase, ca. 1921
Designer: Arthur J. Stone (1847-1938)
Maker: Herbert A. Taylor (1871-1942) at Arthur J. Stone, Silversmith (1901-1937), Gardner, Massachusetts (chasing by Stone)
Silver with gold details
H: 7⅝ in. Wt: 18 oz., 15 dwt.
Inscription: engraved TO / *AJS AND EBS* / 1896-1921 / *FROM THEIR FELLOW WORKMEN/ HAT-BHH-ALH-CWB* / *EHU-ESW* (on underside)
Marks: struck incuse *Stone* conjoining a hammer / STERLING / T
Worcester Art Museum, Worcester, Massachusetts. Gift of Mrs. Arthur J. Stone. 1939.23

For its intrinsic beauty and the story it holds, this vase commands a primary position in the history of American silver. It was presented to Arthur and Elizabeth Stone by Herbert A. Taylor, Benjamin H. Harrison, Arthur L. Hartwell, Charles W. Brown, Earle H. Underwood, and possibly Edwin Sibley Webster,[1] on the occasion of the couple's twenty-fifth wedding anniversary in 1921. Its inscription, which honors fellowship and mutual achievement, documents the fulfilled aspirations of Ruskin, Morris, and Ashbee.

The shop was a working model of Arts and Crafts movement principles, acknowledging the contribution of the individual craftsman. Feeling obliged to continue the apprenticeship system that had benefited him and to credit his employees, Stone hired and trained assistants whose pieces were marked individually with the initial of the hammerer next to Stone's mark. Until 1926, when a mild stroke caused Stone to hire other chasers and designers, he himself generated the shop's designs and did

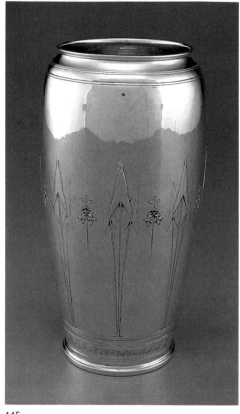

145

the chased ornament, except for line chasing. Profits realized were shared every six months and no workman was ever laid off for lack of work.[2] Many of them began training under him in the after hours of their high-school days and lived close to the shop adjoining Stone's home. Most were Master Craftsmen members of the Boston Society of Arts and Crafts, and three, including Herbert Taylor (who fabricated this vase), received the Society's Medalist award.[3]

A highly cultured individual, Stone had a broad, chiefly self-acquired education and a rich library of design references, but his preferred source for artistic inspiration was nature study.[4] The floral designs that frequently ornament his silver were based on firsthand observation.[5] Gold inlay (such as that seen in the arrowhead blossoms), although infrequent, is a distinguishing characteristic. The spare, ascetic quality of Stone silver insured his shop's success when Arts and Crafts metalwork styles and textures became unfashionable. For reasons both aesthetic and economic (chased and pierced decoration could greatly increase the cost of the shop's silverware), most of its production was unornamented. Suitability, another Stone design discipline, is apparent in his pitchers, whose spouts and handles are placed for comfortable pouring, and whose interiors allow easy hand access for cleaning. The relatively high surface planish set the standard for New England handicraft metalwork. Stone eschewed the Chicago practice of creating more obviously hammer-textured surfaces and marking them "hand-wrought"; he stated in 1934: "The word 'hand-wrought' means much or little of itself. It may stand only for sturdy usefulness, or for exquisite perfection of symmetry and design. It may accompany ignorant, careless workmanship or the skilled intelligence of long experience."[6]

WSB

1. The initials "ESW" among the donors of the vase probably stand for Edwin Sibley Webster, a partner (with Charles A. Stone) in the Boston engineering firm Stone and Webster, which patronized Arthur Stone's shop for commemorative silver.

2. "An American Silversmith," *Bulletin of the Society of Arts & Crafts* 10 (March 1926), pp. 1-2.

3. Taylor, who had been Stone's apprentice in the commercial trade, joined the shop in 1908 and remained until its sale in 1937.

4. In an article discussing this vase, Stone stated: "I believe I am safe in saying that all silversmiths of the present generation have gone to the Greeks for their outlines in hollow ware. And why not? The Greeks went to nature, and nature is, after all, the best source for design." See Anne Webb Karnagham, "Arthur J. Stone, Silversmith," *American Magazine of Art* 17 (June 1926), pp. 298, 300.

5. Stone foraged New England fields and ponds with his friend Charles Morgan and the arrowhead plant chased on this vase was one of their favorite finds. (Elenita C. Chickering to author, January 27, 1986.)

6. *Creative Design in Home Furnishings* 1 (Winter 1934-1935), p. 30.

146
Pitcher, ca. 1910
Shreve & Co. (1852 to present), San Francisco
Silver
H: 9¼ in. W: 5 in. Diam: (of base) 3⁵/₁₆ in. Wt: 16 oz.
Inscription: applied embossed medallion of two dolphins and tridents abreast crown-

146

topped shield enclosing C / C / C (initials unknown)
Marks: struck incuse shields enclosing S, flanking cartouche that frames hanging bell / SHREVE & CO. / STERLING / SAN FRANCISCO
The Brooklyn Museum, H. Randolph Lever Fund. 82.167

The iron hardware of the Middle Ages provided one of the most popular images for evoking archaic craft practices and construction methods of the pre-industrial past in Arts and Crafts furnishings. In the form of strap hinges, latches, and escutcheons – with either real or simulated nails and rivets – such hardware was typically used on furniture, but, hardware-like, motifs also adorned art metalwares and even pottery.[1] The long strap hinges with spade terminals on this piece provide the same visual effect as the abstracted-leaf and elongated-stem forms found on some Potter spoons, Jarvie candlesticks, and Roycroft furniture hardware (nos. 44, 139 and 168). The decorative rivets have

their counterpart, occasionally seen on Mission-style furniture, in pegs that serve no structural purpose.

Strap and rivet ornament applied to sterling silver is notably a product of Shreve & Company. Founded in 1852 as a jewelry shop in San Francisco's pioneer Gold Rush era, the firm soon made commissions from Comstock-lode silver. By 1900 their wares ranged from souvenir spoons to battleship services. Shreve may have been producing silver holloware with strap-and-rivet ornament early in the first decade of the century, but surviving examples mostly date after 1906, when the firm opened a new factory to replace the one lost in the San Francisco earthquake. Augustus F. Rose's widely available manual *Copper Work*, introduced in 1906, was filled with strap-and-rivet ornament and even illustrated pitchers whose handles may have inspired the one seen here; however, a large San Francisco collection of old Spanish wrought-iron locks, keys, and hinges formed by 1903 could also have been the source of inspiration for the ornament.[2] In 1911 Shreve used the strap-hardware motif in its "XIVth Century" flatware pattern.

In producing silver with strap-and-rivet decoration, Shreve usually applied the motifs to its standard holloware forms and only occasional examples, such as this pitcher, reveal the successful marriage of form and ornament. The pitcher's strap, rather than hollow, handle conveys the idea of medieval latch hardware. Its contours play against the pitcher's baluster shape and act as a foil to strap shapes applied to the body and to cutouts in the rim. The curving tails of the dolphins, repeating shapes seen throughout, suggest a yachting association.

WSB

1. An advertisement for Clewell Studios referred to "The hammered and riveted drinking vessels of the Middle Ages reproduced in copper and perfectly lined with porcelain for actual use." See *Town & Country* 63 (November 21, 1908), p. 42, ill.

2. Augustus F. Rose, *Copper Work* (Worcester, Mass.: Davis Press, 1906), pls. 35-37. For the San Francisco collection, see the advertisement for McCann, Belcher & Allen in *House Beautiful* 14 (November 1903), p. xxxi, ill.

147

Coffee set with tray, ca. 1917
Tiffany & Company (1837 to present) New York
Silver and ivory
Coffee pot – H: 6⅜ in. W: (at spout) 5¼ in. D: (at handle) 7¾ in. Wt: (gross) 17 oz., 9 dwt.
Cream pitcher – H: 3 in. W: (at handle) 3¼ in. D: 2¾ in. Wt: 5 oz., 12 dwt.
Sugar bowl with cover – H: 3³⁄₁₆ in. W: (at handles) 4⅜ in. D: 3⅝ in. Wt: 8 oz., 1 dwt.
Tray – H: ¾ in. W: (at handles) 13 in. D: 11¹¹⁄₁₆ in. Wt: 28 oz., 13 dwt.
Marks: struck incuse text as follows:
Coffee pot – TIFFANY & C⁰· / 16968 MAKERS 7570 / STERLING SILVER / 925-1000 / m / SPECIAL HAND WORK and /1½ PINTS
Cream pitcher – TIFFANY & C⁰· / 16968 MAKERS . . . / STERLING SILVER / 925-1000 / m / SPECIAL HAND WORK, and /1½ GILLS
Sugar bowl – TIFFANY & C⁰· / 16968 MAKERS 6584 / STERLING SILVER / 925-1000 / m / SPECIAL HAND WORK, and 2 GILLS
Tray – TIFFANY & C⁰· / 16968 MAKERS 8396 / STERLING SILVER / 925-1000 / m
Yale University Art Gallery, New Haven. Gift of Dorothy Scudder Black in Memory of Henry H. Scudder, B.A. 1917. 1977.34.a-d

In the second decade of the twentieth century large firms and manufacturers such as Tiffany & Company competed in the market for hand-wrought silver tablewares that had been developed by handicraft silversmiths. Most of these art metalsmiths were part of small communal shops established after 1905 in the environs of Boston and Chicago, where patronage had been fostered by their respective arts and crafts societies and museums. The market was slower to develop in New York. Arts and crafts activities there revolved around exhibitions of the National Society of Craftsmen at the National Arts Club, but were no match for the handicraft exhibits and displays found in Boston or Chicago. Although the Metropolitan Museum of Art greatly helped the nation rediscover its handicraft heritage with exhibitions that focused attention on colonial silver and other decorative arts,[1] New Yorkers did not have a museum actively interested in the Arts and Crafts movement. The city's lack of ready access to the work of contemporary Boston and Chicago craftsmen and to art silverware in general was remedied, however, around 1912. The Chicago-based jeweler Lebolt & Company began producing handmade hammer-textured silver

that soon became available at their New York branch, and in 1914 Chicago's Kalo Shop (no. 142) opened a New York outlet for its wares. Simultaneously, the newly founded Little Gallery began its long history of offering New Yorkers handwrought silver tablewares – frequently in the colonial revival style – from leading Massachusetts handicraft silversmiths. Tiffany, too, joined the competition with reproductions of American colonial silver and with silver marked "SPECIAL HAND WORK."

It is unclear when Tiffany began making table silver with such a designation. The drawings for this coffee set were assigned a pattern number that was entered into the Tiffany silver pattern books in 1907 and a tea set of the same design was advertised in *The Craftsman* in 1914.[2] The example shown here was probably not made until about 1917, when it was a wedding present to Dorothy Weeks Scudder. The pieces in the Scudder set are the earliest examples now known to bear the "SPECIAL HAND WORK" mark. Only ten additional works bearing this mark have been found to date and, of these, one – a paneled bowl – has a provenance.[3] All of the examples are meticulously executed, display a hammered surface on extra-heavy-gauge sterling silver, and many reveal telltale signs of hand-raised fabrication such as a center punch.[4] Tiffany & Company's appellation "SPECIAL HAND WORK" was their proud hallmark for unusually substantial and artful silver tablewares made through handicraft processes and offered for sale as an alternative to the art silver tablewares from small shops spawned by the Arts and Crafts movement.

WSB

1. In particular: "Hudson-Fulton" exhibition, 1909; "Silver Used in New York, New Jersey, and the South" exhibition, 1911; and in the installation of silver loaned by Judge Alphonso T. Clearwater, beginning in 1911.
2. *Craftsman*, November 1914, p. 1a., ill.
3. The paneled bowl, said to have been a 1921 wedding present, and a lobed bowl are in a private collection. A coffee set is illustrated in "Art Deco & Art Nouveau" (New York: Sotheby Parke Bernet, November 24, 1978), lot 56; a tall compote is included in "Important Art Nouveau & Art Deco" (New York: Sotheby Parke Bernet, March 27, 1980), lot 273, ill.; a low compote and pitcher appear in "Fine Art Nouveau & Art Deco" (New York: Sotheby's, April 22, 1981), lots 227, 232. ill.; a large round bowl is in the collection of the Art Institute of Chicago; an ice bowl and a second edition of the aforementioned lobed

bowl have been observed by the author in the marketplace. The comparative rarity of the "SPECIAL HAND WORK" mark is underscored by its omission in the standard reference for Tiffany silver: Charles H. Carpenter, Jr., with Mary Grace Carpenter, *Tiffany Silver* (New York: Dodd, Mead, 1978).
4. Scholars have believed that Tiffany put the "SPECIAL HAND WORK" mark on lathe-spun work; see, for example, Charles H. Carpenter, Jr., *Gorham Silver 1831-1981* (New York: Dodd, Mead, 1982), p. 109. However, in addition to the evidence of the objects themselves, Tiffany maintains that 'SPECIAL HAND WORK' refers to the fact that the pieces were hand raised" (from Janet Zapata, Archives of Tiffany & Co., in a letter to the author, April 18, 1986).

VIII.

The Silence stood listening.

148

148

Silence: An Idyl, by Mena A. Pfirshing, 1901
Calligrapher, decorator, and designer: Walt M. DeKalb
Multicolored inks on white paper
13¾ x 10¾ in. (page)
Collection of Richard Blacher

During the early 1870s, William Morris copied and illuminated several manuscripts, some of which were exhibited in the eighties.[1] Like everything else he did, this activity had a far-reaching influence. In 1898 his friend W.R. Lethaby, an architect who was principal of the Central School of Arts and Crafts in London, hired as instructor for a new course in calligraphy the young Edward Johnston;[2] out of this class came the twentieth-century revival of calligraphy. Johnston's first American student was Elizabeth Holden Webb, who later returned to New York City to teach.[3]

Silence: An Idyl is an example of American turn-of-the-century calligraphy. On the vellum binding the title is lettered in red and blue and placed within a matching frame decorated with zoomorphic interlacings that are reminiscent of Hiberno-Saxon manuscripts. The title page, within a ruled border, begins with a large floral-decorated Gothic "S". Each of the eleven text

pages also has a ruled border with large decorated Gothic initials, and the text lettering itself is in Gothic. The most charming feature of these pages is the use of plant motifs placed with the catchwords in the lower right corners. In a few cases flowers with elongated stems are depicted, recalling developments in art contemporary with this manuscript.

ST

1. For a complete description of Morris's calligraphy, see Joseph Dunlap's essay in *William Morris and the Art of the Book* (New York: Pierpont Morgan Library and Oxford University Press, 1976).

2. For the life of Johnston, see Priscilla Johnston, *Edward Johnston* (2d ed., New York: Pentalic Corporation, 1976). Johnston's own classic work is *Writing & Illuminating & Lettering* (London: Pitman, 1906), with many subsequent editions.

3. *2,000 Years of Calligraphy* (Totowa, N.J.: Rowman and Littlefield, 1965), p. 139.

149 (color plate, p. 30)
Ecclesiastes, or the Preacher; and the Song of Solomon, 1902
Printer: Ballantyne Press, London, under the supervision of Charles Ricketts
Designer and illuminator: da Loria Norman (1872-1935)
14 unfoliated printed leaves, 2 manuscript leaves at front; all on vellum
11¼ x 7½ in. (page)
Colophon: *IN THE YEAR OF OUR LORD MCMXX THIS BOOK WAS DESIGNED AND ILLUMINATED BY DA LORIA NORMAN IN HER STUDIO ABOVE THE LAKE AT LYME, CONNECTICUT*
Spencer Collection, New York Public Library, Astor, Lenox and Tilden Foundations

Not since the Renaissance had the making of books assumed such importance as it did in the Arts and Crafts movement. Books are among the principal surviving monuments of the thirteenth and fourteenth centuries, so that illumination (or book painting) came to figure prominently in the nineteenth-century Gothic revival. Henry Noel Humphreys and other antiquarians produced books depicting the glories of medieval illumination, and many manuals appeared offering do-it-yourself instruction.[1] The Arts and Crafts movement continued this trend, with one new addition – a calligraphy revival.

A leading member of this revival was da Loria Norman, born in Kansas. She went to England with her family in the 1880s, studied on the Continent, and returned to America in 1914.[2] Although she had studied to be both a concert pianist and a grand opera singer, she gave up those pursuits for visual art, a field in which she had received no formal training. She worked in media from oil painting to embroidery, but specialized in illumination. Da Loria Norman was influenced by the principles of the Arts and Crafts movement, as shown by her preoccupation with fine materials. She once tried eight sheepskins before finding the right piece of parchment for a particular illumination; for her embroidery she kept Japanese silk in twenty different but almost indistinguishable shades of each color.

Perhaps the most outstanding piece of Norman's work is *Ecclesiastes, or the Preacher; and the Song of Solomon*. Charles Ricketts designed the text and supervised its printing on vellum at the Ballantyne Press in his own unique type, the King's Fount. Ms. Norman then took Ricketts's pages, added two manuscript leaves of her own notes, illuminated the whole, and placed it within a binding created from her own embroidery. (This intricate needlework was shown in 1914 at the Louvre, in a Pre-Raphaelite exhibition entitled "The Britons," as the only contemporary example.) Having doublures (inside covers) of beige morocco leather with gilt dentelles and beige *moiré* endpapers, the binding is reminiscent more of Elizabethan embroidered bindings than of the simpler bindings typical of Arts and Crafts handworkers.

Ms. Norman explained the motives behind her work in notes at the beginning of the book: "The aim of the illuminator has been to stimulate the beholder to search for a spiritual significance, and not present a mere illustration which would excite no effort to study, for usually, literal illustration converts the mind with material expression, whereas symbolism elevates thought to the DIVINE." Stylistically, her illumination also recalls late Renaissance manuscripts as much as it does those of the turn of the century. It is not innovative. Individualist though she was, Norman could have found her inspiration only during this period when medieval crafts were reborn and when the efforts of many infused art with a new spirituality.

ST

1. Henry Noel Humphreys, *The Illuminated Books of the Middle Ages* (London: Longmans, Brown, Green, and Longmans, 1849).

2. All biographical information is taken from a document prepared in 1979 by two granddaughters of da Loria Norman, Cynthia Norman and Lucy de Sanchez.

150 (color plate, p. 31)
Flowers of Song from Many Lands, by Frederick Rowland Marvin, 1902
Publisher: Pafraets Book Company, Troy, New York (printed at the Merrymount Press, Boston)
Designer of binding: Mary Crease Sears (d. 1938)
Binder: Agnes St. John
Green morocco leather with multicolored leather inlays
H: 9⅝ in. W: 7 in. D: 1 in.
The Houghton Library, Harvard University

Mary Crease Sears had wanted to be an architect, but instead studied art in Boston at the Museum of Fine Arts School, went to Paris and London to study bookbinding, and eventually set up her own Boston studio in a row house near the Public Library. There she took private commissions and trained women apprentices. In her teaching she stressed the equal importance of the three main stages of binding: collating, forwarding, and finishing – that is, sewing the leaves in the correct order; adding boards, headbands, and leather covering; and decorating the leather covers. According to one story, a young woman who had applied to Sears for instruction in finishing only, was shown that in her previous work the text blocks on different pages were not in perfect register, and thus she was persuaded to start at the beginning again.[1]

Sears's work was widely recognized for its high quality. She was a Medalist of the Boston Society of Arts and Crafts and was awarded a gold medal at the St. Louis Exposition. *Flowers of Song from Many Lands* received particular praise as a consummate example of the binder's art.[2] The iris and tulip designs on its green morocco covers are composed of more than a thousand pieces of inlaid colored leather. The sumptuous effect derives not only from the richness of coloring but also from the repetition of motifs, a device often used in Arts and Crafts printing.

Sears also worked from historical precedents, as shown by a vellum book for photographs she did for Mrs. John L. Gardner.[3] The brown leather binding is blind-tooled (without gilt) and has silver clasps and bosses, the central clasp on the front cover containing an emerald.

ST

1. Biographical data are taken from Ralph Bergengren, "A Complete Bookbinder," *House Beautiful* 37 (March 1915), pp. 85-89.

2. Eva Lovett, "The Exhibition of the Society of Arts and Crafts, Boston," *International Studio* 31 (March 1907), p. 30.

3. Illustrated in Bergengren 1915, p. 87.

151
The Song of Roland, 1906
Publisher: Houghton, Mifflin, and Company, Boston (printed at Riverside Press, Cambridge)
Designer: Bruce Rogers (1870-1957)
Black and red on white paper, with hand coloring
17½ x 11½ in. (page)
Department of Rare Books and Special Collections, Princeton University Library

Bruce Rogers was born in Lafayette, Indiana, and attended Purdue University from 1886 to 1890; during this period he became interested in bookmaking, design, and illustration. In 1893 he found a job in Indianapolis with the Indiana Illustration Company and began to work for Joseph M. Bowles's periodical *Modern Art*, which had just commenced publication. Bowles was a sensitive editor who anticipated the printing revolution and made *Modern Art* into one of the major vehicles for spreading the doctrine of printing as an art: "the salvation of modern printing can come in only one way, through a reunion of printers and artists."[1]

Rogers always believed that printing was inferior to fine art, and presumably he became a typographer because of some hesitancy about his own artistic abilities. Nevertheless, of the "heroic" generation of American typographers who began their careers under the inspiration of the Arts and Crafts movement, he became the best-known book designer and the first American printing figure to gain a reputation in England as elevated as his domestic one. He must have found Bowles's doctrine a solace, for when Bowles moved *Modern Art* to Boston in 1895, Rogers followed him.

Bowles and Rogers, while still in Indianapolis, collaborated on a volume published in 1895, R.B. Gruelle's *Notes: Critical and Biographical*, proofs of which were actually sent to William Morris for comment. In Boston, Rogers did various work for the local "literary" publishers, but it was for Way and Williams of Chicago that he did his other important Arts and Crafts book, *The Banquet of Plato*, also in 1895. He later designed two typefaces based on Jenson: Montaigne in 1901 and Centaur in 1915.

In 1896 Rogers was hired to work for Houghton, Mifflin's Riverside Press. He supervised the production of several books influenced by the Arts and Crafts movement before being commissioned by George Mifflin in 1900 to design the Riverside Press Limited Editions, a series of volumes for bibliophiles. This series was to be innovative in the employment of "allusive" typography, which uses elements of antique styles to capture the spirit of the age to which the text belongs. According to Rogers: "when a man of general artistic training takes up printing, he is apt to go back over the history and achievement of the art with an eye, not to the technical problems, but to the effects produced . . . when he tries his hand, he will endeavor to reproduce one of the admirable effects he has seen – or rather, perhaps, a combination of several of them."[2]

The Song of Roland, the third offering in the Riverside series of limited editions, was printed in an edition of 220 copies. The work is clothed in Gothic dress, with a splendid opening decoration that evokes stained glass. It shows the fine presswork accomplished under Rogers's supervision and the impeccable taste that he brought to all his work. The prospectus for the book points out that it would be "printed on hand presses . . . . The type is the beautiful French Gothic used in the 'Parlement of Foules,' and the present volume is set in double columns with marginal notes in brown and rubricated folios as page headings. . . . The illustrations are a unique feature of the book. They are seven in number, and are derived from the window of Charlemagne in the Cathedral of Chartres, noted for the beauty of its thirteenth century glass. Mr. Rogers visited Chartres especially to study this window . . . . The compartments of the window picturing events in the Legend of Roland have been carefully drawn and reproduced. The lead lines are printed with the type, and the colors are afterwards filled in by hand in conformity to the color scheme of the window itself."[3]

Rogers left Riverside in 1912 to become a freelance designer working both in America

THE SONG OF ROLAND

I

The Treachery of Ganelon

Charles the King, our great Emperor, has been for seven long years in Spain; he has conquered all the high land down to the sea; not a castle holds out against him, not a wall or city is left unshattered, save Saragossa, which stands high on a mountain. King Marsilie holds it, who loves not God, but serves Mahound, and worships Apollon; ill hap must in sooth befall him. King Marsilie abides in Saragossa. And on a day he passes into the shade of his orchard; there he sits on a terrace of blue marble, and around him his men are gathered to the number of twenty thousand. He speaks to his dukes and his counts, saying: 'Hear, lords, what evil overwhelms us; Charles the Emperor of fair France has come into this land to confound us. I have no host to do battle against him, nor any folk to discomfort his. Counsel me, lords, as wise men and save me from death and shame.' But not a man has any word in answer, save Blancandrin of the castle of Val/Fonde. Blancandrin was among the wisest of the paynims, a good knight of much prowess, discreet and valiant in the service of his lord. He saith to the King: 'Be not out of all comfort. Send to Charles the proud, the terrible, proffer of faithful service and goodly friendship; give him bears and lions and dogs, seven hundred camels and a thousand falcons past the moulting time, four hundred mules laden with gold and silver, that he may send before him fifty full wains; and therewith shall he richly reward his followers. Long has he waged war in this land, it is meet he return again to Aix in France. And do thou pledge thy word to follow him at the feast of Saint Michael, to receive the faith of the Christians, and to become his man in all honour & loyalty. If he would have hostages, send them to him, or ten or twenty, to make good the compact. We will send him the sons of our wives; yea, though it be to death, I will send mine own. Better it were that they lose their lives than that we be spoiled of lands and lordship, and be brought to beg our bread. By this my right hand,' saith Blancandrin, 'and by the beard that the wind blows about my breast, ye shall see the Frankish host straightway scatter abroad, and the Franks return again to their land of France. When each is in his own home, and Charles is in his chapel at Aix, he will hold high festival on the day of Saint Michael. The day will come, and the term appointed will pass, but of us he will have no word nor tidings. The King is proud and cruel of heart, he will let smite off the heads of our hostages, but better it is that they lose their lives than that we be spoiled of bright Spain, the fair, or suffer so great dole and sorrow.' And the paynims cry: 'Let it be as he saith.' So King Marsilie hath ended his counsel; he then called Clarin de Balaguer, Estramarin, and Endropin, his fellow, and Priamon, and Barsan the Bearded, Machiner, and Maheu his uncle, Joimer, and Malbien from over/sea, and Blancandrin; ten of the fiercest he hath called, to make known his will unto them. 'Lords, barons,' he saith, 'go ye to Charlemagne, who is at the siege of the city of Cordova, bearing olive branches in your hands in token of peace and submission. If by your wit ye can make me a covenant with Charles, I will give you great store of gold and silver, and lands and fiefs as much as ye may desire.' 'Nay,' say the paynims, 'of these things we have and to spare.' King Marsilie hath ended his council, & he saith to his men: 'Go ye forth, lords, & bear in your hands

Marsilie takes counsel against Charles

And sends to him ten Ambassadors

and in England, thus becoming the world's first full-time book designer. There was never a particular "Rogers" style in printing, but rather an interesting eclecticism, always informed by Rogers's knowledge of printing history. The limited editions from Riverside made him famous, and he maintained his standards in later periods. Part of the delight in his work stems from his playful use of printers' flowers and other small decorations cast in type metal. A designer of Rogers's seriousness of mind could hardly have indulged in such playfulness had he not started out in the era of Arts and Crafts decoration.

ST

1.   Joseph M. Bowles, "Thoughts on Printing: Practical and Impractical," *Modern Art* 2 (Summer 1894).

2.   Letter from Bruce Rogers to Henry Lewis Bullen, dated November 4, 1916, Rare Book and Manuscript Library, Columbia University.

3.   *The Song of Roland* [Prospectus] n.d., one leaf.

152

The Divine Comedy, by Dante Alighieri, three volumes, 1929
Designer: John Henry Nash (1871-1947)
Black and green inks on white paper
13¾ x 10 in. (page)
Rare Books and Manuscripts Division, New York Public Library, Astor, Lenox, and Tilden Foundations

Thomas James Cobden-Sanderson (1840-1922), founder of the Doves Press, one of the greatest of the English private presses, was the leader of the turn-of-the-century revolution in bookbinding. Doves type, like Morris's Golden type, was modeled by Emery Walker on that of the fifteenth-century Venetian printer Nicolas Jenson, but Doves was lighter in tone than Golden. The layout of the Doves book, unlike those of Kelmscott, included no decoration except for handwritten capitals. Cobden-Sanderson was an eccentric who eventually threw his type into the Thames because he wanted no one else to use it. He could not, however, negate the influence of his style, which succeeded the influence of Morris in America.[1]

The American printer who was to follow the Doves tradition most closely had not yet embarked on the major period of his career. John Henry Nash, born in Canada, moved in 1895 to San Francisco, where he worked for several

different presses before joining Paul Elder in the Tomoyé Press. Following the earthquake of 1906 the partners moved to New York City, returning to San Francisco in 1909. Two years later the partnership broke up and Nash went on to other firms. After he began to work on his own and became one of the best-known printers in the world,[2] he was sought out by wealthy businessmen, notably William Randolph Hearst. At the time Nash printed *The Life and Personality of Phoebe Apperson Hearst* (1928)[3] he was working on *The Divine Comedy* (1929), which took six years to complete and shows his skill at its best: the impeccable presswork, the close composition of the American Type Founders Cloister type, the fine material of Van Gelder paper with a Nash watermark from Holland, vellum bindings protected by cloth bags (rather than the usual slip cases), and the restrained yet highly effective decoration of simple green rulings. The set was included in the Royal Library at Windsor and a presentation copy to the Pope brought forth an apostolic blessing.[4]

In Arts and Crafts printing as a whole, the Doves influence served as a transition between the neo-Gothic imitators of Morris and the neoclassical "Crystal Goblet" (or "printing should be invisible") school of Beatrice Warde and the British typographer Stanley Morison. Miss Warde, an American printing historian living in England, was a persuasive advocate of unobtrusive typography, leaning more toward Renaissance models.[5] The Doves style straddled these two schools. On the one hand, like Morris, it derived its inspiration from fifteenth-century Venice; on the other, it avoided decoration in pursuit of a classical simplicity and serenity unknown to him.

ST

1. "During the last few years the somewhat Gothic feeling of the Kelmscott Press books has been slowly abandoned for the lighter and more classical styles of type – a movement in which The Doves Press, London, has been chiefly instrumental." See Bruce Rogers and D.B. Updike, *The Development of Printing as an Art* (exhibition catalogue; Boston: Society of Printers, 1906), p. 20.

2. Nash's career flourished to the point that one commentator referred to Morris as a Victorian Nash. See Robert D. Harlan, *John Henry Nash: The Biography of a Career* (Berkeley: University of California Press, 1970), pp. 49-50.

3. Printed in a format similar to that of the *Divine Comedy*, the text shows marked contrast between its journalistic slightness and its monumental physical treatment.

4. Ibid, p. 53. A letter from Nash to Henry Lewis Bullen (October 24, 1930) quotes a letter received by F.W. Heron from the book collector A. Edward Newton: "Will you be good enough to tell John Henry Nash that I spent several hours in the Royal Library at Windsor yesterday and the Librarian whom I met several years ago at Cambridge in charge of Pepy's [sic] Library, began talking to me of fine printing and walking over to a shelf took therefrom a copy of Nash's Dante, four vols., and remarked quite casually, 'Now here is a book printed in San Francisco that to my mind is just what a book should be.'" (Rare Book and Manuscript Library, Columbia University).

5. Beatrice Warde, *The Crystal Goblet: Sixteen Essays on Typography* (Cleveland: World, 1956).

153

Sonnets from the Portuguese, by Elizabeth Barrett Browning, 1900
Printer: Elston Press, New York
Designer: Helen Marguerite O'Kane (1879-   )
Black ink on white paper
10¼ x 8 in. (page)
Collection of Eleanor McDowell Thompson

Among the favorite texts for reprinting by private presses at the turn of the century was Elizabeth Barrett Browning's *Sonnets from the Portuguese*. The versions range in visual impact from a starkly unadorned pamphlet known as the "Reading Sonnets" to the supremely dramatic pages of the Elston Press volume.[1]

Little is known about the Elston Press. Clarke Conwell established it in 1900 in New York City, where *Sonnets from the Portuguese* was the first book issued, and moved it in 1901 to New Rochelle. The last book, *A Masque of Love*, appeared in 1904, published by the Chicago book dealer Walter M. Hill. The first volumes were printed in typefaces based on those of William Morris and adorned with lavish decorations by Conwell's wife, Helen Marguerite O'Kane.[2] With the sixth volume, Conwell turned to Caslon type, a much less imposing face, and cut back on the decorations. The later books are as good as the earlier from the point of view of craftsmanship; though possibly in more genteel taste, they are less interesting in their design.

The Elston books have always been appreciated for their impeccable presswork but, ironically, they are now valued for the same art work that earlier critics judged harshly. A contemporary writer found the effect of the type and decorations "somewhat heavy," while the foremost bibliographer of private presses, Will Ran-

I

Proem : Rescue of Dante by Virgil

Time: Morning of Good Friday of the Jubilee year, 1300, Dante being midway on the way to three-score and ten.
Place: The "wandering wood of this life," where Dante comes to himself from that sleep which is spiritual death. To understand the Poet one must "go into the poet's country,"—a country where all material things and transitory wants are looked at sub specie eternitatis. Dante himself is at once an individual and a type of humanity erring, repenting, winning salvation. Virgil is at once the poet whom Dante most admired and the type of human wisdom (philosophy). Beatrice is at once the woman whom Dante loved and the mouthpiece of Divine wisdom (theology). Earth is still the centre of the universe; the sun is a larger planet; astronomy is hardly distinguisht from astrology.

1 WHEN half the journey of our life was done
   I found me in a darkling wood astray,
       because aside from the straight pathway run.
4 Ah me, how hard a thing it is to say
   what was this thorny wildwood intricate
       whose memory renews the first dismay!
7 Scarcely in death is bitterness more great:
   but as concerns the good discovered there
       the other things I saw will I relate.
10 How there I entered I am unaware,
   so was I at that moment full of sleep
       when I abandoned the true thoroughfare.
13 But when I reacht the bottom of a steep
   ending the valley which had overcome
       my courage, piercing me with fear so deep,
16 Lifting mine eyes up, I beheld its dome
   already covered with that planet's light
       which along all our pathways leads us home.
19 Then was a little quieted the fright
   that had been lurking in the heart of me
       throughout the passage of the piteous night.
22 And as the panting castaway, if he
   escape the wave and on the shore arrive
       turns back and gazes on the perilous sea,
25 Even so my spirit, still a fugitive,
   turned back to look again upon the shore
       that never left one person yet alive.
28 My weary frame somewhat refresht, once more
   along the solitary slope I plied
       so that the firm foot ever was the lower.

31 And lo! where but begins the mountainside,
   a leopard light and very swift of pace
       and covered with a gayly spotted hide.
34 Never withdrew she from before my face;
   nay, rather blockt she so my going on
       that oft I turned my footing to retrace.
37 It was about the moment of the dawn;
   uprose the sun and paled the light benign
       of those fair stars which were beside him yon
40 When took they motion first from Love Divine:
   so the sweet season and the time of day
       caused me to augur as a hopeful sign
43 That animal with skin bedappled gay:
   yet not so much but that I felt dismayed
       to see a lion intercept my way.
46 It seemed to me that he toward me made
   with head erected and with hunger raving,
       so that the very air appeared afraid:
49 And a she-wolf, made gaunt by every craving
   wherewith methought she heavy-laden went,
       and much folk hitherto of joy bereaving;
52 She brought on me so much discouragement
   by terror of her aspect that perforce
       I forfeited all hope of the ascent.
55 And as one, interrupted in his course
   of winning, when his fortune is undone
       is full of perturbation and remorse,
58 That truceless beast made me such malison,
   and coming on against me pace by pace
       baffled me back where silent is the sun.
61 While I was falling back to that low place,
   a being was made present to my ken
       who through long silence seemed in feeble case.

LINES 31-58
Just what sins the three beasts typify is disputed. Elsewhere in the Poem the wolf is the type of avarice, by which Dante means all forms of selfish advantage at the expense of others. It is the sin which he most frequently stigmatizes; obviously, therefore, the allegory here cannot be merely personal. If the leopard symbolizes lust, the lion pride, the wolf avarice, the correspondence is sufficiently plain with the grand division of sins in Canto xi into sins of Incontinence, of Violence, and of Fraud.

LINES 38-40
The sun was placed in the sign of the Ram (Aries) at the Creation, and rises now accompanied by the same stars. At Eastertide all nature rises with the risen God; the vernal equinox is the true beginning, not only of the year, but of all things. Our Chaucer afterwards chose the same date for his pilgrimage to Canterbury, when "the yongë Sonne Hath in the Ram his halfë cors yronnë."

LINE 48
Cf. Shakespeare's Henry the Fifth, Chorus I, lines 12-14; and Tennyson's Godiva.

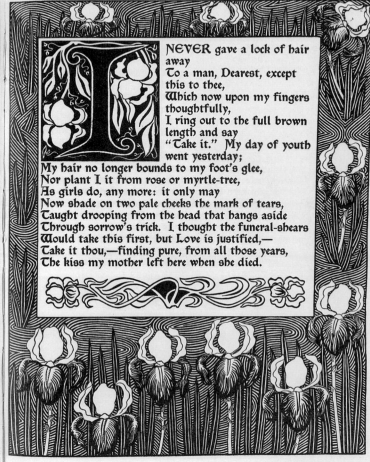

153

som, declared in 1929 that the designed decoration "was hardly up to the other standards of the press."[4] Conwell's presswork is alluded to by a notice laid in *Sonnets from the Portuguese*. It reports that Conwell could not find enough hand-pressmen to finish the book and, lacking enough time to do it himself, had to use a commercial power press: "Mr. Conwell wishes . . . to state that no other book will ever be printed by him except by hand as was his original intention." The great book designer Bruce Rogers wrote in 1948 of Conwell: "He was probably the most meticulous pressman who ever worked in the U.S. – but most of his books were spoiled by the hard, stiff paper he used, and by his wife [H.M. O'Kane]'s illustrations – which are a weak copy of the Birmingham School's style of illustration."

Helen O'Kane, the designer of *Sonnets from the Portuguese*, was twenty-one years old when it was published. Influenced in this book by Art Nouveau as well as by William Morris (and in some of her other work by Aubrey Beardsley and Edward Burne-Jones), she was clearly knowledgeable about the art world of the time, but, given her age, she cannot have had much experience in designing book pages. Her greatest accomplishment lies in creating a book spread as controlled as it is complicated, the resulting tension producing a sensation of un-leashed power. The type used for *Sonnets from the Portuguese* is American Type Founders Satanick, based on Morris's Troy, a semi-Gothic face. Legend has it that the type was called Satanick because Morris said "go to the Devil" when his permission was asked for copying.

All of Conwell's books sold out almost on publication, yet he never made any money and only after a long time did he find out why. His wastage of printed sheets – sheets thrown out for the smallest detectable imperfections – was at least fifty percent of each run.[5]

ST

1. The "Reading Sonnets" is the best known of the forgeries perpetrated by Thomas James Wise, who had them printed secretly by a commercial firm, admittedly not the usual sort of private press. See John Carter and Graham Pollard, *An Enquiry into the Nature of Certain Nineteenth Century Pamphlets* (London: Constable, 1934).

2. Miss O'Kane also did work for trade publishers, for example her decorations for *Pre-Raphaelite Ballads* by William Morris (New York: A. Wessels, 1900).

3. See, for example, Colin Franklin, *The Private Presses* (Chester Springs, Pa.: Dufour, 1969), p. 159.

4. FitzRoy Carrington, "Private and Special Presses," *Book Buyer* 23 (1901), p. 100; and Will Ransom, *Private Presses and their Books* (New York: Bowker, 1929), p. 74.

5. Letter from Bruce Rogers to Thomas A. Larremore, dated March 15, 1948. Department of Special Collections, University of California, Santa Barbara.

154

The Acre of the Earth-Turner, by Tuley Francis Huntington, 1929
Printer: House of Huntington, Palo Alto, California
Designer: Tuley Francis Huntington (1870-1938)
Black and red inks on white paper
8 x 6 in. (page)
School of Library Service Library, Columbia University, New York

The Arts and Crafts movement, with its highly moral philosophy, had among its practitioners certain eccentrics who reached peaks of mysticism in its name. T. J. Cobden-Sanderson of the Doves Bindery and Press was one. Much later and far less known was Tuley Francis Huntington.

Born near Barrington, Illinois, Huntington graduated from Cornell College in Iowa. He taught English for a while in the Milwaukee high school system and eventually moved to California.[1] Between 1900 and 1916 he owned and operated an apricot ranch in Los Altos.[2] He also taught English at Stanford University, wrote an English composition textbook, and edited Coleridge and Milton for publication. When he retired from teaching, he established a private press on the second-floor veranda of his home in Palo Alto.

The House of Huntington, as this press was called, produced three books, all written by Huntington: *The Acre of the Earth-Turner:* (subtitled *and whatso the tale tells of the master's life-days and*

undying in the valley of the orchards and that land of the wondrous sun (1929); *Iron, Rain, and Green*, in "block verse" (1929); and *Jacqueline of Very Near* (1931), a story for his granddaughter – all published unbound in slip cases. The press also put out three issues of a small periodical, *The Lagday Letter* (1932-1934).

The language in these writings is mysterious and arcane, especially for an English professor. The text of *Lagday Letter*, Number 1, opens: "The tale of the Earth Turner is an adventure in audacity. Quite openly, and taking on the narrative treatment of pious propaganda, it satirizes a grotesquery put under ban of silence by craven vacuity." Eventually it becomes clear that the author is against Communism, Capitalism, and the Church. It also becomes clear that he is a latter-day disciple of the Arts and Crafts movement. "To build a book that shall be artfully different, and beautiful too in certain subtle trifles . . . the author, the artist, and the printer shall be one and the same man . . . . The master writes the books he prints, he sets up each letter of the text and each type-ornament, he oils and inks the press, and he turns and holds the wheel to gather the lingering pressure that produces the black type-block of the page perpetual."

In *The Acre of the Earth-Turner*, Huntington declared himself against the trade printing of the day with its gray type and narrow pages and the dehumanized atmosphere of the high-speed shop. The book was published in an edition of forty numbered and signed copies, printed in Goudy's Italian Old Style on Kelmscott paper, and priced expensively at $25. Fifty copies of *Iron, Rain, and Green* were printed in black and four colors on Crane's Old Book rag paper; the typeface was Grebe Koch Antique. This type was used again in *Jacqueline of Very Near*, published in an edition of twenty-seven copies on Tuscany handmade paper and priced even more expensively at $60.

Huntington's typography is not as eccentric as his language, but it is unusual in some details, such as the placement of folios (page numbers) in the lower outer corners of the text block, causing at least one cataloguer to call *The Lagday Letter* "unpaged" and at least one reader to wonder at the absence of corresponding footnotes. Indeed, Huntington's pages are always solid blocks with large Morris-like margins and are beautifully printed on fine papers. His use of color is warm and subtle and his arrangement of the typographic decorations striking.

Huntington evokes not Morris but the Cubistic side of Art Deco, with an abstract hint of American Indian motifs. *The Acre of the Earth-Turner* displays a close-set page in the Venetian-style type associated with Kelmscott, influenced by art movements after World War I. The text includes references to contemporary events and people, such as Herbert Hoover, couched in archaic language. These strange combinations, visual and linguistic, are oddly touching, despite the impenetrability of the writing.

ST

1. Louise Farrow Barr, *Presses of Northern California and their Books 1900-1933* (Berkeley: Book Arts Club, University of California, 1934), p. 51.

2. *New York Times*, May 5, 1938, p. 23.

155

The Essay on Nature, by Ralph Waldo Emerson, 1902-1903
Printer: Alwil Shop, Palisades, New York
Designer: Frank B. Rae, Jr.
Black, red, and green inks on white paper
8½ x 5¼ in. (page)
Rare Book and Manuscript Library, Columbia University, New York

Frank B. Rae, Jr., was the first art editor for the Blue Sky Press and produced some of its most appealing designs. He joined the press in 1900 after a brief stay with the Roycrofters in East Aurora, only to leave the Chicago area the same year to settle in Ridgewood, New Jersey, where he founded the Alwil Shop.[1]

One of his outstanding books is Emerson's *Essay on Nature*. Printed on only one side of the sheet, the text is in American Type Founders Jenson, with a red floriated initial at its opening and "Nature" as a running title in red on each page within half borders composed of a branch, rose, and leaves in green. Three-color printing was seldom done during this period and indeed was disdained by many printers as being obtrusively colorful. In this modest format, however, the result is pleasant and unpretentious.

In his own way, Rae attempted to realize some of Morris's ideals that had been neglected by others. For example, in 1901 he wrote: "In book-making, I think that one step in confirming . . . freedom of craftsmanship is to do away,

HAPPY ARE THEY THAT THINK RIGHT THOUGHTS, FOR THEY SHALL FIND THE LIFE THAT IS GOOD AND BEAUTIFUL ⬥ ⬥

HAPPY ARE THEY THAT SPEAK TRUE WORDS, FOR THEY SHALL STAND ERECT IN SPEECH EVEN AS THEY STAND ERECT IN ✳ ✳ THOUGHT ⬥ ⬥ ⬥ ⬥ ⬥

HAPPY ARE THEY THAT DO ✳ THE WORK OF THE HANDS, FOR THEY SHALL LIVE & LOVE THE LAW AND EAT OF THE WHEAT OF THEIR OWN ✳ HARVESTS ⬥ ⬥ ⬥ ⬥ ⬥

THE PAGES OF THE ⬥⬥⬥ ✳✳✳ SIXTEEN SAYINGS

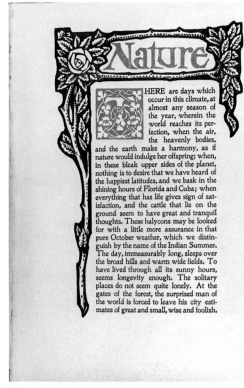
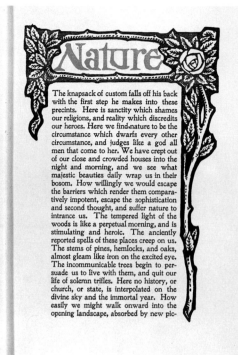

155

so far as may be, with the formality now existing between publisher and patron, to establish a sympathy and friendship between the man who makes and the man who loves beautiful books."[2] To this call for humanizing the book even beyond the work of the artisan, Rae added his own perspective, revering Morris while refusing to imitate his adherence to the fifteenth century: "We have arrived long since at a place where machines would enslave our very souls – true. The hope of the handicrafts is to prove the sullen sameness of products delivered by machine, thus to awaken interest in the truer work – and that is well. But in the fight for better work, more human vital work, it appears to me a defeat of the purpose to cast all the progress of the years to air, and begin in a servile imitating of work now gone and dead."[3]

ST

1. He continued to design for Blue Sky, and two of its proprietors, Noble and Stevens, gave him manuscripts to print. Paul Kruty, "The Blue Sky Press of Hyde Park, 1899-1907," *Chicago History* 11 (Fall - Winter 1982), pp. 146-147.

2. Quoted in Thomas Wood Stevens, *The Unsought Shrine* (Ridgewood: Alwil, 1901).

3. Frank B. Rae, Jr., "Setters of Types," *Impressions Quarterly* 3 (March 1902).

156

Empedocles on Etna: A Dramatic Poem, by Matthew Arnold, 1900
Printer: Thomas Bird Mosher (1852-1923), Portland, Maine
Designer: Thomas Bird Mosher
Black ink on white paper, with hand coloring
8⅝ x 6 in. (page)
Collection of Jean-François Vilain and Roger S. Wieck

For his open flaunting of the International Copyright Law of 1891, passed the same year in which he began publishing, Thomas Bird Mosher was called the "Passionate Pirate."[1] Mosher was fond of contemporary English writers and tended to issue their books without asking permission or paying the royalties called for by the new law, although he did often pay small sums to these authors. The passion came from his overwhelming love of literature and fine printing. His ability to combine the two enthusiasms in a long series of titles published at modest prices is what makes him an enduring figure in the history of American bookmaking. Mosher's small volumes, like those of Elbert Hubbard (see no. 170), sold widely throughout the country, bringing avant-garde ideas and carefully devised formats to many middle-class homes.

In accordance with Mosher's customary choice of Aesthetic writers, his format was not typically in an Arts and Crafts mold. Like many others in the Aesthetic movement, he preferred sixteenth-century Renaissance models, derived from Chiswick Press imprints. His volumes were usually small, with centered title pages, old-style Roman type, a good amount of white space on the page, and Renaissance arabesque-floral decoration used sparingly in headpieces, tailpieces, and an occasional initial. The books were bound in board or flexible covers and printed on imported handmade paper by commercial printers in Portland, Maine, under Mosher's supervision.

Mosher was born in Biddeford, Maine. His father, a sea captain who took his teenage son with him on voyages, insisted that he read only good literature while at sea, so that, despite the lack of much formal education, Mosher grew up with developed literary sensibilities. This taste, though primarily Aesthetic, did not exclude the Arts and Crafts movement. Mosher was fond of William Morris and published many of his writings. At least two of Mosher's books have a Kelmscott design. He issued

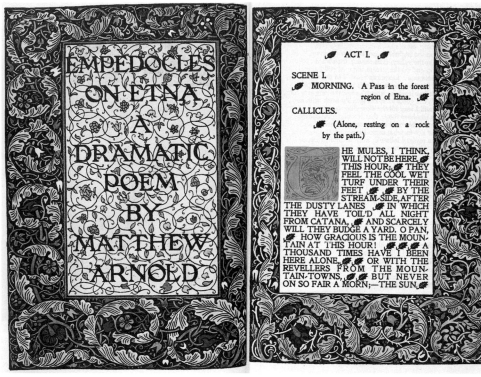

156

157 (color plate, p. 32)
Poster for Bradley His Book, 1896
Printer: Wayside Press, Springfield,
Massachusetts
Artist: Will H. Bradley (1868-1962)
Woodcut: black, red, blue, green, and yellow
inks on white paper
48 x 34 in.
Museum of Fine Arts, Boston. Lee M. Friedman
Fund. 1969 (69.1152)

Will Bradley excelled in two of the genres that
added much color and excitement to the turn
of the century's artistic life. The 1896 poster for
the periodical *Bradley His Book* reflects the contemporary craze for both posters and "little
magazines." Bradley, in fact, owed a good part
of his early fame to the posters he did for Stone
and Kimball's *Chap-Book*, the periodical that
launched the little magazine movement in
1894. The first of Bradley's posters in this journal was "Twins" (May 1894). Criticized for its
draftsmanship and praised for its startling originality, this poster helped to initiate the American poster craze.

In the 1890s, book and periodical publishers
introduced the use of posters for advertising
new titles or issues. Businesses such as bicycle
manufacturers also commissioned posters,
which, like fine prints, were sometimes put out
in limited numbered editions; there were also
magazines devoted entirely to posters. Bradley's interest in the form did not survive the
fashion; the poster for *Bradley his Book* is one of
his last. Yet in the two years of his involvement
with the genre he became "a really considerable figure in the history of the poster."[1] A
typical contemporary comment was: "Bradley's
position in the poster world is a most unique
and interesting one, for he has expressed for
Americans the eccentric phase in modern art of
which [Aubrey] Beardley's work is certainly the
source. Bradley's work has much original flavor,
though he weaves with the same wonderful line
and often uses masses of solid black or white
with telling effect, as does his English
prototype."[2]

So brief were the lives of many little
magazines during the craze that any listing of
new periodicals was out of date by the time of
publication.[3] Stone and Kimball's *Chap-Book*
lasted from 1894 to 1898. It combined avant-
garde content with a format that harked back to
the crude eponymous chap-books carried by
itinerant peddlers in earlier times. Within the

Dante Gabriel Rossetti's *Hand and Soul* in 1899 on
Kelmscott paper, with American Type Founders ornaments and Jenson text. In 1900 he
produced Matthew Arnold's *Empedocles on Etna*
in 450 copies on Kelmscott paper at $2.50 and
in fifty copies on Japan vellum at $5. As with the
Rossetti, initials are in red, a practice abandoned by Morris, and the sheets were dry-
pressed to take out the indentation of the type,
a practice abhorred by Morris. Yet the effect is
convincingly Morrisian. The influence of
Charles Rickett's Vale Press books is also apparent in the use of white space and a scattered leaf
ornament.

The present copy has been colored by hand,
either by a former owner or by a member of a
group such as the Craftsman's Guild, established in Boston in 1900.[2] The fashion of hand
coloring is reminiscent of some of Hubbard's
books. These humble representatives of the
Gothic-revival interest in medieval illumination

are engaging despite their relative simplicity. In
a Mosher book, normally cool and remote, the
color is doubly appealing.

After Mosher's death, his publishing enterprise was continued for a while by his secretary,
Flora Lamb, but without the intensity of its
creator. Mosher had disseminated his books
wider than any private press, while investing in
them a degree of personal conviction no trade
publisher could possibly emulate.

ST

1. Norman H. Strouse, *The Passionate Pirate* (North Hills,
Pa.: Bird and Bull Press, 1964).

2. "A little group of art workers calling itself 'The
Craftsman's Guild,' has recently established a business
home at 21 Cornhill in Boston and is commanding
attention by its efforts toward the revival of the early
book and missal illuminating of the monastic period."
See "The Craftsman's Guild," *Publishers' Weekly* 58 (September 8, 1900), p. 486.

context of the Arts and Crafts movement, this combination hit just the right note. Bradley's own magazine was also fresh in literary and artistic content. *Bradley His Book*, which ran for seven numbers (1896-1897), is perhaps the most brilliantly printed of all the little magazines, utilizing color to an extent and in ways not matched elsewhere. The present poster demonstrates this command of color, depicting a woman resembling those found later in *War is Kind* (see no. 46), with a peacock so fashionable at the time.

ST

1. Bevis Hillier, *Posters* (New York: Stein and Day, 1969), p. 8.

2. Mabel Key, "The Passing of the Poster," *Brush and Pencil* 4 (April 1899), pp. 17-18.

3. See F. W. Faxon, "Ephemeral Bibelots," *Bulletin of Bibliography* 3 (1903), pp. 72-74, 92, 106-107, 124-126.

158

Whiting Paper Company notebook cover, ca. 1895
Artist: Will H. Bradley (1868-1962)
Green, mustard, orange and black on white paper
19⅞ x 9¼ in.
Mark: BRADLEY (printed at upper left)
Private Collection

From the beginning, Will Bradley was involved with both fine book work and with commercial printing. His early advertisements showed even more of a Morris influence than his books. Whereas his floral borders for the title page spread of Richard Doddridge Blackmore's *Fringilla, or Tales in Verse* (Cleveland: Burrows Brothers, 1895) are from Kelmscott, they are almost overpowered by the large black masses and swirling lines of the Beardsleyesque frontispiece and title decoration. In the 1896 prospectus for the periodical *Bradley His Book*, the picture is shrunk so much in relation to the border as to produce a Morrisian air. The same is true of the Whiting Paper Company notebook cover of about 1895.

This piece of printing also shows Bradley's mastery of color. American printers during the eighties had achieved brilliantly colored advertisements under the influence of both the Aesthetic movement and the developing technology of color printing, but never before had American typography seen such powerful effects as in Bradley's work. A contemporary

158

commented: "His card in many colors for the Whiting Paper Company is one of the best – if not the best – thing of the kind he has done . . . these are most skillful and professional decorations, peculiarly subtle and rich. I understand that Mr. Bradley trusts no longer to the ordinary pressman to match the colors in his designs, but now has a $750 press of his own, and sends the printer *proofs in printers' inks* from which to work."[1]

After the turn of the century, Bradley did less book work, but his commercial work gained even more influence with the widespread popularity of the *American Chap-Book*. This periodical, issued in twelve numbers from September 1904 to August 1905, was commissioned by the American Type Founders Company to advertise its own wares to American printers. The issues contained many decorations of Bradley's, which he used lavishly to illustrate his essays on design. By this time his style had become less reminiscent of Morris. Borders are less often used, and the Gothic horror of vacant space has been tempered by a judicious use of tinted papers as background. The Arts and Crafts roots are still evident, however, in the close placement of repeated elements, the heavy, rounded lines, and the general emphasis on decoration and color.

The *American Chap-Book* influenced a whole generation of printers, as did Bradley's work in redesigning periodicals. More than any other artist, he was responsible for bringing the artistic vision of Morris to the grass-roots level. The Kelmscott influence eventually affected not only elite private presses but also metropolitan trade publishers and even some jobbing printers in small towns.

ST

1. [J. M. Bowles], "Echoes," *Modern Art* 4 (Spring 1896), n.p.

III

Spreading the Reform Ideal

Spreading the Crafts: The Role of the Schools

Wendy Kaplan

It was the "most democratic of art movements," the American Civic Association declared in 1906, in the wake of the rapid spread of Arts and Crafts ideals across the country.[1] Americans were subscribing to dozens of periodicals devoted to Arts and Crafts concerns, joining hundreds of Arts and Crafts societies, and taking classes at a bewildering variety of summer schools, night schools, design schools, and settlement houses. They also viewed the works of craftsmen from all over the world at international expositions (see no. 6) and at exhibitions sponsored by societies and schools. These agents of dissemination affected amateurs as well as professionals, consumers and appreciators as well as makers.

After a brief overview of books, periodicals, and Arts and Crafts societies, this essay focuses on the role of education in spreading Arts and Crafts ideology – and practice. Manual training programs in the public schools and the British-inspired methodology taught at American design schools, topics not covered elsewhere in this catalogue, were crucial in shaping an understanding of the crafts among artists, art workers, hobbyists, and the general public.

John Ruskin and William Morris had a wide audience in America; publishers reprinted their books many times, and societies, settlements, and university extension programs offered reading groups devoted to them. Newspapers, libraries, and societies published reading lists to instruct Arts and Crafts enthusiasts as to where they could turn for enlightenment. The American Civic Association's list, issued in 1906, suggested books by or about Morris, among them *Hopes and Fears for Art* and *A Dream of John Ball*; also included was John Ruskin's influential *Stones of Venice*, as were a few studies of the Arts and Crafts movement in America.[2] Reading lists tended to pro-

mote philosophy and ideals of the movement rather than instruction manuals about furnishing one's home. However, books such as Charles Locke Eastlake's *Hints on Household Taste* (1868) were very popular and inspired manufacturers all over the country to adopt rectilinear, Gothic-inspired furniture designs.[3] So prevalent were factory knockoffs, which adapted the style but not the spirit of Eastlake's designs, that in the fourth London edition of the book, the author denounced "American tradesmen [who are] continually advertising what they are pleased to call 'Eastlake' furniture, with the production of which I have had nothing whatever to do, and for the taste of which I should be very sorry to be considered responsible."[4] Eastlake's principles of structural integrity and "honest" construction were still in evidence decades after the publication of his book; for example, Gustav Stickley's use of butterfly joints on the back of a settle of about 1902 (no. 204) can be traced to a design in *Hints on Household Taste* (fig. 1).

Mass communication played an essential role in the transmission of style at the turn of the century. The advent of cheaper printing techniques and especially the development of the halftone (which substantially reduced the cost of illustrations) created a vast new audience for periodicals.[5] Art journals such as *Studio* and *Brush and Pencil* and more general magazines such as *Ladies' Home Journal* and *House and Garden* served as a font of design ideas for architects and craftsmen, and as arbiters of taste for middle-class consumers. The new "shelter" periodicals, especially *House Beautiful* (which declared itself to be the "only magazine in America devoted to Simplicity, Economy, and Appropriateness in the home")[6] and *Bungalow Magazine* (fig. 2), played an important role in promoting the Arts and Crafts ideals of

Fig 1. Design for a dresser, illustrated in Charles Locke Eastlake, *Hints on Household Taste* (London, 1868).

Fig. 2. Cover illustration for *The Bungalow Magazine*, October 1909.

unity of design and vernacular architecture.[7] One of the most successful journals to popularize the philosophy of the movement was the furniture manufacturer Gustav Stickley's *Craftsman* (see pp. 216–218). Stickley's earliest issues were his most idealistic (fig. 3); after the fading of his reformer's zeal – after he stopped touting the socialist message of William Morris – he presented hand-craftsmanship more in terms of individual fulfillment than as a way of altering production methods (fig. 4).

The Arts and Crafts movement was sufficiently established in America by 1904 for an economist to write a detailed account of the revival of handicrafts for the U.S. Bureau of Labor. Max West observed: "There has been in the first place, a rapid organization of arts and crafts societies in the cities, bringing together at meetings and exhibitions the craftsmen in various lines and specimens of their work. . . . [T]he movement has extended to rural communities; arts and crafts societies have been organized even in small villages, and the products of domestic industry are exhibited and sold both at local exhibitions and in the larger exhibitions held in the cities."[8] According to West's broad definition of Arts and Crafts, its components included not only the organizations that went by the name "Society of Arts and Crafts" (which usually offered classes and sold their members' work through exhibitions or permanent salesrooms) but also utopian communities such as Rose Valley and Byrdcliffe as well as social-work activities at Hull House in Chicago and on Indian reservations[9] (see nos. 166, 165, 159, and 160).

Most organizations that called themselves "Arts and Crafts Societies" followed the model established by the society in Boston. Itself patterned upon the Arts and Crafts Exhibition Society in London, the Boston organization initi-

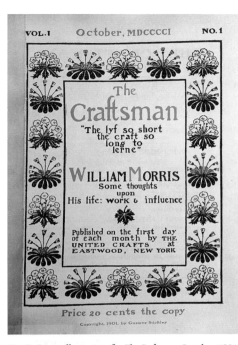

Fig. 3. Cover illustration for *The Craftsman*, October 1901.

Fig. 4. Photographs of amateur work made from Craftsman designs. Illustrated in *The Craftsman*, August 1906.

ated American exhibitions devoted solely to the decorative arts (fig. 5); its "medalist" award was considered one of the highest accolades a craftsman could receive. In order to raise standards as well as to market the products of its members, the Society maintained a salesroom, where objects could be sold only after a jury had found them worthy. Another of its activities was the publication of the influential monthly *Handicraft* (1902-1904),[10] which published essays, book reviews, exhibition announcements, lists of craft services, and quotations from the works of Ruskin, Morris, Ashbee, and Emerson. Its combination of theory, practical information, and exhortation was characteristic of all the crafts magazines at the turn of the century.

The status and financial well-being of the Society, however, was at the expense of some of its original ideals. In the early years a faction led by Arthur Astor Carey (see no. 135) and Mary Ware Dennett was committed to the social ideals of Ruskin and Morris. Mrs. Ware Dennett stated that the "great work to be done [is] the study of the conditions that underlie the production of artistic things," and that the "work of the Society is educational and social first, aesthetic and commercial second."[11] But by 1905 the Society was run more like a business. Led by its president, H. Langford Warren, an architect and Harvard University professor, the membership chose to separate improved standards of craftsmanship from social reform and to remain studiously apolitical. The life of the craftsman would be no concern of theirs; he would be judged solely on the merits of his product. Concluding that "good Art cannot come out of fundamentally bad conditions," Mrs. Ware Dennett resigned from the organization.[12] Her conflict exemplified what many reformers at the time considered

Fig. 5. Interior view of Copley Hall and the display of contemporary handicrafts at the time of the "First Exhibition of the Arts and Crafts," April 5-16, 1897. Archives of the Boston Society of Arts and Crafts, Boston.

to be the failure of the Arts and Crafts movement in both Britain and America. The British journalist A.R. Orage wrote of the division in his own country between the commitment to the ideals of craftsmanship and to the improvement of working conditions: "The traditions' of handicraft have been revived, but nobody who visits the exhibitions of the Arts and Crafts Society in these days [1907] can doubt for an instant that virtue has gone out of the movement. The disappearance of sociological ideas has in fact left the craft ideas of the movement pale and anaemic . . .". What remained was nothing more than a "lamentable series of little Guilds, hole-in-

the-corner institutions, [and] associations for the sale of petty craftwork."[13]

Although Orage's statement was strident and exaggerated, his critique was basically valid. By 1910, the Arts and Crafts movement had lost many of its social ideals (and not all its participants shared them even at the beginning). Because the labor-intensive nature of handwork hindered its competition with factory production, the improvement of the worker's lot through handcraftsmanship could never be attained on a grand scale. The movement, however, could succeed on other levels. Max West considered that perhaps the most far-reaching effect of Arts and

Crafts societies was "not to be in the quantity of handmade goods" but in "the standards of durability and tests set by the craftsmen [that made] their influence felt in improving the quality and design of factory-made goods."[14]

The Arts and Crafts movement affected industrial production most directly through the schools. The Ruskinian ideal of art's uplifting power, combined with the commercial need for skilled designers and craftsmen, produced a system that offered art education on many different levels. There were two basic kinds of programs. One incorporated drawing and handicrafts into the elementary and high school liberal arts curricula. The other aimed to make students at vocational, industrial arts, and design schools into craftsmen and designers who would make American goods competitive with European imports.

Manual training was both a reaction against industrialization and a response to it. Education reformers argued that the development of highly specialized and repetitive activities in factories deprived the worker of joy in labor; handicrafts in the schools would at least give children the pleasure of handcraftsmanship and bring more creativity to their future employment. They would have a better idea of how an object was made and of the design principles behind its construction. Not only would products improve, but children would obtain the moral values associated with handcraftsmanship at the same time they developed skills for future application in industry.

In the years following the Philadelphia Centennial, momentum grew for the establishment of manual arts programs in elementary and high schools. Increased immigration and the advent of compulsory education laws in the 1870s created the need for the kind of school "best suited to develop . . . the mass of our population doing manual labor."[15] According to an article in *International Studio*: "New York was one of the first cities of the United States to introduce the work into the elementary grades. This was done in 1887. By 1890 thirty-seven cities had introduced it. Four years later the number had increased to ninety-five; while ten years later over four hundred counted manual training as part of the regular school work. Now [1909] some form of handwork is to be found nearly everywhere, even in small towns and little country schools."[16]

The purpose of such programs grew out of the Arts and Crafts conviction that working with one's hands at an early age would produce profound spiritual benefits. The American Civic Association and public school officials shared the beliefs of Charles W. Eliot, the president of Harvard University: "The main object in every school should be, not to provide the children with means of earning a livelihood, but to show them how to live a happy and worthy life, inspired by ideals which exalt and dignify both labor and pleasure."[17] Even more explicit about the benefits derived from crafts was a lecture entitled "Possibilities of Manual Training for Moral Ends" given at a conference of school superintendents; it concluded with a quote from Ruskin: "A boy cannot learn to make a straight shaving or drive a fine curve without learning a multitude of other matters which the life of a man could not teach him."[18]

Practical considerations underlay such rhetoric. While few educators believed that public schools should prepare students for actual positions in industry, most maintained that manual training would inculcate the right habits and attitudes toward work. For those fortunate enough not to need industrial employment, exposure to handicrafts would make them more discriminating consumers. They would help to create a market for handcrafted products and select well-made industrial goods over shoddy imitations.

Rich and poor alike could apply the skills acquired in manual training to enhance their own homes. They could stencil their walls, embroider their cushions and hammer out lamps (see nos. 200 and 202). Charles Godfrey Leland, who introduced manual training to the Philadelphia school system and inspired the creation of the British Home Arts and Industries Association, insisted that the "house beautiful" was available to all. Any home could have "Pompeian floors, carved dados, stenciled walls and ceilings, and plain oak furniture, but still artistic, covered with antique patterns, Spanish stamped and gilt leather, at no greater cost than that of wood, leather, stones, and white or colored washes needed."[19]

The overriding theme in all the contemporary literature was utility; the lessons taught at school should be used in the home or for future employment; art should be applied to everyday life. Both public and professional design schools rejected as useless the long tradition of copying the "antique." They replaced copybooks with real models and practice exercises with designs that would actually be executed. "Design for use" was the motto, and the result was an avalanche of student-made furniture, wall hangings, curtains, pillows, bookbindings, picture frames, embroidery, and weavings. *The Craftsman* and other magazines constantly applied William Morris's dictate "Have nothing in your houses that you do not know to be useful, or believe to be beautiful"[20] to the making of objects. As one article asserted: "Manual training should mean the training which will enable one not only to make a well constructed article of practical utility, but also a piece beautiful to look upon."[21]

The Arts and Crafts belief in the dignity of work and joy in labor was closely linked with progressive educational philosophy – with John Dewey's commitment to integration of mind and body, thought and action, classroom and society. The psychologist G. Stanley Hall's recapitulation theory of child development, with its emphasis on children's natural proclivity toward the decorative arts, also fitted well with Arts and Crafts convictions.[22] *The Craftsman, International Studio, Art and Progress, The Chautauquan*, and *Manual Training Magazine* often quoted Dewey's and Hall's ideas. These periodicals condemned "the divorce between the hand and the brain which is destructive of any genuine integral education."[23] The reformers declared that handicraft was to be united with aesthetics, applied with fine arts, and all the arts united with the study of more traditional subjects such as history, literature, and math. Reflecting their idealism, the art historian and educator Florence Levy pronounced: "Art is no longer considered a non-essential 'frill,' but an important method of teaching. It is not 'art for art's sake' merely, but 'art for life's sake.'"[24]

Educators were joined by manufacturers in advocating the establishment of industrial art schools – the former because it would produce better craftsmen and designers; the latter because it would result in more competitive products. The ceramics teacher Charles Binns (no. 177) noted that before such institutions were established "Handicraft and design were divorced, technical instruction was unknown."[25] An article in *Art and Progress* summed up the general lament: "We have trained master mechanics and not master-craftsmen; we have developed artists and not arti-

sans with the result that our manufacturers are lacking in artistic quality and trained workmen in artistic pursuits are foreigners."[26]

Just as the poor quality of British products at the 1851 Crystal Palace Exposition provided the catalyst for the development of the National Art Training Schools, so too, after similar performances at expositions, did Americans demand improved standards of commercial production through education.[27] The establishment of American art museums also followed the English precedent of the South Kensington Museum (renamed the Victoria and Albert Museum in 1899), whose purpose was to provide industrial designers with inspiration from the best objects from the past. The motto on the original seal of the Boston Museum of Fine Arts, "Art/Education/Industry," indicates the seriousness with which museums took the responsibility for improving national design standards. A similar commitment was stated in the charter of the Metropolitan Museum of Art in New York, which referred to one of the museum's functions as the "application of arts to manufacturers and practical life."[28] Henry Watson Kent, appointed supervisor of museum instruction in 1907, later declared that the Metropolitan's programs had "showed that a museum . . . might be a really practical place for the artists and designers of the future to see what others of their various arts and crafts have done and to learn how to make these same things fit into our modern life and needs. . . . This is exactly what Ruskin and William Morris in England wanted, what in the Machine Age people were puzzled about, and what it seemed to some of us a museum of art should teach its public."[29] One such program was an annual exhibition of American industrial art, at which the requirement for objects displayed was

that they be inspired by those in the museum's collections (see no. 132).

The founding of art schools with museum affiliations also followed an English example: the South Kensington Museum's National Schools of Design. "Affording instruction in the Fine Arts" was part of the Boston Museum of Fine Arts charter, and classes were begun six months after the Museum opened in July of 1876.[30] Classes in decorative design began in 1884 and by the turn of the century had acquired an important place in the school's curriculum.

Schools affiliated with art museums, which included training for industrial as well as fine arts careers, opened all over the country. For example, the School of the Art Institute of Chicago was one of the most significant. Louis J. Millet taught decorative design and architecture there from 1891 to 1918 and influenced a generation of craftsmen with his emphasis on improving the design of objects made for everyday use.[31]

Students of industrial art could find numerous other choices for their instruction. The Pratt Institute (founded in 1887) offered courses in metalwork, furniture, design, weaving, and other crafts, as well as in the fine arts; the Massachusetts Normal School specialized in training art teachers; the California College of Arts and Crafts (see no. 175) was devoted solely to the industrial arts. Universities such as Columbia and Syracuse offered industrial art programs in addition to the traditional liberal arts curriculum and universities, in particular, responded to the need for professionally trained ceramists: the programs at the New York State School of Clay-Working and Ceramics at Alfred University and at Newcomb College (see nos. 177, 178, and 179) were among the most renowned.[32]

Most American design schools derived their method of instruction from the approach established by Sir Henry Cole at the National Art Training Schools, which Cole had taken over in 1852 and transferred to South Kensington in 1863. With branches established throughout England, the National Art Training Schools taught that good design was based on the stylization of forms. There were detractors, however, which prompted on both continents a fundamental debate concerning the nature of ornamentation. The battle between the champions of conventionalized versus naturalistic decoration illustrates the great diversity of reform ideals even when consensus existed about what changes were necessary.

Most reformers shared the conviction that objects must be faithful to the material from which they were made, that they should never result from historical copying, and that their decoration must be inspired by nature. Discussing design reformers in an essay of 1878 entitled "The Growth of Conscience in the Decorative Arts," the American architect Henry Van Brunt declared: "They are all arrayed against imitations, against producing in one material forms invented for another, against concealment of devices of construction, in short, against sham work of any kind."[33] The reformers could agree on what was false; the problem arose in determining what was true. They were unified in their belief that nature should be the primary source of design inspiration, but bitterly divided about how nature should be depicted.

The designers Owen Jones and Christopher Dresser, who were associated with the Henry Cole circle, along with Charles Locke Eastlake – a popularizer of the same design principles – were the most influential advocates of conventionalized decoration. In *The Grammar of Ornament* (first published in 1856) Owen Jones listed thirty-seven "propositions"

concerning decoration. One of his major points – "All ornament should be based upon a geometrical construction" – was emphasized by an illustration of several varieties of flowers in plan and elevation.[34] Eastlake summed up the moral basis of conventionalized design in stating: "The art of the decorator is to typify, not represent, the works of nature . . . decorative art is degraded when it passes into a direct imitation of nature."[35] Because the decorator was in effect pretending that, for example, a flower could grow on the leg of a table, such imitations were considered false representation. Three-dimensional designs on wallpapers or carpets were especially insidious since surface coverings are, by nature, two-dimensional.

Just as designers were not to copy nature in exact detail, so too were they forbidden to follow historical precedent absolutely. *The Grammar of Ornament* was a compendium of designs from all over the world (fig. 6), but all were stylized according to Jones's "Propositions." His disciple Christopher Dresser wrote: "I have insisted upon the study of historic ornament as a necessary part of the education of an ornamentalist, but I have not done so with the view of his being enabled thereby to produce an imitation . . . no past style is precisely suited to our wants."[36]

Jones's *Grammar of Ornament* and Dresser's many publications, especially *Principles of Decorative Design* (fig. 7), were as influential in America as they were in Britain. Reprinted many times in both countries, they became standard reference works in design schools and in craftsmen's personal libraries.[37] More than Jones, Dresser became well known through his designs for manufacturers as well as through his writings. Trained as a botanist, he studied the structure of natural forms and translated them into abstract designs that could be taught in

Fig. 6. Plate 4: "Egyptian No. 1.," from Owen Jones, *The Grammar of Ornament* (London, 1856).

schools and were adaptable to industrial production as well.

The facility with which conventionalized design could be rendered indicates the economic motivation behind the reformers' moral indignation. As suggested earlier, Henry Cole took over the Schools of Art and founded a Department of Practical Arts in response to Britain's poor showing at the Crystal Palace exposition; schools that would produce competent industrial designers were considered the necessary antidote to the superiority of European, and particularly French, imports. Since French designs were naturalistic, it suited the needs of manufacturers very well if conventionalized designs, whose geometric forms were far better suited to machine production, were also considered aes-

Fig. 7. Stylized ornamentation from Christopher Dresser, *Principles of Decorative Design* (London, Paris, and New York, 1873).

thetically preferable to naturalistic decoration.[38]

Insistent that art must be transcribed literally from nature, John Ruskin led the opposition to conventionalized ornamentation. He despised South Kensington because he believed that in the very establishment of departments such as Practical Arts lay an immoral separation of the decorative and the fine arts. Rather than unite the arts, Ruskin saw coursework in rules for decoration as further isolating the applied from the fine arts. He decried the attempts to wed art and industry as ignoble materialism, stating: "The tap root of all this mischief is in the endeavour to make money by designing for manufacture. No student who makes this his primary objective will be able to design at all; and the very words 'School of Design' involve the profoundest of art fallacies.

Drawing may be taught by tutors, but Design only by Heaven; and to every scholar who thinks to sell his inspiration, Heaven refuses his help."[39]

Ruskin rejected the Cole circle's method of instruction for the same reason that he rejected classical art – both resulted in a rigidity and a standardization that deadened human creativity. In a collection of lectures entitled *The Two Paths* (1859), the only book Ruskin devoted solely to the decorative arts, he railed against ornamentalists who "endeavor to substitute mathematical proportions for the knowledge of life they do not possess and the representation of life of which they are incapable."[40] The consequences of following stylization in preference to naturalism were made clear in the first lecture, "The Deteriorative Power of Conventional Art Over Nature." Since "the people who practice it are cut off from all possible sources of healthy knowledge or natural delight," conventionalized decoration "is destructive of whatever is best and noblest in humanity."[41]

Jones, Dresser, and Ruskin all believed that art had a moral power and a moral responsibility. Ruskin, however, saw deviation from recording the direct observation of nature as a violation of truth; whereas Jones and Dresser, in their belief that geometry was the fundamental law of nature, saw a greater truth in stylization. While Ruskin's point of view was extremely influential in America, it was the principles of South Kensington that were followed in American design schools.

In 1871 the city of Boston hired Walter Smith to be both director of drawing instruction for the city and state director of art education. Then headmaster of the government design school in Leeds, Smith had been recommended for the position in Massachusetts by his former teacher Sir Henry Cole.[42] By establishing

a curriculum for teacher training at the Massachusetts Normal School of Art, Smith spread South Kensington methodology throughout America. Other programs he introduced – exhibitions of both student and professional work, free night schools for adults, and drawing classes in public schools – were adapted by many states.[43]

In addition to English reform principles and economic expediency, the influence of Japanese art was the third important factor behind the emergence of conventionalized design in American schools. Christopher Dresser openly acknowledged his debt to the Orient; the transmission of the Japanese aesthetic to England and America is evident in a lecture Dresser gave at the Philadelphia Centennial in which he praised a robe he had viewed "in the Japanese court of the Vienna Exhibition" as "the finest dress that I have ever seen. The pattern . . . consisted of many colored flowers. . . . The flowers were not foreshortened or shaded, but were treated as flat surface . . . no merely imitative treatment of flowers could possibly have conveyed the thought of summer so well as this conventional treatment did."[44]

A great champion of Japanese design principles, Arthur Wesley Dow was one of the most influential teachers in America at the turn of the century (see no. 172). Former curator of Japanese Art at the Museum of Fine Arts in Boston, an instructor at the Pratt Institute in Brooklyn, and a noted painter, Dow was appointed director of fine arts at Teachers College, Columbia University, in 1904. The Japanese had been the greatest inspiration in his work and he believed their aesthetic of "rhythm and harmony, in which modeling and nature-imitation are subordinate"[45] was the fundamental principle behind all good art.

While Ruskin had maintained that stylization would separate the fine arts

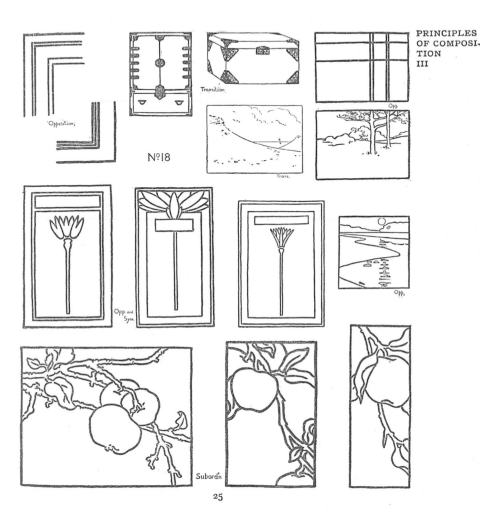

PRINCIPLES
OF COMPOSI·
TION
III

Fig. 8. Page from Arthur Wesley Dow, Composition: *A Series of Exercises in Art Structure for the Use of Students and Teachers* (New York, 1899).

from the decorative arts by establishing a different set of standards for the latter, Dow argued the opposite position – that abstraction was most appropriate not only for decorative arts but for the fine arts as well. In his book *Composition* (fig. 8), Dow asserted that the basic elements of design were line, color, and *notan* (the Japanese term for the arrangement of dark and light). He further refined his definition by including the concepts of opposition, transition, subordination, repetition, and symmetry.[46] Dow believed that just as in painting, true creativity in the production of pottery, furniture, weaving, or prints would emerge after mastering the principles of composition, not from literal representation.

Students and teachers from all over the country came to study with Dow and returned to spread his design philosophy at their own institutions. For example, Mary Sheerer, who taught decoration at the Newcomb College pottery (see no. 179), studied with Dow at his summer school in Ipswich; Isabelle Percy West took Dow's precepts to the California College of Arts and Crafts (see no. 175). She later recounted: "Art schools then taught only drawing, painting and sculpture in a dry, academic way. When I heard of Mr. Dow's work in design and composition I knew that was exactly what I wanted. Mr. Meyer and Mr. Nahl explained their exciting plans for a new kind of art school and asked me if I would teach the course I was taking in design and composition after my graduation. Of course I was flattered and delighted for, like all his students, I was thrilled with Mr. Dow's approach and eager to share all I'd learned."[47]

The relationship between education and the Arts and Crafts movement has been subject to debate, with some historians maintaining that reforms in education constituted a different reaction to industrialization.[48] Considering the British system, this distinction has some validity, but in America educational reform and the crafts were integrally linked, especially through manual training programs. American teachers incorporated Arts and Crafts rhetoric about unity of design and joy in labor, and piously invoked the twin gods of Ruskin and Morris.

The training of the handcraftsmen and that of the industrial designer were not seen as diametrically opposed; Americans were less ambivalent than the English about the relationship between craft and industry. Even in England, Walter Crane quoted approvingly a trade journal opinion that "the arts and crafts movement has been the best influence upon machine industry during the past ten years."[49] Americans took to heart Crane's goal that the role of design schools was to "turn our artists into manufacturers and our manufacturers into artists."[50] Thus, educators saw no contradiction between championing both the handcrafted and the improvement of the mass-produced; the latter could also find a place in the Arts and Crafts movement.

1. Mrs. M.F. Johnson, "Arts and Crafts," Leaflet No. 10, Department Pamphlet No. 4-I, American Civic Association, Department of Arts and Crafts, 1906, p. 1 (from files at the Art Association of Richmond, Indiana).

2. Ibid., p. 3.

3. First published in England in 1868, *Hints on Household Taste* appeared in seven American editions between 1872 and 1883.

4. Quoted in Simon Jervis, "Eastlake, Charles Locke" in *The Penguin Dictionary of Design and Designers* (Harmondsworth [U.K.] and New York: Penguin, 1984), p. 169.

5. Frank Luther Mott, *A History of American Magazines*, vol. 4 (Cambridge: Harvard University Press, 1957), p. 3.

6. Ibid., vol. 5, p. 155.

7. Mary Corbin Sies, "The Shelter Magazine and Standards of American Domestic Architectural Taste in the East and Midwest, 1897-1917," unpublished paper presented to the Ninth Biennial Convention, American Studies Association, Philadelphia, November 1983. See also idem, "American Country House Architecture in Context: The Suburban Ideal of Living in the East and Midwest: 1877-1917" (Ph.D. diss., University of Michigan, Ann Arbor, 1987).

8. Max West, "The Revival of Handicraft in America," U.S. Bureau of Labor, *Bulletin* 55 (November 1904), pp. 1597-1598.

9. Ibid., pp. 1601, 1616-1617, and 1619-1621.

10. For an excellent account of the Boston Society of Arts and Crafts as well as other societies, see Eileen Boris, *Art and Labor: Ruskin, Morris, and the Craftsman Ideal in America* (Philadelphia: Temple University Press, 1986), pp. 32-52. The most comprehensive account is Beverly Kay Brandt, "Mutually Helpful Relations: Architects, Craftsmen and the Society of Arts and Crafts, Boston" (Ph.D. diss., Boston University, 1985).

11. Quoted in Brandt 1985, pp. 199 and 201.

12. Ibid., p. 200.

13. A.R. Orage, "Politics for Craftsmen," *Contemporary Review* 91 (June 1907), pp. 783, 787.

14. West 1904, p. 1622. For the development of mass production, see David Hounshell, *From the American System to Mass Production, 1800-1932* (Baltimore: Johns Hopkins University Press, 1984).

15. Florence N. Levy, "Craft Classes in the Public Schools," *International Studio* 35 (October 1908), p. 121.

16. "Manual Art in Elementary Schools," *International Studio* 38 (April 1909), p. 74.

17. Quoted in Johnson 1906, p. 5.

18. Quoted in R. Charles Bates, "Possibilities of Manual Training for Moral Ends," speech summarized in *Manual Training Magazine* 11 (April 1901), pp. 169-170.

19. Quoted in Boris 1986, p. 84. Boris's chapter 5, "Schooling Taste" (pp. 82-98), provides an outstanding analysis of manual training in public·schools.

20. Quoted in *William Morris & Kelmscott* (London: Design Council, 1981), p. 85.

21. Jacob I. Milsner, "Craftsmanship in the New York Schools," *Craftsman* 5 (December 1903), pp. 305-306. For more about the rejection of the antique, see Emil Larch, "New Departure in Study of Architectural Design," *Brush and Pencil* 8 (August 1901), pp. 253-254.

22. For Dewey's educational theories, see John Dewey, *The School and Society* (New York: McClure, Phillips & Co., 1900). Concerning Hall, see Boris 1986, p. 84.

23. Oscar Lovell Triggs, "A School of Industrial Art," *Craftsman* 3 (January 1903), p. 216.

24. Florence N. Levy, "Art Education in the Elementary Public Schools of New York," *Art and Progress* 1 (February 1910), p. 121.

25. Charles Binns, "Education in Clay," *Craftsman* 4 (June 1903), p. 160.

26. "Industrial Art," *Art and Progress* 4 (January 1913), p. 840.

27. As Florence Levy pointed out, "The Centennial at Philadelphia in 1876 and subsequent expositions were of the greatest service in raising standards of public taste." See Levy 1910, p. 119.

28. Henry Watson Kent, *What I Am Pleased to Call My Education* (New York: Grolier Club, 1949), p. 153.

29. Ibid., pp. 158-159.

30. H. Winthrop Peirce, *History of the School of the Museum of Fine Arts, Boston* (Boston: Museum of Fine Arts, 1930), p. 68. See also Walter Muir Whitehill, *Museum of Fine Arts, Boston: A Centennial History*, vol. 1 (Cambridge: Harvard University Press, 1970).

31. Sharon S. Darling, *Chicago Metalsmiths* (Chicago: Chicago Historical Society, 1977), pp. 38-39.

32. The variety of options for manual and industrial arts training in New York alone is demonstrated by a list of schools compiled in Coy L. Ludwig, *The Arts and Crafts Movement in New York State* (Hamilton, N.Y.: Gallery Association of New York State, 1983), pp. 24-25.

33. William A. Coles, ed., *Architecture and Society: Selected Essays of Henry Van Brunt* (Cambridge: Harvard University Press, 1969), p. 116.

34. Owen Jones, *The Grammar of Ornament* (London: Day and Son, 1856), p. 5.

35. Charles Locke Eastlake, *Hints on Household Taste* (New York: Dover Publications, 1969; reprint of 1878 edition, first published 1868), p. 132.

36. Christopher Dresser, *Studies in Design* (London: Cassell, Petter, Galpin, 1876), p. 13.

37. For example, Jones's *Grammar of Ornament* and Dresser's *Art of Decorative Design* were in the library of the silversmith Arthur Stone (see nos. 143-145), as were books by Ruskin and A.W.N. Pugin. The books from Arthur Stone's library are now at the Museum of Fine Arts, Boston.

38. For an excellent analysis of the economic factors behind design reform as well as the conventionalized versus naturalistic controversy, see Catherine Lynn, "Decorating Surfaces: Aesthetic Delight, Theoretical

Dilemma" in Doreen Bolger Burke et al., In Pursuit of Beauty: America and the Aesthetic Movement (New York: Metropolitan Museum of Art and Rizzoli, 1986).

39. Quoted in Gillian Naylor, The Arts and Crafts Movement (London: Studio Vista Publishers, 1971), p. 22.

40. John Ruskin, The Two Paths, Being Lectures on Art and Its Application to Decoration and Manufacture, vol. 10 of Works of John Ruskin (Kent [U.K.]: George Allen, 1884, first published 1859), pp. 22-23. The Two Paths was reprinted nineteen times in America between 1859 and 1892.

41. Ibid., pp. 10, 13.

42. For an extended discussion of Smith, see Diane Korzenik, Drawn to Art: A Nineteenth Century American Dream (Hanover, N.H., and London: University Press of New England, 1985), pp. 154-161.

43. Boris 1986, pp. 83-84.

44. Christopher Dresser, "Art Industries," Penn Monthly 8 (January 1877), pp. 21-22.

45. Arthur Wesley Dow, Composition: A Series of Exercises in Art Structure for the Use of Students and Teachers (New York: Doubleday, Page, 1913; first published in 1899 under the title Composition: A Series of Exercises Selected from a New System of Art Education.), p. 76.

46. Frederick C. Moffatt, Arthur Wesley Dow (1857-1922) (Washington, D.C.: National Collection of Fine Arts, Smithsonian Institution, 1977), p. 84.

47. James Schevill, "The Early Years," California College of Arts and Crafts Newsletter, Winter 1965, p. 2.

48. Peter Stansky, Redesigning the World: William Morris, the 1880's and the Arts and Crafts, (Princeton: Princeton University Press, 1985), pp. 24, 25-29. Concerning the same subject, Alan Crawford wrote: "Unlike the rationalist designers of the mid-nineteenth century, such as Owen Jones, Arts and Craftsmen set great store by the quality of direct observation, and tried to render nature recognisably, not as some notional geometric essence." See Alan Crawford, ed., By Hammer and Hand: The Arts and Crafts Movement in Birmingham (Birmingham [U.K.]: Birmingham Museums and Art Gallery, 1984), p. 15.

49. Walter Crane, Ideals in Art (London: G. Bell and Sons, 1905), p. 30.

50. Quoted in Isabelle Anscombe and Charlotte Gere, Arts and Crafts in Britain and America (New York: Rizzoli, 1978), p. 64.

159

Paradise Lost, by John Milton, 1902
Printer: Doves Press, Hammersmith, England
Designer of binding: Ellen Gates Starr (1859-1940)
H: 9⁷⁄₁₆ in. W: 6¹³⁄₁₆ in. D: 1⁷⁄₁₆ in.
Marks: signed and dated E G S 1905
The University of Chicago Library. Gift of Helen Gunsaulus.

The bibliophile and publisher W. Irving Way pointed out that American women were not as quick as their European counterparts to take up hand bookbinding.[1] By the late nineties, however, a movement was taking shape; and by 1910, many women had enrolled in training courses, not just in metropolitan centers but also in smaller cities and even by correspondence.

The earlier movement in England, though beset by difficulties, had been even stronger: "It is evident that by 1900 bookbinding was widely accepted as a craft for women, and that many were actively involved in it."[2] The rise of the movement there was attributable in part to Thomas James Cobden-Sanderson's revival of hand binding. As the story goes, when he once wondered aloud what craft he could take up, Jane Morris suggested bookbinding. The Doves Bindery, which Cobden-Sanderson subsequently established, became renowned for the novelty of designs that swept aside the cobwebs of historicism. He went on to found the equally famous Doves Press, but his influence on binding, spread by his students as well as his admirers, did not diminish.

One of these students was an American woman, Ellen Gates Starr, who became one of the luminaries of turn-of-the-century American binding. After an early career as a teacher, Miss Starr helped in 1889 to found Hull House in Chicago with her friend Jane Addams. Her subsequent years of lecturing on art did not satisfy her, and in 1897 she went to England, where she served for over a year as an apprentice to Cobden-Sanderson. She is quoted as saying, "I began to feel that it was not enough to talk about and explain beautiful and well-made things which have been done long ago, and that it would be a great deal better to make something myself, ever so little, thoroughly well, and beautiful of its kind."[3] Returning to Hull House, she set up a bindery, trained apprentices of her own, bound books on commission, and dis-

159

played widely at Arts and Crafts exhibitions all over the country.

Miss Starr's Paradise Lost, an early effort, is not particularly reminiscent of Cobden-Sanderson. Its design is more elaborate than her later products. She stresses visual allusions to the text, as: "it must be felt that an indisputable appropriateness – and that not the servile grouping of self-evident similars which led Morris to damn all mere appropriateness – is implicit in the use of clover leaves and blossoms for the simple pastoral of 'Daphnis and Chloe,' the passion-flower and its vine for 'In Memoriam,' the lily and its bending bud and stalk for 'The Idylls of the King,' and the oak leaves and acorns for the 'Life of Abraham Lincoln.'"[4] The stylized ovate leafage of her Paradise Lost may represent Milton's Tree of Life or Tree of Knowledge, or simply the Garden of Eden.

> Laurel and Mirtle, and what higher grew
> Of firm and fragrant leaf; on either side
> Acanthus, and each odorous bushie shrub
> Fenc'd up the verdant wall; each beauteous flower,
> Iris all hues, Roses, and gessamin
> Rear'd high this Flourisht heads between.
> (Book IV)

Like so many other artists who started out in the Arts and Crafts period, Ellen Gates Starr absorbed the exuberance of the time into her early work, only to assume later a more restrained and perhaps less interesting classicism. She lived to regret having become a binder, for the selling of her books to the rich as luxury items betrayed her socialist ideals, but she was a leading pioneer in a craft that itself pioneered the advancement of employment for women.

ST

1. W. Irving Way, "Women and Bookbinding Again," *House Beautiful* 3 (February 1898), pp. 76-81.
2. Anthea Callen, *Women Artists of the Arts & Crafts Movement, 1870-1914* (New York: Pantheon, 1979), p. 196.
3. Quoted in Wallace Rice, "Miss Starr's Bookbinding," *House Beautiful* 12 (June 1902), p. 13.
4. Rice 1902, p. 14.

160
Table mat, ca. 1905
Sybil Carter Indian Lace Association
Made at an Indian reservation, Oneida, Wisconsin
Linen bobbin-made lace on linen plain weave; two rows of deflected-element embroidery
L: 12 ½ in. W: 17 ¼ in.
Cooper-Hewitt Museum, the Smithsonian Institution's National Museum of Design, New York. Gift of Mrs. Bayard Cutting in memory of Miss Mary Parsons. 1943-44-4

Sybil Carter (died 1908), a missionary with the Protestant Episcopal Church, introduced lacemaking classes for the Ojibwa Indians on the White Earth Reservation in Minnesota in 1890.[1] Unlike others whose purpose was to preserve a native American craft, her concerns were to provide an economically disadvantaged group with manual skills and to create a marketable product. She offered patterns as well as lessons in technique and in 1904 the Sybil Carter Indian Lace Association was formed.[2] Providing teachers' salaries and raw materials for the workers and handling the marketing of the finished articles, the Association sold laces and embroideries at their small shop in New York and held prestigious annual sales in private houses there and in Boston, Pittsburgh, and Philadelphia. At one such sale in the home of Mrs. Bayard Cutting in 1904, every piece was sold, with receipts totaling $1,000 and orders

160

were taken for another $1,200 worth of laces and embroideries.[3]

Patterns provided by the Association were usually adaptations of seventeenth-century Italian models, many of them resulting in altar or communion cloths commissioned for use in churches. The Indian origin of the laces is only occasionally apparent in pieces that incorporate into the design squaws with papooses, hunting braves, teepees, and canoes.

Needlework produced by the Sybil Carter Indian Lace Association was exhibited frequently in this country and in Europe, and won gold medals at the 1900 Paris International Exhibition, the 1901 Pan-American Exposition (in Buffalo, New York), the 1905 Exposition Universelle (in Liège, Belgium), and the 1906 International Exhibition in Milan. A Grand Prize was awarded at the Louisana Purchase Exposition of 1904 and the Highest Award was conferred at the Australia Exhibition of Women's Work in 1907.

GM

1. On the reservations, interest in lacemaking expanded and by 1908 there were several hundred lacemakers in the United States who were members of the Sioux, Seneca, Onondaga, Oneida, Piute, and Hopi tribes, in addition to the Ojibwa.
2. Although Sybil Carter died in 1908, the association bearing her name continued to function for almost twenty years more until it was dissolved in 1926. For further discussion of the association, see Kate C. Duncan, "American Indian Lace Making," *American Indian Art Magazine* 5 (May 1980), pp. 28-35.
3. See handwritten note on printed invitation in the Cooper-Hewitt textile department research file.

161
Coverlet, 1920-1930
Berea Fireside Industries, Berea, Kentucky
"Overshot" (cotton plain weave with continuous supplementary wool weft)
L: (of warp) 109 in. W: (of weft; two loom widths sewn together) 69 in.
Berea College Appalachian Museum, Berea, Kentucky

161

Berea College was established as a free school in an area of economic hardship in rural Kentucky. In 1893 a recently appointed president, Dr. William Frost, became aware of traditional bedcovers used in local mountain cabins and recognized their appeal, especially for people in the northern states, where the Industrial Revolution had broken the handweaving tradition.[1] Since devotées of the Arts and Crafts movement preferred textiles woven at home or as part of a cottage industry, Dr. Frost often took old coverlets with him on trips to attract funding and publicity for the college. To assure a continuing supply of new coverlets for Berea's marketing objectives, however, it was necesssary to improve the skills of the mountain people, whose facility had declined;[2] coverlets (or "kivers," in the vernacular) failed to match properly when two narrow-width loom lengths were seamed together. Within a few years, students' families responded to the idea of weaving coverlets in order to earn money for education, and a program known as the Fireside Industries of Berea was set up with woodworking and other handcrafts included as well as weaving.[3]

The design of this "overshot" coverlet, identified as "Lover's Knot" by the Appalachian Museum, is one of many patterns varied by changes in the threading or treadling procedures. It was woven with a white cotton plain weave and a deep-blue supplementary weft for the overshot. All four edges were turned under and hemmed.

GM

1. Descendants of Celtic and Saxon immigrants in Appalachia were said to have passed on weaving skills in an unbroken line from generation to generation. See the following articles in *House Beautiful*: Katherine Louise Smith, "A Mountain Fireside Industry" (May 1902), pp. 406-409; Mabel Tuke Priestman, "Coverlet Weaving in the South" (January 1907), pp. 256-257; Frances Harper "A Penelope of the Carolina Mountains" (May 1917), pp. 385 and 412.

2. Smith 1902, pp. 406-409.

3. For further discussion of weaving in the southern mountains, see Allen Eaton, *Handicrafts of the Southern Highlands* (New York: Russell Sage Foundation, 1937).

162

Chalice veil, ca. 1915
Scuola d'Industrie Italiane, New York
Linen embroidery on linen plain weave; cut-
work, withdrawn-element work, and deflected-
element work
L: 23 ½ in. W: 23 ½ in.
Cooper-Hewitt Museum, the Smithsonian Insti-
tution's National Museum of Design, New York.
Gift of Scuola d'Industrie Italiane through Mrs.
Gino Speranzo. 1943-41-1A

One of the phenomena associated with the
international Arts and Crafts movement was the
establishment of needlework and craft schools
under the patronage of wealthy and influential
people. This seemed to occur most frequently
in Italy, which in turn influenced the schools of
other countries. The goal of the Scuola
d'Industrie Italiane (School of Italian Work) on
Macdougal Street in New York was "to improve
the condition of Italian immigrant women and
their Italian-American daughters and to encourage the manufacture of old-time laces and
embroideries."[1]

The New York school was based on the
model of the Industrie Femminile Italiane (Italian Women's Work), which had spread successfully throughout Italy. Carolina Amari, a Florentine involved in several aspects of the work in
Italy, was invited to New York in 1905 to organize the classes. The assortment of patterns she
brought, both new and antique, were copied to
serve as guides for the students. They used
openwork embroidery techniques to make a
variety of domestic as well as ecclesiastic linens;
their works were on display in the 1906 Milan
International Exhibition (unfortunately, these
were among the numerous pieces destroyed by
fire) and, the following year, at the Society of
Arts and Crafts in Boston. The Needle and
Bobbin Club, a New York club of collectors and
connoisseurs, featured an advertisement for the
school in its first bulletin, published in 1916.[2]
The notice, always the upper left quarter page at
the front of the magazine, appeared in each
issue thereafter until 1926.[3] Ironically, 1926 was
the year the Sybil Carter Indian Lace Association disbanded and the Society of Blue and
White Needlework of Deerfield ceased
production.

This chalice veil – a faithful copy of an antique piece in the Metropolitan Museum of Art
in New York – is worked with a design of open
crosses alternating with shields; the crosses are

in withdrawn-element work, the shields in cut-
work with needle-made fillings of looping, and
the inner borders are in deflected-element
work. The veil is part of a set of linen that
includes a caporal, a bourse and an altar cover.

GM

1. Eva Lovett, "An Italian Lace School in New York,"
International Studio 29 (July 1906), p. xii.
2. *Bulletin of the Needle and Bobbin Club* 1 (December
1916), p. ii.
3. During those ten years the address of the school
changed four times: from Macdougal Street to King
Street in 1919, to a room number in the Anderson
Galleries in 1923, and finally to an address on East 54th
Street in 1925.

163

Covered vase, 1913-1916
Arequipa Pottery (1911-1918), Fairfax,
California
Buff earthenware, wheel-thrown with excised
and pierced decoration, covered with medium-
green glossy glaze
H: (with cover) 16¼ in. Diam: 11¹³⁄₁₆ in.
Marks: incised *Arequipa/California/J.J.x.x.* (on
bottom)
Label: *AREQUIPA/CALIFORNIA* in banner across
stylized tree next to vase (on paper under
cover)
National Museum of American History, Smithsonian Institution, Gift of Eri and Phyllis Richardson. 1982.806.1

The Arequipa Pottery was founded in 1911 on
the model established by the Marblehead Pottery (see no. 115).[1] Dr. Philip King Brown saw it
as a way to provide craft therapy for his patients
recuperating from the early stages of tuberculosis; sale of the pottery would help finance their
hospitalization at the Arequipa Sanatorium. At
both Marblehead and Arequipa the pottery was
first instituted as adjunct to a medical facility
and then divorced from it financially early on,
but similarities end here. The Marblehead Pottery was organized to include a small regular
work force. At Arequipa, however, the majority
of the decorators were patients for whom the
average length of convalescence was only four
or five months, so few could produce consistently good work over a long period of time.
Similarly, Arthur Baggs (see no. 116) managed
the operation at Marblehead during its entire
thirty-two-year lifetime, while at Arequipa man-

agers changed often. Whereas Baggs could provide stable long-term planning and a product
with a consistent style, each of the managers at
Arequipa left his own imprint in terms of technology and style.

Frederick Hurten Rhead (see nos. 183 and
191), the first pottery director, developed the
use of local clays and introduced glazes and
decorative techniques he had perfected at the
Avon and Weller potteries in Ohio. Although
the activities of pottery decoration were undoubtedly healing for the patients,[2] the financial success necessary to continue the artistic
work was less assured. Rhead found it difficult
to get ceramics into production at the same
time that the organization was struggling to
separate the commercial pottery from the sanatorium, and he left in July 1913.

Albert L. Solon, the second director, came to
Fairfax with credentials as impressive as
Rhead's. His upbringing in a family of English
potters, training at the Victoria Institute, apprenticeship in an English tile factory, and tenure as a chemist in the southern California
clayworking industry prepared him for the difficult tasks at Arequipa. Solon continued to experiment with materials and techniques that
could be developed commercially by an ever-
changing staff of decorators of uneven talent.
Whereas Rhead had concentrated on matte
glazes and raised "squeeze-bag" decoration,
Solon chose glossy glazes and carved decoration. The covered vase shown here is a good
example of the materials, techniques, and
mode of operation instituted by Solon: a
predominantly local clay body was thrown by
an experienced potter, motifs in a Moorish
style designed by a professional artist (perhaps
Solon himself) were carved into the damp clay
surface (probably by one of the more accomplished convalescents), and the piece was covered with a brilliant monochromatic glaze. In
addition to improving internal operations, Solon opened new markets by experimenting
with tile production. His display of pottery for
the 1915 Panama-Pacific Exposition, which included the opportunity to watch the convalescents at work, won a Gold Medal.

When Solon left in the spring of 1916 to teach
in San Jose, Fred H. Wilde, also trained in the
English tile industry, took over the operation.
Under his direction the technology and markets for tiles were developed further and the
pottery's translations of Spanish designs be-

163

came popular with home builders. Economic difficulties during the first World War, however, forced the Arequipa Pottery to close in 1918, whereas the sanatorium continued until 1957.

EPD and BRD

1. For information about the Arequipa Pottery, see Paul Evans, *Art Pottery of the United States: An Encyclopedia of Producers and Their Marks* (New York: Charles Scribner's Sons, 1974), pp. 17-21; Robert W. Blasberg, "Arequipa Pottery," *Western Collector* 6 (October 1968), pp. 7-10; and Hazel V. Bray, *The Potter's Art in California, 1885-1955* (Oakland: Oakland Museum, 1980), pp. 13-14.

2. Eloise Roorbach, "Art as a Tonic," *Craftsman* 24 (June 1913), pp. 343-346.

164 (color plate, p. 33)
Vase, 1915
Paul Revere Pottery (1911-1942) of the Saturday Evening Girls' Club, Boston/Brighton, Massachusetts
Decorator: Sarah Gelner (1894-1982)
Buff earthenware, wheel-thrown with incised irises in purples, blues, and greens against dark-blue sunset sky on pale yellow ground
H: 8¾ in. Diam: 7½ in.
Marks: painted S E G/JUNE 8, 1915 with artist's initials *SG* in vertical broken rectangle below (on bottom)
Collection of Marilee B. Meyer

In 1899, Mrs. James J. Storrow, a member of the board of managers of the North Bennett Industrial School, became interested in a group for high-school-age girls who met at the North End Branch of the Boston Public Library on Saturday evenings for lectures, readings, music, dance, and crafts. The library provided such cultural activities to benefit the Italian and Jewish girls of poor immigrant families in this neighborhood near the Old North Church. Dues were "paid in time . . . one hour's service per week from each of its members . . ."[1]

At the suggestion of Edith Guerrier, librarian at the North End Branch and supervisor of the Saturday Evening Girls' Club, and her friend Edith Brown, a pottery was established in 1907. Girls who worked there earned extra money for schooling; some were preparing to make the potter's craft a life's work. In 1912, Mrs. Storrow purchased a house at 18 Hull Street in Boston, where their wares were sold from "The Bowl Shop" of the Paul Revere Pottery. These small quarters were abandoned in 1915, when Mrs.

Storrow built a pottery on Nottingham Road in Brighton, designed by Edith Brown to look like an English country house, surrounded by green lawns, flower beds, and oak trees. Inside, in the workrooms, someone would read aloud to the girls every afternoon as they worked along with a small staff: potter, designer, kilnman, and assistant. Although more than 200 girls were employed in the pottery over the years, only fifteen to twenty were in the shops at any one time. Sarah Gelner, who worked on and off in both Boston and Brighton from 1910 or 1911 until her marriage in 1921, specialized in designs with flowers such as the present example in blues and greens. Because her family was poor she often gave her pottery as gifts to friends and relatives.[2]

Prices for the breakfast, tea, and table sets, vases, tiles, mugs, salt and pepper shakers, milk pitchers, honey pots, lamps, desks sets, and toilet sets for children's use were expensive compared to industrially mass-produced wares, but as Edith Brown affirmed, "there are plenty of people in this country who prefer an article made under the right conditions, and who, therefore, will pay the price such conditions necessitate."[3] Never a profitable operation, the Paul Revere Pottery was nonetheless a successful social experiment. Mrs. Storrow subsidized the project until it closed in 1942, two years before her death.[4]

EPD and BRD

1. Margaret Pendleton, "Paul Revere Pottery," House Beautiful 32 (January 1912), p. 74.

2. Information about Sarah Gelner was kindly provided by her daughter, Barbara Rimer.

3. Pendleton 1912, p. 74. According to this source: "Nothing could be more appropriate for the breakfast table for a country house or bungalow, when the dining-room is finished and furnished in oak, than pieces made up from this pottery."

4. As part of her goal to provide the decorators with a healthy, balanced alternative to the factory, Mrs. Storrow also donated the use of a summer camp in Gloucester.

165 (color plate, p. 34)
Linen press cabinet, ca. 1904
Byrdcliffe Colony, Woodstock, New York
Panel designer: Zulma Steele
Oak with tulip poplar panels; brass hardware
H: 55 in. W: 41 in. D: 18 ¾ in.
Marks: *Byrdcliffe* and 1904 within octagon encircling stylized lily burned into panel
Collection of Mr. and Mrs. Mark Willcox

In 1902 Ralph Radcliffe Whitehead (1854-1929), heir of a wealthy British industrialist, founded the Byrdcliffe Colony as a place where like-minded individuals could escape "the slavery of our too artificial and too complex life, to return to some way of living which requires less of material apparatus."[1] With Hervey White, a writer and socialist, and Bolton Brown, a painter and professor of art at Stanford University, Whitehead hoped to establish a community of independent craftsmen in the natural, healthful, and inspirational surroundings of the countryside. Although the ideal of cooperation and shared goals was encouraged at the colony, Whitehead was very selective about the craftsmen who should participate in the community's activities. He could exercise such control because Byrdcliffe was never financially self-sufficient and depended on Whitehead's inherited fortune.

The colony was meant to provide the healthy environment necessary in which to lead a life based upon the combination of intellectual and manual labor. Whitehead wrote in *Handicraft* magazine: ". . . art itself can never be strong and sane till the gulf which separates the artist from the mechanic . . . has been bridged."[2] His philosophy evolved from an intimate association with John Ruskin, with whom he studied at Oxford, later traveling with him to Italy. Whitehead tried to form colonies there and in Austria, no doubt inspired by Ruskin's attempt at an artistic community with the Guild of St. George.[3]

Continuing to travel in Europe, Whitehead was apprenticed to a woodworker in Berlin while obtaining a divorce from his first wife. In 1892, newly married to an American, Jane Byrd McCall, he bought land in Santa Barbara, California, where he and his wife built an elaborate Tuscan villa. Several years later a school was built on the grounds so that their two sons might learn the manual arts.

In 1901, with Hervey White and Bolton Brown, Whitehead renewed the search for the

site of his long-awaited colony. Brown discovered the Woodstock property, which Whitehead noted had beauty, healthfulness, and accessibility – requirements for his version of a colony of craftsmen.[4] Ground was broken in 1902 with the erection of dwelling houses for Whitehead and Brown, a studio, dormitory, and dining hall; the buildings were constructed of local materials, designed to fit into the wooded surroundings. Artists and craftsmen came as both teachers and pupils, staying for varying amounts of time and producing painting, pottery, furniture, textiles, and metalwork.[5]

Although it is doubtful that all the Byrdcliffe furniture, about fifty pieces, was produced during one season, most of it is dated 1904.[6] The pieces were simple and rectilinear, made usually of poplar or quartered oak. It is unclear who designed the basic forms; possibly Canadian designer Dawson Watson is responsible for some and Whitehead for others. Many of the floral designs that characterize Byrdcliffe furniture were created by two former Pratt Institute students, Zulma Steele and Edna Walker. These women followed Ruskin's advice in using natural motifs of local plant life as sources for their work. The artists' nature studies from Woodstock flora and fauna were then conventionalized, as seen on this chest. Full-size drawings were transferred to wooden panels and the design, once carved, was stained with transparent colors similar to the flowers' natural shades; other wood surfaces remained untouched.[7] The actual construction of the furniture was carried out in the woodworking shop, overseen by a local carpenter, Fordyce Herrick.

Furniture from Byrdcliffe was not a profitable venture. Most of it was sold in New York, and transportation of large and often unwieldy pieces was difficult. Since intricate handwork made the furniture prohibitively expensive, much of it remained in Whitehead's house unsold.[8] Thus, in 1905, Whitehead closed the woodworking shops and encouraged the development of other crafts such as pottery, weaving, and framemaking.

Byrdcliffe was short-lived as an artists' colony. Hermann Dudley Murphy remained only one session, and when Bolton Brown was dismissed he set up studios nearby, a practice soon followed by others. Hervey White left in 1904, founding his own community for musicians, writers, and intellectuals only three miles away. Birge Harrison, the painter who replaced

Brown, also left in that year and, with his departure, Byrdcliffe began to fade.[9] Harrison set up
an art school in Woodstock that soon attracted
the Art Students' League to the town, and it is
clear that the presence of Byrdcliffe brought to
Woodstock the artists who established the later
colonies and groups for which Woodstock became renowned. For a while, Byrdcliffe continued to attract famous visitors such as Jane Addams and C.R. Ashbee, but by 1915 it was a
private estate kept by Whitehead. When he
died in 1929, Jane Whitehead moved to Byrdcliffe permanently, renting out the buildings to
summer visitors and selling off parts of the
estate. After Jane's death in 1952, their son Peter
kept the campus until his death in 1976.

JSB

1. Ralph Radcliffe Whitehead, "A Plea For Manual
Work," *Handicraft* 2 (June 1903), pp. 69-70.

2. Ibid., p. 71.

3. Robert Edwards, "Byrdcliffe: Life by Design," in
Byrdcliffe Arts and Crafts Colony, Life by Design (Wilmington:
Delaware Art Museum, 1984), p. 2. See also Robert
Edwards, "The Utopias of Ralph Radcliffe White-
head," *Antiques* 127 (January 1985), pp. 260-276.

4. Whitehead 1903, p. 73.

5. During the first season in 1903, Hermann Dudley
Murphy, a landscape painter who functioned as dean
of the school, taught painting and framemaking. Elizabeth Penman and Edith Hardenburgh taught pottery
during the second season. Ellen Gates Starr exhibited
her work at the Boston Society of Arts and Crafts in
1907 as a Byrdcliffe artist. (See Edwards 1984, pp. 8-9.)

6. Ibid., p. 10.

7. Ibid.

8. Ibid.

9. Alf Evers, *The Catskills: From Wilderness to Woodstock*
(Garden City, N.Y.: Doubleday, 1972), p. 632.

166
Library table, ca. 1902
Designer: Will Price (1861-1916)
Maker: The Rose Valley Shops, Rose Valley,
Pennsylvania
Oak
H: 29½ in. W: 66 in. D: 39½ in.
Marks: branded rose and *V* encircled with buck-
led belt; inscribed *Rose Valley Shops* (inside upper
end rail of table support)
Collection of Robert Edwards

In 1901 with the financial assistance of Edward
Bok and other prominent Philadelphians, the
architect Will Price and his associates founded

166

the Rose Valley community for the "manufacture of structures, articles, materials and products involving artistic handicraft."[1] Symbolically,
Price selected the ruins of a failed industrial
enterprise – the Rose Valley mills – as the location for his utopian experiment. Between 1901
and 1906, craftsmen working there produced
furniture, bookbindings, and pottery.

Handcraftsmanship was central to Price's philosophy. The Rose Valley furniture shop consisted of four to six workers who made carved
furniture in the Gothic, Renaissance, and Colonial styles, often with interlocking tenons that
made it possible for the pieces to be dismantled
easily. The craftsmen did use some power
machinery, however, for Price believed that
machines were "tools with which a thinking
man may work, shaping the product with his
own volition."[3]

After exhibiting at the Louisiana Purchase
Exposition in 1904, Rose Valley received more
commissions and several new sales outlets – the
Society of Arts and Crafts in Boston and the
Guild of Arts and Crafts in New York among

them.[4] Two years later, most of the crafts enterprises in Rose Valley, including the furniture
shop, had either dispersed or closed; for
another decade the residents maintained the
community's cultural activities such as theater
and music.

CZ

1. This was noted in the incorporation papers of July
17, 1901.

2. Among the power tools used were the handsaw, the
circular saw, and the mortising machine. See Will Price
as cited in William Ayres, ed., *A Poor Sort of Heaven, a Good
Sort of Earth: The Rose Valley Arts and Crafts Experiment*
(Chadds Ford, Penna.: Brandywine River Museum,
1983), p. 54.

3 . Will Price, "Do We Attack the Machine?," as cited in
Ayres 1983, p. 54.

4. Until this time, the shop had been soliciting commissions solely through the architectural office of Price and
McLanahan in Philadelphia and through *House and Gardens* and Rose Valley's magazine *The Artsman*. See Will
Price, "Is Rose Valley Worth While?," as cited in Ayres,
1983, p. 57.

167 (color plate, p. 35)
Crib, 1922
Frank Jeck (dates unknown), Bryn Athyn,
Pennsylvania
Cherry and remnants of velvet hangings
H: 64½ in. W: 44¼ in. D: 24¼ in.
Collection of Lachlan Pitcairn

Located just north of Philadelphia, the Swedenborgian community of Bryn Athyn was established in 1897 as a religious and educational center of the Church of the New Jerusalem. The founders separated from other Swedenborgians in an effort to ensure the continuity of their more rigorous commitment to principles of rational spiritualism.[1] In establishing a separatist community, the Church leaders agreed on the importance of creating a house of worship worthy of their truer faith in God. Looking back to the medieval cathedral as the ultimate unification of religious faith, artistic beauty, and social harmony, they turned in 1912 to the Boston firm of Cram and Goodhue, the leading American designer of Gothic churches. Ralph Adams Cram provided initial sketches, working drawings, and a quarter-inch scale model of a structure in the Perpendicular style; he also suggested that the community establish a guild system to provide such decorative features as stained-glass windows, ironwork, and wood carving[2] and that the building be contracted out exactly as designed in order that his presence not be required on the site.

Raymond Pitcairn, the major benefactor for the project and also a lawyer, rejected Cram's original proposal in favor of a more organic plan of design and construction. Being one of the earliest collectors and having assembled an extensive architectural library, with the advice of such experts as Arthur Kingsley Porter, Pitcairn himself was quite knowledgeable about medieval art.[3] Under the influence of Porter, he emphasized the importance of planning and fashioning work on site as the building progressed. This fundamental philosophical difference removed Cram from overall control of the design and construction and limited his role to that of occasional visitor.

Pitcairn took Cram's basic plan and modified it in both proportions and details. The draftsmen provided designs that were then tested, piece by piece, in full-scale models. They were thus not the ultimate designers but merely participants in one of the six guilds – for drafting, modeling, stone carving, woodworking, metal,

and stained glass – set up to build the cathedral. In an effort to maintain integrity in performance and quality in the final product, each was housed in its own shop adjacent to the construction site.[4] The Cram-based Gothic cathedral was completed in 1919, at which time Pitcairn was already planning a wing to include a tower and council hall in the Romanesque style of the twelfth century. Having come to favor this less refined, rougher style in the late teens, Pitcairn collected many examples of Romanesque stained glass and carving to serve as inspiration for the second phase of the cathedral. The Council Hall and Ezekiel Tower were begun in 1920 and finished in 1926.

This particular crib was made by Frank Jeck, a Czechoslovakian woodworker who worked on the Romanesque part of the cathedral.[5] Drawing ideas from the Pitcairn library and collection, Jeck decorated the piece with certain decorative features of the early style: the geometrically cross-hatched tympanums on the rails, the towers with windows capped by semicircular windows, the trefoil arches in the gables of the tester frame, and the carved fabric folds in the rails, which closely resemble the folds of clothing on Romanesque sculpture. The tympanums and the towers echo the variety of decorative details seen throughout the cathedral.[6] Furnished originally with velvet hangings (blue on the outside and yellow on the inside), the crib had fabric as a dust ruffle along the lower edge of the side and foot testers, as an encompassing headcloth, along the inside of the railing, and within the roof panels.

The present piece offers clear evidence of the difference between what Samuel Yellin referred to as natural texture and disfigurement.[7] Even in the medieval period, small timbers such as the posts and rails of the crib would have been sawed or rived to approximate dimensions and then finished with jack and smoothing planes.[8] Only on larger architectural beams was it appropriate to prepare the stock with broad axes or adzes. For the posts of this crib, Jeck used an adze to shape the timbers, endowing them with irregularities similar to hand-hammered metal. Emphasizing appearance and effect rather than process, his method shows how the romanticism of the reform movement could draw upon historically inappropriate technology to produce a desired aesthetic.

ESC

1. For a good introduction to the Swedenborgian faith, see Marguerite Beck Block, *The New Church in the New World* (New York: Henry Holt, 1932).

2. The most thorough study of the development and building of the cathedral is Bruce Glenn, *Bryn Athyn Cathedral: The Building of a Church* (Bryn Athyn, Pennsylvania: Bryn Athyn Church of the New Jerusalem, 1971).

3. Pitcairn's interest in medieval art is chronicled in *Radiance and Reflection: Medieval Art from the Raymond Pitcairn Collection* (New York: Metropolitan Museum of Art, 1982).

4. Many of the craftsmen, such as the Italian stonecutters, were immigrants who commuted daily by train from Philadelphia.

5. Interview with Lachlan Pitcairn, December 21, 1985.

6. This emphasis on variation was inspired by the scholarship of William Goodyear, Curator of Medieval Art at the Metropolitan and then at the Brooklyn Museum.

7. Part of Yellin's critique of contemporary perceptions of handwork is transcribed in Jack Andrews, "Samuel Yellin, Metalworker," reprinted from *Anvil's Ring* (Summer 1982), p. 7.

8. The most thorough discussion of medieval furniture is in Penelope Eames, "Furniture in England, France and the Netherlands from the Twelfth to the Fifteenth Century," *Furniture History* 13 (1977).

168
Cellaret, ca. 1910
Roycroft, East Aurora, New York
Oak; copper trimmings
H: 34 ¼ in. W: 40 in. D: 19 ½ in.
Mark: incised Roycroft symbol (R in circle with cross), on left side
Collection of Tazio Nuvolari

Few American crafts communities were run as socialistic enterprises, and Roycroft, founded in 1895, was no exception. Its founder, Elbert Hubbard, remarked: "The World of Commerce is just as honorable as the World of Art and a trifle more necessary. Art exists on the surplus that Business Men accumulate."[1] While Roycroft was decidedly a profitmaking venture under his sole ownership and direction, Hubbard did uphold the ideal of satisfaction in labor. A catalogue of 1912 refers to the furniture as similar to the "mission" style of the California monks in its simplicity, beauty, and strength; an advertisement describes the pieces as "Aurora Colonial Designs,"[2] perhaps an effort to emphasize their enduring nature and associate them with a romantic past.

air- and kiln-dried wood, most often of oak but also of ash, walnut, bird's-eye maple, and African or Santo Domingo mahogany. The pieces were given a "secret finish" and waxed rather than varnished. Roycroft's insignia, adopted by Elbert Hubbard in 1895, was a cross and circle used by one of the first bookbinders in the middle ages – a monk named Cassiodorus. Hubbard divided the circle into three parts to signify Faith, Hope, and Love, and added an "R" for Roycroft.[6]

Although Roycroft publications claim that each piece was made by a single craftsman, the furniture, all marked with the company insignia or name, is not individually signed. The literature asserts, furthermore, that each object was made to order, not mass-produced.[7] Considering the amount of machinery available at Roycroft, the amount of goods produced, and the fact that by 1906 over 400 people worked at the community,[8] it is unlikely that every piece of furniture was made to order by a single craftsman.

The cellaret, which appears in the 1906 catalogue, may have been available at an earlier date. It could be purchased in oak, mahogany, or ash, all with handwrought copper fittings made at the community's copper shop. While this example does not carry the bulbous feet of much Roycroft furniture, its simple design and construction is characteristic; the copper fittings, which are also functional, are its only decoration.

JSB

168

1. Felix Shay, *Elbert Hubbard of East Aurora* (New York: William H. Wise, 1926), p. 201.

2. David M. Cathers, *Furniture of the American Arts and Crafts Movement* (New York: New American Library, 1981), p. 94. For information about the Roycroft community, see also Eileen Boris, "Art and Labor: John Ruskin, William Morris, and the Craftsman Ideal in America, 1876-1915" (Ph.D. dissertation, Brown University, 1981); and Robert Edwards, "The Roycrofters," in *Nineteenth Century Furniture: Innovation, Revival and Reform* (New York: *Art and Antiques*, 1982), pp. 104-111.

3. Cathers 1981, p. 91.

4. Charles F. Hamilton, *Roycroft Collectibles* (San Diego: A.S. Barnes, 1980), p. 61.

5. Santiago Cadzow, one of the first cabinetmakers at the shops, designed some furniture and taught woodworking to other Roycrofters. Albert Danner and Albert Buffum both came to the community in the early 1900s; the latter was eventually superintendent of the

During the first decade, the Roycroft shop was small. Furniture was first sold to the public in 1897 and two years later Hubbard began to advertise in his magazine. As demand grew, the community responded with increased manufacture. Twice as many pieces appeared in the 1906 catalogue as in the 1904 issue,[3] and production increased during the second decade of the new century. After Elbert Hubbard and his wife drowned on the *Lusitania* in 1915, the community continued under the leadership of their son Bert, who established Roycroft "departments" in several hundred stores such as Lord

and Taylor and Marshall Field.[4] Despite the growing popularity of Roycroft furniture, the community began to founder after 1919; it suffered greatly during the Depression and finally collapsed in 1938.

There was no one craftsman solely responsible for design of the Roycroft pieces.[5] Throughout the more than twenty years of production, they were characterized by a basic rectilinear form and minimal ornament, many featuring legs tapering to a rounded fat foot. The furniture is constructed with pegs, pins, and mortise-and-tenon joints. Roycrofters used solid furniture shop. An illustrator at Roycroft, Victor Toothaker, also worked as a designer.

6. Nancy Hubbard Brady, *Roycroft Handmade Furniture: A Facsimile of a 1912 Catalogue With Other Related Material Added* (East Aurora, N. Y.: House of Hubbard, 1973), p. 58.

7. Brady 1973, p. 57. Another Roycroft publication containing valuable information is *Catalog of Roycroft Furniture and Other Things* (East Aurora, N. Y.: Roycroft, 1906; reprint ed., New York: Turn of the Century Editions, 1981).

8. Dard Hunter, *My Life with Paper: An Autobiography* (New York: Alfred A. Knopf, 1958), p. 42.

169

Ali-Baba bench, ca. 1906
Roycroft, East Aurora, New York
Oak with white ash slab
H: 17 ¾ in. W: 36 in. D: 15 ¾ in.
Marks: Roycroft symbol incised on outside of two legs
Collection of Robert Edwards

Personal reminiscences of Elbert Hubbard and his writings reveal a witty, sardonic personality and an eccentric humor that sometimes found its way into his craft.[1] By exaggerating the "honest" materials and construction used in making this bench, called "Ali Baba" after a Roycroft handyman so nicknamed, Hubbard satirized the Arts and Crafts quest to return to nature and lead the simple life. The bark is left on the underside of the oak slab seat, so that it retains its character as an uncut log. A polished wood version, which sold for $10 in 1906, is usually shown in the catalogue; this rustic example may be a unique variation.

JSB

1. Felix Shay, *Elbert Hubbard of East Aurora* (New York: William H. Wise, 1926), p. 140.

170

The Holly Tree, by Charles Dickens, 1903 (no. 17 of 100 copies)
Printer: The Roycroft Press, East Aurora, New York
Designer of binding: Louis Herman Kinder (1866-1938)
Binding: green morocco, with gilt tooling and multicolored leather inlays
Paper: Japan Vellum
H: 8¾ in. W: 5⅞ in. D: ½ in.
Marks: stamped with Roycroft symbol – R in circle with cross – and Kinder's initials in circle

169

(on bottom of rear doublure); signed *Elbert Hubbard*
Collection of Richard Blacher

Elbert Hubbard established the Roycroft Press in 1895. Its first book, *The Song of Songs Which is Solomon's*, at $2, is an amateurish and clumsy piece of work compared to the later Roycroft volumes; however it establishes the pseudo-Kelmscott style that the press was to follow for some of its books. Typically, Hubbard's claims for the first book exceeded the realization. The announcement circular averred that "this publication will mark an era in the art of printing in America," whereas one reviewer termed it "odd, curious, interesting ... but ... surely not one of the most beautiful books issued lately in the States."[1]

Hubbard's forte lay in entrepreneurship, not in design. The Roycroft books, though available in only a few select bookstores, were shipped in carloads to American homes. Hubbard's career as a lecturer and his well-publicized entertainment of celebrities at the Roycroft Inn helped to increase sales.

Perhaps the best-known characteristic of Roycroft books was the typical chamois suede binding, disrespectfully known as "window cleaners," "mouse skin," or the technical term "limp ooze." These tended to powder with age, their silk doublures becoming shabby, thus causing some discontent with Roycroft volumes. The $2 cost, however, was quite an inexpensive price for an artistically produced book.

Hubbard also offered books in paper wrappers, paper boards, three-quarter leather, flexible leather, modeled leather, vellum, and morocco. Some of the finest bindings rose to very high prices. One Roycroft catalogue has a photograph of *An American Bible* captioned "The finest of the Roycroft Modeled-Leather books. Price, $300.00 a Single Copy."[2] Another catalogue has a page entitled "Fine Bindings," with a list of fourteen titles ranging in price from $10 to $100. The introductory heading states: "The following books are bound in the highest style of the Bookbinder's Art, by our Mr. Louis H. Kinder and pupils; we believe that no finer or

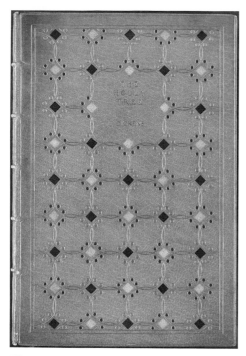

170

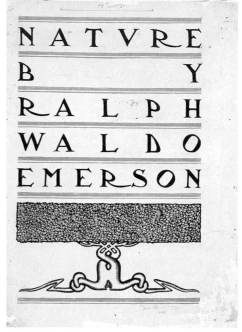

171b

and *Fine Bookbinding in America: A Chapter in the History of the Roycroft Shop* (Newtown, Pa.: Bird and Bull Press, 1985).

5. Ibid., p. 117.

171 a and b
Drawing for *Nature*, by Ralph Waldo Emerson, 1905
Printer: The Roycroft Press, East Aurora, New York
Designer: Dard Hunter (1883-1966)
Red and black inks on white paper
Book – H: 8⅛ x 5¼ in. (page)
Drawing – H: 14⅝ x 9¼ in.
Boice Lydell, The Roycroft Arts Museum, East Aurora, New York

A number of accomplished artists worked at the Roycroft Press as illustrators and book designers. The most famous were W.W. Denslow, best known as the illustrator of *The Wizard of Oz*, and Dard Hunter, who was to become a world authority on hand papermaking.

Hunter came to East Aurora in 1903 from Chillicothe, Ohio, where his father owned a newspaper and had given his son an interest in fine printing by showing him a Kelmscott Press book and telling him about William Morris. Hunter also became interested in Elbert Hubbard through his brother's reading of *The Philistine* and settled for East Aurora instead of England. He remained there off and on until 1910, when he moved to Vienna to study graphic art and then to London to work as a designer. Later, he founded his own Mountain House Press, and his travels took him all over the world to observe papermaking techniques. Hunter has been much revered for his "one-man books," in which he carried the Arts and Crafts ideal of unity of workmanship to its apex. For these books he wrote the text, designed and cast the type, and composed and printed the copy on paper he had made himself. As he observed, "the book should be the work of one man alone. In this way, and only this, will the volume be truly his."[1]

Hunter's masterpieces for Roycroft are often cited as *Justinian and Theodora* (1906) and *White Hyacinths* (1907). Both books have double title pages with floral motifs, whose elongated, rectilinear lines reflect the Viennese Secessionists and the Glasgow style. Through reading art magazines, Hunter had become aware of European movements even before his first trips abroad. Yet, despite all their visible influences, his own contributions to Art Nouveau and the Arts and Crafts movement remain uniquely American.

Hunter's designs for Emerson's *Nature*, published by the Roycroft Press in 1905, are among the most interesting of his accomplishments in East Aurora. The title page, with its spaced lettering in black, red rules, and stylized tree with red fruits and twisted roots, as well as the similar tailpieces used throughout, are reminiscent of Will Bradley's work (see nos. 46, 157, and 158). In contrast, the section openings have red capital letters placed against more realistically depicted landscapes. The distinctive work inspired one art historian to comment: "There is a clarity to Hunter's designs that is lacking in earlier Roycroft books . . . . He has discarded all obvious references to layout and to the typography of sixteenth-century Venice. . . . Instead, Hunter arranges a series of sensitively related squares and rectangles and organizes the type and decorations within these spaces in relation to the page as a whole."[2]

Although he retained an affection and respect for Hubbard, Hunter later believed that his years in East Aurora had not been his most

better work has ever been done in America – all are hand-tooled after special designs. Those who order first will get the books."[3]

Hubbard, knowing that European craftsmanship excelled in this handicraft, was glad to get Kinder, a German who worked for him from about 1897 to late 1911. Kinder was something of a scholar as well; in 1893 he had published an English translation of Josef Halfer's *The Process of the Marbling Art*, and in 1901 he founded a short-lived magazine with practical information for binders.[4] Kinder's work exemplifies the best-quality design produced by the Roycrofters. The binding of *The Holly Tree* is said to be "the only one of Kinder's thus far located which bears his identifying mark. This attests to his particular pride in it."[5]

ST

1. [J.M. Bowles], "Echoes," *Modern Art* 4 (April 1896), unpaged.

2. *The Roycroft Catalog 92: Books, Leather and Copper* (East Aurora: Roycrofters, 1912), p. 5.

3. *The Roycroft Books: A Catalog and Some Remarks* (East Aurora: Roycrofters, 1902), p. 10.

4. For a complete survey of Kinder and his work, see Richard J. Wolfe and Paul McKenna, *Louis Herman Kinder*

productive. He wrote in 1958: "Even though the books produced at the Roycroft Shop were bizarre and lacked taste and refinement, they were, nevertheless, a step in the right direction. These books were better made than most of the work done in this country at the time, and people who had never before thought of collecting books began assembling the Roycroft issues. Mr. Hubbard probably had more influence in the development of book-collecting than any other person of his generation."[3]

ST

1. Dard Hunter, "The Lost Art of Making Books," *Miscellany* 2 (1915), p. 6.

2. Robert Koch, "Elbert Hubbard's Roycrofters as Artist-Craftsmen," *Winterthur Portfolio* 3 (1967), p. 81.

3. Dard Hunter, *My Life with Paper* (New York: Knopf, 1958), p. 43.

172 a, b and c
Ipswich Prints, First Set, 1902 (copyright 1901)
Textile design from a Japanese collection of ancient patterns
Marsh Island
Lily - Coloured drawing
Arthur Wesley Dow (1857-1922), Ipswich, Massachusetts
Ink and engraving on paper
Textile and *Lily,* 8 x 7 in.; *Marsh Island,* 7 x 8 in.
Marks: (on *Lily*) *AWD* monogram with landscape
Society for the Preservation of New England Antiquities, Boston

Arthur Wesley Dow was an artist and teacher whose theories revolutionized art education in the United States at the turn of the century. His seminal book *Composition: A Series of Exercises Selected from a New System of Art Education* (1899) guided generations of students and teachers in developing the judgment and design knowledge that Dow believed were fundamental to great art. A proponent of the Arts and Crafts movement, he advanced theories in support of the democratization of art, the unification of fine arts and crafts, and the development of a unique American aesthetic.

Born in Ipswich, Massachusetts, Dow trained locally and in Paris. In 1891 he met Ernest F. Fenollosa, then curator of Oriental art at the Boston Museum of Fine Arts and formerly head of the Tokyo Fine Arts Academy and the Imperial Museum. Fenollosa introduced Dow to Japanese art through the paintings and prints he

172b

had assembled for the Museum's collection.[1] Condemning French academic art as imitative, the two men saw Eastern and Western art coming together through a new American style they called "synthesism,"[2] and Dow soon began applying Japanese design principles to paintings of his favorite subjects: New England landscape scenes and floral motifs. He proposed that line, mass, and color be used in a careful building process to create "beauty" (defined as "elements of difference harmonized by elements of unity")[3] and to make a product greater than its single components.

As Dow's devotion to the ideal of synthesism grew, his commitment to dissemination also increased. He advocated art education to insure "a powerful, distinctly American School," and zealously made instruction a priority.[4] In 1895 Dow became an instructor at Pratt Institute in Brooklyn, where he taught "structural" principles in classes of life drawing, painting, design, and art education. Two years later he was also teaching at the Art Students League in New York and serving as curator of Oriental art at the Museum of Fine Arts in Boston. In 1904 Dow accepted the position of Director of Fine Arts at Teachers College, Columbia University. As department head, he was able to build a curriculum and hire instructors to uphold his theories. *Composition* was used as the basic text, its popularity reflected by the fact that twenty editions were in print by 1938.

Although disdained by professional painters, Dow succeeded in converting a nation of school teachers, pupils, craftsmen, and amateur artists to the Japanese art of rhythm and harmony.[5] His influence spread with great rapidity through his pupils, many of whom taught in public and art schools throughout the United States. Isabelle Percy West was recruited to teach at the newly founded California College of Arts and Crafts even before her graduation from Columbia in 1905,[6] and another student, Mary Scovel, established a curriculum based on his theories for the Chicago Art Institute.[7] Max Weber, Dow's pupil at Pratt, and Georgia O'Keeffe, who studied with him at Columbia, often acknowledged the fundamental role of his teachings in the development of their art.[8] Dow also lectured extensively in strategic locations that would best disseminate his theories. His reputation spread abroad, prompting the

English Art Teacher's Association to send a representative to Columbia to study his work at first hand.

During the summers from 1900 to 1906 Dow returned to Ipswich, where he instructed small groups of students and received inspiration for his own work. In 1900 he founded the influential Ipswich Summer School of Art to encourage application of the principles of composition to simple handcrafted metalwork, woodblock prints, pottery, baskets, and textiles.[9] Using a foot-powered press there, Dow printed 800 copies of the first of three packets of "Ipswich Prints." He was initially interested in manipulating the printing press and inks to create painterly compositions, but soon realized the added value of the medium in expanding the resources for classroom color study. The present example – one of three from a set of six prints – reflected Dow's interest in the local landscape as a design source that complemented both Japanese principles and Arts and Crafts ideals. Dow instructed students to treat the landscape first as a design, afterward as a picture; he saw flowers as providing a great variety of line and proportion, making them convenient subjects for elementary composition. Advocating abstract design, Dow wrote, "All the lines and areas must be related one to another by connections and placings, so as to form a beautiful whole. Not a picture of a flower is sought . . . but rather an irregular pattern of lines and spaces . . . ."[10] Dow intended that the prints help young students "find joy in the common things about [them]," arguing that "our American life needs more appreciation of the simple beauty of nature."[11]

JCS

1. In 1895 Fenollosa organized an exhibition of Dow's woodblock prints. See *Special Exhibition of Color Prints Designed, Engraved and Printed by Arthur W. Dow* (Boston: Museum of Fine Arts, 1895), p. [1].

2. Frederick C. Moffatt, *Arthur Wesley Dow (1857-1922)* (Washington, D.C.: National Collection of Fine Arts, Smithsonian Institution, 1977), p. 49.

3. Arthur Wesley Dow, *Composition: A Series of Exercises in Art Structure for the Use of Students and Teachers* (New York: Doubleday, Doran, 1938), p. 22; first published in 1899 under the title *Composition: A Series of Exercises Selected from a New System of Art Education.*

4. Arthur Wesley Dow, "Ipswich as It Should Be," *Ipswich Chronicle,* May 9, 1891, quoted in Moffatt 1977, p. 50.

5. See Moffatt 1977, p. 90.

6. James Schevill, "The Early Years – The Idea of a College," *California College of Arts and Crafts* 59 (Winter 1965), p. 2.

7. See Moffatt 1977, p. 91.

8. See ibid., pp. 83, 129.

9. The school's influence was exceptionally widespread, attracting art teachers from all parts of the United States. See Sylvester Baxter, "Handicraft and its Extension at Ipswich" *Handicraft* 1 (February 1903), p. 252.

10. Dow 1938, p. 62.

11. Quoted from Dow's notes to instructors, accompanying *Ipswich Prints, First Set,* p. [3].

173

Cover design for Agatha's Unknown Way, by "Pansy" (Mrs. Isabella Macdonald Alden), 1898
School of the Museum of Fine Arts, Boston
Designer: Olive Lothrop Grover
Relief print in green and yellow inks on textured cream paper
7¼ x 4¾ in.
School of the Museum of Fine Arts, Boston

The School of the Museum of Fine Arts, Boston, was founded in 1877 by William Morris Hunt and John La Farge. A class in decoration was introduced in 1884; its twenty-five pupils met three afternoons a week. Although their designs were intended to meet the needs of manufacturers, students were encouraged to "work free from the trend to commercialism."[1] The young artisans strove to "see as an artist and feel as a poet" while designing wallpapers, carpets, bookcovers, silverware, jewelry, and stained glass.[2]

In 1894 Olive Lothrop Grover came from Winnetka, Illinois, to study at the school. Like many women of her day, she sought a fulfilling career in the arts. While a student at the school, she was taught the craft of cover decoration and became a successful "decorative designer" even before her studies were completed. Two of her best book covers, *Shadows* (1897) by M.A. DeWolf Howe and *The Round Rabbit* (1898) by Agnes Lee, were published by Copeland and Day. Her book cover for *Agatha's Unknown Way,* written by the children's author Isabella Macdonald Alden and published in 1898 by Fleming H. Revell, illustrates the conventionalized

173

designs often employed by Ms. Grover and characteristic of the period.[3]

ST and JD

1. H. Winthrop Pierce, *The History of the School of the Museum of Fine Arts, Boston, 1877-1927* (Boston: T.O. Metcalf Co., 1930).

2. Ibid.

3. The design is found in Scrapbook no. 2 of the School of the Museum of Fine Arts, Boston (1885-1905), p. 73. Grover also designed bookplates, some of which can be seen on p. 72 of the same scrapbook. Several of her binding designs were used by Copeland and Day. See Nancy Finlay, *Artists of the Book in Boston, 1980-1920* (Cambridge, Houghton Library, 1985), p. 91.

174

Table mat, 1908
Lydia Bush-Brown (1887-1984)
Block-printed cotton plain weave with silk embroidery (including satin, back, and knot stitches) plus couching
L: 32 in. W: 16 in.
Cooper-Hewitt Museum, the Smithsonian Institution's National Museum of Design. Gift of Lydia Bush-Brown Head. 1977-77-3

174

The daughter of Margaret Lesley and Henry Bush-Brown, both accomplished artists, Lydia Bush-Brown made this table mat while a student at the Pratt Institute of Fine and Applied Arts in Brooklyn.[1] Among her teachers were Salome and Ralph Helm Johonnot, who had earlier studied art in Vienna.[2]

Apart from weaving the foundation cloth, Miss Bush-Brown was responsible for the entire production of the mat. She made the design, cut and finished the woodblocks, printed the cloth, embellished the design with embroidery, and hemmed the textile. The combination of two different techniques – block printing and embroidery – on selected portions of the design is characteristic of the period; it had been used earlier by Candace Wheeler and the Associated Artists.

After Miss Bush-Brown had completed her training at Pratt, she went on to take lessons in batik from Charles Pellew in Washington, D.C. She achieved recognition for her "silk murals" in numerous exhibitions and articles in the contemporary press in the 1920s and 1930s.[3]

GM

1. Mabel Tuke Priestman, *Art and Economy in Home Decoration* (New York: John Lane, 1908).

2. Maud A. Harrow, "Is Pattern Beauty?," *House and Garden* 29 (May 1916), p. 35.

3. See *House Beautiful* (August 1924), cover and pp. 109-111; and *Good Furniture* (April 1927, pp. 189-190; and August 1928, pp. 104-110).

175a and b

Print chest and wall cabinet, 1915
Designer and carver: Margery Wheelock (ca. 1890-ca. 1967) under the direction of Frederick H. Meyer (1872-1961)
Makers: alumni of the California School of Arts and Crafts,[1] Berkeley
Oak with wrought-copper hinges and door pulls
Chest – H: 35¼ in. W: 39½ in. D: 12½ in.
Wall cabinet – H: 20 in. W: 74 in. D: 10½ in.
Marks: carved Gothic letters *CSAC* and *1915* (on undershelf of wall cabinet)
The Oakland Museum, Courtesy of the California College of Arts and Crafts

After his furniture studio was destroyed in the San Francisco earthquake of 1906, Frederick H. Meyer founded one of the first craft schools on the west coast,[2] the School of the California Guild of Arts and Crafts. Meyer's dream for practical education in design, mechanical drawing, and commercial arts and crafts, as well as teacher training, became a reality when a reporter for the *San Francisco Call* mistakenly published his preliminary ideas as definite plans for a manual arts program and students responded.[3] Beginning as a summer program with forty-five students and three teachers,[4] the institution quickly outgrew its three-room studio in Berkeley and moved into larger facilities in Oakland in 1922. Among the courses taught were woodcarving, drawing, composition, design, and drawing from the antique. In the next years, jewelry making, weaving, embroidery, and pottery were added to the curriculum along with courses in the fine arts.

The school demonstrated its work with a model studio in the Palace of Education at the Panama-Pacific International Exposition in 1915.

Almost all of the furniture in the studio, including a portfolio rack, pedestal, model stand and chair, easel, drafting table and chair, and this print chest and hanging cabinet,[5] was designed by Margery Wheelock.[6] Despite this promising beginning, Miss Wheelock, like many women who trained in the applied arts, did not pursue a professional career in design. Instead, she assisted her husband and fellow graduate of the program, Harry St. John Dixon (see no. 138), with metalwork designs and did bookwork for his shop in San Francisco.[7]

CZ

1. In 1908, the name changed from the School of the California Guild of Arts and Crafts to the California School of Arts and Crafts. Renamed the California College of Arts and Crafts in 1936 (although it had been officially a college since 1922), it continues to train students in the fine and applied arts today. For more information about the school and its teachers, see Margaret Penrose Dhaemers, "California College of Arts and Crafts, 1907-1944" (master's thesis, Mills College, 1967).

2. The Mark Hopkins Institute of Art and Throop Polytechnic Institute in Pasadena were other early programs in the applied arts in California.

3. James Schevill, "The Early Years: The Idea of a College," *California College of Arts and Crafts Review* (Winter 1965; originally published in December 1953), pp. 1-3. German by birth, Meyer had moved to California when he was sixteen. Finding western schools inadequate for training, he went east to Cincinnati and the Industrial Art School in Philadelphia and abroad to the Königliche Akademischen Hochschule in Berlin for training, before returning to teach and work in California. Meyer contributed to *School Arts Magazine* and *Sierra Educational News* and served as director of the California College of Arts and Crafts until 1944.

4. Perham W. Nahl and Isabelle Percy West, Meyer's friends from the Mark Hopkins Institute (where he was a professor of applied art from 1902 to 1906), were among his first teachers. Mrs. West had studied design and composition with Arthur Wesley Dow at Columbia University (see no. 172).

5. Catalogue of California School of Arts and Crafts (Spring 1915), pp. 8-9.

6. Others contributing to the studio were students named Dinsdale, Abell, and Harry St. John Dixon and instructor Herman Steinbrun. The display was one of eight model rooms in the Department of Fine and Applied Arts, and was awarded a gold medal. See Timothy J. Anderson, Eudorah M. Moore, and Robert W. Winter, eds., *California Design 90* (Santa Barbara: Peregrine Smith, 1980), p. 63.

7. Margery Wheelock's daughter, Sarah Dixon-Roberts, noted this information in an interview with Hazel Bray of The Oakland Museum in June 1983.

175a and b

176

176

Vase, 1900
Susan S. Frackelton (1848-1932), Milwaukee
Stoneware, wheel-thrown and salt-glazed with
cobalt-blue underglaze over incised decoration
of irises on white slip
H: 6¼ in. Diam: 5 in.
Marks: incised *S Frackelton* (S superimposed over
F)/1900 (on bottom)
Museum of the State Historical Society of Wis-
consin. Gift of Mrs. Herman G. Seely. 1958.1321

Born into a wealthy Milwaukee family and educated in private schools, Susan Frackelton
seems to have been drawn to ceramic decoration through her husband's business in wholesale china and glass importing and through her
father's brickyards.[1] In the early 1870s she studied painting in Milwaukee with Heinrich Vian-
den and by 1877 had established Frackelton's
China Decorating Works as an adjunct to her
husband's business. Mrs. Frackelton's experiments with stoneware began in 1874. While
contemporaries were trying sophisticated clays
and glazes, she chose humble local stoneware
clays for the body, traditional cobalt blue for the
decoration, and the age-old method of glazing
with common salt during the firing process.
Firing was done at first in vacant areas of local

brick kilns and later in traditional stoneware
potteries in Minnesota and Ohio. "To her belongs the credit of elevating the common salt-
glazed stoneware to a place beside the finer
ceramic wares in this country," wrote the eminent American ceramics historian Edwin AtLee
Barber in 1901.[2]
Of Mrs. Frackelton's many exhibitions during
the last two decades of the 1800s, the Paris
Exposition of 1900 brought the greatest critical
acclaim; even the exacting German critics noticed her work as being of "special interest
. . . an unusually important attempt to revive the
grey stoneware of Rhenish character with applied ornaments and flowers done in a modern
manner."[3] The present vase was exhibited
there with the National League of Mineral Painters' display.[4] Unlike English or Rhenish art
stoneware of the period, which includes geometric design, landscape scenes, or flora and
fauna rendered in the Aesthetic mode, Frackelton drew individual plant motifs in semi-
naturalistic style, abstracting the decorative
qualities of the natural models without obliter-
ating their identities. Typical of her best work in
stoneware, this vase also exhibits her tendency
to present the design on an airy field, whereas
foreign decorators more often filled the entire
surface.
Mrs. Frackelton's many contributions to the
ceramic arts in America were widely acknowledged. During the 1880s she concentrated on
simplifying china painting as an amateur activity: she developed and marketed odorless
china colors; published the first edition of her
decorating manual, *Tried by Fire*, in 1886; and in
1886 and 1888 patented a portable gas-fired
kiln.[5] Her efforts to establish local schools of art
in Milwaukee (1888) and Detroit (1890) met
with much less success than other endeavors.
But failure on the local level forced Mrs. Frackelton into the national scene. She founded the
National League of Mineral Painters in 1892 as a
way to promote education and competition on
a larger scale. In 1902, Mrs. Frackelton moved
permanently to Chicago, where she produced
book illuminations and lectured on a wide
variety of arts and crafts.

EPD and BRD

1. For more information, see George A. Weedon, Jr.,
"Susan S. Frackelton and the American Arts and Crafts
Movement" (master's thesis, University of Wisconsin,
Milwaukee, 1975).

2. Edwin AtLee Barber, *The Pottery and Porcelain of the
United States*, 2nd ed. (New York: G.P. Putnam, 1901), p.
512.

3. "Frackelton Blue and Grey," *Keramic Studio* 3 (December 1901), p. 166. In addition to Rhenish stoneware, Mrs. Frackelton may have had in mind as a
model the English revival of decorated gray salt-glazed
stoneware by Doulton & Company, begun in 1871.

4. When shown in Paris, this vase had a cover. For
illustration and discussion of it, see "Mrs. Frackelton's
Work," *Art Amateur* 44 (January 1901), pp. 51-52.

5. In 1894, the Frackelton Dry Water Colors received a
special award at the Exposition Universelle d'Anvers,
Antwerp, Belgium; see Susan Frackelton, *Tried by Fire*,
1st ed. (New York: D. Appleton, 1886); 1886 patent no.
349,935, 1888 patent no. 386,395.

177

Vase, 1915
Charles Fergus Binns (1857-1934), Alfred, New
York
Stoneware, wheel-thrown and decorated in
overall striated glossy glaze shading from green
at base to blue at neck
H: 9⅛ in. Diam: 7¼ in.
Marks: incised C.F. B. / 15 within circle (on
bottom)
The Art Institute of Chicago, Gift of the Atlan
Ceramic Club. 1916.436

Charles Binns spent the first half of his career
working for a commercial pottery – England's
Worcester Royal Porcelain Works, where his
father was superintendent.[1] After many years of
service in all aspects of the operation there,
Binns retired at the age of forty and secured in
1899 a position as the first director for the new
school of industrial arts in Trenton, New Jersey.
His accomplishments recommended him for
the position as first director of the New York
School of Clayworking and Ceramics in Alfred,
founded in 1900 to provide practical and academic training for those who wished to have a
career in ceramics. But Binns's conception of
such a career was not the standard one of
working in a commercial factory or even in an
art pottery, where labor was divided. At Alfred,
his students learned control of the whole artistic process from conception to finished piece.
As the first to teach this approach, Binns is
considered the "father" of modern studio
ceramics.[2]
Binns's role as a teacher was not limited to
the classrooms and studios of industrial arts
schools, however. He wrote extensively, pub-

177

1. For more about Binns, see Susan R. Strong, "The Searching Flame: Charles Fergus Binns," *American Ceramics* 1 (Summer 1982), pp. 44-49.

2. Binns's most famous early students included Arthur Baggs of the Marblehead Pottery (see nos. 115 and 116), Paul Cox of the Newcomb Pottery (see no. 179), Adelaide Alsop Robineau (see nos. 108 and 109), Mary Chase Perry (see no. 114), Elizabeth Gray Overbeck (see no. 111), and R. Guy Cowan (whose Cowan Pottery in Rocky River, Ohio, attempted to unite the work of potter-designers with production techniques).

3. For Binns's definitive essay on ceramics as fine art, see "The Art of Manufacture and the Manufacture of Art," *American Ceramic Society Bulletin* 2 (1923), pp. 55-59.

4. Charles F. Binns, ed., *Ceramic Technology* (London: Scott Greenwood, 1897); and Charles F. Binns, *The Potter's Craft: A Practical Guide for the Studio and Workshop* (New York: D. Van Nostrand Company, 1st ed. 1910, and 2nd ed., revised and enlarged, 1922).

5. For a description of Binns's method, see J.F. McMahon, "Charles Fergus Binns," *American Ceramic Society Bulletin* 17 (1938), pp. 175-176.

6. For more about the Atlan Ceramic Art Club, see Sharon S. Darling, *Chicago Ceramics & Glass* (Chicago: Chicago Historical Society, 1979), pp. 17-27.

lishing numerous articles on technique and criticism for periodicals such as *Keramic Studio*, the *American Magazine of Art*, and the *Bulletin* of the American Ceramic Society.[3] In addition, his books *Ceramic Technology* and *The Potter's Craft* are still considered classics.[4] His fervent commitment to professional standards was shown in his dedication to the American Ceramic Society; he was one of its founders in 1899 and held many offices in the organization over the years.

The vase shown here is typical of Binns's later work done in Alfred and serves as a good example of his mature craftmanship. Influenced, no doubt, by Oriental aesthetics, he felt that the glaze and shape of a piece were the most important; decoration was unnecessary if the other two were executed in harmony.[5] This work was acquired by the Art Institute of Chicago through the Atlan Ceramic Art Club, an organization of prominent women china painters in the Chicago area.[6] It was chosen from the pieces displayed by Binns at the Fifteenth Annual Exhibition of Applied Art and Original Designs for Decoration held at the Art Institute in 1916.

EPD and BRD

178 (color plate, p. 36)
Lamp, 1904
Newcomb Pottery (1895-1940), New Orleans
Decorator: Mary Given Sheerer (1865-1954)
White earthenware, wheel-thrown with incised white irises and green, blue-green, and blue slips covered with a glossy transparent glaze; shade – six panels of glass beads strung on wire and attached to wire mesh with irises in white, two shades of green, medium blue, and yellow
H: (to top of chimney) 21 in.
H: (of shade) 6¼ in. H: (of base) 8¾ in.
W: (of shade) 14⅜ in. W: (of base) 8 in.
Marks: incised artist's cipher M.S. enclosed by line at top and bottom; impressed X, W, and ciphers NC and JM; registration number VV82 painted in blue (on bottom)
Collection of Sonia and Walter Bob

In 1894 Ellsworth Woodward began the pottery program at the H. Sophie Newcomb Memorial College, founded in 1886 as the women's coordinate of Tulane University.[1] Educated at the Massachusetts Normal Art School and the Rhode Island School of Design, Woodward established the commitment to education in the handicrafts that was a hallmark of Newcomb's art program. Mary Given Sheerer, trained in

drawing, painting, and sculpture at the Art Academy in Cincinnati and the Art Students League in New York, was hired to direct the pottery, which was to provide employment for young women who had been trained at Newcomb. Art industries had not developed in the south as they had in the north; the pottery would give economic meaning to art education. "The whole thing was to be a southern product, made of southern clays, by southern artists, decorated with southern subjects!" wrote Sheerer in 1899.[2]

Students of the college were allowed to use the pottery's facilities for study, but most of the work sold was produced by graduate students and professional decorators who had been through the Newcomb art program. At first the decorators were paid on a piecework basis as was the practice in industrial potteries: money was received by the decorator when the piece was sold and the cost of materials was deducted from the sales price. Late in 1900 it was decided to pay the decorator for each piece made regardless of whether it survived the kiln to be sold. Even so, wages were not high and the pottery closed during academic holidays.

Despite Woodward's declared intention of training women for industrial art, a conservative attitude toward women's roles was reflected in the fact that a man was consistently hired to be the potter; furthermore, course work was aimed primarily at training women to be designers and decorators. Notwithstanding the number of American women who had grown from decorating to clayworking,[3] instruction in the total ceramics process was not added to the college art program until much later.

From the foundation established by Woodward in the pottery project, the art program grew to include a wide variety of materials. Classes in embroidery and needlework taught by Gertrude Roberts Smith (see no. 180) began in 1902. The metalwork program and stained-glass production grew out of the need for lampshades to coordinate with pottery lamp bases.[4] Beaded shades were also made briefly in 1904-1905 – an idea conceived by Mary Sheerer. The lamp shown here was exhibited at the 1904 Louisiana Purchase Exposition, where the exquisitely beaded shade drew attention.[5] The irises on the shade are identified as Iris *"Louisiana"* by the single red beads that appear on each blossom in imitation of the stray red flecks of nature's model.

EPD and BRD

1. Factual information in this entry is based generally on the contents of Jessie Poesch, *Newcomb Pottery: An Enterprise for Southern Women, 1895-1940* (Exton, Pa.: Schiffer Publishing, 1984). See also Suzanne Ormond and Mary E. Irvine, *Louisiana's Art Nouveau: The Crafts of the Newcomb Style* (Gretna, La.: Pelican, 1976).

2. Mary G. Sheerer, "Newcomb Pottery," *Keramic Studio* 1 (November 1899), p. 151.

3. Examples of women decorators who had become clayworkers by 1902 include Adelaide Alsop Robineau (nos. 108 and 109), Susan Frackelton (no. 176), and Mary Louise McLaughlin (no. 107).

4. Harriet Joor, "The Art Industries of Newcomb College," *International Studio* 41 (July 1910), pp. 8, 10, 12, and 14; this lamp with beaded shade is illustrated on p. 38.

5. The lamp arrived in St. Louis too late to be approved by the jury of selection, but Woodward induced F.A. Whiting, superintendent of applied arts, to include Sheerer's lamp among entries for final judging. In his letter to Whiting Woodward described the lamp as "the most distinguished product of the Newcomb Pottery up to date" and went on to praise the beaded shade as being "unique" and "one of the most satisfactory and permanent workmanlike bits of handicraft that I have yet seen from any source." Despite Woodward's insistent support for the lamp, it did not receive an award. See Jody Blake, "Fair Years for Newcomb Pottery: 1900-1915," Department of Art, Newcomb College, May 1983, pp. 26-28.

179 (color plate, p. 37)
Vase, 1909
Newcomb Pottery (1895-1940), New Orleans
Decorator: Sarah Agnes Estelle Irvine (1887-1970)
Earthenware, wheel-thrown with irises modeled in low relief; dark blue slips covered with transparent matte glaze
H: 13⅜ in. Diam: 7¾ in.
Marks: incised cipher *SI*; impressed ciphers *NC* and *JM*, *W*; registration number *DH66* painted in blue (on bottom)
Private Collection, courtesy of The Metropolitan Museum of Art

Newcomb Pottery is characterized by decoration inspired by the southern landscape rendered in cool colors on elegant forms. Its distinctive appearance was dictated in large part by local conditions. The Louisiana climate made it difficult to paint in slip on unfired clay (the technique developed in Cincinnati); thus, a bis-

quit firing was required.[1] Furthermore, the colors of slips chosen – green, blue, yellow, and black – were those that produced the most consistent results.

Apart from technical considerations, art instruction at the College was equally crucial to the development of a Newcomb style. Mary Sheerer, who managed the daily operations and instructed the students in pottery decoration, believed that underglaze painting required "simple, big designs and firm drawing."[2] She was a follower of Arthur Wesley Dow's principles (based on the Japanese style of abstraction from nature) and his philosophy of instruction as recorded in his book *Composition*, available to the Newcomb students.[3] Between 1900 and 1906, Miss Sheerer and several of her students took Dow's famous summer course at Ipswich, Massachusetts, and carried his bold designs – heavy lines defining broad color zones – into the decoration of Newcomb pottery (see no. 178). By 1910, however, Dow's art had changed to reflect a pronounced tonalism typical of the period, and Newcomb wares, likewise, came to be characterized by a naturalistic style. Transparent, matte, and semi-matte glazes, developed by Paul Cox to enhance the new romanticism, were used almost exclusively after 1911.[4]

Yet another factor contributing to the homogeneity of Newcomb wares was the longevity of its personnel. Nearly all pottery made from 1896 to 1927 was thrown by Joseph Meyer, and some artists worked there for many years. Sarah [Sadie] Irvine, who decorated this vase, was on the staff from 1908 to 1952. "I was accused of doing the first oak-tree decoration, also the first moon. I have surely lived to regret it," wrote Miss Irvine. "Our beautiful moss-draped oak trees appealed to the buying public . . . . And oh, how boring it was to use the same motif over and over and over . . . ."[5]

While such consistency underlay the stability essential to Newcomb's success, it also led to a product perceived as rather stale by some connoisseurs. Work submitted for display in 1929 at the new Cranbrook Academy of Art was declined because George Booth "desires to represent modern tendencies."[6] In the early 1930s Juanita Gonzalez, who trained at Newcomb College and then in New York with Alexandre Archipenko, attempted to introduce the symbolism and freedom of expression characteristic of contemporary studio potters, but the innovations were lost on the consumer: "We've tried to change before, but the public hasn't let

us. They demand the oak trees which are so typical of Louisiana that they bring back memories."[7]

EPD and BRD

1. The process afforded a clear surface for decorating with colored slips and solved the problem of differential shrinkage between the raw clay body and slips during firing. The clay used was local in origin with admixtures of other American clays. See Jessie Poesch, *Newcomb Pottery: An Enterprise for Southern Women, 1895-1940* (Exton, Pa.: Schiffer Publishing, 1984).

2. Mary G. Sheerer, "Newcomb Pottery," *Keramic Studio* 1 (November 1899), p. 152.

3. Arthur Wesley Dow, *Composition: A Series of Exercises Selected from a New System of Art Education* (New York: Baker and Taylor Company, 1899). See also Poesch 1984, pp. 26-28, for further discussion of Dow's method and its influence at Newcomb Pottery.

4. "While the effects thus produced are pleasant and inviting," commented Charles F. Binns (see no. 177), "there are still some who believe that the luscious surface of a brilliant glaze is more appropriate for the method of treatment. Nevertheless, the trend of present taste is undoubtedly towards the texture quality." (See "Pottery in America," *American Magazine of Art* 7 [February 1916], p. 133.) Although 1911 is the year identified for Cox's development of a consistently successful transparent matte glaze, such glazes were used intermittently before that date. This vase is, therefore, an early example of the new texture.

5. Robert W. Blasberg, "The Sadie Irvine Letters: A Further Note on the Production of Newcomb Pottery," *Antiques* 100 (August 1971), pp. 250-251. These transcriptions of Miss Irvine's letters include a description of her working method.

6. Correspondence from H.P. Macomber, Secretary of the Department of Art, Cranbrook Academy of Art, to Ellsworth Woodward, January 1930, quoted in Poesch 1984, p. 77.

7. Lota Lee Troy, Newcomb Pottery director, quoted in article in [New Orleans] *Item*, March 2, 1932, quoted in Poesch 1984, p. 84.

180
Table runner, 1905-1915
Marie Delavigne (d. 1963) of the Art School of the H. Sophie Newcomb Memorial College, New Orleans
Silk embroidery (running [darning] stitch) on linen plain weave
L: 108 in. W: 21 in.
Marks: embroidered *NC* and *MD*
Collection of Sonia and Walter Bob

180 (detail)

Although produced in smaller quantity than pottery, the crafts of embroidery, weaving metalwork, bookbinding, printing, and calligraphy were all part of the Newcomb College program. Gertrude Roberts Smith (1869-1962), supervisor of the textile crafts at the college, was a painter and potter as well. She had come in 1893 to help build the art school and was a significant presence there for forty years. Miss Roberts's mastery of several crafts reflected the interdisciplinary nature of the Newcomb curriculum; in fact, the combination of pottery, embroidery, and jewelry earned the college the Grand Prize at the 1915 San Francisco Panama-Pacific International Exposition.[1]

Marie Delavigne needed both imagination and technical skill to execute this table runner in only one stitch – the running (or darning) stitch. She also displayed ingenuity in the clarity of the design – oak trees in a retreating landscape – and in the color composition: bright hues of chartreuse, pink, and orange contrasted with the background blues and greens (shades associated with Newcomb pottery).

It appears that the fabric was woven on a loom with a maximum width of fifteen inches,

the measurement of the central piece (it is bordered by two side pieces three inches wide). To conceal the strong vertical lines of the selvages, Miss Delavigne planned the embroidery design to occur where the fabric is seamed together. She finished the runner with cotton twill tape at each end.

GM

1. "The Newcomb Art School," *American Magazine of Art* 10 (October 1919), p. 480.

181

Four tiles, ca. 1911-ca. 1923
Batchelder Tile Company (1909-1932, with various partners), Pasadena and Los Angeles
Designer: Ernest A. Batchelder (1875-1957)
Earthenware, molded and finished by hand; washed in blue
H: 6 in. W: 6 in. D: 1¼ in. to 3¼ in.
Marks: *BATCHELDER/PASADENA* (impressed on bottom)
Collection of Robert Winter

Ernest A. Batchelder's philosophy of education reflected the heart of the Arts and Crafts move-

ment. "We learn by doing," he declared in the preface to his 1910 manual *Design in Theory and Practice.* "In setting mind and hand to the solution of a definite problem, we meet and overcome questions which no amount of reading can foresee. We may attend lectures and indulge in critical discussions of design in terms of language; we may become well versed in the history of art, and in biographical data pertaining to the lives of artists; yet find ourselves far removed from any true appreciation of the work of the past, or quite at a loss when confronted by a simple problem in constructive design demanding artistic invention."[1]

A native of New Hampshire, Batchelder studied at the Massachusetts Normal School in Boston and the School of Arts and Crafts at Birmingham, England.[2] His association with Denman W. Ross, design professor at Harvard University and donor of a substantial collection of Asian arts to the Boston Museum of Fine Arts, encouraged Batchelder's enthusiasm for teaching the theory and practice of design. He organized the Handicraft Guild in Minneapolis in 1902 and taught summer courses there from 1903 to 1908. Between 1904 and 1909 he was in charge of the department of arts and crafts at the Throop Polytechnic Institute (now California Institute of Technology) in Pasadena.[3]

Batchelder put his theory of "doing" to work in 1909 in a small building for kiln and shop behind his house in Pasadena. This backyard pottery was to be the basis for a school of design and handicrafts, but it became a major tile manufactory when it was moved to an industrial section of Pasadena in 1912 to accommodate a rapid increase in business.[4] Tiles were molded from designs worked out on paper, but company literature stressed reliance on the "sympathetic interpretation of the designs at the hands of Mr. and Mrs. Ingels" in the modeling shop where the original molds were made.[5] Bearing out Batchelder's philosophy that "our salvation is to be sought not in borrowing from Europe,"[6] many of the tiles mirror the California locality, especially those depicting rolling landscapes, winding roads, poplars, live oaks, and various fauna. But many others are based on foreign motifs such as the Tudor rose, Viking ships, knights, castles, and Mayan iconography. These corbel tiles, for example, depict musicians in medieval garb playing simple instruments. They were designed early in the firm's history, but must have remained popular be-

181

cause they were still included in the 1923 company catalogue for $3.60 each.[7]

EPD and BRD

1. Ernest A. Batchelder, *Design in Theory and Practice* (New York: Macmillan, 1910) p. vi. This book is a compilation of a series of articles that appeared originally in *The Craftsman* magazine between 1907 and 1909. Batchelder was also the author of *The Principles of Design* (Chicago: Inland Printer, 1904).

2. For more about Batchelder, see Elva Meline, "Art Tile in California: The Work of E.A. Batchelder," *Spinning Wheel* 27 (November 1971), pp. 8-10 and 65; and Hazel V. Bray, *The Potter's Art in California, 1885 to 1955* (Oakland, Calif: Oakland Museum, 1980), p. 12.

3. Mabel Urmy Seares, "Ernest Batchelder and His Tiles," *International Studio* 58 (April 1916), p. 54.

4. Eventually the tiles, made in Los Angeles, were available across the country through display rooms in Chicago, New York, San Francisco, and Los Angeles, and from distributors in smaller cities.

5. Ernest A. Batchelder, *A Little History of Batchelder Tiles* (Los Angeles: Batchelder-Wilson Company, 1925), p. 2.

6. Batchelder 1910, p. vii.

7. According to Robert Winter, corbel tiles of this pattern were used on the pergola of Greene and Greene's Cordelia Culbertson House in Pasadena, built in 1911; see also *Batchelder Tiles: A Catalog of Hand Made Tiles* (Los Angeles: Batchelder-Wilson Company, 1923), p. 31.

182

Vase, 1914
University City Porcelain Works (1912-1915), University City, Missouri
Designer: Taxile Doat (1851-1938)
Porcelain, molded in gourd shape and covered with white crystalline glaze
H: 10 in. W: 3¼ in.
Marks: stamped cipher UC in green/ 1914 / cipher TD (on bottom)
University City Public Library Archives, University City, Missouri

One of the most talented of the foreign ceramists who came to the United States and contributed to the Arts and Crafts movement was the Frenchman Taxile Doat. Born at Albi (Tarn) in 1851, Doat studied ceramics technology at the Ecole des Arts Décoratifs in Limoges and sculpture at the Ecole des Beaux-Arts in Paris. In 1878 he began working at the national manufactory of Sèvres, where he remained until 1906.[1] His achievements in the *pâte-sur-pâte* decoration[2] won gold medals at several international expositions, and he was knighted by the French government. After 1898 he maintained a personal studio at Sèvres for his own experimentation and designs, while continuing to execute works for the national manufactory.

In 1903 a series of articles on high-fired ceramics by Doat was translated and published by Samuel and Adelaide Alsop Robineau in their monthly *Keramic Studio*; in 1905 the articles were combined in a single volume entitled *Grand Feu Ceramics*.[3] Four years later Edward G. Lewis, a founder-promoter of the American Woman's League and the Peoples [sic] University at University City, Missouri, offered Doat the directorship of the pottery division at the Academy of Art. Doat accepted the challenge and joined the Robineaus, Frederick H. Rhead (nos. 183, 191), Kathryn E. Cherry (no. 184), and others on a distinguished faculty.

The choice of porcelain as a product of the University City kiln[4] owed something to porcelain's prestige value, but it was also based on the discovery in 1903 of a vein of pure kaolin (the key ingredient of porcelain) by workmen digging water-main trenches nearby. Edward Lewis

182

and his wife Mabel had then begun experimenting with porcelain in a converted chicken house, using Doat's book as a guide.[5]

In spite of the excellent wares produced at University City, which included some spectacular exhibition pieces by Doat, the financial condition of the American Woman's League suffered with the U.S. government's investigation of Lewis for mail fraud. In 1911 the Robineaus returned to New York and Rhead left University City to direct the new Arequipa Pottery in California, but Doat was persuaded to remain and, with new assistants, continued to produce porcelains for the reorganized University City Porcelain Works. Emphasis in this later period was on molded jars, containers, and vases that could be more quickly and cheaply manufactured. The present vase is a fine example of these molded wares from the late years of the operation and was designed by Doat after similar Sèvres and other French models in gourd and vegetal shapes. In 1915, Doat ended his employment with Lewis and returned to his beloved Villa Kaolin at Sevres, where he lived until his death in 1938.

BRD and EPD

1. *Hard Porcelains and Grès Flammés Made at University City, Mo.* (University City, Mo.: University City Porcelain Works, 1914), n.p.

2. The technique involves painting thin layers of porcelain slip on top of each other to create a cameo-like relief design against a contrasting porcelain ground.

3. Taxile Doat, *Grand Feu Ceramics: A Practical Treatise on the Making of Fine Porcelain and Grès Flammés*, translated by Samuel E. Robineau with an essay by Prof. Charles F. Binns (Syracuse: Keramic Studio Publishing Co., 1905).

4. The first successful kiln was fired on April 2, 1910. A crystalline-glazed plaque by Taxile Doat bearing the inscription "THE FIRST OBJECT OF CERAMIC ART DRAWN FROM THE KILNS OF UNIVERSITY CITY. 2 APRIL 1910." is preserved at the University City Public Library.

5. See *Hard Porcelains and Grès Flammés*, n.p.

183 (color plate, p. 38)
Vase, 1911
University City Pottery (1910-1912), University City, Missouri
Designer: Frederick Hurten Rhead (1880-1942)
Buff earthenware, wheel-thrown with incised decoration of a stylized woodland landscape in matte glazes of blue, green, and white
H: 17½ in. Diam: 4¾ in.

Marks: incised cipher *UC* enclosing ciphers *AWL* and *FHR* [?]; 1911; 1020 (on bottom)
P.G. Pugsley & Son Antiques, San Francisco

Frederick Rhead's career, like that of many potters, followed a peripatetic course (see nos. 163 and 191).[1] After several years as art director at the Roseville Pottery, Rhead left in 1908 to join a friend, William P. Jervis, who was operating his own pottery on Long Island, New York. The next year, however, he accepted an invitation to teach pottery at the Art School of the Peoples [sic] University for the American Woman's League at University City, Missouri.[2] His decision was prompted partly by a desire to leave the artistic constraints of large commercial potteries like Weller and Roseville and accept the opportunity to work with Taxile Doat, the famous French ceramist hired to be Director of the Division of Ceramics. In addition to planning the studio pottery correspondence courses and supervising the installation of equipment for the new school, he began writing a craft pottery textbook.[3]

While Mrs. Robineau and Doat concentrated on porcelain production at University City, Rhead specialized in earthenware and low-fired ceramics. Most of his pottery during this period features deeply incised designs drawn in a stylized manner, such as in this tall vase with swirling tree branches and mushrooms on a woodland floor. Many vases and tiles also depict peacocks or flowers in a style reminiscent of nineteenth-century English Aesthetic movement book illustration. Agnes Rhead frequently helped her husband with the decorating, but the designs were his.[4]

As a result of financial and legal problems with the American Woman's League and its founder, Edward G. Lewis, Rhead was forced to leave University City in 1911 along with the Robineaus and others.[5] His wealth of experience helped him find employment almost immediately, however; in California he first directed the new Arequipa Pottery (see no. 163) and then, in 1913, his own pottery at Santa Barbara. When the latter operation proved to be unprofitable, Rhead returned to the midwest and served for ten years as director of the research department of the American Encaustic Tiling Company and fifteen years as art director of the Homer Laughlin China Company. The "Fiesta" line of dinnerware he designed for that firm, with its modern shapes and bright monochromatic glazes, is the best remembered of

Rhead's commercial work. In 1934 his professional achievements earned him the Charles Fergus Binns Medal from the New York State College of Ceramics at Alfred.

BRD and EPD

1. Sharon Dale, *Frederick Hurten Rhead: An English Potter in America* (Erie, Pa.: Erie Art Museum, 1986).

2. Rhead's association with Samuel and Adelaide Alsop Robineau extended back to 1903, when he began submitting designs for ceramic decoration to their *Keramic Studio* monthly. See Peg Weiss, ed., *Adelaide Alsop Robineau: Glory in Porcelain* (Syracuse: Syracuse University Press in association with Everson Museum of Art, 1981), pp. 93-115. This section, written by F.H. Rhead, is entitled "The University City Venture" and was edited by Paul Evans.

3. Frederick Hurten Rhead, *Studio Pottery* (University City, Mo.: Peoples University Press, 1910).

4. The ambiguous artist's cipher on the present vase may be interpreted as *FHR* or *AR* (for Agnes Rhead).

5. For details, see personal correspondence, F.H. Rhead to Taxile Doat, October 15, 1911, on letterhead of the Arequipa Sanitorium, Fairfax, California. Collection of University City Public Library.

184

Vase, ca. 1910 - 1913
Delinières & Co., Limoges
Decorator: Kathryn Evelyn Cherry (1871-1931), working for the American Woman's League at the University City Pottery (1910-1912), University City, Missouri
Porcelain, molded and decorated over glaze in black stylized floral pattern
H: 12¼ in. Diam: 8⅞ in.
Marks: underglaze green printed *D & C⁰ / FRANCE; A.W.L. / K.E.C. / U.C.*, painted in black and glazed (on bottom)
Collection of Betty and Robert A. Hut

The career of Kathryn Cherry is one of the success stories among the many remarkable midwestern women within the Arts and Crafts movement. Born Kathryn Evelyn Bard in 1871 in Quincy, Illinois, she attended Washington University School of Fine Arts in St. Louis, New York School of Arts, and the Pennsylvania Academy of Fine Arts in Philadelphia. She also studied abroad for a year before marriage to William W. Cherry, M.D., in 1892.[1] Her art education subsequently included the study of china painting with Marshall Fry and with Adelaide Alsop Robineau (see nos. 108 and 109), who later reminisced: "It was about the time of the birth of *Keramic Studio* (1899) that Mrs. Cherry came to

184

Mrs. Robineau's studio in New York for a few lessons in what was then the only conventional work, raised paste-enamel and lustre. Since then she has so far outstripped her teacher, both in design and execution of overglaze decoration, that if the latter returned to this field, which she deserted fifteen years ago, she would need to take lessons of her pupil."[2]

In fact, Mrs. Cherry became a very influential teacher. She was an instructor in overglaze painting and decoration at the Alfred (New York) University Summer School beginning in 1901 and a frequent contributor of designs to *Keramic Studio* through the years. In 1910 she began teaching and directing a correspondence course in china painting for the Division of Ceramics of the Art Academy of the Peoples [sic] University, endowed by the American Woman's League at University City, Missouri, a suburb of St. Louis.[3]

Mrs. Cherry was one of the most prominent of the relatively few women who managed to make a profession of china painting. She combined an active teaching career with the marketing of her own line of china colors through *Keramic Studio* and the Robineau Pottery. The present vase is a departure from her most typical stylized china decoration, which usually featured bright colorful enamels like those on Dorothea Warren O'Hara's bowl (no. 113). It also illustrates the frequent dependence of American decorators on imported porcelain blanks, in spite of the availability of American porcelain.

BRD and EPD

1. *Who Was Who in America*, vol. 1 (Chicago: Marquis Who's Who, 1960), p. 215.

2. Adelaide Alsop Robineau, "Mrs. Kathryn E. Cherry," *Keramic Studio* 18 (March 1917), p. 178.

3. *The Art Academy of the Peoples University* (University City, Mo.: Peoples University Press, 1910).

185

Covered cup, 1914
Douglas Donaldson (1882-1972), Los Angeles
Silver, parcel-gilt, *champlevé* enamels, opal, moonstones, turquoise, emeralds, and peridots
H: 8 ⅜ in. Diam: 3 5/16 in. Wt: (gross) 22 oz., 10 dwt.
Inscription: engraved Harvard shield enclosing *VE RI / TAS* flanked by ribbon framing motto *CHRISTO ET* and *ECCLESIAE* (on exterior); engraved *HARVARD / FRESHMAN / SINGING / CUP* (on underside)

185

Marks: engraved *Douglas Donaldson 1914* Harvard University. 587.1928

Douglas Donaldson is one of several mid-western Arts and Crafts teacher-practitioners who followed a path from Minneapolis to Los Angeles. The group's common origin was the Handicraft Guild of Minneapolis to which Donaldson came from Joliet, Illinois, as a twenty-five-year-old student in 1907. That he was already accomplished in the disciplines he would make his life work is suggested by his consignor-member status at the Detroit Society of Arts and Crafts and the catalogue record of copper jewelry he exhibited as a member of the National Society of Craftsmen.[1] He is known to have studied under James H. Winn, the prominent handicraft jeweler, and undoubtedly attended the 1907 summer classes in metalwork and jewelry at the Guild taught by Winn.

Donaldson's teaching career probably began in the summer of 1909 at the Guild. By this time he had been a pupil of the nation's foremost teacher of enameling, Laurin H. Martin, and this craft was a feature of his copper jewelry and holloware sent by the Guild to the Art Institute of Chicago's annual Arts and Crafts exhibitions of 1908 and 1909. In 1909 Donaldson and Nelbert Murphy (Chouinard) followed their teacher Ernest A. Batchelder (see no. 181) to Batchelder's newly established school of design and handicraft on the Pasadena Arroyo Seco.[2] From 1912 to 1919 Donaldson headed the art department of Manual Arts High School of Los Angeles. A report of the summer session he held in 1915 listed "Hammer work, repousse work, etching, coloring processes, gilding, stone polishing, and casting [as] some of the processes taken up in the metalwork and jewelry classes. . . ."[3] In 1919 Donaldson began teaching metalwork, jewelry, and decorative design classes at Otis Art Institute in Los Angeles, and, about 1921, with his wife, Louise Towle Donaldson – his former pupil at the Handicraft Guild of Minneapolis – established a studio in Hollywood. There, from the mid-1920s he conducted annual summer courses emphasizing design and color theory.[4]

Donaldson's skills as a silversmith, enameler, and jeweler are joined in this chalice-shaped cup to a degree rarely seen in American work. Made for the 1915 Panama-California Exposition in San Diego, it reflects the *tour de force* character of objects made for public spectacle and not for everyday life. Following the Exposition's closing, the cup became the highlight of an exhibition of California crafts Donaldson organized to travel to Los Angeles, Buffalo, Boston, New York City, and Chicago.[5] Before completing the tour, it was purchased – for $400 – from the Boston Society of Arts and Crafts as a trophy for Harvard College's inter-dormitory singing contest.[6]

Passages of the ornament on the cup relate closely to Batchelder examples, especially the motifs on the base, which can be traced to a Coptic weaving.[7] The horizontal panels of the jeweled band follow Bachelder's advice: "Then see if you can strike a few well-curved lines having a common growing point and related by a movement in harmony with the movement represented by . . . the flower heads."[8] Despite significant losses of enamel, enough of the colors remain to demonstrate Donaldson's mastery of the medium. Enamels ornament the base, the six panels of the pedestal, and the four bird plaques of the jeweled band. Hues of light green, turquoise, yellow, rust, navy, and purple were carefully chosen for interactive effects, as were those of the cabochon stones.

WSB

1. Archives of American Art, *Papers of the Detroit Society of Arts and Crafts*, roll 281, frames 942, 952; and *Arts and Crafts Exhibition* (New York: National Arts Club in collaboration with National Society of Craftsmen, 1907), pp. 15, 44.

2. An article of Donaldson's, "The Making of Metal Lamp Shades" (*Palette and Bench* 2 [February 1910], pp. 109-111), reveals that much of the design influence of his Guild work is traceable to Batchelder through the latter's progressive text *Design in Theory and Practice* ([New York: Macmillan, 1910], p. 252, fig. 148).

3. Antony Anderson, "Art and Artists: Summer School," *Los Angeles Times* (July 11, 1915), sec. 3, p. 4, col. 6. Student metalwork from the school appears in "Examples of Nineteenth Century American Craftsmanship," *Century Magazine* 95 (January 1918), p. 456, ill.

4. The radical and brilliant use of color in costumes and scenery by Léon Bakst for the Ballet Russes in Paris in 1909 exerted considerable influence on designers such as Donaldson and his colleague Rudolph F. Schaeffer.

5. "California Exhibition of Applied Arts Under the Auspices of the Los Angeles Arts and Crafts Club" (brochure); see also "Art at Home and Abroad: Wide Variety in Group of Current Exhibitions," *New York Times* (April 4, 1916), sec. 5, p. 15.

6. The author is indebted to Louise Ambler for the purchase-price information.

7. Batchelder 1910, p. 244, fig. 137; facing p. 243, pl. 61.

8. Ibid., p. 191.

186

Box, 1911-1914
Theodore Hanford Pond (1872-1933),
Baltimore
Silver
H: 3 in. W: 3⅞ in. D: 3⅞ in. Wt: 6 oz., 7 dwt.
Marks: struck incuse *POND* / circular shop mark of dragonfly enclosed by *KWO-NE-SHE* and *HAND/ WROUGHT / STERLING*
Private Collection

Campaigning for handicraft as an art rather than simply a manual vocation, Theodore H. Pond – writer, lecturer, educator, craftsman, and museum director – played a major role in directing the course of arts and crafts education in America from the turn of the century until his death.

186

Among the many crafts he practiced, he was best known as a silversmith and work from his studio appeared at major exhibitions in New York, Chicago, and Buffalo.[1]

Born to American missionary parents in Beruit, Pond spent his youth in Europe and the Middle East before coming to America and attending Pratt Institute from 1888 to 1892. For the next three or four years he was employed by Louis C. Tiffany as a designer of stained glass and interior decorations. By 1896 Pond was on the faculty of the Rhode Island School of Design, which he left in 1902 to organize and superintend a department of applied and fine arts at the Mechanics Institute in Rochester. He went in 1908 to Baltimore to create and head a department of design and applied arts at the Maryland Institute. There, from 1911 to 1914, he organized and directed The Pond Applied Art Studios, whose emblem this box bears.[2]

Two major principles of the Arts and Crafts movement are embodied in the box. First, its fabrication reflects Pond's belief that a silversmith should be able to carry out his work from beginning to end.[3] Second, its form and ornament derive from nature: the *repoussé* and chasing on the cover suggest the petals of a hibiscus; the flower's contours inspired the shape of the box. A broad range of metalworking techniques – seaming, extrusion, soldering, and hinge fabrication – are displayed in the piece.

Being labor-intensive, boxes were not a staple of the professional silversmith. For the enamel and metal handicrafter, however, they were a favorite vehicle for artistic expression (see nos. 129, 131, and 187), and this box, which lacks the unlabored look of repetitive handwork, is probably unique. The form relates to a dish of 1900 by C.R. Ashbee[4] and, in fact, Pond's teaching methods reflect the English ideals of integrating design theory and practice and paying a fair wage for the work produced. As *Arts & Decoration* said of Pond's Applied Art Studios in 1913: "In the school a system of apprenticeship, such as is in vogue in England, is followed and a charge for instruction is made to male apprentices. A portion of the day is spent in the study of theoretical design and the remainder in practical shop work. A graduated scale of pay has been arranged whereby students become wage earners after the first three months."[5]

WSB

1. For more information about Pond, see Warren Wilmer Brown, "Theodore Hanford Pond, Craftsman," *International Studio* 47 (September 1912), pp. XLIII-XLV, ill.; and Theodore Hanford Pond, "The Handicrafts in Connection with Art Training," *Handicraft* 3 (September 1910), pp. 195-201. For an example of Pond's extensive participation at one exhibition, see *Exhibition of Old and Modern Handicraft* (Baltimore: Handicraft Club of Baltimore, 1913), pp. 34-36 and unpaged illustrations.

2. See the studio's advertisement in *Handicraft* 5 (August 1912), p. 81. The meaning of the emblem's words "KWO-NE-SHE" are unknown.

3. Theodore Hanford Pond, "The Craft of the Silversmith," *Arts & Crafts Magazine* 3 (April 1913), pp. 113-115.

4. Rowland and Betty Elzea, *The Pre-Raphaelite Era, 1848-1914* (Wilmington: Wilmington Society of Fine Arts, 1976), p. 149, nos. 6-43, ill.

5. "What the Art Schools are Doing," *Arts & Decoration* 3 (April 1913), p. 209.

187

Box, ca. 1910
The Handicraft Guild of Minneapolis
Copper, amethysts, and silk lining
H: 2¼ in. Diam: 5 in.
Marks: struck incuse *HANDICRAFT GUILD / MINNEAPOLIS*
Collection of Jennifer Braznell

The Handicraft Guild of Minneapolis, founded by Ernest Batchelder in 1902, was one of many organizations that played an important part in spreading reform in taste, design, and craft.[1] Work by its craftsmen was widely circulated in

187

1. The Guild began with a salesroom where members' work was sold on commission. In 1905 summer school sessions were begun in which Batchelder's classes in composition and design complemented practical application taught by experienced craftsmen. A year-round school program probably began in 1906 and a new building designed to house studios for various crafts opened about 1908. See "Society Biographies: The Handicraft Guild, Minneapolis," *Handicraft* 3 (December 1910), pp. 341-342; and Elva Meline, "Art Tile in California, The Work of E.A. Batchelder," *Spinning Wheel* 27 (November 1971), p. 8.

2. Fred D. Crawshaw stated in his introduction to *Metal Spinning: Practical Instruction in a Fascinating Art* (Chicago: Popular Mechanics, 1909), pp. 9-10: "Like so many others of the old-time crafts, the one of metal spinning has partially come into disuse because of commercial competition . . .[i.e., produced with a stamp or press] . . . . Sometimes, however, where only a comparatively few articles of any particular shape are desired, they are spun instead of stamped out, to save the cost of the dies . . . . From the stand point of the craftsman, metal spinning is a craft which is highly desirable of attainment and which may replace beaten-metal work in some cases, or, in many cases, be used in connection with it." Crawshaw illustrated a covered box, with contours similar to this example (p. 45) but a near match to a Guild box illustrated by Elizabeth A. Chant in "The Summer Session of the Handicraft Guild," *Palette and Bench* 1 (October 1908), p. 24.

3. Payne's book (published by Manual Arts Press, Peoria, in 1914) and *Copper Work* by the Rhode Island School of Design instructor Augustus F. Rose (published by Davis Press, Worcester, Massachusetts, in 1906) were the most influential American publications devoted to metalwork. The only others known at the time were the modest volumes from Popular Mechanics Company of Chicago's crafts handbook series, such as Fred D. Crawshaw's *Metal Spinning* (1909) and John Adams's *Metal Work and Etching* (1910).

exhibitions and was even retailed in Philadelphia and New York. Best known for metalwork, jewelry, and pottery, the Guild also produced leatherwork, bookbinding, woodwork, woodcarving, and woodblock printing.

Although metal spinning – the process by which this box's base and cover were made – is a machine-fabrication method popularly acknowledged as distinct from handicraft, it may well have been taught at the Guild.[2] Alternatively, there may have been outside suppliers of spun metalwares upon which members practiced the rudimentary *repoussé*, chasing, and stone-setting skills seen here. (Such a practice would have been analogous to china painting on manufactured blanks, a popular Arts and Crafts movement pastime.) Typical of the Guild's metalwares of about 1910, the box retains a lavender silk lining and was probably intended for jewelry.

Arthur Payne chose the cover of this box, or an identical one, to illustrate chasing in his publication *Art Metalwork with Inexpensive Equipment*, one of the most comprehensive American texts to disseminate information about metalworking techniques for manual training in schools or home workshops.[3] In his preface Payne noted: "All of the designs and practically all of the work used as illustrations in this book are the products of students who worked in classes of twenty or more under ordinary school conditions."

WSB

188

Fabric sample, ca. 1920
Edward Worst (1866-1949), after traditional pattern
"Overshot" (cotton plain weave with continuous supplementary wool wefts)
L: (of warp) 40 in. W: (of weft; selvage to selvage) 29 in.
Chicago Historical Society

Arts and Crafts exhortations to return to a simpler way of life – one without excessive ornamentation and one in which the essential structure of objects was visible – created a climate that encouraged the revival of handloom weaving. Just as emphasis was placed on the way a chair was put together, with joinery apparent, the interaction of vertical warps and horizontal wefts of textiles was meant to be seen. Among those who helped to disseminate basic weaving skills to a wider audience was Edward Francis Worst, the author of several books[1] and a teacher of manual arts. Through his efforts, woodwork, metalwork, and home-economics classes became part of the public-school curriculum in Chicago.

Born in Lockport, Illinois, Edward Worst had traveled extensively in Scandinavia and northern Europe in the years before the First World War to learn more about the craft of weaving and fiber production. Like many exponents of the Arts and Crafts movement in the northern and eastern United States, he valued the process of study and experimentation as much as quality in the finished product. By contrast, conditions in the south forced an emphasis on weaving for profit. Lucy Morgan, a graduate of Berea College, with whom Worst founded the Penland School of Handicrafts in North Carolina, asked for his help "in restoring old patterns and [in changing] colors in order that their product might be more saleable for the American home."[2]

Although Worst taught continually, he never stopped his own weaving. Fascinated with the patterns of colonial coverlets, he analyzed their structure, prepared weavers' diagrams (called "drafts"), and later wove his own examples, such as the present piece – probably an exercise to test a pattern or try out a color scheme.

GM

1. Worst's best-known work, published in 1918, was *Foot-Power Loom Weaving* (Milwaukee: Bruce Publishing Company). Originally intended as a manual for use in the school system, the book is considered a classic for handloom weavers. For further discussion of his life, see Olivia Mahoney, *Edward F. Worst, Craftsman and Educator* (Chicago: Chicago Historical Society, 1985).

2. Quoted in Mahoney 1985, p. 34. The school grew out of Lucy Morgan's earlier organization, the Penland Weavers and Potters.

IV

Reform of the Home

House and Home in the Arts and Crafts Era: Reforms for Simpler Living

Cheryl Robertson

Arts and Crafts practitioners were often progressive, sometimes revolutionary, in their designs for open-plan houses and furnishings derived from the lines and colors of the natural environs rather than eclectic combinations of details borrowed from European historical styles. However, such changes in the outward trappings of domestic architecture and decoration did not imply a fundamental change in relations and rituals within the family domicile. Turn-of-the-century intellectuals and artist-craftsmen dismissed the formal, over-stuffed parlor suites of the Gilded Age as *passé*; yet they retained – indeed reinforced – the Victorian cult of domesticity.

Post-Civil-War social trends – notably increased opportunities for female education and paid employment in the cities, as well as the introduction of fashionable apartment houses or residential hotels offering possibilities for communal cooking, cleaning, and laundry services – countermanded certain cherished underpinnings of American civilization.[1] Jeffersonian republicanism and Jacksonian democracy had established deep-seated convictions about the rural freehold as originator of civic virtue and the upstanding citizen as the product of a private, single-family dwelling situated in the countryside. A.J. Downing, America's most famous architectural spokesman for bourgeois aspirations in the early Victorian period, addressed those issues explicitly in the preface to his treatise *The Architecture of Country Houses* (1850).[2] Downing gave three reasons to explain why his countrymen needed housing fabricated in accord with the suburban models presented in his book. First, a rural architecture composed of "smiling lawns and tasteful cottages" was a powerful promoter of order and culture. Second, the individual home featuring "com-

munings with nature and the family" fostered the best kind of character development, marked by a pure spirit and superior intellectual powers. Third, the country home was a moral exemplar more effectual than any preachings inculcated by churches, schools, or other societal institutions. The preface concluded with a definition of the readership as persons of all classes interested in "the beauty, convenience, or fitness of a house in the country."

Arts and Crafts spokesmen, concerned particularly with the middle-class home – as opposed to other reformers who focused on tenement housing or immigrant assimilation – revived Downing's premises and encapsulated them in a catchy phrase, "the simple life." Its key elements were retreat from the city, centrality of the family, moral education through artistic appreciation, and self-improvement by means of home beautification. A sampling of writings on simplified living by Charles Wagner, William Gray Purcell, Charles Keeler, and Ray Stannard Baker demonstrates the essential conservatism of ideologues associated with the Arts and Crafts movement. They subscribed to Downing's tenets but repackaged them in the up-to-date guise of the bungalow furnished with natural materials and handmade accessories chosen or crafted by the full-time professional homemaker.

The Simple Life: Theory and Practice

Charles Wagner, a French Protestant minister and founder of the Union for Moral Action, undertook an American lecture tour in 1904 at the behest of Theodore Roosevelt. The president said of the pastor's publication *The Simple Life* (1901) that he knew of "no other book . . . which contains so much that we of America ought to take to our hearts." Indeed, the American public had taken

Wagner to heart as soon as *The Simple Life* was in print. It was a best-seller in 1901.[3]

What in Wagner's message took Americans by storm? His preachings on moral rectitude and discipline as the backbone of human progress encouraged individualized expression of religious sentiment in lieu of adherence to sectarian dogma. The key was simplicity, defined as a state of mind unrelated to external trappings. Beneath a rich man's finery, a joyous, altruistic heart could beat; conversely, a beggar was not simple if he dreamed of idleness and sensual excesses. Hence, the American middle class were not required to jettison physical comfort to follow Wagner, but they need not "keep up with the Joneses" to validate their social worth.

Wagner had grown up with his Alsatian peasant grandparents and then pursued advanced study in Paris and Strasbourg. Homesick and spiritually disconsolate in those university years, he found renewed faith in a return to the tranquil fields and traditions of his childhood. One of Wagner's essays portrayed the New World experience as an analogue of his youthful loss of innocence and subsequent self-renewal: "In spite of all appearances to the contrary, both by tradition and by temperament, America loves simplicity. She knows what she owes to it; she feels that if she should escape from the influence of this vital and regenerative force, the scepter would depart from her. She takes account of the fact that young and powerful nations become contaminated with startling rapidity when in contact with corruption to which long habitude has accustomed older civilizations."[4]

Wagner credited women with a natural grace and homey aesthetic that put "witchery into a ribbon and genius into a stew."[5] This phrase, with annotations, resurfaced in Orison Swett Marden's lengthy inquiry into the state of American womanhood and the home.[6] Marden underscored the alchemist abilities of wives and mothers in transforming even a bare attic into a happy, loving household. The interior decorator Mabel Tuke Priestman, who published widely in American periodicals sympathetic to Arts and Crafts goals and products, added her influential voice to the Wagnerian chorus.[7] Quoting the Frenchman in her *Art and Economy in Home Decoration* (1910), she warned moderate-income readers against ostentatious display. Harmony and simplicity were Priestman's objectives, evidenced in handicrafts and creative decorating schemes expressive of the "human beauty" of the female hand and mind.

Certainly Wagner's notion of democracy in matters of the spirit and his championship of sincerity and resourcefulness held strong appeal for a middle class anxious about its economic prospects and uncertain of the relationship between consumerism and respectability. The case of Henry and Frances James and their daughter Helen is a telling one.[8] In 1887, Henry, a lawyer in St. Paul, Minnesota, platted a country suburb named Newport Park and built a rambling, turreted house for his family there. As Henry struggled to turn a profit from his investments, Frances endeavored to stretch each dollar spent on her interiors. She selected cheesecloth draperies and contemplated redying them when they looked tired. She made a barrel into a chair, upholstered homemade furniture in durable corduroy and created a simple *étagère* from a cheap pine music stand, ebonized and fitted with a plush curtain. Despite the couple's ambitions and economies, the Jameses had to move to less expensive quarters in St. Paul at the close of the nineteenth century.

Whereas necessity had spurred her mother's talent for transmuting cheapness into beauty, Helen James Sommers chose the same aesthetic for reasons of self-esteem and fulfillment. Having married a scion of a St. Paul mercantile family in 1909, she relished the challenge of making an integrated, artistic composition from an assemblage of ordinary household objects. In August of 1909, she wrote that her husband "... adopts my ways without a protest, candles & bare table & all." A month later she enthused: "It is such fun to try to make the house a harmonious whole; with the wicker furniture & simple curtains, it will be simplicity & sunniness itself."[9]

While Helen Sommers did not patronize the Minneapolis architectural office of Purcell, Feick, and Elmslie (see no. 198), their supporters were discriminating clients of her ilk, who esteemed inventiveness over luxury. The partnership made a specialty of designing and equipping artful but moderately priced compact houses. Purcell developed a larger Prairie practice than did Frank Lloyd Wright, probably owing in part to his adherence to the challenges and discipline expressed in these lines about his own house, planned in 1907: "To now produce a building that would satisfy the conscience, not violate the integrity of the 'form and function' world, not 'copy' and do it all within an iron ring of fixed cost – that was not so easy."[10]

Purcell cultivated friendships with the craftsmen who turned his sketches into brick, stucco, timber, and glass, and he was proud that these laborers sometimes called on him to design their own residences. In a description of commissions for 1910, Purcell recorded one from Ed Goetzenberger, a tinsmith, for whom the architect created a rather severe house with plain wall surfaces like neutral mounts against which flowers, a gay awning, and the changing tonalities of sunlight and shadow provided natural, organic decoration.

Throughout his life, Purcell identified himself as a woodsman, a product of the "pioneer life" he experienced during boyhood summers spent in a log cabin built by his grandfather. In "Back to the Woods," published in *Inland Architect* six years before his death, Purcell criticized resort cottages, popular since the late nineteenth century, where boulders and bark abounded and the refrigerator was camouflaged behind rough pine planks. His concluding paragraph provides both a distillation of simple life precepts and an autobiographical insight into how self-sufficient citizens could be reared despite increasingly urbanized conditions. Periodic forays into the wilds would yield enduring memories and habits: "Here [in the forest] we are in a free world. We build with primitive materials which are close to their origin, which still carry Nature's loving fingerprints and odors. It is essential that we establish all our patterns and workmanship as an appreciation of the love of order and pride in hand skills. Living close to Nature, we are offered an opportunity to understand true wealth. We can, if so inclined, partake of her Intelligence because, in the forest, we become an integral part of sentient Nature. To overemphasize in our forest buildings the rockiness of rocks or the barkiness of wood, shows us to be preoccupied with very superficial matters while missing the great rhythms and wonders of the Mother who bore us and who still hopes we may reflect some of her deep wisdom."[11]

Most Purcell clients lived in suburbs, not wilderness tracts; yet he and his architectural colleagues were able to fabricate "insurgent" domiciles in which the outdoors and indoors were integrated. Purcell houses sat close to the earth; their low-lying roofs paralleled the horizontality of the prairies. Bands of casement windows, and/or window walls functioning as mini-conservatories, made a garden of the living quarters. Wild flora and fauna bloomed on murals or in colorful, geometricized wall stencils and embroidered textiles. Open, interpenetrating interior spaces gave a sense of spaciousness and evoked the undifferentiated living hall of the Anglo-Saxon colonists. Raised hearths, derived from prototypes Purcell had seen in Swedish folk farmhouses, beckoned the fire-loving family to sheltered intimacy.

In the California architect Bernard Maybeck, Purcell discerned an artist, like his mentor Louis Sullivan, who sought to uplift the human spirit through functionalist buildings that were in harmony with the landscape (see nos. 75 and 76). Purcell was delighted by a visit in 1913 to Maybeck's home – a brown-shingled affair with a broad redwood slab door, set amid a flower-filled yard bordered by a vine-covered fence. Inside he found a very tall fireplace and chimney, exposed beams, a shed-slope ceiling, and doors and windows that framed the summer sunset sky. As the moon rose, Purcell noted: "It shone through the bay window at our backs, and a spar of its light caught the side of Mr. Maybeck's head and beard in soft outline. The square of moonlight on the floor filled the room with shadowless shadow. A soft breeze from the brown hills pressed through the house and gently billowed the tall curtain of the high door. It made and remade patterns of fabric folds on the steps. This one-sided room with its interior space shaped like the outside of a chizel [sic] was strange to me. But now it really came to life – changing its patterns, color, light effects – until at last it seemed time for me to go."[12]

Just such qualities had earlier inspired the poet-naturalist Charles Keeler to choose Maybeck as the architect of his Berkeley residence (1895) and to dedicate to him a treatise on healthful living and household decoration. The book, *The Simple Home*, was the bible of the Hillside Club (see no. 75), a local civic-improvement society dedicated to the promotion of picturesque houses and tree-lined streets adapted to the contours of the landscape; the organization was one of Keeler's – and Maybeck's – favorite projects. In 1898, a year after the club's inception, Keeler formed a handicraft group among the membership; in their own home Keeler and his wife produced furniture for sale. Another joint effort was book printing in the manner of William Morris's Kelmscott Press.[13]

An emphasis on the handwrought was a central thesis permeating the chapters on gardening, house building, and home furnishing in Keeler's volume on domestic simplification. His own library, however, was a medley not of straight lines and clean surfaces but of carved furniture and richly patterned carpets (fig. 1). It demonstrated his special respect for Near and Far Eastern decorative arts, in which ornament grew out of construction and mechanical production had made few inroads. In *The Simple Home*, Keeler recommended Oriental rugs, distinguished by hand-knotting and natural dyes. For furniture he praised Chinese teakwood, and for lighting festive lanterns of Chinese, Japanese, or Moorish origin. Regarding ceramic accessories, Keeler believed "the Chinese and Japanese are the master potters." Other "useful ornaments" were hanging Japanese baskets for plants and handicrafts by primitive peoples – South Sea island fans or American Indian baskets – which shared in the Japanese aesthetic of natural materials conventionally treated.

Fig. 1. Charles Keeler's library during his residency at Highland Place house, Berkeley, California, 1895-1907. Bernard Maybeck architect, 1895. Illustrated in Charles Keeler, *The Simple Home* (1979 reprint of 1904 edition published by Paul Elder, San Francisco).

Keeler argued so eloquently for the hand-crafted home environment because it was supposed to create the proper setting for fulfillment of incorporeal needs: "Of all reforms needed in the life of the home, that of the relation of the man to his family is most pressing. Modern materialism demands of far too many men an unworthy sacrifice. That the wife and children may live in ostentation the man must be a slave to business, rushing and jostling with the crowd in the scramble for wealth. A simpler standard of living will give him more time for art and culture, more time to live."

Another writer and social commentator, Ray Stannard Baker, knew about materialistic avarice and the dark side of metropolitan life from personal experience as a muckraker journalist for *McClure's* magazine. In 1906, he began a series of first-person country-life sketches under the *nom de plume* David Grayson.[14] The first six volumes of Gray-son's folksy musings, written over some twenty years, are consistent in their promotion of a return to the land to cultivate the individuality and diversity suffocated by the conformist business world. Broken in body and soul by a feverish urban pace, Grayson healed his frayed nerves by walking in fresh plowed furrows, sitting in quiet thickets, and drinking in the smell of cows at milking. His adventures were followed avidly not by rural dwellers but by readers who, like Baker himself, were cut off from daily contact with the life force of the soil. Two million copies of the stories were sold in America, the British Commonwealth, and in several foreign translations.

Grayson's most incisive account of the meaning of simplified living and its pitfalls appeared in chapter 12, "A Woman of Forty-Five," of *Great Possessions* (1917).[15] The woman in question was the fictional Mary Starkweather, the "sole dependable representative of the Rich" in Grayson's community. She made a cottage of her barn in order to escape the crowded furnishings, overloaded mantels, and plethoric bookcases in the old family manse. When David Grayson paid a visit to investigate the new lodgings, he encountered Mary in the process of discarding things that she declared had enslaved her. Grayson portrayed sympathetically this pageant of divestiture: "I saw her from time to time that summer and she seemed, and I think she was, happier than she had been before in her whole life. Making over her garden, selecting the 'essential books,' choosing the best pictures for her rooms, even reforming the clothing of the boys, all with an emphasis upon perfect simplicity – her mind was completely absorbed."

Mary's husband Richard was less sanguine about the new domesticity. He commented that he did not know what his wife wanted their children to do in the cottage, or where he should sit, because Mary had not yet determined in what chair he would look the most decorative! Later, Richard confided that the simple life was getting more complicated every day. By mid-December Grayson received a note from Mary Starkweather about a discovery she wanted to share. Grayson went to the converted barn, where he found a notice instructing callers to come to the main house. There Mary confessed: "I am trying to be honest with myself, David. Honest above everything else. That's fundamental. It seems to me I have wanted most of all to learn how to live my life more freely and finely . . . . I thought I was getting myself free of things when, as a matter of fact, I was devoting more time to them than ever before – and, besides that, making life more or less uncomfortable for Dick and the children. So I've taken my courage squarely in my hands and come back here into this blessed old house, this blessed, ugly, stuffy old home – I've learned *that* lesson."[16] Mary Starkweather had realized that self-conscious pursuit of material simplification did not yield the expected simple-life benefits. The final words that David Grayson ascribed to Mary were a definition of simple living as a by-product of some great interest, so absorbing that one forgets himself into simplicity. Though couched in homey prose, Grayson's conclusion was congruent with Thorstein Veblen's warning about simplicity – equated with discriminating taste, household industry, and handmade objects – degenerating into yet another demonstration of conspicuous consumption.[17]

It is no accident that Grayson's reformed simple-lifer is a woman. A disturbing question arises in reviewing Purcell's focus on pioneering, Keeler's on sacrificial devotion to the family, and Wagner's on female service in the humble abode: did the simple life promulgated by men to uplift men shift additional burdens onto women's shoulders?

An Aesthetic of Economy: Gender Implications

Even a quick perusal of homemaking books and of articles on household economics and beautification in shelter magazines demonstrates that women yearned for a less complex existence. However, the female definition of simplified living focused, for the most part, on liberation from drudgery, reduction of hours spent on routine housekeeping tasks, and relief from inept, unreliable servants. A convenient house was the middle-class woman's dream – systematically planned, filled with labor-saving appliances and stripped of nonessential dust-catching adornments. The interests of the progressive woman lay not in the

strenuous life Theodore Roosevelt urged on his countrymen but in the "effective life" described by Ellen H. Richards, first president of the American Home Economics Association.[18] Efficiency, she explained, was the keynote to domestic success, and its implementation depended upon the transplantation of engineering principles practiced in large manufacturing concerns to individual residences. *Household Engineering* (1920) was, in fact, the title of a book by Christine Frederick, whose schedules and standard practices for tasks ranging from bathroom care to dressmaking had been unveiled in the *Ladies' Home Journal* in 1912.[19] Her model home was characterized by built-in furniture and a neat clustering of hall, dining, and living areas to save steps.

Certainly Ms. Frederick would have approved *Suburban Life*'s "house that Jack built," with Jill's help, for a modest $2,000.[20] The hallway was central, with bedroom, bath, and kitchen opening onto it. A space-saving feature of the bedroom was a graduated set of drawers built under the stairway. At the back of the living room an artistic grille hid the furnace, installed upstairs to avoid countless trips to the basement. Behind it, a two-foot-square space held a chute for coal; an outside window permitted coal to be put in from the delivery wagon; a revolving furnace pan precluded shaking and dumping, thereby eliminating dust and dirt. A mechanical novelty was the sliding partition between kitchen and living room. Jill set the table in the kitchen with dishes from a built-in cabinet, then pushed a button to swing both the china cupboard and dining table into the living room; a shelf under the cupboard held platters and bowls or soiled plates. After the meal the revolving wall conveyed the dishes back to the compact "kitchenette," depositing them next to the sink to expe-

dite washing. Attached to the sink was a stationary tub, the top of which formed a drain board. Built into the wall, only a footstep away, was a glazed kitchen cabinet with the unusual addition of a window in the back, to prevent gloom from settling into this sparkling machine shop of a servantless housewife.

One measure of the widespread acceptance of the diminutive "Pullman" kitchen, sometimes seen in tandem with the dining alcove, was its inclusion as a standard feature in mail-order catalogues of low-cost building plans and prefabricated houses during the 1920s. "Aladdinette Homes" advertised small apartment-sized kitchens, which halved the time normally spent near the cook stove and banished three-fifths of the arduous chores associated with food preparation. Pacific Portable Construction Company promoted cozy combination breakfast-nook kitchens, hung with Sanitas, an easily cleaned paper endorsed (along with linoleum) by professional home economists. Still, the modern kitchen, whether custom-designed or mass-produced, was supposed to conjure up a cherished cultural memory of the New England fireside. *Country Life in America* approved the streamlined kitchen of an architect's wife, exemplary in conserving human energy but ". . . if the description pictures it as a cheerless laboratory, planned with scientific skill and so chemically cleaned as to render it stripped of every bit of the homely cheer so dear to all our hearts, the writer does it wrong. The aluminum kettle sings as cheery a song as any iron ancestor of old. The brisk little alarm clock ticks away merrily on the annunciator. Simpkins, the venerable yellow cat, stretches her comfortable length, and dozes and yawns at the glowing coals under the grate; a troop of noisy, hungry country boys and girls swoop in, intent on plunder, and the old kitchen spirit

Fig. 2. "The Kitchen of an Architect's Wife," illustrated in *Country Life in America*, October 1916.

hovers over it all, the same yesterday, today, and forever" (fig. 2).[21] A Windsor chair and braided rug completed the picture of colonial snugness preserved despite accommodation to time-saving innovations.

Likewise, Isabel McDougall's perfected kitchen included rag rugs, preferably made at home as a rainy-day project for mother and children.[22] Instructions for the fabrication of these variegated textiles and for other handiwork – tooled leather, batiked fabrics, pierced-metal lamp shades, and appliquéd table runners, to name a few – were a regular feature of the shelter and women's periodicals like *House and Garden*, *American Homes and Gardens*, *House Beautiful*, *Beautiful Homes*, *The Craftsman*, *Ladies' Home Journal*, and *Good Housekeeping*. In *How to Make Rugs* (1900), Candace Wheeler asserted that a resurgence of domestic manufactures was a predictable outgrowth of the reduction of household labor owing to mechanical inventions; Ellen H. Rich-

ards, drawing similar conclusions, wanted her scientific managers to devote their increased free time not to social work or careers but to aesthetic pursuits capable of rendering the home a more attractive place than the club.[23] Perhaps the most significant factor in the revival of female domestic crafts was the symbolic coupling of industrial and preindustrial homemakers. Artists and writers of the late nineteenth and early twentieth century demonstrated a preoccupation with the figure of the grandmother and a belief that women possessed certain enduring qualities – "the eternal feminine" – linking them to the past.[24] The spinning wheel, an omnipresent interior decoration after the turn of the century, was the attribute of Revolutionary War mothers who kept the home fires burning. Homespun stood for the virtues of patriotism, frugality, and production.

Americans acknowledged some truth in Grace Van Everen Stoughton's conten-

tion that finished goods of mills and factories were more uniform in character and superior in quality to home output.[25] Nonetheless, they remained ambivalent about woman's contemporary role as a consumer of store-bought commodities rather than a producer of home-made staples. Handicraft projects eased the transition, for they served simultaneously to sharpen judgments about workmanship in the marketplace and to bind a new generation of women to their do-it-yourself progenitors. By embellishing a factory-made tablecloth with embroidery, or purchasing an unfinished set of chairs that she stained and pyroengraved on the crest rails, the modern housewife could give the ready-made a homemade look.

Stenciling received much attention in both periodicals and advice books about interior decoration.[26] Few tools were required, a host of materials from wood and plaster to leather and cloth could be so decorated, virtually limitless permutations in color and design were possible, and even large mass-produced objects like sideboards and bedsteads could be dressed in a handmade guise by the addition of a stenciled scarf or spread. Homemade furniture, running the gamut from small stands to large combination pieces like a billiard-table davenport, was more often a male pursuit. A number of magazines catered to women by printing directions for painted wall friezes and curtain borders, but they also appealed to male readers with departments variously titled "The Handicraftsman," "For the Amateur Craftsman," and "Home Training in Cabinet Work."[27] The professional man needed the therapy of a basement workshop, so the argument went, where the substitution of manual for mental labor would prove relaxing and gratifying.[28]

Sexual differentiation in craft pastimes was matched by distinctions in styles, forms, and room usage within the home. Whereas Victorian residences had been planned in accord with the doctrine of separate spheres, Arts and Crafts disciples sought to reduce the segregation while retaining differentiation. For example, although neither was off-limits to other family members, the bedroom and the kitchen were female regions. In both rooms hygiene was paramount; thus white – the badge of the housewife-turned- sanitary-engineer – predominated in color schemes for walls and fitments. Ivory-enameled woodwork and furniture were frequent choices in chamber decoration for reasons of taste as well as ease in cleaning. A.F. and B. Jackson's *How to Select Furnishings for the Home* stressed the feminine refinement of such bedroom equipage: "Enameled furniture has become very popular for the bedroom principally because it is the one room in the house above all others where the woman's taste reigns supreme. The daintiness of the delicate tints of enameled furniture appeals to her."[29] The diminutive Adamesque swags that adorned the Jacksons' painted suite were a variant of the eighteenth-century imagery noted previously *vis-à-vis* the kitchen. Other colonial references suitable for sleeping-room schemes were rag rugs and pieces in Sheraton or other styles made from mahogany, a wood having "a certain feminine elegance."[30]

Oak, on the other hand, seemed more muscular, the perfect wood for a Morris chair (no. 205), deemed quintessentially male in its strong lines and substantial cushioning. The settle (no. 204), too, met the male standard of sturdiness, with rustic overtones. In his 1898 catalogue, Joseph P. McHugh illustrated reading chairs based on Morris recliners and convertible table-settles captioned with masculine epithets evocative of Old England.[31] Featuring hinged box

seats doubling as chests, McHugh's "King Arthur" and "Vicarage" settles were practical trappings for the den. For such a room – a chamber set aside for smoking, gaming, and the private conversations of men – the multipurpose table-settle, sometimes with receptacles for papers, books, and a smoker's outfit incorporated beneath the ample armrests, was admirably adapted.[32] Its space-saving qualities were especially appreciated when a billiard table figured among the den appointments. The so-called gentleman's game enjoyed a resurgence as urban dwellers moved to the country and sought means for discouraging their sons from the pursuit of pleasure in saloons.[33]

Since man's true sphere was the out-of-doors, a fox-hunting frieze, snowshoes, fishing rods and other mementos of sport and physical culture might bedeck the fireplace mantel and walls, sturdily sheathed in wood, denim, or corduroy. The scarlet and mulberry hues prevalent in East Indian madras and Baghdad hangings accented window and door openings. Instead of the luxurious Oriental curios found in smoking rooms of the 1880s and early '90s, decorators advocated American Indian crafts, redolent of savage spirituality: "The Indian room and the den seem to be fitted for each other, especially if the occupant is given to hunting and fishing in the Rockies or the woods of Maine and Canada. The solid, masculine character of most Indian decoration fits well into the den, and there are a great many things in the way of tobacco jars, pipe-racks, and smokers' conveniences done in Indian style. Tabourettes and small stands in Mission are available, with buckskin and Indian-tanned thongs used instead of nails and wedges."[34]

In the popular mind, Indians were linked with California's missionizing

monks, whose stuccoed courtyard buildings and heavy rectilinear furniture were relics of a romanticized colonial past wherein women were bit players.[35] The Macey Company of Grand Rapids, Michigan, cited the "old Spanish Fathers" in publicity for its Mission line imbued with "the spirit of the ancient monastery pieces" but modified enough to be "just the thing for furnishing a den or library." The Macey Book Cabinets catalogue of 1913 devoted a full-page engraving to a boxy sectional bookcase, displayed front and center, in a sympathetic library vignette distinguished by a beamed ceiling, partially wainscoted walls, a cruciform candle sconce, a leather-upholstered Morris chair, and such Indian artifacts as a globular jar, a hide-covered drum, a print of a chief in feathered regalia, and a rug made or inspired by Navajo weavers (see no. 208).[36]

Mrs. Henry Pittker of St. Louis, Missouri, heeded the advice of retailers and interior designers in her selections for the masculine retreats of library and den (figs. 3 and 4).[37] The walls of the former were treated with a green garden frieze, in artful contrast to the prevailing tone of dull red carried out in the Oriental rugs and Spanish roan leather upholstery on Gustav Stickley's Craftsman furniture. Art-glass shades adorned the substantial library chandelier and the blocky copper electroliers of the den. Textiles – susceptible to fading and retention of dust, dirt, and smoke – were minimized in this card room, their replacements being durable linoleum and a red wallpaper with the texture of burlap. The unpatterned paper was capped by a brilliant Indian frieze, complementing the clean lines and curved cutouts of the Limbert Arts and Crafts furniture ensemble. At the opposite end of the spectrum was Mrs. Pittker's reception room, a glimpse of which is

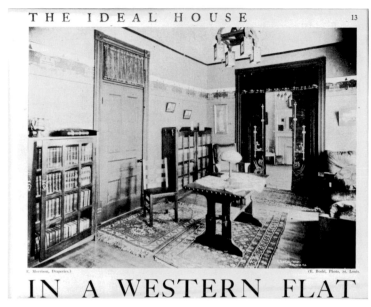

Fig. 3. Henry Pittker library, St. Louis, Missouri, with furnishings selected by his wife; pictured in *The Ideal House*, November 1906.

Fig. 4. Henry Pittker card room and den, St. Louis, Missouri, with linoleum floor covering, Limbert furniture, and other decorations selected by his wife; illustrated in *The Ideal House*, November 1906.

seen in the library photograph. Here daintiness prevailed in silk velour portières and lambrequins, rose-bordered walls tinted a delicate apple-green, and a Hepplewhite suite finished in gold leaf.

In fact, the reception-room parlor and its attendant feminine finery were endangered species in the opening decade of the twentieth century. The successors were an ample, informal living room and decorations identified with the virility of the smoker's sanctum.[38] Were it not for the caption "An Artistic Living Room," one might assume the massive andirons and high-back settle shown in fig. 5 were accoutrements in a cozy den. By 1905, tastemaking journals and decorating manuals began to advocate the Mission style for bedchambers and dining rooms as well as dens and libraries. Although *The Ideal House* magazine for November 1906 declared "Mission is a 'masculine' style," a previous issue in the same year had called "Mission-and-Arts-and-Crafts" a "home style."[39] It lacked a bit in daintiness and femininity, the unnamed author admitted, but he concluded that one could live contentedly and wholesomely in a completely Mission-decorated dwelling. The last stanza of a poem published three years later in *Furniture, A Magazine of Education for the Home* bore lighthearted testimony to female enthusiasm for the stalwart furnishings:

'Parlor suites' are in wretched taste,
    Eleanor says with a final air,
And the paltry tables that long disgraced
    Homes of wealth must be stowed somewhere.
A kitchen stool and a mat well placed–
    Lo, the finish correct and bare,
Of Mission furniture, plain and chaste![40]

Fig. 5. "An Artistic Living-Room," pictured in *Suburban Life*, September 1909. The caption reads: "Here is a room which will make a strong appeal to masculinity . . . . A room like this is not difficult to provide in almost any house at comparatively small expense. The fireplace and mantel command prompt attention, and the high-back settle, so constructed as to be an integral part of the room makes an immediate appeal, with its suggestions of warmth and comfort."

Fig. 6. Inglenook of living hall, John Hays Hammond's bungalow, *Lookout Hill*, Gloucester, Massachusetts. Designed by architects Wheelright and Haven in accord with the client's criteria of comfort, attractiveness, economy of maintenance, and harmony with the surroundings. One of seven photographs of the dwelling from *American Homes and Gardens*, May 1908.

The final couplet of the second stanza is ironic, for it appears that Eleanor, not her husband, is the devotee of a manly aesthetic:

I ache all day from my shoulders down,
For Mission furniture's hard – if chaste!

Ambiguities about gender implications of furniture forms were stated explicitly in "The Household" department of *American Homes and Gardens* of October 1905.[41] Entitled "Furniture for Men," the article announced "sex in furniture" as "a new idea" and listed shaving stands and cellarettes as the prime male objects. In the second tier were lounging chairs, settles, davenports, "bachelor" chiffoniers, and auto valets. However, women could own and use these objects: "Then come lounging chairs, club chairs and all sorts of comfortable seats,

which, we may be sure, the women will value as highly as any man, but which have a very high place in any scheme devised for masculine comfort."

The trend toward increased usage of male-associated artifacts by all members of the family in all rooms of the early-twentieth-century house might be interpreted as a retrograde step for women. While the nineteenth-century notion of separate spheres had limited women's aspirations and activities outside the four walls of the house, feminine autonomy, even superiority, in domestic concerns had been validated. Now "effeminate" was a pejorative adjective attached to discredited Victorian values in home decoration.[42] The Roycrofter Alice Hubbard worried about men's usurping of female prerogatives in the household:

"Men have successfully invaded the home and taken away not only most of the drudgery but also the work that involved action of head, hand and heart – the vital quality in the work of the housewife has gone."[43] Yet she observed that women had launched a counter-invasion of the worlds of art, business, and the professions. On a triumphant note, she postulated a forthcoming egalitarian society wherein men and women, interdependent, "shoulder to shoulder," accomplished the "world's work."

Alice Hubbard's views and the lifestyle of the Roycroft community were hardly typical of theory or practice in domestic arrangements throughout bourgeois America. Still, home economists, although wedded to traditional beliefs in the sanctity of the nuclear family and the containment of women in the home, shared Hubbard's vision to some extent. The professionalization of housework paved the way for a meeting of minds between husbands and wives. If women practiced housewifery in accord with the efficient methods of the factory or office, would not they and their husbands share the same aesthetic standard for the household? Simplified living, understood as convenience and economy in decoration as well as finances, was an androgynous goal exemplified in the unpretentious, rationally planned bungalow house and furnishings.

The Bungalow: Natural, Convenient, Cheap, and Thoroughly Arts and Crafts

The origin of the bungalow lay in seventeenth-century India, where the English had modified the thatched hut of Bengal to serve as a rest house in the tropics. This Anglo-Indian hybrid was the "irreducible minimum of accommodation" for peripatetic traders, administrators, and military personnel of the British empire in Asia.[44] Characterized by a one-story plan with center hall, a broad extended roof, and a wraparound veranda, it was a primitive shelter intended to maximize ventilation and minimize exposure to the sun. The earliest American bungalow (1880) was also a refuge from the sun, though hardly unassuming in scale and amenities. This clapboarded two-and-a-half-story residence at Monument Beach on Cape Cod did incorporate the generous porch and horizontal lines of its tropical progenitor.[45]

The first generation of American bungalows, defined as a summer or weekend retreat, often combined the comfortable repose of the seaside resort with the rugged ambiance of another Victorian vacation haunt – the mountain camp. Owners were successful urban denizens who had the means to escape periodically from the environmental irritants and social formalities of the city. *Indoors & Out* noted in a 1907 issue, "the word bungalow . . . [conveys] a sense of roughing it a bit, living more or less in the open air for pleasure, [and] a hint at extemporised conveniences with a suspicion of Bohemianism and a laxity of conventional conduct."[46]

A case study of John Hays Hammond's Gloucester [Massachusetts] bungalow (fig. 6) serves as a compendium of architectural and decorative formulas favored by prosperous adherents of the simple life.[47] Built upon a rocky precipice, the fieldstone foundation, balustrade, and chimney, along with the weathered-shingle siding, seemed an organic extension of the seaside cliffs. Inside, hunting and boating trophies evoked a genteel version of the strenuous life. The spacious central living room contained a magnificent moose head on the chimney breast, a polar-bear-pelt floor covering, a mantel-shelf display of yachting cups won by the Hammond brothers, and a fireside footrest recycled from the rib of a ship wrecked off the New England coast. Tribal artifacts – Indian baskets and blankets and Zulu shields – added a note of "native" exoticism and reinforced the primitive tone set by hefty six-by-eight-inch hewn rafters overhead. The wainscoted walls consisted of a simple vertical sheathing of the studs with ceiling boards of North Carolina pine, stained moss-green. Gray-greens and browns, being the dominant background colors in nature, were thought to soothe the senses, much as ruddy embers of a wood fire purportedly induced calmness and regenerative introspection.[48]

The focal point of the forty-by-twenty-five-foot living hall, itself the main feature of the Hammond resort, was a massive fireplace composed of seventy-five tons of two-foot-thick undressed stones covering the entire western end of the room. Here was material testimony to Henry H. Saylor's conviction: "A Bungalow without a fireplace would be almost as much an anomaly as a garden without flowers – and as cheerless. Perhaps you have heard of the man whose definition of a home was, 'a fireplace boxed in.' It is even more fitting as applied to a bungalow."[49] The sturdy, rude construction, interrupted by small leaded casement windows and a cavernous hearth opening "large enough for roasting a row of ducks, a fat buck or a bear steak in the true medieval manner such as Sir Walter Scott describes," paid homage to the distant Anglo-Saxon past.[50] Flanked by two heavy red-cushioned settles with built-in bookcases above, this chimney corner offered the same kind of comfortable isolation sought in the placement and accoutrements of the citified den.

In fact, *Bungalow Magazine* asserted that a fireside inglenook could replace the den in a compact dwelling in which economy in floor space and furnishings expenditures was a prime consideration.[51] The same article eulogized the poetic expression that flowered in the atmosphere of the hearth and, indeed, some bungalow owners actually carved verses on the mantel. Contributors to homemaking periodicals gave advice about suitable fireplace mottoes and rhymes, such as Thackeray's rendering of a sixteenth-century Ronsard sonnet, replete with "old time" and "eternal feminine" imagery:

> Some winter night shut snugly in
> Beside the faggots in the hall,
> I think I see you sit and spin
> Surrounded by your maidens all.[52]

Dispensers of domestic advice in the

Arts and Crafts period connected the hearth explicitly with family unity. Phrases like "domestic altar," "family altar," and "domestic center of civilization" found material expression in bungalow plans wherein the living room, frequently with dais-hearth, served as the hub for all household activities, and partitions were removed wherever feasible. The concept was well illustrated in the Hammond bungalow, where the sun parlor functioned as part of the living room and a balcony loft minimized the separation between upstairs and downstairs. The purpose of such an open arrangement was to bring the family circle physically closer, thereby promoting greater mutuality and toleration.[53]

Vacation bungalows like the Hammonds's, which emphasized decorative schemes based on little-refined raw materials and hand workmanship, had significant urban-industrial and class implications. On the surface, the bungalow purported to be an anti-city, do-it-yourself, primitive dwelling. However, nature became captivating when it had been tamed; simple living was meaningful insofar as one enjoyed a surplus of material goods; reforms in the workplace along individualistic, handicraft lines were unprofitable without a leisure class of committed consumers. The do-it-yourselfism suggested by log cabins, animal pelts, and bark-covered furniture was often an illusion, since rustic artifacts, including small buildings, were readily available through mail-order catalogues or stores. Simple built-in shelves and plank tables or benches, which would seem likely candidates for amateur handiwork, were often commissioned from local carpenters.[54] Seen in terms of cultural geography, the vacation bungalow and its equipage represented a transformation of the landscape from productive farm commu-

nities to consumptive, private recreation homes. The Arcadian dream was precisely that, as James Burly saw in describing an Adirondack camp as the setting for "playing" at canoeing, fishing, and hunting.[55]

In California the bungalow took on not only a different look – with redwood timbers fashioned in a hybrid Japanese-Swiss style or stucco evocative of Spanish colonial adobe *casas* – but a variant meaning as an informal abode used as a primary residence. California's mild climate, picturesque scenery, and decentralized settlement pattern were admirably suited to year-round occupancy of rambling, open-air residences. The term "California bungalow" came to stand for all American houses designed to accentuate the charm of outdoor life.[56] Privacy was less a matter of closeting the inhabitants within four walls than of strategic plantings and luxuriant gardens that extended the boundaries of the house into the adjoining landscape. Sleeping porches provided for the family's physical well-being, especially the prevention or cure of tuberculosis by means of sunlight and fresh air. The "ultimate" bungalow by Charles and Henry Greene for the Gambles of Pasadena has been called an "apotheosis of the sleeping porch."[57]

Family solidarity found expression in the transplanting and metamorphosis of the Victorian cottage porch from an accretion on the front of the residence, in full view of neighbors and passersby on the street, to a full-blown outdoor living room at the side or back. One shelter magazine contributor maintained that the porch, not the fireplace, symbolized the unity of the nature-loving family: "... the porch should really be the first thing considered, and if after this is designed there is room left for the house, so much the better .... [Here] one takes a siesta out of doors, or lingers in the

half light of the evening to say the intimate things that the sun, for all its shining, never quite brings forth. Even in the city, life is made more endurable in the summer by a porch that is properly secluded, and in the country it means infinitely more."[58]

Many alterations were made to the bungalow in its transplantation to England and dissemination throughout the Commonwealth and the United States, but the enveloping veranda persisted, sometimes turned outside-in. On the Pacific coast, Spanish mission and bungalow attributes sometimes intermingled to produce a patio house in a U-shape, with the chain of rooms opening onto a central courtyard. The modish multipurpose porch for dozing, dining, and socializing had colonial-revival overtones too. New England yeoman pioneers were generally perceived to have had a close relationship with nature, expressed in homesteads that lacked rigid boundaries between indoors and out; two hundred years later, the open-air living room was a means to that end.[59]

The decorator Hazel Adler saw the porch as the fundamental module for a domestic architecture devoted to appreciation of nature's sublimity; she discussed rooms consisting mostly of windows and French doors opening onto balconies or lower verandas.[60] A model for her was the California home of the architect Irving Gill, wherein stark white walls were a backdrop for the ever-changing colors of prismatic window reflections. On equipage for the indoor-outdoor house, she commented: "Obviously heavy furniture, elaborate draperies or rugs, and countless trivial decorative objects would be out of keeping with the natural backgrounds of which these rooms are so largely composed, so their furnishing has come to resemble more and more that of their proto-

Fig. 7. Sunroom published in *American Homes and Gardens*, August 1908.

type[,] the enclosed porch."

The well-equipped porch was a medley of blossoming plants and plant materials processed for use as furniture, floor coverings, hangings, and decorations. Pleasing color schemes were created with potted ferns or palms, window boxes of trailing periwinkle and nasturtiums, long-blooming begonias, and scarlet geraniums, the latter "doubly agreeable with mission furniture and the sombre colors of Oriental rugs."[61] A fumed-oak swing and Oriental rug figured among the equipment of a 1908 *American Homes & Gardens* porch-sunroom, glassed in to permit year-round enjoyment (fig. 7). Native American rugs augmented the theme of craftsmanship, as did splint-bottomed hickory or rattan and willow seating forms. Willow products, along with their wicker (no. 207) and prairie-grass relatives, were near-perfect encapsulations of the Arts and Crafts aesthetic.[62] Being handwrought from strong reeds or branches, each piece was unique. Colors ranged from buff-brown to marsh-green; the simple outlines were unpretentious and not derivative of any period style. Tables and chairs were durable but light, making lifting for housecleaning easy. Furthermore, the pieces met sanitary standards, for a light scrubbing with water removed dirt.

Other plant fibers were equally suitable for porch textiles.[63] Mourzouk cocoa matting or Crex wire-grass carpets were inexpensive, clean, and stout-wearing. For sun shades, Japanese reed-work might be employed; homespun linen, unbleached muslin, or India-print cottons were well-advised choices for side curtains and lounging pillows. Casement cloth, denim, burlap, and related canvases, such as the jute-and-flax combination marketed by Gustav Stick-

ley, were good alternatives, owing to their coarse-woven appearance and durability. With the addition of a broad table, perhaps of yellowish-gray rough birch harmonizing with the hues and unpolished textures of the other appointments, to hold ". . . a few, but not too many, magazines, one or two novels of the better sort, and several volumes of essays and poems," the hospitable porch was ready for occupancy.[64]

In the case of one- or two-room tent bungalows in which shades and awnings became the walls – made of canvas, stretched on frames and hinged for maximum ventilation – the porch and its equipment were, in effect, the house. These tent-houses were utilized as temporary habitations, but their relatives, portable and prefabricated bungalows, could be adapted as primary dwellings. Writing in *House Beautiful*, Hanna Tachau explained the allure: "We all of us have it in us to be tent-dwellers, campers out, if you will, but the restraining walls of cities have slowly, inexorably closed us in, shutting out the free sweep of an unbounded horizon and limitless sky and the joy that comes from breathing untainted air."[65]

With the advent of the electric street-car in the late 1880s and early '90s, white-collar employees and professionals could have their own bit of nature in the suburbs while commuting daily to urban vocations.[66] Besides its health advantages, a suburban plot was less costly than real estate in a densely populated city. The bungalow itself was a bargain: the compact plan and structural simplicity facilitated mass production. Moreover, the home economists' Pullman kitchen and breakfast nook eased the housewife's burden in the one-servant or servantless household, and the arrangement of rooms on one floor eliminated steps. (Besides, the one-story plan made additions easy when family size increased.) Wall beds folding into ventilated closets, and having the appearance of a buffet or a desk and bookcase when not in use, turned dens or even living rooms into guest rooms when the occasion demanded. The numerous built-in furnishings saved dollars as well as space – an important consideration for middle-class families earning $1,500 to $5,000 a year.[67]

The meaning of the term "bungalow," transposed from forest to suburbs, was first and foremost "inexpensive." Since the self-built bungalow could be constructed for as little as $400 and furnished for a minimal $150, it was affordable to the salaried class, which "has so enormously increased of late years because of the great consolidation of business interests that the final adjustment has not been made. The one fact of uncertain tenure of position and uncertain promotion has profoundly affected living conditions, ownership of the family abode, and incidentally marriage."[68] The home-owning desire of the bourgeoisie was the theme of an ode to the bungalow by Mary R. St. Clair:

Now our table's piled with volumes
  Varying in size and hue,
From small "Cottage Homes" in
yellow
  To the "Ready Built" in blue.
And we ponder o'er each chapter,
What's the reason? Don't you know
That the day is fast approaching
When we'll build our bungalow?[69]

Bungalow books and catalogues, published over some twenty years beginning about 1905, satisfied a yearning for the union of the artful and the useful in moderately priced single-family dwellings. Most of these latter-day versions of nineteenth-century architectural pattern books were really advertising literature for companies that supplied complete sets of bungalow drawings for a few dollars. The Los Angeles "Bungalow

Man" Henry L. Wilson printed generic designs – with dimensions, cost, plans, and illustrations – in *The Bungalow Magazine*, a monthly launched in March of 1909. He compiled them in *The Bungalow Book* of 1910, including "a short sketch of the evolution of the bungalow from its primitive crudeness to its present state of artistic beauty and cozy convenience."[70] A successor, *Bungalow Magazine*, headed by Jud Yoho of Seattle, had nearly twice the circulation of *The Craftsman*.[71] Like Stickley's publication, which featured verbal and visual details of "Craftsman" homes, *Bungalow Magazine* offered a bungalow of the month with complete working drawings. These served to promote Yoho's construction firm, Craftsman Bungalow Company. Other house schemes came from the readers, to whom the following call was directed in the first editorial: "To all who are interested in beauty, comfort, convenience and economy in the home, the editor extends an earnest invitation to contribute photographs, descriptions, original ideas or suggestions, of unique arrangements, designs and 'beauty spots' of their houses."[72] The Prairie-style façade of "A Beauty from the South," highlighted in the issue for January of 1914, was indeed original and unique for its locale in El Paso, Texas. However, its interior (fig. 8), considered along with three others drawn respectively from Wilson's *Bungalow Book* (fig. 9), the Los Angeles Investment Company's *Practical Bungalows* (fig. 10), and the Sherwin-Williams Company's *Cottage Bungalow* (fig. 11), typifies the major design principles and artistic icons of the Arts and Crafts suburban bungalow home.

The most striking aspect of the four images is their emphasis on horizontal lines – "inanimate personifications of hospitality" and symbolic of repose, according to Henry L. Wilson.[73] Exposed

ceiling beams subordinate height to width; projecting mantel shelves interrupt vertical planes of fireplace masonry, much as nearly continuous picture moldings and/or plate rails overshadow the flat wainscoting halted four or five feet above the baseboard. *Bungalow Magazine* called readers' attention to the plaster rail girdling the four walls of B.F. Stevens's combined living-dining room: "This feature is worth special praise, giving as it does, a mark of continuity, and emphasizing the length and size of the rooms together."[74] Most bungalow plans treated living room, dining area, and den-inglenook *en suite*, interrupting but not halting the horizontal flow of space with sliding doors or buttressed openings, the flanks of which doubled as bookcases or settles. Built-in window seats underscored horizontal window sills, as did net, cretonne, or raw silk curtains, curtailed at the sill. Windows were usually casements grouped side by side and sheltered on the exterior by broad overhanging eaves. Rectilinear table scarves might highlight the horizontal expanse of living- or dining-room tables, although these "center[s] of modern family life" were often left unadorned to reveal the wood figure.[75]

Banishment of superfluous ornament, in favor of enrichment achieved by color contrasts, texture, and constructional elements inherent in the working of raw materials, is the second theme of the four bungalow illustrations. Buffets, benches, even lamps might be conceived as part of the architectural fabric: witness the Stevens light standards, which serve as an unintimidating, yet stately portal separating areas for eating and entertaining. Lead cames fastening glass panes together could be both functional and ornamental, as in the glazed cabinets pictured by the Los Angeles Investment Company and in Wilson's dining room. Similarly, Wilson's hang-

Fig. 8. Bungalow of B.F. Stevens, illustrated and described as " . . . a living example of high art at 'less cost,'" by *Bungalow Magazine*, January 1914. Trost & Trost, architects, El Paso, Texas.

Fig. 10. Living room no. 595, shown in the seventh bungalow-book edition of Los Angeles Investment Company's *Practical Bungalows*, 1912. The company delivered a full set of house blueprints, from among thousands of plans in stock, for $5. The Architectural Department promised designs for individual features at moderate prices.

Fig. 9. Dining room no. 727, from Henry L. Wilson's *Bungalow Book* (5th ed., Chicago, 1910). Also illustrated in *The Bungalow Magazine*, December 1909, for "A Five-Room Brick Bungalow – total cost, $2,100."

Fig. 11. One of two model living-room schemes by the Decorative Department of Sherwin-Williams Paints and Varnishes, from *Cottage Bungalow* (Cleveland, ca. 1910). The free portfolio, consisting of color plates for seven interiors, a verandah, and three exterior perspectives, was advertised in *The International Studio* (November 1910) and *Ladies' Home Journal* (April 1, 1911) as "the most complete and most practical decorative plan ever offered."

ing electrolier, virtually indistinguishable from a Gustav Stickley model pictured in *Craftsman Homes*, derives its quaint arabesque patterning from hammered copper. The glass bead or prism borders on the shade might seem an affectation, but they were a means to refract and radiate light, sometimes in an iridescent, spectral display.[76] Mottled, opalescent art glass produced a kindred glowing effect, which complemented the red-gold luster and surface irregularities of beaten copper, whether utilized for lighting devices, bowls, or fireplace hoods. Rough-cast brick and sandy tinted plaster, set off by casings and furniture of coarse-grained oak, contributed additional texture and reiterated an amber-russet color scheme.

The texts accompanying these pictures and countless others in the bungalow literature make it clear that reds and yellows juxtaposed with mossy greens and browns, representing an equalizing of warm and cool colors of nature, were the most desirable for relating the bungalow interior to the landscape and for effecting a balanced mental state among the occupants. For the magazine *Indoors & Out*, Florence Williams reported on color harmonies in California bungalows: "The colors, too, are carefully chosen, one color scheme often being used for the entire bungalow, – a soft green stain for the outside with a lighter tone of the same color for all the inside woodwork, a frieze of tan burlap, dark red brick fireplaces and touches of bright yellow in the curtains and cushions, just four blending colors everywhere through the house, repeating so quietly the tones of the surrounding hills and trees . . . ."[77] The crimson or scarlet dyes of Near Eastern and American Indian rugs might be offset by verdant leafage in a tapestry wallpaper or the gray-green patina of bronze statuary and other metal accessories. The grass

cloth or burlap specified by Wilson for his dining-room walls was enlivened by a red-and-green stenciled frieze of poinsettias, the winter flower of southern California.[78] As might be expected from a paint company, Sherwin-Williams gave detailed directions on chromatic harmonies for a cottage-bungalow living room, illustrated in color. Their wall stencil consisted of an olive-toned central design matching the olive leather recommended for furniture upholstery and the panels of a folding screen. The peripheral squares of the stencil design, painted in yellow and burnt sienna muted with white, picked up the orange accent of the inglenook bricks, window treatment, and some of the pillows covered in "copper cloth."

The furniture ensemble chosen by Sherwin-Williams illustrates an often-overlooked but omnipresent aspect of Arts and Crafts interiors – historicism as seen in actual antiques or composite revivals. The side chair next to the inglenook features a banister back and blocky turned stiles and legs copied from American seating forms dating to the early eighteenth century. So too the bulbous turnings and spiral twists of the Stevens dining table recall the William and Mary era, also known as "Jacobean" or "Flanders" in twentieth-century trade literature.[79] The circular dining table shown by the Los Angeles Investment Company is a descendant of the Empire pillar-and-claw center table, while one of the Stevens living-room chairs sports the tablet crest and the scrolled sweeping arms of a Sheraton armchair joined with the plank seat and spindle supports of a Windsor. Period pieces or adaptations might be mixed with modern furniture and woodwork without violating the dictum of unity in decoration. For instance, the decorator Dorothy Tuke Priestman advocated combinations of Morris chairs and

wicker and colonial-style furnishings in a single interior, since all conformed to a common formula of simple design.[80] Like other contemporary designers, she felt that the suites of matched furniture so common in Victorian homes stifled individuality and achieved not harmony but sameness.

An advertisement of July 1903 in *The House Beautiful* for Dexter Brothers' "Boston Furniture Reproductions of Old New England Models . . . [for] Cottage, Camp, and Bungalow" becomes more meaningful when related to Alice Peyton's analysis "Simplicity as an Ideal."[81] She praised William Morris for his pioneering efforts to convert people to greater sincerity in artistic expression, and she commended Mission furniture for its revolt against Victorian fussiness. Yet she cautioned against Mission faddishness and championed colonial pieces for their enduring embodiment of Morrisian principles. Ms. Peyton recommended the use of a William and Mary highboy not because it was period furniture imbued with genealogical or patriotic sentiment; rather, she said, "Because it is both useful and beautiful it possesses the perennial charm which fits it to become a worthy and permanent part of our household furnishings. Such is the invincible combination of qualities which makes of mere chairs and tables and cabinets, heirlooms to be passed from one generation to the next."

The search for perennial beauty in objects that simultaneously conveyed refined aspirations and humble marks of craftsmanship also informed the selection of sculpture and other *objets d'art*. Such ornamental devices were considered essential to the cultural education of the family, but their quantity and arrangement were to be strictly controlled. Casts like the one occupying the Sherwin-Williams inglenook were recommended for placement against a chimney breast; when tinted with a concoction of burnt umber, turpentine, and beeswax, the color and texture of the plaster blended with the brickwork. Similarly, a fireplace corner designed by Mabel Tuke Priestman consisted of an oaken-beam mantel with corbeled shelf, below which was inserted a plaster cast of Aurora, stained yellow-green in this instance.[82] The fireplace facing of dull-orange tiles suited the simple Mission lines of the woodwork and furniture, she reported, while the Aurora and a stag's head added interest to the "extremely simple" room.

Reproductions of Greek and Renaissance subjects, ranging from statuettes of the Winged Victory and Venus de Milo to reliefs of Madonnas and busts of Dante, might exist happily alongside a fifteenth-century Italian majolica plate, a Hispano-Moresque jug, an antique Persian bowl, a bit of old Delft and Chinese porcelain, or a Japanese Satsuma, Kaga, or Kyoto vase.[83] While the exact type and origin of ceramics displayed on the plate rails of the Wilson and Stevens interiors are not specified, one would expect some to be Oriental blue-and-white porcelain. Canton ginger jars and willow-patterned tablewares were prized both for their traditional designs in cobalt blue and their historical association with the "colonial" China trade. Fine Japanese pottery and porcelain, whether Imari blue-and-white or green-glazed, were highly valued accessories because they personified an artistry based on classic forms and abstracted natural decoration. Of equal stature was American art pottery produced in this vein.

The four bungalow schemes bear little direct impress from Japan; still, they all demonstrate the kind of Oriental sensitivity explicated by Florence Morse: "Our habits of life, our climate, and our

social conditions make it impossible that in our own abodes we should copy closely a Japanese model. Indeed, we ought to copy closely no model at all, but compose a home interior from our own tastes and necessities. Yet we should profit greatly by an adoption of the Japanese spirit, which has no false standards of display, which does not sacrifice to convention, which encourages individual taste and skill, which denies that the old is undesirable because it is old, or the new worthy because it is new, which lavishes expense only on objects intrinsically beautiful and lasting, and which insists on freedom, cleanliness, simplicity, and grace as the essentials of household art."[84]

The Simple and Artistic Home: A Universal Goal

Japanese standards held particular appeal for artists acutely aware of their outward surroundings, as did the bungalow with its emphasis on proportion, color harmony, and organic relation to the natural environs. Writing on the Greene brothers, who made a specialty of Nipponese "chalets" (nos. 68 and 69), Arthur C. David generalized that American bungalows owed more to Japanese sources than to vernacular structures in the tropics.[85] Henrietta P. Keith published "The Trail of Japanese Influence in our Modern American Architecture" in *The Craftsman* (July 1907), and for her 1909-1910 edition of *Practical Studies in Interior Decoration and Furnishing*, she commenced a chapter on the bungalow interior with the comment: "Everything one story is dubbed a bungalow, and, shades of the Orient!"[86] Just ten to fifteen years before, Keith claimed, the bungalow had been limited to woodland locations or served as a rustic retreat for "eccentric" artists.

How the artist, the bungalow, and Jap-

anese traditions came together to produce the simple and artistic home is well illustrated by *Cro Nest*, the abode of the architect Claude Fayette Bragdon, who practiced in Rochester, New York (see no. 195).[87] Bragdon had received his training in the office of Bruce Price, who designed the initial *japonesque* resort cottages at Tuxedo Park. His other talents included lecturing, writing, illustrating, publishing, and creating theater sets and costumes. According to a close associate, Harvey Ellis, he was a founder and guiding spirit of the Rochester Arts and Crafts Society, for which he produced the cover designs of its exhibition catalogues.

Cro Nest was a two-story house "along bungalow lines," encased in gray shingles appropriate for its site on the brow of a tree-covered hillside.[88] Even the shutters were unobtrusive with a coat of leaf-green paint to match the summer foliage. The stair hall (fig. 12) displayed Japanese properties in its unadorned banisters and soft green-stained woodwork of cypress, a durable wood favored in Japan for its grain striations. On the yellow walls were hung Japanese color prints and some French posters, illuminated by a Japanese hanging lamp with melon-shaped shade of orange paper. Rare Japanese prints and cypress woodwork reappeared in the twenty-one-by-twenty-five-foot living room, and the motif of a crow perched on a grapevine (appearing first in the stained glass of the front door) was a unifying device throughout the house. Bragdon's hearth (fig. 13) functioned in a way analogous to the *tokonoma* – the place of highest honor in a Japanese home – wherein a scroll painting or calligraphic exercise was mounted on the wall and a flower vase on a low stand placed on the raised floor of the alcove. The mantel shelf of *Cro Nest* was adorned with a *cloisonné* vase and a blue Grueby example containing

Fig. 12. Stair hall at *Cro Nest*. Claude Bragdon, architect, Rochester, New York. Photographed by his sister Mary Bragdon and published in *Good Housekeeping*, May 1904.

Fig. 14. Living room looking toward the dining room at *Cro Nest*. The lamp is a green Grueby example; window curtains throughout are green denim. Shades of blue predominate in rugs, *portières*, and tiles, complementing burnt-orange tinted walls. Photographed by Mary Bragdon and published in *Good Housekeeping*, May 1904.

Fig. 13. Living-room fireplace at *Cro Nest*. Photographed by Mary Bragdon and published in *Good Housekeeping*, May 1904.

Fig. 15. Living room, looking toward the hall, at *Cro Nest*. Photographed by Mary Bragdon and published in *Good Housekeeping*, May 1904.

peacock feathers, along with a few prized antiquities, notably an Etruscan lamp and a drawing by an early Italian master in an old carved and gilded Spanish frame. By the fireplace, a green Grueby lamp shed light on a small, understated table matched in form and plainness by the dining table visible through the glass doors (fig. 14). The restraint demonstrated in the *Cro Nest* interiors established a tone not of asceticism but of reverence. Alfred H. Granger sensed a kindred atmosphere in Frank Lloyd Wright's studio, where a choice bit of plaster, an apt motto, or a floral arrangement provided ". . . the right sort of inspiration, which recognizes the wondrous beauty of the works of the past, while at the same time it lives in the world of to-day and cares for its simplest flowers."[89]

Early-twentieth-century architects borrowed numerous concepts from traditional Japanese architecture, such as vertical board-and-batten construction, *irimoya* (gable and hip) roofs, open timberwork, lattice details, multi-use interior spaces, flexible room dividers, and open-air galleries.[90] Nipponese dwellings had few stationary partitions inside, and exterior *shoji* screens could be slid open to make the grounds an integral part of the household decoration. Bragdon adapted these spatial concepts to the rigorous climate of upstate New York. A large plate-glass window in the living room framed a view of a sundial with the distant city behind, and the sliding partition between living and dining areas was glazed. Thus, the woodland vista beyond the dining-room bay window could always be appreciated by occupants of rattan or oak chairs in the living room (fig. 15). Both rooms shared a sympathetic design scheme so that they might appear as a unit when the doors were opened. In the angle formed by the living and dining spaces

was a piazza, protected by screens in the summer to serve as an outdoor dining nook, and glass-enclosed in winter to form a "palm room," or sun parlor. A treetop piazza adjoined the owners' rooms in the upper story.

The house along bungalow lines, incorporating select *japonesque* principles of construction, spatial fluidity, and integration of the building and its environs, enjoyed favored status in Arts and Crafts communities. Of Ralph Whitehead's Byrdcliffe near Woodstock, New York (see no. 165), Poultney Bigelow reported in October 1909: ". . . here within the last five years has arisen one bungalow after another, each the home of artists in one form or another, painter or sculptor, weaver or dyer, metalworker or wood-carver, in short, here is a city of the forest where every tree is a soul in sympathy with the workers under its branches."[91] A desire for communion with the out-of-doors may explain Byrdcliffe's architectural divergence from the local Catskill farmhouse intended to insulate the inhabitant from nature's wintry blasts. In any case, the bungalows were simple shelters in the spirit of the California chalets of Bernard Maybeck and Greene and Greene. They were sided with unfinished boards and equipped with wooden porches and balconies overhung by spreading roofs. The open stairway in the living hall of Whitehead's own *White Pines* reiterated decorative elements found in Bragdon's entryway: plain posts and banisters, flat door jambs and moldings, Japanese prints, and the suspended melon lantern.

At the summer colony of Arden, situated on 162 wooded acres outside Wilmington, Delaware, young campers and families lived in bungalows erected by the community from trees felled and sawed on the property. Mabel Tuke Priestman documented the thirty-

bungalow village of sixty inhabitants, devoted to the principles of the single-tax proponent Henry George, in *American Homes and Gardens*.[92] She illustrated one private interior, captioned "The 'Owl's Nest,' a Japanese Bungalow," and described communal facilities for dining at the inn and for craft activities at *Red House*. The clubhouse was named in honor of the home Philip Webb had designed for William Morris, whose preachings on the joy of manual labor informed Arden's founding mentors, Frank Stephens and William L. Price. Price's phrase "The art that is life. . .," borrowed from *Artsman* magazine for the title of the present book, seems a fitting motto for Arden adherents, whom Mrs. Priestman identified as ". . . doctors, literary socialists and employers of labor hobnobbing in the most friendly way with the working man, who brings his children to spend a Sunday, knowing that he will have the hand of good fellowship extended to him and a hearty invitation to come again."

Although class distinctions were by no means eradicated after the turn of the century, social reformers ranging from single-tax communitarians and country-life adherents to home economists, civic-minded architects, and interior decorators contributed in their various crusades to the popularization and partial realization of A.J. Downing's suburban utopia. *The Architecture of Country Houses* had espoused the egalitarian precept of universal home ownership in a rural setting; yet different sorts of dwellings were prescribed for working men, farmers, and the leisured, educated class. Like the Victorian doctrine of separate spheres, which stressed mutuality but circumscribed sex roles, Downing's tripartite housing model emphasized moral parity even as it legitimized the existing class structure. Downing was adept at promoting Ruskinian theories of the beautiful and useful in architecture in layman's terms for an American audience.[93] However, the task of effecting material and behavioral change fell to his Arts and Crafts successors. They did convince at least segments of the wealthy that harmony and fitness rather than accumulation and opulence were essential criteria for a rich domestic life. Concerning the house of moderate cost, Kate Greenleaf Locke maintained: "Its ofttimes quaint simplicity and undoubted artistic completeness attracts the rich man who is tired of living for show, and he builds a house of modest pretensions simply because it appeals to his artistic instincts and because of its 'home' suggestion." She continued, in regard to the bungalow: "It appeals to a wide circle and several classes because when it is furnished luxuriously and used conventionally there is yet in its atmosphere a delightful flavor of Bohemianism and the liberty and originality that camp life and studio life permits, and yet when it is furnished with extreme simplicity it may (if sufficiently artistic in its treatment) outrank the most expensive conventional house."[94] In fact, the bungalow combined the attributes of taste, rusticity, and economy that Downing had ascribed respectively to the villa, farmhouse, and cottage. This democratization of domestic architecture evidenced in "classless" bungalows embellished with do-it-yourself crafts and/or quality – as opposed to multiple – furnishings was a cardinal achievement of the American Arts and Crafts movement.

1. Regarding female education and the dissatisfaction of the "educated American drudge," see Katherine Busbey, *Home Life in America* (London: Methuen, 1910), pp. 106-112. Apartment-hotels and other multifamily housing are discussed in Gwendolyn Wright, *Building the Dream: A Social History of Housing in America* (New York: Pantheon Books, 1981), pp. 138-140, 148-151.

2. A.J. Downing, *The Architecture of Country Houses* (New York: D. Appleton, 1850), pp. v-vi.

3. Roosevelt is quoted in David E. Shi, *The Simple Life: Plain Living and High Thinking in American Culture* (New York: Oxford University Press, 1985), p. 183. Wagner's *Simple Life* appears on the "better"-seller list compiled by Frank Luther Mott in *Golden Multitudes: The Story of Best Sellers in the United States* (New York: R.R. Bowker, 1947), p. 324.

4. Charles Wagner, "The Simple Life in America," Mary L. Hendee, trans., *Outlook* 81 (December 30, 1905), p. 1065.

5. Charles Wagner, *The Simple Life*, Mary L. Hendee, trans. (New York: McClure, Phillips, 1902), 5th ed., p. 148.

6. Orison Swett Marden, *Woman and Home* (New York: Thomas Y. Crowell, 1915), 3rd printing, pp. 310-312.

7. Mabel Tuke Priestman, *Art and Economy in Home Decoration* (New York: John Lane Co., 1910), pp. 17-18.

8. See Joan M. Seidl, "Consumers' Choices, A Study of Household Furnishing, 1880-1920," *Minnesota History* 48 (Spring 1983), pp. 185-186. Seidl's study is based on personal papers of midwestern householders deposited at the Minnesota Historical Society.

9. Ibid., pp. 186, 195.

10. William Gray Purcell, "Parabiography, 1907," p. 4. This and other writings and drawings by Purcell are housed at the Northwest Architectural Archives, University of Minnesota in Minneapolis. Regarding the success of the Purcell, Feick, and Elmslie partnership, see H. Allen Brooks, *The Prairie School* (Toronto, 1972; reprinted, New York: W.W. Norton, 1976), p. 131.

11. William Gray Purcell, "Back to the Woods," *Inland Architect* 2 (August 1959), pp. 8-10.

12. William Gray Purcell, "Bernard Maybeck, Poet of Building: His Battle with the Book," pp. 1-2, 4. This typewritten manuscript, a second draft, is dated July 10, 1949, and bears the notation "Written for Mrs. Harwell Harris." It is part of the Documents Collection at the College of Environmental Design, University of California, Berkeley.

13. The Hillside Club Papers and Keeler Family Papers are at Bancroft Library, University of California, Berkeley. For an account of the bookmaking and furniture enterprises of Charles and Louise Keeler, see Dimitri Shipouhoff, "Introduction" to Charles Keeler, *The Simple Home* (Santa Barbara: Peregrine Smith, 1979; reprint of 1904 edition published by Paul Elder, San Francisco), pp. xxxi-xxxii.

14. For details about Ray Stannard Baker's career and his alter ego David Grayson, see *American Chronicle: The Autobiography of Ray Stannard Baker [David Grayson]* (New York: Charles Scribner's Sons, 1945), pp. 213-219, 228-248; Robert C. Bannister, Jr., *Ray Stannard Baker: The Mind and Thought of a Progressive* (New Haven: Yale University Press, 1966), pp. ix-xi, 108-125; Walter A. Dyer, *David Grayson: Adventurer* (Garden City, N.Y.: Doubleday, Page, 1926), p. 18; John E. Semonche, *Ray Stannard Baker: A Quest for Democracy in Modern America, 1870-1918* (Chapel Hill: University of North Carolina Press, 1969), pp. vii-viii, 160-193.

15. David Grayson, *Great Possessions* (Garden City, N.Y.: Doubleday, Page, 1917), pp. 155-175.

16. Ibid., p. 172.

17. Thorstein Veblen, *Theory of the Leisure Class* (1899; reprinted New York: Penguin, 1983), pp. 156-162.

18. Ellen H. Richards, *The Cost of Shelter* (New York: John Wiley & Sons, 1913), pp. 49-50.

19. See David P. Handlin, *The American Home: Architecture and Society, 1815-1915* (Boston: Little, Brown, 1979), pp. 419, 422-423; and Susan Strasser, *Never Done: A History of American Housework* (New York: Pantheon Books, 1982), pp. 214-219.

20. See Margaret H. Pratt, "The House That Jack Built," *Suburban Life* 14 (May 1912), p. 321. For another example of a rationally planned house outfitted with mechanical aids, see Russell Fisher, "A House Designed for Housekeeping," *Country Life in America* 29 (February 1916), p. 38.

21. Katherine L. Sullivan, "The Kitchen of an Architect's Wife," *Country Life in America* 30 (October 1916), p. 42. Modern scientifically planned kitchens are illustrated in *Aladdin Homes*, catalog no. 33 (Bay City, Mich.: Aladdin Company, 1921), p. 105; *Pacific Houses, Ready-Cut and Factory-Built* (Los Angeles: Pacific Portable Construction Company, 1918), pp. 23, 75; *Pacific's Book of Homes*, vol. 25 (Los Angeles: Pacific Portable Construction Company, 1925), pp. 151-152; and Edna D. Day, "Model Kitchen That Saves Time and Steps," *Beautiful Homes* 1 (February 1909), p. 13.

22. Isabel McDougall, "An Ideal Kitchen," *House Beautiful* 13 (December 1902), p. 31.

23. Candace Wheeler, *How to Make Rugs* (New York: Doubleday, Page, 1902), p. 13; and Richards 1913, p. 56.

24. See Celia Betsky, "Inside the Past: The Interior and the Colonial Revival in American Art and Literature, 1860-1914," *The Colonial Revival in America*, Alan Axelrod, ed. (New York: W.W. Norton for Winterthur Museum, 1985), pp. 171, 178-179.

25. Grace Van Everen Stoughton, "Scientific Training as Applied to the Household," *House Beautiful* 15 (December 1903), p. 63.

26. Alice M. Kellogg reported: "With so much popular attention given to stenciling (which seems to be taking the place of china painting, embroidery and pyrography) a wide range of usefulness is opened in home arts." (See *American Homes and Gardens* 6 [April 1909], p. 145.) Dorothy Tuke Priestman listed minimal skill, low cost, enrichment of inexpensive materials, washability

of stenciled material, and broad scope for original designs and color effects as the "five good reasons [that] of all the handicrafts stenciling appeals most to me." (See *Home Decoration* [Philadelphia: Penn Publishing Co., 1909], p. 156.)

27. "The Handicraftsman" appeared in *American Homes and Gardens*, "For the Amateur Craftsman" in *Bungalow Magazine*, "Home Training in Cabinet Work" in *The Craftsman*; see also the series of furniture-making articles by Eugene Clute in *Ideal House*, beginning in October of 1906.

28. See Gustav Stickley, *Craftsman Homes* (New York: Craftsman Publishing, 1909), pp. 169-170; Jared Stuyvesant, "Why You Should Have a Workshop and How," *House & Garden* 18 (December 1910), p. 352; and Ira S. Griffith, "Recreation with Tools," *Suburban Life* 10 (January 1910), p. 22.

29. A.F. and B. Jackson, *How to Select Furnishings for the Home* (Grand Rapids: *Good Furniture Magazine*, 1919), pl. 250 verso. See also H.P. Keith, "A Complete Decorative Scheme for Interiors Treated on Mission Lines," *Keith's Magazine on Home Building* 14 (November 1905), p. 317; and Charles Alma Byers, "Modern Bungalow Bedroom, Improvement on the Old Style of Cottage Sleeping Chamber," *Bungalow Magazine* 5 (February 1916), pp. 114-118.

30. For simplicity of design, the Sheraton style was unsurpassed, according to Ekin Wallick (See *Inexpensive Furnishings in Good Taste* [New York: Hearst's International Library Co., 1915], p. 77). A case for the femininity of mahogany, in contrast to oak, is made by Elsie de Wolfe in *The House in Good Taste* (New York: Century Co., 1913), p. 248. Margaret Greenleaf explored the colonial associations of mahogany in "Congenial and Uncongenial Furniture," *House & Garden* 17 (April 1910), p. 141.

31. See *Some Pictures of Quaint Things Which are Sold At the Sign of the "Popular Shop," and a Few Words about Making the House Beautiful with Homely Material* (New York: Joseph P. McHugh & Co., 1898), unpaged. The settle is contrasted with the "effeminate" drawing-room couch in A.J. Edwards, "Practical Application of Decorative Art: Hints from Many Sources," *House Beautiful* 4 (October 1898), pp. 177-178. For a concise secondary analysis of the Morris chair as symbol of manly comfort, see Eileen Boris, *Art and Labor: Ruskin, Morris, and the Craftsman Ideal in America* (Philadelphia: Temple University Press, 1986), pp. 58-60.

32. Dorothy Biddle featured a table-settle with built-in shelves at the ends, designed by E.H. Ascherman *en suite* with other smoking-room furniture (see "The Planning of Ideal Rooms," *Arts and Decoration* 1 [November 1910], p. 25). Concerning the appropriateness of table-settles as den furniture, see Alice M. Kellogg, *Home Furnishing, Practical and Artistic* (New York: Frederick A. Stokes, 1905), p. 53; and William Martin Johnson, "The House Practical – Fifth Article: Dens and Cozy Corners," *Ladies' Home Journal* 16 (May 1899), p. 27.

33. "Far Sighted Architects Suggest a Billiard Room," *Modern Homes* 1 (March 1915), p. 25; for an example of a combined smoking-card-billiard-room-den, see Gaylord Howe, "A Playroom for the Whole Family," *Suburban Life* 5 (September 1907), pp. 134-136. On combating the temptations of saloons, see Oliver Coleman, "Taste," *House Beautiful* 12 (September 1902), pp. 243-244.

34. "American Indian Decoration," *Ideal House* 2 (July 1906), pp. 9-11; see also Kellogg 1905, pp. 51-52. John Kendrick Bangs identified men as outdoor animals in "The Man of the House: He Wants What He Wants When He Wants It," *Suburban Life* 10 (January 1910), p. 26. General discussions of wall coverings, ornaments, and textiles for the den are found in James Arthur, "Let's Have a Den," *Suburban Life* 3 (December 1906), p. 273; "Papering the Bungalow," *The Bungalow Magazine* 2 (April 1909), p. 60; and "Peeps into Modern Homes," *Artistic Home Ideas* 1 (January 1902), p. 21.

35. Regarding the romance of the California missions (and promoter Charles Lummis), see Kevin Starr, *Inventing the Dream: California Through the Progressive Era* (New York: Oxford University Press, 1985), pp. 82-89.

36. *Macey Book Cabinets – Sectional – For the Home*, catalog no. 1213P (Grand Rapids, Mich.: Macey Company, 1913), p. 29; and *Christmas Gifts* (Grand Rapids: Fred Macey Co., n.d.), unpaginated. Both trade catalogues are in the Romaine Collection, University of California, Santa Barbara.

37. "In a Western Flat," *Ideal House* 3 (November 1906), pp. 12, 14.

38. See Allen W. Jackson, *The Half-Timber House: Its Origin, Design, Modern Plan, and Construction* (New York: Robert M. McBride & Co., 1929; reprint of 1912 edition), pp. 48-49; Kate Greenleaf Locke, "The Interior Details of the Bungalow and Its Furnishings," *American Homes and Gardens* 6 (December 1909), p. 477; Maria Parloa, *Home Economics* (New York: Century Co., 1898), pp. 38-39.

39. "The Art of Color," *Ideal House* 3 (November 1906), p. 25; "A Home Style," *Ideal House* 1 (January 1906), p. 7.

40. *Furniture, A Magazine of Education for the Home* 1 (July 1909), p. 15.

41. "Furniture for Men," *American Homes and Gardens* 1 (October 1905), p. 259.

42. See Charles Eastlake, *Hints on Household Taste* (1st American ed., Boston: James R. Osgood & Co., 1872), p. 167. Homes conceived by women lacked discipline, proportion, and reason, according to Samuel Howe, in "Visit to the House of Mr. Stickley," *Craftsman* 3 (December 1902), pp. 164-165.

43. Alice Hubbard, *Woman's Work, Being an Inquiry and an Assumption* (East Aurora, N.Y.: Roycrofters, 1908), pp. 132-133, 135.

44. J. Lockwood Kipling, "The Origin of the Bungalow," *Country Life in America* 19 (February 1911), pp. 308-309.

45. See Clay Lancaster, "The American Bungalow," *Art Bulletin* 40 (September 1958), pp. 239-240.

46. See Anthony D. King, *The Bungalow: The Production of a Global Culture* (London: Routledge & Kegan Paul, 1984), p. 137.

47. See Mary H. Northend, "Two New England Bungalows," *American Homes and Gardens* 5 (May 1908), pp. 169-173, 179.

48. See "Concerning Choice in Color," *Craftsman* 1 (December 1901), unpaged; Fred Hamilton Daniels, *The Furnishing of a Modest Home* (Worcester, Mass.: Davis Press, 1908), p. 40; Una Nixon Hopkins, "The Decoration of Our Homes," *Keith's Magazine on Home Building* 29 (February 1913), p. 80. The hypnotic and therapeutic qualities of the wood fire are treated by Henry H. Saylor in *Making a Fireplace* (Philadelphia: McBride, Nast, 1913), p. 1.

49. Henry H. Saylor, *Bungalows* (Philadelphia: John C. Winston Co., 1911), p. 135. A similar opinion about the fireplace as primary requisite for the bungalow is found in Charles Alma Byers, "Designing the Bungalow Fireplace," *Bungalow Magazine* 3 (September 1914), p. 549.

50. See John Taylor Boyd, Jr., "The Informal Fireplace," *Country Life in America* 30 (May 1916), p. 32.

51. "Inglenooks," *Bungalow Magazine* 6 (May 1917), p. 293.

52. See Alice Van Leer Carrick, "Happy Hours by the Fireplace," *House Beautiful* 44 (September 1918), p. 190. Excerpts from Emerson, Burns, and Browning were recommended by Harriet Woodward Clark in "The Relation of the Fireplace to the Home," *Suburban Life* 6 [January 1908], p. 22). Other verses are proposed by E.N. Vallandigham in "Some Fireplace Mottoes," *Indoors & Out* 3 (December 1906), pp. 133-136.

53. Phraseology about the hearth as altar sanctifying the institution of the family appears in Carrick 1918, p. 190; and Edward N. Vallandigham, "The Fireplace in the Home," *Indoors & Out* 1 (December 1905), pp. 131, 136. Ways in which house plans and family interaction affect one another are elaborated in Dorothy E. Smith, "Household Space and Family Organization," *Pacific Sociological Review* 14 (January 1971), pp. 58, 67; Robert C. Twombly, "Saving the Family: Middle Class Attraction to Wright's Prairie House, 1901-1909," *American Quarterly* 27 (March 1975), pp. 67-69; and Barbara Laslett, "The Family as a Public and Private Institution: An Historical Perspective," *Journal of Marriage and the Family* 35 (August 1973), p. 486.

54. Eleanor Allison Cummins treated carpenter-built furniture in "Furnishing the Country House," *Keith's Magazine on Home Building* 25 (June 1911), p. 418. An excellent example of a trade catalogue featuring objects with a "do-it-yourself" look is *Rustic Work* (New York: Rustic Construction Works, ca. 1910), 24 pp.

55. James Burly, "A Comfortable Camp in the Woods," *House & Garden* 25 (June 1914), p. 449.

56. Robert Winter, "The Common American Bungalow," in *American Domestic Vernacular Architecture: Home Sweet Home*, Charles W. Moore, Kathryn Smith, and Peter Becker, eds. (New York: Rizzoli for Craft and

Folk Art Museum, Los Angeles, 1983), p. 99; Lancaster 1958, p. 243.

57. Robert Winter, *The California Bungalow* (Los Angeles: Hennessey & Ingalls, 1980), p. 58. Sleeping porches were publicized regularly in the popular magazine press from about 1908 to 1920; see, for example, L.S. Metcalfe, "Outdoor Bedrooms Easily Constructed," *Beautiful Homes* 3 (February 1910), p. 6; and "The Sleeping Porch is Now Considered Indespensible [sic]," *Modern Homes* 1 (December 1914), p. 7.

58. Judson Litchfield, "The Porch," *House Beautiful* 8 (June 1900), p. 392. Regarding the expanded size and secluded siting of porches, see also Sarah Leyburn Coe, "Making the Most of the Porch," *House & Garden* 20 (June 1912), p. 31.

59. See Handlin 1979, pp. 352-353.

60. Hazel H. Adler, *The New Interior: Modern Decoration for the Modern Home* (New York: Century Co., 1916), p. 227.

61. Eleanor Allison Cummins, "On Decoration and Furnishing," *Keith's Magazine on Home Building* 13 (February 1913), p. 102.

62. Wicker or willow furnishings were standard in period illustrations of porches. Good compilations of wicker-willow advantages and attributes are Katharine Newbold Birdsall, "The Willow and Wicker Furniture Family," *House & Garden* 17 (May 1910), pp. 177-178; and D.D. McCall, "The Use and Beauty of Willow Furniture," *Arts and Decoration* 1 (March 1911), p. 221. For information about prairie-grass products, see *The Twentieth Century Ideal Furniture Made from the Prairie Grass of America* (New York: Ludwig Bauman & Co., ca. 1905), unpaged.

63. The most complete statements about carpets, curtains, and other textiles for porches are in Adler 1916, p. 229; "Porch Furniture," *House Beautiful* 13 (April 1903), p. 354; and H.J. Slater, "Furnishing Bungalow Porches," *The Bungalow Magazine* 1 (May 1909), p. 87.

64. Rough birch furniture is recommended by Florence Finch Kelly in "How to Furnish a Bungalow - IV," *Indoors & Out* 4 (August 1907), p. 217. The quotation about books on a porch table is in "Porch Furniture" 1903, p. 354.

65. Hanna Tachau, "Why Not a Sleeping Porch for Everyone?" *House Beautiful* 45 (May 1919), p. 284. Tent-bungalow examples are in Saylor 1911, pp. 31, 33; and Winter 1980, p. 58.

66. The suburbanization of the bungalow is covered in Winter 1983, p. 99; and King 1984, pp. 140-142.

67. Regarding the cheapness of built-in features, when included in the home-building contract, see Margaret Greenleaf, "Built-in Conveniences for the House," *House & Garden* 16 (November 1909), p. 178; and Henry H. Saylor, ed., *Distinctive Homes of Moderate Cost* (New York: McBride, Winston, 1910), p. 59. Income and membership in the middle class are discussed by Ruth Schwartz Cowan in *More Work for Mother* (New York: Basic Books, 1983), p. 155; and Daniel Horowitz, "Frugality or Comfort: Middle-Class Styles of Life in the

Early Twentieth Century," *American Quarterly* 37 (Summer 1985), p. 247.

68. Richards 1913, p. 105. For testimony on the popularity of the low-cost bungalow, see Wilson Eyre, "The Purpose of the Bungalow," *Country Life in America* 19 (February 1911), p. 305; Henrietta P. Keith and Eleanor A. Cummins, *Practical Studies in Interior Decoration and Furnishing* (2nd ed., Minneapolis: M.L. Keith, 1909-1910), pp. 151, 153; King 1984, p. 144; and James Johnson, "Furnishing a Portable House for $150," *House & Garden* 16 (July 1909), pp. 24-25. Henry L. Wilson described a $2,800 bungalow furnished for $550 in "Furnishing a California Bungalow," *The Bungalow Magazine* 1 (April 1909), pp. 56-58.

69. Mary R. St. Clair, "Our Bungalow," *Bungalow Magazine* 6 (November 1917), p. 647.

70. Quoted in King 1984, p. 144.

71. Circulation statistics are drawn from *American Newspaper Annual and Directory* (Philadelphia: N.W. Ayer & Sons, 1915). Ayer reported a circulation of 40,000 for *Bungalow Magazine*, 22,500 for *Craftsman*. *Bungalow Magazine* (1 [September 1912], p. 5), had projected a circulation of 50,000 by 1915.

72. D.E. Hooker, "Editorial," *Bungalow Magazine* 1 (August 1912), p. 5. *Bungalow Magazine* ceased publication after March of 1918. The Library of Congress owns the 1913 and 1916 editions of Yoho's *Craftsman Bungalows* mail-order catalogues, as well as Yoho's and Merritt's 1920 offering, *Colonial Homes: A Collection of the Latest Designs Featuring the New Colonial Bungalow.*

73. See "'Horizontality' of Lines Symbolic of Hospitality," *The Bungalow Magazine* 1 (November 1909), p. 258.

74. "A Beauty from the South," *Bungalow Magazine* 3 (January 1914), p. 21.

75. See Althea Harwin, "Table as Center of Modern Family Life," *Beautiful Homes* 4 (August 1910), p. 10. Ample living-room tables, as well as bookcases built into buttresses between en-suite rooms, window seats, wainscoting, beamed ceilings, and chair, picture, and plate rails, are discussed in the series "A Grammar of House Planning" from *The Bungalow Magazine* (note "Chapter Two – The Living Room" and "Chapter Three – The Dining Room," vol. 1 [August - September 1909], pp. 179-187, 214-217). Casement windows and curtaining are discussed in John A. Knowles, "Casement Windows, Their Artistic and Practical Value for the Home Builder," *Keith's Magazine on Home Building* 25 (May 1911), p. 312; and "A Casement Window," *Craftsman* 4 (June 1903), pp. 205-208.

76. "Lights and Shades in Modern Houses," *Artistic Home Ideas* 3 (May 1903), p. 129.

77. Florence Williams, "Homes in the Land of Sunshine," *Indoors & Out* 4 (August 1907), p. 205. See also *The Home Beautiful* (Chicago: Martin Senour Co., 1900), [p. 3]; and *Artistic Interiors, Muresco Home Decorative Interior Suggestions* (New York: Blanchard Press for Benjamin Moore & Co., n.d.), p. 7.

78. "A Five-Room Brick Bungalow," *The Bungalow Magazine* 1 (December 1909), p. 283.

79. See Maude Gleason, "Flanders Furniture and Its New Popularity," *Suburban Life* 11 (August 1910), p. 95; and "Homecraft Furniture" in *Aladdin Houses*, catalogue no. 27, (Bay City, Mich.: North American Construction Co., 1915), p. 42.

80. Priestman 1909, p. 39. The mixing of colonial pieces with chairs that "have the simple lines of Mission, but with curvature introduced" is recommended in "Simple Furniture," *Ideal House* 2 (March 1906), p. 13. Karl Theodore Opperman discouraged the use of upholstered ensembles in favor of combinations of old English armchairs and Windsors with Arts and Crafts pieces. (See "Decorating and Furnishing the Bungalow," *Suburban Life* 12 [January 1911], p. 168.) For additional testimony against sets of like pieces for living-room decoration, see Daniels 1908, p. 53.

81. See *Arts & Decoration* 7 (October 1917), p. 573. The remarkable congruence of Mission, colonial, and late-seventeenth-century European styles is summed up in an advertisement from W.F. Halstrick of Chicago, appearing in *House Beautiful* 7 (November 1900), p. 706. A Mission armchair with horizontal slat back is captioned: "A hand-made reproduction of an Antique Dutch Chair finished in Flemish Oak, with cane or leather seat. Solidly built on the true colonial lines...."

82. Priestman 1910, pp. 114-115. Plaster casts are also treated in "An Inexpensive City House Decorated by Samuel Howe," *House Beautiful* 14 (August 1903), p. 143; Daniels 1908, p. 102; and Kellogg 1905, p. 235.

83. See "Bric-A-Brac or What You Will," *House Beautiful* 5 (January 1899), p. 82. See also Henry H. Kennard, "What Should Go Above the Mantel," *House & Garden* 26 (November 1914), pp. 294-295; and Margaret Greenleaf, "Decorating and Furnishing the Small House," *Ideal Homes* 1 (October 1909), p. 7, as examples of articles specifying Canton jars and willow dishes. Japanese blue-and-white ware is endorsed by Minerva L. Power in "An Attractive Dining-Room in a City Flat," *Architect and Engineer of California* 9 (May 1907), p. 83; and by H.P. Keith in "A Complete House Decorative Scheme," *Keith's Magazine on Home Building* 13 (May 1905), p. 306. Regarding the classic simplicity of Japanese pottery, see Katherine Pope, "The Vase in the Home," *House & Garden* 17 (February 1910), p. 76.

84. Florence Morse, "About Furnishings," in *Household Art*, Candace Wheeler, ed. (New York: Harper & Bros., 1893), pp. 176-177.

85. David is quoted in Clay Lancaster, *The American Bungalow, 1880-1930* (New York: Abbeville Press, 1985), p. 122.

86. Keith and Cummins 1909-1910, p. 151. The same introduction had appeared in a 1905 article for *Keith's Magazine on Home Building* in conjunction with a complete bungalow decorative scheme based on Japanese motifs and materials. (See H.P. Keith, "A Complete

House Decorative Scheme – For Bungalow Design,"
Keith's Magazine on Home Building 13 [May 1905], p. 304.)

87. For Bragdon biography, see Coy L. Ludwig, *The Arts and Crafts Movement in New York State, 1890s-1920s* (Hamilton, N.Y.: Gallery Association of New York State, 1983), pp 78-79; and Lawrence Wodehouse, *American Architects from the Civil War to the First World War* (Detroit: Gale Research Co., 1976), p. 28.

88. The phrase "along bungalow lines" was used for houses of more than one story that retained the snugness and earth-hugging spirit of the bungalow (see Saylor 1911, p. 43). For *Cro Nest*, see Claude Bragdon, "An Architect's House," *Good Housekeeping* 38 (May 1904), pp. 484-488. Descriptions of the plan and furnishings are from this article.

89. Alfred H. Granger, "An Architect's Studio," *House Beautiful* 7 (December 1899), pp. 39-40. See also David Grayson's account of a Japanese nobleman who ornamented his house with a single vase at a time in order to fully comprehend its lesson of beauty (*A Day of Pleasant Bread* [Garden City, N.Y.: Doubleday, Page, 1926; reprint of 1908 edition from Phillips Publishing], p. 14).

90. See "The Influence of the Japanese House," in Siegfried Wichmann, *Japonisme: The Japanese Influence on Western Art in the 19th and 20th Centuries* (New York: Harmony Books, 1981), pp. 358-369. For further discussion of Japanese houses and of Japanese features adapted to American bungalows (especially those conceived by Greene and Greene), see Clay Lancaster, *The Japanese Influence in America* (New York: Walton H. Rawls, 1963), pp. 66-68, 122-124.

91. Poultney Bigelow, "The Byrdcliffe Colony of Arts and Crafts," *American Homes and Gardens* 6 (October 1909), pp. 389 and 391; regarding wooden buildings at Byrdcliffe and the decoration of Whitehead's personal residence, *White Pines*, see Robert Edwards, "Byrdcliffe: Life by Design," in *The Byrdcliffe Arts & Crafts Colony* (Wilmington: Delaware Art Museum, 1984), pp. 7-8.

92. Mabel Tuke Priestman, "The Summer Camp at Arden," *American Homes and Gardens* 5 (May 1908), pp. 180-183.

93. See Jan Cohn, *The Palace or the Poorhouse: The American House as a Cultural Symbol* (East Lansing: Michigan State University Press, 1979), p. 68.

94. Kate Greenleaf Locke, "Furnishing and Decorating Houses of Moderate Cost," *House & Garden* 11 (June 1907), pp. 219, 223.

A More Reasonable Way to Dress

Sally Buchanan Kinsey

To Gustav Stickley in his role as editor of *The Craftsman* and as a major voice of the American Arts and Crafts movement, beauty, comfort, and simplicity in dress were "as much a part of progress as is a wise style in architecture, or an athletic physical standard for the growth of women, or the right use of machinery in handicraft work." The enlightened view of *The Craftsman* in 1907 benefited from a half-century of intense dress-reform advocacy by concerned men and women who were allied with wider issues such as healthfulness of family and community and aesthetic improvement of civic and domestic environments.[1] In her plea for the elevation of "housewifery" to the status of an art or science, Catherine Beecher, pioneer of the scientific housekeeping movement, suggested that the adoption of comfortable, functional house apparel was essential to the efficient management of a home and appropriate to the role of women as guardians of culture. Among the "true rules of grace and beauty" in her book, first published in 1842, is a forthright precept on suitability: "Any mode of dress, not suited to the employment, the age, the season, or the means of the wearer is in bad taste."[2] It is a statement that would be echoed into the twentieth century by *The Craftsman* and other Arts and Crafts theorists.

Related to the urge for functionalism was the concern for physical well-being. Voicing a plea shared with many physicians, Miss Beecher deplored the bondage induced by "murderous contrivances of the corset shop" and the ills they fostered, especially the poorly developed rib cages that in turn forced many women to endure respiratory problems, immature digestive systems, and undue difficulties in childbearing. Mary E. Tillotson, a nineteenth-century historian of the American dress reform movement and a lifelong advocate of

"science costume," recalled that in her delicate youth she was released from her corset and tight clothing to wear a "grandmother suit" made by her sisters: cotton drawers made like trousers took the place of petticoats and the skirt was nine inches from the floor. This reform dress, she was convinced, restored her to good health. In her history of the American movement, she noted that female physicians and hydropathists were particularly aware of the consequences of lacing tight, as it was commonly described in fashion journals. One practitioner who was consumptive in her youth, a Dr. Stobridge of Cortland, New York, was "cured" by the reform of her dress and years later was to be found wearing a "science costume" in her infirmary in order to influence "corset-caged victims" under her care.[3]

The dress-reform movement was from its inception directed to the growing middle class, the men and women who would in a later generation benefit from the *Craftsman* point of view. Their sensibilities were affronted on occasion by the radical imagery of trouser-clad vociferous females, as with the Bloomerists of the early 1850s; this became a hindrance to the true purpose of the movement – the improvement of life – a concept that was at the core of Arts and Crafts design as well. In writing her history, Mary Tillotson noted tartly that to identify the symbol of an important idea such as dress reform by a person's name (Bloomer) was not only inadequate but misguiding. An objective term was more appropriate as nomenclature, hence "science costume" was the term Mrs. Tillotson and others used to convey the reform principles of "freeing tortured bodies . . . to redeem their native qualities, restore them to nature's intent, qualify them for the liberty, equality and joy that the universe declares is their heritage."[4] Tunic and

Fig. 1. Ladies' Dress Reform Meeting, Boston, 1874

The Emancipation Suit.

Patented Aug. 3, 1875.

Price, plain, $3.00; trimmed, $4.50.

Believing that much of the ill-health of woman is attributable to ill-constructed and too weighty clothing, the "EMANCIPATION SUIT" has been arranged, with the intention of producing an undergarment which, by its peculiar fitness and styles of manufacture, will prove acceptable and conducive to the health of all who may wear it.

It may be made of cotton, linen, or any fabric adapted to the habit of the wearer. It is made in one entire article of dress, (or the drawers can be made separate, to button on,) and supplies the place of *chemise, drawers, corset and corset cover.*

The study has been to produce a hygienic garment, viz. :

To free the breast from compression and irritation.

To equalize warmth and weight of clothing.

To free the waist line from ligature and excessive heating, and by the arrangement of buttons, support the clothing upon the shoulders.

In taking waist measures, give exact size of waist.

Fig. 2. Emancipation Suit, from Alice Fletcher Dress Reform Depot Catalog. Private Collection

trouser ensembles were merely symbols of what one reformist, Abba G. Woolson, expressed as the hope for "a revolution in the structure" of dress, with the most significant reforms to take place in the attitude of men and women toward the clothes they wore.[5]

The dress-reform movement in America was formalized at a convention held in upstate New York in 1855, with the assistance of Dr. James C. Jackson, a physician and hydropathist. The new National Dress Association, so named in 1856 ("Reform" was added later), attracted followers through a newsletter posted by Dr. Jackson, and with *Sibyl*, a dress-reform journal edited by Dr. Lydia Hasbrouck.[6] In the 1850s and '60s dress reform was practiced for grateful patients at water-cure resorts and "therapeutic academies," and comfortable gymnasium apparel was introduced at private "health colleges." The formal association dissolved in the Civil War era but in the late 1860s dress reform was endorsed by influential organizations such as the New England Women's Club in Boston and Sorosis in New York; it also began to attract national attention.

A spirit of inventiveness and an emphasis on health, comfort, and utility prevailed within the innovative garments proposed by concerned reformists. At the World Health Convention in New York in 1864, Mrs. M. M. Jones advocated pantaloons supported by shoulder suspenders and covered with a "hygienic" smock that resembled a bungalow apron, the favorite work costume of many Arts and Crafts women in the twentieth century.[7] In the 1870s Mrs. Tillotson's Anti-Fashion Society in Vineland, New Jersey, promoted improved underwear and work suits for more efficient housekeeping; in California, the journalist Marietta Stow established the National Social Science Sisterhood to encourage the wearing of a "Triple S"

costume with functional skirtage at knee length.[8] In Boston interest in dress reform increased (see fig. 1); patterns and garments respecting hygienic principles were sold at a dress-reform bureau by Mrs. Woolson, a professor of *belles lettres* who lectured on the importance of art education as an aid to proper selection of garments. Her organization sponsored a symposium of female physicians who spoke on the evils of contemporary costume and published their lectures in 1874 under the title *Dress as It Affects the Health of Women*.[9] Reaching an even larger population, the Alice Fletcher Dress Reform Depot in New York offered by mail order an assortment of reform undergarments including union suits of knit cashmere or merino wool for men, women, and children; shoulder-yoke stocking supporters for women and children; and a woman's "Emancipation Suit" intended to replace four customarily worn items: chemise, drawers, corset, and corset cover (fig. 2).[10]

Thus, approaching the Centennial, the objectives of dress reform were being conveyed to a wider public through merchandising and publications. Reform dress was worn by some adventurous women at the Philadelphia Centennial Exhibition in 1876 and a number of reform garments were on display, including designs approved by the Dress Reform Committee of the New England Women's Club for construction based on four hygienic principles: "no ligatures, uniform temperature, lightness of weight, and suspension from the shoulder."[11] The Alice Fletcher Depot won a Centennial medal for its designs. During the height of Centennial activity in 1875 and 1876, the American Free Dress League, formed in 1874 with the aid of the Anti-Fashion Society, held two conventions in Philadelphia. At the meeting in 1876 the League adopted resolutions that suggest affinities with those formed five years later by the Rational Dress Society of Great Britain; indeed, they may have been shared with a founder of that society, Mrs. King, when she visited Vineland, New Jersey, in the 1880s.[12] The resolutions confirmed the proposition that costume for both sexes is important for health and harmony; they also appealed to "thinking men and women" to reject the excesses of fashion and to wear only clothing designed on scientific principles and therefore "conducive to health, comfort and freedom." Certainly these were primary concerns as the dress reform movement gathered international attention.

Nor would aesthetics be ignored; dress-reform pamphlets and self-help manuals that abounded in the late nineteenth century are compatible with the noblest theories of Arts and Crafts design. The author of one such discourse on dress selection, Ethel C. Gale, emphasized that to be well dressed it is not necessary to seek extremes of high fashion, but it is essential to consider form, color, and fabric and to heed the importance of healthfulness as well as neatness, affordability, and suitability to occupation. She railed against the popular penchant for wearing expensive but shabby finery as house apparel, for a women could not be considered well dressed when attired with inappropriate garments. Women were advised to ignore the exaggerations in pattern and color of the popular Rococo revivals, for these too soon become "grotesque . . . [while] plain goods are never out of date." The plain goods that Mrs. Gale preferred were washable textiles such as "butcher's linen" and "oatmeal cloth" (rough cotton) suited to the construction of housekeeping smocks, aprons, and wrappers, to be sewn by machine with the aid of a pattern from Butterick or McCall. A more elegant plain textile

Fig. 3. American woman, ca. 1878. Photograph by Carter, Worcester, Massachusetts. Private Collection

for public wear was a "nun's cloth," a sheer wool-and-silk blend that could be purchased in the subdued tones of "cloister brown," gray, and black, as well as in pastels. The softness of nun's cloth and the ease of draping allowed free movement (fig. 3) and a comfortable bosom while remaining true to the fashionable *cuirasse* bodice, which might be defined by a Fletcher Dress Reform Corset Waist instead of a steel-ribbed "Hercules." All was to be accomplished in good taste, for an important concern of the true dress reformist – ever mindful of the onus of Bloomerism – was that any reformation should take place within the boundaries of social acceptability.[13]

Home economists continued to warn in graphic terms of the hazards to a woman of fashion who chose to remain faithful to the tradition of a small waist. Now the appeal was often on aesthetic grounds: "She will weaken her circula-

tion, she will make her hands red, she will incur headache, she will crack her voice, and she will ruin her digestion, all to produce a malformation which wise men regard with pity," wrote the authors of *Home and Health and Home Economics*.[14] Such vehement admonishments could go unheeded for formal parties and public occasions, especially by American women who were seeking to emulate fashionable European society. But as Mrs. Woolson hoped, a quiet "revolution in the structure" was beginning to take place, especially an increasing public awareness of the evils of lacing tight and of ill-formed clothing designed to distort the wearer's natural "symmetry" (a Victorianism for "body proportion").[15] For thinking women attuned to self-improvement, the home became a laboratory for dress reform.

In the afterglow of Centennial awakening, lighter corsetings were worn under morning wrappers and housekeeping smocks, and soon under gowns for reception dress. Modern women increasingly adopted looser lacings under fashionable princess-line tea gowns and kimonos. In a novel of New York life, *The Age of Innocence*, Edith Wharton provided a vivid description of the impact of such simplicity in the drawing rooms of the 1870s, where it was customary for ladies who received in the evening to wear "close-fitting armor of whaleboned silk" with ruffles and long sleeves. Here the house guest, Madame Olenska, flaunting tradition, was attired in a dramatic flowing velvet robe fashioned with a mandarin collar and wide, loose sleeves that bared the arm to the elbow in the manner of a kimono. The caller Newland Archer, himself a member of drawing-room society, found the effect "bold . . . but undeniably pleasing."[16] Celebrated actresses in this golden age of theater, such as Sarah Bernhardt, Ellen Terry, and Lillie Langtry

– all of whom toured America in the eighties – preferred to receive in such flowing costumes and contributed to their popularity.[17] The reigning beauty queen of the American stage in that decade, Mary Anderson, was renowned for her Grecian proportions and uncorseted loveliness. Even the *maître* of couture confectionery, Charles Frederick Worth, sanctioned the simplicity of a kimono over the princess style for evenings at home.[18] In the minds of many women, kimono styles were an identification with artistic attitudes and the Pre-Raphaelites, for the medieval themes and *japonaiserie* of the wider Rossetti circle continued to capture the fancy of Americans long after the original Brotherhood disbanded, and the ideal that simplicity is the foundation of all art, expressed by William Morris in his work, was well known in this country in the eighties.[19]

When Oscar Wilde brought his reform message to over 90 cities throughout North America in 1882, he found audiences with heightened appreciation for the beauties of the Japanese style in dress and interiors, as well as eager receptivity to his plea that they seek further inspiration from designs of ancient civilizations – especially the Greek – and in the homespun comforts of early American colonists. In his lectures and later in essay form, Wilde, a staunch dress reformist and champion of the tea gown, urged women to return to classic principles of drapery, with costuming hung from the shoulders rather than impeding the waistline with cumbersome bulk and weight. Lacing tight should be rejected in favor of naturalism. Ornamentation, if used at all, should be handwork of quality and permanence, "as in the old days."[20] Thus, the Wildean outlook of the wearer of a modern tea gown of the 1880s and 1890s is symbolized by a generous waist-line to accommodate the symmetry of reform undergarments, possibly including a soft cotton corset with stitched panels rather than stays – or even a Fletcher Emancipation Suit. The gown would be draped loosely and the weight of it suspended from the shoulders; perhaps it would be distinguished by Old English hand-smocking, which was enjoying a revival of popularity (no. 190). Because of the "cut-in-one" construction (bodice and skirt are cut in continuous panels) of the shoulder-to-hem line, the tea gown eliminated waistline pressure and was a style well suited for reform corseting and for wear during pregnancy.[21]

Among the major beneficiaries of dress reform were children who would become adults in the Arts and Crafts era.[22] As the home became the center of enlightened dress, reforms were taking place in society's attitude toward children and their education. Girls and boys were beginning to be regarded less as imperfect miniature adults. More attention was directed to the child's individuality, and sex differentiation became more conspicuous in the clothing of very young children, who had traditionally been attired in dresses – boys and girls alike – until formal schooling began. In matters of dress reform, their particular requirements for movement and growth were addressed with seriousness; often their attire united the best principles of utility, simplicity, and beauty. A custom of middle-class America in the late nineteenth century called for children to be presented briefly to family and friends at tea time, when the youngsters' budding talents in music, art, and language were displayed. For such an occasion, children could be dressed in the newest fashions, or in reform items that would have been too forward for adult tastes. It was a clever economic move, for to make a reform statement with children's dress was less costly than attempting it for adults. Aesthetically it was a way to indicate, perhaps through the choice of a practical Kate Greenaway smock, one's embrace of reform principles, even if they were not displayed on the adult self.[23] And so, the young girl of the eighties, groomed with ideas of progress, might become the bicycling collegiate of the nineties and a self-assured Gibson Girl at the turn of the century.

Dress for men underwent serious appraisal also. Mrs. Woolson had noted that the uniformity and sober suiting of the Industrial Revolution male was an insult to women's aesthetic tastes: "By what privilege, we ask, do they ignore their bounden allegiance to art and daily afflict our sense of the graces of form and charms of color by the attire they adopt? Have not our eyes rights in this matter?"[24] The monotonous regularity of male attire was boring even to males. In his well-known *Hints on Household Taste*, which went into six editions in America by 1881, Charles Eastlake called for comfort and variety, emphasizing that formal dress was particularly in need of reform, for at a dinner table it was hardly possible to distinguish the host from a clergyman from a butler.[25] Wilde, who thought western miners were the only well-dressed men in America, agreed with Eastlake that a return to the comfortable and picturesque was needed.[26] Aching brows under weighty stovepipes could be assuaged by a return to the aesthetic of olden times (that is, the eighteenth century) and by the adoption of country dress for city wear. Again, the first evidence that such hints were being taken seriously came from the home, where young boys still in curls might be introduced to reform comforts with sailor suits of durable fabrics such as plain-weave cotton "crash," or Indian Head, one of the first

Fig. 4. Young boy, ca. 1885. Photograph. Private Collection

Fig. 5. Elbert Hubbard, 1904. Photograph. Private Collection

and most popular of American utility textiles (fig. 4). At the turn of the century, as a young adult, he would favor the country tweeds and easy tailoring of the American craftsmen's sack suit, so often preferred by Arts and Crafts figures such as Gustav Stickley, Elbert Hubbard (fig. 5), and Frank Lloyd Wright, in rustic contrast to the sober suitings of conservative gentry.

In this period of rapid population growth and urbanization, middle-class American families sought new opportunities for the enjoyment of nature. Outdoor sports were avidly indulged: archery, lawn tennis, badminton, and boating in summer; ice skating and sledding in winter. Croquet was so popular across the country that manufacturers sold sets with candle holders on the wickets for night play. "Wash goods" for sport – linen blazers for men, tennis aprons for women – were offered by mail order, a service that was increasingly in demand as the population moved west. Hiking, hunting, and mountain climbing were popular for mixed groups of male and female friends. For such strenuous activities makers of specialized costuming recognized the advantages to women of the once-notorious pantaloon styles.[27] One ensemble, marketed in England as the Rocky Mountain Travelling Costume, was composed of Turkish leglettes covered by a tunic and a calf-length divided skirt, to be worn with ankle-concealing gaiters for warmth and modesty.[28] Citified versions of this style were offered through a popular dress-reform journal, *The Jenness-Miller Magazine*, published in New York from 1889. The journal's American Costume, a wool tunic covering a divided skirt, was endorsed by dress reformists who convened at the World's Columbian Exposition in Chicago in 1893.[29] Other interpretations of this comfortable apparel, suggesting ap-

propriateness for bicycling and country outings, appear in many fashion journals and beauty manuals of the era, and it was considered a suitable uniform for most "scientific" physical culture. By the turn of the century, utility tunics and divided skirts of heavy-duty drill or duck had gained acceptance for resort wear, representing a victory of sorts for bloomer advocates and for dedicated reformists who had always hoped to inspire a more realistic and practical approach toward dress. Clearly, the New Woman was emerging.[30] Her simplicity, suitability, and practicality of dress represented a modern approach to life. The concept of dress reform became associated with acceptable role models – the sportswoman, the college woman, the progressive homemaker – and as historian Lois Banner observed: "Who could resist the tide of change when even the *Ladies' Home Journal*, the venerable organ of middle-class female opinion, in 1893 endorsed the right of women to choose their own clothes on the basis of comfort?"[31]

The acceptance of dress reform in the guise of practical, functional, and simplified apparel is to be noted in the objectives of new self-improvement organizations such as the midwestern Society for the Promotion of Physical Culture and Correct Dress, organized in 1888 and endorsed by the Chicago Women's Club. Papers presented at meetings of the Society included the topics "Bondage of Conventional Dress" and "A Plea for the Natural." In an attempt to "reinstate the ideal proportions of classic sculpture as the correct standard of womanly form," each member was urged to supply herself with a photograph of the Venus de Milo, and to strive for the ideal through diet and exercise. Only then would she attempt the design of apparel. Principles of art, health, and utility were to be consulted, and fashion books ignored, for the emphasis was on the expression of one's individuality through carefully considered choices of address. Women who sought this were not cranky reformers.[32] Indeed, principles of dress design and selection began to be introduced into domestic arts curricula for schools and colleges – for example, in the newly formed New York College for the Training of Teachers (1889), which became Teachers College in 1892 and an affiliate of Columbia University in 1898. It worked closely with the Industrial Education Association, also started in the 1880s, to provide apparel design instruction in public schools.[33] Domestic arts education for the young was expected to reap multiple rewards: with the mastery of the skills of apparel design for sartorial economy and comfort, it taught problem-solving and the understanding of handcraft. Most important to *The Craftsman*, which advocated grouping apparel design with bookbinding and carpentry, what young designers learned to do well with their hands would help them to understand "the dignity of manual labor."[34]

What styles of apparel might the novice designer learn to create? Some authors on dress, as in *Beauty of Form and Grace of Vesture*, echoing Eastlake and Wilde, suggested that the most suitable costuming for the new century should be a revival of loosely girded Empire-waist fashions from the Federal period, an era of freedom in dress. Such styles, inspired by "our grandmothers" but popularly known as "Josephine looks," were distinctly in contrast to the wasp waists and hourglass silhouettes of 1890s couture and forecast the classical-revival gowns in vogue internationally during the late Edwardian years.[35] Other experts, such as Helen Lathrop Gilbert Ecob, a nationally recognized writer on dress and beauty, favored medieval gowns of the type popularized by Liberty of London at the turn of the century

Fig. 6. The "comfort principle," illustrated in *The Well-Dressed Woman . . .*, by Helen Ecob (New York, 1892).

and often interpreted by American dressmakers for at-home attire. Mrs. Ecob was an advocate of divided skirts for day wear and sport but she appreciated the freedom and simplicity of Pre-Raphaelite themes in dress, with their attendant comfort and ease of movement allowing essential elements of grace and self-possession to be expressed.[36] Clever designers could combine the relaxed Empire waistline and the soft flow of a kirtle (medieval tunic) to create a languorous air worthy of Jane Morris and then add a convenient utility pocket in the tradition of an *aumônière* (alms purse) as an appropriate accessory to hold needlework (fig. 6). The work pocket or wall pocket (to hold an alma-

nac) was a typical first project for novice textile and apparel designers; designs for these colorful and useful accessories appeared in many homemaking and manual arts journals at the turn of the century and were used as practice pieces for embroidery and basic design.

As utility, simplicity, and beauty – three principles that united reformists, designers, and teachers – became elements of American apparel, the phrase "dress reform" was used with caution. In concept it was to be a sincere concern of the Art and Crafts movement; as a spokesman writing in an early issue of *The Craftsman* acknowledged, "to learn what to wear is as essential as to know what to eat."[37] But if it meant ever-changing frills and fancies, fashion should be considered a hindrance to the simple life. Early on, *The Craftsman* adopted a firm yet democratic stance, rejecting alliances with *outré* styles: "This question of good dressing is much simpler than 'reforms' and 'movements.' It does not need to force a woman to 'take a stand' and in any ostentatious way differ from the prevailing modes; all that is necessary is for her to study her own color scheme, to understand the merits and faults of her own body, to select for that body the clothes that are just suited in line and color, to avoid useless ornamentation, and to see to it that the color, texture and cut of her clothes are suited to her occupation in life."[38] If that occupation included motherhood, the "New Homemaker" was especially obligated to set an example of artistic and comfortable dress and to select garments for her children that would allow them to be led "to Nature, to imaginative ideas, to art and her own companionship," wrote the silversmith Janet Payne Bowles in *The Craftsman* in 1904 (see no. 130).[39] For a young American homemaker who accepted these tenets (fig. 7), the simplicity of her house dress

Fig. 7. *An Interesting Story.* Photograph by Mrs. W.W. Pearce, from *Western Camera Notes,* November 1903, p. 266

and attitude of relaxation is in striking contrast to the imposing Edwardian *grande-dame* who is the usual symbol of the era. It is easy to believe that the companionable young mother, enjoying her children in the fresh air and garden setting of a modern bungalow, may herself have been a fortunate daughter of the 1880s in a Kate Greenaway smock. Now her choice of dress for her own children and herself will consider comfort and utility. Her morning attire will perhaps be a plainly cut, smock-like wrapper or sacque intended for comfort but also to be pleasing to her family; hence the choice of cotton lawn printed with "neat" flowers (as the Sears and Roebuck catalogues distinguished small floral prints from larger fancy designs). In the afternoon, for leisurely activities such as visiting or reading, she might choose a porch dress of striped cotton (no. 189) that could be covered with a bungalow apron (utility kimono) if kitchen chores were necessary. Just as she had done in an earlier era, her children would benefit from this enlightened approach to dress. The Arts and Crafts years were ones of unusual freedom in children's apparel and with a strong concern for their health and growth. Washable, sturdy play

clothes – rompers, smocks, and Russian suits (bloomer and tunic combination) – were of practical storm serge (tough wool) for winter and gingham for summer; they may be viewed as a forecast of the simplicity and functionalism these Arts and Crafts children would prefer as adults in the 1920s. Certainly *The Craftsman* approved of this approach to children's dress, saying that in teaching a child the path to appropriate attire, a mother teaches the best philosophy of life and cultivates taste and "a beauty that is associated with health and sanity."[40]

This concern for the reasonable life motivated *The Craftsman* approach to apparel design – "plain clothes for plain occasions" – as toward all applied arts. In his noteworthy essay of 1906 on the industrial age, "Use and Abuse of Machinery," Stickley observed that the sewing machine as a labor-saving device took away from the work ethic as much as it brought, for it encouraged desires for insensitive overelaboration in costume design.[41] Possibly such thinking impelled him to establish a fashion department for the journal, the better to promote a new "Philosophy of Dress." Some readers were mystified by this dimension. Within an essay of 1907 describing a way to sew "practically indestructible" linen shirtwaists that "will not go out of style, for they have no extravagant modishness to begin with," *The Craftsman* addressed a vexed subscriber's query – "What have fashions to do with handicrafts or fine arts?" – by replying: "If we are going to simplify life, simplicity is not for one phase and extravagance for another. It is of no use to build houses of the kind that reduce labor, and make dresses of the kind that use up all the hours we have saved in our wise architecture . . . useful, beautiful clothes, are, in fact, one kind of handicraft, and any instruction about

the making of them has as much a place in *The Craftsman* as cabinet work or basketry or book binding."[42] Still, the consideration of dress within the pages of a craft manual was not without criticism from some bewildered readers; one subscriber took exception to the shirtwaist essay and pleaded, "Tell us of the philosophy of life, cut out fashions," to which the determined editor replied that dress as expression of character and personality was, like one's home and friends, "inevitably woven in the woof of life." The goal of *The Craftsman* philosophy of dress was not to present the silly subject of fashion, but to contribute to a "better and more reasonable way of living."[43]

The Craftsman was not alone in philosophizing on the subject of dress. Perhaps not again has the subject been treated with such high intentions by so many sincere individuals. Alice Hubbard, wife of "The Fra," numbered among the many who directed serious consideration to the relationship of dress to identity when she wrote in 1908: "Woman is so great when she is honestly herself that she need not attempt to be anyone else. She can and will evolve a far better mode of dress than is now used by any one. Her clothing will be so adapted to the needs of the body in its work, that the subject will be only a small item in her mind and leave time and energy for things of more benefit to herself. But in the meantime we gain nothing by imitation."[44] The threat of imitation was a concern shared with other writers, designers, and teachers. Eva Olney Farnsworth, an educator from Minnesota, expressed this firmly in 1915: "Art requires absolute truth. No sham or false appearance is permitted." To Mrs. Farnsworth, imitation "is always a sham and is never artistic. A true and self-reliant individuality in dress, based upon true rules of art, will produce a costume at once suitable and becoming to the wearer."[45] But how to achieve individuality without flamboyance in dress? Across America, eager journalists were willing to offer advice. Belle Armstrong Whitney, writing for the Good Health Publishing Company of Battle Creek, Michigan, advised women to demand quality in fabric and to select styles that would endure for the life of the garment. In her plea for "sane thrift" Mrs. Whitney invoked the spirit of William Morris and the Arts and Crafts movement when she wrote in 1916; "We need useful clothes for comfort. We need beautiful clothes to develop and satisfy our love of beauty." In a practical, *Craftsman*-like vein, she suggested choosing clothes that are reasonable in cost and are easy to put on and take off – legitimate areas of concern in Mrs. Whitney's day, as modish garments often strained the purse while relying for effect upon a labyrinth of gathers, fasteners, and appended drapery.[46]

Because of these concerns for quality and convenience, the art of apparel design was approached scientifically and seriously. Rules of design were as exacting as those for a metalsmith or a homebuilder, and carried forth the best motives of Morris and the early dress reformers. In her manual of instruction forthright Mrs. Farnsworth cited parallels: "Dress, like architecture, is based upon practical requirements and can only be true and logical when it meets these requirements." The practical requirements concerning the figure meant to Mrs. Farnsworth that clothing must allow freedom and graceful action if it was to be considered artistic.[47] Many architects of the era would have appreciated her analogy. Frank Lloyd Wright, with the aid of a creative seamstress, enjoyed designing dresses for his wife that reveal, in their sturdy and unadorned geometry, structural similari-

ties with his architecture.[48] Claude Bragdon, a designer of theater costumes as well as buildings, urged the study of that "temple" of the human figure, for "the correlation between the house and its inhabitant, and the body and its consciousness is everywhere close. . . . Architectural beauty, like human beauty, depends upon a proper subordination of parts to the whole, [and] a harmonious interrelation between these parts."[49] Before solving artistic problems, however, a designer needed to stimulate creative powers. The household arts curriculum in use at Teachers College of Columbia University from around 1910 stressed the study of architecture, sculpture, and historic costume in books and prints and at museums, the theater, and opera. The design should solve the problems of freedom of movement and suitability to purpose and surroundings; most of all, it should express the personality of the wearer. The textbook warned that this last consideration is a rigorous challenge, for a designer needed skill to detect and appreciate the unique qualities of the individual and to emphasize them without conspicuousness. Simplicity is ever the keynote; overelaboration is the mark of the amateur.[50]

Social reformers in this era of radical moves toward female emancipation hoped that as women developed self-assurance they would "become superior to the passion for ornament,"[51] or at least that they would be able to tame it. But it was also an era when many women, especially from immigrant families, had a strong propensity for the ornamental needle arts, having perhaps learned the traditional skills from older women in the extended family. Only about ten percent of married women worked outside of the home; for the others there were many opportunities to practice one's needle skills on proj-

ects for home or personal beautification. Since the average wage in America at this time was around twenty-two cents an hour, it was economical to purchase and hand-finish a partially constructed item of apparel. A typical offering from Wanamaker stores' mail-order catalogue of 1911 offered a cotton blouse, stamped for embroidery and with the finishing threads included, for $1.30; a completed version cost ten dollars.[52] The concern for proper use of ornament was intense at all levels of design and theory. Domestic arts handbooks for students urged them to plan for harmonious ornament at the first stages of design: *The Craftsman* rejected out of hand "silly, over-ornamental, over-fitted, sparkling useless dress" and manuals like that of Mrs. Farnsworth, directed to the homemaker-designer, specified that the correct ornament must reveal itself as an integral finishing touch to the structure of the costume.[53] Hence, the washable coarse lace or Irish crochet on a porch dress (no. 189) should be constructed as a flat band within the fabric of the garment, rather than be used as a flounce as it would have been in the 1890s (no. 30), for the concept of the house dress had changed. No longer a hostess gown, it was more in the nature of garb for a modern-day *châtelaine*, the medieval keeper of the storehouse and head of the household not only in matters of economy but in culture as well.

Because judicious use of ornament was sanctioned as an appropriate finishing touch, the basic costume design needed to be a structure of simplicity, likened to a painter's – or embroiderer's – canvas. To the satisfaction of dress reformists, gone were the complicated underarm fastenings on cross-draped bodices over armorial superstructures. Coarse-thread embroidery and soutache (braid) of washable silk or cotton were best worked in flat areas to enhance an interesting architectural element of the design, such as an asymmetrical neckline closure (no. 190), and color contrasts were subtle rather than harsh. Earth tones – "willow," "bamboo," "parsley" – embroidered on natural linens and cottons were regarded as the most compatible combinations for harmony with the greenery, basketry, and mission oak of a bungalow interior. Visual unity between one's apparel and one's interior was an essential aesthetic, wrote Estelle Izor, author of *Costume Design and Home Planning*.[54] The harmony of the total effect relied upon one's informed choices of dress and furnishings, in order that inhabitant and setting might favor each other. Simplicity – as expected – was the keynote to effective design. If one was not artistically inclined, wrote Mrs. Izor, then "an honest, frank use of plain, inexpensive material worth the price paid for it reflects more credit on the wearer and the community in which she lives than all the showey finery and shoddy jewelry that she can wear."

The fears of some theorists for the dangers of over-ornamentation did not keep others from encouraging a spirit of adventure in the New Homemaker. Students of dress design were, not surprisingly, urged to consult the work of European designers for inspiration, for patterns by the houses of Paquin, Lucille, and others were regularly offered within the pages of journals such as *Woman's Home Companion*.[55] Jane Fales's manual for college students in the household arts curriculum at Columbia mentions in particular the important French *couturier* Paul Poiret and his search for greater simplicity and original detail through the study of historic dress.[56] In the second decade of the new century, the acceptance by Americans of the influence of European designers

represents a marked change from the rejection typical of a few years earlier, when floridly attired continentals were viewed by Mrs. Ecob (who preferred a quieter artistic dress) as "enemies of the home" wearing "vulgar and sensual [fashions that] appeal to the lower nature."[57] (Even in 1910, the seeking of inspiration in *haute couture* would bring a frown to *The Craftsman*, which worried unduly about the power of advertising and "butterfly women who think mainly of clothes" with their adverse influences upon American women who have "homes to keep, children to bring up and friends to love."[58])

Further inspiration (and one of which *The Craftsman* approved) for color schemes and construction could be derived from the study of Japanese textiles;[59] student designers and homemakers were urged to interpret the subtle colorations and simplicity of line in order to avoid extremes of construction and decoration. "Kimono" had endured in the jargon of dress design, but a term that might once have suggested a tea gown (to Mrs. Wharton's Newland Archer in the 1870s) was now more likely to describe popular treatment for a variety of apparel. Instructions for machine-sewn kimono wrappers, kimono waists (blouses), and kimono sacques for infants were given in women's journals and sewing handbooks. Teachers College manual included directions for converting a tailored shirtwaist to a kimono waist, a task well placed in the advanced category of costume skills.[60] The straight lines and broad surfaces of the many versions of kimono styling were well suited to structural bands of ornament and inset panels of lace (no. 34). Manuals that adhered to reform principles of construction often suggested variations on the princess theme, because this long-time favorite shared with kimono styling a provision for free-

Fig. 8. *Abastenia Eberle: American Sculptor*. Photograph by Clarence White, from "People Who Interest Us: Abastenia Eberle, Sculptor of National Tendency," *Craftsman* 18 (1910), pp. 474-475

Fig. 9. *Structural Unity*. Illustration by Rachel Taft Dixon from *Costume Design and Home Planning*, by Estelle Peel Izor (New York, 1916)

dom of movement.[61] The result could be a subtle and artistic blending of Pre-Raphaelite and Oriental elements, as in a costume worn by the sculptor Abastenia Eberle (fig. 8). Her generous kimono bodice is uninhibiting of waistline and hipline and offers an opportunity for decorative yet structural ornament, thus satisfying the requirements of good Arts and Crafts design as well as the precepts of dress reform. Miss Eberle is wearing the kimono over a house dress, its slender sleeves delicately embroidered at the cuffs, effecting a twentieth-century interpretation of the medieval gown and kirtle (loose overdress covering a long-sleeved tunic) so revered by the Pre-Raphaelites. Miss Eberle's choice of costume, appropriately artistic yet honest in its presentation of structural ornament, would have earned the approval of many dress-reform theorists, including the stringent, homespun Stickley in whose journal Miss Eberle was featured. Her ensemble is a study in the achievement of graceful action advocated by Mrs. Farnsworth, and in unity, that most desired state, "a consistent relation of all forms with a reason for each," as Mrs. Izor wrote to her students.[62] The designs she suggested to exemplify this state of general harmony are interpretations of kimono and princess effects by Rachel Taft Dixon (fig. 9) certain to appeal to the Arts and Crafts aesthetic of home-makers and craftswomen.

The best examples of Arts and Crafts apparel, in which can be numbered the dress of Miss Eberle and the designs of Mrs. Dixon, represent a unity of hand and machine skills (for, despite the fears of *The Craftsman*, women overcame the dangers of ill-used ornament inherent in the sewing machine) and most important, the unity of wearer with surroundings. The well-dressed, i.e., appropriately dressed Arts and Crafts woman provided what the author Emily Bur-

bank termed in 1917 "the vital spark" to animate the environment.[63] To the concerned woman of the new century, as designer and consumer, the right of choice was primary. The key was self-education. Appropriateness was the watchword. And, wrote Mrs. Izor, ". . . the final test will be the affirmative answer to . . ., 'Is it beautiful? Is it suitable to wear?'"[64] That so many American women could answer a positive "Yes," in the spirit of dress reform and the ideals of the Arts and Crafts movement, was assurance that Mrs. Woolson's hoped-for "revolution in the structure" was in progress.

1. See "Shirt-Waists from a Craftsman Point of View," *Craftsman* 11 (February 1907), p. 651.; Rabbi Joseph Leiser, "Simplicity: A Law of Nature," *Craftsman* 2 (August 1902), p. 228.

2. See Catherine E. Beecher, *A Treatise on Domestic Economy, For the Use of Young Ladies at Home and at School* (rev. ed.; New York: Harper and Brothers, 1849), pp. 116-117.

3. See Mary E. Tillotson, *History ov [sic] the First Thirty-five Years ov [sic] the Science Costume Movement in the United States of America* (Vineland, N. J.: Weekly-Independent Book and Job Office, 1885), pp. 13-56. Mrs. Tillotson was a spelling reformist and the original document quoted in this essay was written in "reform" style (for example, "physician" is spelled "fizishun") but, for purposes of clarity, direct references to Tillotson will use standard English. Her writings on dress reform were known in England; see *The Rational Dress Society's Gazette* 1 (London: Hatchards, 1888), p. 7.

4. See Tillotson 1885, pp. 16-20.

5. Abba Louisa (Goold) Woolson, ed., *Dress-Reform, a Series of Lectures Delivered in Boston, on Dress as It Affects the Health of Women* (Boston: Roberts Brothers, 1874), p. vii. Amelia Jenks Bloomer, a temperance advocate and editor (with her husband as publisher) of a reform journal, *The Lily*, adopted in 1851 a style of tunic and "Turkish" pantaloons similar to those being worn by her friend Elizabeth Smith Miller, the daughter of the abolitionist Gerrit Smith, and by Mrs. Miller's cousin Elizabeth Cady Stanton. Others who wore this ensemble included the reformer Lucy Stone, the actress Fanny Kemble, the journalist Jane Cunningham Croly, and Dr. Mary Edwards Walker. Mrs. Bloomer found that the attire attracted so much attention on the streets of Seneca Falls, New York, she employed it in the manner of a theatrical costume to draw crowds to her temperance speeches. In a few years she abandoned it for that very reason: her trousers and "kilt" (her term) were compelling more notice than her oratory, especially when she wore the attire in Britain. Mrs. Bloomer noted philosophically: "With us, the dress was but an incident, and we were not willing to sacrifice greater questions to it." See D. C. Bloomer, *Life and Writings of Amelia Bloomer* (Boston: Arena Publishing Company, 1895), p. 70.

6. See Tillotson 1885, pp. 16-20; idem, *Progress vs. Fashion. An Essay on the Sanitary and Social Influences of Women's Dress* (Vineland, N. J., 1873), pp. 22-24. Dr. Jackson, a hydropathist, headed a water-cure resort in the Finger Lakes region of New York State. The cure included sleeping in wet bandages and partaking of Dr. Jackson's new cereal, "Granula." Female patients were obliged to wear reform dress – pantaloons covered by tunics, corsetless – during their visits. Dr. Jackson held a Hygienic Festival in the early 1850s at which 150 editors and reformers, including Amelia Bloomer and Elizabeth Cady Stanton, were in attendance. (See Eva Loyster, comp., "Glen Haven Sanitorium and Water Cure" [unpublished paper, Skaneateles Historical Society, n. d.].) For Dr. Jackson's views on dress, see

James C. Jackson, M.D., *Consumption: How to Prevent It, and How to Cure It* (Boston: B. Leverett Emerson, 1862), pp. 212-223; and *How to Treat the Sick Without Medicine* (Dansville, N.Y.: Austin, Jackson and Company, 1877), pp. 61-81.

Dr. Hasbrouck adopted reform dress in 1849 and wore it throughout her life. In the pages of *Sibyl*, which she edited until its demise in 1864, she advocated "hygeopathy," a system of healthy living. She practiced hydropathy, advocated women's suffrage, and was president of the National Dress Reform Association during 1863 and 1864. See Tillotson 1885, p. 16; and Robert McHenry, ed., *Famous American Women* (New York: Dover Publications, 1980), p. 180.

7. See Mrs. M. M. Jones, *Women's Dress, Its Moral and Physical Relations: Being an Essay Delivered Before the World's Health Convention, New York City, Nov., 1864* (New York: Miller, Wood and Co., 1865), pp. 12-29.

8. For the Anti-Fashion Society and the Social Science Sisterhood, see Tillotson 1885, pp. 24-51.

9. The dress reform bureau of Mrs. Woolson was at 4 Hamilton Place, Boston. Participating in her lecture series were: Mary J. Safford-Blake, M.D., lecturing on hygienic and aesthetic undergarments; Caroline E. Hastings, M.D., on the evils of corseting for young girls and babies; Mercy B. Jackson, M.D., on proper weight distribution of attire; and Arvilla B. Haynes, M.D., on the effect of clothing on respiration and circulation. (See Woolson 1874.)

10. The Alice Fletcher company, established in 1874, manufactured and sold dress-reform garments at 6 East Fourteenth Street in Manhattan. See *Hygienic Undergarments for Ladies and Children*, mail-order catalogue (New York: Alice Fletcher, n.d. [after 1878]).

11. See Deborah J. Warner, "The Women's Pavilion," in *1876: A Centennial Exhibition*, Robert C. Post, ed. (Washington, D. C.: Smithsonian Institution, 1976), p. 165.

12. Activities of the American Free Dress League are described in Tillotson 1885, pp. 34-43; the principles of the Rational Dress Society of Great Britain are described in their *Gazette* of 1888, p. 1. For an account of the Society's activities, see Stella Mary Newton, *Health, Art and Reason: Dress Reformers of the 19th Century* (London: John Murray, 1974). Mrs. King, one of the organizers of the British society, was received courteously when she visited American cities in the early 1880s, attired in "narrow and very comfortable trousers." See Tillotson 1885, p. 52.

13. See Ethel C. Gale, *Hints on Dress: or What to Wear, When to Wear It, and How to Buy It* (New York: G. P. Putnam and Sons, 1872), pp. 22-38. Terms and descriptions for textiles of the period may be found in *The Dictionary of Needlework: An Encyclopaedia of Artistic, Plain and Fancy Needlework* (London: L. Upcott Gill, 1882) and in *American Fabrics and Fashions, Encyclopedia of Textiles* (3rd ed.; Englewood Cliffs, N. J.: Prentice-Hall, 1980), p. 181. Descriptions of textiles vary with the resource. For example, nun's cloth can be all-wool bunting (*Needlework* 1882) or a wool-silk blend (*Textiles* 1980).

14. C. H. Fowler and W. H. DePuy, *Home and Health and Home Economics: A Cyclopedia of Facts and Hints for All Departments of Home Life, Health and Domestic Economy* (New York: Phillips and Hunt, 1880), p. 198.

15. "Symmetry" was a term used by Gale (see note 13).

16. Edith Wharton, *The Age of Innocence* (New York: D. Appleton, 1920; reprinted, Charles Scribner's Sons, 1968), pp. 105-106.

17. On actresses in America, see Lois W. Banner, *American Beauty* (New York: Alfred A. Knopf, 1983), pp. 106-153; Cornelia Otis Skinner, *Madame Sarah* (Boston: Houghton-Mifflin, 1967); Roger Manvell, *Ellen Terry* (New York: G. P. Putnam's Sons, 1968); Lillie Langtry (Lady de Bathe), *The Days I Knew* (New York: George H. Doran, 1925); and Mary Anderson, *A Few Memories* (New York: Harper and Brothers, 1895).

18. Charles Frederick Worth devised a kimono-sleeve costume in the 1860s, and variations became popular in the United States. See Ishbel Ross, *Taste in America* (New York: Thomas Y. Crowell, 1967), p. 191; and Stella Blum, ed., *Victorian Fashions and Costumes from Harper's Bazaar: 1867-1898* (New York: Dover Publications, 1974).

19. Examples of Morris's work were shown at the Philadelphia Centennial Exhibition of 1876. See Linda Parry, *William Morris Textiles* (New York: Viking Press, 1983), p. 19; and William Morris, Lecture on Textiles, July 11, 1884 (London: pamphlet published for the International Health Exhibition, 1884).

20. Oscar Wilde's American lectures were later published as essays. One entitled "The Practical Application of the Principles of the Aesthetic Theory to Exterior and Interior House Decoration, With Observations upon Dress and Personal Ornaments" appeared as the essay called "House Decoration." See Oscar Wilde, *Miscellanies*, vol. 14 of *The First Collected Edition of the Works of Oscar Wilde, 1908-1922*, Robert Ross, ed. (15 vols.; London: Methuen, 1908; reprinted 1969), pp. 279-290.

21. The problems caused by lacing tight during the childbearing years are described in John S. Haller and Robin M. Haller, *The Physician and Sexuality in Victorian America* (Chicago: University of Illinois Press, 1974), pp. 168-174.

22. American attitudes toward children are described in Harvey Green, *The Light of the Home* (New York: Pantheon Books, 1983). See also Elizabeth Ewing, History of Children's Costume (New York: Charles Scribner's Sons, 1977), pp. 80-111.

23. The renewed interest in smocks and smocking is discussed in Barbara Baines, *Fashion Revivals* (London: Batsford, 1981), pp. 88-90. Kate Greenaway's influence is mentioned in Elizabeth Aslin, *The Aesthetic Movement* (New York: Frederick A. Praeger, 1969), pp. 163-164; and in Alison Adburgham, *Liberty's: A Biography of a Shop* (London: George Allen and Unwin, 1975), pp. 55-56.

24. Woolson 1874, p. 48.

25. Charles L. Eastlake, *Hints on Household Taste* (London: Longmans, Green, 1878; reprinted, New York: Dover Publications, 1969), pp. 262-264.

26. Wilde, lecture of 1882 in *Miscellanies* 1908, p. 285.

27. Foster Rhea Dulles, *A History of Recreation: America Learns to Play*, 2nd ed. (New York: Appleton-Century-Crofts, 1965), p. 192; see also Donald J. Mrozek, *Sport and American Mentality: 1880-1910* (Knoxville: University of Tennessee Press, 1983); and Harvey Green, *Fit for America: Health, Fitness, Sport, and American Society* (New York: Pantheon Books, 1986).

28. The Rocky Mountain costume was displayed at the International Health Exhibition in London in 1884, and termed useful but "far removed from the beautiful," and required a wearer to be "bold." See Ada S. Ballin, *The Science of Dress in Theory and Practice* (London: Sampson, Low, Marston, Searle and Rivington, 1885), p. 183.

29. Annie Jenness Miller, editor of *The Jenness-Miller Magazine*, was a member of the National Council of Women and their Committee on Dress Reform, to recommend suitable attire for attending the World's Columbian Exposition in Chicago in 1893. Several "walking dresses," including the Jenness-Miller "rainy day dress or so-called American Costume," were endorsed and it was hoped that a large number of female fairgoers would wear them, "ready to incur the possibility of a slight temporary martyrdom in the interests of so desirable a cause." See "Dress Reform at the World's Fair," *Review of Reviews* 7 (April 1893), pp. 312-316. See also Jeanne Madeline Weimann, *The Fair Women* (Chicago: Academy Chicago, 1981), pp. 531-537.

30. The term "New Woman" was used by the novelist Sarah Grand (Frances E. Clark) in an essay of 1894 for the *North American Review*, to describe a woman who had "improved herself so as to be in every way the best companion for man, and without him the best fitted for a place of usefulness in the world." See Gillian Kersley, *Darling Madame: Sarah Grand and Devoted Friend* (London: Virago Press, 1983), pp. 76-77. See also Gail Cunningham, *The New Woman and the Victorian Novel* (New York: Harper & Row, 1978).

31. Lois W. Banner, *Women in Modern America: A Brief History* (New York: Harcourt Brace Jovanovich, 1974), pp. 25-26; Catherine Clinton, *The Other Civil War: American Women in the Nineteenth Century* (New York: Hill and Wang, 1984); and Helen Lefkowitz Horowitz, *Alma Mater: Design and Experience in the Women's Colleges from Their Nineteenth-Century Beginnings to the 1930s* (New York: Alfred A. Knopf, 1984).

32. Frances Mary Steele and Elizabeth Livingston Steele Adams, *Beauty of Form and Grace of Vesture* (New York: Dodd, Mead, 1892), pp. 25 and 225-227.

33. Dolores Hayden, *The Grand Domestic Revolution* (Cambridge: MIT Press, first paperback ed., 1982), pp. 124-126; Ellen Condliffe Lagemann, *A Generation of Women* (Cambridge: Harvard University Press, 1979), pp. 19-28; and Julie A. Matthaei, *An Economic History of Women in America* (New York: Schocken Books, 1982).

34. *Craftsman* attitudes regarding manual arts training are explained in "Industrial Art in Public Schools," *Craftsman* 22 (April-September 1912), p. 346. See also S. Horace Williams, "The Educative Value of Manual Training," *Manual Training Magazine* 11 (1910), pp. 36-44.

35. Steele and Adams 1892, pp. 208-211.

36. Helen Lathrop (Gilbert) Ecob, *The Well-Dressed Woman: A Study in the Practical Application to Dress of the Laws of Health, Art and Morals* (New York: Fowler and Wells, 1892), p. 200. For a suggested costume-design curriculum, see Helen G. Ecob, "A New Philosophy of Fashion," *Chautauquan* 31 (September 1900), p. 608. For mention of Mrs. Ecob and a drawing of her in aesthetic dress, see *Review of Reviews* 1893, p. 316.

37. Leiser 1902, p. 228.

38. "Dress and Its Relation to Life," *Craftsman* 11 (November 1906), pp. 269-270.

39. Bowles 1904, p. 65.

40. "The Right to Beauty," *Craftsman* 12 (April 1907), p. 130.

41. Gustav Stickley, "Use and Abuse of Machinery," *Craftsman* 11 (November 1906), p. 205.

42. "Shirt-Waists from a Craftsman Point of View," *Craftsman* 11 (February 1907), pp. 648-654 (a woodfiber tint of linen was recommended for this project; see p. 652).

43. "Raising the Standard of Dressmaking," *Craftsman* 12 (May 1907), p. 252.

44. Alice Hubbard, *Woman's Work, Being an Inquiry and an Assumption* (East Aurora, N.Y.: Roycrofters, 1908), pp. 66-67. Her husband, Elbert (fig. 5), was no stranger to the hazards of the natural look, having on one occasion been refused a room at the Waldorf-Astoria when the room clerk mistook him for a weatherbeaten rustic. See Freeman Champney, *Art and Glory* (New York: Crown Publishers, 1968), pp. 92-93.

45. Eva Olney Farnsworth, *The Art and Ethics of Dress: As Related to Efficiency and Economy* (San Francisco: Paul Elder, 1915), p. 20.

46. Belle Armstrong Whitney, *What to Wear: A Book for Women* (Battle Creek, Mich.: Good Health, 1916), pp. 16-17.

47. Farnsworth 1915, p. 9.

48. David A. Hanks, *The Decorative Designs of Frank Lloyd Wright* (New York: E. P. Dutton, 1979), pp. 24-25.

49. Claude Bragdon, *Architecture and Democracy* (New York: Alfred A. Knopf, 1918), p. 208.

50. The curriculum in use at Columbia was later published by an assistant professor of household arts and director of the Department of Textiles and Clothing at Teachers College. See Jane Fales, *Dressmaking: A Manual for Schools and Colleges* (New York: Charles Scribner's Sons, 1917), pp. 252-255.

51. W. L. George, *Woman and Tomorrow* (New York: D. Appleton, 1913), p. 24.

52. John Wanamaker, *Spring and Summer Catalog* (New York, 1911), pp. 116-117.

53. "The Right to Beauty," *Craftsman* 12 (April 1907), p. 124; Farnsworth 1915, pp. 15-16.

54. Estelle Peel Izor, *Costume Design and Home Planning* (New York: Mentzer, Bush, 1916), p. 67. The publication was used in Indianapolis schools to instruct students in a "sane, sensible, well-balanced attitude toward dress" and to help them attain a standard for the "wise selection of the innumerable common things that their daily life compels them to use" (p. ix).

55. Margaret McKenna-Friend ("Paris Fashion News by Cable," *Woman's Home Companion* [March 1917], p. 58) offered words from French couturiers on the new silhouette for spring: "The straight line, with one or two slight deviations, is the correct line." The same issue included a design for a tailored suit by Madame Paquin of Paris, exclusively for the magazine. Patterns for "French" designs were offered by many pattern companies and publishers, for example "L'Art de la Mode," a catalogue issued monthly by Morse-Broughton Company, 3 East 19th Street, New York.

56. Fales 1917, p. 255.

57. *Chautauquan* 31 (September 1900), p. 604.

58. "Paris Fashions and American Women," *Craftsman* 17 (January 1910), p. 465. Stickley's attitude persisted into the second decade; see "The Slaves of This Century," *Craftsman* 26 (April 1914), pp. 120-121.

59. For the study of Japanese textiles, see "The Right to Beauty," *Craftsman* 12 (April 1907), p. 132; see also Fales 1917, p. 255.

60. See Fales 1917, p. 265.

61. See Farnsworth 1915, pp. 13-14; Izor 1916, p. 17.

62. For "unity," see Izor 1916, pp. 87-88.

63. Emily Burbank, *Woman as Decoration* (New York: Dodd, Mead, 1917), p. xi. To this author, the goal was "distinct individuality" (p. 25). The term "decoration" was more complimentary than it would be in the 1980s.

64. Izor 1916, p. 41.

century participated actively in "homekeeping" even when hired help was possible, and was careful to dress appropriately. No longer was her house dress an elegant silk-and-lace confection, paraded at tea time. Now it was a high standard of healthfulness, cleanliness, and harmony to which the New Family aspired. For a morning of child care and gardening, a gingham smock or apron would be worn over a modest "tub dress" (washable work dress). In the afternoon, reading and handcrafts or conversation with friends would be indulged within the health-giving environment of a sun porch or pergola. For these pastoral pleasures, the homemaker would be garbed comfortably in a fresh, cheerful, printed-cotton "porch dress," a statement of simplicity and practicality.

Porch dresses were available by mail order or from dressmakers and dry goods stores. They were also often homemade from a commercial pattern that would include instructions for ornaments such as the button detail seen on this example. Washability was essential because this apparel was worn at a time of day when household duties could intervene. Therefore, cotton or linen lawn, mull (sheer muslin), and "tub silk" (a woven cotton-silk blend) were popular, as were embellishments of durable cotton or linen lace, Irish crochet, and "coarse thread" embroidery. It was attire that had been carefully selected to include decorative touches, for the Arts and Crafts homemaker, while seeking to create an impression of serious regard for her domestic responsibilities, would also wish to display her appreciation and talent for the needle arts. If her sewing skills were insufficient, help was at hand. Journals such as *The Craftsman*, *The Designer*, and *Woman's Home Companion* were among many that regularly published advice and instructions.

The homemaker might well seek encouragement from May Morris, the daughter and disciple of William Morris: "Design is the very soul and essence of beautiful embroidery, as it is of every other art, exalted or humble."[2] The menial purpose of the project should not encourage lowered standards of craftsmanship, for if the needle artist "pursues her craft with due care, and one might even say with enthusiasm, . . . she will not only taste that keen pleasure which everyone feels in creative work, however unpretending, but the product will be such as others will be careful to preserve; this in itself being an incentive to good work."[3]

Following May Morris's advice to "avoid confusion and indistinctness of detail,"[4] the seamstress of this dress worked horizontal rows of satin stitch across the bodice, creating an architectonic lattice effect that, punctuated by button motifs and conspicuous French knots, suggests a modern interpretation of a Greek bead-and-reel motif. The inclusion of lace hints at a more recent tradition for house dresses, but now the lace is treated as a flat panel (rather than as a ruffle) and the skirt insert is placed off-center with a bit of blue embroidery to bring it into the total decorative scheme. This costume is a charming example of old and new ideas, and possesses the "life and meaning" and the "feeling for beauty" that May Morris found in well-planned work of "definite utility."[5]

SK

1. "Raising the Standard of Dressmaking: Let the Thinkers Be Workers," *Craftsman* 12 (May 1907), p. 251.
2. May Morris, *Decorative Needlework* (London: Joseph Hughes, 1893), p. 79.
3. Ibid., Dedicatory Note, n.p.
4. Ibid., p. 120.
5. Ibid., Dedicatory Note, n.p.

190
Arts and Crafts dress, 1910-1916
Origin unknown
Unbleached linen hopsacking, silk embroidery, all by hand
H: 56 in. W: (around waistline) 26 in.
Collection of Mary Kane and Ted Hendrickson

Natural textiles and muted colors were popular for Arts and Crafts apparel and interiors. "It is a sign of the improving taste of the age that colors are so largely banished," wrote Helen Ekin Starrett in 1907, and "a great gain when a young woman or anyone else can wear clothes without being conscious of them."[1] As with good manners, "the truly refined dress will never admit of obtrusive display of any kind," she advised, noting the comment of a courtly young man who reminisced over his meeting with a cultured young woman: "I am sure that she was well dressed, for I did not notice anything she had on."[2]

Quiet harmony of dress, personality, and environment was a goal to be achieved, if one hoped to rise above mere fashion. Natural silks, cottons, and linens in colors with poetic names – "wild thyme," "lichen," "withered leaf"[3] –

189

189
Porch dress, 1900-1910
Origin unknown
Cotton; machine-sewn seams, hand-sewn finishes
H: 59½ in. W: (across shoulders) 13¾ in.
Margaret Woodbury Strong Museum, Rochester. 81.202

"With the kitchen commodious and bright and filled with a blue and white cleanness, what unusually pretty, even picturesque, costumes belong to it," wrote *The Craftsman*."[1] The reform-minded woman of the early twentieth

190

medieval English embroidery), so fervently admired by Morris. The leaf-like meanders and the "glittering leafage"[4] were favorite themes for braid appliqué, as they were for other Arts and Crafts endeavors (see nos. 17 and 165).

In the late nineteenth century, a reformation of taste in America led women away from layers of weighted silks toward linens, cottons, and wild silks, which were celebrated for their natural textures. On this dress, the tactility of raw linen is enhanced by an open plain weave (or tabby weave) with a random slub (variation of thread thickness) to create the rustic effect of hopsacking, a favorite Arts and Crafts textile. Traditionally, hopsacking is defined as a utility textile woven of rough jute or hemp, to create the goods known commercially as burlap. In the Arts and Crafts era, however, "hopsacking" was a term – along with "huckaback" and "homespun" – to identify a variety of coarse-textured linen, cotton, and wool much in favor for apparel and furnishings. A garment of unbleached linen the color of a withered leaf, perhaps enhanced as is this example, by hand-crafted leaf-like ornament, was durable, unpretentious, and seen as compatible with the friendly oak and basketry of an Arts and Crafts interior. In an interview of 1903, a young American actress, Ethel Barrymore, described her preference for the effect: "Put good work into the most ordinary material and you have a pretty dress. I once had a dress made of hopsacking . . . . I had it well made and well cut, and it was as much admired as any dress I ever had . . . . It isn't always easy to get a dress simple, I know, but when you do, just see what you have: the most artistic thing you can get in the way of a gown. Really, I just hate conspicuousness in dress . . . . a perfectly simple dress, well made, always makes a good-looking girl the more charming, and makes a homely girl look better."[5] Her words rang true, certainly, to American men and women who honored the design-reform tenets of comfort, utility, and simplicity.

SK

1. Helen Ekin Starrett, *The Charm of Fine Manners* (Philadelphia: J.B. Lippincott, 1907), pp. 104-105. Mrs. Starrett was the principal of a private school for girls.
2. Ibid., p. 108.
3. James Chittick and E.A. Posselt, *A Glossary of Silk Terms* (New York: Cheney Brothers, 1915), pp. 77-82.
4. William Morris, "The History of Pattern Designing," Lecture 5 of *Lectures on Art Delivered in Support of the Society for the Protection of Ancient Buildings* (London: Macmillan,

1882), p. 150. Especially fond of the acanthus motif, Morris stated: "No form of ornament has gone so far, or lasted so long as this."
5. Gustav Kobbé, *Famous Actors and Actresses and Their Homes* (Boston: Little, Brown, 1903), pp. 46-50.

191
Jardinière, 1903
Avon Faience Company (1902-1905), Division of Wheeling Potteries Company (1902-1908), Tiltonville, Ohio
Designer: Frederick Hurten Rhead (1880-1942)
Buff earthenware, molded with decoration outlined in white slip with glossy glazes in medium blue, dark green, and medium brown; legend in white slip at top reads: WINTER·THE·KING·/ ·OF·INTIMATE·DELIGHTS·/·FIRE-SIDE·ENJOYMENTS· /·HOMEBORN·HAPPINESS
H: 11½ in. Diam: 19¼ in.
Marks: *Rhead* (incised on side); 1903 / *Avon* within irregular cartouche over *W. Pt's Co.* (incised on bottom)
Private Collection

Frederick Hurten Rhead was born in 1880 at Hanley in the Staffordshire district of England, the eldest son of a noted ceramist, Frederick Alfred Rhead.[1] Educated in the Stoke-on-Trent Government Art School and the Wedgwood Institute in Burslem, he received degrees in design, modeling, and painting. His first practical experience in the ceramics industry came as apprentice to his father at the Brownfield Pottery and Wileman & Co.; soon he was teaching at the Longton Art School and at age nineteen was named art director at Wardle & Co., Washington Works, Hanley. These early opportunities in the field of ceramics presaged Rhead's career in the United States, where he distinguished himself as a potter, educator, author, and art director for several American art potteries and tableware manufacturers (see nos 163 and 183).

Rhead worked first in this country with a fellow Englishman, William P. Jervis, at the Avon Faience Company.[2] In 1902 Jervis had been named manager of the Vance Faience Company, which manufactured colonial-revival wares and a new line of art pottery. Late in 1902 the firm's name was changed to the Avon Faience Company, a subsidiary of the Wheeling Potteries Company, and early in 1903 Rhead joined the company as a decorator and designer. A major

were selected for afternoon apparel on those occasions when a homemaker might, in the privacy of her inglenook, share with a friend her taste for Japanese prints, her appreciation for the work of William Morris and his American disciples, or her own efforts at handcrafts. Such a dress as this might have been sewn by the wearer from a puchased pattern. The asymmetrical design allowed a single side panel of harmonious ornament, at once more artistic and less distracting than the usual mirror-image frontal treatment of this era. Sea-foam green soutache braid of silk was laid on the surface by hand couching, a traditional embroidery technique that reaches back to *Opus Anglicanum* (early

191

192
Frieze of three tiles, 1907-1910
Rookwood Pottery Company (1880-1960),
Cincinnati
Buff terra-cotta, press-molded with raised design of house in landscape; covered with brick-red and dark- and light-green matte glazes
H: (for each tile) 16 in. W: 16 in.
Private Collection

Tiles pressed with relief decoration and covered with glossy monochromatic glazes began to be made in America in the 1870s. Companies like the Low Art Tile Works (see no. 9) manufactured them until the end of the century, when the fashion for dead- or matte-finish glazes on flat surfaces began to emerge.[1] Matte glazes were recommended for tiles because of the "soft, mellow way" they reflected light in a room, a "way that is very restful to the eyes, and blends harmoniously with the woodwork, rugs, draperies, and other furnishings of an interior."[2]

Experimentation with matte glazes began at Rookwood in 1896 and by the end of 1900 matte-glazed art pottery was being sold and some architectural tile work had been tried. Rookwood's manager and principal stockholder, William W. Taylor, was convinced to pursue architectural tiles as one solution to lagging sales of art pottery, which had been its main product since 1880 (see nos. 32 and 55). Competition from other art potteries increased as they continued to copy Rookwood's successful line or offer stylish alternatives to Rookwood's painterly, conservative standard. In 1903 Taylor expanded the Rookwood plant in order to accommodate the growing architectural department.[3]

Although Rookwood received its greatest publicity in trade journals for major public installations, the company also developed a line of stock designs for smaller settings in public buildings and private homes. These patterns, first published in a catalogue of August 1907, included the present example offered as no. 1227Y: "Outline English Landscape," a frieze of five tiles, in single colors for $5 or $6 each or rendered in several colors (as here) for $10 each.[4] The original pattern of the frieze extended for two more tiles on the left, giving a broader sweep to the cloud formations and landscape in the background and ending at the left with some smaller trees in the foreground. The tiles appear again in the 1909 catalogue,

contribution to the work produced at Avon was the introduction of the English tube-lining technique of decorating, whereby thick clay slip is trailed onto a pot to form intricate linear designs. The raised lines of slip also served to contain colored glazes in a manner similar to *cloisonné* enameled metal.

This jardinière displays to advantage the technique and style of Rhead's early work. White clay slip was used to embellish the piece with pine cones, trees, and snow and to draw a domestic sentiment.[3] The influence of the tube-lined decoration was soon felt at the larger Weller Pottery, where Rhead worked for a short time after leaving Avon in 1903; the most successful line he introduced there was called "Weller Faience" and featured slip-trailed and -painted designs. By 1904, employed at the Roseville Pottery, Rhead once again initiated the

stylized tube-lined designs so popular in England; some shapes, including this jardinière, were copied from his designs for Avon.

BRD and EPD

1. "Frederick Hurten Rhead," *Bulletin of the American Ceramic Society* 21 (December 1942), p. 306.

2. For more about Avon Faience Company, see Paul Evans, *Art Pottery of the United States* (New York: Charles Scribner's Sons, 1974), pp. 303-306.

3. Adapted from William Cowper, "The Winter's Evening," in *The Task*, book 4 (1784), lines 139-140: "I crown thee King of intimate delights,/Fire-side enjoyments, home-born happiness."

192

"Outline English Landscape." Tile frieze illustrated in
Illustrations and Price List of Stock Designs in Decorated Tiles,
Mantel Facings and Complete Mantels (Cincinnati: 1907). Col-
lection of the Cincinnati Historical Society. Rookwood
Pottery Company, Architectural Department.

combined with a second series to form a longer frieze of repeating pattern, as for a border.[5]

The method of making tiles such as these was to press coarse damp stoneware clay into molds having the outline of the design inside. Unlike the deep intaglio relief of earlier tiles like Low's, the newer style was meant to show a relatively flat, smooth surface. The slightly raised outline provided barriers for containing colors.

EPD and BRD

1. For more information about the American art-tile industry, see Thomas P. Bruhn, *American Decorative Tiles, 1870-1930* (Storrs: William Benton Museum of Art, University of Connecticut, 1979).

2. "Decorative Tile-Making: A Modern Craft and its Ancient Origins," *Craftsman* 25 (May 1914), p. 615.

3. Architectural faience, added at Rookwood to keep pace with changing tastes in the ceramics market, was never as profitable as art pottery. Profit margins in the architectural department were always slim in order to offer competitive prices. The largest numbers of sales were recorded for the years 1907 to 1913, but these figures declined gradually until 1920 and abruptly thereafter. For more information about Rookwood's architectural faience and garden pottery, see Herbert Peck, *The Book of Rookwood Pottery* (New York: Crown Publishers, 1968), pp. 161-168.

4. *Architectural Department. Illustrations and Price List of Stock Designs in Decorated Tiles, Mantel Facings and Complete Mantels* (Cincinnati: Rookwood Pottery Company, 1907), pp. 9 and 16.

5. *Architectural Department. Illustrations and Price List of Stock Designs in Decorated Tiles, Mantel Facings and Complete Mantels* (Cincinnati: Rookwood Pottery Company, 1909), pp. 9 and 30.

193 (cover and color plate, p. 39)
Wallpaper frieze, 1900-1905
H.B.H. Company (origin unknown)
Block-printed paper
L: 18½ in. W: 46½ in.
Marks: *HBH* and 364 (style number)
Cooper-Hewitt Museum, the Smithsonian Institution's National Museum of Design, New York. Gift of Paul Franco. 1938-50-16

Borders were an important ingredient in the Arts and Crafts design repertoire and were used frequently in various media: solidly colored rugs, table runners, curtains or portières, and books. In the absence of stenciled designs or wallpaper friezes – which appeared often in multiple combinations (see no. 49) – walls were "bordered" by a picture rail one or two feet below the ceiling line.

The use of landscape friezes, depicting woodland or rural scenes with strongly romantic overtones, is documented by a design of Gustav Stickley that was published in *The Craftsman*.[1] The drawing shows the fireplace corner of a living room that has a deep landscape frieze with a repeating pattern at the top of the wall. Dominating the room full of hallmarks of the period – a doorway opening with portières, a deeply bordered rug, furniture, and a considerable amount of brick and wood – the frieze is said to be "so definitely decorative, the wall spaces below are left absolutely plain and the structural features are also severely simple in character."

The purple, pink, gold, and murky olive-green colors of this landscape frieze – part of the fashionable palette in use in the United States at the turn of the century – help to date the paper to 1900-1905.

GM

1. See *Craftsman* 5 (July 1906), p. 524.

194
Wallpaper panel and border, 1907
Allen-Higgins Company, Worcester, Massachusetts
Roller-printed paper
L: 27½ in. W: 19½ in.
L: (of repeat) 15 in.
Marks: *Allen-Higgins Co.* and 0702 (style number)[1]
Society for the Preservation of New England Antiquities, Boston. 1974.3652-C

The Allen-Higgins Company, a firm that aggressively sought the Arts and Crafts market, advertised regularly in the trade magazine *Wallpaper News and Interior Decorator*, as well as in consumer-directed publications such as *The Craftsman*. Both the text and the illustrations in the advertisements changed frequently enough so that a good record exists of the company's products.[2] In *Wallpaper News* Allen-Higgins claimed: "Our 0407 is one of the few papers on the market made especially to match Mission furniture and this class of furnishing"[3]; an ad in *The Craftsman* stated: "We are making odd and distinctive things to match Craftsman furniture and general furnishings."[4]

With its colors of olive-green, yellow, and dark brown, this paper would be very appropriate with the dark stained oak of Arts and Crafts furniture and half-paneled walls. Also available from Allen-Higgins was a series of related papers including friezes, narrow borders, and a solid olive-green unpatterned paper. The homeowner could assemble various combinations according to the requirements of his rooms.

GM

1. Because the style numbers advanced in regular sequence from lower to higher, this paper can be dated to the autumn of 1907.

2. Allen-Higgins, founded in 1899, also sold grass cloths, fabrics to match wallpapers, and varnished tiles.

3. Advertisement in *Wallpaper News and Interior Decorator* 27 (May 1906), p. 10.

4. Advertisement in *Craftsman* 15 (October 1908), p. xl.

195 (color plate, p. 40)
Elevations of living room (west and east sides, north and south ends) for Nathan Stein summer house, Ontario Beach, New York, 1897-1899
Architect: Bragdon and Hillman (Claude Fayette Bragdon [1866-1946] and James Constable Hillman [1863-1932])
Watercolor and ink on paper
16⅞ x 28⅛ in.
University of Rochester Library (Department of Rare Books and Special Collections)

The transcendental air of the American Arts and Crafts movement appealed particularly to individuals such as Claude Bragdon, who had interests in mystical occultism. He became the most noteworthy American architectural follower of Theosophy, which inspired European artists such as Mondrian and Kandinsky. Born in Oberlin, Ohio, Bragdon lived in a number of midwestern locations before winding up in Rochester working for Charles Ellis and later Harvey Ellis. He traveled in Europe in 1894 and then set up his own practice in Rochester. With Ellis he helped establish the Rochester Arts and Crafts Society and wrote several articles for *The Craftsman*. Architecturally Bragdon worked in a number of idioms, including log cabin, Secession, colonial revival, and the bungalow. (He contributed a $3,000 bungalow to the *Ladies' Home Journal* series of inexpensive houses [see no. 197].)[1] For him the architectural essence of the home could be summed up in "three talismanic words . . . Simplicity, Coherence, and Individuality."[2]

194

The Nathan Stein house was a low, bungalow-like structure covered on the exterior with shingles. The veranda posts were oak saplings with the bark and branch stubs left on. In an article contemporaneous with the Stein house, Bragdon described an interior consisting "of little else than one great living room and its appendages." He designed it as a unit, with colors and furniture harmonizing. High wainscoting of boards lapped one over the other and a prominent shelf made the room predominantly horizontal. The wall above the wainscoting was "covered with burlaps, painted a dull gold color"[3]; motifs in the frieze were based upon Japanese sword guards. The interior rendering was amazingly precise and certainly relates in presentation and style to Bragdon's mentor Harvey Ellis (see no. 196). Its highlights of ornament, details, and texture also recall interiors by M.H. Baillie Scott for the Duke of Hesse in Darmstadt. Bragdon's cabinet with its extensive top shelf support is especially reminiscent of Scott.[4] The chairs and built in settle in the rendering may have been influenced by the English designer George Walton.

Bragdon's architectural career continued until about World War I, coupled with an increasingly consuming interest in spiritualism. Ultimately he moved to New York City and took up stage-set design. Although he gave up designing buildings, he convinced Louis Sullivan to reprint "Kindergarten Chats" as a book and continued to write on architecture.

RGW

1. Harvey Ellis, "Claude Fayette Bragdon," *Brochure Series of Architectural Illustration* 3 (October 1897), p. 157. For information on the subject I am indebted to Jean France of the University of Rochester, who has a long study of Bragdon in progress. See also Erville Costa, "Claude F. Bragdon, Architect, State Designer, and Mystic," *Rochester History* 29 (October 1967), pp. 1-20.

2. Claude Bragdon, "The Architecture of the Home," *House Beautiful* 16 (June 1904), p. 10.

3. Idem, "A Bungalow," *House Beautiful* 2 (November 1897), p. 158.

4. I am indebted to Jean France for these observations. Scott's renderings were published in *Building News* of July 23, 1897, and republished in James D. Kornwolf, *M.H. Baillie Scott and the Arts and Crafts Movement* (Baltimore: Johns Hopkins University Press, 1972), pp. 164-165. See also M.H. Baillie Scott, "Decoration and Furniture for the New Palace, Darmstadt," *Studio*, March 1899, pp. 107-115.

196

196

Architectural drawing of library and conservatory for Joseph T. Cunningham house, Rochester, 1900 (project never built)
Architect: Harvey Ellis (1852-1904)
Ink and watercolor on paper
19½ x 34⅛ in.
Inscription: *Section of Library and Conservatory for Mr. Joseph T. Cunningham – Charles S. Ellis and Harvey Ellis Architects Rochester, N.Y. 1900* (upper right corner)
The Margaret Woodbury Strong Museum, Rochester

The close connection between the Aesthetic movement, the colonial revival, and the Arts and Crafts can be seen in the work of Harvey Ellis. A peripatetic individual, Ellis worked in architects' offices in upper New York state, Saint Paul, Saint Louis, and perhaps other cities in the 1880s and 1890s. Between bouts of alcoholism, he created a very personalized version of the Richardson Romanesque, the Queen Anne, and the modernized colonial. Working as a draftsman, Ellis seldom received credit as a designer but, as William Gray Purcell remem-

bered, "His name was known to everyone who read an architectural magazine from 1880 to well past 1900 for his remarkable fine pen drawings."[1]

Born in Rochester, New York, Ellis would return periodically to work with his brothers, also architects, in Rochester. His training was casual: a semester at West Point and varying periods in architects' offices in New York, Albany, and elsewhere. He traveled to Europe in the early 1870s and later, during visits to the American southwest, became impressed with Pueblo and Mission architecture. In 1894 Ellis returned to Rochester and became active in art circles, helping to found the Rochester Arts and Crafts Society in 1897, one of the first in the United States. Mysticism and religious exotica attracted him and he converted to Catholicism about this time.

Shortly after Ellis's return to Rochester in the mid-1890s, his drawing style changed markedly as a result of an obsession with Japanese prints.[2] His student Claude Bragdon (see no. 195) observed that Ellis had "studied his little collec-

tion of prints to such purpose that he came to see things *à la Japonais*, in terms of pattern and denuded shadow . . . . What Japanese art really did for Harvey Ellis was to emancipate his color sense . . . ."[3]

Ellis's shift in orientation can be seen in his rendering for the Cunningham library and conservatory.[4] The flat bands of color and plain wall surfaces owe much to Japanese prints as well as to Glasgow and Vienna. The structural character of architecture is borne out in the woodwork and the sense of shelter is dramatized by the high-beamed ceiling and hearth, which contrasts with ample fenestration and contact with nature through potted plants in the conservatory. Except for the chair all the furniture is built in. Reflecting the continuing English influence, a large Pre-Raphaelite mural or tapestry of a gowned figure hangs over the mantel and the copper-hooded hearth.

RGW

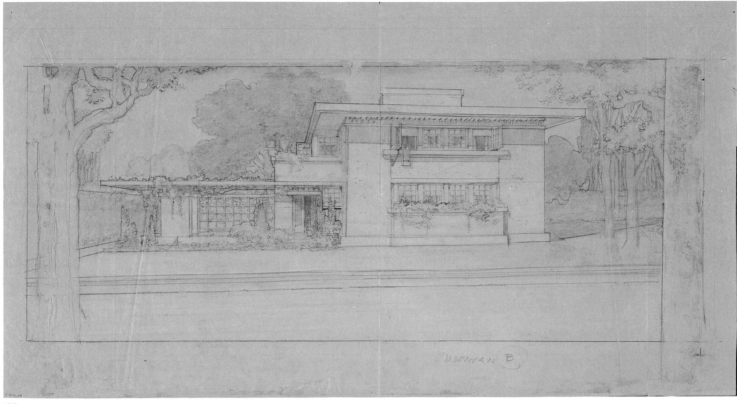

197

1. William G. Purcell, "Forgotten Builders – The Nation's Voice," *Northwest Architect* 8 (June-July 1944), p. 5. For biography see Jean France et al., *A Rediscovery – Harvey Ellis: Artist, Architect* (Rochester: Memorial Art Gallery, University of Rochester, 1972); Roger Kennedy "Long, Dark Corridors: Harvey Ellis," *Prairie School Review* 5, nos. 1 and 2 (1968), pp. 5-18.

2. In 1897 he combined Japanese prints with modern French posters in an exhibition for the Rochester Art Club.

3. Claude Bragdon, "Harvey Ellis: A Portrait Sketch," *Architectural Review* 15 (December 1908), p. 178; reprinted in *Prairie School Review* 5, nos. 1 and 2 (1968), pp. 19-25.

4. Coy L. Ludwig, *The Arts and Crafts Movement in New York State, 1890s-1920s* (Oswego: Gallery Association of New York State, 1983), pp. 75-76.

197
Development drawing for "A Fireproof House for $5,000," 1906[1]
Architect: Frank Lloyd Wright (1867-1959)
Renderer: Marion Mahony (1871-1962)
Pencil on tracing paper
15 x 27⅝ in.
Inscription: MM monogram (lower left)
The Frank Lloyd Wright Memorial Foundation, *Taliesin West*, Scottsdale, Arizona

A major concern of the Arts and Crafts movement was well-designed and economical housing for the middle class. The intention was to provide an alternative to the mass-produced, poorly designed speculator housing rapidly filling American suburbs. One of the chief promoters of this reform was Edward Bok (1863-1930), editor of *The Ladies' Home Journal*, a homemaker magazine oriented toward Arts and Crafts. Bok seized upon the idea of commis-

sioning reputable architects to provide model house plans to his readers at a nominal fee. Initially architects balked, but beginning in 1895 he published a series of houses in the Queen Anne, colonial revival, and other styles, estimated to cost between $3,500 and $7,000. After 1900 more prominent architects – including Hugh Garden, Elmer Grey, Claude Bragdon, Ralph Adams Cram, Robert Spencer, and Frank Lloyd Wright – contributed plans. In his autobiography Bok wrote – in the third person – about his intentions: "Bok felt a keen desire to take hold of the small American house and make it architecturally better. He foresaw, however, that the subject would finally include small gardening and interior decoration." Publishing designs of all types with the intention of uplifting American taste, he received praise from Theodore Roosevelt: "Bok is the only man I ever heard of who changed, for the better, the architecture of an entire nation, and he did it so quickly and yet so effectively that we didn't know it was begun before it was finished."[2]

The three houses Frank Lloyd Wright contributed to Bok's magazine were published in February and July of 1901 and April of 1907. His $5,000 fireproof model, easily the most famous, spawned a host of imitators across the country and greatly influenced followers in the Prairie School (no. 198). The source was the plain foursquare boxy house that had been used in America since the mid-nineteenth century.[3] In Wright's design the corners are emphasized by substantial piers and windows are banked; a broad low-hipped roof caps the composition, tying it to the ground. A pergola, terrace, and window boxes bring nature close and, inside, the central chimney divides the living and dining spaces. Wright suggested that the house was to be built of monolithic concrete with steel reinforcing, but this was never done. Instead, the two known variants – the Hunt House in La Grange, Illinois (1907), and the Stockman house in Mason City, Iowa (1908) – were erected on a wood stud frame with lath and stucco covering. The rendering by Marion Mahony is unusual in the somewhat stiff quality of the house and in the attention she gave to the foliage.

RGW

1. The drawing was published in *Ladies' Home Journal* of April 1907.

2. Edward Bok, *The Americanization of Edward Bok: An Autobiography* (New York: Pocket Books, 1965 [first published in 1920]), pp. 171, 179. See also Alice M. Bowsher, "Edward Bok's Attempt to Promote Good Design in the Suburbs: An Analysis of Architecture Illustrated in the *Ladies' Home Journal*" (master's thesis, University of Virginia, 1977).

3. H. Allen Brooks, "Percy Dwight Bentley at La Crosse," *Prairie School Review* 9, no. 3 (1972), pp. 6-8; and Richard Guy Wilson and Sidney K. Robinson, *The Prairie School in Iowa* (Ames: Iowa State University Press, 1977), pp. 6-7. See also "The Work of Tallmadge and Watson, Architects" *Western Architect* 22 (December 1915), reprinted in H. Allen Brooks, ed., *Prairie School Architecture; Studies from 'The Western Architect'* (Toronto: University of Toronto Press 1975), pp. 268-289.

198
Presentation drawing: perspective view and plans for "A Home Type for F.W. Bird and Son, East Walpole, Massachusetts," 1908 (project never built)
Architects: William Gray Purcell (1880-1965) and George Feick, Jr. (1881-1945)
Renderer: William Gray Purcell
Ink on paper
18 x 17½ in.
Northwest Architectural Archives, University of Minnesota, Minneapolis

William Purcell's interest in developing an economical alternative to the middle-class mass-produced builder's house prompted his entry in the competition sponsored by F.W. Bird and Son, a manufacturer of building papers and shingles. The Bird Company's product, a tar paper, would be used on the lower section, cut in broad bands and covered by batten boards placed horizontally; Bird shingles would cover the narrow band of the upper floor. While the entry did not win the competition, recognition came to its architects later: the basic house form with some alterations, such as a gabled roof, was built by Purcell and Elmslie in several locations.[1]

Both the U-shaped plan and the square form with the low-rising hipped roof of the Bird competition house were inspired by Frank Lloyd Wright's $5,000 house scheme. There are also similarities linking the rendering style with the flat foliage to Marion Mahony's drawing for Wright (nos. 85 and 197).

RGW

1. David Gebhard, "William Gray Purcell and George Grant Elmslie and the Early Progressive Movement in American Architecture from 1900 to 1920" (Ph.D. dissertation, University of Minnesota, 1957), p. 116. For a house influenced by the Bird house, see Purcell's A.B.C. Dodd house of 1910-1911 in Charles City, Iowa, illustrated in Richard Guy Wilson and Sidney K. Robinson, *The Prairie School in Iowa* (Ames: Iowa State University Press, 1977), pp. 56-57.

199 (color plate, p. 41)
Presentation perspective: "Casas Grandes" project for Homer Laughlin, Hollywood, California, ca. 1912-1915 (project never built)
Architect: Irving John Gill (1870-1936)
Watercolor and ink on cardboard
13 x 22½ in.
Architectural Drawing Collection, University of California, Santa Barbara

Irving Gill's interest in multifamily housing projects was twofold: he was committed to the idea that architecture could reform the way people lived, and he knew that the economic benefits of his hollow tile and concrete construction could be realized only by mass production. Of his numerous schemes for housing projects, only a few were built. Some early designs, such as Lewis Court in Sierra Madre (1910) and Echo Park Court in Los Angeles (1912), owed their form to the bungalow courts of Pasadena (fig. 2), although stylistically they were Gill's own. His austere two-story Horatio West Court in Santa Monica (1919) also has a bungalow court plan.[1] The housing project he worked on for several years for Homer Laughlin, a Los Angeles businessman, is a creative departure.

If the forms of the structures in "Casas Grandes" have any sources, it could be southwestern pueblos and perhaps Mediterranean villages. Also, there might be some remote Tibetan aspect, as can be seen in the nearly contemporary Taylor house by Louis Christian Mullgardt (no. 77). Going far beyond the bungalow court or the Mission style, Gill reduced all functions to cubic masses; two, three, and four floors are submerged into batter-walled concrete structures. The method of access to each of the units is unclear and gives the project an unreal, mysterious air. Inhabitants would either be reformed in such a dwelling or they would move out.

The purely sensual aspect of the rendering, with its varied colors, brings into question the assertion that Gill was unconcerned with architectural drawings and presentations.[2]

RGW

1. For background see Esther McCoy, *Five California Architects* (New York: Reinhold Publishing, 1960), pp. 59-101.

2. David Gebhard and Deborah Nevins, *200 Years of American Architectural Drawings* (New York: Watson-Guptill, 1977), p. 54. A plot plan for a different site also exists at Santa Barbara; it is signed by Frank Lloyd Wright, Jr., and is dated 1912.

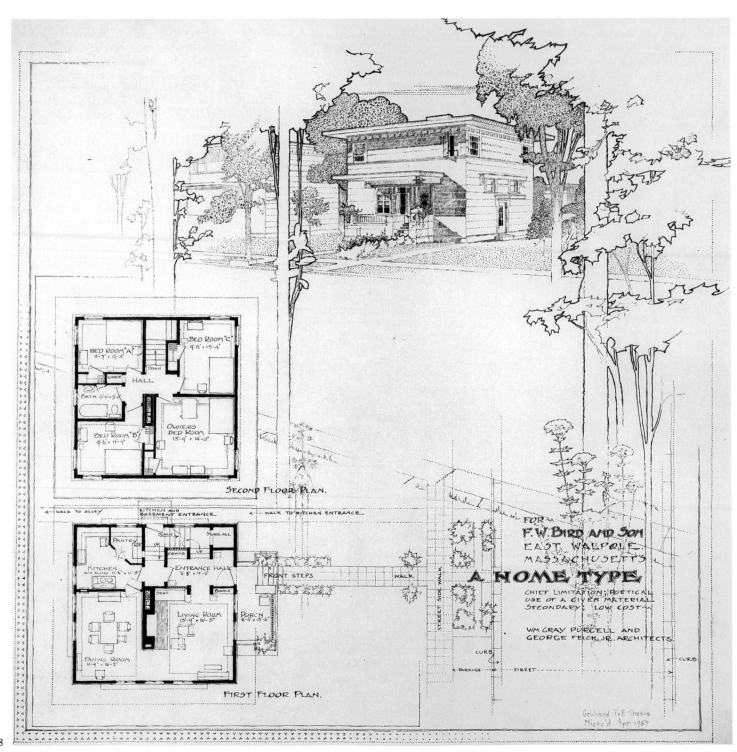

SECOND FLOOR PLAN.

BED ROOM "A"
11'-7" x 9'-4"

BED ROOM "C"
9'-8" x 13'-4"

DOWN

LINEN   HALL

BATH 6'-0" x 5'-0"

OWNERS
BED ROOM
13'-9" x 14'-0"

BED ROOM "B"
9'-6" x 11'-7"

WALK TO ALLEY   KITCHEN AND
BASEMENT ENTRANCE   WALK TO KITCHEN ENTRANCE

PANTRY
ICE

STORE-ALL

DOWN

UP

COATS

UP

KITCHEN
with pantry 11'-6" x 11'-3"

ENTRANCE HALL
6'-8" x 11'-6"

FRONT STEPS   WALK

SEAT   BOOKS

LIVING ROOM
13'-9" x 16'-8"

PORCH
6'-6" x 13'-6"

DINING ROOM
11'-4" x 16'-7"

FIRST FLOOR PLAN.

FOR
F. W. BIRD AND SON
EAST WALPOLE
MASSACHUSETTS

A HOME TYPE

CHIEF LIMITATION: POETICAL
USE OF A GIVEN MATERIAL
SECONDARY: LOW COST

WM. GRAY PURCELL AND
GEORGE FEICK, JR. ARCHITECTS

STREET SIDE WALK

CURB   CURB

PARKING   STREET

Gebhard T+E Thesis
Micro'd Apr. 1957

198

200 (color plate, p. 42)
Cushion cover, early 20th century
Embroiderer: Annie May Hegeman, New York
City (after a design by Morris & Co., London)
Cotton embroidery (running stitch) on cotton
plain weave
L: 27½ in. W: 27¼ in.
Cooper-Hewitt Museum, the Smithsonian Institution's National Museum of Design. Gift of
Annie May Hegeman. 1936-5-3

The widespread influence of William Morris is
apparent especially through the products of his
interior-design firm. Offering embroidery patterns at sales outlets in Europe and the United
States, "[Morris] provided an opportunity for
many people to acquire designs, their price
(especially if bought in kit form) being much
cheaper than for-the-wall hangings, bed-covers
and portières . . . . The designs were available in
three different stages of completion: as background fabric marked with the design to be
embroidered entirely at home, with the embroidery already started as a guide, or, if desired, all the work could be done in the Morris
& Co. workshops."[1]

This cushion cover, embroidered by Annie
May Hegeman in a non-directional design, belongs to the first category; traces of the blue
pigment that guided her hand can be seen
under the finished work. The palette, with
many pale colors, is not typical of Morris & Co.
and may represent the taste of Miss Hegeman.
A New Yorker who assembled a small collection of clothing accessories and unusual needlework, she created numerous embroideries
following the design of others. The use of the
running (or darning) stitch alone in an embroidery is characteristic of early-twentieth-century
work.

GM

1. Linda Parry, *William Morris Textiles* (London: Weidenfeld and Nicolson, 1983), p. 29.

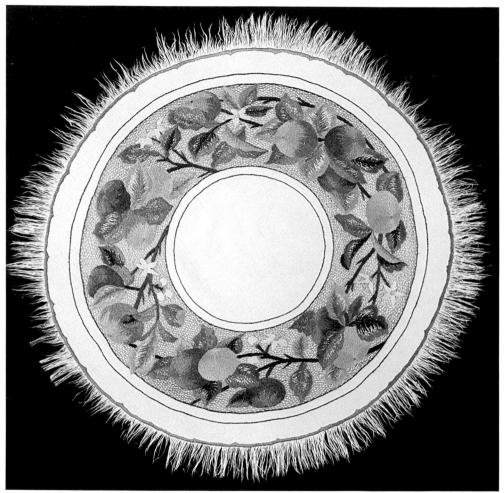

201

201

Embroidered mat, ca. 1912-1916
Designer: George Fenety (1854-1933), Boston
Maker: Anna Macbeth Robertson (1840-1927)
Boston
Silk embroidery (including running, stem,
satin, knot, and buttonhole stitches) on linen
plain weave
Diam: 29½ in.
Private Collection

Common to every home in the early twentieth
century, tea cloths, pillow and tray covers, and
small table mats could be purchased in an unfinished state as designs upon cloth, often with
embroidery silks included in the package.[1] The
decoration of this mat – a wreath of oranges
within a strongly defined border – shows the
influence of earlier English artists, notably Walter Crane.

The designer, George W. Fenety, was born in
Nova Scotia and moved to Boston sometime
before 1878. He was a potter at the Chelsea
Keramic Art Works for several years but, in the
catalogues of the Boston Society of Arts and
crafts exhibitions from 1899 to 1903, he is listed
for his textiles.[3] Some years later, in 1916,
Fenety advertised in the first issue of the *Needle
and Bobbin Bulletin* with the statement "special
designs begun for finishing at home."[4] Marked
on the fabric with a spiked wheel, his outline
had to be covered completely with embroidery
since the blue pigment did not wash out. The
background, in what is variously called running
stitch or darning stitch, is very characteristic of
Arts and Crafts needlework.

The current owner of this cloth, a member of

the embroiderer's family, has recounted that at the beginning of each summer, her female relatives purchased a supply of marked patterns from Fenety and did the embroidery in their summer homes.

GM

1. Candace Wheeler, "The Art of Stitchery," *House Beautiful* 5 (April 1899), p. 196.
2. In 1878, when George Fenety was twenty-four years old, he donated three pieces of Chelsea Art Pottery to the Museum of Fine Arts.
3. *Exhibition of the Society of Arts & Crafts*, Copley Hall, Boston, April 4-15, 1899, p. 37.
4. *Bulletin of the Needle and Bobbin Club* 1 (December 1916), p. 34.

202

Lantern, ca. 1910
Attributed to Forest Craft Guild (1907-1917), Grand Rapids
Patinated brass and mottled glass
H: 18½ in. W: 8⅝ in. D: 7½ in.
Collection of Andrew S. Braznell

In 1910 Mabel Tuke Priestman illustrated this lantern, or an identical one, with other metalwares made by students of the Forest Craft Guild in her book *Handicrafts in the Home*.[1] It comes from a large body of surviving Arts and Crafts metalwork that documents the popularity of handicraft in everyday life. An essential aspect of arts and crafts classes, manual training was emphasized increasingly after World War I as occupational therapy to rehabilitate handicapped veterans. Because of their strong decorative value and quaintness, lanterns were an appealing intermediate project for amateurs, putting to practical use a knowledge of mathematics and composing patterns, as well as developing facility in handling a variety of hand tools. This one involved cutting, bending, piercing, embossing, drilling, soldering, and toning, which, except for riveting and etching, are the primary metalworking operations; it did not require annealing or more difficult raising or seaming processes.[2] Openings in the roof permit the lantern to be lit by a candle, recalling the popular outdoor Japanese lanterns of the era. Green art-glass inserts completed the piece.

Forest Emerson Mann (1879-1959), a student at Pratt Institute in the late 1890s, taught arts and crafts at Chautauqua and Dayton before founding the Forest Craft Guild in Grand Rapids in 1907.[3] A year later Mrs. Priestman described the enterprise: "For some time Mr. Mann was conducting a School of Applied Arts, in Grand Rapids, and was so impressed with the good work he was able to get from his pupils that he opened a co-operative shop, where many of his former pupils are associated with him . . . . In conducting the workshop inexperienced men and women are trained to do the designing and . . . carrying out the work upon the jewelry, wrought metal, and leather work . . . . Although it has been in operation less than two years, it gives employment to eight workers, who sup-

202

ply the local salesroom and the dealers in the various cities where the products are for sale."[4] Forest Craft Guild advertised in *The Craftsman*[5] and in 1914 had a New York City outlet in Gustav Stickley's Craftsman Building.

WSB

1. *Handicrafts in The Home* ([Chicago: A.C. McClurg, and London: Methuen, 1910], pp. 6-11, 22-23, ill.) was a publication addressed to women at home and tailored to the broad interest in handicraft as a leisure activity often pursued for commercial reward. Mrs. Priestman also showed a Guild lamp and shade (whose mottled glass matches that in this lantern) and book racks nearly identical to some known to the author marked "FOREST / CRAFT / GUILD."
2. See Frank G. Sanford, *The Art Crafts For Beginners* (New York: Century Co., 1904), pp. 107-123. Mrs. Priestman advised that a lantern be made first in pasteboard so as to practice in cheap material before making the attempt in metal. (See "The Craft of Hammering and Piercing Metal," *American Homes and Gardens* 6 (December 1909), pp. 463-464, ill.).
3. By early 1904 Mann had located in Grand Rapids, where he became director of the Society of Arts and Crafts and taught classes in design, composition, and technical processes, including pottery as well as metalsmithing. See Irene Sargent, "The Feldspar Group of Minerals as Treated in the Jewelry of Forest E. Mann," *Keystone* 27 (April 1906), pp. 568a-568d, ill.; obituary, *Grand Rapids Press* (April 14, 1959), p. 25.
4. Mabel Tuke Priestman, "Arts and Crafts – Where a Problem is Being Solved," *House Beautiful* 24 (November 1908), pp. 126-127, ill. Mrs. Priestman was probably in error in writing that Mann's shop was known as the Grand Rapids School of Applied Arts. Known as Forest Craft Guild, it is listed in Grand Rapids city directories from 1908 to 1917. See also Mrs. Priestman's "Cut Brass Work," *International Studio* 36 (January 1909), pp. XCIX-C, ill.
5. *Craftsman* 15 (November 1908), p. xxxii, ill.

203

Armchair, ca. 1900-1910
New Jersey
Curly maple
H: 45 in. W: 25¼ in. D: 24¼ in.
Private Collection

Seeking the fulfillment of individual accomplishment in an increasingly complex industrial society, amateur craftspeople, in particular, benefited from the work-with-your-hands, do-it-yourself ethos of the Arts and Crafts movement. Their needs were addressed by the furniture designs published regularly in *The Craftsman* and by articles on how-to-make Mission furniture,

203

204

which appeared in many periodicals. *The House Beautiful* of 1905 noted that "The furniture is so plain and easy to construct that it is not a difficult matter to make most any article designed as the joints are all easily made and the tools required will be a plane, saw, hammer, mallet, bit and brace, several chisels, and the various other small tools that make up a working set."[1] Popular Mechanics Press in Chicago published a series of how-to Arts and Crafts books in 1909 and H.H. Windsor's *Mission Furniture: How To Make It* also provided detailed drawings and directions for these rectilinear furniture forms.[2]

This example is one of a set of two armchairs and two sidechairs made in the home workshop of a woodworker in New Jersey. Awkward in proportion, they emulate the popular Mission five-slat-back form.

CZ

1. "Home Made Mission Furniture," *House Beautiful* 17 (January 1905), p. 11.

2. H.H. Windsor, *Mission Furniture: How to Make It*, 3 vols. (Chicago: Popular Mechanics Company, 1909, 1910, 1912; reprint ed. Dover Publications, 1980).

204

Settle, ca. 1903
Craftsman Workshops, Eastwood (Syracuse),
New York (1899-1916)
Oak
H: 65⅞ in. W: 57 in. D: 20 in.
Marks: large red decal of joiner's compass with
Stickley outlined below (on back, top center)
Collection of Mr. and Mrs. John M. Angelo

This settle was made for the foyer of Gustav
Stickley's house on Columbus Avenue in Syracuse.[1] Like the corner cupboard (no. 101), also
made for his own use, this piece is not illustrated in the Craftsman furniture catalogues and
was probably a custom design.[2] Except for the
raised butterfly splines on the back, the Gothic
arches on the sides, and composition of oak
rather than poplar or pine, this settle is very
much like its colonial predecessor. The form
witnessed a revival in popularity during the
1870s and 1880s, when it became an integral part
of the Queen Anne inglenook and center for
family gatherings around the fireplace.

CZ

1. According to Stickley's grandson Peter Wiles (personal communication, January 8, 1987), there was also a
settle in the dining room and possibly one in the
breakfast room. For a sketch of the dining room, illustrating the former, see "A Visit to Mr. Stickley's House,"
Craftsman 3 (December 1902), p. 168.

2. A few other examples of this settle are known to
exist; the placement of the butterfly splines, as well as
the profile of the sides, varies on them, suggesting
custom design in each case. One was illustrated in *The
Craftsman* in September 1903 and another (published as
plans for a high-back hall settle, without the butterfly
splines and Gothic arches) in June 1906.

205 (color plate, p. 43)

Morris chair, ca. 1912
Craftsman Workshops, Eastwood (Syracuse),
New York (1899-1916)
Oak with leather cushions (upholstery not
original)
H: 40 in. W: 32⅝ in. D: 37½ in.
Marks: branded joiner's compass and *Stickley* (on
back of back seat rail)
Collection of Edgar O. Smith

Developed by Morris and Company in the
1860s, the "Morris chair" appealed to the Victorian fascination with adjustable furniture and
love of comfort. It became one of the most
popular forms for the living room or den in the

1890s and was manufactured by virtually every
furniture company.[1] In 1902 *The American Cabinet
Maker and Upholsterer* reported: "It must be understood that this chair remained in obscurity until
twelve to fifteen years ago, when some manufacturer proceeded to make a small line of them, to
retail at a popular price. This started the ball
rolling, and the demand for them has never
ceased to increase. Large factories with hundreds of workmen make nothing but Morris
chairs, all striving to get the most improved
chair, and one that will be most favored by the
public."[2]
Gustav Stickley began manufacturing Morris
chairs around 1901. He published this design as
part of his "Lessons in Craftsman Cabinet Work"
in 1909.[3]

CZ

1. As late as 1918 over fifty firms continued to manufacture the form. See *The Grand Rapids Furniture Record Directory
of Furniture Manufacturers* (Grand Rapids: Periodical Publishing Company, 1918), pp. 133-134.

2. "Morris Chairs," *American Cabinet Maker and Upholsterer*
65 (February 1, 1902), p. 18. The form was so popular
that both Crofts and Reed and the Larkin Soap Company offered free Morris chairs with the purchase of
$10 or more of their products. (See *Ladies Home Journal*,
May 1902, p. 44; and January 1905, p. 37.)

3. See *Craftsman* 17 (December 1909), pp. 336-339.

206

Booktable, ca. 1910
L. and J.G. Stickley, Fayetteville, New York (1902-
present)
Oak
H: 29 in. W: 26⅞ in. D: 26⅞ in.
Mark: "Handcraft" decal of wooden screw
clamp (on underside of top)
Collection of Mr. and Mrs. K. Conrad Harper
(courtesy of the Jordan-Volpe Gallery, New York)

This design derives from the popular nineteenth-century revolving bookcase form. Gustav
Stickley published a similar "combination table
and encyclopedia bookcase" with ornamental
slats in 1909.[1]

CZ

1. See Gustav Stickley, *Craftsman Homes* (New York:
Craftsman Publishing Company, 1909), p. 178.

206

207

Armchair, ca. 1907 - ca. 1913
Marketer: Craftsman Workshops, Eastwood
(Syracuse), New York
Willow (upholstered cushions not original)
H: 40 in. W: 33 in. D: 26¼ in.
Collection of D.P. Magner, Arts and Crafts,
Brooklyn

Capitalizing on the popularity of wicker at the
turn of the century, Gustav Stickley introduced a
rectilinear style of "Craftsman Willow Furniture" built along the sturdy lines of his oak
furniture. By 1904 he was illustrating wicker of
this type in *The Craftsman*;[1] by 1907 he was marketing it.[2] Stickley suggested that a room should
have at least one or two pieces of willow furniture, as "it affords so exactly the relief that is
necessary to lighten the general effect of the
darker and heavier oak pieces."[3] Craftsman
Workshops wicker was sold unfinished or
stained unevenly with a soft green or deep
golden brown to add to the natural look of the
fiber. The cushions were upholstered with a
Craftsman canvas, linen crash, chintz, or
cretonne.
Stickley's willow designs resemble Austrian
work by Hans Vollmer (a student of Josef Hoffmann).[4] Other Austrian artists, Koloman Moser
and Leopold Bauer, and German designers such
as Peter Behrens had been doing this "humble
basket-work" since the late 1890s.

CZ

207

1. A wicker armchair with rectilinear lines is illustrated in *The Craftsman* 7 (November 1904), p. 215.

2. See "Craftsman Willow Furniture," *Craftsman* 12 (July 1907), pp. 477-480.

3. *Catalogue of Craftsman Furniture* (Syracuse: Gustav Stickley), 1910.

4. See A.S. Levetus, "Modern Austrian Wicker Furniture," *International Studio* 21 (February 1904), pp. 323-328.

208

Navajo blanket, 1875-1890
American southwest
Wool (tapestry-woven plain weave)
L: 67 in. W: 52½ in.
North Andover Historical Society, North Andover, Massachusetts. Gift of Caroline S. Rogers and Abbot Stevens, from the Samuel Dale Stevens Collection. 38.4

Navajo blankets – used as rugs by Arts and Crafts collectors – were prized for the fact that they were woven by native Americans on simple looms they made themselves. They were no less appealing for the romantic idea, then current in the popular press, that their designs were symbolic.[1] On this blanket, for example, the four tassels at the corners were thought to represent the four corners of the earth and the white-tipped crosses were regarded as a representation of Spider Woman – a spirit who, by legend, descended from the mountains to teach the Navajo to weave.

Demand for such blankets during the late nineteenth century resulted in rapid production and a consequent decline in quality.[2] This example, woven before the Indian came to produce blankets specifically for the tourist trade, was bought in 1919 by Samuel Dale Stevens (1859-1922), a partner in M.T. Stevens & Sons, a textile manufacturing firm. Stevens acquired antique textile tools and woven coverlets in addition to fine textiles, and left his collection to the Merrimack Valley Textile Museum. He was also a pioneer collector of American decorative arts – holdings that can be found today in the North Andover Historical Society.

GM

1. The decline in quality has been addressed by several authors, including Mary Hunt Kahlenberg and Anthony Berlant, *The Navaho Blanket* (Los Angeles: Praeger, 1972), p. 25; and Charles Avery Amsden, *Navaho Weaving* (Santa Ana: Fine Arts Press, 1934), p. 189. See also Kate Peck Kent, *Navajo Weaving, Three Centuries of*

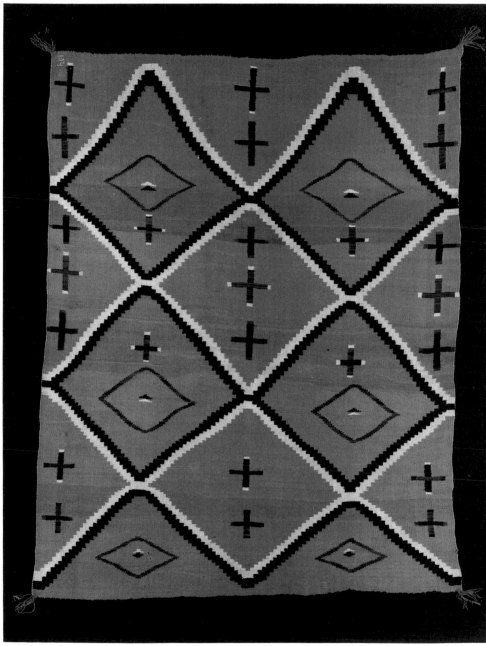

208

Change (Santa Fe: School of American Research Press, 1985). As yet another consequence of the demand for Navajo blankets, at least one manufacturer (in Philadelphia) was producing in 1902 what was described as a "close reproduction of the real Indian product." (See *Upholstery Dealer and Decorative Furnisher* 1 [January 1902], p. 64.)

2. References to Navajo symbolism, sometimes contradictory, can be found in Harriet Geithmann, "Blanketry in Navajo-Land," *House Beautiful* 62 (November 1927), p. 556; U.S. Hollister, *The Navajo and the Blanket* (publisher unknown; Denver, 1903), pp. 114, 115; and George Wharton James, *Indian Blankets and Their Makers* (Chicago: A.C. McClurg 1914), pp. 60-64.

209

Pair of "Princess" candlesticks, 1911-1915
Designer: probably Karl E. Kipp (active ca. 1908-1931), The Tookay Shop (1911-1915), East Aurora, New York
Copper
H: 8 in.
Marks: (on each) struck incuse cipher of circle enclosing addorsed letters KK
Collection of James and Janeen Marrin

By about 1905 a popular market for art metalwares had been developed through arts and crafts exhibitions, articles discussing interior decoration, and the illustrated advertisements of various retailers, notably Gustav Stickley. In this favorable economic climate Elbert Hubbard saw such metalware accessories as an appropriate complement to other Roycroft Industries wares (see nos. 168-171), his flourishing publishing enterprise having by then expanded to include an inn and shops producing various allied book crafts, tooled leather work, sculpture, furniture, and an array of souvenir and gift items. Hubbard's ingenious and relentless sales pitch – "Made with our head, hand and heart" – beguiled the Chautauquans and the Babbitts of America's middle class and, combined with innovative mail-order techniques, made Roycroft "art copper" prevalent nationwide.

In 1909 Hubbard charged Karl Kipp, an employee in the Roycroft bindery who had arrived the previous year, with establishing an art copper department. Kipp, who had been a banker, achieved instant success, but, for reasons unknown, he left in 1911 to establish his own art metal enterprise – The Tookay Shop – taking at least one of Hubbard's metalworkers with him.[1] "Princess" candlesticks of this type were repeated monthly in The Tookay Shop advertise-

209

base was a favorite device of Josef Hoffmann and his circle for vases, clocks, and especially columnar-base tables. The spindly verticals recall Mackintosh designs and are an aspect of the rectilinear Glasgow-Vienna style; hammer-textured surfaces, widely favored for metalwares at the time, appeared frequently in Wiener Werkstätte work of about 1905, with which Kipp would have been familiar through his early period at Roycroft. There the full range of Secessionist designs were readily accessible to him through their publication in *Dekorative Kunst, Deutsche Kunst und Dekoration,* and *The International Studio,* as well as other art publications. When Dard Hunter, a fellow Roycrofter, returned from Vienna during the summer of 1909, Kipp had just begun setting up the art copper department. Hunter left the Roycrofters six months later, but the two became friends and Hunter obviously found Kipp an enthusiastic ally for Secessionist-style designs.[6]

WSB

1. The Roycrofter Walter U. Jennings helped Kipp establish The Tookay Shop; see Charles F. Hamilton, *Roycroft Collectibles* (San Diego and New York: A.S. Barnes & Company, and London: Tantivy Press, 1980), pp. 61, 88.

2. *House Beautiful* 3 (December 1912), p. viii. The shop's name stemmed from Karl Kipp's initials, which appear in the advertisement in the cipher he used to mark his metalwork.

3. Hamilton 1980, p. 63.

4. See Nancy Hubbard Brady, ed., *The Book of the Roycrofters, Being a Catalog of Copper, Leather, and Books* (facsimile of two catalogues), 1909-1916 (East Aurora, N.Y.: House of Hubbard, 1977), pp. 16, 53, ill.; pp. 71, 83, ill.

5. Candle shades, a popular domestic accessory, may well have been used with "Princess" candlesticks. In 1908 a candlestick with shade, close to the Kipp and Secessionist designs, appeared in "Candle and Lamp Shades," *The Good Housekeeping Home and Handicraft Book* (New York, Chicago, and Springfield, Mass.: Phelps Publishing Co., 1908), p. 42, fig. 5.

6. Foreign periodicals at Roycroft are cited in Dard Hunter, *My Life with Paper* (New York: Alfred A. Knopf, 1958), pp. 35, 43. For the Secessionist influence Hunter brought to Roycroft, see Robert Koch, "Elbert Hubbard's Roycrofters as Artist-Craftsmen," *Winterthur Portfolio* (1967), pp. 80-82.

ments in *House Beautiful* from October 1912 to February 1913 and were offered at $3.50 a pair or singly at $2.[2] The accompanying text emulated Hubbard, noting that ". . . the things made by Karl Kipp are entirely hand-wrought and therefore can not be duplicated." Following Hubbard's demise aboard the *S.S. Lusitania* in May 1915, Elbert Hubbard II succeeded his father, persuaded Kipp to return, and immediately set upon establishing countrywide Roycroft outlets – 320 by 1924 – where their art copper was sold.[3] The "Princess" candlestick became part of Roycroft's copper line and was illustrated in its 1919 and 1926 catalogues as model 403 at $5 a pair, a forty-three-percent increase from Kipp's 1913 price.[4]

The candlestick embodies the Vienna Secessionist style that characterizes many of Kipp's designs.[5] By 1905 the chamfered rectangular

210

Smoking set, ca. 1912-ca. 1920
Niloak Pottery (1909-1946), Benton, Arkansas
Blue, red, brown, and tan clays, combined and wheel-thrown in marbleized pattern
Tray – H: 1¼ in. Diam: 11¼ in.
Humidor – H: 6⅝ in. Diam: 5¼ in.
Cigarette container – H: 3⅛ in. Diam: 2⅞ in.
Marks: *NILOAK* in art letters (impressed on bottom of each piece)
Collection of Kenneth R. Trapp

Like William H. Fulper (see no. 124), Charles Hyten understood that the market for utilitarian stoneware was passing with the turn of the new century; but while Fulper attacked the problem from the point of surface and form, Hyten examined the clay body itself and developed a pottery entirely new for the period. Trained in his father's Eagle Pottery to make crocks and jugs, Hyten used his knowledge of clay chemistry to combine several different local clays in a distinctive product called "Niloak" for the art-pottery market.[1] The variegated line was designated "Mission" in order to appeal to home furnishers who decorated in that popular style. Before forming the vessels, each clay was combined with additional ingredients so that the coefficients of expansion matched and the pieces did not break apart in the drying and firing stages. The various colored clays were then combined, but not mixed; when turned on the potter's wheel the colors swirled together in a unique pattern. Finished pieces were fired at a high temperature and polished to a silky texture afterward.

Although Niloak pottery was not produced in the same kind of studio setting as most artwares of the Arts and Crafts mode, it was intended to serve the same market. By 1912 the wares were offered nationally to fine art shops and collectors through shelter magazines. Forms, predominantly classical or Oriental,[2] included small bowls, candlesticks, pitcher and tankard sets, steins, punchbowl and cup sets, fern dishes, clocks, and vases made in a variety of sizes adaptable as lamps. In the company trade catalogue of about 1920 this smoking set, including the tray, humidor, match holder, cigarette container and ashtray, sold for $8; without the tray it could be bought for $6.

EPD and BRD

1. *The Niloak Pottery,* trade catalogue, n.d. ca. 1920. For more information about the pottery, see Paul Evans, *Art Pottery of the United States* (New York: Charles

210

Marks: *TECO* impressed vertically three times (on bottom of base)
Luther Collection

"A lamp of Teco ware in itself sets off a room, gives that fine, dainty, delicate hint of color that is so pleasing to the eye, and soothing to the nerves," noted a writer for *The Craftsman* in 1904. "We are a nervous people, made so by our strenuous life. In our quieter moments we should so surround ourselves with objects of subdued tone, beautiful form and generally pleasing appearance, that they will have a direct and soothing influence . . . ."[1] Thus, for only $40 the middle-class homemaker could purchase utility, beauty, and sedation for her family.[2]

The product catalogue notes the pottery's "chasteness of design and harmony of decoration, its new and unique glaze, its velvety glossless finish and soft moss green, crystalline color, celebrated for its delicate shadings and richness of tones,"[3] all of which are shown to great advantage in the base of this lamp designed by the architect William B. Mundie.[4] As a draftsman for (and later partner of) William LeBaron Jenney, Mundie worked on many major buildings in Chicago during his long career there.[5] He was one of several famous Chicago architects engaged by William Gates (see no. 121), originator and manufacturer of the Teco Art Pottery, to design vases, jardinières, and lamp bases. As in this lamp base, Mundie's designs were usually based on intersecting circles and rectangles.

The shade was produced by the firm of Giannini and Hilgart, which had been in the art-glass business in Chicago since 1899.[6] Fritz Hilgart was a glass stainer; Orlando Giannini, trained as a sculptor in Cincinnati, executed art glass commissions for Frank Lloyd Wright and other Chicago architects.

By commissioning designs for his artwares from Chicago artists Gates made the Prairie style available to homeowners across the country through mail-order catalogues and advertisements in popular shelter magazines.

EPD and BRD

1. "Teco Pottery and the Holidays," *Craftsman* 7 (November 1904), p. 234.

2. *Teco Art Pottery* (Terra Cotta, Ill.: Gates Potteries, 1904), p. 2 for illustration and p. 13 for price.

3. Ibid., p. 9.

4. *Teco Pottery* (Chicago: Campbell Company, 1906), no. 271, illustrates the base as "Classic jardiniere" by W.B.

Scribner's Sons, 1974), pp. 189-192; and Ralph and Terry Kovel, *The Kovels' Collector's Guide to American Art Pottery* (New York: Crown Publishers, 1974), pp. 128-133.

2. The name "Niloak," which is "kaolin" spelled backwards, was intended to evoke the glories of ancient Chinese porcelain. Kaolin (not present in significant amounts, if at all, in Niloak's "Mission" ware) was one of the two most important ingredients in the Chinese formula for porcelain, which is considered the acme of clay bodies.

211

Lamp, ca. 1905
Base – Gates Potteries (ca. 1885-ca. 1922), Terra Cotta, Illinois
Designer: William B. Mundie (1863-1939)
Shade – Giannini and Hilgart (1899-present), Chicago
Designer: Orlando Giannini (1861-1928)

Base – Buff earthenware, molded and covered overall with medium-green crystalline matte glaze
Shade – green and blue stained glass; copper fittings
H: (including base and shade) 17 in. W: (of shade) 10½ in.

211

Mundie. The base could be purchased separately for $10 as a vase or jardinière. See also *Teco Art Pottery* 1904, pp. 10 and 15.

5. Henry F. Withey and Elsie Rathburn Withey, *Biographical Dictionary of American Architects (Deceased)* (Los Angeles: New Age Publishing Co., 1956), p. 434.

6. For more about Giannini and Hilgart, see Sharon Darling, *Chicago Ceramics and Glass* (Chicago: Chicago Historical Society, 1979), p. 120 and passim. For reference to Giannini as designer of this shade, see *Teco Pottery* 1906, no. 16, in which the shade is shown with a different base. Yet another base appears with this shade in *Teco Art Pottery* 1904 (p. 2), which illustrates the present base with a different shade designed by Giannini. Although no Teco catalogue shows the present combination of shade and base, the match occurs in *International Studio* 23 (1907), p. CCCLXIV, with the shade assigned to the Chicago metalsmith Robert Jarvie. Jarvie's production of lanterns was recorded during the period, but he is not known to have made art-glass shades. Since Jarvie sold the work of other craftsmen alongside his own in his shop, it is likely that the reporter was confused as to the actual maker.

212

Tile setting: The Arkansas Traveler, 1986[1]
Moravian Pottery and Tile Works (1898-present, with interruptions between 1960 and 1974), Doylestown, Pennsylvania
Designer: Henry Chapman Mercer (1856-1930)
Red earthenware, press-molded and covered with glossy colored glazes; set in mortar
H: 55 in W: 72 in.
Marks: cipher of conjoined MOR incorporated in various elements of design
Moravian Pottery and Tile Works, Bucks County Department of Parks and Recreation, Doylestown, Pennsylvania

Archaeologist, museum curator, antiquarian, folklorist, and tile-maker, Henry Chapman Mercer was a man of many talents and had the financial freedom to indulge them.[2] Born into a prominent Bucks County, Pennsylvania, family, he trained for law at the University of Pennsylvania, but his earlier education at Harvard University under Charles Eliot Norton had more to do with mature interests. During the 1880s Mercer's fascination with archaeology and local history developed, and he was attracted to pottery as one of the many local crafts he investigated. Even at this late date the making of traditional redware vessels had survived on a small scale in Bucks County. In his determination to keep this craft alive, Mercer apprenticed to a local potter, but was unable to

master quickly the skills necessary to produce holloware. He turned to tiles as an alternative and with the advice of industrial and art potters was able to devise methods whereby the product would be uniform while retaining many handmade qualities.

Many of Mercer's earliest tiles were small with simple patterns and little or no applied color. The work appealed to consumers and critics for "the quaint medieval designs rudely carved and irregular in effect."[3] Isabella Stewart Gardner chose Mercer's tiles as paving for her house in Boston and regional architects such as Ralph Adams Cram and Bertram Goodhue, Will Price, Irving Gill, Ward Wellington Ward, and Wilson Eyre included them in their projects.

Mercer quickly grew tired of the plain tiles and believed "he might as well make soap if they were the sole product of the pottery."[4] In 1906 he began to develop "brocade" and "mosaic" murals, many based on stories, historical events, and legends that were instructive as well as attractive. *The Arkansas Traveler*, a "brocade" mural, was produced after 1916. It pictures seven scenes from the popular nineteenth-century folk song in which a traveler from the city seeks directions, food, and shelter from a rural fiddler and his family living in a rustic cabin with a leaky roof. Suspicious at first, the fiddler happily shares his food and humble abode after the traveler plays for him the second part of a tune of which the fiddler knows only the first part. The story can be followed in the seven scenes beginning at the lower left and alternating with panels of colonial-revival windows, doors, columns, and latticework.

In an article of 1896 Mercer traced his own interest in the song and legend back some thirty years.[5] It was a theme that continued to haunt him: a sophisticated traveler, lost in the back woods and dependent on the hospitality of the country folk for necessities, was the one person who could teach them the ways they had forgotten. In *The Arkansas Traveler*, Mercer illustrated this interest in preserving and interpreting the rural past for the generations that would carry it forward.

BRD and EPD

1. Designed in 1916, *The Arkansas Traveler* was produced for eleven installations by 1929. The present installation was made from Mercer's original molds in 1986 at his second tile works, designed and built in 1921. The Moravian Pottery and Tile Works has been operated in the spirit of Mercer's original intentions by the Bucks County Department of Parks and Recreation since the early 1970s.

2. For more complete information about Mercer and the Moravian Pottery and Tile Works, see Henry Chapman Mercer, "Notes," *Bucks County Historical Society Collections* 4 (1917), pp. 482-487; Benjamin H. Barnes, *The Moravian Pottery: Memories of Forty-Six Years* (Doylestown, Penna.: Bucks County Historical Society, 1970); and Cleota Reed, *Henry Chapman Mercer and the Moravian Pottery and Tile Works* (Philadelphia: University of Pennsylvania Press, in preparation).

3. "Louisiana Purchase Exposition Ceramics," *Keramic Studio* 6 (April 1905), p. 269.

4. Barnes 1970, p. 6.

5. Mercer's designs for the third and fourth scenes of this surround were based loosely on lithographs published by Currier and Ives in 1870 after paintings by Edward Payson Washburn in 1859. The lithographs were used as illustrations in H.C. Mercer, "On the Track of 'The Arkansas Traveler,'" *Century Magazine* 51 (new series 29, March 1896), pp. 710-711; see p. 707 for the history of his interest in the legend.

Frank Lloyd Wright

Edward S. Cooke, Jr.

Frank Lloyd Wright (1867-1959), the most influential architect of the early twentieth century, executed designs for homes in a new indigenous American style. Arguing for work that reflected contemporary needs rather than past style and that made use of appropriate materials and technology, Wright produced houses that represented total integration of the site, structure, and furnishings. The Arts and Crafts movement, strong in various guises in Chicago, provided Wright with the philosophy, manufacturers, and clientele for developing such a style.

Born in rural Wisconsin, Wright entered the architectural profession in 1887[1] as an apprentice to Joseph Lyman Silsbee, a Chicago architect who worked primarily in the Shingle Style.[2] Sometime after November of that year, Wright left Silsbee's office and began to work for Dankmar Adler and Louis Sullivan (see nos. 83 and 84), who needed extra draftsmen for the Chicago Auditorium commission then underway. As the result of his preparing working drawings from Sullivan's ornamental sketches, Wright gained a solid understanding of the master's approach to design and ornament. About 1890, the principals of the Adler and Sullivan firm, preferring large commercial structures, began to turn small domestic projects over to Wright, who was then the chief draftsman. He spent increasing time on house designs, and was fired by Sullivan eventually in 1893 for accepting commissions outside the office.

When first on his own, Wright worked in a variety of styles, including Shingle, Queen Anne, Old English, and colonial revival. His William Winslow house of 1894, in River Forest, Illinois, resembled the early work of George Washington Maher. Wright's own house, built in 1889 in Oak Park, provides insight into his architectural philosophy. The renova-

tions and additions to this Shingle Style building, which were begun in 1895, foreshadow some of the most important components of his mature work. The kitchen was converted into a dining area distinguished by stark geometric simplicity and totally integrated furnishings: tall-backed chairs appeared almost like screens, solid tables were given rectilinear moldings, and stained-glass windows were placed as friezes above simple paneling. Also anticipating his later Prairie style was a two-story barrel-vaulted playroom with a fireplace mural and indirect lighting. In 1898 Wright added another wing, articulated with banks of windows and a series of posts and lintels, in which he located his studio, office, and library.

Wright's nascent work in his own home manifests his transformation of Sullivan's ideas. Whereas Sullivan sought the abstraction of ornament through the understanding of natural evolution (see no. 84), Wright emphasized the geometric relationships underlying all structures. This mathematical orientation can be traced to a variety of sources – the work of the nineteenth-century French architectural theoretician Viollet-le-Duc, the example of Japanese prints, the friendship of Robert Spencer, and the writings of the Austrian designer Otto Wagner – but Wright developed his own arithmetic philosophy suited to the midwestern environment. Wagner's ideas were especially important: he extolled the benefits of simple and economic designs made from durable and easily worked materials and believed that the structure should provide clear evidence of its materials and mode of construction. Because there were few commercially available choices for suitable furnishings, Wright also began to concern himself with all matters of interior design. His interest in a new indigenous style and in the integration of the constructed environment led him to be one of the founding members of the Chicago Society of Arts and Crafts in 1897.[3]

While committed to the same philosophical goals as other Chicago reformers, Wright disagreed on the means of achieving the intended result. In a talk to the Society in 1901,[4] he explained that the geometric simplicity of his new American style was ideally suited to mechanized production because machines could provide the necessary straight, smooth-surfaced, uniform parts in any desirable quantity. In two articles published in the same year, Wright applied his machine-design theories about new materials and technologies to domestic projects.[5] These articles feature illustrations of low horizontal buildings with wide overhanging eaves, decorated simply with functional trim elements – casement windows, screens, and window boxes; the interior renderings show custom-designed furnishings that repeat the geometry of the structure. Such ideas were given form in the first true Prairie-style houses of 1901, for example the F.B. Henderson house in Elmhurst, Illinois, and the Frank Thomas house in Oak Park.

From 1901 to 1909 Wright designed many houses in the fully developed Prairie style: strong horizontal massing without any basement and with refined horizontal trim, open flexible floor plans, and heavy overhanging roofs (see no. 86). The uncluttered interiors, centered around the fireplace or hearth, featured clean-lined trim and furniture whose rectilinearity endowed the chairs with the appearance of screens and tables and case furniture with the appearance of built-in units. These domestic designs fulfilled Wright's criteria for American architecture in accordance with the technological sophistication and democratic individualism he cited as the salient strengths of the nation in the early twentieth century. Technology permitted new

solutions and possibilities, in Wright's opinion, and should not be used to replicate old styles, to replace appropriate handwork, or to deny the modern age. Rather, architects should learn from the machine and use it to transform natural principles into architectural forms. Democratic individualism prompted Wright to reject any sort of hierarchical room arrangement and to employ large open plans with built-in and movable furniture that permitted flexible organization.[6]

In 1909 Wright became disillusioned with his familial and professional life in suburban Chicago and traveled to Europe with the wife of a former client. He wrote a foreword to a German edition of his portfolio, but did little designing until his return late in 1910. Subsequently he worked in a different manner, most of his domestic designs being uninspired variations of earlier works (for example, the William B. Green house of 1912 in Aurora, Illinois) or semi-cubist, boxy, and self-contained structures (for example, the Emil Bach house of 1915 in Chicago).[7] Many of the commissions of the 1920s were in more distant locations, such as California. Best known are the Aline Barnsdall house of 1920 in Los Angeles and a house of 1923 for Mrs. George Millard in Pasadena. This period of activity was followed by another time of introspection and spiritual renewal from about 1924 until 1936. Yet another exploration began in 1936 with the S.C. Johnson administration building in Racine, Wisconsin, a squarish sort of streamlined structure with large plant-like interior pillars and specially designed cast-aluminum and magnesite furniture. In the same year Wright designed the Herbert Jacobs house, his first Usonian home, which became the prototype for the ranch-type structure so popular in America after World War II. The single-story, L-shaped structure uti-

lized many technological innovations such as radiant slab heat, ready-made walls, and insulation. In the latter part of his life, Wright explored several other stylistic variations: the streamlined geometry of the Marin County Civic Center (1957) in San Rafael, California; the taut surface of the Johnson Research Tower (1946) in Racine; and the triangulation of the Beth Shalom Synagogue (1956) in Elkins Park, Pennsylvania, are but a few key examples.

In more than 700 designs produced during Wright's seventy-year career, he demonstrated a facility for building with the materials and methods appropriate to the time and place. Work in new materials such as fiberglass, synthetic-fiber wall panels, concrete blocks, and pyrex testifies to his adaptability, as do accomplishments within the Arts and Crafts movement, the cubism of the 1920s, the International Style of the 1930s, and the streamlined look after 1945.

1. Much of the biographical data about Wright is drawn from Robert Twombly, *Frank Lloyd Wright: An Interpretive Biography* (New York: Harper & Row, 1973). Other helpful works include H. Allen Brooks, *Frank Lloyd Wright and the Prairie School Tradition* (New York: George Braziller, 1984); Brian Spencer, ed., *The Prairie School Tradition* (New York: Whitney Library of Design, 1985); and David Hanks, *The Decorative Designs of Frank Lloyd Wright* (New York: E.P. Dutton, 1979).

2. Silsbee employed, in addition to Wright, George Grant Elmslie and George Washington Maher (see nos. 90-94 and 217-221).

3. A provocative discussion of Wright's design philosophy that stresses the Austrian influence in particular is Narciso Menocal, "Frank Lloyd Wright and the Question of Style," *Journal of Decorative and Propaganda Arts* 2 (Summer/Fall 1986), pp. 4-19.

4. "The Art and Craft of the Machine," reprinted in Edgar Kaufman, Jr., and Ben Raeburn, eds., *Frank Lloyd Wright: Writings and Buildings* (Cleveland: World Publishing Company, 1960), pp. 55-73.

5. *Ladies' Home Journal*, February and July of 1901.

6. Wright's views are expressed most clearly in Kaufman and Raeburn 1960 and his introduction to *Ausgeführte Bauten und Entwürfe von Frank Lloyd Wright* (Berlin: Ernst Wasmuth, 1910).

7. Wright's work from 1910 until his death is surveyed in Twombly 1973.

The Susan Lawrence Dana House

Begun in 1902 and finished in 1904, the Susan Lawrence Dana house was one of Frank Lloyd Wright's earliest completely designed Prairie-style houses.[1] His largest project at that date, the Dana house cost approximately $125,000 and involved an extensive integrated decorative scheme consisting of stained glass, furniture, lighting fixtures, textiles, wall murals, sculpture, and even fountains. Susan Lawrence Dana, a silver and gold heiress, was an ideal client for Wright. Her wealth, cosmopolitan taste, interest in collecting art, and social prominence provided him with the means to perfect his ideas. The program involved unusual circumstances – the preservation of the Victorian study of the old Lawrence house in the middle of the new structure – but Wright still executed a true Prairie-style house. The brick exterior encases a cross-gabled design with a low overhanging roof, banks of stained glass and casement windows set into stucco or patterned brick walls tucked up under the eaves, and projecting piers at the gable ends. Multileveled interiors consist of brick piers, sand-finished plaster and simple face-board moldings with integrated lighting fixtures, furniture, and textiles.

Wright considered the most important functions of the Dana house to be the display of art work and entertainment of guests. For a gallery/ballroom and a smaller dining room he created an open, two-storied, barrel-vaulted space with indirect lighting, stained glass, and painted murals – all features that he first used in the playroom in his own house. Like George Washington Maher (see nos. 217-221), Wright sought to link the site and the house by means of earthy autumn colors, the consistent use of a local plant – the sumac – and stained glass along the porches, arcades, and walkways. Many of the stained-glass windows throughout the house featured an abstracted sumac plant composed of amber and green glass. The designs of some windows took inspiration from butterflies, wheat, and other midwestern flora.

ESC

1. The Dana house, probably the best preserved of Wright's complete Prairie-style houses, is discussed and illustrated in Richard R. Morse and Ralls Melotte, "The Dana-Thomas House," *Stained Glass* 77, no. 2 (Summer 1982), pp. 138-141; idem, "The Dana-Thomas House: Symbol of a Revolution," *Stained Glass* 77, no. 3 (Fall 1982), pp. 265-268; and David Hanks, *The Decorative Designs of Frank Lloyd Wright* (New York: E.P. Dutton, 1979), pp. 77-80.

213 (color plate p. 44)
Sectional perspective drawing of dining-room interior for Susan Lawrence Dana house, Springfield, Illinois, 1903
Architect: Frank Lloyd Wright (1867-1959), Chicago and Oak Park, Illinois
Pencil, pastels, and washes on brown paper
25 x 20 5/16 in.
Avery Library, Columbia University, New York

This sectional drawing, in which the near wall has been cut away in order to present a clear unobstructed view, shows a unified geometric design. The barrel-vaulted ceiling of the Dana house dining room at the end of the entry stairs echoes the Sullivanesque arch of the entrance and elaborates the sumac motifs of the stained glass in the entry hall. A long hallway with a wall of stained-glass windows links the room to the other highlighted interior space – the gallery-ballroom. Square spindles in the chairs echo the exposed ceiling beams and, along with the brick piers, wooden pilasters, and stained-glass windows, provide vertical emphasis. The upward thrust is balanced by the horizontality of slab-top tables, the crest rails of the chairs, the built-in cabinets, the geometric motifs of the textiles, the frieze and its face-board molding enframement, and the transom window above the frieze. Serving the function of screens, the windows mediate between outside and inside worlds and the chairs, being movable, help to organize the open interior space.

Like the Greenes (see nos. 222-225) and other architects who developed totally integrated designs, Wright cultivated and patronized a number of specialists who could interpret and execute his work. The Dana house frieze was the first of several collaborations between Wright and George Niedecken, a Milwaukee interior designer (see nos. 96-97).[1]

ESC

1. Cheryl Robertson et al., *The Domestic Scene (1897-1927): George M. Niedecken, Interior Architect* (Milwaukee: Milwaukee Art Museum, 1981), pp. 11, 26, 43-48.

214 (color plate, p. 45)
Window for Susan Lawrence Dana house, Springfield, Illinois (1903)
Designer: Frank Lloyd Wright (1867-1959)
Maker: Linden Glass Company, Chicago
Leaded stained glass
H: 46½ in. W: 31½ in.
Richard W. Bock Sculpture Collection, Greenville College, Greenville, Illinois

The Arts and Crafts architect sought to unify form with function, building with surroundings, and materials with design. In the house designed for the Dana family Frank Lloyd Wright made extensive use of glass to achieve this harmony.[1] The intricate stained-glass panels in ceilings and exterior and interior walls throughout served as a means of integrating the building with its natural surroundings. Inasmuch as they extended the house outward and brought the outside in, the windows functioned more as "light screens" than as walls.

Wright believed that windows, like all architectural elements, must be integrated with the building design and its surroundings through unifying motifs drawn from nature. In the Dana House dining room, "prairie-life" appears throughout the decorative scheme in the form of plants and butterflies. Most prevalent in the design of the windows is an abstract sumac leaf reduced to geometric patterns of earth-colored (amber, green, and gold) and clear glass. Wright's choice of light colors and transparency "interferes less with the function of the window and adds a higher architectural note to the effect of *light* itself."[2] Likewise, the functional leadwork is an integral part of the design. Zinc cames are utilized in a variety of widths to hold the glass and define the simple geometric shapes.

Unlike many of his contemporaries, Wright believed that machine technology, when used correctly, did not debase craftsmanship: "The machine can do any kind of glass – thick, thin, colored, textured to order and cheap."[3] The geometrical and straight lines of the Dana house windows were, he believed, best crafted by machinery, and he supervised their production at the Linden Glass Company of Chicago. The firm, which produced the glass for a number of Wright's projects, executed stained-glass windows, mosaics, and lighting fixtures for some of Chicago's most famous public buildings, clubs, and residences. This particular window is one of the "extras" Wright often requested be made for his houses in the event of damage. It was given to the artist Richard Bock, who made the sculpture for the Dana house.[4]

JSB

1. For information about Frank Lloyd Wright stained glass, see Sharon Darling, *Chicago Ceramics and Glass* (Chicago: Chicago Historical Society, 1979); and David Hanks, *The Decorative Designs of Frank Lloyd Wright* (New York: E.P. Dutton, 1979).

2. Frank Lloyd Wright, "In the Cause of Architecture: The Meaning of Materials – Glass," in *Architectural Record* 64 (July 1928), p. 14.

3. Ibid., p. 12.

4. For articles about the Dana house, see Ralls Melotte and Richard Morse, "The Dana-Thomas House: Symbol of a Revolution," *Stained Glass* 77 (Fall 1982), pp. 265-268; and "The Dana-Thomas House," *Stained Glass* 77 (Summer 1982), pp. 138-141.

215 (color plate, p. 46)
Hanging lamp for Susan Lawrence Dana house, Springfield, Illinois (1903)
Designer: Frank Lloyd Wright (1867-1959)
Maker: Linden Glass Company, Chicago
Leaded stained glass
H: 19 in. W: 23½ in. D: 23½ in.
Richard W. Bock Sculpture Collection, Greenville College, Greenville, Illinois

"Glass and light – two forms of the same thing!"[1] Frank Lloyd Wright's comment upon the relationship of material to "function" explains his choice of medium for the lighting fixtures in the Dana House. Four large glass chandeliers were hung in each of four corners of the dining room, achieving a unity with the windows and the glass transom at the north end of the ceiling. Wright chose a prairie nature form, the butterfly, for his motif, the geometric shapes of the insect corresponding with the sumac motif of the windows. The autumn colors – orange, yellow, red, and green – harmonize with the other glass work and with the entire decorative scheme.

This lamp, like the Dana house window (no. 214), is an "extra" that Wright gave to the sculptor Richard Bock.

JSB

1. Frank Lloyd Wright, "In the Cause of Architecture: The Meaning of Materials – Glass," *Architectural Record* 64 (July 1928), p. 16.

216
Dining room chair from Susan Lawrence Dana house, Springfield, Illinois, 1903-1904
Designer: Frank Lloyd Wright (1867-1959), Chicago and Oak Park, Illinois
Maker: possibly John W. Ayers Co., Chicago
Oak; leather, horsehair, cotton, jute, and sheet-metal upholstery[1]
H: 51 in. W: 17⅞ in. D: 18½ in.
Dana-Thomas Historic Site, the Illinois Historic Preservation Agency

Frank Lloyd Wright first formulated his design for a tall-backed dining chair in 1895 for the dining-room renovations of his own house in Oak Park. The form consisted of a very straight rectilinear frame with turned twisted spindles between the rear seat rail and a thick crest rail and with a turned finial at the top of each rear post – characteristics related somewhat to eighteenth-century slatted turned chairs and to those of the Boston architect H.H. Richardson. Wright developed the chair particularly for his new dining room, designing the crest to echo the horizontal strength of the paneling below the window frieze; twisted spindles gave the appearance of a screen.[2] The idea explored originally for Wright's own house was then adapted for use in public commissions. For the Joseph Husser house of 1899, which was not a Prairie-style structure, the finials were eliminated and square-sectioned slats were substituted for turned slats; the rear legs flared both at the top and at the foot. For the Dana chairs, Wright made additional refinements, eliminating the flaring of the upper rear leg.[3]

Wright's tall-backed chair not only fulfilled an interest in architectonic furniture that served to break up open space and organize activity; it also took advantage of the latest technology. Reacting against the misuse of mechanized woodworking tools to replace or imitate appropriate handwork, Wright stressed the importance of linking simplified designs and new techniques. He felt that the markings, texture, and color of wood were intrinsic artistic qualities and that carving "tortured" the material, stripping it of its natural beauty. "By its wonderful cutting, shaping, smoothing, and repetitive capacity" the machine provided clean, strong forms that would be affordable to more than the rich.[4] Even the upholstery of the Dana chair reflects this interest in new practical technologies. A sheet-metal plate nailed to the slip-seat frame replaces the more traditional jute or linen webbing. The upholsterer also used a prefabricated fox edge – a strip of jute-wrapped cord nailed around the upper edge of the frame – instead of a stitched edge, and combined horsehair and cotton for the seat's filling. Such conventions reduced costs and made work more predictable.

Wright's talks in Chicago and at the Craftsman Building in New York may have inspired other versions of this form: both the Tobey Company of Chicago (in 1901) and Gustav Stickley (in 1904) produced similar tall-backed spindle chairs.[5]

ESC

1. The plastic casters are not original.

2. See Anne Farnam, "H.H. Richardson and A.H. Davenport: Architecture and Furniture as Big Business in America's Gilded Age," in Paul Debabian and William Lipke, eds., *Tools and Technologies: America's Wooden Age* (Burlington: University of Vermont, 1979), p. 85. Wright used turned spindles for a built-in screen in the George Blossom house of 1892. David Hanks, *The Decorative Designs of Frank Lloyd Wright* (New York: E.P. Dutton, 1979), p. 28.

3. He used the same chair type for the P.A. Beachy house in Oak Park in 1906. See Hanks 1979, pp. 35-37; and *Frank Lloyd Wright: Art in Design* (New York: Hirschl and Adler Modern, 1983), p. 25.

4. Frank Lloyd Wright, "The Art and Craft of the Machine," reprinted in Edgar Kaufman, Jr., and Ben Raeburn, eds., *Frank Lloyd Wright: Writings and Buildings* (Cleveland: World Publishing Company, 1960), pp. 65-66.

216

5. Sharon Darling, *Chicago Furniture: Art, Craft, & Industry, 1833-1983* (New York: W.W. Norton, 1984), p. 239; *House Beautiful* 20, no. 5 (October 1904), p. 16; and John Crosby Freeman, *The Forgotten Rebel: Gustav Stickley and His Craftsman Mission Furniture* (Watkins Glen, N.Y.: Century House, 1966), p. 16.

George Washington Maher

Edward S. Cooke, Jr.

George Washington Maher (1864-1926) received his architectural training not in school but through the more traditional apprenticeship in a number of drafting rooms. Most influential to his development was the time he spent working for Sullivan and Adler and for J.L. Silsbee. Louis Sullivan inspired an interest in natural ornament and a commitment to the philosophy of architecture; Silsbee gave him a solid foundation in the Shingle Style. Like Frank Lloyd Wright and George Grant Elmslie, who also worked for both Sullivan and Silsbee, Maher was devoted to the systematic composition of design and to the total integration of harmonious parts. He and his contemporaries enjoyed their greatest patronage in the affluent suburbs of Chicago and in growing upper-midwestern towns like Winona, Minnesota.[1]

When Maher began to work on his own in 1888, he continued to design residences according to Silsbee's style, characterized by rock-faced foundations, low and wide fenestration, long overhanging roofs, and short massive chimneys. Such substantial structures closely resembled the domestic work of H.H. Richardson, whose example, Maher claimed, served as an inspiration for American architects to develop their own styles, different from the stale historical styles of the Europeans.[2]

In 1897, with the design for the John Farson house in Oak Park, Illinois, Maher conceived, independent of his mentors,[3] what he called the "motif rhythm theory." To unify the exterior and interior he focused upon the visible decorative details: "There must be evolved certain leading forms that will influence the detail of the design; these forms crystallize during the progress of planning and become the motifs that bind the design together. These motifs are susceptible to repetition, varying in proportion and ornateness as the various situations arise." In the Farson house Maher combined honeysuckle motifs and carved lion's heads in various media throughout the building.[4]

There were several inherent shortcomings in Maher's concept. He himself recognized the possibility of overkill with excessive repetition: "Each effect, whether it be the mantel, stair railing or decoration of the house, becomes related as a result of this method of design. There is no limit to the use of this motif treatment, excepting that of fitness for the place intended, and the restraint necessary on the part of the designer in order to obtain sobriety and character in the composition." Yet another problem was the difficulty of generating unique designs for each client and location. It was far easier to repeat existing combinations, for example, the Voysey-like rectangular structure and lotus and poppy motifs used on numerous buildings.[5]

Beginning about 1905, with his Corbin and Irwin houses, Maher veered away from the overwhelming monumentality and elaborate carving of earlier work and began to design with a lighter hand, emphasizing architectural details and favoring geometric patterns rather than excessive floral decoration. Maher's changed aesthetic can be attributed to the influence of the German and Austrian exhibits at the 1904 St. Louis World's Fair, which he visited with Robert Spencer, and to the growing British architectural press, which published the designs of M.H. Baillie Scott, C.F.A Voysey, and their contemporaries. Many of Maher's residential structures for the period of 1905 to 1915 combine Voysey-influenced domestic forms with a midwestern horizontality. His indebtedness to Voysey, and to German designers, can be seen also in the furniture and fabrics used to decorate the interiors of these houses.[6]

In the early 1910s Maher provided a number of designs for residences and larger buildings in southern Minnesota, but World War I brought this period of activity to a close. After the war, he focused most of his energy upon community planning rather than on building design.[7]

1. William Rudd, "George W. Maher: Architect of the Prairie School," *Prairie School Review* 1, no. 1 (1964), p. 5; H. Allen Brooks, *The Prairie School: Frank Lloyd Wright and His Midwest Contemporaries* (New York: W.W. Norton, 1976), p. 34; and Sharon Darling, *Chicago Furniture: Art, Craft, & Industry, 1833-1933* (New York: W.W. Norton, 1984), p. 249.

2. George Washington Maher, "Originality in American Architecture," reprinted in *Prairie School Review* 1, no. 1 (1964), pp. 12-15; and H. Allen Brooks, "The Early Work of the Prairie Architects," *Journal of the Society of Architectural Historians* 19, no. 1 (March 1960), pp. 2-4.

3. The Farson house possessed some of the monumental qualities of Richardson's work – especially the heavy roof and deep porch – but differed in its low horizontality and open floor plan.

4. George Maher, "An Architecture of Ideas," reprinted in *Tiller* 2, no. 4 (March/April 1984), p. 46; and Darling 1984, pp. 250-252.

5. Maher 1984, p. 46; and Gary Hollander, "Rockledge: A Summer House Designed by George W. Maher," *Tiller* 1 (July/August 1983), p. 11.

6. Brooks 1976, pp. 105-109. Gustav Stickley emphasized the importance of German design in "The German Exhibit at the Louisiana Purchase Exposition," *Craftsman* 6 (1904), pp. 489-506. Examples of the British architectural press are Charles Holme, ed., *Modern British Domestic Architecture* (London: Studio, 1901) and several books written by Lawrence Weaver.

7. Rudd 1964, p. 10.

Rockledge

In 1912 George Washington Maher designed *Rockledge*, (see p. 95, figs. 36 and 37) a summer residence near Homer, Minnesota, for E.L. King, a successful pharmaceutical businessman. Sited just beneath a cliff along the Mississippi River, *Rockledge* was one of Maher's finest designs in the Voysey style in which he worked after 1905. The U-shaped building featured stucco exterior walls set off by wooden trim, canted buttresses, banded casement windows, and uninterrupted eaves, all characteristics of the modern English domestic style. Maher combined these English features with certain American conventions. He made the form more horizontal than had been customary in England, added sleeping porches, and used terra-cotta instead of slate or tile for the roof. On the inside Maher followed the practices of other midwestern architects such as Wright, establishing a very open floor plan with large rooms, wide doorways, and extensive fenestration to provide scenic views of the grounds about the house.[1]

Rockledge was a clear example of Maher's motif-rhythm theory. To link the building to its site, he drew upon color and floral motifs: the earthy browns of the cliff, the greens of the foliage, and the varied orange hues of the coral lilies that grew wild on the location. The terra-cotta roof blended with the lily colors and the brown-stained trim echoed the earth of the cliff face. Inside, the rugs combined dull oranges, earthy browns, and greenish-browns, while the furniture was finished with a greenish-brown stain. Maher domesticated the lily by including it in stained-glass panels for the lamps and sconces and in the drapery and upholstery fabrics.

A dependence upon architectonic and geometric formulas characterizes much of Maher's work after 1905. The segmental arch with short flanges set upon canted buttresses is the main unifying device for *Rockledge*. It was used for the entrance portico, the crest rails of the furniture, the lintels above the fireplaces, the crest rails of the lamps, the finials of the fireplace tools, the ends of the trestle table, the furniture escutcheons, and even for the layout of the terraces. The idea may derive from Voysey, whose 1903 design for the Walters house has the same feature for its hooded entrance porch.[2]

A second architectural feature found throughout the house was trapezoidal guttae, used either as capitals on posts or as applied decorative drops. Maher placed guttae in many places: on the eaves of the building, the capitals of the interior columns, and the radiator grilles; under the mantels; and as capitals on most of the furniture. The use of guttae as independent capitals or as decorative applications may have been inspired by the work of Bruno Möhring, a German designer who exhibited at the St. Louis Fair. The architectonic form and height of Maher's furniture also suggests the influence of German designers.[3] A third unifying device was the cross-hatched grid pattern, found on the rugs, radiator covers, fireplace screens, and ceiling light fixtures.

ESC

1. Gary Hollander, "Rockledge: A Summer House Designed by George W. Maher," *Tiller* 1, no. 6 (July/August 1983), pp. 10-16. See also the illustrations in H. Allen Brooks, ed., *Prairie School Architecture: Studies from "The Western Architect"* (New York: Van Nostrand Reinhold, 1983), pp. 177-80; and in *Frank Lloyd Wright and Viollet-le-Duc: Organic Architecture and Design from 1850 to 1950* (Chicago: Kelmscott Enterprises, 1986), p. 63. Maher's indebtedness to English work is best illustrated by David Gebhard, *Charles F.A. Voysey, Architect* (Los Angeles: Hennessey and Ingalls, 1975); and James Kornwolf, *M.H. Baillie Scott and the Arts and Crafts Movement* (Baltimore: Johns Hopkins Press, 1972).

2. Gebhard 1975, p. 154.

3. *Deutsches Kunstgewerbe St. Louis 1904* (Berlin: Ernst Wasmuth, 1904), esp. pp. 27, 32, and 69.

217 (color plate, p. 47)
Armchair from E.L. King house, Rockledge, Homer, Minnesota, ca. 1912
Designer: George Washington Maher (1864-1926), Chicago
Oak and leather
H: 45¾ in. W: 25¼ in. D: 22½ in.
Collection of Robert Edwards

Almost every Prairie architect who designed furniture developed a tall-backed chair with full-height central splat. This version, one of a pair, is distinctive because it is less severely rectilinear than those designed by Frank Lloyd Wright (see no. 216) or William Purcell and George Elmslie (see no. 93). Although loosely reminiscent of William-and-Mary-style leather examples and Chinese chairs, the Maher pieces manifest closer ties to the Secessionist style and to the work of C.F.A. Voysey. The Austrian influence can be seen in the segmental arch and the constructivist sides in which the wide panel with flanking columns beneath the arms is decorative rather than structural. Voysey's influence is most evident in the canted stiles whose thicker dimension is oriented toward the front.[1] With its architectonic qualities – wide substantial base, tapered stiles, and segmental pediment replete with cornice moldings made and guttae – the chair conforms admirably to Maher's unified-design criteria; its greenish-brown finish links it to other components of the *Rockledge* furnishing scheme.

The construction reveals the work of a very efficient furniture-making shop that made use of current technology without sacrificing quality. Most of the decoration was achieved through sawed profiles and moldings made with a powered shaper, which enabled the craftsman to spend time cutting joints rather than using doweled joints or nailed construction. The upholstery reflects the same attention to efficient work: under the leather cover of the slip seat is jute webbing, and a chaff filling.[2]

ESC

1. Cheryl Robertson et al., *The Domestic Scene (1897-1927): George M. Niedecken, Interior Architect* (Milwaukee: Milwaukee Art Museum, 1981), pp. 49-55; and David Gebhard, *Charles F.A. Voysey, Architect* (Los Angeles: Hennessey & Ingalls, 1975).
2. Such short cuts can be found also in the work of L. & J.G. Stickley and other commercial furniture makers. See Edward S. Cooke, Jr., and Andrew Passeri, "Spring Seats of the Nineteenth Century," in *Upholstery in America and Europe from the Seventeenth Century to World War I* (forthcoming).

218
Tall case clock from E.L. King house, Rockledge, Homer, Minnesota, ca. 1912
Designer: George Washington Maher (1864-1926), Chicago (works by Walter H. Durfee, Providence, R.I.)
Oak; copper, silk curtains, brass
H: 80 in. W: 31½ in. D: 15 in.
Collection of Robert Edwards

The tall case clock, characterized by an imposing case, hooded bonnet, and long pendulum and weights (accessible and often visible behind a front-facing door) was primarily an artifact of the late eighteenth and early nineteenth century. After that date, shelf clocks, patented timepieces, and watches became the preferred means of keeping time,[1] and, except for inherited examples endowed with personal significance, the tall case clock fell out of favor. George Washington Maher incorporated into this colonial form the unifying features of *Rockledge*: the canted stiles, guttae-topped pilasters, and the guttae on the face.[2] Similarities to a smaller clock, also from *Rockledge*, and registered in 1912, provided a date for the furnishings of the house.[3]

ESC

1. David Landes, *A Revolution in Time* (Cambridge: Belknap Press of Harvard University Press, 1983), esp. pp. 308-337; and Edwin Battison and Patricia Kane, *The American Clock, 1725-1865* (Greenwich, Conn.: New York Graphic Society, 1973), pp. 10-20.
2. Several other designers like George Elmslie and L. and J.G. Stickley also transformed the traditional timepiece by packaging it in a shell that incorporated the salient features of their own personal stylistic vocabulary. See Stephen Gray, ed., *The Mission Furniture of L. & J.G. Stickley* (New York: Turn of the Century Editions, 1983), p. 135; and Robert Judson Clark, ed., *The Arts and Crafts Movement in America, 1876-1916* (Princeton: Princeton University Press, 1972), p. 64.
3. Work order 86208, Chelsea Clock Company, Boston, Massachusetts.

218

219 (color plate, p. 48)
Table lamp from E.L. King house, Rockledge, Homer, Minnesota, ca. 1912
Designer: George Washington Maher (1864-1926), Chicago
Brass, bronze, stained glass, lead (patina not original)
H: 16¼ in. W: 21¾ in. D: 11⅞ in.
Collection of Robert Edwards

This table lamp sat originally upon a trestle table in the center of the reception room just inside the entrance to *Rockledge*.[1] Given its prime location, Maher spared no expense in incorporating almost all of the unifying motifs and colors of the house in his intricate design. The wild lily, the colors of the glass, and the original patinated finish of the brass linked the lamp to the exterior; the canted buttresses, columns with beveled bases and guttae capitals, and the segmental arches with flanges echoed the architectural motifs of the interior.

ESC

1. Illustrations of the interior are published in H. Allen Brooks, ed., *Prairie School Architecture: Studies from "The Western Architect"* (New York: Van Nostrand Reinhold, 1983), p. 179.

220
Andirons from E.L. King house, Rockledge, Homer, Minnesota, ca. 1912
Designer: George Washington Maher (1864-1926), Chicago
Brass and iron
H: 21½ in. W: 8½ in. D: 26½ in.
Collection of Mr. and Mrs. Henry E. Fuldner

By the early twentieth century the development of heating stoves and central heating diminished the importance and suitability of woodburning fires. Although the fireplace with andirons to support logs was reduced to a romantic symbol, several designers such as Frank Lloyd Wright, Purcell and Elmslie, and George Niedecken did design andirons.[1] This particular pair provided suitable accents for Maher's rhythm motif at *Rockledge*; the segmental arch of the base and the guttae capital could be seen throughout the house. If the andirons were used in the billiard room, such motifs had a more immediate reference point: the fireplace there featured guttae under the mantel and a segmental arch in the chimney breast.[2]

ESC

1. Robert Judson Clark, ed., *The Arts and Crafts Movement in America, 1876-1916* (Princeton: Princeton University Press, 1972), p. 64; Sharon Darling, *Chicago Metalsmiths* (Chicago: Chicago Historical Society, 1977), pp. 72-73; and Cheryl Robertson et al., *The Domestic Scene (1897-1927): George M. Niedecken, Interior Architect* (Milwaukee: Milwaukee Art Museum, 1981), p. 79.

2. H. Allen Brooks, ed., *Prairie School Architecture: Studies from "The Western Architect"* (New York: Van Nostrand Reinhold, 1983), p. 180.

220

221

Rug from E.L. King house, Rockledge, Homer, Minnesota, ca. 1912
Designer: George Washington Maher (1864-1926), Chicago
Knotted wool
L: 76 in. W: 58 in.
Collection of Allan Sacks and Barbara Taff

Several rugs woven with a geometric grid pattern survive from *Rockledge.*[1] Compared with guttae and canted buttresses, the rugs' cross-hatching provided a gentler unifying rhythm. This rug, with a moss-green field and olive border has a separate geometric pattern in the middle of the field.[2] The random color striations of the border resemble the effect of hand-dyed and hand-knotted yarns, but the rug was probably machine-made. Other designers, for example, George Niedecken, had rugs made by the firms of Bolletin and Thompson of New York and T.A. Chapman of Milwaukee.[3]

ESC

1. *Important Arts and Crafts, Art Nouveau and Art Deco* (Christie's catalogue, December 10-11, 1982), pp. 34-35.

2. Several of the other floor coverings had a mottled salmon and brown field with green borders.

3. Cheryl Robertson et al., *The Domestic Scene (1897-1927): George M. Niedecken, Interior Architect* (Milwaukee: Milwaukee Art Museum, 1981), p. 59.

221

Charles Sumner Greene and Henry Mather Greene

Edward S. Cooke, Jr.

The brothers Charles Sumner Greene (1868-1957) and Henry Mather Greene (1870-1954) have been designated as the preeminent west coast architects who worked according to Arts and Crafts principles. Their mature work of the early twentieth century emphasized such aspects of design as honest wood construction, buildings integrated with furnishings and landscape, and concern with the beauty of the materials. In the opinion of the English Arts and Crafts leader C.R. Ashbee, expressed in 1909: "C. Sumner Greene's work [is] among the best there is in this country. Like [Frank] Lloyd Wright the spell of Japan is on him. He feels the beauty and makes magic out of the horizontal line, but there is in his work more tenderness, more subtlety, more self-effacement than in Wright's work. . . . He took us to his workshops where they were making, without exception, the best and most characteristic furniture I have seen in this country."[1] Recent scholarship on the Greenes has accepted Ashbee's judgment and corroborated their design as the ultimate expression of American Arts and Crafts.[2] However, a close examination of the brothers' careers and an analysis of their products helps us to understand more thoroughly the context in which the Greenes worked and to identify their production more accurately as a selective adaptation of Arts and Crafts ideals.

The Greene brothers became interested in matters of design and materials through their education at Calvin Milton Woodward's Manual Training School in St. Louis, the first of its kind in America. They drew from this background later in their careers, when they began to design furnishings as well as houses.[3] Next the brothers embarked upon architectural training at the Massachusetts Institute of Technology: a two-year program consisting of the standard courses on design,

the orders of architecture, and the history of ornament. After graduation in 1891 and two more years in Boston, the Greenes moved to California, where their parents had just settled, and established an architectural practice in Pasadena. Their work during the 1890s reflects a wide variety of styles, including colonial revival, Dutch revival, Queen Anne, Shingle, and Mission.[4]

At the beginning of the twentieth century, the work of the Greenes shifted noticeably. Charles Greene's honeymoon trip to England in the spring of 1901 familiarized him with the natural beauty of English vernacular houses and with those of such leading architects as C.F.A. Voysey. Upon his return to Pasadena, he and his brother began to follow more closely the latest designs published in *International Studio*. They also began to subscribe to *The Craftsman* and work in a Craftsman architectural style. The James A. Culbertson house in Pasadena (1902) was their first true Arts and Crafts design. Over the next four or five years the brothers created many relatively inexpensive bungalows characterized by shingle-clad exteriors, clinker brick and cobblestone-boulder masonry, deeply overhanging roofs, horizontal bands of casement windows, and sleeping porches. Although the forms were derived almost entirely from home designs illustrated in *The Craftsman*, the Greenes did add elements of Oriental art. Their conception of framing timbers and some of their decorative details were inspired by the Japanese, especially by the Ho-o-den exhibit of joinery at the World's Columbian Exposition in 1893. The brothers learned a great deal from their friend John C. Bentz, a local dealer in Oriental antiques and Charles, in particular, collected Oriental books, prints, and furniture.[5]

Toward the end of 1906, the Greenes refined their designs further, developing what has been called "Ultimate Bungalows,"[6] and their reputation attracted several wealthy clients whose money and interests allowed the architects to realize their own ideas for integrated architecture. Thereafter, the Greenes no longer relied on existing commercially available furnishings but instead upon specific trusted craftsmen such as Peter and John Hall (nos. 222-223), Emile Lange (no. 37), and the Art Metal Company (no. 224) to execute custom work according to their exacting standards. Greene designs still owed much of their inspiration to Craftsman and Japanese styles, but their collaborators – contributing buildings, furniture, lighting fixtures, leaded glass, hardware, fireplace tools, carpets, curtains, fabric, and garden pottery – also influenced the final product. In making the transition from Craftsman simplicity to total design, however, the Greenes concerned themselves to such an extent with refined details that their interior accessories became a self-indulgent exercise far removed from the more pragmatic technical side of the workmanship.[7] Although the Greenes' collaborators used efficient techniques, the architects called for labor-intensive decoration such as inlay and chasing and preferred to implement new forms and solutions each time. This prevented craftsmen from establishing limited-production runs.

The Greene designs from 1907 to 1909 received critical acclaim from their professional peers and were published in *Architectural Record* and *Western Architect*. However, the compulsive attention to details – qualities that attracted the attention of the architectural press – did not attract new clients. By 1910 the Greenes had acquired a reputation for being too costly and too slow and the decline in commissions made it necessary for them to offer designs in the various popular styles of the second decade of the century – Mission and English country houses. Instead of redwood and fir houses characterized by angularity and straight lines, the Greenes worked in stucco, cement, and plaster to produce structures with softer lines.

In 1916, Charles Greene moved to Carmel, California, and settled among the community of painters, poets, and photographers there. Within this supportive, artistic circle, he was able to pursue at his own pace a labor-intensive quest for beautiful, integrated designs. Henry remained in charge of the Pasadena office, but his work was confined primarily to additions and alterations. In the 1920s the Greenes' architectural activity slowed significantly; no new published designs appeared after 1922.[8] It was not until after World War II, when a craft revival emphasized craftsmanship and materials, that the work of the Greenes began again to receive critical attention.

1. As quoted in Randell Makinson, *Greene & Greene: Furniture and Related Designs* (Santa Barbara: Peregrine Smith, 1979), p. 150.

2. For example, see ibid; and Randell Makinson, *Greene & Greene: Architecture as a Fine Art* (Santa Barbara: Peregrine Smith, 1977).

3. Alan Marks, "Greene and Greene: A Study in Functional Design," *Fine Woodworking* 12 (September 1978), p. 41.

4. Makinson 1977, pp. 34-63.

5. Ibid., pp. 55-149; and Robert Winter, "The Arroyo Culture," in *California Design 1901* (Santa Barbara: Peregrine Smith, 1980), p. 27.

6. The "ultimate bungalows" included those for Robert R. Blacker (1907), Freeman A. Ford (1907), and David B. Gamble (1908) in Pasadena; Charles M. Pratt (1909) in Nordhoff; William R. Thorsen (1909) in Berkeley; and Earle C. Anthony (1909) in Los Angeles. See Makinson 1977, pp. 150-187.

7. For a thoughtful analysis of several different levels of craftsmanship, from practical to romantic, see David Pye, *The Nature and Art of Workmanship* (London: Cambridge University Press, 1968).

8. Makinson 1977, pp. 188-266.

The Robert R. Blacker House

The house that Charles and Henry Greene designed for Robert R. Blacker in 1907 was the first and largest of the brothers' bungalows between 1907 and 1909.[1] Located on the most prestigious lot of the Oak Knoll section of Pasadena, the Blacker estate consisted of a main house, garage, gardener's cottage, greenhouse, and pergola. The long, heavy timber work (particularly prominent on the angled *porte cochère*), the numerous porch railings, and the interior hanging lanterns mark the Blacker house as the most Oriental of all the Greene structures. Even its location at a corner of the property emphasized the Eastern influence. The siting allowed an expansive natural garden, complete with lake, that seemed to roll from the terraces of the house. With a budget exceeding $100,000, the Greenes were able to execute an ambitious plan linking the outside and the inside and to establish a coherent interior-furnishing plan.

While the shell was made simply of clinker brick, Oregon pine, cedar shakes, and malthoid (an asbestos-based material used for roofing), the interior was finished more lavishly. Mahogany and teak paneling accented by ebony and mahogany pegging and detailing predominated, with even the hanging lanterns given smoothly finished mahogany frames. The friezes in the living and dining rooms were decorated with modeled plaster and the living-room plaster ceiling was covered with gold leaf, producing a soft indirect light. Much of the furniture was embellished with carving and inlay.

Each room had its own set of unifying details. Lily pads in various materials – plaster, leaded glass, and brass – decorated the living-room ceiling, lanterns, and firescreen.[2] Several distinguishing features linked the furniture of this room: double brackets (used at the knees of the legs and at the upper corners of windows and doors), straight legs with slight carved recesses at the feet, ebony inlaid cloud lifts behind the drawer pulls and along the crest rail of the sofa, and a tree-like inlay of fruitwood with copper and silver branches. Here the forms combined Oriental and Georgian styles, whereas in the master bedroom they related more closely to the work of C.F.A. Voysey and Charles Rennie Mackintosh. The massing of the chiffonier and the abstracted quality of the rocking-chair splat and its cloud inlay (used in all the furniture of this set) recall English and Scottish influence.

ESC

1. The Blacker house is illustrated and discussed in Randell Makinson, *Greene & Greene: Architecture as a Fine Art* (Santa Barbara: Peregrine Smith, 1977), pp. 150-155; and idem, *Greene & Greene: Furniture and Related Designs* (Santa Barbara: Peregrine Smith, 1979), pp. 58-67, 100.

2. For a period photograph of the Blacker living room and the preliminary drawings of its furniture, see Makinson 1979, pp. 58-59.

222 (color plate, p. 49)
Writing table from Robert R. Blacker house, Pasadena, 1907
Designers: Charles Sumner Greene (1868-1957) and Henry Mather Greene (1870-1954)
Maker: Peter Hall Manufacturing Company, Pasadena
Mahogany, ebony, and laminated wood; fruitwood, copper, and silver inlay
H: (of table section) 29½ in. W: (of table section) 50½ in. D: (of table section) 26½ in.
H: (of desk section) 17⅝ in. W: (of desk section) 47¾ in. D: (of desk section) 17⅜ in.
Collection of Richard Anderson and Richard Anderson II

For the past fifteen years scholars and collectors have revered the houses and furnishings designed by Charles and Henry Greene during their "ultimate bungalow" period, from 1907 through 1909. The oiled mahogany, square ebony plugs, smooth workmanship, and carved

Blacker house living room, ca. 1910. Collection of Robert Judson Clark.

and inlaid decoration of the Blacker writing table typifies the Greenes' work at this time, as distinct from the Tichenor desk (no. 70) produced during the Craftsman phase of their career.

The aesthetic of work such as this desk can be attributed to the Greenes' growing confidence in their work, the wealth of patrons who were willing to fund their total designs, and – to a greater degree than has been recognized – collaboration with trusted craftsmen. The furniture from the "ultimate bungalow" period was all made by Peter and John Hall, sons of a Swedish-trained cabinetmaker, who first began to work with the Greenes in 1905.[1] Admiring their renovation work, the Greenes helped the Halls to set up their own shop.[2] It was the Halls' introduction of mahogany to the Greenes that gave their furniture an appearance distinct from that of most other Arts and Crafts furniture makers, who preferred native woods such as oak and pine.[3]

Other distinguishing features were the extensive use of table-sawed construction and slotted screw fastening – early manifestations of what has become known popularly as Scandinavian design[4] as opposed to dovetail, mortise-and-tenon, dado, and doweled construction favored by native craftsmen. The Scandinavian approach, which emphasized construction-based work and industrial simplicity, combined with the Greenes' interest in details and total design to produce clean, pleasing forms.

The Blacker writing table is a particularly good example of the Halls' contribution to the Greene and Greene aesthetic. The finger joints on the desk section, the half-blind tongue and rabbet joints of the drawer fronts, and the dado joint of the drawer backs were achieved with a table saw.[5] At each end of the table surface the Halls attached a batten that was grooved to fit over an end-grain tongue and was secured with screws countersunk through rectangular slots. This construction – concealed with an ebony spline and rectangular ebony plugs – allowed the wood of the top to expand and contract across the grain without splitting or warping.[6] It is a technique not found on any earlier American examples.

The Halls' shop practices also affected relationships between different parts. They shaped the components first, then used the table saw to cut joints, and then assembled the components. These parts did not always fit in the same flush

222 (detail)

plane, a design decision that eliminated the time-consuming practice of paring joints for a tight fit and provided a certain amount of surface variety to the piece of furniture.

ESC

1. Information about the Halls is drawn from Randell Makinson, *Greene & Greene: Furniture and Related Designs* (Santa Barbara: Peregrine Smith, 1979), pp. 34-98; and Alan Marks, "Greene and Greene: A Study in Functional Design," *Fine Woodworking* 12 (September 1978), pp. 40-45.

2. The first furniture commission for the Hall shop was the Henry M. Robinson house in Pasadena. Although some of the Robinson furniture continued to reflect the Craftsman influence, that of the living and dining rooms differed in its Chinese forms and mahogany primary woods.

3. Cabinetmakers prefer mahogany to oak or ash because of its good weight-strength ratio, few imperfections, consistent grain structure, ease of working, and capacity to take an even stain. See Bruce Hoadley, *Understanding Wood: A Craftsman's Guide to Wood Technology* (Newtown, Conn: Taunton Press, 1980).

4. According to Tage Frid (personal communication, May 1986), these same technical concerns were stressed in furniture making in Scandinavia in the 1920s. Frid himself was trained in Denmark in the early 1920s and, in fact, the Greene and Greene furniture made by the Halls, especially the drawers, has a feeling very similar to Frid's work.

5. Another feature of the Greenes' furniture from this period – the bridle joint – was also a table-sawed joint. For a good introduction to this joinery, see Tage Frid, *Tage Frid Teaches Woodworking – Joinery: Tools and Techniques* (Newtown, Conn.: Taunton Press, 1979). The illustration of the Hall shop in Makinson 1979 (p. 57) points up the importance of the circular table saw to that firm. In other views of custom shops from the same period, joiners' benches predominated.

6. For a discussion of this technique, see Marks 1978, p. 43.

224

223 (color plate, p. 50)
Armchair from Robert R. Blacker house, Pasadena, 1907
Designers: Charles Sumner Greene (1868-1957)
and Henry Mather Greene (1870-1954)
Maker: Peter Hall Manufacturing Company,
Pasadena
Mahogany and ebony; fruitwood, silver, and
copper inlay
H: 34⅛ in. W: 24³⁄₁₆ in. D: 19³⁄₁₆ in.
Collection of Max Palevsky

The seating forms from the Blacker living room
are unified by a number of design features. The
knee brackets and downward-stepped handrests
link the armchairs and the couch; the Georgian
back splat and crest-rail design are common to
the side chairs, armchairs, and rocking chair;
and all the forms have naturalistic inlay of
fruitwood, silver, and copper. The armchair, in
particular, illustrates the various components of
the Greenes' design. In its proportions and
overly engineered look the piece resembles Chinese furniture; its crest rail and medial stretcher
are akin to the Stickley Craftsman style; and its
splat recalls English Georgian.

Charles Greene's decorative touch appears in
the inlay and soft piercing of the splat, and the
millwork foundations of the Hall brothers shop
are equally evident. The arms were attached in
the easiest fashion by screwing them in place
from the side and a single piece of mahogany
serves for the arm and handrest. The Halls
avoided the danger of shortgrain by setting an
ebony spline within table-sawed bridle joints in
the arm and front post. This eliminated the necessity of cutting and fitting a second piece of
wood to connect the two parts.

ESC

224
Firescreen from Robert R. Blacker house, Pasadena, 1914
Designers: Charles Sumner Greene (1868-1957)
and Henry Mather Greene (1870-1954)
Maker: Art Metal Company, Los Angeles
Cast bronze and chased sheet bronze
H: 28 in. L: (open) 57¾ in.
Private Collection

Although no invoice survives for this firescreen,
it can be attributed to the Art Metal Company
with certainty and dated 1914 on the evidence of
a bill for a similar example.[1] Both were photographed in the same shop setting.[2] The lag
between the construction of the house and the
purchase of the firescreen may indicate that the
Greenes' interiors were not finished all at once.
Possibly the initial emphasis was on furniture,
with the other accessories acquired as time or
money permitted. Another explanation could

be that the Greenes had not discovered a reliable source for bronze work up to their standards
prior to 1914.

ESC

1. The second is a firescreen for the William Thorsen
house.
2. Letter to the author from Randell Makinson, June 4,
1986.

225
Rocking chair from Robert R. Blacker house, Pasadena,
1907
Designers: Charles Sumner Greene (1868-1957)
and Henry Mather Greene (1870-1954)
Maker: Peter Hall Manufacturing Company,
Pasadena
Mahogany and ebony; silver, copper, fruitwood,
and mother-of-pearl inlay
H: 39½ in. W: 26 in. D: 30 in.
Los Angeles County Museum of Art, Museum
Acquisition Fund

For the master bedroom of the Blacker house,
the Greenes developed a design program that
drew inspiration from C.F.A. Voysey and Charles
Rennie Mackintosh.[1] The bifurcated splat and
especially the abstract inlay of this rocking chair
resemble the work of the Glaswegian designer.
The broad overhanging top and the stacked
massing of a chiffonier with matching inlay from
the same room further affirm the relationship to
Voysey and Mackintosh.

ESC

1. David Gebhard, *Charles F.A. Voysey, Architect* (Los Angeles: Hennessey & Ingalls, 1975); and Robert Macleod,
Charles Rennie Mackintosh: Architect and Artist (London: Collins, 1983).

225

Index

Photograph Credits

Unless otherwise noted, all photography was done by the Department of Photographic Services at the Museum of Fine Arts, Boston.

David Aldrich   p. 113, fig. 11
The Art Institute of Chicago   nos. 5, 19, 134, 140, 177
Athenaeum of Philadelphia   no. 26; p. 225, fig. 4
Avery Architectural and Fine Arts Library, Columbia University   nos. 59, 213
Dirk Bakker   nos. 20, 114, 129
Bildarchiv Foto Marburg   p. 87, fig. 15; p. 89, fig. 21
Bild-Archiv der Osterreichischen Nationalbibliothek   p. 90, fig. 23
Robert J. Bitondi   no. 33, 63
Mary and Leigh Block Gallery, Northwestern University no. 89
E. Irving Blomstrann   no. 22
Richard W. Bock Sculpture Collection, Greenville College nos. 214, 215
Boston Public Library   p. 106, fig. 4; p.122, fig. 25
Simeon Braunstein   p. 33, figs. 30, 31
The Brooklyn Museum   no. 146
Bert L. Brown   p. 119, fig. 22
Will Brown   nos. 21, 50, 212
The Burnham Library, The Art Institute of Chicago   p. 122, fig. 26
Geremy Butler Photography   p. 82, fig. 9
California Historical Society   p. 34k9, fig. 10
Martin Charles   p. 106, fig. 3
Chicago Architectural Photography Company   p. 79, fig. 2
Chicago Historical Society   nos. 84, 87, 188; p. 228, fig. 10
Christie, Manson & Woods International, Inc.   no. 42
Church of the New Jerusalem of San Francisco   p. 124, fig. 28
Cincinnati Historical Society   no. 192a
Columbia University Library   nos. 11, 18, 154, 155
Leland Cook   no. 38
Charles L. Criscuolo   no. 52
Lynn Diane DeMarco   nos. 28, 32, 53, 92, 98, 103, 110, 117, 133, 168, 178, 180, 184, 191, 192, 204, 205, 206, 207
Detroit Institute of Arts   no. 13
Rick Echelmeyer   nos. 35, 51, 71, 95, 104, 106, 165, 166, 167, 169, 203, 217, 218; p. 224, figs. 1-3; p. 226, figs. 5-8; p. 227, fig. 9; p. 229, fig. 11; p. 231, fig. 12; p. 232, fig. 13; p. 233, fig. 19
Richard Eells   no. 96, 97, 101, 220
Cook Ely   p. 118, fig. 21

M. Lee Fetherree   no. 79, 80, 175 a,b, 210
Ron Forth   nos. 6, 14
Frankenberry, Laughlin and Constable Advertising   no. 88
Courtney Frisse   nos. 108, 195
Richard Goodbody   no. 39
Greene and Greene Library, Gamble House, University of Southern California   p. 104, fig. 2
Harvard University   no. 185
Helga Photo Studio   no. 4
Hessisches Landesmuseum   p. 87, fig. 17
Historic American Building Survey, Library of Congress   p. 110, fig. 9
Houghton Library, Harvard University   no. 2; p. 113, fig. 12
Hull House Collection Archives, University of Illinois p. 58, fig. 6
Henry E. Huntington Library and Art Gallery   p. 79, fig. 4
Scott Hyde   nos. 49, 160, 162, 174, 193, 200
Indianapolis Museum of Art   no. 130
Kendall School of Design   p. 232, figs. 15, 16; p. 233, figs. 17, 18
Sally Kinsey   p. 359, figs. 1-2; p. 360, fig. 3
Franco Khoury   no. 221
Ralph and Terry Kovel   p. 232, fig. 14
Kunstbibliothek, Stiftung Preussischer Kulturbesitz   p. 81, fig. 8
Bedford Lemere   p. 84, fig. 13
Library of Congress   p. 114, fig. 14; p. 116, figs. 16-19; p. 118, fig. 20; p. 212, fig. 1; p. 213, fig. 2; p. 339, fig. 1; p. 343, figs. 3,4; p. 344, figs. 5,6; p. 347, fig. 7; p. 349, fig. 8
Los Angeles County Museum of Art, Photographic Services   nos. 115, 137, 181, 209, 223, 224, 225
Gilbert Mangin   p. 91, fig. 26
Georg Mayer   p. 90, fig. 24
Michael McKelvey   no. 123
The McKim, Mead, and White Collection, Museum of the City of New York   p. 79, fig. 3
Metropolitan Museum of Art   nos. 8, 40, 43, 47, 48, 127, 178
Minneapolis Institute of Arts   nos. 36, 94
Eric Mitchell   no. 55
William Morris Gallery   p. 81, fig. 7
Museum of Fine Arts of Houston   no. 66
National Museum of American History, Smithsonian Institution   nos. 109, 163
New York Public Library   nos. 149, 152; p. 363, fig. 6
Northwest Architectural Archives, University of Minnesota   no. 90, 91, 198
The Oakland Museum   p. 98, fig. 43
Frederick Law Olmsted National Historic Site   p. 126, figs. 29, 30
University of Pennsylvania   nos. 23, 24, 25

Princeton University, Department of Art and Archaeology   p. 82, fig. 10; p. 84, fig. 12; p. 85, fig. 14; p. 87, fig. 16; p. 88, figs. 18-20; p. 90, figs. 22, 25; p. 92, figs. 27, 28; p. 93, figs. 29, 32; p. 94, fig. 33, 34; p. 95, figs. 35, 36, 37; p. 97, fig. 41; p. 299, fig. 1
Princeton University Library   nos. 17, 46, 151
Marvin Rand   nos. 37, 70
Robert Reiter   no. 183
Rhode Island School of Design Museum of Art   no. 27; p. 112, fig. 10
The University of Rochester Library, Department of Rare Books and Special Collections   p. 352, figs. 12, 13, 14, 15
Bill Rose   no. 72
San Diego Historical Society   no. 74
The Schlesinger Library, Radcliffe College   p. 59, fig. 7
Bill Selley   no. 182
Society for the Preservation of New England Antiquities   no. 172, 194
Southern Illinois University at Edwardsville   no. 83
Stanford University Archives   p. 79, fig. 1
State Historical Society of Wisconsin   no. 176
N.L. Stebbins, Society of Arts and Crafts, Boston   p. 300, fig. 5
Margaret Woodbury Strong Museum   nos. 34, 189, 196
Syracuse University   p. 364, fig. 7; p. 366, figs. 8,9
George Thomas   p. 103, fig. 1; p. 120, fig. 23
University of California at Berkeley, Architectural Documents Collection, College of Environmental Design   nos. 75, 76; p. 96, figs. 38, 40; p. 98, fig. 42
University of California at Riverside, Field Collection   p. 124, fig. 27
University of California at Santa Barbara, Architectural Drawing Collection   nos. 73, 81, 82, 199
University of Chicago Library   no. 159
University of Pennsylvania   nos. 23, 24, 25
Victoria and Albert Museum   p. 54, fig. 3; p. 55; fig. 4; p. 56, fig. 5; p. 80, fig. 5; p. 81, fig. 6
Richard Guy Wilson   p. 110, figs. 6-8; p. 121, fig. 24
Henry Francis du Pont Winterthur Museum Library, Collection of Printed Books   p. 341, fig. 2; p. 349, figs. 9, 11
Frank Lloyd Wright Foundation, Copyright © 1960   nos. 85, 86
Yale University Art Gallery (Joseph Szaszfai)   nos. 135, 147